Catalog of American ID Numbers 1960-69

Compiled by the Staff of Cars & Parts Magazine

Published by
Amos Press Inc.
911 Vandemark Road
Sidney, Ohio 45365

Publishers of

Cars & Parts
The Magazine Serving the Car Hobbyist

Collector Car Annual

Collectible Trucks

Cars & Parts Legends Series
Muscle Cars of the '60s/'70s

Catalog of American ID Numbers 1970-79

Salvage Yard Treasures
A Guide to America's Salvage Yards

Distribution by Motorbooks International Publishers and Wholesalers
P.O. Box 2, Osceola, WI 54020 USA

Printed and bound in the United States of America

Library of Congress Cataloging-In-Publication Date
ISBN 1-880524-01-5

Revised: September 1991

ACKNOWLEDGEMENTS

The staff of *Cars & Parts* Magazine devoted more than a year to the revision of the Catalog of American Car ID Numbers 1960-69. It has been a labor-intensive project which required assistance from hundreds of car collectors, clubs, researchers, and a tremendous amount of interviewing and photography at car shows, swap meets and auctions.

This book wouldn't have been possible without very special help from the following:

Motor Vehicle Manufacturers Association

Dan Kirchner - Researcher

Tom Hinson - Computer Programmer

Automotive History Collection of the Detroit Public Library

In addition, a special thank you is extended to Greg Donahue, Chuck Kuhn, Barbara Hillick, Jeff Kennedy, and others who helped enormously in specific areas.

Catalog of American Car I D Numbers 1960-69

Compiled by the Staff of Cars & Parts Magazine

Revised: September 1991

SUBJECT	SECTION / PAGE

The information contained in The Catalog of American ID numbers 1960-69 was compiled from a variety of sources including original manufacturers' catalogs (when available) and official published shop manuals. The *Cars & Parts* staff and researchers made every attempt to verify the information contained herein. However, many manufacturers made changes from year-to-year and model-to-model, as well as during mid-year production. And, in some instances, conflicting information and reports surfaced during the course of our in-depth research. As a result, *Cars & Parts* does not guarantee the absolute accuracy of all data presented in this ID catalog.

INTRODUCTION

Authentication has become such a critical issue within the old car hobby that the need for a comprehensive, accurate and dependable identification guide has become quite apparent to anyone involved in buying, selling, restoring, judging, owning, researching or appraising a collector car. With this in-depth and detailed ID guide, the staff of *Cars & Parts* magazine has compiled as much data as possible on the years and makes covered to help take the fear out of buying a collector car.

Deciphering trim codes, verifying vehicle identification numbers (VIN), interpreting body codes and authenticating engine numbers will become a much easier process with this guide at your side. Putting this information at your fingertips has not been a simple task, but one worth the tremendous time and money spent on its production.

Each car manufacturer used a different system of identification and changed its system almost annually in the '60s. The *Cars & Parts* staff has developed the most consistent information possible from year to year for each manufacturer. Some data are not presented due to lack of availability, space, time considerations, and the researchers' inability to verify sources.

Each corporation, division, year, model, VIN, body plate and engine number required decisions about what to print. The staff of *Cars & Parts* is justifiably proud of this book and invites your comments. Additional information is especially welcome.

The information contained in the Catalog of American ID Numbers 1960-69 was compiled from a variety of sources including original manufacturers' catalogs (when available) and official published shop manuals. The *Cars & Parts* staff and researchers made every attempt to verify the information contained herein. However, many manufacturers made changes from year-to-year and model-to-model, as well as during mid-year production. And, in some instances, conflicting information and reports surfaced during the course of our in-depth research. As a result, *Cars & Parts* does not guarantee the absolute accuracy of all data presented in this ID catalog.

HOW TO USE THIS CATALOG

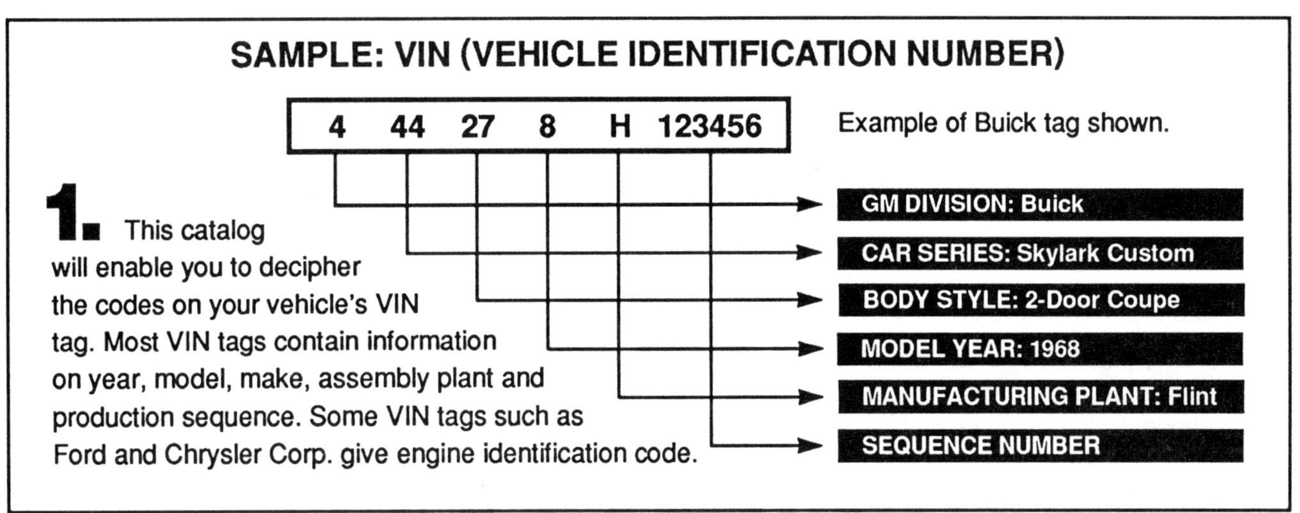

1. This catalog will enable you to decipher the codes on your vehicle's VIN tag. Most VIN tags contain information on year, model, make, assembly plant and production sequence. Some VIN tags such as Ford and Chrysler Corp. give engine identification code.

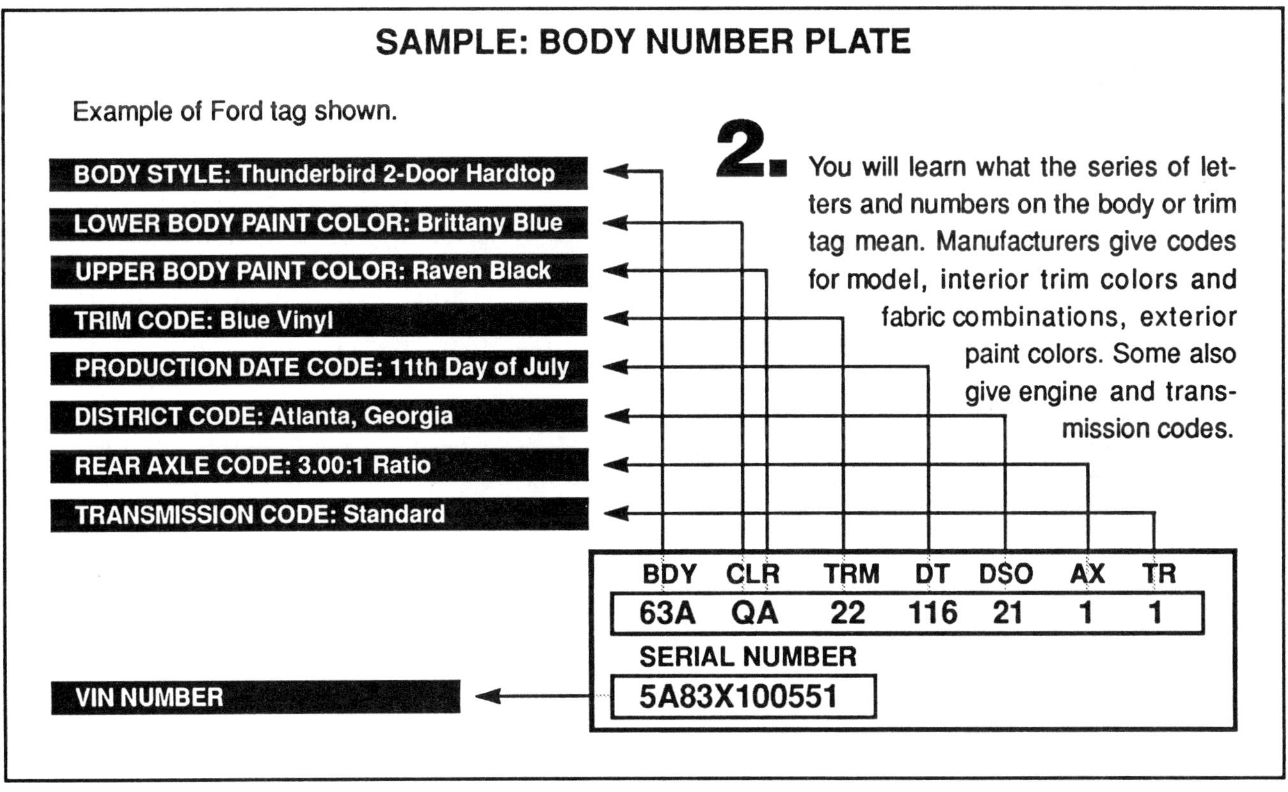

2. You will learn what the series of letters and numbers on the body or trim tag mean. Manufacturers give codes for model, interior trim colors and fabric combinations, exterior paint colors. Some also give engine and transmission codes.

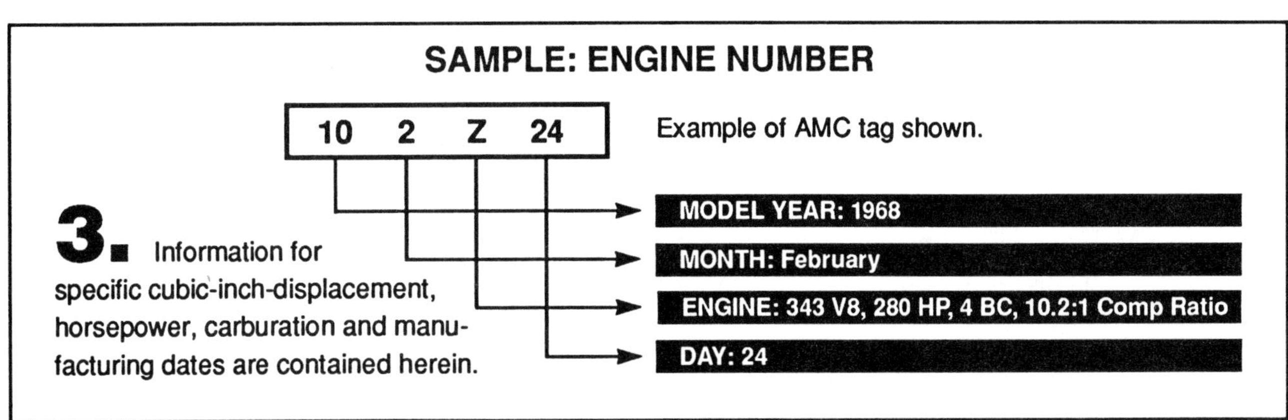

3. Information for specific cubic-inch-displacement, horsepower, carburation and manufacturing dates are contained herein.

1960 AMC RAMBLER

1960 AMC RAMBLER

1960 AMC RAMBLER AMERICAN

1960 AMC RAMBLER AMERICAN

VEHICLE IDENTIFICATION NUMBER

AMC
B-10551

Commonly referred to as the VIN NUMBER, this series of numbers is stamped on a plate attached to the right wheelhouse panel.

THE FIRST DIGIT: Identifies the body class

BODY CLASS	CODE
Rebel 8	A
American 6	B
Rambler 6	C
Ambassador 8	H

LAST SIX DIGITS: Represent the basic production numbers

BODY NUMBER PLATE

A unit body number plate is riveted to the left front body hinge pillar above the lower hinge. Included are the body, model, trim, paint code and car code numbers which indicate the date of manufacture.

AMERICAN MOTORS CORP.
DETROIT MICH.

BODY NO. 3218
MODEL NO. 6018-2
TRIM NO. 42
PAINT NO. 15-72
E-10911

EXAMPLE:

3218	Production Sequence
60	Model Year (1960)
18-2	Body Style (4-Door Wagon)
42	Trim
15	Body Color
72	Roof Color

AMERICAN	CODE
2-Dr. Business Coupe-D	6002
2-Dr. Wagon-D	6004
2-Dr. Wagon-S	6004-1
4-Dr. Wagon-C	6304-2
4-Dr. Sedan-D	6005
4-Dr. Sedan-S	6005-1
4-Dr. Sedan-C	6005-2
2-Dr. Club Sedan-D	6006
2-Dr. Club Sedan-S	6006-1
2-Dr. Club Sedan-C	6006-2

RAMBLER CLASSIC 6	CODE
4-Dr. Sedan-D	6015
4-Dr. Sedan-S	6015-1
4-Dr. Sedan-C	6015-2
4-Dr. Wagon-D	6018
2-Dr. Wagon-S	6018-1
4-Dr. Wagon-C	6018-2
4-Dr. 2 Seat Wagon-S	6018-3
4-Dr. 2 Seat Wagon-C	6018-4
4-Dr. Hardtop Sedan-C	6019-2

RAMBLER REBEL V-8	CODE
4-Dr. Sedan-D	6025
4-Dr. Sedan-S	6025-1
4-Dr. Sedan-C	6025-2
2-Dr. Wagon-S	6028-1
2-Dr. Wagon-C	6028-2
2-Dr. Wagon-S	6028-3
4-Dr. Wagon-C	6028-4
4-Dr. Hardtop Sedan-C	6029-2

RAMBLER AMBASSADOR	CODE
4-Dr. Hardtop Wagon-C	6083-2
4-Dr. Sedan-D	6085
4-Dr. Sedan-S	6085-1
4-Dr. Sedan-C	6085-2
4-Dr. Wagon-D	6088
4-Dr. Wagon-S	6088-1
4-Dr. Wagon-C	6088-2
4-Dr. Wagon-S	6088-3
4-Dr. Wagon-C	6088-4
4-Dr. Hardtop Sedan-C	6089-2

D-Deluxe
S-Super
C-Custom

THE TRIM NUMBER furnishes the key to trim color and material for each model series.

AMERICAN TRIM

COLOR	CLOTH	VINYL	LEATHER	CODE
Gray	•	•		T001,T002
Gray		•		T011,T012
Blue	•	•		T003
Blue		•		T013
Green	•	•		T004
Green		•		T014
Red/Gray	•	•		T005
Red/Gray		•		T015

RAMBLER/REBEL TRIM

COLOR	CLOTH	VINYL	LEATHER	CODE
	•	•		T021,T041
	•	•		T027,T047
	•	•		T028,T048
	•	•		T029,T049
	•	•		T042,T022
Blue	•	•		T043,T023
Blue		•		T053,T033
Green	•	•		T044,T024
Green		•		T054,T034
Red	•	•		T045,T025
Red		•		T055,T035
	•	•		T046
		•		T031,T051
		•		T037,T057
		•		T038,T058
		•		T039,T059
		•		T052,T032
		•		T056

AMBASSADOR TRIM

COLOR	CLOTH	VINYL	LEATHER	CODE
Gray	•	•		T062,T064
Gray		•		T072
Blue	•	•		T063,T074
Blue		•		TO73
Red/Gray	•	•		T065
Red/Gray		•		T075

AMBASSADOR CUSTOM TRIM

COLOR	CLOTH	VINYL	LEATHER	CODE
Gray	•	•		T067,T068
Gray		•		T077,T078
Pink	•	•		T069
Pink		•		T079
Gold	•	•		T081
Gold		•		T091
Aqua	•	•		T082
Aqua		•		T092
Blue	•	•		T083
Blue		•		T093
Green	•	•		T084
Green		•		T094
Red	•	•		T085
Red		•		T095
	•	•		T086
		•		T096
White/Gray	•	•		T087,T088
White/Gray		•		T097,T098
Yellow/Gray	•	•		T089
Yellow/Gray		•		T099

THE PAINT CODE furnishes the key to the paint colors used on the car. A two-number code indicates the color of the car. A two-tone car has two sets of numbers. The first number is the body color, the second is the roof color.

COLOR	CODE
Classic Black	P1
Alamo Beige	P4
Autumn Yellow	P5
Lt. Chatsworth Green	P8
Lt. Placid Blue	P10
Oriental Red	P13
Aqua Mist Metallic	P15
Med. Westchester Green	P18
Med. Sovereign Blue	P19
Lt. Dartmouth Gray	P20
Med. Harvard Gray	P21
Echo Green Metallic	P23
Auburn Red Metallic	P24
Festival Rose	P25
Frost White	P72
Cinnamon Bronze	P94

ENGINE NUMBER

The engine code number is located on a machined surface of the engine block or stamped on a tag. These engines are marked with a code identifying the year, month, engine letter code, and day of manufacture. In the machining of cylinder blocks and crankshafts, it is sometimes necessary to machine the cylinder bores to .010" oversize, and the crankshaft main bearing journals or crank pins to .010" undersize.

EXAMPLE:

2	2	A	24
1960	Month	Code	Day

ENGINE NO.	NO. CYL.	CID	HORSE-POWER	COMP. RATIO	CARB
A	6	195.6	90	8.0:1	Holley 1 BC
C	6	195.6	127	8.7:1	Holley 1 BC
			138*		2 BC
E	8	327	250	8.7:1	Holley 2 BC
F	8		270	9.7:1	4 BC

* Optional 138 @ 4500 RPM with 2 BC

1961 AMC RAMBLER

1961 AMC RAMBLER

1961 AMC RAMBLER AMBASSADOR

1961 AMC RAMBLER AMBASSADOR

1961 AMC RAMBLER AMERICAN

1961 AMC RAMBLER AMERICAN

VEHICLE IDENTIFICATION NUMBER

AMC
B-221001

Commonly referred to as the VIN NUMBER, this series of numbers is stamped on a plate attached to the right wheelhouse panel.

THE FIRST DIGIT: Identifies the body class

Rebel 8	A
American 6	B
Rambler 6	C
Ambassador 8	H

LAST SIX DIGITS: Represent the basic production numbers

BODY NUMBER PLATE

A unit body number plate is riveted to the left front body hinge pillar above the lower hinge. Included are the body, model, trim, paint code and car code numbers which indicate the date of manufacture. The model number identifies the body style.

AMERICAN MOTORS CORP.
DETROIT MICH.

BODY NO. 3218
MODEL NO. 6118-2
TRIM NO. 125
PAINT NO. 30-72
E-000001

EXAMPLE:

3218	Production Sequence
61	Model Year (1961)
18-2	Body Style (4-Door Wagon)
125	Trim
30	Upper Body Color
72	Lower Body Color

AMERICAN	CODE
2-Dr. Business Coupe-D	6102
2-Dr. Wagon-D	6104
2-Dr. Wagon-S	6104-1
4-Dr. Wagon-C	6104-2
4-Dr. Sedan-D	6105
4-Dr. Sedan-S	6105-1
4-Dr. Sedan-C	6105-2
4-Dr. Sedan-C	6106-5
2-Dr. Club Sedan-D	6106
2-Dr. Club Sedan-S	6106-1
2-Dr. Club Sedan-C	6106-2
2-Dr. Convertible-C	6107-2
2-Dr. Convertible-C	6107-5
4-Dr. Sta. Wagon-D	6108
4-Dr. Sta. Wagon-S	6108-1
4-Dr. Sta. Wagon-C	6108-2

RAMBLER CLASSIC 6	CODE
4-Dr. Sedan-D	6115
4-Dr. Sedan-S	6115-1
4-Dr. Sedan-C	6115-2
4-Dr. Sedan-C	6115-5
4-Dr. Wagon-D	6118
4-Dr. Wagon-S, 2-Seat	6118-1
4-Dr. Wagon-C, 2-Seat	6118-2
4-Dr. Wagon-S, 4-Seat	6118-3
4-Dr. Wagon-C, 4-Seat	6118-4

RAMBLER CLASSIC 8	CODE
4-Dr. Sedan-D	6125
4-Dr. Sedan-S	6125-1
4-Dr. Sedan-C	6125-2
4-Dr. Sedan-C	6125-5
2-Dr. Wagon-S, 2-Seat	6128-1
2-Dr. Wagon-C, 2-Seat	6128-2
2-Dr. Wagon-S, 3-Seat	6128-3
5-Dr. Wagon-C, 3-Seat	6128-4

RAMBLER AMBASSADOR V-8	CODE
4-Dr. Sedan-D	6185
4-Dr. Sedan-S	6185-1
4-Dr. Sedan-C	6185-2
4-Dr. Sedan-C	6185-5
4-Dr. Wagon-S, 2-Seat	6188-1
4-Dr. Wagon-C, 2-Seat	6188-2
5-Dr. Wagon-S, 3-Seat	6188-3
5-Dr. Wagon-C, 3-Seat	6188-4

D-Deluxe
S-Super
C-Custom

THE TRIM NUMBER furnishes the key to trim color and material for each model series.

AMERICAN TRIM

COLOR	CLOTH	VINYL	LEATHER	CODE
Gray	•	•		T102
Gray		•		T112
Blue	•	•		T103
Blue		•		T113
Green	•	•		T104
Green		•		T114
Red/Gray	•	•		T105
Red/Gray		•		T115

CUSTOM TRIM

COLOR	CLOTH	VINYL	LEATHER	CODE
Gray/Black	•	•		T128
Gray/Black		•		T138
Red/Black	•	•		T129
Red/Black		•		T139
Beige/Brown	•	•		T141
Beige/Brown		•		T151
Aqua/Black	•	•		T142
Aqua/Black		•		T152
Blue	•	•		T143
Blue		•		T153
Green	•	•		T145
Green		•		T154
Green/Black	•	•		T146
Green/Black		•		T156
	•	•		T149
		•		T159

AMERICAN CUSTOM CONVERTIBLE TRIM

COLOR	CLOTH	VINYL	LEATHER	CODE
Silver		•		T127
Red		•		T137
Beige		•		T140
Aqua		•		T147
Blue		•		T148
Green		•		T150
Red		•		T157
Gray		•		T158
Yellow		•		T160

RAMBLER CLASSIC TRIM

COLOR	CLOTH	VINYL	LEATHER	CODE
Gray	•	•		T121,T122
Gray		•		T131,T132
Blue	•	•		T123
Blue		•		T133
Green	•	•		T124
Green		•		T134
Red/Black	•	•		T125
Red/Black		•		T135
Gold	•	•		T126
Gold		•		T136

AMBASSADOR TRIM

COLOR	CLOTH	VINYL	LEATHER	CODE
Gray/Black	•	•		T162
Gray/Black		•		T172
Blue	•	•		T163
Blue		•		T173
Green	•	•		T164
Green		•		T174
Red/Black	•	•		T165
Red/Black		•		T175
Beige	•	•		T166
Beige		•		T176

AMBASSADOR CUSTOM TRIM

COLOR	CLOTH	VINYL	LEATHER	CODE
Gray/Black	•	•		T168
Gray/Black		•		T178
Red/Black	•	•		T169,T185
Red/Black		•		T179,T195
Beige	•	•		T181
Beige		•		T191
Aqua/Black	•	•		T182
Aqua/Black		•		T192
Blue	•	•		T183
Blue		•		T193
Green	•	•		T184
Green		•		T194
Green/Black	•	•		T186
Green/Black		•		T196
Yellow/ Black	•	•		T189
Yellow/ Black		•		T199

THE PAINT CODE furnishes the key to the paint colors used on the car. A two-number code indicates the color of the car. A two-toned car has two sets of numbers. The first number is the body color, the second is the roof color.

COLOR	CODE
Classic Black	P1
Alamo Beige	P4
Chatsworth Green	P8
Aqua Mist Metallic	P15
Echo Green Metallic	P23
Valley Green Metallic	P26
Sonata Blue	P27
Berkeley Blue Metallic	P28
Whirlwind Tan Metallic	P29
Briarcliff Red	P30
Inca Silver Metallic	P31
Waikiki Gold	P32
Jasmine Rose	P33
Fire Glow Red Metallic	P34
Frost White	P72

ENGINE NUMBER

The engine code number is located on a machined surface of the engine block or stamped on a tag. These engines are marked with a code identifying the year, month, engine letter code, and day of manufacture. In the machining of cylinder blocks and crankshafts, it is sometimes necessary to machine the cylinder bores to .010" oversize, and the crankshaft main bearing journals or crank pins to .010" undersize.

EXAMPLE:

3	2	A	24
1961	Month	Code	Day

ENGINE NO.	NO. CYL.	CID	HORSE-POWER	COMP. RATIO	CARB
A	6	195.6	90	8.0:1	Holley 1 BC
B	6	195.6	125	8.7:1	Holley 1 BC
C	6	195.6	127	8.7:1	Holley 1 BC
			138*		2 BC
			215		4 BC
E	8	327	250	8.7:1	Holley 2 BC
F	8	327	270	9.7:1	Holley 4 BC

* Optional 138 @ 4500 RPM with 2 BC

1962 AMC RAMBLER

1962 AMC RAMBLER

1962 AMC RAMBLER AMBASSADOR

1962 AMC RAMBLER AMBASSADOR

1962 AMC RAMBLER AMERICAN

1962 AMC RAMBLER AMERICAN

1962 AMC

VEHICLE IDENTIFICATION NUMBER

AMC
B-375001

Commonly referred to as the VIN NUMBER, this series of numbers is stamped on a plate attached to the right wheelhouse panel.

THE FIRST DIGIT: Identifies the body class

BODY CLASS	CODE
American 6	B
Classic 6	C
Ambassador 8	H

LAST SIX DIGITS: Represent the basic production numbers

BODY NUMBER PLATE

A unit body number plate is riveted to the left front body hinge pillar above the lower hinge. Included are the body, model, trim, paint code and car code numbers which indicates the date of manufacture. The model number identifies the body style.

AMERICAN MOTORS CORP.
DETROIT MICH.

BODY NO. 324151
MODEL NO. 6218-2
TRIM NO. T264
PAINT NO. P37
E-00000

EXAMPLE:

324151	Production Sequence
62	Model Year (1962)
18-2	Body Style (4-Door Wagon)
T264	Trim
P37	Paint

AMERICAN	CODE
2-Dr. Business Coupe-D	6202
2-Dr. Convertible 400	6207-5
2-Dr. Wagon-D	6204
2-Dr. Wagon-C	6204-2
4-Dr. Wagon-D	6208
4-Dr. Wagon-C	6208-2
4-Dr. Wagon 400	6208-5
4-Dr. Sedan-D	6205
4-Dr. Sedan-C	6205-2
4-Dr. Sedan 400	6205-5
2-Dr. Club Sedan-D	6206
2-Dr. Club Sedan-C	6206-2
2-Dr. Club Sedan 400	6206-5

RAMBLER CLASSIC	CODE
4-Dr. Sedan-D	6215
4-Dr. Sedan-C	6215-2
4-Dr. Sedan 400	6215-5
4-Dr. Wagon-D	6218
4-Dr. Wagon-C	6218-2
4-Dr. Wagon-C, 3-Seat	6218-4
4-Dr. Wagon 400	6218-5
4-Dr. Club Sedan-D	6216
4-Dr. Club Sedan-C	6216-2
4-Dr. Club Sedan 400	6216-5

AMBASSADOR	CODE
4-Dr. Sedan-D	6285
4-Dr. Sedan-C	6285-2
4-Dr. Sedan 400	6285-5
2-Dr. Club Sedan-D	6286
2-Dr. Club Sedan-C	6286-2
2-Dr. Club Sedan 400	16286-5
4-Dr. Wagon-D	6288
4-Dr. Wagon-C	6288-2
5-Dr. Wagon 400	6288-5
5-Dr. Wagon 400	6288-6

D-Deluxe
S-Super
C-Custom

THE TRIM NUMBER furnishes the key to trim color and material for each model series.

AMBASSADOR 400 TRIM

COLOR	CLOTH	VINYL	LEATHER	CODE
Silver	•	•		T292,T242
Blue	•	•		T293,T243
Green	•	•		T294,T244
Red	•	•		T295,T245
Copper	•	•		T296,T246
Aqua	•	•		T298,T248
Gold	•	•		T299,T249

AMBASSADOR CUSTOM TRIM

COLOR	CLOTH	VINYL	LEATHER	CODE
Silver	•	•		T282
Blue	•	•		T283
Green	•	•		T284
Red	•	•		T285
Copper	•	•		T286

RAMBLER CLASSIC 400 TRIM

COLOR	CLOTH	VINYL	LEATHER	CODE
Silver	•	•		T272,T242
Blue	•	•		T273,T243
Green	•	•		T274,T244
Red	•	•		T275,T245
Copper	•	•		T276,T246
Aqua	•	•		T278,T248
Gold	•	•		T279,T249

RAMBLER CLASSIC TRIM

COLOR	CLOTH	VINYL	LEATHER	CODE
Silver	•	•		T262,T252*
Blue	•	•		T263
Green	•	•		T264
Red	•	•		T265
Copper	•	•		T266

*Deluxe only

RAMBLER AMERICAN 400 TRIM

COLOR	CLOTH	VINYL	LEATHER	CODE
Silver	•	•		T222,T242
Silver		•		T232*
Blue	•	•		T223,T243
Blue		•		T233*
Green	•	•		T224,T244
Green		•		T234*
Red	•	•		T225,T245
Red		•		T235*
Copper	•	•		T226,T246
Copper		•		T236*
Aqua	•	•		T228,T248
Aqua		•		T238*
Gold	•	•		T229,T249
Gold		•		T239*

*Convertible only

RAMBLER CUSTOM/DELUXE TRIM

COLOR	CLOTH	VINYL	LEATHER	CODE
Silver	•	•		T212,T202*
Blue	•	•		T213
Green	•	•		T214
Red	•	•		T215
Copper	•	•		T216

THE PAINT CODE furnishes the key to the paint colors used on the car. A two-number code indicates the color of the car. A two-toned car has two sets of numbers. The first number is the body color, the second is the roof color.

COLOR	CODE
Classic Black	P1
Aqua Mist Metallic*	P15
Sonata Blue	P27
Briarcliff Red	P30
Inca Silver Metallic	P31
Jasmine Rose*	P33
Baron Blue Metallic	P35
Glen Cove Green	P36
Elmhurst Green Metallic	P37
Algiers Rose Copper Metallic	P38
Villa Red Metallic*	P39
Majestic Blue Metallic	P40
Corsican Gold Metallic*	P41
Sirocco Beige	P42
Frost White	P72

* 400 only

ENGINE NUMBER

The engine code number is located on a machined surface of the engine block or stamped on a tag. These engines are marked with a code identifying the year, month, engine letter code, and day of manufacture. In the machining of cylinder blocks and crankshafts, it is sometimes necessary to machine the cylinder bores to .010" oversize, and the crankshaft main bearing journals or crank pins to .010" undersize.

EXAMPLE:

4	2	A	24
1962	Month	Code	Day

ENGINE NO.	NO. CYL.	CID	HORSE-POWER	COMP. RATIO	CARB
A	6	195.6	90	8.0:1	Holley 1 BC
B	6	195.6	125	8.7:1	Holley 1 BC
C	6	195.6	127	8.7:1	Holley 1 BC
			138*		2 BC
E	8	327	250	8.7:1	Holley 2 BC
F	8	327	270	9.7:1	Holley 4 BC

* Optional 138 @ 4500 RPM with 2 BC

1963 AMC RAMBLER AMBASSADOR

1963 AMC RAMBLER AMBASSADOR

1963 AMC RAMBLER AMERICAN

1963 AMC RAMBLER AMERICAN

1963 AMC RAMBLER CLASSIC

1963 AMC RAMBLER CLASSIC

VEHICLE IDENTIFICATION NUMBER

AMC
B-100551

Commonly referred to as the VIN NUMBER, this series of numbers is stamped on a plate attached to the right wheelhouse panel.

THE FIRST DIGIT: Identifies the body class

BODY CLASS	CODE
American 6	B
Rambler Classic 6	G
Ambassador 8	H
Classic V8	Z

LAST SIX DIGITS: Represent the basic production numbers

BODY NUMBER PLATE

A unit body number plate is riveted to the left front body hinge pillar above the lower hinge. Included are the body, model, trim, paint code and car code numbers which indicate the date of manufacture. The model number identifies the body style.

AMERICAN MOTORS CORP.
DETROIT MICH.

BODY NO. 243511
MODEL NO. 6318-2
TRIM NO. 362
PAINT NO. 72
E-000001

EXAMPLE:

243511	Production Sequence
63	Model Year (1963)
18-2	Body Style (4-Door Wagon)
362	Trim
72	Paint

AMERICAN	CODE
2-Dr. Business Coupe 220	6302
2-Dr. Sta. Wagon 220	6304
2-Dr. Sta. Wagon 330	6304-2
4-Dr. Sedan 220	6305
4-Dr. Sedan 330	6305-2
4-Dr. Sedan 440	6305-5
2-Dr. Club Sedan 220	6306
2-Dr. Club Sedan 330	6306-2
2-Dr. Club Sedan 440	6306-5
2-Dr. Convertible 440	6307-5
4-Dr. Sta. Wagon 220	6308
4-Dr. Sta. Wagon 330	6308-2
4-Dr. Sta. Wagon 440	6308-5
2-Dr. Hardtop 440	6309-5
2-Dr. Hardtop 440H	6309-7

CLASSIC V-6/V-8	CODE
4-Dr. Sedan 550	6315
4-Dr. Sedan 660	6315-2
4-Dr. Sedan 770	6315-5
2-Dr. Club Sedan 550	6316
2-Dr. Club Sedan 660	6316-2
2-Dr. Club Sedan 770	6316-5
4-Dr. Sta. Wagon 550	6318
2-Dr. Sta. Wagon 660	6318-2
4-Dr. Sta. Wagon 660	6318-4
4-Dr. Sta. Wagon 770	6318-5

AMBASSADOR	CODE
4-Dr. Sedan 800	6385
4-Dr. Sedan 880	6385-2
4-Dr. Sedan 990	6385-5
2-Dr. Club Sedan 800	6386
2-Dr. Club Sedan 880	6386-2
2-Dr. Club Sedan 990	6386-5
4-Dr. Sta. Wagon 800	6388
4-Dr. Sta. Wagon 880	6388-2
4-Dr. Sta. Wagon 990	6388-5
4-Dr. Sta. Wagon 990	6388-6

THE TRIM NUMBER furnishes the key to trim color and material for each model series.

AMERICAN TRIM

COLOR	CLOTH	VINYL	LEATHER	CODE
Silver/ Black	•	•		T312,T302*
Blue	•	•		T313
Aqua	•	•		T314
Red	•	•		T315
Ivory	•	•		T316

*220 only

AMERICAN 440/440-H TRIM

COLOR	CLOTH	VINYL	LEATHER	CODE
Silver/ Black	•	•		T322,T342
Blue	•	•		T323,T343
Aqua	•	•		T324,T344
Red	•	•		T325,T345
Gold	•	•		T326,T346
Coral	•	•		T327,T347

AMERICAN CONVERTIBLE TRIM

COLOR	CLOTH	VINYL	LEATHER	CODE
Silver/ Black		•		T332
Blue		•		T333
Aqua		•		T334
Red		•		T335
Gold		•		T336
Coral		•		T337

RAMBLER CLASSIC 550 TRIM

COLOR	CLOTH	VINYL	LEATHER	CODE
Silver/ Black	•	•		T352
Blue	•	•		T353
Aqua	•	•		T354

RAMBLER CLASSIC 660 TRIM

COLOR	CLOTH	VINYL	LEATHER	CODE
Silver/ Black	•	•		T362
Blue	•	•		T363
Aqua	•	•		T364
Red	•	•		T365
Ivory	•	•		T366

RAMBLER CLASSIC 770 TRIM

COLOR	CLOTH	VINYL	LEATHER	CODE
Silver/ Black	•	•		T372,T342
Blue	•	•		T373,T343
Aqua	•	•		T374,T344
Red	•	•		T375,T345
Gold	•	•		T376,T346
Coral	•	•		T377,T347

AMBASSADOR 880 TRIM

COLOR	CLOTH	VINYL	LEATHER	CODE
Silver/ Black	•	•		T382
Blue	•	•		T383
Aqua	•	•		T384
Red	•	•		T385
Gold	•	•		T386

AMBASSADOR 990 TRIM

COLOR	CLOTH	VINYL	LEATHER	CODE
Silver/ Black	•	•		T392,T342
Blue	•	•		T393,T343
Aqua	•	•		T394,T344
Red	•	•		T395,T345
Gold	•	•		T396,T346
Coral	•	•		T397,T347

RAMBLER CLASSIC 550 TRIM

COLOR	CLOTH	VINYL	LEATHER	CODE
Silver/ Black	•	•		T352
Blue	•	•		T353
Aqua	•	•		T354

RAMBLER CLASSIC 660 TRIM

COLOR	CLOTH	VINYL	LEATHER	CODE
Silver/ Black	•	•		T362
Blue	•	•		T363
Aqua	•	•		T364
Red	•	•		T365
Ivory	•	•		T366

RAMBLER CLASSIC 770 TRIM

COLOR	CLOTH	VINYL	LEATHER	CODE
Silver/ Black	•	•		T372,T342
Blue	•	•		T373,T343
Aqua	•	•		T374,T344
Red	•	•		T375,T345
Gold	•	•		T376,T377
Coral	•	•		T377,T347

AMBASSADOR 880 TRIM

COLOR	CLOTH	VINYL	LEATHER	CODE
Silver/ Black	•	•		T382
Blue	•	•		T383
Aqua	•	•		T384
Red	•	•		T385
Gold	•	•		T386

AMBASSADOR 990 TRIM

COLOR	CLOTH	VINYL	LEATHER	CODE
Silver/ Black	•	•		T392,T342
Blue	•	•		T393,T343
Aqua	•	•		T394,T344
Red	•	•		T395,T345
Gold	•	•		T396,T346
Coral	•	•		T397,T347

THE PAINT CODE furnishes the key to the paint colors used on the car. A two-number code indicates the color of the car. A two-tone car has two sets of numbers. The first number is the body color, the second is the roof color.

COLOR	CODE
Classic Black	P1
Briarcliff Red	P30
Majestic Blue Metallic	P40
Corsican Gold Metallic	P41
Sceptre Silver Metallic	P43
Bahama Blue	P44
Cape Cod Blue Metallic	P45
Palisade Green	P46
Aegean Aqua Metallic	P47
Calais Coral Metallic	P48
Valencia Ivory	P49
Concord Maroon Metallic	P50
Frost White	P72

ENGINE NUMBER

The engine code number is located on a machined surface of the engine block or stamped on a tag. These engines are marked with a code identifying the year, month, engine letter code, and day of manufacture. In the machining of cylinder blocks and crankshafts, it is sometimes necessary to machine the cylinder bores to .010" oversize, and the crankshaft main bearing journals or crank pins to .010" undersize.

EXAMPLE:

5	2	A	24
1963	Month	Code	Day

ENGINE NO.	NO. CYL.	CID	HORSE-POWER	COMP. RATIO	CARB
B,C	6	195.6	125	8.7:1	1 BC
B,C	6	195.6	138	8.7:1	2 BC
A	6	195.6	90	8.0:1	1 BC
E	8	327	250	8.7:1	2 BC
F	8	327	270	9.7:1	4 BC
G	8	287	198	8.7:1	2 BC

1964 AMC RAMBLER AMBASSADOR

1964 AMC RAMBLER AMBASSADOR

1964 AMC RAMBLER AMERICAN

1964 AMC RAMBLER AMERICAN

1964 AMC RAMBLER CLASSIC

1964 AMC RAMBLER CLASSIC

VEHICLE IDENTIFICATION NUMBER

AMC
B-155001

Commonly referred to as the VIN NUMBER, this series of numbers is stamped on a plate attached to the right wheelhouse panel.

THE FIRST DIGIT: Identifies the body class

BODY CLASS	CODE
American 6	B
Rambler 6 Classic	G
Ambassador 8	H
Classic V8	Z

LAST SIX DIGITS: Represent the basic production numbers

BODY NUMBER PLATE

A unit body number plate is riveted to the left front body hinge pillar above the lower hinge. Included are the body, model, trim, paint code and car code numbers which indicate the date of manufacture. The model number identifies the body style.

AMERICAN MOTORS CORP.
DETROIT MICH.

BODY NO. R 000001
MODEL NO. 6415-2
TRIM NO. 472
PAINT NO. 72
E-000001

EXAMPLE:

000001	Production Sequence
64	Model Year (1964)
15-2	Style (4-Dr. Sedan)
472	Trim
72	Paint

AMERICAN	CODE
2-Dr. Convertible 440	6407-5
2-Dr. Wagon 220	6408
4-Dr. Wagon 330	6408-2
4-Dr. Sedan 220	6405
4-Dr. Sedan 330	6405-1
4-Dr. Sedan 440	6405-2
2-Dr. Club Sedan 220	6406
2-Dr. Club Sedan 330	6406-2
2-Dr. Hardtop 440	6409-5
2-Dr. Hardtop 440H	6409-7

RAMBLER CLASSIC	CODE
4-Dr. Sedan 550	6415
4-Dr. Sedan 660	6415-2
4-Dr. Sedan 770	6415-5
4-Dr. Wagon 550	6418
2-Dr. Wagon 660	6418-2
4-Dr. Wagon 770	6418-5
2-Dr. Club Sedan 550	6416
2-Dr. Club Sedan 660	6416-2
4-Dr. Club Sedan 770	6416-5
2-Dr. Hardtop 770	6419-5
2-Dr. Hardtop Typhoon 770	6419-7

AMBASSADOR	CODE
4-Dr. Wagon 990	6488-5
4-Dr. Sedan 990	6485
2-Dr. Hardtop 990	6489-5
2-Dr. Hardtop 990H	6489-7

THE TRIM NUMBER furnishes the key to trim color and material for each model series.

AMERICAN 220/330 TRIM

COLOR	CLOTH	VINYL	LEATHER	CODE
Silver/ Black	•	•		T432,T422*
Blue	•	•		T433
Green	•	•		T434
Red	•	•		T435
Gold	•	•		T436
Turquoise	•	•		T438

* 220 Only

AMERICAN 440/440-H TRIM

COLOR	CLOTH	VINYL	LEATHER	CODE
Silver/ Black	•	•		T442
Black	•	•		T441
Blue	•	•		T443
Green	•	•		T444
Red	•	•		T445
Gold	•	•		T446
Maroon	•	•		T447
Turquoise	•	•		T448

RAMBLER CLASSIC 550 TRIM

COLOR	CLOTH	VINYL	LEATHER	CODE
Silver/ Black	•	•		T452
Blue	•	•		T453
Green	•	•		T454

RAMBLER CLASSIC 660 TRIM

COLOR	CLOTH	VINYL	LEATHER	CODE
Silver/ Black	•	•		T462
Blue	•	•		T463
Green	•	•		T464
Red	•	•		T465
Gold	•	•		T466
Turquoise	•	•		T468

RAMBLER CLASSIC 770 TRIM

COLOR	CLOTH	VINYL	LEATHER	CODE
Silver/ Black	•	•		T472
Black	•	•		T471
Blue	•	•		T473
Green	•	•		T474
Red	•	•		T475
Gold	•	•		T476
Maroon	•	•		T477
Turquoise	•	•		T478

AMBASSADOR 990/990-H TRIM

COLOR	CLOTH	VINYL	LEATHER	CODE
Silver/ Black	•	•		T492
Black	•	•		T491
Blue	•	•		T493
Green	•	•		T494
Red	•	•		T495
Gold	•	•		T496
Maroon	•	•		T497
Turquoise	•	•		T498

THE PAINT CODE furnishes the key to the paint colors used on the car. A two-number code indicates the color of the car. A two-tone car has two sets of numbers. The first number is the body color, the second is the roof color.

COLOR	CODE
Classic Black	P1
Solar Yellow Metallic	P13A
Sceptre Silver Metallic	P43
Rampart Red	P51
Sentry Blue Metallic	P52A
Forum Blue	P53
Woodside Green Metallic	P54A
Westminster Green	P55
Aurora Turquoise	P56
Lancelot Turquoise Metallic	P57
Bengal Ivory	P58
Emperor Gold Metallic	P59
Contessa Rose Metallic	P60A
Vintage Maroon Metallic	P61
Frost White	P72

ENGINE NUMBER

The engine code number is located on a machined surface of the engine block or stamped on a tag. These engines are marked with a code identifying the year, month, engine letter code, and day of manufacture. In the machining of cylinder blocks and crankshafts, it is sometimes necessary to machine the cylinder bores to .010" oversize, and the crankshaft main bearing journals or crank pins to .010" undersize.

EXAMPLE:

6	2	A	24
1964	Month	Code	Day

ENGINE NO.	NO. CYL.	CID	HORSE-POWER	COMP. RATIO	CARB
B	6	195.6	125	8.7:1	1 BC
B	6	195.6	138	8.7:1	2 BC
C	6	195.6	127	8.7:1	1 BC
C	6	195.6	138	8.7:1	2 BC
A	6	195.6	90	8.0:1	
L	6	232	145	8.5:1	1 BC
G	8	287	198	8.7:1	2 BC
E	8	327	250	8.7:1	2 BC
F	8	327	270	9.7:1	4 BC

1965 AMC RAMBLER AMBASSADOR

1965 AMC RAMBLER AMBASSADOR

1965 AMC RAMBLER AMERICAN

1965 AMC RAMBLER AMERICAN

1965 AMC RAMBLER CLASSIC

1965 AMC RAMBLER CLASSIC

VEHICLE IDENTIFICATION NUMBER

AMC
H100551

Commonly referred to as the VIN NUMBER, this series of numbers is stamped on a plate attached to the right wheelhouse panel.

THE FIRST DIGIT: Identifies the body class

BODY CLASS	CODE
Ambassador 8-287	E
Ambassador 8-327	H
American 6-196	P
American 6-199	Q
American 6-232	W
Classic 6-199	J
Classic 6-232	L
Classic 8-287	Z
Classic 8-327	U
Marlin 6	2
Marlin 8-287	3
Marlin 8-327	4
Ambassador 6-232	S

LAST SIX DIGITS: Represent the basic production numbers

BODY NUMBER PLATE

A unit body number plate is riveted to the left front body hinge pillar above the lower hinge. Included are the body, model, trim, paint code and car code numbers which indicate the date of manufacture. The model number identifies the body style.

AMERICAN MOTORS CORP.
DETROIT MICH.

BODY NO. 000005
MODEL NO. 6505-2
TRIM NO. 532
PAINT NO. P1-72
E-000005

EXAMPLE:

000005	Production Sequence
65	Model Year (1965)
05-2	Style (4-Dr. Sedan)
532	Trim
P1-72	Color

AMERICAN	CODE
4-Dr. Sta. Wagon 220	6508
4-Dr. Sta. Wagon 330	6508-2
4-Dr. Sedan 220	6505
4-Dr. Sedan 330	6505-2
4-Dr. Sedan 440	6505-5
2-Dr. Club Sedan 220	6506
2-Dr. Club Sedan 330	6506-2
2-Dr. Convertible 440	6507-5
2-Dr. Hardtop 440	6509-5
2-Dr. Hardtop 440H	6509-7

RAMBLER CLASSIC	CODE
4-Dr. Sedan 550	6515
4-Dr. Sedan 660	6515-2
4-Dr. Sedan 770	6515-5
4-Dr. Sta. Wagon 550	6518
4-Dr. Sta. Wagon 660	6518-2
4-Dr. Sta. Wagon 770	6518-5
2-Dr. Club Sedan 550	6516
2-Dr. Club Sedan 660	6516-2
4-Dr. Convertible 770	6517-5
2-Dr. Hardtop 770	6519-5
2-Dr. Hardtop 770H	6519-7

AMBASSADOR	CODE
4-Dr. Sedan 880	6585-2
4-Dr. Sedan 990	6585-5
4-Dr. Sta. Wagon 880	6588-2
4-Dr. Sta. Wagon 990	6588-5
2-Dr. Club Sedan 880	6586
4-Dr. Convertible 990	6587-5
2-Dr. Hardtop 990	6589-5
2-Dr. Hardtop 990H	6589-7

MARLIN	CODE
2-Dr. Fastback	6559-7

THE TRIM NUMBER furnishes the key to the trim color and material for each model series.

AMERICAN TRIM

COLOR	CLOTH	VINYL	LEATHER	CODE
Black/Gray	•	•		T522
Black/White	•	•		T532
Blue	•	•		T533
Green	•	•		T534
Red	•	•		T535
Taupe	•	•		T536
Aqua	•	•		T537

AMERICAN 440/440-H TRIM

COLOR	CLOTH	VINYL	LEATHER	CODE
Black	•	•		T541
Blue	•	•		T543
Green	•	•		T544
Red	•	•		T545
Cordo./ Taupe	•	•		T546
Aqua	•	•		T547
Black/White	•	•		T548

RAMBLER CLASSIC 550 TRIM

COLOR	CLOTH	VINYL	LEATHER	CODE
Black/White	•	•		T552
Blue	•	•		T553
Aqua	•	•		T557

RAMBLER CLASSIC 660 TRIM

COLOR	CLOTH	VINYL	LEATHER	CODE
Black/White	•	•		T562
Blue	•	•		T563
Green	•	•		T564
Red	•	•		T565
Cordo./ Taupe	•	•		T566
Aqua	•	•		T567

RAMBLER CLASSIC 770/770-H TRIM

COLOR	CLOTH	VINYL	LEATHER	CODE
Black	•	•		T571
Blue	•	•		T573
Green	•	•		T574
Red	•	•		T575
Cordo./ Taupe	•	•		T576
Aqua	•	•		T577
Black/ White	•	•		T578

AMBASSADOR 880 TRIM

COLOR	CLOTH	VINYL	LEATHER	CODE
Black/White	•	•		T582
Blue	•	•		T583
Green	•	•		T584
Red	•	•		T585
Cordo./ Taupe	•	•		T586
Aqua	•	•		T587

AMBASSADOR 990/990-H TRIM

COLOR	CLOTH	VINYL	LEATHER	CODE
Black	•	•		T591
Blue	•	•		T593
Green	•	•		T594
Red	•	•		T595
Cordo./ Taupe	•	•		T596
Aqua	•	•		T597
Turquoise	•	•		T598

THE PAINT CODE furnishes the key to the paint colors used on the car. A two-number code indicates the color of the car. A two-tone car has two sets of numbers. The first number is the body color, the second is the roof color.

COLOR	CODE
Classic Black	P1A
Antigua Red	P3A
Mystic Gold Metallic	P4A
Legion Blue	P5A
Viscount Blue Metallic	P5A
Seaside Aqua	P7A
Marina Aqua Metallic	P8A
Atlantis Aqua Metallic	P9A
Montego Rose	P10A
Barcelona Taupe Metallic	P11A
Corral Cordovan Metallic	P12A
Solar Yellow	P13A
Silver Metallic	P14A
Woodside Green Metallic	P54A
Frost White	P72A

ENGINE NUMBER

The engine code number is located on a machined surface of the engine block or stamped on a tag. These engines are marked with a code identifying the year, month, engine letter code, and day of manufacture. In the machining of cylinder blocks and crankshafts, it is sometimes necessary to machine the cylinder bores to .010" oversize, and the crankshaft main bearing journals or crank pins to .010" undersize.

EXAMPLE:

7	2	A	24
1965	Month	Code	Day

ENGINE NO.	NO. CYL.	CID	HORSE-POWER	COMP. RATIO	CARB
L	6	232	145	8.5:1	1 BC
L	6	232	155	8.5:1	2 BC
J	6	199	128	8.5:1	1 BC
A	6	195.6	90	8.0:1	
B	6	195.6	125	8.7:1	
B	6	195.6	138	8.7:1	
G	8	287	198	8.7:1	2 BC
F	8	327	270	9.7:1	4 BC

1966 AMC MARLIN

1966 AMC MARLIN

1966 AMC RAMBLER AMBASSADOR

1966 AMC RAMBLER AMBASSADOR

1966 AMC RAMBLER AMERICAN

1966 AMC RAMBLER AMERICAN

1966 AMC RAMBLER CLASSIC

1966 AMC RAMBLER CLASSIC

VEHICLE IDENTIFICATION NUMBER

AMC
A6KS52B100001

The VIN is stamped and embossed on a stainless steel plate welded to the right front fender under the hood. It consists of the manufacturer's symbol, model year, transmission type, body identity, class of body, series and engine identity, and a sequential production number for each series.

THE FIRST DIGIT: Identifies the division (A for American Motors Corp.)

THE SECOND DIGIT: Identifies the model year (1966)

THE THIRD DIGIT: Identifies the assembly plant

ASSEMBLY PLANT	CODE
Brampton, Ont., CAN	B
Kenosha, WI	K

THE FOURTH DIGIT: Identifies the transmission type

TRANSMISSION	CODE
Automatic Column Shift (3 speed)	A
Floor Shift Automatic (3 speed)	C
Four Speed Floor Shift	F
Overdrive Column Shift (3 speed)	O
Standard Column Shift (3 speed)	S

THE FIFTH DIGIT: Identifies the body type

BODY TYPE	CODE
2-Dr. Wagon	4
4-Dr. Sedan	5
2-Dr. Sedan	6
2-Dr. Convertible	7
4-Dr. Wagon	8
2-Dr. Hardtop	9

THE SIXTH DIGIT: Identifies the model

MODEL	CODE
220/550	0
880	2
440/770/990	5
Rebel, Marlin, DPL, Rogue	7

THE SEVENTH DIGIT: Identifies the series and engine

AMERICAN	CODE
199 CID, OHV 6, 1-BC	A
232 CID, OHV 6, 2-BC	B
290 CID, V-8, 2-BC	C

CLASSIC	CODE
199 CID OHV 6	E
232 CID OHV 6	F
232 CID OHV 6	G
287 CID V-8	H
327 CID V-8	J
327 CID V-8	K

AMBASSADOR	CODE
232 CID, OHV 6, 2-BC	M
287 CID, V-8, 2-BC	N
327 CID, V-8, 2-BC	P
327 CID, V-8, 4-BC (H.C.)	Q

MARLIN	CODE
232 CID, OHV 6, 2-BC	S
287 CID, V8, 2-BC	T
327 CID, V8, 4-BC (H.C.)	U
232 CID, OHV 6, 1-BC	V
327 CID, V-8, 2-BC (L.C.)	W

LAST SIX DIGITS: Represent the basic production number

BODY NUMBER PLATE

A unit body number plate is riveted to the left front door below the door lock and is visible when the door is open. This body plate includes the model, body, trim, paint code, and car built sequence numbers. The model number identifies the body style.

AMERICAN MOTORS CORP.
DETROIT MICH.

BODY NO. A000036
MODEL NO. 6688-5
TRIM NO. 697
PAINT NO. 20
W0000145

EXAMPLE:

A000036	Production Sequence
66	Model Year (1966)
88-5	Body Type (4-Door Wagon)
697	Trim
20	Paint

AMERICAN	CODE
4-Dr. Wagon 220	6608
4-Dr. Wagon 440	6608-5
4-Dr. Sedan 220	6605
4-Dr. Sedan 440	6605-5
2-Dr. Sedan 220	6606
2-Dr. Sedan 440	6606-5
2-Dr. Convertible 440	6607-5
2-Dr. Hardtop 440	6609-5
2-Dr. Hardtop Rogue	6609-7

RAMBLER CLASSIC	CODE
4-Dr. Sedan 550 6615	
4-Dr. Sedan 770	6615-5
4-Dr. Wagon 550	6618
4-Dr. Wagon 770	6618-5
2-Dr. Club Sedan 550	6616
4-Dr. Convertible 770	6617-5
2-Dr. Hardtop 770	6619-5
2-Dr. Hardtop Rebel	6619-7

AMBASSADOR	CODE
4-Dr. Wagon 880	6688-2
4-Dr. Wagon 990	6688-5
4-Dr. Sedan 880	6685-2
4-Dr. Sedan 990	6685-5
2-Dr. Club Sedan 880	6686-2
2-Dr. Convertible 990	6687-5
2-Dr. Hardtop 990	6689-5
2-Dr. Hardtop DPL	6689-7

MARLIN	CODE
2-Dr. Fastback	6659-7

THE TRIM NUMBER furnishes the key to the trim color and material for each model series.

MARLIN TRIM

COLOR	CLOTH	VINYL	LEATHER	CODE
Black	•	•		T691
Red	•	•		T695
Aqua	•	•		T697
White	•	•		T698
Saddle		•		T699

AMERICAN TRIM

COLOR	CLOTH	VINYL	LEATHER	CODE
Blue	•	•		T623
Black/White	•	•		T628
Tan	•	•		T629

AMERICAN 440 TRIM

COLOR	CLOTH	VINYL	LEATHER	CODE
Black	•	•		T641
Blue	•	•		T643
Green	•	•		T644
Red	•	•		T645
Aqua	•	•		T647
Saddle	•	•		T649
White		•		T648

AMERICAN 440/ROGUE

COLOR	CLOTH	VINYL	LEATHER	CODE
Black	•			T641*
Blue	•			T643*
Green	•			T644*
Red	•			T645*
Aqua	•			T647*
White	•			T648*
Saddle	•			T649*

* Convertible only, all vinyl

RAMBLER CLASSIC 550 TRIM

COLOR	CLOTH	VINYL	LEATHER	CODE
Black/White	•	•		T653
Blue	•	•		T658
Tan	•	•		T659

RAMBLER CLASSIC 770 TRIM

COLOR	CLOTH	VINYL	LEATHER	CODE
Black	•	•		T671
Blue	•	•		T673
Green	•	•		T674
Red	•	•		T675
Black/Mauve	•	•		T676
Aqua	•	•		T677
Saddle	•	•		T679

RAMBLER CLASSIC 770/REBEL TRIM

COLOR	CLOTH	VINYL	LEATHER	CODE
Black	•	•		T671*
Black/Mauve	•	•		T676
Blue	•	•		T673*
Green	•	•		T674
Red	•	•		T675*
Aqua	•	•		T677*
White	•	•		T678
Saddle	•	•		T679*

* Rebel only

AMBASSADOR 880 TRIM

COLOR	CLOTH	VINYL	LEATHER	CODE
Blue	•	•		T683
Green	•	•		T684
Red	•	•		T685
Aqua	•	•		T687
Saddle	•	•		T689

AMBASSADOR 990 TRIM

COLOR	CLOTH	VINYL	LEATHER	CODE
Black	•	•		T691
Black/Mauve	•	•		T696
Blue	•	•		T693
Green	•	•		T694
Red	•	•		T695
Aqua	•	•		T697
White	•	•		T698
Saddle	•	•		T699

AMBASSADOR 990/DPL TRIM

COLOR	CLOTH	VINYL	LEATHER	CODE
Black	•	•		T691*
Blue	•	•		T693*
Green	•	•		T694
Red	•	•		T695*
Black/Mauve	•	•		T696
Aqua	•	•		T697*
White	•	•		T698
Saddle	•	•		T699*

* DPL only

THE PAINT CODE furnishes the key to the paint colors used on the car. A two-number code indicates the color of the car. A two-tone car has two sets of numbers. The first number is the body color, the second is the roof color.

COLOR	CODE
Classic Black	1
Antigua Red	3
Brisbane Blue Metallic	15
Britannia Blue Metallic	16
Crescent Green	17
Granada Green Metallic	18
Balboa Aqua	19
Cortez Aqua Metallic	20
Marquessa Mauve Metallic	21
Samoa Gold Metallic	23
Caballero Tan Metallic	24
Apollo Yellow	25
Sungold Metallic	37
Frost White	72

ENGINE NUMBER

The engine code number is located on a machined surface of the engine block or stamped on a tag. These engines are marked with a code identifying the year, month, engine letter code, and day of manufacture. In the machining of cylinder blocks and crankshafts, it is sometimes necessary to machine the cylinder bores to .010" oversize, and the crankshaft main bearing journals or crank pins to .010" undersize.

EXAMPLE:

8	2	A	24
1966	Month	Code	Day

ENGINE NO.	NO. CYL.	CID	HORSE-POWER	COMP. RATIO	CARB
L	6	232	145	8.5:1	1 BC
L	6	232	155	8.5:1	1 BC
J	6	199	128	8.5:1	1 BC
G	8	287	198	8.7:1	2 BC
E	8	327	250	8.7:1	2 BC
F	8	327	270	9.7:1	4 BC
H	8	290	200	9.7:1	2 BC
H	8	290	225	10.0:1	4 BC

1967 AMC MARLIN

1967 AMC MARLIN

1967 AMC RAMBLER AMBASSADOR

1967 AMC RAMBLER AMBASSADOR

1967 AMC RAMBLER AMERICAN

1967 AMC RAMBLER AMERICAN

1967 AMC RAMBLER REBEL

1967 AMC RAMBLER REBEL

VEHICLE IDENTIFICATION NUMBER

AMC
A7KS52B100551

The VIN is stamped and embossed on a stainless steel plate welded to the right front fender under the hood. It consists of the manufacturer's symbol, model year symbol, transmission type, body style, body class, series and engine, and a sequential production number for each series.

THE FIRST DIGIT: Identifies the division(A for American Motors Corp.)

THE SECOND DIGIT: Identifies the model year (1967)

THE THIRD DIGIT: Identifies the assembly plant

ASSEMBLY PLANT	CODE
Brampton, Ont., CAN	B
Kenosha, WI	K

THE FOURTH DIGIT: Identifies the transmission type

TRANSMISSION	CODE
Standard Column Shift (3 speed)	S
Overdrive Column Shift (3 speed)	O
Automatic Column Shift (3 speed)	A
Floor Shift Automatic (3 speed)	C
Four Speed Floor Shift w/console	F
Four Speed Floor Shift Floor Mounted	M

THE FIFTH DIGIT: Identifies the body type

BODY TYPE	CODE
4-Dr. Sedan	5
2-Dr. Sedan	6
2-Dr. Convertible	7
4-Dr. Sta. Wagon	8
2-Dr. Hardtop	9

THE SIXTH DIGIT: Identifies the model

MODEL	CODE
550/220	0
880	2
440/770/990	5
Marlin, DPL, Rogue, SST	7

THE SEVENTH DIGIT: Identifies the series and engine

AMERICAN	CODE
199 CID, OHV 6, 1-BC	A
232 CID, OHV 6, 2-BC	B
290 CID, V-8, 2-BC	C
290 CID, V-8, 4-BC	D
232 CID, OHV 6, 1-BC	E
343 CID, V-8, 4-BC	X

AMBASSADOR	CODE
232 CID, OHV 6, 2-BC	M
290 CID, V-8, 2-BC	N
232 CID, OHV, 1-BC	P
343 CID, V-8, 4-BC (H.C.)	Q
343 CID, V-8, 2-BC	R

REBEL	CODE
232 CID, OHV 6, 1-BC	F
232 CID, OHV 6, 2-BC	G
290 CID, V-8, 2-BC	H
343 CID, V-8, 2-BC	J
343 CID, V-8, 4-BC	K

MARLIN	CODE
232 CID, OHV 6, 2-BC	T
290 CID, V8, 2-BC	U
343 CID, V8, 4-BC (H.C.)	W
232 CID, OHV 6, 1-BC	S
343 CID, V-8, 2-BC (L.C.)	V

LAST SIX DIGITS: Represent the basic production number

BODY NUMBER PLATE

A unit body number plate is riveted to the left front door below the door lock and is visible when the door is open. This body plate includes the model, body, trim, paint code, and car built sequence numbers.

AMERICAN MOTORS CORP.
DETROIT MICH.

BODY NO. 000024
MODEL NO. 6788-5
TRIM NO. 799
PAINT NO. 36
W000032

EXAMPLE:

000024	Production Sequence
67	Model Year (1967)
88-5	Model (4-Dr. Station Wagon)
799	Trim
36	Paint

AMERICAN	CODE
4-Dr. Sedan 220	6705
4-Dr. Sedan 440	6705-5
2-Dr. Sport Sedan 220	6706
2-Dr. Sport Sedan 440	6706-5
2-Dr. Convertible Rogue	6707-7
4-Dr. Sta. Wagon 220	6708
4-Dr. Sta. Wagon 440	6708-5
2-Dr. Hardtop 440	6709-5
2-Dr. Hardtop Rogue	6709-7

RAMBLER REBEL	CODE
4-Dr. Sedan 550	6715
4-Dr. Sedan 770	6715-5
2-Dr. Sport Sedan 550	6716
4-Dr. Convertible SST	6717-7
4-Dr. Sta. Wagon 550	6718
4-Dr. Sta. Wagon 770	6718-5
2-Dr. Hardtop 770	6719-5
2-Dr. Hardtop SST	6719-7

RAMBLER AMBASSADOR — **CODE**

Model	Code
4-Dr. Sedan 880	6785-2
4-Dr. Sedan 990	6785-5
2-Dr. Sport Sedan 880	6786-2
2-Dr. Convertible DPL	6787-7
4-Dr. Sta. Wagon 880	6788-2
4-Dr. Sta. Wagon 990	6788-5
2-Dr. Hardtop 990	6789-5
2-Dr. Hardtop DPL	6789-7

MARLIN — **CODE**

Model	Code
2-Dr. Hardtop	6759-7

THE TRIM NUMBER furnishes the key to trim color and material for each model series.

AMERICAN 220 TRIM

COLOR	CLOTH	VINYL	LEATHER	CODE
Blue	•	•		T723
Black	•	•		T728
Tan	•	•		T729

AMERICAN 440/ROGUE TRIM

COLOR	CLOTH	VINYL	LEATHER	CODE
Black	•	•		T741,T748
Blue	•	•		T743
Green	•	•		T744
Red	•	•		T745
Aqua	•	•		T747
Tan	•	•		T749

RAMBLER REBEL 550 TRIM

COLOR	CLOTH	VINYL	LEATHER	CODE
Blue	•	•		T753
Black	•	•		T753
Tan/Black	•	•		T753

RAMBLER 770/SST/SST CUSTOM TRIM

COLOR	CLOTH	VINYL	LEATHER	CODE
Black	•	•		T771
Blue	•	•		T773
Green	•			T774
Red	•	•		T775
Burgundy	•	•		T776
Aqua	•			T777
White		•		T778
Tan	•	•		T779

AMBASSADOR 880 TRIM

COLOR	CLOTH	VINYL	LEATHER	CODE
Black	•	•		T781
Blue	•	•		T783
Aqua	•			T787
Tan	•	•		T789

AMBASSADOR 990/DPL TRIM

COLOR	CLOTH	VINYL	LEATHER	CODE
Black	•	•		T791
Blue	•	•		T793
Green	•			T794
Red	•	•		T795
Burgundy	•	•		T796
Aqua	•			T797
White		•		T798
Tan	•	•		T799

MARLIN TRIM

COLOR	CLOTH	VINYL	LEATHER	CODE
Black	•	•		T791
Blue	•	•		T793
Red	•	•		T795
Tan	•	•		T799

THE PAINT CODE furnishes the key to the paint colors used on the car. A two-number code indicates the color of the car. A two-tone car has two sets of numbers. The first number is the body color, the second is the roof color.

COLOR	CODE
Classic Black	1
Marina Aqua Metallic	8
Granada Green Metallic	18
Apollo Yellow	25
Strato Blue Metallic	31
Barbados Blue Metallic	32
Royale Blue Metallic	33
Alameda Aqua	34
Yuma Tan Metallic	36
Sungold Metallic	37
Stallion Brown Metallic	38
Matador Red	39
Flamingo Burgundy Metallic	40
Rajah Burgundy Metallic	41
Satin Chrome	42
Hialeah Yellow	58
Pale Green Metallic	59
Frost White	72

ENGINE NUMBER

These engines are marked with a code identifying the year, month, engine letter code, and day of manufacture. The letter contained in the code number denotes the size of the cylinder bore and also the compression rate.

6-cylinder engine number is located on boss adjacent to the distributor.

8-cylinder engine number is located on a tag which is attached to the alternator mounting bracket.

The engines are marked with a code identifying year, month, engine letter code, and day of manufacture.

EXAMPLE:

9	2	A	24
1967	Month	Code	Day

ENGINE NO.	NO. CYL.	CID	HORSE-POWER	COMP. RATIO	CARB
L	6	232	145	8.5:1	
L	6	232	155	8.5:1	
J	6	199	128	8.5:1	
H	8	290	200	9.0:1	2 BC
N	8	290	225	10.0:1	4 BC
Z	8	343	280	10.2:1	4 BC

1968 AMC JAVELIN

1968 AMC JAVELIN

1968 AMC RAMBLER AMBASSADOR

1968 AMC RAMBLER AMBASSADOR

1968 AMC RAMBLER REBEL

1968 AMC RAMBLER REBEL

1968 AMC RAMBLER ROGUE

1968 AMC RAMBLER ROGUE

VEHICLE IDENTIFICATION NUMBER

AMC
A8SO50A100551

The VIN is stamped and embossed on a stainless steel plate welded to the right front fender under the hood. It consists of the manufacturer's symbol, model year, transmission type, body identity, body class, series and engine, and a sequential production number for each series.

THE FIRST DIGIT: Identifies the division (A for American Motors Corp.)

THE SECOND DIGIT: Identifies the model year (1968)

THE THIRD DIGIT: Identifies the transmission type

TRANSMISSION	CODE
Standard Column Shift (3 speed)	S
Overdrive Column Shift (3 speed)	O
Automatic Column Shift (3 speed)	A
Floor Shift Automatic (3 speed)	C
Four Speed Floor Shift w/Console	F
Four Speed Floor Shift Floor Mounted	M

THE FOURTH DIGIT: Identifies the series

SERIES	CODE
American	O
Rebel	1
AMX	3
Javelin	7
Ambassador	8

THE FIFTH DIGIT: Identifies the body type

BODY TYPE	CODE
4-Dr. Sedan	5
2-Dr. Sedan	6
2-Dr. Convertible	7
4-Dr. Sta. Wagon	8
2-Dr. Hardtop	9

THE SIXTH DIGIT: Identifies the body class

BODY CLASS	CODE
550/220	0
Ambassador Base	2
440/770/DPL	5
AMX, Rogue, SST	7

THE SEVENTH DIGIT: Identifies the engine

ENGINE	CODE
199 CID, OHV SIX, 1-BC	A
232 CID, OHV SIX, 1-BC	B
232 CID, OHV SIX, 2-BC	C
290 CID, V-8, 2-BC	M
290 CID, V-8, 4-BC	N
343 CID, V-8, 2-BC	S
343 CID, V-8, 4-BC	T
390 CID, V-8, 2-BC	W
390 CID, V-8, 4-BC	X

LAST SIX DIGITS: Represent the basic production number

BODY NUMBER PLATE

A unit body number plate is riveted to the left front door below the door lock and is visible when the door is open. This body plate includes the model, body, trim, paint code, and car built sequence numbers.

AMERICAN MOTORS CORP.
DETROIT MICH.

BODY NO. W000019
MODEL NO. 6885-5
TRIM NO. 894
PAINT NO. 46A-72A
W0000192

EXAMPLE:

W000019	Production Sequence
68	Model Year (1968)
85-5	Body Type (4-Dr. Sedan)
894	Trim
461A-72A	Paint

AMERICAN	CODE
4-Dr. Sedan 220	6805
4-Dr. Sedan 440	6805-5
2-Dr. Sport Sedan 220	6806
4-Dr. Sta. Wagon 440	6808-5
2-Dr. Hardtop Rogue	6809-7

REBEL	CODE
4-Dr. Sedan 550	6815
4-Dr. Sedan 770	6815-5
2-Dr. Convertible 550	6817
2-Dr. Convertible SST	6817-7
4-Dr. Sta. Wagon 550	6818
4-Dr. Sta. Wagon 770	6818-5
2-Dr. Hardtop 550	6819
2-Dr. Hardtop 770	6819-5
2-Dr. Hardtop SST	6819-7

AMBASSADOR	CODE
4-Dr. Sedan	6885-2
4-Dr. Sedan DPL	6885-5
4-Dr. Sedan SST	6885-7
4-Dr. Sta. Wagon DPL	6888-5
2-Dr. Hardtop	6889-2
2-Dr. Hardtop DPL	6889-5
2-Dr. Hardtop SST	6889-7

JAVELIN	CODE
2-Dr. Hardtop	6859-5
2-Dr. Hardtop SST	6859-7

AMX	CODE
2-Dr. Sport Coupe	6839-7

THE TRIM NUMBER furnishes the key to trim color and material for each model series.

AMERICAN TRIM

COLOR	CLOTH	VINYL	LEATHER	CODE
Gray/White	•	•		T828
Black/White	•	•		T828

AMERICAN 440/ROGUE TRIM

COLOR	CLOTH	VINYL	LEATHER	CODE
Blue	•	•		T843
Green	•	•		T844
Red	•	•		T845
Black/White	•	•		T848

AMX TRIM

COLOR	CLOTH	VINYL	LEATHER	CODE
Black		•		T831
Tan		•		T832
Red		•		T835

JAVELIN TRIM

COLOR	CLOTH	VINYL	LEATHER	CODE
Black		•		T831
Black/White		•		T838

JAVELIN SST TRIM

COLOR	CLOTH	VINYL	LEATHER	CODE
Black	•	•		T831
Tan	•	•		T832
Red	•	•		T835

REBEL 550 TRIM

COLOR	CLOTH	VINYL	LEATHER	CODE
Black	•	•		T851
Blue	•	•		T853
Red	•	•		T855

REBEL 770 TRIM

COLOR	CLOTH	VINYL	LEATHER	CODE
Black	•	•		T871
Blue	•	•		T873
Green	•	•		T874
Gold	•	•		T876
Russet	•			T879

REBEL SST TRIM

COLOR	CLOTH	VINYL	LEATHER	CODE
Black	•	•		T871
Blue	•	•		T873
Green	•	•		T874
Gold	•	•		T876
Russet	•	•		T879

AMBASSADOR TRIM

COLOR	CLOTH	VINYL	LEATHER	CODE
Black	•	•		T881
Blue	•	•		T883
Red	•	•		T885

AMBASSADOR DPL TRIM

COLOR	CLOTH	VINYL	LEATHER	CODE
Black	•	•		T891
Blue	•	•		T893
Green	•	•		T894
Gold	•	•		T896
Russet	•	•		T899

AMBASSADOR SST TRIM

COLOR	CLOTH	VINYL	LEATHER	CODE
Black	•	•		T891
Blue	•	•		T893
Green	•	•		T894
Gold	•	•		T896
Russet	•	•		T899

THE PAINT CODE furnishes the key to the paint colors used on the car. A two-number code indicates the color of the car. A two-tone car has two sets of numbers. The first number is the body color, the second is the roof color.

COLOR	CODE
Classic Black	P1A
Matador Red	P39A
Saturn Blue Metallic	P43A
Caravelle Blue Metallic	P44A
Blazer Blue Metallic	P45A
Laurel Green Metallic	P46A
Rally Green Metallic	P47A
Tahiti Turquoise Metallic	P48A
Lanedo Tan Metallic	P49A
Calcutta Russet Metallic	P50A
Scarab Gold Metallic	P52A
Turbo Silver Metallic	P54A
Hialeah Yellow	P58A
Frost White	P72A

ENGINE NUMBER

These engines are marked with a code identifying the year, month, engine letter code, and day of manufacture. The letter contained in the code number denotes the size of the cylinder bore and also the compression rate.

6-cylinder engine number is located on panel adjacent to the distributor.

8-cylinder engine number is located on a tag which is attached to the front of the right valve cover.

EXAMPLE:

10	2	A	24
1968	Month	Code	Day

ENGINE NO.	NO. CYL.	CID	HORSE-POWER	COMP. RATIO	CARB
L	6	232	145	8.5:1	
M	6	232	155	8.5:1	
J	6	199	128	8.5:1	
P	6	199		8.5:1	
H	8	290	200	9.0:1	2 BC
N	8	290	225	10.0:1	4 BC
S	8	343	235	9.0:1	2 BC
Z	8	343	280	10.2:1	4 BC
W	8	390	425	11.2:1	4 BC

1969 AMX

1969 AMX

1969 AMC JAVELIN

1969 AMC JAVELIN

1969 AMC RAMBLER AMBASSADOR

1969 AMC RAMBLER AMBASSADOR

1969 AMC RAMBLER REBEL

1969 AMC RAMBLER REBEL

1969 AMC RAMBLER ROGUE

1969 AMC RAMBLER ROGUE

VEHICLE IDENTIFICATION NUMBER

AMC
A9S050A100551

The VIN is stamped and embossed on a stainless steel plate welded to the right front fender under the hood. It consists of the manufacturer's symbol, model year, transmission type, body identity, body class, series and engine identity, and a sequential production number for each series.

THE FIRST DIGIT: Identifies the division (A for American Motors Corp.)

THE SECOND DIGIT: Identifies the model year (1969)

THE THIRD DIGIT: Identifies the transmission type

TRANSMISSION CODE	
Standard Column Shift (3 speed)	S
Overdrive Column Shift (3 speed)	O
Automatic Column Shift (3 speed)	A
Floor Shift Automatic (3 speed)	C
Four Speed Floor Shift Floor Mounted	M

THE FOURTH DIGIT: Identifies the series

SERIES	CODE
American Rambler	O
Rebel	1
AMX	3
Javelin	7
Ambassador	8

THE FIFTH DIGIT: Identifies the body type

BODY TYPE	CODE
4-Dr. Sedan	5
2-Dr. Sedan	6
4-Dr. Sta. Wagon	8
2-Dr. Hardtop	9

THE SIXTH DIGIT: Identifies the body class

BODY CLASS	CODE
Rambler, Rebel Base	0
Ambassador Base	2
440, Javelin, DPL	5
AMX, Rogue, SST	7

THE SEVENTH DIGIT: Identifies the engine

ENGINE	CODE
199 CID, OHV SIX, 1-BC	A
232 CID, OHV SIX, 1-BC	B
232 CID, OHV SIX, 2-BC	C
290 CID, V-8, 2-BC	M
290 CID, V-8, 4-BC	N
343 CID, V-8, 2-BC	S
343 CID, V-8, 4-BC	T
390 CID, V-8, 2-BC	W
390 CID, V-8, 4-BC	X

LAST SIX DIGITS: Represent the basic production number

BODY NUMBER PLATE

A unit body number plate is riveted to the left front door below the door lock and is visible when door is open. This body plate includes the model, body, trim, paint code, and car built sequence numbers.

AMERICAN MOTORS CORP.
DETROIT MICH.

BODY NO. 000006
MODEL NO. 6906
TRIM NO. 928
PAINT NO. 77-72
E000009

EXAMPLE:

000006	Production Sequence
69	Model Year (1969)
06	Body Type (2-Dr. Sport Sedan)
928	Trim
77-72	Paint

AMERICAN RAMBLER	CODE
4-Dr. Sedan 220	6905
4-Dr. Sedan 440	6905-5
2-Dr. Sport Sedan 220	6906
4-Dr. Sta. Wagon 440	6908-5
2-Dr. Hardtop Rogue	6909-7

REBEL	CODE
4-Dr. Sedan	6915
4-Dr. Sedan SST	6915-7
4-Dr. Sta. Wagon	6918
4-Dr. Sta. Wagon SST	6918-7
2-Dr. Hardtop	6919
2-Dr. Hardtop SST	6919-7

AMBASSADOR	CODE
4-Dr. Sedan	6985-2
4-Dr. Sedan DPL	6985-5
4-Dr. Sedan SST	6985-7
4-Dr. Sta. Wagon	6988-5
4-Dr. Sta. Wagon SST	6988-7
2-Dr. Hardtop DPL	6989-5
2-Dr. Hardtop SST	6989-7

JAVELIN	CODE
2-Dr. Hardtop	6979-5
2-Dr. Hardtop SST	6979-7

AMX	CODE
2-Dr. Sports Coupe	6939-7

THE TRIM NUMBER furnishes the key to trim color and material for each model series.

AMX TRIM

COLOR	CLOTH	VINYL	LEATHER	CODE
Charcoal		•	•	931
Platinum		•		932
Red		•		935
Saddle		•	•	936

JAVELIN TRIM

COLOR	CLOTH	VINYL	LEATHER	CODE
Charcoal		•		961
Parchment		•		968

JAVELIN SST TRIM

COLOR	CLOTH	VINYL	LEATHER	CODE
Charcoal	•	•		961
Platinum	•	•		962
Blue	•	•		963
Red	•	•		965
Beige	•	•		966

RAMBLER TRIM

COLOR	CLOTH	VINYL	LEATHER	CODE
Blue	•	•		923
Parchment	•	•		928

RAMBLER 440 TRIM

COLOR	CLOTH	VINYL	LEATHER	CODE
Charcoal	•	•		941
Blue	•	•		943
Green	•	•		944
Red		•		945

RAMBLER/ROGUE TRIM

COLOR	CLOTH	VINYL	LEATHER	CODE
Charcoal	•	•		941
Blue	•	•		943
Green	•			944
Red	•	•		945

REBEL TRIM

COLOR	CLOTH	VINYL	LEATHER	CODE
Charcoal		•		951
Blue	•	•		953
Beige	•	•		956
Avocado	•	•		957

REBEL SST TRIM

COLOR	CLOTH	VINYL	LEATHER	CODE
Platinum	•	•		972
Blue	•	•		973
Red		•		975
Brown	•	•		976
Avocado	•	•		977
Yellow		•		979

AMBASSADOR TRIM

COLOR	CLOTH	VINYL	LEATHER	CODE
Charcoal		•		981
Blue	•	•		983
Beige	•	•		986
Avocado	•	•		987

AMBASSADOR/DPL TRIM

COLOR	CLOTH	VINYL	LEATHER	CODE
Charcoal	•	•		991
Blue	•	•		993
Red		•		995
Beige	•	•		996
Avocado	•	•		997

AMBASSADOR/SST TRIM

COLOR	CLOTH	VINYL	LEATHER	CODE
Charcoal		•		991
Platinum	•			992
Blue	•	•		993
Red		•		995
Beige		•		996
Avocado	•			997
Yellow		•		999
Brown	•			996

THE PAINT CODE furnishes the key to the paint colors used on the car. A two-number code indicates the color of the car. A two-tone car has two sets of numbers. The first number is the body color, the second is the roof color.

COLOR	CODE
Big Bad Blue	P2
Big Bad Orange	P3
Big Bad Green	P4
Flat Black	P7
Bright Red	P9
Bright Blue	P10
Matador Red	P39A
Ascot Gray	P62
Castillian Gray Metallic	P63
Beale St. Blue Metallic	P64
Regatta Blue Metallic	P65
Alamosa Aqua Metallic	P68
Surf Green Metallic	P70
Hunter Green Metallic	P71
Frost White	P72A
Willow Green Metallic	P75
Pompeii Yellow	P76
Butternut Beige Metallic	P77
Cordoba Brown Metallic	P78
Bittersweet Orange Metallic	P79
Black Mink Metallic	P80
Bright White	P88

ENGINE NUMBER

These engines are marked with a code identifying the year, month, engine letter code, and day of manufacture. The letter contained in the code number denotes the size of the cylinder bore and also the compression rate.

6-cylinder engine number is located on the panel adjacent to the distributor.

8-cylinder engine number is located on a tag which is attached to the front of the right valve cover.

EXAMPLE:

11	2	A	24
1969	Month	Code	Day

ENGINE NO.	NO. CYL.	CID	HORSE-POWER	COMP. RATIO	CARB
M	6	232	145	8.5:1	1 BC
L	6	232	155	8.5:1	2 BC
J,P	6	199	128	8.5:1	
H	8	290	200	9.0:1	2 BC
N	8	290	225	10.0:1	4 BC
S	8	343	235	9.0:1	2 BC
Z	8	343	280	10.2:1	4 BC
W	8	290	315	10.2:1	4 BC
	8	290	425	10.2:1	4 BC

1960 BUICK

1960 BUICK

VEHICLE IDENTIFICATION NUMBER

BUICK
4G1101555

Commonly referred to as the VIN NUMBER, this series of numbers and letters is stamped on a plate attached to the left front door hinge pillar.

FIRST DIGIT: Identifies the series

SERIES	CODE
LeSabre	44
Invicta	46
Electra	47
Electra 225	48

SECOND DIGIT: Identifies the model year (1960)

THIRD DIGIT: Identifies the assembly plant

ASSEMBLY PLANT	CODE
Flint, MI	1
South Gate, CA	2
Linden, NJ	3
Kansas City, KS	4
Wilmington, DE	5
Atlanta, GA	6
Framingham, MA	7
Arlington, TX	8

LAST 6 DIGITS: Represent the basic production numbers

BODY NUMBER PLATE

Complete identification of each body is provided by a plate riveted to the cowl at the left of center under the hood.

BUICK DIV. GENERAL MOTORS
FLINT, MICH.

STYLE 60 4439 BODY FB 1032
TRIM 420 PAINT AA
ACC. BFGIU

BODY BY FISHER

EXAMPLE:

60	Model Year (1960)
4	GM Division (Buick)
4	Series (LeSabre)
39	4-Door Hardtop
FB	Flint, Michigan
1032	Production Sequence
420	Trim
A	Lower Body Color
A	Upper Body Color

THE STYLE NUMBER is a combination of the year, division, series, and body style.

LESABRE	CODE
Sedan, 2-Door	4411
Hardtop, 2-Door	4437
Hardtop, 4-Door	4439
Estate Wagon, 4-Door, 2-Seat	4435
Estate Wagon, 4-Door, 3-Seat	4445
Convertible, 2-Door	4467
Sedan, 4-Door	4419

1960 BUICK

INVICTA	CODE
Sedan, 4-Door, 6 Window	4619
Estate Wagon, 4-Door, 6 Passenger	4635
2-Door Hardtop Coupe, 2-Door	4637
Hardtop Sedan, 4-Door, 4 Window	4639
Estate Wagon, 4-Door, 3 Seats	4645
Convertible Coupe, 2-Door	4667

ELECTRA	CODE
Sedan, 4-Door	4719
Hardtop Coupe, 2-Door	4737
Hardtop Sedan, 4-Door	4739

ELECTRA 225	CODE
Riviera Sedan, 4-Door	4829
Hardtop Sedan, 4-Door	4839
Convertible Coupe, 2-Door	4867

THE BODY NUMBER is the production serial number of the body. The prefix letter denotes the plant in which the body was built.

ASSEMBLY PLANT	CODE
Flint, MI	FB
South Gate, CA	BC
Linden, NJ	BL
Kansas City, KS	BK
Wilmington, DE	BW
Atlanta, GA	BA
Framingham, MA	BF
Arlington, TX	BT

THE TRIM NUMBER furnishes the key to trim color and material for each model series.

LESABRE TRIM COLOR	CLOTH	VINYL	LEATHER	CODE
Green		•		400,405
Green	•			401
Blue		•		410,415
Blue	•			411
Gray		•		420,425
Gray	•			421
Fawn		•		430,435
Fawn	•			431
Maroon		•		445
Red		•		460
Red	•			471

INVICTA TRIM COLOR	CLOTH	VINYL	LEATHER	CODE
Green		•		600
Green	•			601,602,605
Blue		•		610
Blue	•			611,612,615
Blue			•	616,619
Gray		•		620,624
Gray	•			621,622,625
Fawn		•		630
Fawn	•			631,632,635
Fawn			•	636,639
Maroon	•			641,642,645
Maroon			•	646,649
Turquoise		•		650
Turquoise	•			651,652
Red		•		660,664
Tan			•	695

ELECTRA TRIM COLOR	CLOTH	VINYL	LEATHER	CODE
Green	•			701,702
Blue	•			711,712
Gray	•			721,722
Fawn	•			731,732
Maroon	•			741
Turquoise	•			751,752

ELECTRA 225 TRIM COLOR	CLOTH	VINYL	LEATHER	CODE
Green	•			801
Blue			•	810,819
Blue	•			811
Fawn			•	830,839
Fawn	•			833
Maroon			•	840,849
Turquoise			•	850,859
Red			•	860,869
Black			•	880,889
Black	•			883

THE PAINT CODE furnishes the key to the paint colors used on the car. A two-letter code indicates the bottom and top colors respectively.

COLOR	CODE
Sable Black	A
Gull Gray	B
Arctic White	C
Silver Mist	D
Chalet Blue	H
Lucerne Green	K
Titian Red	L
Casino Cream	M
Cordovan	N
Pearl Fawn	P
Tahiti Beige	R
Turquoise	T
Tampico Red	V
Midnight Blue	W
Verde Green	X

ENGINE NUMBER

Along with the VIN number, the engine block is stamped with an engine production code. The code has a series of letters that identifies the engine and a numeric production date code. The production code is stamped on the right side of the engine block.

LESABRE

ENGINE NO.	NO. CYL.	CID	HORSE-POWER	COMP. RATIO	CARB	TRANS
3G	8	364	210	8.5:1	2 BC	MAN
L3G	8	364	235	9.0:1	2 BC	AUTO
3G	8	364	250	10.25:1	2 BC	AUTO
3G	8	364	300	10.25:1	4 BC	AUTO

INVICTA & ELECTRA

ENGINE NO.	NO. CYL.	CID	HORSE-POWER	COMP. RATIO	CARB	TRANS
4G	8	401	325	10.25:1	4 BC	AUTO

1/4-inch dash "-" following code indicates .010 oversize cylinder bore.

1961 BUICK

1961 BUICK

1961 BUICK

1961 BUICK SKYLARK

1961 BUICK SKYLARK

1961 BUICK SPECIAL

1961 BUICK SPECIAL

1961 BUICK

VEHICLE IDENTIFICATION NUMBER

BUICK
4H1001555

Commonly referred to as the VIN NUMBER, this series of numbers and letters is stamped on a plate attached to the left front door hinge pillar. Also stamped on the top surface of the engine block forward of the valve cover on the left side.

FIRST DIGIT: Identifies the series

SERIES	CODE
Special	0
Special Deluxe	1
Skylark	3
LeSabre	4
Invicta	6
Electra	7
Electra 225	8

SECOND DIGIT: Identifies the model year (1961)

THIRD DIGIT: Identifies the assembly plant

ASSEMBLY PLANT	CODE
Flint, MI	1
South Gate, CA	2
Linden, NJ	3
Kansas City, KS	4
Wilmington, DE	5
Atlanta, GA	6
Arlington, TX	8

LAST 6 DIGITS: Represent the basic production sequence numbers

BODY NUMBER PLATE

Complete identification of each body is provided by a plate riveted to the cowl at the left of center under the hood.

BUICK DIV. GENERAL MOTORS
FLINT, MICH.

STYLE 61-4719 BODY FB 3321
TRIM 732 PAINT AA
ACC. BFGIU

BODY BY FISHER

EXAMPLE:

61	Model Year (1961)
4	GM Division (Buick)
7	Series (Electra)
19	4-Door Sedan
FB	Flint, Michigan
3321	Production Sequence
732	Trim
A	Lower Body Color
A	Upper Body Color

THE STYLE NUMBER is a combination of the year, division, series, and body style.

SPECIAL	CODE
Sedan, 4-Door	4019
Sedan, 2-Door	4027
Station Wagon, 4-Door, 2-Seat	4035
Station Wagon, 4-Door, 3-Seat	4045

SPECIAL DELUXE	CODE
Sedan, 4-Door	4119
Station Wagon, 4-Door, 2-Seat	4135

SKYLARK	CODE
Coupe, 2-Door	4317

LESABRE	CODE
Sedan, 2-Door	4411
Estate Wagon, 4-Door, 2-Seat	4435
Hardtop, 2-Door	4437
Hardtop, 4-Door	4439
Estate Wagon, 4-Door, 3-Seat	4445
Convertible, 2-Door	4467
Sedan, 4-Door	4469

INVICTA	CODE
Hardtop Coupe, 2-Door	4637
Hardtop Sedan, 4-Door	4639
Convertible, 2-Door	4667

ELECTRA	CODE
Sedan, 4-Door	4719
Hardtop Coupe, 2-Door	4737
Hardtop Sedan, 4-Door	4739

ELECTRA 225	CODE
Riviera Sedan, 4-Door	4829
Convertible, 2-Door	4867

THE BODY NUMBER is the production serial number of the body. The prefix letter denotes the plant in which the body was built.

ASSEMBLY PLANT	CODE
Flint, MI	FB
South Gate, CA	BC
Linden, NJ	BL
Kansas City, KS	BK
Wilmington, DE	BW
Atlanta, GA	BA
Arlington, TX	BT

THE TRIM NUMBER furnishes the key to trim color and material for each model series.

SPECIAL TRIM

COLOR	CLOTH	VINYL	LEATHER	CODE
Green	•	•		001
Green		•		005
Blue	•	•		011
Blue		•		015
Gray	•	•		021
Gray		•		025
Fawn	•	•		031
Fawn		•		035
Red		•	•	065

SPECIAL DELUXE TRIM

COLOR	CLOTH	VINYL	LEATHER	CODE
Green	•	•		101
Green		•		105
Blue	•	•		111
Blue		•		115
Gray	•	•		121
Gray		•		125
Fawn	•	•		131
Fawn		•		135
Turquoise	•	•		151
Turquoise		•		155
Red		•		165
Black/Red	•	•		181

SKYLARK TRIM

COLOR	CLOTH	VINYL	LEATHER	CODE
Blue	•	•		113,117
Gray	•	•		123,127
Fawn	•	•		133,137

LESABRE TRIM

COLOR	CLOTH	VINYL	LEATHER	CODE
Green	•	•		401,406
Green		•		405,400
Blue	•	•		411,416
Blue		•		410,415
Gray	•	•		421
Fawn	•	•		431,436
Fawn		•		430,435
Saddle		•	•	443
Turquoise		•		455
Turquoise	•	•		456
Red	•	•		466
Red		•		460,465
Black/Red	•	•		481
Cream		•		490

INVICTA TRIM

COLOR	CLOTH	VINYL	LEATHER	CODE
Green	•	•		601
Green		•		600
Blue	•	•		611
Blue		•		610,617
Gray	•	•		621
Fawn	•	•		631
Fawn		•		630,637
Saddle		•	•	643
Turquoise	•	•		651
Turquoise		•		650
Red		•	•	663
Red		•		660
Maroon	•	•		661
Maroon		•		667
Black		•	•	683
Cream		•		690

ELECTRA TRIM

COLOR	CLOTH	VINYL	LEATHER	CODE
Green	•	•		702
Blue	•	•		712
Gray	•	•		722
Fawn	•	•		732
Turquoise	•	•		752
Maroon	•	•		762

ELECTRA 225 TRIM

COLOR	CLOTH	VINYL	LEATHER	CODE
Green	•	•		801
Blue	•	•		811
Blue		•	•	810,819
Gray	•	•		821
Gray		•	•	820,829
Fawn	•	•		831
Fawn		•	•	830,839
Turquoise	•	•		851
Turquoise		•	•	850
Red		•	•	860,869

THE PAINT CODE furnishes the key to the paint colors used on the car. A two letter code indicates the bottom and top colors respectively.

PAINT	CODE
Granada Black	A
Arctic White	C
Newport Silver	D
Venice Blue	E
Laguna Blue	F
Bimini Blue	H
Dublin Blue	J
Kerry Green	K
Rio Red	L
Sun Valley Cream	M
Cordovan	N
Turquoise	P
Phoenix Beige	R
Desert Fawn	T
Tampico Red	V

 1961 BUICK

ENGINE NUMBER

Along with the VIN number, the engine block is stamped with an engine production code. The code has a prefix series of letters and numbers that identifies the engine and year, then a four digit numeric production sequence code. The production code is stamped on the right front of the engine block opposite the VIN number. When viewed from the front of the engine, the number is upside down.

SPECIAL & DELUXE

ENGINE NO.	NO. CYL.	CID	HORSE-POWER	COMP. RATIO	CARB	TRANS
H	8	215	155	8.8:1	2 BC	M/A
H	8	215	185	10.25:1	4 BC	M/A
LH	8	215	NA	7.6:1	2 BC	M/A

SKYLARK

ENGINE NO.	NO. CYL.	CID	HORSE-POWER	COMP. RATIO	CARB	TRANS
H	8	215	185	10.25:1	4 BC	M/A

LESABRE

ENGINE NO.	NO. CYL.	CID	HORSE-POWER	COMP. RATIO	CARB	TRANS
3H	8	364	250	10.25:1	2 BC	AUTO
3H	8	364	300	10.25:1	4 BC	AUTO
L3H	8	364	235	9.0:1	2 BC	AUTO

INVICTA & ELECTRA

ENGINE NO.	NO. CYL.	CID	HORSE-POWER	COMP. RATIO	CARB	TRANS
4H	8	401	325	10.25:1	4 BC	AUTO
L4H	8	401	NA	8.75:1	4 BC	AUTO

1/4-inch dash "-" following code indicates .010" oversize cylinder bore.

1962 BUICK

1962 BUICK

1962 BUICK SPECIAL

1962 BUICK SPECIAL

VEHICLE IDENTIFICATION NUMBER

BUICK
4I1001555

Commonly referred to as the VIN NUMBER, this series of numbers and letters is stamped on a plate attached to the left front door hinge pillar, and stamped on the top surface of the engine block forward of the valve cover on the left side.

FIRST DIGIT: Identifies the series

SERIES	CODE
Special	0
V-6	A
Special Deluxe	1
Skylark	3
LeSabre	4
Invicta	6
Electra 225	8

SECOND DIGIT: Identifies the model year (1962)

THIRD DIGIT: Identifies the assembly plant

ASSEMBLY PLANT	CODE
Flint, MI	1
South Gate, CA	2
Linden, NJ	3
Kansas City, KS	4
Wilmington, DE	5
Atlanta, GA	6
Arlington, TX	8

LAST SIX DIGITS: Represent the basic production numbers

BODY NUMBER PLATE

Complete identification of each body is provided by a plate riveted to the cowl at the left of center under the hood.

BUICK DIV. GENERAL MOTORS
FLINT, MICH.

STYLE 62 4819 BODY FB 3321
TRIM 813 PAINT AA
ACC. BFGIU

BODY BY FISHER

EXAMPLE:

62	Model Year (1962)
4	GM Division (Buick)
8	Series (Electra 225)
19	4-Door Sedan
FB	Flint, Michigan
3321	Production Sequence
813	Trim
A	Lower Body Color
A	Upper Body Color

THE STYLE NUMBER is a combination of the year, division, series, and body style.

SPECIAL	CODE
Sedan, 4-Door	4019
Sedan, 2-Door	4027
Station Wagon, 4-Door, 2-Seat	4035
Station Wagon, 4-Door 3-Seat	4045
Convertible, 2-Door	4067

1962 BUICK

SPECIAL DELUXE	CODE
Sedan, 4-Door	4119
Station Wagon, 4-Door, 2-Seat	4135
Convertible, 2-Door	4167

SKYLARK	CODE
Coupe, 2-Door	4347
Convertible, 2-Door	4367

LESABRE	CODE
Sedan, 2-Door	4411
Hardtop, 4-Door	4439
Hardtop, 2-Door	4447
Sedan,4 Door	4469

INVICTA	CODE
Estate Wagon, 4-Door, 2-Seat	4635
Hardtop Sedan, 4-Door	4639
Estate Wagon, 4-Door, 3-Seat	4645
Hardtop, 2-Door	4647
Convertible, 2-Door	4667
Option Wildcat	

ELECTRA 225	CODE
Sedan, 4-Door	4819
Riviera Sedan, 4-Door	4829
Sedan Hardtop, 4-Door	4839
Hardtop, 2-Door	4847
Convertible, 2-Door	4867

THE BODY NUMBER is the production serial number of the body. The prefix letter denotes the plant in which the body was built.

ASSEMBLY PLANT	CODE
Flint, MI	FB
South Gate, CA	BC
Linden, NJ	BL
Kansas City, KS	BK
Atlanta, GA	BA
Arlington, TX	BT

THE TRIM NUMBER furnishes the key to trim color and material for each model series.

SPECIAL TRIM COLOR	CLOTH	VINYL	LEATHER	CODE
Green	•	•		001
Blue	•	•		011
Blue		•		015,010
Silver	•	•		021
Silver		•		024,025
White	•	•		031
Fawn	•	•		031
Fawn		•		035,030
Red		•		075,070

SPECIAL DELUXE TRIM COLOR	CLOTH	VINYL	LEATHER	CODE
Green	•	•		101
Green		•		105
Blue	•	•		111
Blue		•		115
Silver	•	•		121
Silver		•		125
Fawn	•	•		131
Fawn		•		135
Rose	•	•		161
Red		•		175

SKYLARK TRIM COLOR	CLOTH	VINYL	LEATHER	CODE
Blue	•	•		113
Blue		•		118,117
Silver	•	•		123
White		•		126,127
Fawn	•	•		133-138
Gold	•	•		143
Rose	•	•		163
Red		•		178,177
Black		•		188,187
Saddle		•		197

LESABRE TRIM COLOR	CLOTH	VINYL	LEATHER	CODE
Blue	•	•		411
Silver	•	•		421
Fawn	•	•		431
Aqua	•	•		451
Rose	•	•		461
Black		•		484

INVICTA TRIM COLOR	CLOTH	VINYL	LEATHER	CODE
Green		•		605,603
Green	•	•		602
Blue		•		615,613
Blue		•		618,614
Blue	•	•		616,611,612
Silver	•	•		622
White		•		628,624
Fawn		•		635,633,638
Fawn		•		634,639
Fawn	•	•		636,631,632
Gold		•		644
Aqua		•		655,653,654,655
Aqua	•	•		651
Rose	•	•		661
Rose		•		664
Red		•		675,673,678
Red		•		674,679
Red	•	•		676
Red		•	•	677
Black		•	•	687
Saddle		•	•	697

ELECTRA 225 TRIM

COLOR	CLOTH	VINYL	LEATHER	CODE
Green	•	•		803,801,802
Blue	•	•		813,811,812
Blue		•	•	810,819
Silver	•	•		823,821,822
White		•	•	826,827
Fawn	•	•		833,831,832
Gold	•	•		842
Gold		•	•	840
Rose	•	•		862
Rose		•	•	860
Red		•	•	878,870,879
Black		•	•	880
Saddle		•	•	898,890,899

THE PAINT CODE furnishes the key to the paint colors used on the car. A two-letter code indicates the bottom and top colors respectively.

COLOR	CODE
Regal Black	A
Arctic White	C
Silver Cloud	D
Cadet Blue	E
Marlin Blue	F
Glacier Blue	H
Willow Mist	J
Cameo Cream	M
Burgundy	N
Teal Mist	P
Aquamarine	Q
Desert Sand	R
Fawn Mist	T
Cardinal Red	V
Camelot Rose	X

ENGINE NUMBER

Along with the VIN number, the engine block is stamped with an engine production code. The code has a prefix series of letters and numbers that identifies the engine and year, then a four digit numeric production sequence code. On the V-8 engines, the production code is stamped on the right front of the engine block opposite the VIN number. On the V-6 engine, the number is on the front of the block below the left cylinder head gasket.

SPECIAL

ENGINE NO.	NO. CYL.	CID	HORSE-POWER	COMP. RATIO	CARB	TRANS
6I	6	198	135	8.8:1	2 BC	M/A
I	8	215	155	9.0:1	2 BC	M/A
LI	8	215	145	7.6:1	2 BC	M/A
HI	8	215	190	11.0:1	4 BC	M/A

SPECIAL DELUXE

ENGINE NO.	NO. CYL.	CID	HORSE-POWER	COMP. RATIO	CARB	TRANS
I	8	215	155	9.0:1	2 BC	M/A
LI	8	215	145	7.6:1	2 BC	M/A
HI	8	215	190	11.0:1	4 BC	M/A

SKYLARK

ENGINE NO.	NO. CYL.	CID	HORSE-POWER	COMP. RATIO	CARB	TRANS
HI	8	215	190	11.0:1	4 BC	M/A

LESABRE

ENGINE NO.	NO. CYL.	CID	HORSE-POWER	COMP. RATIO	CARB	TRANS
2I	8	401	280	10.25:1	2 BC	AUTO
L2I	8	401	265	9.0:1	2 BC	AUTO
4I	8	401	325	10.25:1	4 BC	AUTO
L4I	8	401	315	8.75:1	4 BC	AUTO

INVICTA, ELECTRA 225 & WILDCAT

ENGINE NO.	NO. CYL.	CID	HORSE-POWER	COMP. RATIO	CARB	TRANS
4I	8	401	325	10.25:1	4 BC	AUTO
L4I	8	401	315	8.75:1	4 BC	AUTO

1963 BUICK

1963 BUICK

1963 BUICK RIVIERA

1963 BUICK RIVIERA

1963 BUICK SPECIAL

1963 BUICK SPECIAL

1963 BUICK

VEHICLE IDENTIFICATION NUMBER

BUICK
4J1001555

Commonly referred to as the VIN NUMBER, this series of numbers and letters is stamped on a plate attached to the left front door hinge pillar, and stamped on the top surface of the engine block forward of the valve cover on the left side.

Exception: 4700 Series — the number is on the right cowl under the hood.

FIRST DIGIT: Identifies the series

SERIES	CODE
Special V-8	0
Special V-6	A
Special Deluxe V-8	1
Special Deluxe V-6	B
Skylark	3
LeSabre	4
Wildcat	6
Riviera	7
Electra 225	8

SECOND DIGIT: Identifies the model year (1963)

THIRD DIGIT: Identifies the assembly plant

ASSEMBLY PLANT	CODE
Flint, MI	1
South Gate, CA	2
Linden, NJ	3
Kansas City, KS	4
Wilmington, DE	5
Atlanta, GA	6
Arlington, TX	8

LAST 6 DIGITS: Represent the basic production numbers

BODY NUMBER PLATE

Complete identification of each body is provided by a plate riveted to the cowl at the left of center under the hood.

BUICK DIV. GENERAL MOTORS
FLINT, MICH.

STYLE 63 4347 FB 2707 BODY
TRIM 178 CC PAINT
ACC. BFGIU

BODY BY FISHER

EXAMPLE:

63	Model Year (1963)
4	GM Division (Buick)
3	Series (Skylark)
47	2-Door Coupe
FB	Flint, Michigan
2707	Production Sequence
178	Trim
C	Lower Body Color
C	Upper Body Color

THE STYLE NUMBER is a combination of the year, division, series, and body style.

SPECIAL	CODE
Sedan, 4-Door	4019
Sedan, 2-Door	4027
Station Wagon, 4-Door, 2-Seat	4035
Station Wagon, 4-Door, 3-Seat	4045
Convertible, 2-Door	4067

SPECIAL DELUXE	CODE
Sedan, 4-Door	4119
Station Wagon, 4-Door, 2-Seat	4135

SKYLARK	CODE
Coupe, 2-Door	4347
Convertible, 2-Door	4367

LESABRE	CODE
Sedan, 2-Door	4411
Estate Wagon, 4-Door, 2-Seat	4435
Hardtop, 4-Door	4439
Estate Wagon, 4-Door, 3-Seat	4445
Coupe, 2-Door	4447
Convertible, 2-Door	4467
Sedan, 4-Door	4469

INVICTA	CODE
Estate Wagon, 4-Door, 2-Seat	4635

WILDCAT	CODE
Hardtop Sedan, 4-Door	4639
Coupe, 2-Door	4647
Convertible, 2-Door	4667

RIVIERA	CODE
Sports Coupe, 2-Door	4747

ELECTRA 225	CODE
Sedan, 2-Door	4819
Riviera Sedan, 4-Door	4829
Hardtop, 4-Door	4839
Coupe, 2-Door	4847
Convertible, 2-Door	4867

THE BODY NUMBER is the production serial number of the body. The prefix letter denotes the plant in which the body was built.

ASSEMBLY PLANT	CODE
Flint, MI	FB
South Gate, CA	BC
Linden, NJ	BL
Kansas City, KS	BK
Wilmington, DE	BW
Atlanta, GA	BA
Arlington, TX	BT

THE TRIM NUMBER furnishes the key to trim color and material for each model series.

SPECIAL TRIM

COLOR	CLOTH	VINYL	LEATHER	CODE
Aqua		•		085,055
Aqua	•	•		051
Black		•		016,085,080
Blue	•	•		011
Blue		•		076,015,010
Red		•		079,075,070
Red/Black	•	•		071
Rose		•		036
Sandlewood	•	•		031
Sandlewood		•		039,035,030

SPECIAL DELUXE TRIM

COLOR	CLOTH	VINYL	LEATHER	CODE
Aqua	•	•		151
Aqua		•		155
Black		•		185
Blue	•	•		111
Blue		•		115
Red		•		175
Red/Black	•	•		171
Rose	•	•		161
Sandlewood	•	•		131
Sandlewood		•		135
Saddle		•		195

SKYLARK TRIM

COLOR	CLOTH	VINYL	LEATHER	CODE
Aqua	•	•		157
Black		•		188,189
Blue	•	•		117
Blue		•		119
Red		•		178,179
Rose	•	•		167
Sandlewood	•	•		137
Sandlewood		•		139
Saddle		•		198,199
White		•		148,149

LESABRE TRIM

COLOR	CLOTH	VINYL	LEATHER	CODE
Aqua	•	•		451,452
Aqua		•		455
Black		•		485
Blue	•	•		411,412
Blue		•		415,416,410
Red	•	•		471
Red		•		475,476
Red		•		470,479
Red/Black	•	•		472,471
Rose	•	•		462,461
Rose		•		460
Sandlewood	•	•		431,432
Sandlewood		•		435,436
Sandlewood		•		430,439
Saddle		•		495,490

WILDCAT TRIM

COLOR	CLOTH	VINYL	LEATHER	CODE
Black		•		687,689
Black		•		681-688
Blue	•	•		615
Blue		•		619
Red		•		677,671
Red		•		678,679
Rose	•	•		665
Sandlewood	•	•		635
Sandlewood		•		637,631,638
Saddle		•		697,691
Saddle		•		698,699
White		•		649

RIVIERA TRIM COLOR	CLOTH	VINYL	LEATHER	CODE
Black	•	•		787
Black		•	•	788
Blue	•	•		717
Blue		•	•	718
Blue		•		716
Red		•	•	778
Sandlewood	•	•		737
Sandlewood		•		736
Saddle		•	•	798
Silver		•	•	728
Silver		•		726
White		•	•	748

ELECTRA TRIM COLOR	CLOTH	VINYL	LEATHER	CODE
Aqua	•	•		851,856
Black		•	•	888,880,889
Blue	•	•		811,816
Blue		•	•	810
Red		•	•	878,870,879
Sandlewood	•	•		831,836
Sandlewood		•	•	830
Saddle		•	•	898,899
Silver	•	•		821,826
White		•	•	849

THE PAINT CODE furnishes the key to the paint colors used on the car. A two letter code indicates the bottom and top colors respectively.

COLOR	CODE
Regal Black	A
Arctic White	C
Silver Cloud	D
Spruce Green	E
Marlin Blue	F
Willow Mist	J
Burgundy	N
Teal Mist	P
Twilight Aqua	Q
Desert Sand	R
Bronze Mist	S
Fawn Mist	T
Granada Red	V
Diplomat Blue	W
Rose Mist	X

ENGINE NUMBER

Along with the VIN number, the engine block is stamped with an engine production code. The code has a prefix series of letters and numbers that identifies the engine and year, then a four digit numeric production sequence code. On the V-8 engines, the production code is stamped on the right front of the engine block opposite the VIN number. On the V-6 engine, the number is on the front of the block below the left cylinder head gasket.

SPECIAL & SPECIAL DELUXE

ENGINE NO.	NO. CYL.	CID	HORSE-POWER	COMP. RATIO	CARB	TRANS
JL	6	198	135	8.8:1	2 BC	M/A
JZ	6	198	NA	NA	2 BC	M/A
JM	8	215	155	9.0:1	2 BC	M/A
JP	8	215	145	7.6:1	2 BC	M/A
JN	8	215	200	11.0:1	4 BC	M/A

SKYLARK

ENGINE NO.	NO. CYL.	CID	HORSE-POWER	COMP. RATIO	CARB	TRANS
JN	8	215	200	11.0:1	4 BC	M/A

LESABRE

ENGINE NO.	NO. CYL.	CID	HORSE-POWER	COMP. RATIO	CARB	TRANS
JR	8	401	280	10.25:1	2 BC	M/A
JS	8	401	265	9.0:1	2 BC	M/A
JT	8	401	325	10.25:1	4 BC	M/A
JU	8	401	315	8.75:1	4 BC	M/A

WILDCAT & INVICTA

ENGINE NO.	NO. CYL.	CID	HORSE-POWER	COMP. RATIO	CARB	TRANS
JT	8	401	325	10.25:1	4 BC	AUTO
JU	8	401	315	8.75:1	4 BC	AUTO

ELECTRA 225

ENGINE NO.	NO. CYL.	CID	HORSE-POWER	COMP. RATIO	CARB	TRANS
JT	8	401	325	10.25:1	4 BC	AUTO
JU	8	401	315	8.75:1	4 BC	AUTO

RIVIERA

ENGINE NO.	NO. CYL.	CID	HORSE-POWER	COMP. RATIO	CARB	TRANS
JT	8	401	325	10.25:1	4 BC	AUTO
JV	8	401	315	8.75:1	4 BC	AUTO
JW	8	425	340	10.25:1	4 BC	AUTO

1964 BUICK

1964 BUICK

1964 BUICK RIVIERA

1964 BUICK RIVIERA

1964 BUICK SPECIAL

1964 BUICK SPECIAL

VEHICLE IDENTIFICATION NUMBER

BUICK
4K1001555

Commonly referred to as the VIN NUMBER, this series of numbers and letters is stamped on a plate attached to the left front door hinge pillar, and stamped on the top surface of the engine block forward of the valve cover on the left side.

FIRST DIGIT: Identifies the series

SERIES	CODE
Special V-8	0
Special V-6	A
Special Deluxe V-8	1
Special Deluxe V-6	B
Skylark V-8	3
Skylark V-6	C
LeSabre	4
Wildcat	6
Riviera	7
Electra 225	8

SECOND DIGIT: Identifies the model year (1964)

THIRD DIGIT: Identifies the assembly plant

ASSEMBLY PLANT	CODE
Flint, MI	1
South Gate, CA	2
Fremont, OH	3
Kansas City, KS	4
Wilmington, DE	5
Atlanta, GA	6
Baltimore, MD	7
Kansas City, MO	8

LAST SIX DIGITS: Represent the basic production numbers

BODY NUMBER PLATE

Complete identification of each body is provided by a plate riveted to the cowl at the left of center under the hood.

BUICK DIV. GENERAL MOTORS
FLINT, MICH.

STYLE 64 4819 BODY FB 3321
TRIM 677 PAINT A
ACC. BFGIU

BODY BY FISHER

EXAMPLE:

64	Model Year (1964)
4	GM Division (Buick)
8	Series (Electra 225)
19	4-Door Sedan
FB	Flint, Michigan
677	Trim
A	Color
3321	Production Sequence

THE STYLE NUMBER is a combination of the year, division, series, and body style.

SPECIAL	CODE
Sedan, 2-Door	4027
Station Wagon, 4-Door, 2-Seat	4035
Convertible, 2-Door	4067
Sedan, 4-Door	4069

SPECIAL DELUXE	CODE
Sedan, 2-Door	4127
Station Wagon, 4-Door, 2-Seat	4135
Sedan, 4-Door	4169

SKYLARK	CODE
Coupe, 2-Door	4337
Convertible, 2-Door	4367
Sedan, 4-Door	4369

SKYLARK SPORTWAGON CUSTOM	CODE
Station Wagon, 4-Door, 2-Seat	4355
Station Wagon, 4-Door, 3-Seat	4365

SKYLARK SPORTWAGON STANDARD	CODE
Station Wagon, 4-Door, 2-Seat	4255
Station Wagon, 4-Door, 3-Seat	4265

LESABRE	CODE
Hardtop, 4-Door	4439
Hardtop, 2-Door	4447
Convertible, 2-Door	4467
Sedan, 4-Door	4469
Estate Wagon, 4-Door, 2-Seat	4635
Estate Wagon, 4-Door, 3-Seat	4645

WILDCAT	CODE
Hardtop Sedan, 4-Door	4639
Hardtop, 2-Door	4647
Convertible, 2-Door	4667
Sedan, 4-Door	4669

RIVIERA	CODE
Sports Coupe, 2-Door	4747

ELECTRA "225"	CODE
Sedan, 4-Door	4819
Sedan, 4-Door, Pillarless	4829
Hardtop, 4-Door	4839
Coupe, 2-Door	4847
Convertible, 2-Door	4867

THE BODY NUMBER is the production serial number of the body. The prefix letter denotes the plant in which the body was built.

ASSEMBLY PLANT	CODE
Flint, MI	FB
South Gate, CA	BC
Fremont, OH	
Kansas City, KS	BK
Wilmington, DE	BW
Atlanta, GA	BA
Baltimore, MD	
Kansas City, MO	

THE TRIM NUMBER furnishes the key to the trim color and material for each model series.

SPECIAL TRIM COLOR	CLOTH	VINYL	LEATHER	CODE
Black		•		028
Black	•	•		092
Blue	•	•		001
Blue		•		021
Fawn	•	•		003
Fawn		•		023,013
Red		•		027,087
Saddle		•		029
Silver	•	•		002
White		•		084

SPECIAL DELUXE TRIM COLOR	CLOTH	VINYL	LEATHER	CODE
Black		•		128
Blue		•		121,111
Blue	•	•		101
Fawn	•	•		103
Fawn		•		113
Green	•	•		100
Maroon		•		117
Red		•		197,127
Saddle		•		129
Silver	•	•		102
White		•		194

SPORTWAGON TRIM COLOR	CLOTH	VINYL	LEATHER	CODE
Black		•		028
Blue		•		021
Red		•		027
Saddle		•		029

SKYLARK TRIM COLOR	CLOTH	VINYL	LEATHER	CODE
Black		•		158,168,148
Blue	•	•		131
Blue		•		151,171,141
Fawn	•	•		133
Green		•		150,170,160
Green	•	•		130
Maroon		•		177
Maroon	•	•		137
Red		•		147,157,167
Saddle		•		159,179
Saddle		•		169,149
White		•		154,174
White		•		184,164

LESABRE TRIM COLOR	CLOTH	VINYL	LEATHER	CODE
Black		•		448
Blue	•	•		401,411
Blue		•		421,471,441
Fawn	•	•		403,413
Fawn		•		423,473,443
Green	•	•		400
Maroon	•	•		417
Maroon		•		427,477
Red		•		447,487
Saddle		•		489
Silver	•	•		402
White		•		484

LESABRE ESTATE WAGON TRIM COLOR	CLOTH	VINYL	LEATHER	CODE
Black		•		438
Blue	•	•		461
Blue		•		431
Fawn	•	•		463
Fawn		•		433
Maroon	•	•		467
Maroon		•		437
Saddle		•		439

WILDCAT TRIM COLOR	CLOTH	VINYL	LEATHER	CODE
Black		•		688,658
Black		•		448,698
Blue	•	•		401,411
Blue		•		421,471
Blue		•		691,441
Fawn	•	•		403,413
Fawn		•		423,473,443
Green	•	•		400
Maroon	•	•		417
Maroon		•		427,274,477
Red		•		687,697
Red		•		447,487
Saddle		•		689,659
Saddle		•		699,489
Silver	•	•		402
White	•	•		694,484

 1964 BUICK

RIVIERA TRIM

COLOR	CLOTH	VINYL	LEATHER	CODE
Black		•		608,628
Blue	•	•		611
Blue		•		601,621
Fawn	•	•		613
Fawn		•		603
Green	•	•		610
Red		•		607
Saddle		•		629
Silver		•		602
White		•		624

ELECTRA TRIM

COLOR	CLOTH	VINYL	LEATHER	CODE
Black		•	•	678,668
Blue	•	•		631,641
Blue		•	•	661
Fawn	•	•		633,643
Green	•	•		630,640
Red		•	•	677,667
Saddle		•	•	679,669
Silver	•	•		632,642
White		•	•	674

THE PAINT CODE furnishes the key to the paint colors used on the car. A two-letter code indicates the bottom and top colors respectively.

COLOR	CODE
Regal Black	A
Arctic White	C
Silver Cloud	D
Marlin Blue	F
Wedgewood Blue	H
Surf Green	J
Sunburst Yellow	K
Claret Mist	L
Coral Mist	N
Teal Mist	P
Desert Beige	R
Bronze Mist	S
Tawny Mist	T
Granada Red	V
Diplomat Blue	W

ENGINE NUMBER

Along with the VIN number, the engine block is stamped with an engine production code. The code has a prefix series of letters and numbers that identifies the engine and year, then a four digit numeric production sequence code. The production code is stamped on the right front of the engine block opposite the VIN number.

SPECIAL, SPECIAL DELUXE & SKYLARK

ENGINE NO.	NO. CYL.	CID	HORSE-POWER	COMP. RATIO	CARB	TRANS
KH	6	225	155	9.0:1	1 BC	M/A
KJ	6	225	NA	7.6:1	1 BC	M/A
KL	8	300	210	9.0:1	2 BC	M/A
KM	8	300	NA	7.6:1	2 BC	M/A
KP	8	300	250	11.0:1	4 BC	M/A
KR	8	300	NA	NA	4 BC	M/A

LESABRE & SKYLARK SPORTWAGONS

ENGINE NO.	NO. CYL.	CID	HORSE-POWER	COMP. RATIO	CARB	TRANS
KL	8	300	210	9.0;1	2 BC	M/A
KM	8	300	NA	7.6:1	2 BC	M/A
KP	9	300	250	11.0:1	4 BC	M/A

LESABRE ESTATE WAGON, WILDCAT

ENGINE NO.	NO. CYL.	CID	HORSE-POWER	COMP. RATIO	CARB	TRANS
KT	8	401	325	10.25:1	4 BC	M/A
KV	8	401	NA	8.75:1	4 BC	M/A
KW	8	425	340	10.25:1	4 BC	M/A
KX	8	425	360	10.25:1	2-4 BC	M/A

ELECTRA 225

ENGINE NO.	NO. CYL.	CID	HORSE-POWER	COMP. RATIO	CARB	TRANS
KT	8	401	325	10.25:1	4 BC	M/A
KV	8	401	NA	8.75:1	4 BC	M/A
KW	8	425	340	10.25:1	4 BC	M/A
KX	8	425	360	10.25:1	2-4 BC	M/A

RIVIERA

ENGINE NO.	NO. CYL.	CID	HORSE-POWER	COMP. RATIO	CARB	TRANS
KW	8	425	340	10.25:1	4 BC	M/A
KX	8	425	360	10.25:1	2-4 BC	M/A

1965 BUICK

1965 BUICK

1965 BUICK RIVIERA

1965 BUICK RIVIERA

VEHICLE IDENTIFICATION NUMBER

BUICK
444275H001555

Commonly referred to as the VIN NUMBER, this series of numbers and letters is stamped on a plate attached to the left front door hinge pillar, and stamped on the engine block.

FIRST DIGIT: Identifies the GM Division (Buick)

SECOND AND THIRD DIGITS: Identify the series

SERIES	CODE V-6	CODE V-8
Special	33	34
Special Deluxe	35	36
Sportwagon	42	
Skylark	43	44
LeSabre	52	
LeSabre Custom	54	
Wildcat	62	
Wildcat Deluxe	64	
Wildcat Custom	66	
Electra	82	
Electra Custom	84	
Riviera	94	

FOURTH AND FIFTH DIGITS: Identify the body style

Body style	Code
2-Door Coupe	27
4-Door 2-Seat Station Wagon	35
2-Door Hardtop Coupe	37
4-Door Hardtop	39
2-Door Hardtop Coupe	47
4-Door 2-Seat Sportwagon	55
4-Door 3-Seat Sportwagon	65
2-Door Convertible	67
4-Door Sedan	69

SIXTH DIGIT: Identifies the model year (1965)

SEVENTH DIGIT: Identifies the assembly plant

ASSEMBLY PLANT	CODE
Flint, MI	H
South Gate, CA	C
Fremont, OH	Z
Kansas City, KS	X
Wilmington, DE	Y
Atlanta, GA	D
Baltimore, MD	B
Kansas City, MO	K
Bloomfield, MI	V

LAST 6 DIGITS: Represent the basic production numbers

BODY NUMBER PLATE

Complete identification of each body is provided by a plate riveted to the cowl at the left of center under the hood.

BUICK DIV. GENERAL MOTORS
FLINT, MICH.

ST 65-44427 H 001555 BODY
TR 108 AC PAINT

BODY BY FISHER

EXAMPLE:

65 Model Year (1965)
4 GM Division (Buick)
44 Series (V-8 Skylark)
27 2-Door Coupe
H* Flint, Michigan
001555 Production Sequence
108 Trim
A Lower Body Color
C Upper Body Color
* Same assembly plants and codes as used on the VIN plate.

THE STYLE NUMBER is a combination of the year, division, series, and body style.

SPECIAL V-6	CODE
Coupe, 2-Door, Thin Pillar	3327
Station Wagon, 4-Door, 2-Seat	3335
Convertible, 2-Door	3367
Sedan, 4-Door, Thin Pillar	3369

SPECIAL V-8	CODE
Coupe, 2-Door, Thin Pillar	3427
Station Wagon, 4-Door, 2-Seat	3435
Convertible, 2-Door	3467
Sedan, 4-Door, Thin Pillar	3469

SPECIAL DELUXE V-6	CODE
Station Wagon, 4-Door, 2-Seat	3535
Sedan, 4-Door, Thin Pillar	3569

SPECIAL DELUXE V-8	CODE
Station Wagon,4-Door, 2-Seat	3635
Sedan, 4-Door, Thin Pillar	3669

SPORTWAGON V-8	CODE
Station Wagon, 4-Door, 2-Seat	4255
Station Wagon, 4-Door, 3-Seat	4265

SKYLARK V-6	CODE
Coupe, 2-Door, Thin Pillar	4327
Coupe Hardtop, 2-Door	4337
Convertible, 2-Door	4367
Sedan, 4-Door, Thin Pillar	4369

SKYLARK V-8	CODE
Coupe, 2-Door, Thin Pillar	4427
Coupe Hardtop, 2-Door	4437
Convertible, 2-Door	4467
Sedan, 4-Door, Thin Pillar	4469

* Option Grand Sport

SPORTWAGON CUSTOM V-8	CODE
Station Wagon, 4-Door, 2-Seat	4455
Station Wagon, 4-door, 3-Seat	4465

LESABRE	CODE
Coupe Hardtop, 2-Door	5237
Hardtop, 4-Door	5239
Sedan, 4-Door, Thin Pillar	5269

LESABRE CUSTOM	CODE
Coupe Hardtop, 2-Door	5437
Hardtop, 4-Door	5439
Convertible, 2-Door	5467
Sedan, 4-Door, Thin Pillar	5469

WILDCAT	CODE
Coupe Hartop, 2-Door	6237
Hardtop, 4-Door	6239
Sedan, 4-Door, Thin Pillar	6269

WILDCAT DELUXE	CODE
Coupe Hardtop, 2-Door	6437
Hardtop, 4-Door	6439
Convertible, 2-Door	6467
Sedan, 4-Door, Thin Pillar	6469

WILDCAT CUSTOM	CODE
Coupe Hardtop, 2-Door	6637
Hardtop, 4-Door	6639
Convertible, 2-Door	6667

ELECTRA	CODE
Hardtop Coupe, 2-Door	8237
Hardtop, 4-Door	8239
Sedan, 4-Door, Semi Thin Pillar	8269

ELECTRA CUSTOM	CODE
Hardtop Coupe, 2-Door	8437
Hardtop, 4-Door	8439
Convertible, 2-Door	8467
Sedan, 4-Door,Thin Pillar	8469

RIVIERA	CODE
Hardtop Coupe, 2-Door	9447

* Option Grand Sport

1965 BUICK

THE TRIM NUMBER furnishes the key to the trim color and material for each model series.

SPECIAL TRIM

COLOR	CLOTH	VINYL	LEATHER	CODE
Black		•		028,088,118
Blue	•	•		001
Blue		•		021,111
Fawn	•	•		003
Ivory		•		024
Red		•		027,087
Saddle		•		029
Silver	•	•		002

SPECIAL DELUXE TRIM

COLOR	CLOTH	VINYL	LEATHER	CODE
Aqua	•	•		106
Black		•		118
Blue		•		121,111
Blue	•	•		101
Fawn	•	•		103
Green	•	•		100
Green		•		120
Red		•		127
Saddle		•		129,119

SPORTWAGON TRIM

COLOR	CLOTH	VINYL	LEATHER	CODE
Blue		•		021
Green		•		020
Red		•		027
Saddle		•		029

SKYLARK TRIM

COLOR	CLOTH	VINYL	LEATHER	CODE
Aqua	•	•		136
Black	•	•		108,138,188
Black		•		198,148,158
Blue	•	•		101,131
Blue		•		191,151
Blue		•		141,171
Fawn	•	•		103,133
Green	•	•		130
Green		•		140
Ivory		•		154
Red		•		157,147,197
Saddle		•		199,159,149

LESABRE TRIM

COLOR	CLOTH	VINYL	LEATHER	CODE
Blue	•	•		401
Fawn	•	•		403
Green	•	•		400
Silver	•	•		402

LESABRE CUSTOM TRIM

COLOR	CLOTH	VINYL	LEATHER	CODE
Aqua	•	•		416
Black	•	•		418
Black		•		428,478
Black		•		448,488
Blue	•	•		411
Blue		•		421,441
Fawn	•	•		413
Red		•		427,447,487
Saddle		•		429,449

WILDCAT TRIM

COLOR	CLOTH	VINYL	LEATHER	CODE
Blue	•	•		401
Fawn	•	•		403
Green	•	•		400
Silver	•	•		402

WILDCAT CUSTOM TRIM

COLOR	CLOTH	VINYL	LEATHER	CODE
Aqua	•	•		416
Black		•		428,478
Black		•		448,488
Black	•	•		418
Blue	•	•		411
Blue		•		421,441
Fawn	•	•		413
Red		•		427,447,487
Saddle		•		429,449

WILDCAT CUSTOM TRIM

COLOR	CLOTH	VINYL	LEATHER	CODE
Black		•		658,678
Blue		•		671,651
Green		•		654,674
Ivory		•		674
Red		•		657,677
Saddle		•		679,659

ELECTRA TRIM

COLOR	CLOTH	VINYL	LEATHER	CODE
Aqua	•	•		636
Blue	•	•		631
Fawn	•	•		633
Green	•	•		654,674
Silver	•	•		632

ELECTRA CUSTOM TRIM

COLOR	CLOTH	VINYL	LEATHER	CODE
Black		•		698,688
Blue	•	•		641
Blue		•		691
Fawn	•	•		643
Gray	•	•		642
Green	•	•		640
Green		•		690
Ivory		•		694
Red		•		697
Saddle		•		699,689

RIVIERA TRIM

COLOR	CLOTH	VINYL	LEATHER	CODE
Black	•	•		618
Black		•		608,628
Blue	•	•		611
Blue		•		601
Fawn	•	•		613
Green	•	•		610
Green		•		620
Ivory		•		624
Saddle		•		609,629

THE PAINT CODE furnishes the key to the paint colors used on the car. A two-letter code indicates the bottom and top colors respectively.

COLOR	Code
Regal Black	A
Arctic White	C
Astro Blue	D
Midnight Blue	E
Seafoam Green	H
Verde Green	J
Turquoise Mist	K
Midnight Aqua	L
Burgundy Mist	N
Flame Red	R
Sahara Mist	S
Champagne Mist	T
Shell Beige	V
Bamboo Cream	Y
Silver Cloud	Z

Note: Code letter can be found on the Fisher Body Number Plate.

ENGINE NUMBER

Along with the VIN number, the engine block is stamped with an engine production code. The code has a series of letters that identifies the engine and a numeric production date code. The production code is stamped on the right side of the engine block.

SPECIAL, SPECIAL DELUXE & SKYLARK

ENGINE NO.	NO. CYL.	CID	HORSE-POWER	COMP. RATIO	CARB	TRANS
LH	6	225	155	9.0:1	1 BC	M/A
LJ	6	225	NA	7.6:1	1 BC	M/A
LL	8	300	210	9.0:1	2 BC	M/A
LM	8	300	NA	8.75:1	2 BC	M/A
LP	8	300	250	10.25:1	4 BC	M/A

SPORTWAGON & LESABRE

ENGINE NO.	NO. CYL.	CID	HORSE-POWER	COMP. RATIO	CARB	TRANS
LL	8	300	210	9.0;1	2 BC	M/A
LM	8	300	NA	8.75:1	2 BC	M/A
LP	8	300	250	10.25:1	4 BC	M/A

SKYLARK GRAND SPORT

ENGINE NO.	NO. CYL.	CID	HORSE-POWER	COMP. RATIO	CARB	TRANS
LR	8	400	325	10.25:1	4 BC	M/A
NA	8	400	NA	8.75:1	4 BC	M/A

WILDCAT

ENGINE NO.	NO. CYL.	CID	HORSE-POWER	COMP. RATIO	CARB	TRANS
LT	8	401	325	10.25:1	4 BC	M/A
LV	8	401	NA	8.75:1	4 BC	M/A
LW	8	425	340	10.25:1	4 BC	M/A
LX	8	425	360	10.25:1	2-4 BC	M/A

ELECTRA & RIVIERA

ENGINE NO.	NO. CYL.	CID	HORSE-POWER	COMP. RATIO	CARB	TRANS
LT	8	401	325	10.25;1	4 BC	AUTO
LV	8	401	NA	8.75:1	4 BC	AUTO
LW	8	425	340	10.25:1	4 BC	AUTO
LX	8	425	360	10.25:1	2-4 BC	AUTO

1966 BUICK ELECTRA

1966 BUICK LESABRE

1966 BUICK RIVIERA

1966 BUICK RIVIERA

1966 BUICK SKYLARK

1966 BUICK SPECIAL

1966 BUICK WILDCAT

1966 BUICK WILDCAT

VEHICLE IDENTIFICATION NUMBER

BUICK
444076H101555

Commonly referred to as the VIN NUMBER, this series of numbers and letters is stamped on a plate attached to the left front door hinge pillar, and stamped on the engine block.

FIRST DIGIT: Identifies the GM Division (Buick)

SECOND AND THIRD DIGITS: Identify the series

SERIES	CODE V-6	CODE V-8
Special	33	34
Special Deluxe	35	36
Skylark	43	44
Sportwagon	42	
Sportwagon Custom	44	
Skylark Grand Sport	46	
LeSabre	52	
LeSabre	54	
Wildcat	64	
Wildcat Custom	66	
Electra	82	
Electra Custom	84	
Riviera	94	

FOURTH AND FIFTH DIGITS: Identify the body style

Sport Coupe, 2-Door, Pillar Post	07
Sport Coupe, 2-Door, Hardtop	17
Station Wagon, 4-Door, 2-Seat	35
Hardtop Coupe, 2-Door	37
Sedan Hardtop, 4-Door	39
Sportwagon, 4-Door, 2-Seat	55
Sport Coupe Hardtop, 2-Door	57
Sportwagon, 4-Door, 3-Seat	65
Convertible, 2-Door	67
Sedan, 4-Door, Pillar Post	69
Sport Coupe Hardtop, 2-Door	87

SIXTH DIGIT: Identifies the model year (1966)

SEVENTH DIGIT: Identifies the assembly plant

ASSEMBLY PLANT	CODE
Flint, MI	H
South Gate, CA	C
Fremont, OH	Z
Kansas City, KS	X
Wilmington, DE	Y
Atlanta, GA	D
Baltimore, MD	B
Kansas City, MO	K
Bloomfield, MI	V
Oshawa, Ont., CAN	I

LAST 6 DIGITS: Represent the basic production numbers

BODY NUMBER PLATE

Complete identification of each body is provided by a plate riveted to the cowl at the left of center under the hood.

BUICK DIV. GENERAL MOTORS
FLINT, MICH.

ST 66-44407 H 101555 BODY
TR 188 AC PAINT
ACC. BFGIU

BODY BY FISHER

EXAMPLE:

66	Model Year (1966)
4	GM Division (Buick)
44	Series (V-8 Skylark)
07	2-Door Sport Coupe
H*	Flint, Michigan
101555	Production Sequence
188	Trim
A	Lower Body Color
C	Upper Body Color

* Same assembly plants and codes as used on the VIN plate.

THE STYLE NUMBER is a combination of the year, division, series, and body style.

SPECIAL V-6	CODE
Coupe, 2-Door, Thin Pillar	3307
Station Wagon, 4-Door, 2-Seat	3335
Convertible, 2-Door	3367
Sedan, 4-Door, Thin Pillar	3369

SPECIAL V-8	CODE
Coupe, 2-Door, Thin Pillar	3407
Station Wagon, 4-Door, 2-Seat	3435
Convertible, 2-Door	3467
Sedan, 4-Door, Thin Pillar	3469

SPECIAL DELUXE V-6	CODE
Coupe, 2-Door, Thin Pillar	3507
2-Door Coupe Hardtop	3517
Station Wagon, 4-Door, 2-Seat	3535
Sedan, 4-Door, Thin Pillar	3569

SPECIAL DELUXE V-8	CODE
Coupe, 2-Door, Thin Pillar	3607
Coupe Hardtop, 2-Door	3617
Station Wagon, 4-Door, 2-Seat	3635
Sedan Thin Pillar, 4-Door	3669

SPORTWAGON V-8	CODE
Station Wagon, 4-Door, 2-Seat	4255
Station Wagon, 4-Door, 3-Seat	4265
Station Wagon, 4-Door, 2-Seat	4455
Station Wagon, 4-Door, 3-Seat	4465

SKYLARK V-6	CODE
Coupe, 2-Door, Thin Pillar	4307
Coupe Hardtop, 2-Door	4317
Hardtop, 4-Door	4339
Convertible, 2-Door	4367

SKYLARK V-8	CODE
Coupe, 2-Door, Thin Pillar	4407
Coupe Hardtop, 2-Door	4417
Hardtop, 4-Door	4439
Convertible, 2-Door	4467

SKYLARK GRAND SPORT	CODE
Coupe, 2-Door, Thin Pillar	4607
Coupe Hardtop, 2-Door	4617
Convertible, 2-Door	4667

LESABRE	CODE
Coupe Hardtop, 2-Door	5237
Hardtop, 4-Door	5239
Sedan, 4-Door, Thin Pillar	5269

LESABRE CUSTOM	CODE
Coupe Hardtop, 2-Door	5437
Hardtop, 4-Door	5439
Convertible, 2-Door	5467
Sedan, 4-Door, Thin Pillar	5469

WILDCAT	CODE
Coupe Hardtop, 2-Door	6437
Hardtop, 4-Door	6439
Convertible, 2-Door	6467
Sedan, 4-Door, Thin Pillar	6469

WILDCAT CUSTOM	CODE
Coupe Hardtop, 2-Door	6637
Hardtop, 4-Door	6639
Convertible, 2-Door	6667

ELECTRA	CODE
Coupe Hardtop, 2-Door	8237
Hardtop, 4-Door	8239
Sedan, 4-Door, Semi-Thin Pillar	8269

ELECTRA CUSTOM	CODE
Coupe Hardtop, 2-Door	8437
Hardtop, 4-Door	8439
Convertible, 2-Door	8467
Sedan, 4-Door, Semi-Thin Pillar	8469

RIVIERA	CODE
Coupe Hardtop, 2-Door	9487

THE BODY NUMBER is the production serial number of the body. The prefix letter denotes the plant in which the body was built.

THE TRIM NUMBER furnishes the key to the trim color and material for each model series.

SPECIAL TRIM

COLOR	CLOTH	VINYL	LEATHER	CODE
Aqua		•		126
Black	•	•		108,408
Black		•		448,128
Blue		•		111,121
Blue	•	•		101
Lt. Fawn		•		113
Fawn	•	•		103
Red		•		117

SPECIAL DELUXE TRIM

COLOR	CLOTH	VINYL	LEATHER	CODE
Aqua		•		166,126
Aqua	•	•		146
Black		•		138,168,128
Blue		•		131,161,121
Blue	•	•		141
Lt. Fawn		•		133,163
Fawn	•	•		143
Red		•		167,137
Saddle		•		139

SKYLARK TRIM

COLOR	CLOTH	VINYL	LEATHER	CODE
Aqua		•		166
Aqua	•	•		156
Black	•	•		188
Black		•		168,198,185
Blue	•	•		181,151
Blue		•		161,191
Lt. Fawn		•		163,193,182
Fawn	•	•		183,153
Green	•	•		150
Red		•		167,197

SPORTWAGON TRIM

COLOR	CLOTH	VINYL	LEATHER	CODE
Black		•		178
Blue		•		161,171
Lt. Fawn		•		133
Green		•		170
Red		•		137,177
Saddle		•		179

SKYLARK GS TRIM

COLOR	CLOTH	VINYL	LEATHER	CODE
Aqua		•		166
Black		•		168,198
Blue		•		161,191
Lt. Fawn		•		163,193
Red		•		167,197

LESABRE TRIM

COLOR	CLOTH	VINYL	LEATHER	CODE
Black	•	•		408
Blue	•	•		401
Fawn	•	•		403
Green	•	•		400

1966 BUICK

LESABRE CUSTOM TRIM

COLOR	CLOTH	VINYL	LEATHER	CODE
Aqua	•	•		416
Aqua		•		426
Black		•		428,478
Blue	•	•		411
Blue		•		421
Lt. Fawn		•		423
Fawn	•	•		413
Red	•	•		417
Red		•		427
Saddle		•		429

WILDCAT TRIM

COLOR	CLOTH	VINYL	LEATHER	CODE
Aqua	•	•		416
Aqua		•		426
Black		•		428,478
Blue	•	•		411
Blue		•		421
Lt. Fawn		•		423
Fawn	•	•		413
Red	•	•		417
Red		•		427
Saddle		•		429

WILDCAT CUSTOM TRIM

COLOR	CLOTH	VINYL	LEATHER	CODE
Aqua		•		456
Black		•		458,498
Blue		•		451
Lt. Fawn		•		453,493
Red		•		457

ELECTRA TRIM

COLOR	CLOTH	VINYL	LEATHER	CODE
Aqua	•	•		636
Black	•	•		678
Blue	•	•		631
Fawn	•	•		633
Green	•	•		630
Slate	•	•		632

ELECTRA CUSTOM TRIM

COLOR	CLOTH	VINYL	LEATHER	CODE
Black	•	•		698
Black		•		698,688
Blue	•	•		641
Blue		•		691
Lt. Fawn		•		693,683
Fawn	•	•		643
Green	•	•		640
Red		•		697
Slate	•	•		642

RIVIERA TRIM

COLOR	CLOTH	VINYL	LEATHER	CODE
Aqua		•		656
Black		•		608,658
Black		•		668,618
Black	•	•		628
Blue		•		601,651,611
Lt. Fawn		•		603,653,663
Green		•		610
Plum	•	•		627
White		•		614
Bronze		•		617

THE PAINT CODE furnishes the key to the paint colors used on the car. A two-letter code indicates the bottom and top colors respectively.

COLOR	CODE
Regal Black	A
Riviera Gunmetal	B
Arctic White	C
Astro Blue	D
Midnight Blue	E
Blue Mist	F
Riviera Gold	G
Seafoam Green	H
Verde Green	J
Turquoise Mist	K
Shadow Turquoise	L
Riviera Red	M
Burgundy Mist	N
Flame Red	R
Riviera Champagne	S
Saddle Mist	T
Riviera Plum	U
Shell Beige	V
Silver Mist	W
Riviera White	X
Cream	Y
Riviera Silver Green	Z

ENGINE NUMBER

Along with the VIN number, the engine block is stamped with an engine production code. The code has a series of letters that identifies the engine and a numeric production date code. The production code is stamped on the right side of the engine block.

SPECIAL, SPECIAL DELUXE, SKYLARK

ENGINE NO.	NO. CYL.	CID	HORSE-POWER	COMP. RATIO	CARB	TRANS
MH	6	225	160	9.0;1	2 BC	M/A
MK	6	225	NA	7.6:1	2 BC	M/A
ML	8	300	210	9.0:1	2 BC	M/A
MM	8	300	NA	7.6:1	2 BC	M/A
MB	8	340	260	10.25:1	4 BC	M/A
MC	8	340	NA	7.6:1	2 BC	M/A

SPORTWAGON & LESABRE

ENGINE NO.	NO. CYL.	CID	HORSE-POWER	COMP. RATIO	CARB	TRANS
MA	8	340	220	9.0:1	2 BC	M/A
MC	8	340	NA	7.6:1	2 BC	M/A
MB	8	340	260	10.25:1	4 BC	M/A

SKYLARK GRAND SPORT

ENGINE NO.	NO. CYL.	CID	HORSE-POWER	COMP. RATIO	CARB	TRANS
MR	8	400	325	10.25:1		

WILDCAT

ENGINE NO.	NO. CYL.	CID	HORSE-POWER	COMP. RATIO	CARB	TRANS
MT	8	401	325	10.25:1	4 BC	M/A
MV	8	401	NA	8.75:1	4 BC	M/A
MW	8	425	340	10.25:1	4 BC	M/A
MZ	8	425	360	10.25:1	2-4 BC	M/A

ELECTRA

ENGINE NO.	NO. CYL.	CID	HORSE-POWER	COMP. RATIO	CARB	TRANS
MT	8	401	325	10.25:1	4 BC	AUTO
MV	8401	NA	8.75:1	4 BC	AUTO	
MW	8	425	340	10.25:1	4 BC	AUTO

RIVIERA

ENGINE NO.	NO. CYL.	CID	HORSE-POWER	COMP. RATIO	CARB	TRANS
MT	8	401	325	10.25:1	4 BC	AUTO
MV	8	401	NA	8.75:1	4 BC	AUTO
MW	8	425	340	10.25:1	4 BC	AUTO
MZ	8	425	360	10.25:1	2-4 BC	AUTO

1967 BUICK ELECTRA

1967 BUICK LESABRE

1967 BUICK RIVIERA

1967 BUICK RIVIERA

1967 BUICK SKYLARK

1967 BUICK SKYLARK

1967 BUICK SPECIAL

1967 BUICK SPECIAL

1967 BUICK WILDCAT

1967 BUICK WILDCAT

VEHICLE IDENTIFICATION NUMBER

BUICK
444 077 H101555

Commonly referred to as the VIN NUMBER, this series of numbers and letters is stamped on a plate attached to the left front door hinge pillar, and stamped on the engine block.

FIRST DIGIT: Identifies the GM Division (Buick)

SECOND AND THIRD DIGITS: Identify the series

SERIES	CODE
Special	33
Special Deluxe	35
Special Deluxe Wagon	36
GS 340	40
Skylark	43 & 44
Sportwagon	44
GS 400	46
LeSabre	52
LeSabre Custom	54
Wildcat	64
Wildcat Custom	66
Electra	82
Electra Custom	84
Riviera	94

FOURTH AND FIFTH DIGITS: Identify the body style

Sport Coupe, 2-Door	07
Sport Coupe, 2-Door Hardtop	17
Station Wagon, 4-Door, 2-Seat	35
Hardtop Coupe, 2-Door	37
Sedan Hardtop, 4-Door	39
Sportwagon, 4-Door, 2-Seat	55
Sport Coupe Hardtop, 2-Door	57
Sportwagon, 4-Door, 3-Seat	65
Convertible Coupe, 2-Door	67
Sedan, 4-Door	
Pillar Post	69
Sport Coupe Hardtop, 2-Door	87

SIXTH DIGIT: Identifies the model year (1967)

SEVENTH DIGIT: Identifies the assembly plant

ASSEMBLY PLANT	CODE
Flint, MI	H
South Gate, CA	C
Fremont, OH	Z
Kansas City, KS	X
Wilmington, DE	Y
Atlanta, GA	D
Baltimore, MD	B
Kansas City, MO	K
Bloomfield, MI	V
Oshawa, Ont., CAN	I

LAST 6 DIGITS: Represent the basic production numbers

BODY NUMBER PLATE

Complete identification of each body is provided by a plate riveted to the cowl at the left of center under the hood.

BUICK DIV. GENERAL MOTORS
FLINT, MICH.

ST 67-44417 H 101555 BODY
TR 188 AC PAINT

BODY BY FISHER

EXAMPLE:

67	Model Year (1967)
4	GM Division (Buick)
44	Series (Skylark)
17	2-Door Hardtop Coupe
H*	Flint, Michigan
101555	Production Sequence
188	Trim
A	Lower Body Color
C	Upper Body Color

* Same assembly plants and codes as used on the VIN plate.

THE STYLE NUMBER is a combination of the year, division, series, and body style.

SPECIAL	CODE
Coupe, 2-Door, Thin Pillar	3307
Station Wagon, 4-Door, 2-Seat	3335
Sedan, 4-Door, Thin Pillar	3369

SPECIAL DELUXE	CODE
Coupe, 2-Door	3517
Station Wagon, 4-Door	3635
Sedan 4-Door, Thin Pillar	3569

SKYLARK	CODE
Coupe, 2-Door, Thin Pillar*	4307
Coupe Hardtop, 2-Door	4417
Hardtop, 4-Door	4439
Convertible, 2-Door	4467
Sedan, 4-Door, Thin Pillar	4469

* Option California GS

SPORTWAGON	CODE
Station Wagon, 4-Door, 2-Seat	4455
Station Wagon, 4-Door, 3-Seat	4465

G.S. 340	CODE
Coupe, 2-Door	4017

G.S. 400	CODE
Coupe, 2-Door, Thin Pillar	4607
Coupe Hardtop, 2-Door	4617
Convertible, 2-Door	4667

LESABRE	CODE
Hardtop, 4-Door	5239
Sedan, 4-Door, Thin Pillar	5269
Coupe Hardtop, 2-Door	5287

* Option 400

LESABRE CUSTOM	CODE
Hardtop, 4-Door	5439
Convertible, 2-Door	5467
Sedan, 4-Door, Thin Pillar	5469
Coupe Hardtop, 2-Door	5487

* Option 400

WILDCAT	CODE
Hardtop, 4-Door	6439
Convertible, 2-Door	6467
Sedan, 4-Door, Thin Pillar	6469
Coupe Hardtop, 2-Door	6487

* Option GS

WILDCAT CUSTOM	CODE
Hardtop, 4-Door	6639
Convertible, 2-Door	6667
Coupe Hardtop, 2-Door	6687

* Option GS

ELECTRA	CODE
Hardtop, 4-Door	8239
Coupe Hardtop, 2-Door	8257
Sedan, 4-Door, Thin Pillar	8269

ELECTRA CUSTOM	CODE
Hardtop, 4-Door*	8439
Coupe Hardtop, 2-Door	8457
Convertible, 2-Door	8467
Sedan, 4-Door, Thin Pillar	8469

* Option Limited

RIVIERA	CODE
Coupe Hardtop, 2-Door	9487

* Option GS

THE BODY NUMBER is the production serial number of the body. The prefix letter denotes the plant in which the body was built.

THE TRIM NUMBER furnishes the key to trim color and material for each model series.

SPECIAL TRIM

COLOR	CLOTH	VINYL	LEATHER	CODE
Black	•	•		108
Black		•		118,138
Blue	•	•		111,131
Blue		•		101
Lt. Fawn		•		114,134
Saddle	•	•		103
Red		•		117

SPECIAL DELUXE TRIM

COLOR	CLOTH	VINYL	LEATHER	CODE
Aqua	•	•		146
Aqua		•		166
Black	•	•		188,148
Black		•		138,168
Blue	•	•		181,141
Blue		•		131,161
Lt. Fawn		•		134,164
Saddle	•	•		183,143
Saddle		•		133

SKYLARK TRIM

COLOR	CLOTH	VINYL	LEATHER	CODE
Aqua		•		166
Black	•	•		188,158,185
Black		•		168,198
Blue	•	•		181,151
Blue		•		161,191
Lt. Fawn	•	•		184
Lt. Fawn		•		164,194
Saddle	•	•		153,183
Saddle		•		163
Maroon	•	•		157
Red		•		167,197

SPORTWAGON & GS 400 TRIM

COLOR	CLOTH	VINYL	LEATHER	CODE
Black		•		178
Blue		•		171
Green		•		170
Saddle		•		173
Red		•		177

WILDCAT TRIM

COLOR	CLOTH	VINYL	LEATHER	CODE
Aqua		•		196
Black		•		185,198
Blue		•		191
Lt. Fawn		•		184,194
Saddle		•		193
Red		•		197

LESABRE TRIM

COLOR	CLOTH	VINYL	LEATHER	CODE
Black	•	•		408
Blue	•	•		401
Green	•	•		400
Saddle	•	•		403

LESABRE CUSTOM TRIM

COLOR	CLOTH	VINYL	LEATHER	CODE
Aqua	•	•		416
Aqua		•		426
Black		•		428,478
Blue	•	•		411
Blue		•		421
Saddle	•	•		413
Saddle		•		423
Maroon	•	•		417
Red		•		427

WILDCAT TRIM

COLOR	CLOTH	VINYL	LEATHER	CODE
Aqua	•	•		416
Aqua		•		426
Black		•		428,478
Blue	•	•		411
Blue		•		421
Saddle	•	•		413
Saddle		•		423
Maroon		•		417
Red		•		427

WILDCAT CUSTOM TRIM

COLOR	CLOTH	VINYL	LEATHER	CODE
Aqua		•		456
Black		•		428,458,498
Blue		•		421,451
Lt. Fawn		•		454
Saddle		•		423
Red		•		457

ELECTRA 225 TRIM

COLOR	CLOTH	VINYL	LEATHER	CODE
Aqua	•	•		636
Black	•	•		638
Black		•		678
Blue	•	•		631
Lt. Fawn		•		674
Saddle	•	•		633

ELECTRA CUSTOM TRIM

COLOR	CLOTH	VINYL	LEATHER	CODE
Black	•	•		648
Black		•		698,688
Blue	•	•		641
Blue		•		691
Lt. Fawn	•	•		644
Lt. Fawn		•		694
Green	•	•		640
Saddle		•		693
Maroon	•	•		647
Red		•		697

RIVIERA TRIM

COLOR	CLOTH	VINYL	LEATHER	CODE
Aqua		•		656
Black		•		608,668
Black		•		658,618
Black	•	•		628
Blue	•	•		651
Lt. Fawn	•	•		624
Lt. Fawn		•		604,664
Green		•		610
Saddle		•		653
Plum		•		619
Ivory		•		612

THE PAINT CODE furnishes the key to the paint colors used on the car. A two-letter code indicates the bottom and top colors respectively.

COLOR	CODE
Regal Black	A
Riviera Turquoise	B
Arctic White	C
Sapphire Blue	D
Midnight Blue	E
Blue Mist	F
Gold Mist	G
Green Mist	H
Verde Green	J
Aquamarine	K
Shadow Turquoise	L
Burgundy Mist	N
Platinum Mist	P
Apple Red	R
Champagne Mist	S
Ivory	T
Riviera Plum	U
Riviera Charcoal	V
Riviera Fawn	W
Riviera Red	X
Riviera Gold	Z

ENGINE NUMBER

Along with the VIN number, the engine block is stamped with an engine production code. The code has a series of letters that identifies the engine and a numeric production date code. The production code is stamped on the right side of the engine block.

SPECIAL, SPECIAL DELUXE (EXCEPT WAGON) & SKYLARK COUPE

ENGINE NO.	NO. CYL.	CID	HORSE-POWER	COMP. RATIO	CARB	TRANS
NH	6	225	160	9.0:1	2 BC	M/A
NL	8	300	210	9.0:1	2 BC	M/A
NM	8	300	NA	7.6:1	2 BC	M/A
NB	8	340	260	10.25:1	4 BC	M/A

SPECIAL DELUXE WAGON, SKYLARK (EXCEPT COUPE & 4-DR. HT)

ENGINE NO.	NO. CYL.	CID	HORSE-POWER	COMP. RATIO	CARB	TRANS
NL	8	300	210	9.0:1	2 BC	M/A
NM	8	300	NA	7.6:1	2 BC	M/A
NB	8	340	260	10.25:1	4 BC	M/A

SKYLARK 4-DR HT, SPORTWAGON, LESABRE

ENGINE NO.	NO. CYL.	CID	HORSE-POWER	COMP. RATIO	CARB	TRANS
NA	8	340	220	9.0:1	2 BC	M/A
NX	8	340	NA	8.1:1	2 BC	M/A
NB	8	340	260	10.25:1	4 BC	M/A

GS 340

ENGINE NO.	NO. CYL.	CID	HORSE-POWER	COMP. RATIO	CARB	TRANS
NB	8	340	260	10.25:1	4 BC	M/A

GS 400

ENGINE NO.	NO. CYL.	CID	HORSE-POWER	COMP. RATIO	CARB	TRANS
NR	8	400	340	10.25:1	4 BC	M/A

WILDCAT, ELECTRA 225, RIVIERA

ENGINE NO.	NO. CYL.	CID	HORSE-POWER	COMP. RATIO	CARB	TRANS
ND	8	430	360	10.25:1	4 BC	AUTO
MD	8	430	360	10.25:1	4 BC	AUTO
NE	8	430	NA	8.75:1	4 BC	AUTO

1968 BUICK ELECTRA

1968 BUICK ELECTRA

1968 BUICK LESABRE

1968 BUICK LESABRE

1968 BUICK RIVIERA

1968 BUICK SPECIAL

1968 BUICK SKYLARK

1968 BUICK SKYLARK

1968 BUICK WILDCAT

1968 BUICK WILDCAT

VEHICLE IDENTIFICATION NUMBER

BUICK
444378H101555

Commonly referred to as the VIN NUMBER, this series of numbers and letters is stamped on a plate attached to the left front door hinge pillar, and stamped on the engine block.

FIRST DIGIT: Identifies the GM Division (Buick)

SECOND AND THIRD DIGITS: Identify the series

SERIES	CODE
Special Deluxe	33
G.S. 350	34
Special Deluxe Wagon	34
Skylark	35
Skylark Custom	44
G.S. 400	46
Sportwagon	44
LeSabre	52
LeSabre Custom	54
Wildcat	64
Wildcat Custom	66
Electra 225	82
Electra 225 Custom	84
Riviera	94

FOURTH AND FIFTH DIGITS: Identify the body style

2-Door Coupe	27
4-Door 2-Seat Station Wagon	35
2-Door Hardtop Coupe	37
4-Door Hardtop	39
4-Door 2-Seat Sportwagon	55
2-Door Hardtop Coupe	57
4-Door 3-Seat Sportwagon	65
Convertible	67
4-Door Sedan	69
2-Door Hardtop Coupe	87

SIXTH DIGIT: Identifies the model year (1968)

SEVENTH DIGIT: Identifies the assembly plant

ASSEMBLY PLANT	CODE
Flint, MI	H
South Gate, CA	C
Fremont, OH	Z
Kansas City, KS	X
Wilmington, DE	Y
Atlanta, GA	D
Baltimore, MD	B
Kansas City, MO	K
Bloomfield, MI	V
Oshawa, Ont., CAN	I

LAST 6 DIGITS: Represent the basic production numbers

BODY NUMBER PLATE

Complete identification of each body is provided by a plate riveted to the cowl at the left of center under the hood.

BUICK DIV. GENERAL MOTORS
FLINT, MICH.

ST 68-44437 H 101555 BODY
TR 138 AC PAINT

BODY BY FISHER

EXAMPLE:

68	Model Year (1968)
4	GM Division (Buick)
44	Series (Skylark Custom)
37	2-Door Hardtop Coupe
H*	Flint, Michigan
101555	Production Sequence
138	Trim
A	Lower Body Color
C	Upper Body Color

* Same assembly plants and codes as used on the VIN plate.

THE STYLE NUMBER is a combination of the year, division, series, and body style.

SPECIAL DELUXE	CODE
Coupe, 2-Door, Thin Pillar*	3327
Sedan, 4-Door, Thin Pillar	3369
Station Wagon, 4-Door, 2-Seat	3435

* Option California GS

G.S. 350	CODE
Hardtop Coupe, 2-Door	3437

SKYLARK	CODE
Hardtop Coupe, 2-Door	3537
Sedan, 4-Door, Thin Pillar	3569

SKYLARK CUSTOM	CODE
Hardtop Coupe, 2-Door	4437
Hardtop Sedan, 4-Door	4439
Convertible	4467
Sedan, 4-Door	4469

SPORTWAGON	CODE
Station Wagon, 4-Door, 2-Seat	4455
Station Wagon, 4-Door, 3-Seat	4465

G.S.400	CODE
Hardtop Coupe, 2-Door	4637
Convertible	4667

* Option 400

LESABRE	CODE
Hardtop, 4-Door	5239
Sedan, 4-Door, Thin Pillar	5269
Coupe Hardtop, 2-Door	5287

* Option 400

LESABRE CUSTOM	CODE
Hardtop, 4-Door	5439
Convertible, 2-Door	5467
Sedan, 4-Door, Thin Pillar	5469
Coupe Hardtop, 2-Door	5487

* Option 400

WILDCAT	CODE
Hardtop, 4-Door	6439
Sedan, 4-Door, Thin Pillar	6469
Hardtop Coupe, 2-Door	6487

WILDCAT CUSTOM	CODE
Hardtop, 4-Door	6639
Convertible, 2-Door	6667
Hardtop Coupe, 2-Door	6687

ELECTRA 225	CODE
Hardtop, 4-Door	8239
Hardtop Coupe, 2-Door	8257
Sedan, 4-Door	8269

ELECTRA 225 CUSTOM	CODE
Hardtop, 4-Door*	8439
Hardtop Coupe, 2-Door	8457
Convertible, 2-Door	8467
Sedan, 4-Door	8469

* Option Limited

RIVIERA	CODE
Hardtop Coupe, 2-Door	9487

* Option GS

THE BODY NUMBER is the production serial number of the body. The prefix letter denotes the plant in which the body was built.

THE TRIM NUMBER furnishes the key to the trim color and material for each model series.

SPECIAL DELUXE TRIM

COLOR	CLOTH	VINYL	LEATHER	CODE
Black	•	•		108
Black		•		198
Blue		•		191,101,111
Gold	•	•		103
Parchment		•		194,114
Buckskin		•		113

GS 350 TRIM

COLOR	CLOTH	VINYL	LEATHER	CODE
Black		•		118,178
Blue		•		111,171
Green		•		170
Buckskin		•		173
Parchment		•		114
White		•		172

SKYLARK TRIM

COLOR	CLOTH	VINYL	LEATHER	CODE
Black	•	•		128
Black		•		118,168
Blue	•	•		121
Blue		•		111,161
Green	•	•		120
Green		•		160
Gold	•	•		123
Parchment		•		114
White		•		162

SKYLARK CUSTOM TRIM

COLOR	CLOTH	VINYL	LEATHER	CODE
Black	•	•		138
Black		•		168,178,158
Blue	•	•		131,141
Blue		•		161,171
Green	•	•		140
Green		•		160,170
Buckskin		•		173,163
Gold		•		133,143
Maroon	•	•		147,137
White		•		162,172,152
Red		•		167

SPORTWAGON TRIM

COLOR	CLOTH	VINYL	LEATHER	CODE
Black		•		188
Blue		•		181
Green		•		180
Buckskin		•		183
Red		•		187

GS 400 TRIM

COLOR	CLOTH	VINYL	LEATHER	CODE
Black		•		158,178
Blue		•		171
Green		•		170
Buckskin		•		173
White		•		152,172

LESABRE TRIM

COLOR	CLOTH	VINYL	LEATHER	CODE
Black	•	•		408
Blue	•	•		401
Green	•	•		400
Gold	•	•		403
Maroon	•	•		407

LESABRE CUSTOM/WILDCAT TRIM

COLOR	CLOTH	VINYL	LEATHER	CODE
Black		•		428,478
Blue	•	•		411
Blue		•		421
Green	•	•		410
Green		•		420
Buckskin		•		423
Gold	•	•		413
Maroon	•	•		417
Red		•		427

WILDCAT CUSTOM TRIM

COLOR	CLOTH	VINYL	LEATHER	CODE
Black	•	•		468
Black		•		458,498
Blue	•	•		461
Blue		•		451
Green		•		450
White		•		452
Red		•		457

ELECTRA 225 TRIM

COLOR	CLOTH	VINYL	LEATHER	CODE
Black	•	•		608
Black		•		618
Blue	•	•		601
Gold	•	•		603
Parchment		•		614

ELECTRA 225 CUSTOM TRIM

COLOR	CLOTH	VINYL	LEATHER	CODE
Black	•	•		628,658
Black		•		638,668
Blue	•	•		621,651
Blue		•		631
Green	•	•		620
Buckskin		•		633
Gold	•	•		654
Maroon	•	•		627
Red		•		637

RIVIERA TRIM

COLOR	CLOTH	VINYL	LEATHER	CODE
Black	•	•		685
Black		•		675,698
Black		•		678,688
Blue		•		691
Green		•		690,680
Buckskin		•		693,683
Parchment		•		672,674
Gold	•	•		684
White		•		682

THE PAINT CODE furnishes the key to the paint colors used on the car. A two-letter code indicates the bottom and top colors respectively.

COLOR	CODE
Regal Black	A
Midnight Teal	B
Arctic White	C
Blue Mist	D
Deep Blue Metallic	E
Teal Blue Mist	F
Ivory Gold Mist	G
Aqua Mist	K
Med. Teal Blue Mist	L
Burnished Saddle	M
Maroon Metallic	N
Tarpon Green Mist	P
Scarlet Red	R
Olive Gold Metallic	S
Desert Beige	T
Charcoal Metallic	V
Silver Beige Mist	W
Buckskin	X
Cameo Cream	Y
Inca Silver Mist	Z

ENGINE NUMBER

Along with the VIN number, the engine block is stamped with an engine production code. The code has a series of letters that identifies the engine and a numeric production date code. The production code is stamped on the right side of the engine block.

SPECIAL DELUXE SKYLARK (EXCEPT STATION WAGON)

ENGINE NO.	NO. CYL.	CID	HORSE-POWER	COMP. RATIO	CARB	TRANS
NA	6	250	155	8.5:1	2 BC	M/A
PO	8	350	230	9.0:1	2 BC	M/A
PW	8	350	NA	7.6:1	2 BC	M/A
PP	8	350	280	10.25:1	4 BC	M/A

SKYLARK CUSTOM & SPECIAL DELUXE WAGON

ENGINE NO.	NO. CYL.	CID	HORSE-POWER	COMP. RATIO	CARB	TRANS
PO	8	350	230	9.0:1	2 BC	M/A
PW	8	350	NA	7.6:1	2 BC	M/A
PP	8	350	280	10.25:1	4 BC	M/A

GS 350

ENGINE NO.	NO. CYL.	CID	HORSE-POWER	COMP. RATIO	CARB	TRANS
PP	8	350	280	10.25:1	4 BC	M/A

SPORTWAGON

ENGINE NO.	NO. CYL.	CID	HORSE-POWER	COMP. RATIO	CARB	TRANS
PO	8	350	230	9.0:1	2 BC	M/A
PW	8	350	NA	7.6:1	2 BC	M/A
PP	8	350	280	10.25:1	4 BC	M/A
PR	8	400	340	10.25:1	4 BC	M/A

GS 400

ENGINE NO.	NO. CYL.	CID	HORSE-POWER	COMP. RATIO	CARB	TRANS
PR	8	400	340	10.25:1	4 BC	M/A

LESABRE

ENGINE NO.	NO. CYL.	CID	HORSE-POWER	COMP. RATIO	CARB	TRANS
PO	8	350	230	9.0;1	2 BC	M/A
PW	8	350	NA	7.6:1	2 BC	M/A
PP	8	350	280	10.25:1	4 BC	M/A

WILDCAT, ELECTRA 225 & RIVIERA

ENGINE NO.C	NO. CYL.	CID	HORSE-POWER	COMP. RATIO	CARB	TRANS
PD	8	430	360	10.25:1	4 BC	AUTO
PE	8	430	NA	8.75:1	4 BC	AUTO

1969 BUICK ELECTRA

1969 BUICK GS400

1969 BUICK LESABRE

1969 BUICK LESABRE

1969 BUICK RIVIERA

1969 BUICK SKYLARK

1969 BUICK SPORTWAGON

1969 BUICK WILDCAT

VEHICLE IDENTIFICATION NUMBER

BUICK
444 379 H101555

Commonly referred to as the VIN NUMBER, this series of numbers and letters is stamped on a plate attached to the top of the dash on the driver's side, to be viewed through the windshield outside the car.

FIRST DIGIT: Identifies the GM Division (Buick)

SECOND AND THIRD DIGITS: Identify the series

SERIES	CODE
Special Deluxe	33
Special Deluxe Wagon	34
G.S. 350	34
Skylark	35
Skylark Custom	44
Sportwagon	44
G.S. 400	46
LeSabre	52
LeSabre Custom	54
Wildcat	64
Wildcat Custom	66
Electra 225	82
Electra 225 Custom	84
Riviera	94

FOURTH AND FIFTH DIGITS: Identify the body style

2-Door Coupe	27
4-Door 2-Seat Station Wagon	35
4-Door 2-Seat Wagon	36
2-Door Hardtop Coupe	37
4-Door Hardtop	39
4-Door 2-Seat Sportwagon	56
2-Door Hardtop Coupe	57
4-Door 3-Seat Sportwagon	66
Convertible	67
4-Door Sedan	69
2-Door Hardtop Coupe	87

SIXTH DIGIT: Identifies the model year (1969)

SEVENTH DIGIT: Identifies the assembly plant

ASSEMBLY PLANT	CODE
Flint, MI	H
South Gate, CA	C
Fremont, OH	Z
Kansas City, KS	X
Wilmington, DE	Y
Atlanta, GA	D
Baltimore, MD	B
Kansas City, MO	K
Bloomfield, MI	V
Oshawa, Ont., CAN	I

LAST 6 DIGITS: Represent the basic production numbers

BODY NUMBER PLATE

Complete identification of each body is provided by a plate riveted to the cowl at the left of center under the hood.

BUICK DIV. GENERAL MOTORS
FLINT, MICH.

ST 69-44437 H 101555 BODY
TR 178 AC PAINT

BODY BY FISHER

EXAMPLE:

69	Model Year (1969)
4	GM Division (Buick)
44	Series (Skylark Custom)
37	2-Door Hardtop Coupe
H*	Flint, Michigan
101555	Production Sequence
178	Trim
A	Lower Body Color
C	Upper Body Color

* Same assembly plants and codes as used on the VIN plate.

THE STYLE NUMBER is a combination of the year, division, series, and body style.

SPECIAL DELUXE	CODE
Coupe, 2-Door, Thin Pillar	3327
Sedan, 4-Door, Thin Pillar	3369
Station Wagon, 4-Door, 2-Seat	3435
Station Wagon, 4-Door, 3-Seat	3436

G.S. 350	CODE
Hardtop Coupe, 2-Door	3437

SKYLARK	CODE
Hardtop Coupe, 2-Door	3537
Sedan, 4-Door, Thin Pillar	3569

SKYLARK CUSTOM	CODE
Hardtop Coupe, 2-Door	4437
Convertible, 2-Door	4467
Hardtop, 4-Door	439
Sedan, 4-Door, Thin Pillar	4469

SPORTWAGON	CODE
Station Wagon, 4-Door, 2-Seat	4456
Station Wagon, 4-Door, 3-Seat	4466

G.S. 400	CODE
Hardtop Coupe, 2-Door	4637
Convertible, 2-Door	4667

LESABRE	CODE
Hardtop Coupe, 2-Door	5237
Hardtop, 4-Door	5239
Sedan, 4-Door, Thin Pillar	5269

LESABRE CUSTOM	CODE
Hardtop Coupe, 2-Door	5437
Hardtop, 4-Door	5439
Convertible, 2-Door	5467
Sedan, 4-Door, Thin Pillar	5469

WILDCAT	CODE
Hardtop Coupe, 2-Door	6437
Hardtop, 4-Door	6439
Sedan, 4-Door, Thin Pillar	6469

WILDCAT CUSTOM	CODE
Hardtop Coupe, 2-Door	6637
Hardtop, 4-Door	6639
Convertible, 2-Door	6667

ELECTRA 225	CODE
Hardtop Coupe, 2-Door	8257
Hardtop, 4-Door	8239
Sedan, 4-Door, Thin Pillar	8269

ELECTRA 225 CUSTOM	CODE
Hardtop Coupe, 2-Door	8457
Hardtop, 4-Door	8439
Convertible, 2-Door	8467
Sedan, 4-Door, Thin Pillar	8469

THE BODY NUMBER is the production serial number of the body. The prefix letter denotes the plant in which the body was built.

THE TRIM NUMBER furnishes the key to the trim color and material for each model series.

SPECIAL DELUXE TRIM

COLOR	CLOTH	VINYL	LEATHER	CODE
Black	•	•		108
Black		•		118,128
Blue	•	•		101
Blue		•		111,121
Buckskin	•	•		103
Buckskin		•		126
Parchment		•		114,124
Pearl		•		125

GS 340 TRIM

COLOR	CLOTH	VINYL	LEATHER	CODE
Black		•		128,188
Blue		•		121,188
Buckskin		•		186
Parchment		•		124
Pearl		•		185

SKYLARK TRIM

COLOR	CLOTH	VINYL	LEATHER	CODE
Black	•	•		138
Black		•		128,178
Blue	•	•		131
Blue		•		121,171
Buckskin	•	•		133
Buckskin		•		176
Green	•	•		130
Green		•		170
Parchment		•		124
Pearl		•		175

SKYLARK CUSTOM TRIM

COLOR	CLOTH	VINYL	LEATHER	CODE
Black	•	•		148
Black		•		178,188,168
Blue	•	•		141,151
Blue		•		171,181,191
Buckskin	•	•		143,153
Buckskin		•		176,186
Buckskin		•		166,196
Burgundy	•	•		157,147
Burgundy		•		187
Green	•	•		150,140
Green		•		170,190
Parchment		•		164
Pearl		•		175,185,195

GS 400 TRIM

COLOR	CLOTH	VINYL	LEATHER	CODE
Black		•		168,188
Buckskin		•		186
Burgundy		•		187
Parchment		•		164
Pearl		•		185

LESABRE TRIM

COLOR	CLOTH	VINYL	LEATHER	CODE
Black	•	•		408
Blue	•	•		401
Buckskin	•	•		403
Burgundy	•	•		407
Green	•	•		400

LESABRE CUSTOM & WILDCAT TRIM

COLOR	CLOTH	VINYL	LEATHER	CODE
Black		•		428,438
Blue	•	•		411
Blue		•		421
Buckskin	•	•		413
Buckskin		•		426
Burgundy		•		427
Green	•	•		410,400
Pearl		•		425

WILDCAT CUSTOM TRIM

COLOR	CLOTH	VINYL	LEATHER	CODE
Black	•	•		468
Black		•		458,478
Blue		•		451
Buckskin		•		453
Parchment	•	•		464
Parchment		•		455
Pearl		•		455

ELECTRA TRIM

COLOR	CLOTH	VINYL	LEATHER	CODE
Black	•	•		608
Black		•		618
Blue	•	•		601
Buckskin	•	•		603
Parchment		•		614

ELECTRA CUSTOM TRIM

COLOR	CLOTH	VINYL	LEATHER	CODE
Black	•	•		648,628
Black		•		638,639,658
Blue	•	•		641,621
Blue		•		631,632
Buckskin		•		633,636
Burgundy		•		637
Green	•	•		620
Green		•		630
Parchment	•	•		644,624

RIVIERA TRIM

COLOR	CLOTH	VINYL	LEATHER	CODE
Black	•	•		678
Black		•		669,688
Black		•		668,698
Blue		•		691
Buckskin		•		686
Burgundy		•		687
Green		•		680
Gold		•		692
Parchment	•	•		674
Parchment		•		666,664,694
Pearl		•		685

THE PAINT CODE furnishes the key to the paint colors used on the car. A two-letter code indicates the bottom and top colors respectively.

COLOR	CODE
Cameo Cream	40
Polar White	*50
Twilight Blue Poly	51
Signal Red	*52
Crystal Blue Poly	53
Turquoise Mist Poly	55
Verde Green Poly	57
Lime Green Poly	59
Burnished Brown Poly	61
Champagne Mist Poly	63
Trumpet Gold Poly	65
Burgundy Mist Poly	67
Silver Mist Poly	69
Embassy Gold Poly	**75
Antique Gold Poly	77
Regal Black	*10
Azure Blue	**80
Sunset Silver Poly	**81
Olive Beige	**82
Deep Gray Mist Poly	**83
Copper Mist Poly	**85
Fire Glow Orange Poly	***Q

* Striping colors
** Specific Riviera colors
*** Spring color

ENGINE NUMBER

Along with the VIN number, the engine block is stamped with an engine production code. The code has a series of letters that identifies the engine and a numeric production date code. The production code is stamped on the right side of the engine block.

SPECIAL DELUXE SKYLARK (EXCEPT WAGON)

ENGINE NO.	NO. CYL.	CID	HORSE-POWER	COMP. RATIO	CARB	TRANS
NA	6	250	155	8.5:1	2 BC	M/A
RO	8	350	230	9.0:1	2 BC	M/A
RW	8	350	NA	8.0:1	2 BC	M/A
RP	8	350	280	10.25:1	4 BC	M/A

SPECIAL DELUXE WAGON & SKYLARK CUSTOM

ENGINE NO.	NO. CYL.	CID	HORSE-POWER	COMP. RATIO	CARB	TRANS
RO	8	350	230	9.0:1	2 BC	M/A
RW	8	350	NA	8.0:1	2 BC	M/A
RP	8	350	280	10.25:1	4 BC	M/A

SPORTWAGONS

ENGINE NO.	NO. CYL.	CID	HORSE-POWER	COMP. RATIO	CARB	TRANS
RO	8	350	230	9.0:1	2 BC	M/A
RW	8	350	NA	8.0:1	2 BC	M/A
RP	8	350	280	10.25:1	4 BC	M/A
RR	8	400	340	10.25:1	4 BC	M/A

GS 350 & CALIFORNIA GS

ENGINE NO.	NO. CYL.	CID	HORSE-POWER	COMP. RATIO	CARB	TRANS
RP	8	350	280	10.25:1	4 BC	M/A

GS 400

ENGINE NO.	NO. CYL.	CID	HORSE-POWER	COMP. RATIO	CARB	TRANS
RR	8	400	340	10.25:1	4 BC	M/A
RS	8	400	340	10.25:1	4 BC	M/A
STAGE 1	8	400	350	10.25:1	4 BC	M/A

LESABRE

ENGINE NO.	NO. CYL.	CID	HORSE-POWER	COMP. RATIO	CARB	TRANS
RO	8	350	230	9.0:1	2 BC	M/A
RW	8	350	NA	8.0:1	2 BC	M/A
RP	8	350	280	10.25:1	4 BC	M/A

WILDCAT

ENGINE NO.	NO. CYL.	CID	HORSE-POWER	COMP. RATIO	CARB	TRANS
RO	8	430	360	10.25:1	4 BC	M/A
RE	8	430	NA	8.75:1	4 BC	M/A

ELECTRA 225 & RIVIERA

ENGINE NO.	NO. CYL.	CID	HORSE-POWER	COMP. RATIO	CARB	TRANS
RO	8	430	360	10.25:1	4 BC	AUTO
RE	8	430	NA	8.75:1	4 BC	AUTO

1960 CADILLAC

1960 CADILLAC

VEHICLE IDENTIFICATION NUMBER

CADILLAC
* 60K123456 *

Commonly referred to as the VIN NUMBER, this series of numbers and letters is stamped into the top left frame support next to the radiator support, and enclosed by asterisks. The number is also on the top surface of the engine block, forward of the valve cover on the left side.

FIRST TWO DIGITS: Identify the model year (1960)

THIRD DIGIT: Identifies the body style

BODY STYLE	CODE
Eldorado Biarritz	E
Eldorado Seville	H
Convertible	F
Sixty-Two Coupe	G
Sixty-Two Sedan, 6-Window	K
Sixty-Two Sedan, 4-Window	A
Coupe DeVille	J
Sedan DeVille, 6-Window	L
Sedan DeVille, 4-Window	B
Fleetwood Sixty Special	M
Fleetwood Seventy-Five Sedan	R
Fleetwood Seventy-Five Limousine	S
Eldorado Brougham	P
Commercial Chassis	Z

LAST 6 DIGITS: Represent the basic production numbers

BODY NUMBER PLATE

Complete identification of each body is provided by a plate riveted to the cowl at the left of center under the hood.

CADILLAC DIV. GENERAL MOTORS CORP.
DETROIT, MICHIGAN

STYLE 60 - 6229 BODY FW-4
TRIM 12 PAINT 10
TOP 2 ACC. CEKMNSKY

BODY BY FISHER

EXAMPLE:

60	Model Year (1960)
62	Series
29	Body Type (6-Window Sedan)
FW-4	Factory Identification
12	Trim
10	Paint
2	Top Material Color

THE STYLE NUMBER is a combination year and body style.

SERIES 62	CODE
Eldorado Biarritz	6467
Eldorado Seville	6437
Convertible	6267
Sixty-Two Coupe	6237
Sixty-Two Sedan, 6-Window	6229
Sixty-Two Sedan, 4-Window	6239
Coupe DeVille	6337
Sedan DeVille, 6-Window	6329
Sedan DeVille, 4-Window	6339

SERIES 60	CODE
Fleetwood Sixty Special	6029

1960 CADILLAC

SERIES 75	CODE
Fleetwood "75" Sedan	6723
Fleetwood "75" Limo	6733
Eldorado Brougham	6929
Commercial Chassis	6890

THE TRIM NUMBER furnishes the key to trim color and material for each model series.

SERIES 62 TRIM

COLOR	CLOTH	VINYL	LEATHER	CODE
Black				30
Black				20
Black				21
Black				11
Silver				40
Gray				31
Gray				22,92
Gray				12
Gray				41
Blue				33
Blue				23,93
Blue				13
Blue				43,53
Plum				34
Plum				44
Fawn				35
Fawn				45
Turquoise				36
Turquoise				46
Green				37
Green				27,94
Green				17
Green				47,57
Saddle				25
Red				28
Red				29
Red				19
Red				59
White				50
White				10
Pink				54
Beige				55
Beige				15
Mauve				58

SERIES 60 TRIM

COLOR	CLOTH	VINYL	LEATHER	CODE
Black	•		•	60
Gray	•		•	61
Gray	•			71
Blue	•		•	63
Blue	•			72
Plum	•		•	64
Fawn	•		•	65
Turquoise	•		•	66
Green	•		•	67
Tan	•			74
Gray/White			•	95
Blue/White			•	96
Green/White			•	97

SERIES 75 TRIM

COLOR	CLOTH	VINYL	LEATHER	CODE
Gray	•		•	80,81,90
Fawn	•		•	84,85

THE PAINT CODE furnishes the key to the paint colors used on the car. A two number code indicates the color of the car. A two-tone car has two sets of numbers.

COLOR	CODE
Ebony (Black)	10
Olympic White	12
Platinum Gray	14
Aleutian Gray	16
Hampton Blue	22
Pelham Blue	24
York Blue	26
Arroyo Turquoise	29
Inverness Green	32
Glencoe Green	36
Beaumont Beige	44
Palomino	45
Fawn	46
Persian Sand	48
Pompeian Red	50
Lucerne Blue	94
Carrara Green	96
Champagne	97
Sienna Rose	98
Heather	99

CONVERTIBLE TOP COLOR

COLOR	CODE
White	1
Black	2
Lt. Gold	4
Med. Blue	5
Lt. Sandalwood	6
Med. Pink	7
Lt. Blue	8

ENGINE NUMBER

The serial number of all 1960 Cadillac engines is stamped on the lower left hand side of the cylinder block, between the two welch plugs, just above the edge of the oil pan. This number is also stamped on top of the frame, on the left hand side bar just behind the radiator, and on the lubrication plate attached to the front face of the left door lock pillar. The engine serial number on the frame is placed between two stars.

Each Cadillac engine carries an engine unit number prefix, which indicates the type of engine, followed by numbers in numerical sequence, denoting the order in which engines were built, regardless of type, starting with number 1. The letters L.C. are added as a suffix to the engine unit number on all engines built to low compression specifications. Engines assembled with .010" oversized pistons may be identified by an asterisk stamped on the block ahead of the engine unit number.

The unit number on all engines is stamped on the bell housing portion of the crankcase behind the left hand cylinder block, directly above the cast rib, and numbered at right angles with the crankshaft.

SERIES 60,62 (EXCEPT 6437,6467)

ENGINE NO.	NO. CYL.	CID	HORSE-POWER	COMP. RATIO	CARB
06X	8	390	325	10.5:1	4 BC
06K	8	390	325	10.5:1	4 BC

SERIES ALL (EXCEPT COMMERICAL CHASSIS)

ENGINE NO.	NO. CYL.	CID	HORSE-POWER	COMP. RATIO	CARB
OQX	8	390	345	10.5:1	3-2 BC
OQK	8	390	345	10.5:'	3-2 BC

SERIES 75 COMMERCIAL CHASSIS

ENGINE NO.	NO. CYL.	CID	HORSE-POWER	COMP. RATIO	CARB
O7X	8	390	325	10.5:1	4 BC
O7K	8	390	325	10.5:1	4 BC

1961 CADILLAC

1961 CADILLAC

VEHICLE IDENTIFICATION NUMBER

CADILLAC
* 61K123456 *

Commonly referred to as the VIN NUMBER, this series of numbers and letters is stamped into the top left frame support next to the radiator support, and enclosed by asterisks. The number is also on the top surface of the engine block, forward of the valve cover on the left side.

FIRST TWO DIGITS: Identify the model year (1961)

THIRD DIGIT: Identifies the body style

BODY STYLE	CODE
Sixty-Two Sedan 4-Window	A
Sixty-Two Sedan Short Deck	C
Sixty-Two Sedan 6-Window	K
Sixty-Two Coupe	G
Sixty-Two Convertible	F
Sedan DeVille 4-Window	B
Sedan DeVille 6-Window	L
Coupe DeVille	J
Eldorado Biarritz	E
Sixty Special Sedan	M
Fleetwood Sedan 9-Passenger	R
Fleetwood Imperial Limosine	S
Commercial	Z

LAST 6 DIGITS: Represent the basic production numbers

BODY NUMBER PLATE

Complete identification of each body is provided by a plate riveted to the cowl at the left of center under the hood.

CADILLAC DIV. GENERAL MOTORS CORP.
DETROIT, MICHIGAN

STYLE 61 - 6229 BODY FW-4
TRIM 20 PAINT 12
TOP 2 ACC. CEKMNSKY

BODY BY FISHER

THE STYLE NUMBER is a combination year and body style.

EXAMPLE:

61	Model Year (1961)
62	Series
29	Style (6-Window Sedan)
FW-4	Factory Identification
20	Trim
12	Paint

SERIES 62	CODE
Sixty-Two Sedan, Short Deck	6299
Eldorado Biarritz	6367
Convertible	6267
Sixty-Two Coupe	6237
Sixty-Two Sedan, 6-Window	6229
Sixty-Two Sedan, 4-Window	6239
Coupe DeVille	6337
Sedan DeVille, 6-Window	6329
Sedan DeVille, 4-Window	6339

SERIES 60	CODE
Fleetwood Sixty Special	6039

SERIES 75	CODE
Fleetwood "75" Sedan	6723
Fleetwood "75" Limo	6733
Commercial Chassis	6890

THE TRIM NUMBER furnishes the key to trim color and material for each model series.

SERIES 62 TRIM

COLOR	CLOTH	VINYL	LEATHER	CODE
Black	•			30
Black			•	20,21,11
Black	•		•	40
Gray	•			31
Gray	•		•	41
Blue	•			33
Blue			•	23,13
Blue	•		•	43
Plum	•			34
Fawn	•			35
Fawn	•		•	45
Turquoise	•			36
Turquoise	•		•	46
Turquoise			•	16
Green	•			37
Green			•	27
Green	•		•	47
Rose	•			39
Rose	•		•	49
Sandalwood			•	24,14
Sandalwood	•		•	44
Saddle			•	25
Maroon			•	28,29,19
White			•	10
Copper			•	15
Mauve			•	18

SERIES 60 TRIM

COLOR	CLOTH	VINYL	LEATHER	CODE
Black	•		•	60
Gray	•		•	61
Gray	•			71
Blue	•		•	63
Blue	•			72
Sandalwood	•		•	64
Fawn	•		•	65
Fawn	•			75
Turquoise	•		•	66
Green	•		•	67
Rose	•		•	69

SERIES 75 TRIM

COLOR	CLOTH	VINYL	LEATHER	CODE
Gray	•		•	80,81,90
Fawn	•		•	84,85

THE PAINT CODE furnishes the key to the paint colors used on the car. A two number code indicates the color of the car. A two tone car has two sets of numbers.

COLOR	CODE
Ebony Black	10
Olympic White	12
Platinum	14
Aleutian Gray	16
Bristol Blue	22
Dresden Blue	24
York Blue	26
San Remo Turquoise	29
Concord Green	32
Lexington Green	34
Granada Green	36
Laredo Tan	44
Tunis Beige	46
Fontana Rose	48
Pompeian Red	50
Nautilus Blue	94
Jade	96
Aspen Gold	97
Topaz	98
Shell Pear	99

CONVERTIBLE TOP COLOR

COLOR	CODE
White	1
Black	2
Lt. Gold	4
Med. Blue	5
Lt. Sandalwood	6
Med. Pink	7
Lt. Blue	8

ENGINE NUMBER

The serial number of all 1961 Cadillac engines is stamped on the lower left hand side of the cylinder block, between the two welch plugs, just above the edge of the oil pan. This number is also stamped on top of the frame, on the left hand side bar just behind the radiator, and on the lubrication plate attached to the front face of the left door lock pillar. The engine serial number on the frame is placed between two stars.

Each Cadillac engine carries an engine unit number prefix, which indicates the type of engine, followed by numbers in numerical sequence, denoting the order in which engines were built, regardless of type, starting with number 1. The letters L.C. are added as a suffix to the engine unit number on all engines built to low compression specifications. Engines assembled with .010" oversized pistons may be identified by an asterisk stamped on the block ahead of the engine unit number.

The unit number on all engines is stamped on the bell housing portion of the crankcase behind the left hand cylinder block, directly above the cast rib, and numbered at right angles with the crankshaft.

SERIES 60 & SERIES 62

ENGINE NO.	NO. CYL.	CID	HORSE-POWER	COMP. RATIO	CARB
16X	8	390	325	10.5:1	4 BC
16K	8	390	325	10.5:1	4 BC

SERIES 75

ENGINE NO.	NO. CYL.	CID	HORSE-POWER	COMP. RATIO	CARB
17X	8	390	325	10.5:1	4 BC
17K	8	390	325	10.5:1	4 BC

1962 CADILLAC

1962 CADILLAC

VEHICLE IDENTIFICATION NUMBER

CADILLAC
* 62K123456 *

Commonly referred to as the VIN NUMBER, this series of numbers and letters is stamped into the top left frame support next to the radiator support, and enclosed by asterisks. The number is also on the top surface of the engine block, forward of the valve cover on the left side.

FIRST TWO DIGITS: Identify the model year (1962)

THIRD DIGIT: Identifies the body style

BODY STYLE	CODE
Sixty-Two Sedan, 4-Window	A
Sedan DeVille, 4-Window	B
Sixty-Two Sedan, Short Deck	D
Eldorado Biarritz	E
Sixty-Two Convertible	F
Sixty-Two Coupe	G
Coupe DeVille	J
Sixty-Two Sedan, 6-Window	K
Sedan DeVille, 6-Window	L
Fleetwood Sixty Special Sedan	M
Sixty-Two Sedan, 4-Window	N
Fleetwood "75" Sedan, 9-Pass.	R
Fleetwood "75", Limosine	S
Commercial	Z

LAST 6 DIGITS: Represent the basic production numbers

BODY NUMBER PLATE

Complete identification of each body is provided by a plate riveted to the cowl at the left of center under the hood.

CADILLAC DIV. GENERAL MOTORS
CORP.
DETROIT, MICHIGAN

STYLE 62 - 6229 BODY FW-4
TRIM 30 PAINT 10-50
TOP 2 ACC. CEKMNSKY

BODY BY FISHER

EXAMPLE:

62	Model Year (1962)
62	Series
29	6-Window Sedan
FW-4	Factory Identification
30	Trim
10-50	Paint
2	Top Material Color

THE STYLE NUMBER is a combination year and body style.

SERIES 62	CODE
Eldorado Biarritz	6367
Convertible	6267
Sixty-Two Coupe	6247
Sixty-Two Sedan, 6-Window	6229
Sixty-Two Sedan, 4-Window	6239
Coupe DeVille	6347
Sedan DeVille, 6-Window	6329
Sedan DeVille, 4-Window	6339
Sixty-Two Sedan, Short Deck	6289
Sixty-Two Sedan, 4-Window, Park Avenue	6389

SERIES 60	CODE
Fleetwood Sixty Special	6039

1962 CADILLAC

SERIES 75 **CODE**

Fleetwood "75" Sedan 6723
"75" Limousine 6733
Commercial Chassis 6890

THE TRIM NUMBER furnishes the key to trim color and material for each model series.

SERIES 62 TRIM

COLOR	CLOTH	VINYL	LEATHER	CODE
Black	•			30
Black	•		•	40,12
Black			•	21,51,11
Gray	•			31
Gray	•		•	41
Blue	•			33
Blue			•	23,13
Blue	•		•	43
Sandalwood	•			34
Sandalwood			•	26,54,14
Gold	•			35
Gold			•	24
Gold	•		•	45
Turquoise	•			36
Turquoise	•		•	46
Turquoise			•	16
Green	•			37
Green			•	27
Green	•		•	47
Rose	•			39
Rose	•		•	49
White			•	20,28
White			•	50,10
Saddle			•	25,15
Red			•	29,59,19
Pink			•	18

SERIES 60 TRIM

COLOR	CLOTH	VINYL	LEATHER	CODE
Black	•		•	60
Gray	•		•	61
Gray	•			71
Blue	•		•	63
Fawn	•		•	65
Fawn	•			75
Turquoise	•		•	66
Green	•		•	67
Rose	•		•	69
Maroon	•			79

SERIES 75 TRIM

COLOR	CLOTH	VINYL	LEATHER	CODE
Gray	•			80,81,90
Gray	•		•	80,81,90
Fawn	•			84,85
Black	•		•	84,85

THE PAINT CODE furnishes the key to the paint colors used on the car. A two-tone car has two sets of numbers.

COLOR **CODE**

White 1
Black 2
Concord Blue 3
Sandalwood 4
Med. Saddle Tan (Bronze) 5
Pink (Heather) 8
Red 9
Ebony Black 10
Olympic White 12
Nevada Silver 14
Aleutian Gray 16
Newport Blue 22
Avalon Blue 24
York Blue 26
Turquoise 29
Sage 32
Granada Green 36
Sandalwood 44
Maize 45
Driftwood Beige 46
Laurel 48
Pompeian Red 50
Burgundy 52
Silver "Fire-Frost" 61
Gold "Fire-Frost" 64
Neptune Blue 94
Pinehurst Green 96
Victorian Gold 97
Bronze 98
Heather 99

CONVERTIBLE TOP COLOR

COLOR **CODE**

White 1
Black 2
Lt. Gold 4
Med. Blue 5
Lt. Sandalwood 6
Med. Pink 7
Lt. Blue 8

1962 CADILLAC

ENGINE NUMBER

The serial number of all 1962 Cadillac engines is stamped on the lower left hand side of the cylinder block, between the two welch plugs, just above the edge of the oil pan. This number is also stamped on top of the frame, on the left hand side bar just behind the radiator, and on the lubrication plate attached to the front face of the left door lock pillar. The engine serial number on the frame is placed between two stars.

Each Cadillac engine carries an engine unit number prefix, which indicates the type of engine, followed by numbers in numerical sequence, denoting the order in which engines were built, regardless of type, starting with number 1. The letters L.C. are added as a suffix to the engine unit number on all engines built to low compression specifications. Engines assembled with .010" oversized pistons may be identified by an asterisk stamped on the block ahead of the engine unit number.

The unit number on all engines is stamped on the bell housing portion of the crankcase behind the left hand cylinder block, directly above the cast rib, and numbered at right angles with the crankshaft.

SERIES 60 & SERIES 62

ENGINE NO.	NO. CYL.	CID	HORSE-POWER	COMP. RATIO	CARB
26X	8	390	325	10.5:1	4 BC
26K	8	390	325	10.5:1	4 BC

SERIES 75

ENGINE NO.	NO. CYL.	CID	HORSE-POWER	COMP. RATIO	CARB
27X	8	390	325	10.5:1	4 BC
27K	8	390	325	10.5:1	4 BC

1963 CADILLAC

1963 CADILLAC

VEHICLE IDENTIFICATION NUMBER

CADILLAC
* 63K123456 *

Commonly referred to as the VIN NUMBER, this series of numbers and letters is stamped into the top left frame support next to the radiator support, and enclosed by asterisks. The number is also on the top surface of the engine block, forward of the valve cover on the left side.

FIRST TWO DIGITS: Identify the model year (1963)

THIRD DIGIT: Identifies the body style

BODY STYLE	CODE
Sedan DeVille, 4-Window	B
Sedan DeVille, 4-Window, Park Avenue	D
Eldorado Biarritz	E
Convertible	F
Sixty-Two Coupe	G
Coupe DeVille	J
Sixty-Two Sedan, 6-Window	K
Sedan DeVille, 6-Window	L
Fleetwood Sixty Special	M
Sixty-Two Sedan, HT, 4-Window	N
Fleetwood "75" Sedan, 9-Pass.	R
Fleetwood "75", Limosine	S
Commercial	Z

LAST 6 DIGITS: Represent the basic production numbers

BODY NUMBER PLATE

Complete identification of each body is provided by a plate riveted to the cowl at the left of center under the hood.

CADILLAC DIV. GENERAL MOTORS CORP.
DETROIT, MICHIGAN

STYLE 63 - 6229 BODY FW-4
TRIM 30 PAINT 10-12
TOP 2 ACC. CEKMNSKY

BODY BY FISHER

EXAMPLE:

63	Model Year (1963)
62	Series
29	Style (6-Window Sedan)
FW-4	Factory Identification
30	Trim
10	Lower Body Color
12	Upper Body Color
2	Top Material Color

THE STYLE NUMBER is a combination year and body style.

SERIES 62	CODE
Eldorado Biarritz	6367
Convertible	6267
Sixty-Two Coupe	6257
Sixty-Two Sedan, 6-Window	6229
Sixty-Two Sedan, 4-Window	6239
Coupe DeVille	6357
Sedan DeVille, 6-Window	6329
Sedan DeVille, 4-Window	6339
Sixty-Two Sedan, Park Avenue	6389

SERIES 60	CODE
Fleetwood Sixty Special	6039

1963 CADILLAC

SERIES 75	CODE
Fleetwood "75" Sedan	6723
"75" Limousine	6733
Commercial Chassis	6890

THE TRIM NUMBER furnishes the key to trim color and material for each model series.

SERIES 62 TRIM

COLOR	CLOTH	VINYL	LEATHER	CODE
Black	•			30
Black			•	21,51,11
Black	•		•	40
Gray	•			31
Gray	•		•	41
Blue	•			32,33
Blue			•	23,13
Blue	•		•	42,43
Sandalwood	•			34
Sandalwood			•	24,54,14
Sandalwood	•		•	44
Turquoise	•			36
Turquoise	•		•	46
Green	•			37
Green			•	27,27B
Green	•		•	47
Rose	•			39
Rose	•		•	49
White			•	20,28,50
White			•	10,18
Tan			•	25
Red			•	29,59,19
Tan			•	15
Beryl			•	16
Emerald			•	17

SERIES 60 TRIM

COLOR	CLOTH	VINYL	LEATHER	CODE
Black	•		•	60
Black			•	71
Gray	•		•	61
Gray			•	72
Dk. Blue	•		•	62
Blue	•		•	63
Sandalwood	•		•	64
Sandalwood			•	74
Beige	•		•	65
Beige			•	75
Turquoise	•		•	66
Green	•		•	67
White			•	70
Red			•	79

SERIES 75 TRIM

COLOR	CLOTH	VINYL	LEATHER	CODE
Gray	•			80,81,90
Fawn	•			84,85
Beige	•		•	84F,85F

THE PAINT CODE furnishes the key to the paint colors used on the car. A two number code indicates the color of the car. A two-tone car has two sets of numbers.

COLOR	CODE
Ebony Black	10
Aspen White	12
Nevada Silver	14
Cardiff Gray	16
Benton Blue	22
Basque Blue	24
Somerset Blue	26
Turino Turquoise	29
Basildon Green	32
Brewster Green	36
Bahama Sand	44
Fawn	46
Palomino	47
Briar Rose	48
Matador Red	50
Royal Maroon	52
Silver Frost	92
Frost Aquamarine	94
Frost Green	96
Frost Gold	97
Frost Red	98

CONVERTIBLE TOP COLOR

COLOR	CODE
White	1
Black	2
Lt. Gold	4
Med. Blue	5
Lt. Sandalwood	6
Med. Pink	7
Lt. Blue	8
Silver Blue	9

1963 CADILLAC

ENGINE NUMBER

The serial number of all 1963 Cadillac engines is stamped on the lower left hand side of the cylinder block, between the two welch plugs, just above the edge of the oil pan. This number is also stamped on top of the frame, on the left hand side bar just behind the radiator, and on the lubrication plate attached to the front face of the left door lock pillar. The engine serial number on the frame is placed between two stars.

Each Cadillac engine carries an engine unit number prefix, which indicates the type of engine, followed by numbers in numerical sequence, denoting the order in which engines were built, regardless of type, starting with number 1. The letters L.C. are added as a suffix to the engine unit number on all engines built to low compression specifications. Engines assembled with .010" oversized pistons may be identified by an asterisk stamped on the block ahead of the engine unit number.

The unit number on all engines is stamped on the bell housing portion of the crankcase behind the left hand cylinder block, directly above the cast rib, and numbered at right angles with the crankshaft.

SERIES 60 & SERIES 62

ENGINE NO.	NO. CYL.	CID	HORSE-POWER	COMP. RATIO	CARB
36X	8	390	325	10.5:1	4 BC
36K	8	390	325	10.5:1	4 BC

SERIES 75

ENGINE NO.	NO. CYL.	CID	HORSE-POWER	COMP. RATIO	CARB
37X	8	390	325	10.5:1	4 BC
37K	8	390	325	10.5:1	4 BC

1964 CADILLAC

1964 CADILLAC

VEHICLE IDENTIFICATION NUMBER

CADILLAC
* 64K123456 *

Commonly referred to as the VIN NUMBER, this series of numbers and letters is stamped into the top left frame support next to the radiator support, and enclosed by asterisks. The number is also on the top surface of the engine block, forward of the valve cover on the left side.

FIRST TWO DIGITS: Identify the model year (1964)

THIRD DIGIT: Identifies the body style

BODY STYLE	CODE
Sedan DeVille, 4-Window	B
Eldorado	E
DeVille Convertible	F
Sixty-Two Coupe	G
Coupe DeVille	J
Sixty-Two Sedan, 6-Window	K
Sedan DeVille, 6-Window	L
Fleetwood Sixty Special	M
Sixty-Two Sedan, HT, 4-Window	N
Fleetwood "75" Sedan, 9-Pass.	R
Fleetwood "75" Limousine	S
Commercial	Z

LAST 6 DIGITS: Represent the basic production numbers

BODY NUMBER PLATE

Complete identification of each body is provided by a plate riveted to the cowl at the left of center under the hood.

CADILLAC DIV. GENERAL MOTORS CORP.
DETROIT, MICHIGAN

STYLE 64 - 6229 BODY FW-4
TRIM 30 PAINT 10-12
TOP 2 ACC. CEKMNSKY

BODY BY FISHER

EXAMPLE:

64	Model Year (1964)
62	Series
29	Body Type (6-Window Sedan)
FW-4	Factory Identification
30	Trim
10	Lower Body Color
12	Upper Body Color
2	Top Material Color

THE STYLE NUMBER is a combination of year and body style.

FLEETWOOD	CODE
Sixty-Two Sedan, 6-Window	6039
Eldorado Convertible	6367

SERIES 62	CODE
Sixty-Two Sedan, 6-Window	6229
Sixty-Two Sedan, 4-Window	6239
Sixty-Two Coupe	6257

DEVILLE	CODE
Convertible	6267
Sedan, 6-Window	6329
Sedan, 4-Window	6339
Coupe	6357

SERIES 75	Code
Fleetwood "75" Sedan	6723
"75" Limousine	6733
Commercial Chassis	6890

THE TRIM NUMBER furnishes the key to trim color and material for each model series.

FLEETWOOD TRIM

COLOR	CLOTH	VINYL	LEATHER	CODE
Black	•		•	60
Black			•	81
Gray	•		•	61
Gray	•			71
Blue	•		•	62
Lt. Blue	•		•	63
Sandalwood	•		•	64
Sandalwood			•	84
Beige	•		•	65
Beige	•			75
Turquoise	•		•	66
Green	•		•	67
White			•	80
Red			•	89

FLEETWOOD ELDORADO CONVERTIBLE TRIM

COLOR	CLOTH	VINYL	LEATHER	CODE
White			•	10
Black			•	11
Blue			•	13
Sandalwood			•	14
Tan			•	15
Aquamarine			•	16
Green			•	17
Red			•	19

FLEETWOOD 75 TRIM

COLOR	CLOTH	VINYL	LEATHER	CODE
Gray	•			90
Lt. Gray	•			91,92
Lt. Gray	•		•	90,91,92
Beige	•			94,95
Beige	•		•	94F,95F
Black	•		•	90,91,92
Black	•		•	94,95

SIXTY-TWO SERIES TRIM

COLOR	CLOTH	VINYL	LEATHER	CODE
Black	•			30
Gray	•			31
Blue	•			32
Lt. Blue	•			33
Sandalwood	•			34
Turquoise	•			36
Green	•			37

DEVILLE TRIM

COLOR	CLOTH	VINYL	LEATHER	CODE
White			•	20,28,50
Black			•	21,51
Black	•		•	40
Blue	•		•	42
Lt. Blue			•	23
Lt. Blue	•		•	43
Sandalwood			•	24,54
Sandalwood	•		•	44
Tan			•	25
Lime			•	26
Lime	•		•	48
Green			•	27
Green	•		•	47
Red			•	29,59
Gray	•		•	41
Turquoise	•		•	46

THE PAINT CODE furnishes the key to the paint colors used on the car. A two number code indicates the color of the car. A two tone car has two sets of numbers.

COLOR	CODE
Ebony Black	10
Aspen White	12
Nevada Silver	14
Cardiff Gray	16
Beacon Blue	22
Spruce Blue	24
Somerset Blue	26
Turino Turquoise	29
Seacrest Green	32
Lime	34
Nile Green	36
Bahama Sand	44
Sierra Gold	46
Palomino	47
Matador Red	50
Royal Maroon	52
Firemist Blue	92
Firemist Aquamarine	94
Firemist Green	96
Firemist Saddle	97
Firemist Red	98

CONVERTIBLE TOP COLOR

COLOR	CODE
White	1
Black	2
Aquamarine	3
Lt. Lime	4
Sandalwood	6
Lt. Blue	8
Silver Blue	9

1964 CADILLAC

ENGINE NUMBER

The serial number of all 1964 Cadillac engines is stamped on the lower left hand side of the cylinder block, between the two welch plugs, just above the edge of the oil pan. This number is also stamped on top of the frame, on the left hand side bar just behind the radiator, and on the lubrication plate attached to the front face of the left door lock pillar. The engine serial number on the frame is placed between two stars.

Each Cadillac engine carries an engine unit number prefix, which indicates the type of engine, followed by numbers in numerical sequence, denoting the order in which engines were built, regardless of type, starting with number 1. The letters L.C. are added as a suffix to the engine unit number on all engines built to low compression specifications. Engines assembled with .010" oversized pistons may be identified by an asterisk stamped on the block ahead of the engine unit number.

The unit number on all engines is stamped on the bell housing portion of the crankcase behind the left hand cylinder block, directly above the cast rib, and numbered at right angles with the crankshaft.

DEVILLE, FLEETWOOD SIXTY-SPECIAL & ELDORADO

ENGINE NO.	NO. CYL.	CID	HORSE-POWER	COMP. RATIO	CARB
44X	8	429	340	10.5:1	4 BC
44K	8	429	340	10.5:1	4 BC

SIXTY-TWO SERIES

ENGINE NO.	NO. CYL.	CID	HORSE-POWER	COMP. RATIO	CARB
46X	8	429	340	10.5:1	4 BC
46K	8	429	340	10.5:1	4 BC

FLEETWOOD SEVENTY-FIVE, COMMERICAL CHASSIS

ENGINE NO.	NO. CYL.	CID	HORSE-POWER	COMP. RATIO	CARB
47X	8	429	340	10.5:1	4 BC
47K	8	429	340	10.5:1	4 BC

1965 CADILLAC

1965 CADILLAC

VEHICLE IDENTIFICATION NUMBER

CADILLAC
* N5100001 *

Commonly referred to as the VIN NUMBER, this series of numbers and letters is stamped into the top surface of the frame R/H side rail, forward of the front coil suspension. (May be obscured by rubber splash shield.) This number is also located on the rear portion of the block behind the left cylinder bank.

FIRST DIGIT: Identifies the body style

BODY STYLE	CODE
Sedan DeVille, 4-Window	B
Eldorado Convertible	E
DeVille Convertible	F
Calais Coupe	G
Coupe DeVille	J
Calais Sedan	K
Sedan DeVille, 6-Window	L
Fleetwood Sixty Special (Fleetwood Brougham Option)	M
Calais Hardtop Sedan	N
Fleetwood "75" Sedan	R
Fleetwood "75" Limousine	S
Commercial	Z

SECOND DIGIT: Identifies the model year (1965)

LAST SIX DIGITS: Represent the basic production numbers

BODY NUMBER PLATE

Complete identification of each body is provided by a plate attached to the top surface of the shroud, left under the hood, near the cowl.

CADILLAC DIV. GENERAL MOTORS
CORP.
DETROIT, MICHIGAN
09C
ST 65 - 68369 FWD 192345 BODY
TR 346 40 PAINT
AEYKMSNL

BODY BY FISHER

EXAMPLE:

65	Model Year (1965)
68369	Body Style (4-Dr. Sedan)
FWB*	Factory Identification
192345	Production Sequence
346	Trim
40	Lower Body Color

* Is unavailable at the time of printing

THE STYLE NUMBER is a combination of the year and body style.

CALAIS SERIES	CODE
Calais Hardtop Sedan	68239
Calais Coupe	68257
Calais Sedan	68269

DEVILLE SERIES	CODE
Hardtop Sedan DeVille	68339
Coupe DeVille	68357
DeVille Convertible	68367
Sedan DeVille	68369

FLEETWOOD SERIES

	CODE
Sixty Special*	68069
Eldorado Convertible	68467
"75" Sedan	69723
"75" Limousine	69733
Commercial Chassis	69890

* Option Brougham

THE TRIM NUMBER furnishes the key to the trim color and material for each model style.

CALAIS TRIM

COLOR	CLOTH	VINYL	LEATHER	CODE
Black	•			210
Gray	•			216
Lt. Blue	•			220
Blue	•			226
Turquoise	•			228
Green	•			230
Sandalwood	•			241

DEVILLE TRIM

COLOR	CLOTH	VINYL	LEATHER	CODE
Black	•		•	310
Black			•	351
Gray	•		•	319
Lt. Blue	•		•	320
Lt. Blue			•	360
Blue	•		•	326
Turquoise	•		•	328
Green	•		•	230
Green			•	370
Sandalwood	•		•	341
Sandalwood			•	381
Bronze	•		•	346
White			•	352
White/Blue			•	353
White/Red			•	354
White/Turquoise		•	355	
Red			•	388

FLEETWOOD TRIM

COLOR	CLOTH	VINYL	LEATHER	CODE
Black	•		•	011
Black			•	051
Gray	•		•	016
Gray	•			018
Lt. Blue	•		•	020
Lt. Blue	•			021
Blue	•			026
Turquoise	•		•	028
Green	•			030
Sandalwood	•		•	041
Sandalwood			•	081
Beige	•			044
White			•	052
White/Blue			•	053
White/Red			•	054
White/Turquoise		•	055	
Red			•	088

ELDORADO CONVERTIBLE TRIM

COLOR	CLOTH	VINYL	LEATHER	CODE
Black			•	451
White/Black			•	452
White/Red			•	454
Gray-Blue			•	461
Blue-Green			•	476
Sandalwood			•	481
Tan			•	483
Red			•	488

FLEETWOOD 75 TRIM

COLOR	CLOTH	VINYL	LEATHER	CODE
Lt. Gray	•			716
Lt. Gray	•		•	716G
Gray	•			719
Gray	•		•	718G
Gray/Gray	•			718
Blue	•			726
Blue	•		•	726M
Beige	•			744
Black/Gray	•		•	716,718
Black/Blue			•	726

THE PAINT CODE furnishes the key to the paint colors used on the car. A two number code indicates the color of the car. A two tone car has two sets of numbers.

COLOR	CODE
Sable Black	10
Aspen White	12
Starlight Silver	16
Ascot Gray	18
Hampton Blue	20
Tahoe Blue	24
Ensign Blue	26
Alpine Turquoise	28
Cascade Green	30
Inverness Green	36
Cape Ivory	40
Sandalwood	42
Sierra Gold	44
Samoan Bronze	46
Matador Red	48
Claret Maroon	49
Peacock Firemist	90
Sheffield Firemist	92
Jade Firemist	96
Saddle Firemist	97
Crimson Firemist	98

CONVERTIBLE TOP COLOR

COLOR	CODE
White	1
Black	2
Blue	3
Brown	5
Sandalwood	6

ENGINE NUMBER

The serial number of all 1965 Cadillac engines is stamped on the lower left hand side of the cylinder block, between the two welch plugs, just above the edge of the oil pan. This number is also stamped on top of the frame, on the left hand side bar just behind the radiator, and on the lubrication plate attached to the front face of the left door lock pillar. The engine serial number on the frame is placed between two stars.

Each Cadillac engine carries an engine unit number prefix, which indicates the year of the engine followed by numbers in numerical sequence, denoting the order in which engines were built, regardless of type, starting with number 1. The letters L.C. are added as a suffix to the engine unit number on all engines built to low compression specifications. Engines assembled with .010" oversized pistons may be identified by an asterisk stamped on the block ahead of the engine unit number.

The unit number on all engines is stamped on the bell housing portion of the crankcase behind the left hand cylinder block, directly above the cast rib, and numbered at right angles with the crankshaft.

CADILLAC ENGINE

ENGINE NO.	NO. CYL.	CID	HORSE-POWER	COMP. RATIO	CARB	TRANS
5	8	429	340	10.5:1	4 BC	AUTO

1966 CADILLAC

1966 CADILLAC CALAIS

1966 CADILLAC CALAIS

1966 CADILLAC DE VILLE

1966 CADILLAC DE VILLE

1966 CADILLAC FLEETWOOD

1966 CADILLAC FLEETWOOD

VEHICLE IDENTIFICATION NUMBER

CADILLAC
* N6100001 *

Commonly referred to as the VIN NUMBER, this series of numbers and letters is stamped into the top surface of the frame R/H side rail, forward of the front coil suspension. (May be obscured by rubber splash shield.) This number is also located on the rear portion of the block behind the left cylinder bank.

FIRST DIGIT: Identifies the model number

BODY STYLE	CODE
Sedan DeVille Hardtop	B
Fleetwood Sedan	D
Eldorado Convertible	E
DeVille Convertible	F
Calais Coupe	G
Coupe DeVille	J
Calais Sedan	K
Sedan DeVille 6-Window	L
Fleetwood Sixty Special Sedan	M
Calais Hardtop Sedan	N
Fleetwood Brougham Sedan	P
Fleetwood "75" Sedan	R
Fleetwood "75" Limousine	S
Commercial	Z

SECOND DIGIT: Identifies the model year (1966)

LAST SIX DIGITS: Represent the basic production numbers

BODY NUMBER PLATE

Complete identification of each body is provided by a plate attached to the top surface of the shroud, left under the hood, near the cowl.

CADILLAC DIV. GENERAL MOTORS CORP.
DETROIT, MICHIGAN
09C
ST 66 - 68369 FWD 192345 BODY
TR 346 12-20 PAINT
PEYKMSNR
BODY BY FISHER

EXAMPLE:

66	Model Year (1966)
68369	Style (4-Dr. Sedan DeVille)
FWD*	Factory Identification
192345	Production Sequence
346	Trim
12	Lower Body Color
20	Upper Body Color

* Is unavailable at the time of printing

THE STYLE NUMBER is a combination of year and body style.

CALAIS	CODE
Hardtop Sedan	68239
Coupe	68257
Sedan	68269

DEVILLE	CODE
Hardtop Sedan	68339
Coupe	68357
Convertible	68367
Sedan	68369

FLEETWOOD	CODE
Sixty Special	68069
Broughman Sedan	68169
Eldorado Convertible	68467
"75" Sedan	69723
"75" Limousine	69733
Commercial Chassis	69890

THE TRIM NUMBER furnishes the key to the trim color and material for each series.

CALAIS TRIM COLOR	CLOTH	VINYL	LEATHER	CODE
Black	•			211
Gray	•			216
Blue	•			226
Turquoise	•			228
Green	•			230
Beige	•			242
Gold	•			244
Copper	•			246

DEVILLE TRIM COLOR	CLOTH	VINYL	LEATHER	CODE
Black	•		•	311
Black			•	351
Gray	•		•	316
Blue	•		•	320
Blue			•	360
Turquoise	•		•	328
Turquoise			•	368
Green	•		•	330
Green			•	371
Beige	•		•	342
Gold	•		•	344
Gold			•	384
Copper	•		•	346
White/Black			•	325
White/Blue			•	353
White/Red			•	354
White/Turquoise		•	355	
Saddle			•	383
Red			•	388

1966 CADILLAC

DEVILLE CONVERTIBLE TRIM

COLOR	CLOTH	VINYL	LEATHER	CODE
Black			•	351
White/Black			•	352
White/Blue			•	353
White/Red			•	354
White/Turquoise		•	355	
Blue			•	360
Turquoise			•	368
Green			•	371
Saddle			•	383
Gold			•	384
Red			•	388

FLEETWOOD TRIM

COLOR	CLOTH	VINYL	LEATHER	CODE
Black	•		•	011
Black			•	051
Gray	•			016
Blue	•		•	020,026
Blue	•			021
Blue			•	060
Turquoise	•		•	028
Turquoise	•			029
Green	•			030
Beige	•		•	042
Beige	•			043
Gold	•		•	044
Gold			•	084
Crimson	•			047
White/Black			•	052
White/Blue			•	053
White/Red			•	054
White/Turquoise		•	055	
Saddle			•	083
Red			•	088

ELDORADO CONVERTIBLE TRIM

COLOR	CLOTH	VINYL	LEATHER	CODE
Black			•	451
White/Black			•	452
White/Vermillion		•	457	
White/Blue			•	458
Blue			•	466
Green			•	471
Saddle			•	483
Gold			•	484
Vermillion			•	489

SEVENTY-FIVE TRIM

COLOR	CLOTH	VINYL	LEATHER	CODE
Gray	•		•	716,719
Blue	•		•	721,726
Beige	•		•	743

THE PAINT CODE furnishes the key to the paint colors used on the car. A two-number code indicates the color of the car. In 1966, two-tone was not a factory option.

COLOR	CODE
Sable Black	10
Strathmore White	12
Starlight Silver	16
Summit Gray	18
Mist Blue	20
Marlin Blue	24
Nocturne Blue	26
Caribbean Aqua	28
Cascade Green	30
Inverness Green	36
Cape Ivory	40
Sandalwood	42
Antique Gold	44
Autumn Rust	46
Flamenco Red	48
Claret Maroon	49
Cobalt Firemist	90
Crystal Firemist	92
Tropical Green Firemist	96
Florentine Firemist	97
Ember Firemist	98

CONVERTIBLE TOP COLOR

COLOR	CODE
White	1
Black	2
Blue	3
Brown	5
Sandalwood	6

ENGINE NUMBER

The serial number of all 1966 Cadillac engines is stamped on the lower left hand side of the cylinder block, between the two welch plugs, just above the edge of the oil pan. This number is also stamped on top of the frame, on the left hand side bar just behind the radiator, and on the lubrication plate attached to the front face of the left door lock pillar. The engine serial number on the frame is placed between two stars.

Each Cadillac engine carries an engine unit number prefix, which indicates the year, followed by numbers in numerical sequence, denoting the order in which engines were built, regardless of type, starting with number 1. The letters L.C. are added as a suffix to the engine unit number on all engines built to low compression specifications. Stamped on rear of left cylinder bank below cylinder head.

The unit number on all engines is stamped on the bell housing portion of the crankcase behind the left hand cylinder block, directly above the cast rib, and numbered at right angles with the crankshaft.

CADILLAC ENGINE

ENGINE NO.	NO. CYL.	CID	HORSE-POWER	COMP. RATIO	CARB	TRANS
6	8	429	340	10.5:1	4 BC	AUTO

1967 CADILLAC DE VILLE

1967 CADILLAC DE VILLE

1967 CADILLAC FLEETWOOD BROUGHAM

1967 CADILLAC DE VILLE

1967 CADILLAC FLEETWOOD ELDORADO

1967 CADILLAC FLEETWOOD ELDORADO

VEHICLE IDENTIFICATION NUMBER

CADILLAC
* N7100001 *

Commonly referred to as the VIN NUMBER, this series of numbers and letters is stamped into the top surface of the frame R/H side rail, forward of the front coil suspension. (May be obscured by rubber splash shield.) This number is also located on the rear portion of the block behind the left cylinder bank.

FIRST DIGIT: Identifies the body style

BODY STYLE	CODE
Sedan DeVille Hardtop	B
DeVille Convertible	F
Calais Coupe	G
Fleetwood Eldorado	H
Coupe DeVille	J
Calais Sedan	K
Sedan DeVille 6-Window	L
Fleetwood Sixty Special Sedan	M
Calais Hardtop Sedan	N
Fleetwood Brougham Sedan	P
Fleetwood "75" Sedan	R
Fleetwood "75" Limousine	S
Commercial	Z

SECOND DIGIT: Identifies the model year (1967)

LAST SIX DIGITS: Represent the basic production numbers

BODY NUMBER PLATE

Complete identification of each body is provided by a plate attached to the top surface of the shroud, left under the hood, near the cowl.

CADILLAC DIV. GENERAL MOTORS CORP.
DETROIT, MICHIGAN
09C
ST 67 - 68369 FWD 192345 BODY
TR 351 12-20 PAINT
EXNYSMKIBA
BODY BY FISHER

EXAMPLE:

67	Model Year (1967)
68369	Style (4-Dr. Sedan DeVille)
FWD*	Factory Identification
192345	Production Sequence
351	Trim
12	Lower Body Color
20	Upper Body Color

* Is unavailable at the time of printing

THIS STYLE NUMBER is a combination of the year and body style.

CALAIS SERIES	CODE
Hardtop Sedan	68249
Coupe	68247
Sedan	68269

DEVILLE SERIES	CODE
Hardtop Sedan	68349
Coupe	68347
Convertible	68367
Sedan	68369

FLEETWOOD SERIES	CODE
Sixty Special	68069
Broughman Sedan	68169
Eldorado Convertible	68347
"75" Sedan	69723
"75" Limousine	69733
Commercial Chassis	69890

THE TRIM NUMBER furnishes the key to trim color and material for each model style.

CALAIS TRIM

COLOR	CLOTH	VINYL	LEATHER	CODE
Black	•			211,251
Blue	•			220
Aqua	•			228
Green	•			230
Covert	•			240
Beige	•			244,282

DEVILLE TRIM

COLOR	CLOTH	VINYL	LEATHER	CODE
Black	•		•	311
Black			•	351
Blue	•		•	320
Blue			•	360
Dk. Blue	•		•	326
Aqua	•		•	328
Aqua				
Green	•		•	330
Green				
Covert	•		•	340
Beige	•		•	344
Maroon	•		•	349
White/Black			•	352
White/Blue			•	353
White/Red			•	354
White/Aqua			•	355
Sandalwood			•	382
Saddle			•	385
Red			•	388

DEVILLE CONVERTIBLE TRIM

COLOR	CLOTH	VINYL	LEATHER	CODE
Black			•	351
White/Black			•	352
White			•	353
White/Red			•	354
White/Aqua			•	355
Blue			•	360
Aqua			•	368
Green			•	371
Covert			•	380
Sandalwood			•	382
Saddle			•	385
Red			•	388
Maroon			•	389
Turquoise			•	390

FLEETWOOD TRIM

COLOR	CLOTH	VINYL	LEATHER	CODE
Black	•		•	010,011
Black			•	051
Gray	•			016
Blue	•			021
Blue	•		•	025,026
Blue			•	060
Aqua	•		•	028,029
Green	•			030
Green			•	071
Covert	•		•	040
Beige	•			043
Beige	•		•	044
Maroon	•		•	049
Maroon			•	089
White/Black			•	052
Sandalwood			•	082
Saddle			•	085
Red			•	088

ELDORADO TRIM

COLOR	CLOTH	VINYL	LEATHER	CODE
Black	•			410,411
Black			•	451
Blue	•			426
Blue			•	466
Aqua	•			429
Aqua			•	469
Green	•			431
Green			•	471
Beige	•			444
Maroon	•			449
Maroon			•	489
White/Black			•	452
Sandalwood			•	482
Saddle			•	485
Red			•	488

SEVENTY-FIVE TRIM

COLOR	CLOTH	VINYL	LEATHER	CODE
Gray	•			716,719
Blue	•			721,726
Beige	•			743

THE PAINT CODE indicates the color used, as well as the convertible or roof panel option colors.

COLOR	CODE
Sable Black	10
Grecian White	12
Regal Silver	16
Summit Gray	18
Venetian Blue	20
Marina Blue	24
Admiralty Blue	26
Capri Aqua	28
Pinecrest Green	30
Sherwood Green	36
Persian Ivory	40
Sudan Beige	42
Baroque Gold	43
Doeskin	44
Flamenco Red	48
Regent Maroon	49
Atlantis Blue Firemist	90
Crystal Firemist	92
Tropic Green Firemist	96
Olympic Bronze Firemist	97
Ember Firemist	98

CONVERTIBLE TOP COLOR

White	1
Black	2
Dark Blue	3
Dark Brown	5
Sandalwood	6

ROOF TOP COLOR

White	1
Black	2
Dark Blue	3
Dark Brown	5
Sandalwood	6

ENGINE NUMBER

The serial number of all 1967 Cadillac engines is stamped on the lower left hand side of the cylinder block, between the two welch plugs, just above the edge of the oil pan. This number is also stamped on top of the frame, on the left hand side bar just behind the radiator, and on the lubrication plate attached to the front face of the left door lock pillar. The engine serial number on the frame is placed between two stars.

Each Cadillac engine carries an engine unit number prefix, which indicates year of the engine, followed by numbers in numerical sequence, denoting the order in which engines were built, regardless of type, starting with number 1. The letters L.C. are added as a suffix to the engine unit number on all engines built to low compression specifications. Engines assembled with .010" oversized pistons may be identified by an asterisk stamped on the block ahead of the engine unit number.

The unit number on all engines is stamped on the bell housing portion of the crankcase behind the left hand cylinder block, directly above the cast rib, and numbered at right angles with the crankshaft.

ENGINE NO.	NO. CYL.	CID	HORSE-POWER	COMP. RATIO	CARB	TRANS
7	8	429	340	10.5:1	4 BC	AUTO

1968 CADILLAC DE VILLE

1968 CADILLAC DE VILLE

1968 CADILLAC FLEETWOOD BROUGHAM

1968 CADILLAC FLEETWOOD BROUGHAM

1968 CADILLAC FLEETWOOD ELDORADO

1968 CADILLAC FLEETWOOD ELDORADO

VEHICLE IDENTIFICATION NUMBER

CADILLAC
* N8100001 *

Commonly referred to as the VIN NUMBER, this series of letters and numbers is stamped on a steel plate and riveted to the cowl bar at the lower left corner of the windshield. Also stamped on a pad on the rear upper portion of the cylinder block behind the intake manifold, and on the left side of the transmission case.

FIRST DIGIT: Identifies the body style

STYLE	CODE
Sedan DeVille Hardtop	B
DeVille Convertible	F
Calais Coupe	G
Fleetwood Eldorado	H
Coupe DeVille	J
Sedan DeVille 6-Window	L
Fleetwood Sixty Special Sedan	M
Calais Hardtop Sedan	N
Fleetwood Brougham Sedan	P
Fleetwood "75" Sedan	R
Fleetwood "75" Limousine	S
Commercial	Z

SECOND DIGIT: Identifies the model year (1968)

LAST SIX DIGITS: Represent the basic production numbers

BODY NUMBER PLATE

Complete identification of each body is provided by a plate attached to the top surface of the shroud, left under the hood, near the cowl.

CADILLAC DIV. GENERAL MOTORS CORP.
DETROIT, MICHIGAN
09C
ST 68 - 68367 FWD 123456 BODY
TR 351 12-1 PAINT
BODY BY FISHER

EXAMPLE:

68	Model Year (1968)
68367	Style (DeVille Convertible)
FWD*	Factory Identification
123456	Production Sequence
351	Trim
12	Lower Body Color
1	Convertible Top Color

* Is unavailable at the time of printing

THE STYLE NUMBER is a combination of year and body style.

CALAIS SERIES	CODE
Coupe	68247
Hardtop Sedan	68249

DEVILLE SERIES	CODE
Coupe	68347
Hardtop Sedan	68349
Convertible	68367
Sedan	68369

FLEETWOOD SERIES	CODE
Sixty Special	68069
Broughman	68169
"75" Sedan	69723
"75" Limousine	69733
Commercial Chassis	69890
Eldorado	69347

THE TRIM NUMBER furnishes the key to trim color and material for each model series.

FLEETWOOD TRIM COLOR	CLOTH	VINYL	LEATHER	CODE
Black	•		•	010,011
Black			•	051
Gray	•			016
Blue	•			021
Blue	•		•	026
Blue			•	066
Aqua	•		•	029
Green	•		•	031
Green			•	071
Covert	•		•	040
Beige	•			043
Maroon	•		•	049
Maroon			•	089
White/Black			•	052
Sandalwood			•	082
Saddle			•	085
Red			•	088

CALAIS TRIM COLOR	CLOTH	VINYL	LEATHER	CODE
Black	•			211
Blue	•			226
Aqua	•			229
Green	•			231
Covert	•			240
Beige	•			244
Black	•			251
Sandalwood	•			282

DEVILLE TRIM COLOR	CLOTH	VINYL	LEATHER	CODE
Black	•		•	311
Black			•	351
Blue	•		•	320
Dk. Blue	•		•	326
Dk. Blue			•	366
Aqua	•		•	329
Green	•		•	331
Covert	•		•	340
Beige	•		•	344
Maroon	•		•	349
White/Black			•	352
White/Blue			•	353
White/Red			•	354
Sandalwood			•	382,385
Red			•	388

1968 CADILLAC

DEVILLE CONVERTIBLE TRIM

COLOR	CLOTH	VINYL	LEATHER	CODE
Black			•	351
White/Black			•	352
White/Blue			•	353
White/Red			•	354
Blue			•	366
Aqua			•	369
Green			•	371
Covert			•	380
Sandalwood			•	382
Saddle			•	385
Red			•	388

FLEETWOOD "75" TRIM

COLOR	CLOTH	VINYL	LEATHER	CODE
Gray	•			716,719
Gray	•		•	716G
Blue	•			721
DuBarry	•			726
Beige	•			743
Black/Gray	•		•	716
Black/Gray	•		•	719
Black/Blue	•		•	721,726
Black/Beige	•		•	743

FLEETWOOD ELDORADO TRIM

COLOR	CLOTH	VINYL	LEATHER	CODE
Black	•			410,411
Black			•	451
Blue	•			426
Blue			•	466
Aqua	•			429
Aqua			•	469
Green	•			431
Green			•	471
Covert	•			440
Beige	•			444
Maroon	•			449
White/Black			•	452
White/Blue			•	453
White/Red			•	454
Covert			•	480
Sandalwood			•	482
Saddle			•	485
Red			•	488
Maroon			•	489

THE PAINT CODE furnishes the key to the paint colors used on the car. A two number code indicates the color of the car. A two-tone car has two sets of numbers.

COLOR	CODE
Sable Black	10
Grecian White	12
Regal Silver	16
Summit Gray	18
Arctic Blue	20
Normandy Blue	24
Emperor Blue	26
Caribe Aqua	28
Silver Pine Green	30
Ivanhoe Green	36
Kashmir Ivory	40
Sudan Beige	42
Baroque Gold	43
Chestnut Brown	44
San Mateo Red	48
Regent Maroon	49
Spectre Blue Firemist	90
Topaz Gold Firemist	94
Monterey Green Firemist	96
Rosewood Firemist	97
Madeira Plum Firemist	98

CONVERTIBLE TOP COLORS

White	1
Black	2
Dk. Blue	3
Dk. Brown	4
Sandalwood	5

ROOF PANEL COLORS

White	1
Black	2
Dk. Blue	3
Dk. Brown	4
Sandalwood	5

ENGINE NUMBER

The serial number of all 1968 Cadillac engines is stamped on the lower left hand side of the cylinder block, between the two welch plugs, just above the edge of the oil pan. This number is also stamped on top of the frame, on the left hand side bar just behind the radiator, and on the lubrication plate attached to the front face of the left door lock pillar. The engine serial number on the frame is placed between two stars.

Each Cadillac engine carries an engine unit number prefix, which indicates year of the engine, followed by numbers in numerical sequence, denoting the order in which engines were built, regardless of type, starting with number 1. The letters L.C. are added as a suffix to the engine unit number on all engines built to low compression specifications. Engines assembled with .010" oversized pistons may be identified by an asterisk stamped on the block ahead of the engine unit number.

The unit number on all engines is stamped on the bell housing portion of the crankcase behind the left hand cylinder block, directly above the cast rib, and numbered at right angles with the crankshaft.

ENGINE NO.	NO. CYL.	CID	HORSE-POWER	COMP. RATIO	CARB	TRANS
8	8	472	375	10.5:1	4 BC	AUTO

1969 CADILLAC COUPE DE VILLE

1969 CADILLAC COUPE DE VILLE

1969 CADILLAC FLEETWOOD BROUGHAM

1969 CADILLAC FLEETWOOD BROUGHAM

1969 CADILLAC FLEETWOOD ELDORADO

1969 CADILLAC FLEETWOOD ELDORADO

1969 CADILLAC SEDAN DE VILLE

1969 CADILLAC SEDAN DE VILLE

VEHICLE IDENTIFICATION NUMBER

CADILLAC
* N9100001 *

Commonly referred to as the VIN NUMBER, this series of letters and numbers is stamped on a steel plate and riveted to the cowl bar at the lower left corner of the windshield. Also stamped on a pad on the rear upper portion of the cylinder block behind the intake manifold, and on the left side of the transmission case.

FIRST DIGIT: Identifies the body style

STYLE	CODE
Sedan DeVille Hardtop	B
DeVille Convertible	F
Calais Coupe	G
Fleetwood Eldorado	H
Coupe DeVille	J
Sedan DeVille 6-Window	L
Fleetwood Sixty Special Sedan	M
Calais Hardtop Sedan	N
Fleetwood Brougham Sedan	P
Fleetwood "75" Sedan	R
Fleetwood "75" Limousine	S
Commercial	Z

SECOND DIGIT: Identifies the model year (1969)

LAST SIX DIGITS: Represent the basic production sequence

BODY NUMBER PLATE

Complete identification of each body is provided by a plate attached to the top surface of the shroud, left under the hood, near the cowl.

CADILLAC DIV. GENERAL MOTORS CORP.
DETROIT, MICHIGAN
09C
ST 69 - 68367 FWD 123456 BODY
TR 351 12-J PAINT
BODY BY FISHER

EXAMPLE:

69	Model Year
68367	Style (DeVille Convertible)
FWD*	Factory Identification
123456	Production Sequence
351	Trim
12	Lower Body Color
J	Convertible Top Color

* Is unavailable at the time of printing

THE STYLE NUMBER is a combination of the year and body style.

CALAIS SERIES	CODE
Coupe	68247
Hardtop Sedan	68249

DEVILLE SERIES	CODE
Coupe	68347
Hardtop Sedan	68349
Convertible	68367
Sedan	68369

FLEETWOOD SERIES	CODE
Sixty Special	68069
Broughman	68169
Eldorado	69347
"75" Sedan	69723
"75" Limousine	69733
Commercial Chassis	69890

THE TRIM NUMBER furnishes the key to trim color and material for each model series.

CALAIS TRIM

COLOR	CLOTH	VINYL	LEATHER	CODE
Black	•			211
Blue	•			226
Aqua	•			229
Green	•			231
Flax	•			242,282
Gold	•			244
Black	•			251

DEVILLE TRIM

COLOR	CLOTH	VINYL	LEATHER	CODE
Black	•		•	311
Black			•	351
Blue	•		•	326
Blue			•	366
Aqua	•		•	329
Green	•		•	331
Green			•	371
Flax	•		•	342
Flax			•	382
Gold	•		•	344
Gold			•	384
Cordovan	•		•	346
Cordovan			•	386
Mauve	•		•	347
Mauve			•	387
White/Black			•	352
Red			•	388

DEVILLE CONVERTIBLE TRIM

COLOR	CLOTH	VINYL	LEATHER	CODE
Black			•	351
White/Black			•	352
White/Blue			•	353
White/Red			•	354
Blue			•	366
Green			•	371
Flax			•	382
Gold			•	384
Cordovan			•	386
Mauve			•	387
Red			•	388

FLEETWOOD TRIM

COLOR	CLOTH	VINYL	LEATHER	CODE
Black	•		•	011
Gray	•			016
Blue	•			026
Aqua	•			029
Green	•		•	031
Flax	•			042
Gold			•	046
Cordovan			•	047
Maroon			•	049
Black			•	051
White/Black			•	052
Blue			•	066
Green			•	071
Flax			•	082
Med. Gold			•	084
Dk. Cordovan			•	086
Dk. Mauve			•	087
Med. Red			•	088

FLEETWOOD ELDORADO TRIM

COLOR	CLOTH	VINYL	LEATHER	CODE
Black	•			410,411
Black			•	451
Blue	•			426
Blue			•	466
Aqua	•			429
Green	•			431
Green			•	471
Flax	•			442
Flax			•	482
Gold	•			444
Gold			•	484
Cordovan	•			446
Cordovan			•	486
Mauve	•			447
Mauve			•	487
White/Black				452
Red			•	488

FLEETWOOD "75" TRIM

COLOR	CLOTH	VINYL	LEATHER	CODE
Gray	•			716
Med. Gray	•			719
Med. Blue	•			721
Dk. Blue	•			726
Beige	•			743

THE PAINT CODE furnishes the key to the paint colors used on the car. A two-number code indicates the color of the car. A two-tone car has two sets of numbers.

COLOR	CODE
Sable Black	10
Cotillion White	12
Patina Silver	16
Phantom Gray	18
Astral Blue	24
Athenian Blue	26
Persian Aqua	28
Palmetto Green	30
Rampur Green	36
Colonial Yellow	40
Cameo Beige	42
Shalimar Gold	44
Cordovan	46
Wisteria	47
San Mateo Red	48
Empire Maroon	49
Sapphire Blue Firemist	90
Chalice Gold Firemist	94
Biscay Aqua Firemist	96
Nutmeg Brown Firemist	97
Chateau Mauve Firemist	99

COVERTIBLE TOP COLORS

White	J
Black	B
Dk. Blue	L
Lt. Flax	M
Dk. Cordovan	N

ROOF COVER COLORS

White	J
Black	K
Dk. Blue	L
Lt. Flax	M
Dk. Cordovan	N
Med. Gold	R

ENGINE NUMBER

The serial number of all 1969 Cadillac engines is stamped on the lower left hand side of the cylinder block, between the two welch plugs, just above the edge of the oil pan. This number is also stamped on top of the frame, on the left hand side bar just behind the radiator, and on the lubrication plate attached to the front face of the left door lock pillar. The engine serial number on the frame is placed between two stars.

Each Cadillac engine carries an engine unit number prefix, which indicates year of the engine, followed by numbers in numerical sequence, denoting the order in which engines were built, regardless of type, starting with number 1. The letters L.C. are added as a suffix to the engine unit number on all engines built to low compression specifications. Engines assembled with .010" oversized pistons may be identified by an asterisk stamped on the block ahead of the engine unit number.

The unit number on all engines is stamped on the bell housing portion of the crankcase behind the left hand cylinder block, directly above the cast rib, and numbered at right angles with the crankshaft.

ENGINE NO.	NO. CYL.	CID	HORSE-POWER	COMP. RATIO	CARB	TRANS
9	8	472	375	10.5:1	4 BC	AUTO

1960 CHEVROLET

1960 CHEVROLET

1960 CORVAIR

1960 CORVAIR

1960 CORVETTE

VEHICLE IDENTIFICATION NUMBER

CHEVROLET
01511T101555

Commonly referred to as the VIN NUMBER, this series of numbers and letters is stamped on a plate attached to the left front door hinge pillar.

Corvette VIN is embossed on a stainless steel plate welded to the top of the steering column mast under the hood.

FIRST DIGIT: Identifies the model year (1960)

SECOND AND THIRD DIGITS: Identify the body series

SERIES	CODE
Corvair Standard	05
Corvair Deluxe	07
Corvair Monza	09
Corvette	08
Biscayne 6 cyl.	11
Biscayne 8 cyl.	12
Biscayne Fleetmaster 6 cyl.	13
Biscayne Fleetmaster 6 cyl.	14
Bel Air 6 cyl.	15
Bel Air 8 cyl.	16
Impala 6 cyl.	17
Impala 8 cyl.	18

FOURTH AND FIFTH DIGITS: Identify the body style

STYLE	CODE
2-Dr. Sedan	11
4-Dr. Sedan	19
Utility Sedan	21
Club Coupe	27
2-Dr. Sport Coupe	37
4-Dr. Sport Sedan	39
Convertible	67
4-Dr. Sedan	69
2-Dr. Sta. Wagon, 6-Pass.	15
4-Dr. Sta. Wagon, 6-Pass.	35
4-Dr. Sta. Wagon, 9-Pass.	45

SIXTH DIGIT: Identifies the assembly plant

ASSEMBLY PLANT	CODE
Atlanta, GA	A
Baltimore, MD	B
Flint, MI	F
Janesville, WI	J
Kansas City, MO	K
Los Angeles, CA	L
Norwood, OH	N
Oakland, CA	O
St. Louis, MO	S
Tarrytown, NY	T
Willow Run, MI	W
Framingham, MA	G

THE LAST SIX DIGITS: Represent the basic production numbers

BODY NUMBER PLATE

Complete identification of each body is provided by a plate riveted to the top of the cowl on the left side of the car.
Exception: Corvair body tag is located on the left rear wheel housing inside the engine compartment.

CHEVROLET DIVISION
GENERAL MOTORS CORP.

STYLE No. 60 1511
BODY No. T 101555
TRIM No. 806
PAINT No. 936

BODY BY FISHER

EXAMPLE:

60	Model Year (1960)
1511	Body Style (Bel-Air, 6 cyl.)
T	Assembly Plant (Tarrytown, NY)
101555	Production Sequence
806	Trim
936	Body Color

THE STYLE NUMBER is a combination of the year, series, and body style.

CORVAIR STANDARD	CODE
Club Coupe	527
4-Dr. Sedan	569

CORVAIR DELUXE	CODE
Club Coupe	727
4-Dr. Sedan	769

CORVAIR MONZA	CODE
Club Coupe	927

CORVETTE	CODE
Convertible	867

BISCAYNE	6 CYL	8 CYL
2-Dr. Utility Sedan	1121	1221
2-Dr. Sta. Wagon	1115	1215
4-Dr. Sta. Wagon	1135	1235

FLEETMASTER	6 CYL	8 CYL
2-Dr. Sedan	1311	1411
4-Dr. Sedan	1319	1419

BEL-AIR	6 CYL	8 CYL
2-Dr. Sedan	1511	1611
4-Dr. Sedan	1519	1619
2-Dr. Sport Coupe	1537	1637
4-Dr. Sport Coupe	1539	1639
4-Dr. Sta. Wagon	1535	1635
4-Dr. Sta. Wagon	1545	1645

1960 CHEVROLET

IMPALA	6 CYL	8 CYL
4-Dr. Sedan	1719	1819
2-Dr. Sport Coupe	1737	1837
4-Dr. Sport Sedan	1739	1839
2-Dr. Convertible	1767	1867
4-Dr. Sta. Wagon	1735	1835

THE BODY NUMBER is the production serial number of the body. The prefix letter denotes the plant in which the body was built.

ASSEMBLY PLANT	CODE
Atlanta, GA	A
Baltimore, MD	B
Flint, MI	F
Janesville, WI	J
Kansas City, MO	K
Los Angeles, CA	L
Norwood, OH	N
Oakland, CA	O
St. Louis, MO	S
Tarrytown, NY	T
Willow Run, MI	W
Framingham, MA	G

THE TRIM NUMBER furnishes the key to trim color and material for each model series.

CORVAIR TRIM

COLOR	CLOTH	VINYL	LEATHER	CODE
Gray	•	•		886
Green	•	•		887
Green		•		882
Blue	•	•		888
Blue		•		883
Red	•	•		889
Red		•		881
Black		•		878
Ivory		•		879
Fawn		•		880

BISCAYNE TRIM

COLOR	CLOTH	VINYL	LEATHER	CODE
Gray	•	•		800
Gray		•		801
Green	•	•		817
Green		•		818
Blue	•	•		833
Blue		•		834

FLEETMASTER TRIM

COLOR	CLOTH	VINYL	LEATHER	CODE
Gray		•		804

BEL AIR TRIM

COLOR	CLOTH	VINYL	LEATHER	CODE
Gray	•	•		806
Gray		•		807
Green	•	•		822
Green		•		823
Blue	•	•		838
Blue		•		839
Turquoise	•	•		849
Turquoise		•		850
Copper	•	•		862
Copper		•		863

IMPALA TRIM

COLOR	CLOTH	VINYL	LEATHER	CODE
Black/White	•	•		809,811
Black/White		•		810
Green	•	•		825,827
Green		•		826
Blue	•	•		841,843
Blue		•		842
Turquoise		•		852,853,854
Copper	•	•		865,867
Copper		•		866
Red/White	•	•		873,875
Red/White		•		874

THE PAINT CODE furnishes the key to the paint colors used on the car.

COLOR	CODE
Tuxedo Black	900
Cascade Green	903
Jade Green	905
Horizon Blue	910
Royal Blue	912
Tasco Turquoise	915
Suntan Copper	920
Roman Red	923
Crocus Cream	925
Ermine White	936
Fawn Beige	938
Sateen Silver	940
Shadow Gray	941
Honduras Maroon	948
Ermine White/Tuxedo Black	950
Ermine White/Cascade Green	953
Cascade Green/Jade Green	955
Ermine White/Horizon Blue	960
Horizon Blue/Royal Blue	962
Ermine White/Tasco Turquoise	963
Fawn Beige/Suntan Copper	970
Ermine White/Roman Red	973
Ermine White/Sateen Silver	984
Sateen Silver/Shadow Gray	988

ENGINE NUMBER

All Chevrolet Engines are stamped with a Plant Code, Production Date, and Engine Type Code.

Note:

1. Corvette Engines have the last six digits of the VIN stamped on the block next to the engine number.

2. Corvair Engines are stamped on the top of the block forward of the generator.

3. 8 cylinder engines are stamped on the right front of the engine block.

4. 6 cylinder engines are stamped on the right side of the block at the rear of the distributor.

EXAMPLE:

T	01	01	A
PLANT	MONTH	DAY	CODE

ENGINE PLANTS — **CODE**

Tonawanda .... T
Flint .... F

CORVAIR

ENGINE CODE	NO. CYL.	CID	HORSE-POWER	COMP. RATIO	CARB	TRANS
Y	6	140	80	8.0:1	2-1 BC	MAN
YD	6	140	95	8.0:1	2-1 BC	MAN
Z	6	140	80	8.0:1	2-1 BC	AUTO

CORVETTE

ENGINE CODE	NO. CYL.	CID	HORSE-POWER	COMP. RATIO	CARB	TRANS
CQ	8	283	230	9.5:1	4 BC	MAN
DG	8	283	230	9.5:1	4 BC	AUTO
CT	8	283	245	9.5:1	2-4 BC	MAN
DJ	8	283	245	9.5:1	2-4 BC	AUTO
CU	8	283	270	9.5:1	2-4 BC	MAN
CR	8	283	275	11.0:1	F.I.	MAN
CS	8	283	315	11.0:1	F.I.	MAN
CY	8	283	275	11.0:1	F.I.	MAN
CZ	8	283	315	11.0:1	F.I.	MAN

FLEETMASTER

ENGINE CODE	NO. CYL.	CID	HORSE-POWER	COMP. RATIO	CARB	TRANS
AP	6	235	135	8.25:1	1 BC	MAN
AR	6	235	135	8.25:1	1 BC	MAN
AS	6	235	135	8.25:1	1 BC	MAN
AT	6	235	135	8.25:1	1 BC	MAN
B	6	235	135	8.25:1	1 BC	PG
BE	6	235	135	8.25:1	1 BC	PG

CHEVROLET

ENGINE CODE	NO. CYL.	CID	HORSE-POWER	COMP. RATIO	CARB	TRANS
A	6	235	135	8.25:1	1 BC	MAN
AE	6	235	135	8.25:1	1 BC	MAN
AF	6	235	135	8.25:1	1 BC	MAN
AG	6	235	135	8.25:1	1 BC	MAN
AJ	6	235	135	8.25:1	1 BC	MAN
AK	6	235	135	8.25:1	1 BC	MAN
AM	6	235	135	8.25:1	1 BC	MAN
AZ	6	235	135	8.25:1	1 BC	MAN
B	6	235	135	8.25:1	1 BC	PG
BE	6	235	135	8.25:1	1 BC	PG
BG	6	235	135	8.25:1	1 BC	PG
BH	6	235	135	8.25:1	1 BC	PG
C	8	283	170	8.5:1	2 BC	MAN
CD	8	283	170	8.5:1	2 BC	MAN/OD
CF	8	283	230	8.5:1	4 BC	MAN
CG	8	283	230	8.5:1	4 BC	MAN/OD
CL	8	283	170	8.5:1	2 BC	MAN
CM	8	283	230	8.5:1	4 BC	MAN
D	8	283	170	8.5:1	2 BC	PG
DB	8	283	230	8.5:1	4 BC	PG
DK	8	283	170	8.5:1	2 BC	PG
DM	8	283	230	8.5:1	4 BC	PG
E	8	283	170	8.5:1	2 BC	TG
EB	8	283	230	8.5:1	4 BC	TG
EG	8	283	170	8.5:1	2 BC	TG
EJ	8	283	230	8.5:1	4 BC	TG
F	8	348	250	9.5:1	4 BC	MAN
FA	8	348	280	9.5:1	3-2 BC	MAN
FE	8	348	335	11.25:1	3-2 BC	MAN
FG	8	348	320	11.25:1	4 BC	MAN
FH	8	348	335	11.25:1	3-2 BC	MAN
FJ	8	348	320	11.25:1	4 BC	MAN
G	8	348	250	9.5:1	4 BC	PG
GB	9	349	280	9.5:1	3-2 BC	PG
GD	8	348	280	9.5:1	4 BC	PG
H	8	348	250	9.5:1	4 BC	TG
HA	8	348	280	9.5:1	3-2 BC	TG

1961 CHEVROLET

1961 CORVAIR

1961 CORVETTE

1961 CHEVROLET

1961 CORVAIR

1961 CORVETTE

VEHICLE IDENTIFICATION NUMBER

CHEVROLET
11511T101555

Commonly referred to as the VIN NUMBER, this series of numbers and letters is stamped on a plate attached to the left front door hinge pillar.

Corvair VIN is embossed on a stainless steel plate welded to the left-hand center pillar post facing.

Corvette VIN is embossed on a stainless steel plate welded to the top of the steering column mast under the hood.

FIRST DIGIT: Identifies the model year (1961)

SECOND AND THIRD DIGITS: Identify the body series

SERIES	CODE
Corvair 500	05
Corvair 700	07
Corvair Monza	09
Corvette	08
Biscayne 6 cyl.	11
Biscayne 8 cyl.	12
Biscayne Fleetmaster 6 cyl.	13
Biscayne Fleetmaster 8 cyl.	14
Bel Air 6 cyl.	15
Bel Air 8 cyl.	16
Impala 6 cyl.	17
Impala 8 cyl.	18

FOURTH AND FIFTH DIGITS: Identify the body style

STYLE	CODE
2-Dr. Sedan	11
Utility Sedan	21
Club Coupe	27
2-Dr. Sport Coupe	37
4-Dr. Sport Sedan	39
Convertible	67
4-Dr. Sedan	69
4-Dr. Sta. Wagon, 6-Pass.	35
4-Dr. Sta. Wagon, 9-Pass.	45

SIXTH DIGIT: Identifies the assembly plant

ASSEMBLY PLANT	CODE
Atlanta, GA	A
Baltimore, MD	B
Flint, MI	F
Janesville, WI	J
Kansas City, MO	K
Los Angeles, CA	L
Norwood, OH	N
Oakland, CA	O
St. Louis, MO	S
Tarrytown, NY	T
Willow Run, MI	W
Framingham, MA	G

LAST SIX DIGITS: Represent the basic production numbers

BODY NUMBER PLATE

Complete identification of each body is provided by a plate riveted to the upper right part of the dash panel. Exception: Corvair body tag is located on the left rear wheel housing inside the engine compartment.

CHEVROLET DIVISION
GENERAL MOTORS CORP.

STYLE No. 61 1511
BODY No. T 101555
TRIM No. 806
PAINT No. 936

BODY BY FISHER

EXAMPLE:

61	Model Year (1961)
1511	Body style (Bel Air, 6 cyl.)
T	Assembly Plant (Tarrytown, NY)
101555	Production Sequence
806	Trim
936	Body Color

THE STYLE NUMBER is a combination of the year, series, and body style.

CORVAIR	500	700
Club Coupe	527	727
4-Dr. Sedan	569	769
4-Dr. Sta. Wagon	535	735

CORVAIR MONZA	CODE
2-Dr. Club Coupe	927
4-Dr. Sedan	969

CORVETTE	CODE
Convertible	867

BISCAYNE	6 CYL	8 CYL
2-Dr. Sedan	1111	1211
2-Dr. Utility Sedan	1121	1221
4-Dr. Sta. Wagon	1135	1235
4-Dr. Sta. Wagon,9-Pass.	1145	1245
4-Dr. Sedan	1169	1269
2-Dr. Sedan,Fleetmaster	1311	1411
4-Dr. Sedan,Fleetmaster	1369	1469

BEL-AIR	6 CYL	8 CYL
2-Dr. Sedan	1511	1611
4-Dr. Sedan	1569	1669
2-Dr. Sport Coupe	1537	1637
4-Dr. Sport Coupe	1539	1639
4-Dr. Sta. Wagon	1535	1635
4-Dr. Sta. Wagon, 9-Pass.	1545	1645

1961 CHEVROLET

IMPALA	6 CYL	8 CYL
4-Dr. Sedan*	1769	1869
2-Dr. Sport Coupe*	1737	1837
2-Dr. Sedan*	1711	1811
4-Dr. Sport Sedan*	1739	1839
2-Dr. Convertible*	1767	1867
4-Dr. Sta. Wagon	1735	1835
4-Dr. Sta. Wagon,9-Pass.	1745	1845

* Option Super Sport

THE BODY NUMBER is the production serial number of the body. The prefix letter denotes the plant in which the body was built.

ASSEMBLY PLANT	CODE
Atlanta, GA	A
Baltimore, MD	B
Flint, MI	F
Janesville, WI	J
Kansas City, MO	K
Los Angeles, CA	L
Norwood, OH	N
Oakland, CA	O
St. Louis, MO	S
Tarrytown, NY	T
Willow Run, MI	W
Framingham, MA	G

THE TRIM NUMBER furnishes the key to trim color and material for each model series.

CORVAIR TRIM

COLOR	CLOTH	VINYL	LEATHER	CODE
Green	•	•		831,897
Green		•		832
Blue		•		836
Blue	•	•		837,888,898
Gray	•	•		885,886
Gray	•	•		887,896
Gray		•		895
Red	•	•		889,899

CORVAIR MONZA TRIM

COLOR	CLOTH	VINYL	LEATHER	CODE
Fawn	•	•		816,845
Fawn		•		855,880
Red	•	•		820,846
Red		•		856,881
Green	•	•		821,847,847
Green		•		857,882
Blue	•	•		829,848
Blue		•		858,883
Ivory		•		859,879
Black		•		878
Gray	•	•		830
Gray/Ivory	•	•		844,871
Gray/Black	•	•		870

BISCAYNE TRIM

COLOR	CLOTH	VINYL	LEATHER	CODE
Gray	•	•		800
Gray		•		801
Green	•	•		817
Green		•		818
Blue	•	•		833
Blue		•		834

FLEETMASTER TRIM

COLOR	CLOTH	VINYL	LEATHER	CODE
Gray		•		804

BEL AIR TRIM

COLOR	CLOTH	VINYL	LEATHER	CODE
Gray	•	•		806,807
Blue	•	•		822,823
Blue	•	•		838,839
Turquoise		•		849
Turquoise	•	•		850
Fawn	•	•		862,863

IMPALA TRIM

COLOR	CLOTH	VINYL	LEATHER	CODE
Gray	•	•		809,811
Gray		•		810
Green	•	•		825,827
Green		•		826
Blue	•	•		841,842,843
Turquoise	•	•		852,853,854
Fawn	•	•		865,867
Fawn		•		866
Red/Ivory	•	•		873,875
Red/Ivory		•		874

THE PAINT CODE furnishes the key to the paint colors on the car.

COLOR	CODE
Tuxedo Black	900
Seafoam Green	903
Arbor Green	905
Jewel Blue	912
Midnight Blue	914
Twilight Turquoise	915
Seamist Turquoise	917
Fawn Beige	920
Roman Red	923
Coronna Cream	925
Ermine White	936
Almond Beige	938
Sateen Silver	940
Shadow Gray	941
Honduras Maroon	948
White/Black	950
White/Seafoam Green	953
Seafoam Green/Arbor Green	955
White/Jewel Blue	959
Jewel Blue/Midnight Blue	962
White/Twilight Turquoise	963
Seamist Turquoise/ Twilight Turquoise	965
Arbor Beige/Fawn Beige	970
White/Red	973
White/Silver	984

1961 CHEVROLET

ENGINE NUMBER

All Chevrolet engines are stamped with a plant code, production date, and engine type code.

Note:

1. Corvette engines have the last six digits of the VIN stamped on the block next to the engine number.

2. Corvair engines are stamped on the top of the block forward of the generator.

3. 8 cylinder engines are stamped on the right front of the engine block.

4. 6 cylinder engines are stamped on the right side of the block at the rear of the distributor.

EXAMPLE:

T	01	01	A
PLANT	MONTH	DAY	CODE

ENGINE PLANTS **CODE**

Tonawanda .... T

Flint .... F

CORVAIR

ENGINE CODE	NO. CYL.	CID	HORSE-POWER	COMP. RATIO	CARB	TRANS
Y	6	145	80	8.0:1	2-1 BC	MAN
YC	6	145	80	8.0:1	2-1 BC	MAN
YD	6	145	98	8.0:1	2-1 BC	MAN
YN	6	145	98	9.0:1	2-1 BC	MAN
YL	6	145	80	8.0:1	2-1 BC	MAN
YM	6	145	98	9.0:1	2-1 BC	MAN
ZF	6	145	98	9.0:1	2-1 BC	AUTO
ZG	6	145	98	9.0:1	2-1 BC	AUTO
Z	6	145	80	8.0:1	2-1 BC	AUTO
ZD	6	145	80	8.0:1	2-1 BC	AUTO
YF	6	145	80	8.0:1	2-1 BC	MAN
YH	6	145	80	8.0:1	2-1 BC	MAN
YJ	6	145	98	8.0:1	2-1 BC	MAN
YQ	6	145	98	9.0:1	2-1 BC	MAN
ZB	6	145	80	8.0:1	2-1 BC	AUTO
ZE	6	145	98	8.0:1	2-1 BC	AUTO
ZK	6	145	98	9.0:1	2-1 BC	AUTO
ZH	6	145	80	9.0:1	2-1 BC	AUTO
ZJ	6	145	80	9.0:1	2-1 BC	AUTO

CORVETTE

ENGINE CODE	NO. CYL.	CID	HORSE-POWER	COMP. RATIO	CARB	TRANS
CQ	8	283	230	9.5:1	4 BC	MAN
CR	8	283	275	11.0:1	F.I.	MAN
CS	8	283	315	11.0:1	F.I.	MAN
CT	8	283	245	9.5:1	2-4 BC	MAN
CU	8	283	270	9.5:1	2-4 BC	MAN
DG	8	283	230	9.5:1	4 BC	AUTO
DJ	8	283	245	9.5:1	2-4 BC	AUTO
CY	8	283	275	11.0:1	F.I.	MAN
CZ	8	283	315	11.0:1	F.I.	MAN

CHEVROLET

ENGINE CODE	NO. CYL.	CID	HORSE-POWER	COMP. RATIO	CARB	TRANS
A	6	235	135	8.25:1	1 BC	MAN
AE	6	235	135	8.25:1	1 BC	MAN
AF	6	235	135	8.25:1	1 BC	MAN
AG	6	235	135	8.25:1	1 BC	MAN
AJ	6	235	135	8.25:1	1 BC	MAN
AK	6	235	135	8.25:1	1 BC	MAN
AM	6	235	135	8.25:1	1 BC	MAN
AP	6	235	135	8.25:1	1 BC	MAN
AR	6	235	135	8.25:1	1 BC	MAN
AS	6	235	135	8.25:1	1 BC	MAN
AT	6	235	135	8.25:1	1 BC	MAN
AZ	6	235	135	8.25:1	1 BC	MAN
B	6	235	135	8.25:1	1 BC	PG
BE	6	235	135	8.25:1	1 BC	PG
BG	6	235	135	8.25:1	1 BC	PG
BH	6	235	135	8.25:1	1 BC	PG
C	8	283	170	8.5:1	2 BC	MAN
CD	8	283	170	8.5:1	2 BC	MAN
CF	8	283	230	8.5:1	4 BC	MAN
CG	8	283	230	8.5:1	4 BC	MAN
CL	8	283	170	8.5:1	2 BC	MAN
CM	8	283	230	8.5:1	4 BC	MAN
D	8	283	170	8.5:1	2 BC	PG
DB	8	283	230	8.5:1	4 BC	PG
DK	8	283	170	8.5:1	2 BC	PG
DM	8	283	230	8.5:1	4 BC	PG
E	8	283	170	8.5:1	2 BC	TG
EB	8	283	230	8.5:1	4 BC	TG
EG	8	283	170	8.5:1	2 BC	TG
EJ	8	283	230	8.5:1	4 BC	TG
F	8	348	250	9.5:1	4 BC	MAN
FA	8	348	280	9.5:1	3-2 BC	MAN
FH	8	348	350	11.25:1	3-2 BC	MAN
FJ	8	348	340	11.25:1	4 BC	MAN
FL	8	348	305	11.0:1	4 BC	MAN
GD	8	348	305	11.0:1	4 BC	PG
GE	8	348	250	9.5:1	4 BC	PG
H	8	348	250	9.5:1	4 BC	TG
HA	8	348	280	9.5:1	3-2 BC	TG
Q	8	409	360	11.25:1	4 BC	MAN
QA	8	409	360	11.25:1	4 BC	MAN

1962 CHEVROLET

1962 CHEVROLET

1962 CHEVROLET

1962 CHEVY II

1962 CHEVY II

1962 CORVAIR

1962 CORVAIR

1962 CORVETTE

1962 CORVETTE

 1962 CHEVROLET

VEHICLE IDENTIFICATION NUMBER

CHEVROLET
21511T101555

Commonly referred to as the VIN NUMBER, this series of numbers and letters is stamped on a plate attached to the left front door hinge pillar.

CORVETTE VIN is embossed on a stainless steel plate welded to the top of the steering column mast under the hood.

CORVAIR VIN is embossed on a stainless steel plate welded to the left-hand center pillar post facing.

CHEVY II VIN is embossed on a stainless steel plate welded to the left front door hinge pillar post facing.

FIRST DIGIT: Identifies the model year (1962)

SECOND AND THIRD DIGITS: Identify the body series

SERIES	CODE
Chevy II 4 cyl.	01
Chevy II	02
Chevy II 6 cyl.	03
Chevy II & Nova 6 cyl.	04
Corvair Monza	09
Corvair 500	05
Corvair 700	07
Corvette	08
Biscayne 6 cyl.	11
Biscayne 8 cyl.	12
Bel Air 6 cyl.	15
Bel Air 8 cyl.	16
Impala 6 cyl.	17
Impala 8 cyl.	18

FOURTH AND FIFTH DIGITS: Identify the body style

STYLE	CODE
2-Dr. Sedan	11
4-Dr. Sedan	19
Club Coupe	27
2-Dr. Sport Coupe	37
4-Dr. Sport Sedan	39
Convertible	67
4-Dr. Sedan	69
2-Dr. Sta. Wagon, 6-Pass.	15
4-Dr. Sta. Wagon, 6-Pass.	35
4-Dr. Sta. Wagon, 9-Pass.	45
2-Dr. Sport Coupe	47

SIXTH DIGIT: Identifies the assembly plant

ASSEMBLY PLANT	CODE
Atlanta, GA	A
Baltimore, MD	B
Flint, MI	F
Janesville, WI	J
Kansas City, MO	K
Los Angeles, CA	L
Norwood, OH	N
Oakland, CA	O
St. Louis, MO	S
Tarrytown, NY	T
Willow Run, MI	W
Framingham, MA	G

LAST SIX DIGITS: Represent the basic production numbers

BODY NUMBER PLATE

Complete identification of each body is provided by a plate riveted to the top of the cowl on the left side of the car. Exception: Corvair body tag is located on the left rear wheel housing inside the engine compartment.

CHEVROLET DIVISION
GENERAL MOTORS CORP.

STYLE No. 62 1511
BODY No. T 101555
TRIM No. 839
PAINT No. 936

BODY BY FISHER

EXAMPLE:

62	Model Year (1962)
1511	Body Style (Bel-Air)
T	Assembly Plant (Tarrytown, NJ)
101555	Production Sequence
839	Trim
936	Body Color

THE STYLE NUMBER is a combination of the year, series, and body style.

CORVAIR	500	700
Club Coupe	527	727
4-Dr. Sedan		769
4-Dr. Sta. Wagon		735

CORVAIR MONZA	CODE
2-Dr. Club Coupe*	927
4-Dr. Sedan	969
Convertible*	967

* Option Spyder

CORVETTE	CODE
Convertible	867

CHEVY II 100	4 CYL	6 CYL
2-Dr. Sedan	0111	0211
4-Dr. Sedan	0169	0269
4-Dr. Sta. Wagon	0135	0235

CHEVY II 300	4 CYL	6 CYL
2-Dr. Sedan	0311	0411
4-Dr. Sedan	0369	0469
4-Dr. Sta. Wagon	0345	0445

NOVA 400	CODE
4-Dr. Sedan	0449
2-Dr. Sport Coupe	0437
2-Dr. Convertible	0467
4-Dr. Sta. Wagon	0435
2-Dr. Sedan	0441

BISCAYNE	6 CYL	8 CYL
2-Dr. Sedan	1111	1211
4-Dr. Sedan	1169	1269
4-Dr. Sta. Wagon	1135	1235

1962 CHEVROLET

BEL-AIR	6 CYL	8 CYL
2-Dr. Sedan	1511	1611
2-Dr. Sport Coupe	1537	1637
4-Dr. Sta. Wagon	1535	1635
4-Dr. Sta. Wagon	1545	1645
4-Dr. Sedan	1569	1669

IMPALA	6 CYL	8 CYL
4-Dr. Sedan	1769	1869
4-Dr. Sport Sedan	1739	1839
2-Dr. Convertible*	1767	1867
4-Dr. Sta. Wagon	1735	1835
4-Dr. Sta. Wagon	1745	1845
2-Dr. Sport Coupe*	1747	1847

* Option Super Sport

THE BODY NUMBER is the production serial number of the body. The prefix letter denotes the plant in which the body was built.

ASSEMBLY PLANT	CODE
Atlanta, GA	A
Baltimore, MD	B
Flint, MI	F
Janesville, WI	J
Kansas City, MO	K
Los Angeles, CA	L
Norwood, OH	N
Oakland, CA	O
St. Louis, MO	S
Tarrytown, NY	T
Willow Run, MI	W
Framingham, MA	G

THE TRIM NUMBER furnishes the key to trim color and material for each model series.

CORVAIR TRIM

COLOR	CLOTH	VINYL	LEATHER	CODE
Blue	•	•		731
Aqua	•	•		745,751
Fawn	•	•		756,757
Red	•	•		779,780

CORVAIR MONZA TRIM

COLOR	CLOTH	VINYL	LEATHER	CODE
Blue	•	•		735
Blue		•		732,736
Aqua	•	•		748
Aqua		•		719,755
Fawn	•	•		759
Fawn		•		758,769
Red	•	•		782
Red		•		781,785
Gold	•	•		793
Gold		•		795,799
Black		•		712,715

CHEVY II 100 TRIM

COLOR	CLOTH	VINYL	LEATHER	CODE
Aqua	•	•		752
Aqua		•		754
Fawn	•	•		760
Fawn		•		761,765
Red	•	•		766
Red		•		777

CHEVY II 300 TRIM

COLOR	CLOTH	VINYL	LEATHER	CODE
Blue	•	•		738
Aqua	•	•		749
Fawn	•	•		762
Red	•	•		778

NOVA 400 TRIM

COLOR	CLOTH	VINYL	LEATHER	CODE
Blue	•	•		739
Blue		•		742
Blue/Ivory		•		740,741
Aqua	•	•		750
Aqua		•		753,721
Aqua/Ivory		•		722
Fawn	•	•		763
Fawn		•		766
Fawn/Ivory		•		767,770
Red/Ivory	•	•		772,774
Red/Ivory		•		775,786
Gold	•	•		787
Gold		•		789
Gold/Ivory		•		790,791

BISCAYNE TRIM

COLOR	CLOTH	VINYL	LEATHER	CODE
Aqua	•	•		852
Aqua		•		855
Fawn	•	•		860
Fawn		•		861,865
Red	•	•		876
Red		•		877

BEL AIR TRIM

COLOR	CLOTH	VINYL	LEATHER	CODE
Green	•	•		823
Blue	•	•		839
Aqua	•	•		850
Fawn	•	•		863
Red	•	•		872

IMPALA TRIM

COLOR	CLOTH	VINYL	LEATHER	CODE
Green	•	•		826
Green		•		829,821,827
Blue	•	•		842
Blue		•		836,831,843
Aqua	•	•		853
Aqua		•		847,845,854
Fawn	•	•		866
Fawn		•		870,856,867
Red	•	•		874
Red		•		886,875,879
Gold	•	•		892
Gold		•		894,890,891
Black		•		815,814

THE PAINT CODE furnishes the key to the paint colors on the car.

COLOR	CODE
Tuxedo Black	900
Surf Green	903
Laurel Green	905
Silver Blue	912
Nassau Blue	914
Twilight Turquoise	917
Twilight Blue	918
Autumn Gold	920
Roman Red	923
Coronna Cream	925
Anniversary Gold	927
Ermine White	936
Adobe Beige	938
Satin Silver	940
Honduras Maroon	948
White/Black	950
White/Seafoam Green	953
Surf Green/Laurel Green	955
White/Silver Blue	959
Silver Blue/Nassau Blue	962
White/Twilight Blue	963
Twilight Turquoise/ Twilight Blue	965
Adobe Beige/Autumn Gold	970
White/Red	973
White/Satin Silver	984

ENGINE NUMBER

All Chevrolet Engines are stamped with a Plant Code, Production Date, and Engine Type Code.

Note:

1. Corvette engines have the last six digits of the VIN stamped on the block next to the engine number.

2. Corvair engines are stamped on the top of the block forward of the generator.

3. 8 cylinder engines are stamped on the right front of the engine block.

4. 6 cylinder engines are stamped on the right side of the block at the rear of the distributor.

EXAMPLE:

T	01	01	RC
PLANT	MONTH	DAY	CODE

ENGINE PLANTS	CODE
Tonawanda	T
Flint	F
Canada	C

CORVAIR

ENGINE CODE	NO. CYL.	CID	HORSE-POWER	COMP. RATIO	CARB	TRANS
YC	6	145	80	8.0:1	2-1 BC	MAN
YH	6	145	80	8.0:1	2-1 BC	MAN
YL	6	145	80	8.0:1	2-1 BC	MAN
YN	6	145	102	9.0:1	2-1 BC	MAN
YQ	6	145	102	9.0:1	2-1 BC	MAN
Y	6	145	102	9.0:1	2-1 BC	MAN
YM	6	145	102	9.0:1	2-1 BC	MAN
Z	6	145	80	8.0:1	2-1 BC	AUTO
ZB	6	145	80	8.0:1	2-1 BC	AUTO
ZD	6	145	80	8.0:1	2-1 BC	AUTO
ZH	6	145	84	9.0:1	2-1 BC	AUTO
ZL	6	145	84	9.0:1	2-1 BC	AUTO
ZJ	6	145	84	9.0:1	2-1 BC	AUTO
ZF	6	145	102	9.0:1	2-1 BC	AUTO
ZK	6	145	102	9.0:1	2-1 BC	AUTO
ZG	6	145	102	9.0:1	2-1 BC	AUTO
YR	6	145	150	8.0:1	TURBO	MAN

CORVETTE

ENGINE CODE	NO. CYL.	CID	HORSE-POWER	COMP. RATIO	CARB	TRANS
RC	8	327	250	10.5:1	4 BC	MAN
RD	8	327	300	10.5:1	4 BC	MAN
RE	8	327	340	11.25:1	4 BC	MAN
RF	8	327	360	11.25:1	F.I.	MAN
SC	8	327	250	10.5:1	4 BC	AUTO
SD	8	327	300	10.5:1	4 BC	AUTO

CHEVY II

ENGINE CODE	NO. CYL.	CID	HORSE-POWER	COMP. RATIO	CARB	TRANS
E	4	153	90	8.5:1	1 BC	MAN
EB	4	153	90	8.5:1	1 BC	MAN
EG	4	153	90	8.5:1	1 BC	AUTO
H	6	194	120	8.5:1	1 BC	MAN
HB	6	194	120	8.5:1	1 BC	MAN
HF	6	194	120	8.5:1	1 BC	AUTO

Note: V-8 engines were dealer installed options

CHEVROLET

ENGINE CODE	NO. CYL.	CID	HORSE-POWER	COMP. RATIO	CARB	TRANS
A	6	235	135	8.25:1	1 BC	MAN
AE	6	235	135	8.25:1	1 BC	MAN
AF	6	235	135	8.25:1	1 BC	MAN
AG	6	235	135	8.25:1	1 BC	MAN
AJ	6	235	135	8.25:1	1 BC	MAN
AK	6	235	135	8.25:1	1 BC	MAN
AM	6	235	135	8.25:1	1 BC	MAN
AZ	6	235	135	8.25:1	1 BC	MAN
B	6	235	135	8.25:1	1 BC	MAN
BG	6	235	135	8.25:1	1 BC	MAN
BE	6	235	135	8.25:1	1 BC	MAN
BH	6	235	135	8.25:1	1 BC	MAN
C	8	283	170	8.5:1	2 BC	MAN
CB	8	283	170	8.5:1	2 BC	MAN
CL	8	283	170	8.5:1	2 BC	MAN
CD	8	283	170	8.5:1	2 BC	MAN
D	8	283	170	8.5:1	2 BC	PG
DK	8	283	170	8.5:1	2 BC	PG
R	8	327	250	10.5:1	4 BC	MAN
RA	8	327	250	10.5:1	4 BC	MAN
S	8	327	250	10.5:1	4 BC	PG
SA	8	327	250	10.5:1	4 BC	PG
RB	8	327	300	10.5:1	4 BC	MAN
SB	8	327	300	10.5:1	4 BC	PG
QA	8	409	380	11.0:1	4 BC	MAN
QB	8	409	409	11.0:1	2-4 BC	MAN

1963 CHEVROLET

1963 CHEVROLET

1963 CHEVROLET

1963 CHEVY II

1963 CHEVY II

1963 CORVAIR

1963 CORVAIR

1963 CORVETTE

1963 CORVETTE

1963 CHEVROLET

VEHICLE IDENTIFICATION NUMBER

CHEVROLET
31511T101555

Commonly referred to as the VIN NUMBER, this series of numbers and letters is stamped on a plate attached to the left front door hinge pillar.

CORVETTE VIN is embossed on a stainless steel plate welded to the right side hinge pillar cross-brace under the glove box.

CORVAIR VIN is embossed on a stainless steel plate welded to the left-hand center pillar post facing.

CHEVY II VIN is embossed on a stainless steel plate welded to the left front door hinge pillar post facing.

FIRST DIGIT: Identifies the model year (1963)

SECOND AND THIRD DIGITS: Identify the body series

SERIES	CODE 4 CYL	CODE 6 CYL
Chevy II 100	01	02
Chevy II 300	03	04
Nova 400	-	04

SERIES	CODE
Corvair 500	05
Corvair 700	07
Corvair Monza 900	09
Corvette	08
Biscayne 6 cyl.	11
Biscayne 8 cyl.	12
Bel Air 6 cyl.	15
Bel Air 8 cyl.	16
Impala 6 cyl.	17
Impala 8 cyl.	18

FOURTH AND FIFTH DIGITS: Identify the body style

STYLE	CODE
2-Dr. Sedan	11
4-Dr. Sedan	19
Club Coupe	27
2-Dr. Sport Coupe	37
4-Dr. Sport Sedan	39
Convertible	67
4-Dr. Sedan	69
4-Dr. Sta. Wagon, 6-Pass.	35
4-Dr. Sta. Wagon, 9-Pass.	45

SIXTH DIGIT: Identifies the assembly plant

ASSEMBLY PLANT	CODE
Atlanta, GA	A
Baltimore, MD	B
Flint, MI	F
Janesville, WI	J
Kansas City, MO	K
Los Angeles, CA	L
Norwood, OH	N
Oakland, CA	O
St. Louis, MO	S
Tarrytown, NY	T
Willow Run, MI	W
Framingham, MA	G

LAST SIX DIGITS: Represent the basic production sequence

BODY NUMBER PLATE

Complete identification of each body is provided by a plate riveted to the top of the cowl on the left side of the car.
Exception: Corvair body tag is located on the left rear wheel housing inside the engine compartment.

CHEVROLET DIVISION
GENERAL MOTORS CORP.

STYLE No. 63 1511
BODY No. T 101555
TRIM No. 839
PAINT No. 936

BODY BY FISHER

EXAMPLE:

63	Model Year (1963)
1511	Body Style (Bel-Air)
T	Assembly Plant (Tarrytown, NY)
101555	Production Sequence
839	Trim
936	Body Color

THE STYLE NUMBER is a combination of the year, series, and body style.

CORVAIR	500	700
Club Coupe	527	727
4-Dr. Sedan		769

CORVAIR MONZA 900	CODE
2-Dr. Club Coupe*	927
4-Dr. Sedan	969
Convertible*	967

*Option Spyder

CORVETTE	CODE
Convertible	0867
Sport Coupe	0837

CHEVY II 100	4 CYL	6 CYL
2-Dr. Sedan	0111	0211
4-Dr. Sedan	0169	0269
4-Dr. Sta. Wagon	0135	0235

CHEVY II 300	4 CYL	6 CYL
2-Dr. Sedan	0311	0411
4-Dr. Sedan	0369	0469
4-Dr. Sta. Wagon	0345	0445

NOVA 400	CODE
4-Dr. Sedan	0449
2-Dr. Sport Coupe*	0437
2-Dr. Convertible*	0467
4-Dr. Sta. Wagon	0435

*Option SS

BISCAYNE	6 CYL	8 CYL
2-Dr. Sedan	1111	1211
4-Dr. Sedan	1169	1269
4-Dr. Sta. Wagon	1135	1235

1963 CHEVROLET

BEL-AIR	6 CYL	8 CYL
2-Dr. Sedan	1511	1611
4-Dr. Sedan	1569	1669
4-Dr. Sta. Wagon	1535	1635
4-Dr. Sta. Wagon	1545	1645

IMPALA	6 CYL	8 CYL
4-Dr. Sedan	1769	1869
2-Dr. Sport Coupe*	1747	1847
4-Dr. Sport Sedan	1739	1839
2-Dr. Convertible*	1767	1867
4-Dr. Sta. Wagon	1735	1835
4-Dr. Sta. Wagon	1745	1845

*Option SS

THE BODY NUMBER is the production serial number of the body. The prefix letter denotes the plant in which the body was built.

ASSEMBLY PLANT	CODE
Atlanta, GA	A
Baltimore, MD	B
Flint, MI	F
Janesville, WI	J
Kansas City, MO	K
Los Angeles, CA	L
Norwood, OH	N
Oakland, CA	O
St. Louis, MO	S
Tarrytown, NY	T
Willow Run, MI	W
Framingham, MA	G
Arlington, TX	R

THE TRIM NUMBER furnishes the key to trim color and material for each model series.

CORVAIR TRIM

COLOR	CLOTH	VINYL	LEATHER	CODE
Aqua	•	•		751
Aqua		•		720
Blue	•	•		731
Fawn	•	•		757
Fawn		•		764
Red	•	•		780
Red		•		783

CORVAIR MONZA TRIM

COLOR	CLOTH	VINYL	LEATHER	CODE
Saddle		•		705
Black		•		712
Ivory		•		727
Blue		•		732
Aqua		•		755
Fawn		•		758
Red		•		781

CHEVY II 100 TRIM

COLOR	CLOTH	VINYL	LEATHER	CODE
Aqua	•	•		752
Aqua		•		754
Fawn	•	•		760
Fawn		•		765,761
Red	•	•		776
Red		•		777

CHEVY II 300 TRIM

COLOR	CLOTH	VINYL	LEATHER	CODE
Blue	•	•		738
Aqua	•	•		749
Fawn	•	•		762
Red	•	•		778

NOVA 400 TRIM

COLOR	CLOTH	VINYL	LEATHER	CODE
Saddle	•	•		707
Saddle		•		709,708,710
Blue	•	•		739
Blue		•		742,740,741
Aqua	•	•		750
Aqua		•		753,721,722
Fawn	•	•		763
Fawn		•		767,770
Red	•	•		772
Red		•		774,775,786
Black		•		702,714

BISCAYNE TRIM

COLOR	CLOTH	VINYL	LEATHER	CODE
Aqua/Fawn	•	•		852
Aqua		•		855
Fawn	•	•		860
Fawn		•		861,865
Red	•	•		876
Red		•		877

BEL-AIR TRIM

COLOR	CLOTH	VINYL	LEATHER	CODE
Green	•	•		823
Blue	•	•		839
Aqua	•	•		850
Fawn	•	•		863
Red	•	•		872

IMPALA TRIM

COLOR	CLOTH	VINYL	LEATHER	CODE
Black	•			811
Black		•		814,812,815
Green	•			826
Green		•		829,821,827
Blue	•			842
Blue		•		836,831,843
Aqua	•			853
Aqua		•		847,845,854
Saddle	•			857
Saddle		•		859,858,862
Fawn	•			866
Fawn		•		870,856,867
Red	•			874
Red		•		886,875,879

THE PAINT CODE furnishes the key to the paint colors on the car.

COLOR	CODE
Tuxedo Black	900
Laurel Green	905
Ivy Green	908
Silver Blue	912
Monaco Blue	914
Daytona Blue	916
Azure Aqua	918
Marine Aqua	919
Autumn Gold	920
Ember Red	922
Riverside Red	923
Saddle Tan	932
Cordovan Brown	934
Ermine White	936
Adobe Beige	938
Satin Silver	940
Sebring Silver	941
Palomar Red	948
White/Black	950
White/Laurel Green	954
White/Silver Blue	959
Silver Blue/Monaco Blue	962
White/Azure Aqua	963
Azure Aqua/Marine Aqua	967
Adobe Beige/Autumn Gold	970
Adobe Beige/Saddle Tan	971
Adobe Beige/Cordovan Brown	972
White/Red	973

ENGINE NUMBER

All Chevrolet engines are stamped with a plant code, production date, and engine type code.

Note:

1. Corvette engines have the last six digits of the VIN stamped on the block next to the engine number.

2. Corvair engines are stamped on the top of the block forward of the generator.

3. 8 cylinder engines are stamped on the right side of the block at the rear of the distributor.

EXAMPLE:

I	01	01	RC
PLANT	MONTH	DAY	CODE

ENGINE PLANTS	CODE
Tonawanda	T
Flint	F

CORVAIR

ENGINE CODE	NO. CYL.	CID	HORSE-POWER	COMP. RATIO	CARB	TRANS
YC	6	145	80	8.0:1	2-1 BC	MAN
YL	6	145	80	8.0:1	2-1 BC	MAN
Z	6	145	80	8.0:1	2-1 BC	AUTO
ZD	6	145	80	8.0:1	2-1 BC	AUTO
ZH	6	145	84	9.0:1	2-1 BC	AUTO
YN	6	145	102	9.0:1	2-1 BC	MAN
YM	6	145	102	9.0:1	2-1 BC	MAN
ZF	6	145	102	9.0:1	2-1 BC	AUTO
ZG	6	145	102	9.0:1	2-1 BC	AUTO
YR	6	145	150	8.0:1	TURBO	MAN

CORVETTE

ENGINE CODE	NO. CYL.	CID	HORSE-POWER	COMP. RATIO	CARB	TRANS
RC	8	327	250	10.5:1	4 BC	MAN
RD	8	327	300	10.5:1	4 BC	MAN
RE	8	327	340	11.25:1	4 BC	MAN
RF	8	327	360	11.25:1	F.I.	MAN
SC	8	327	250	10.5:1	4 BC	AUTO
SD	8	327	300	10.5:1	4 BC	AUTO

CHEVY II

ENGINE CODE	NO. CYL.	CID	HORSE-POWER	COMP. RATIO	CARB	TRANS
E	4	153	90	8.5:1	1 BC	MAN
EB	4	153	90	8.5:1	1 BC	MAN
EG	4	153	90	8.5:1	1 BC	AUTO
H	6	194	120	8.5:1	1 BC	MAN
HB	6	194	120	8.5:1	1 BC	MAN
HF	6	194	120	8.5:1	1 BC	AUTO

V-8 Engines were dealer installed options.

CHEVROLET

ENGINE CODE	NO. CYL.	CID	HORSE-POWER	COMP. RATIO	CARB	TRANS
A	6	230	140	8.5:1	1 BC	MAN
AE	6	230	140	8.5:1	1 BC	MAN
B	6	230	140	8.5:1	1 BC	PG
C	8	283	195	9.25:1	2 BC	MAN
CB	8	283	195	9.25:1	2 BC	MAN
CD	8	283	195	9.25:1	2 BC	MAN
CL	8	283	195	9.25:1	2 BC	MAN
D	8	283	195	9.25:1	2 BC	PG
DK	8	283	195	9.25:1	2 BC	PG
R	8	327	250	10.5:1	4 BC	MAN
RA	8	327	250	10.5:1	4 BC	MAN
RB	8	327	300	10.5:1	4 BC	MAN
RK	8	327	300	10.5:1	4 BC	MAN
S	8	327	250	10.5:1	4 BC	PG
SA	8	327	250	10.5:1	4 BC	PG
SB	8	327	300	10.5:1	4 BC	PG
SG	8	327	300	10.5:1	4 BC	PG
QA	8	409	400	11.0:1	4 BC	MAN
QB	8	409	425	11.0:1	2-4 BC	MAN
QC	8	409	340	10.0:1	4 BC	MAN
QG	8	409	340	10.5:1	4 BC	PG
QM	8	427	430	13.5:1	2-4 BC	MAN

1964 CHEVROLET

1964 CHEVROLET

1964 CHEVELLE

1964 CHEVELLE

1964 CHEVY II

1964 CHEVY II

1964 CORVAIR

1964 CORVAIR

1964 CORVETTE

1964 CORVETTE

VEHICLE IDENTIFICATION NUMBER

CHEVROLET
41511T101555

Commonly referred to as the VIN NUMBER, this series of numbers and letters is stamped on a plate attached to the left front door hinge pillar.

CORVETTE VIN is embossed on a stainless steel plate welded to the right side hinge pillar cross-brace under the glove box.

CHEVELLE & CHEVY II VINS are embossed on a stainless steel plate welded to the left front door hinge pillar post facing.

CORVAIR VIN is embossed on a stainless steel plate welded to the left hand center pillar post.

FIRST DIGIT: Identifies the model year (1964)

SECOND AND THIRD DIGITS: Identify the body series

SERIES	CODE 4 CYL	CODE 6 CYL
Chevy II 100	01	02
Nova		04

SERIES	CODE
Corvair 500	05
Corvair 700	07
Corvair Monza 900	09
Monza Spyder	06
Corvette	08

SERIES	CODE 6 CYL	CODE 8 CYL
Biscayne	11	12
Bel-Air	15	16
Impala	17	18
Impala SS	13	14
Chevelle	53	54
Malibu	55	56
Malibu SS	57	58

SERIES	CODE
2-Dr. Sta. Wagon, 6-Pass.	15
4-Dr. Sta. Wagon, 6-Pass.	35
4-Dr. Sta. Wagon, 9-Pass.	45
2-Dr. Sports Coupe	47

FOURTH AND FIFTH DIGITS: Identify the body style

MODEL	CODE
2-Dr. Sedan	11
4-Dr. Sedan	19
Club Coupe	27
2-Dr. Sport Coupe	37
4-Dr. Sport Sedan	39
Convertible	67
4-Dr. Sedan	69

SIXTH DIGIT: Identifies the assembly plant

ASSEMBLY PLANT	CODE
Atlanta, GA	A
Baltimore, MD	B
Flint, MI	F
Framingham, MA	G
Fremont, CA	H
Janesville, WI	J
Kansas City, MO	K
Los Angeles, CA	L
Norwood, OH	N
Oakland, CA	O
Arlington, TX	R
St. Louis, MO	S
Tarrytown, NY	T
Southgate, CA	U
Willow Run, MI	W
Wilmington, DE	Y

LAST SIX DIGITS: Represent the basic production numbers

BODY NUMBER PLATE

Complete identification of each body is provided by a plate riveted to the top of the cowl on the left side of the car.
Exception: Corvair body tag is located on the left rear wheel housing inside the engine compartment.

CHEVROLET DIVISION
GENERAL MOTORS CORP.

ST 64 1511
BODY T 101555
TR 839
PAINT 916-959

BODY BY FISHER

EXAMPLE:

64	Model Year (1964)
1511	Body Style (Bel Air)
T	Assembly Plant (Tarrytown, NY)
101555	Production Sequence
839	Trim
916	Lower Body Color
959	Upper Body Color

THE STYLE NUMBER is a combination of the year, series, and body style.

CORVAIR	500	700
2-Dr. Coupe	527	-
4-Dr. Sedan	-	769

CORVAIR MONZA	600	900
2-Dr. Coupe	627*	927
2-Dr. Convertible	667*	967
4-Dr. Sedan	-	969
*Spyder		

CHEVY II 100	4 CYL	6 Cyl
2-Dr. Sedan	111	211
4-Dr. Sedan	169	269
4-Dr. Sta. Wagon, 2-Seat		235

NOVA	CODE
2-Dr. Sport Coupe	437
2-Dr. Sedan	411
4-Dr. Sedan	469
4-Dr. Sta. Wagon, 2-Seat	435

NOVA SS	CODE
2-Dr. Sport Coupe	447

CORVETTE	CODE
2-Dr. Sport Coupe	0837
Convertible	0867

BISCAYNE	6 CYL	8 CYL
2-Dr. Sedan	1111	1211
4-Dr. Sedan	1169	1269
4-Dr. Sta. Wagon,6-Pass.	1135	1235

BEL-AIR	6 CYL	8 CYL
2-Dr. Sedan	1511	1611
4-Dr. Sedan	1569	1669
4-Dr. Sta. Wagon,6-Pass.	1535	1635
4-Dr. Sta. Wagon,9-Pass.	1545	1645

IMPALA	6 CYL	8 CYL
4-Dr. Sedan	1769	1869
2-Dr. Sport Coupe	1747	1847
4-Dr. Sport Sedan	1739	1839
4-Dr. Sta. Wagon,6-Pass.	1735	1835
4-Dr. Sta. Wagon 9-Pass.	1745	1845
Convertible	1767	1867

IMPALA SS	6 CYL	8 CYL
2-Dr. Sport Coupe	1347	1447
Convertible	1367	1467

CHEVELLE	6 CYL	8 CYL
2-Dr. Sedan	5311	5411
4-Dr. Sedan	5369	5469
2-Dr. Sta. Wagon,2-Seat	5315	5415
4-Dr. Sta. Wagon,2-Seat	5335	5435

MALIBU	6 CYL	8 CYL
4-Dr. Sedan	5569	5669
2-Dr. Sport Coupe	5537	5637
2-Dr. Convertible	5567	5667
4-Dr. Sta. Wagon,2-Seat	5535	5635
4-Dr. Sta. Wagon, 3-Seat	5545	5645

MALIBU SS	6 CYL	8 CYL
2-Dr. Sport Coupe	5737	5837
2-Dr. Convertible	5767	5867

THE BODY NUMBER is the production serial number of the body. The prefix letter denotes the plant in which the body was built.

ASSEMBLY PLANT	CODE
Atlanta, GA	A
Baltimore, MD	B
Flint, MI	F
Framingham, MA	G
Fremont, CA	H
Janesville, WI	J
Kansas City, MO	K
Los Angeles, CA	L
Norwood, OH	N
Arlington, TX	R
St. Louis, MO	S
Tarrytown, NY	T
Southgate, CA	U
Willow Run, MI	W
Wilmington, MI	Y

THE TRIM NUMBER furnishes the key to trim color and material for each series.

CORVAIR TRIM

COLOR	CLOTH	VINYL	LEATHER	CODE
Aqua		•		720
Blue	•	•		731
Red	•	•		751,780
Red		•		783
Fawn	•	•		757
Fawn		•		764

CORVAIR MONZA TRIM

COLOR	CLOTH	VINYL	LEATHER	CODE
Saddle		•		705
Black		•		712
Ivory		•		727
Blue		•		732
Aqua		•		755
Fawn		•		758
Red		•		781

CHEVY II 100 TRIM

COLOR	CLOTH	VINYL	LEATHER	CODE
Aqua	•	•		752
Aqua		•		754
Fawn	•	•		760
Fawn		•		761
Red	•	•		776
Red		•		777

NOVA TRIM

COLOR	CLOTH	VINYL	LEATHER	CODE
Saddle	•	•		701,703
Blue	•	•		734
Blue		•		736
Aqua	•	•		745
Aqua		•		747
Fawn	•	•		768
Fawn		•		769
Red	•	•		791
Red		•		793

BISCAYNE TRIM

COLOR	CLOTH	VINYL	LEATHER	CODE
Aqua	•	•		852
Aqua		•		855
Fawn	•	•		860
Fawn		•		861
Red	•	•		876
Red		•		877

BEL-AIR TRIM

COLOR	CLOTH	VINYL	LEATHER	CODE
Olive		•		823
Blue	•	•		839
Aqua	•	•		850
Fawn	•	•		863
Red	•	•		872

IMPALA TRIM

COLOR	CLOTH	VINYL	LEATHER	CODE
Black	•	•		811
Black		•		814
Olive	•			826
Olive		•		829
Blue		•		836
Blue	•			842
Aqua	•			853
Aqua		•		847
Saddle	•			857
Saddle		•		859
Fawn	•			866
Fawn		•		870
Red	•			874
Red		•		886

IMPALA SS TRIM

COLOR	CLOTH	VINYL	LEATHER	CODE
Silver		•		805
Black		•		815
Blue		•		831
Ivory		•		845
Fawn		•		856
Saddle		•		862
Ivory		•		878
Red		•		879

CHEVELLE TRIM

COLOR	CLOTH	VINYL	LEATHER	CODE
Blue	•	•		738
Aqua	•	•		749
Fawn	•	•		762
Red	•	•		778

MALIBU TRIM

COLOR	CLOTH	VINYL	LEATHER	CODE
Saddle	•	•		707
Saddle		•		709
Blue	•	•		739
Blue		•		742
Aqua	•	•		750
Aqua		•		753
Fawn	•	•		763
Fawn		•		766
Red	•	•		772
Red		•		774

MALIBU SS TRIM

COLOR	CLOTH	VINYL	LEATHER	CODE
Saddle		•		710
Black		•		714
Aqua		•		722
Ivory		•		729
Blue		•		741
Fawn		•		770
Red		•		786

CORVETTE TRIM

COLOR	CLOTH	VINYL	LEATHER	CODE
Red		•		490AB,490AA
Red			•	898FA,898EA
Black			•	898A
Blue		•		490BB,490BA
Blue			•	898KA,898JA
Saddle		•		490CB,490CA
Saddle			•	898DA,898CA

THE PAINT CODE furnishes the key to the paint colors on the car.

COLOR	CODE
Tuxedo Black	900
Meadow Green	905
Bahama Green	908
Silver Blue	912
Daytona Blue	916
Azure Aqua	918
Lagoon Aqua	919
Almond Fawn	920
Ember Red	922
Riverside Red	923
Saddle Tan	932
Ermine White	936
Desert Beige	938
Satin Silver	940
Goldwood Yellow	943
Palomar Red	948
Bahama Green/Meadow Green	952
White/Meadow Green	954
White/Silver Blue	959
Daytona Blue/Silver Blue	960
White/Lagoon Aqua	965
Desert Beige/Saddle Tan	971
Desert Beige/Ember Red	975
Daytona Blue/Satin Silver	982
Azure Aqua/White	988
Desert Beige/Palomar Red	993
Satin Silver/Palomar Red	995

ENGINE NUMBER

All Chevrolet engines are stamped with a plant code, production date, and engine type code.

Note:

1. Corvette engines have the last six digits of the VIN stamped on the block next to the engine number.

2. Corvair engines are stamped on the top of the block forward of the generator.

3. 8 cylinder engines are stamped on the right front of the engine block.

4. 6 cylinder engines are stamped on the right side of the block at the rear of the distributor.

EXAMPLE:

I	01	01	RC
PLANT	MONTH	DAY	CODE

ENGINE PLANTS	CODE
Tonawanda	T
Flint	F

CORVAIR

ENGINE CODE	NO. CYL.	CID	HORSE-POWER	COMP. RATIO	CARB	TRANS
YC	6	164	95	8.25:1	2-1 BC	MAN
YL	6	164	95	8.25:1	2-1 BC	MAN
YN	6	164	110	9.25:1	2-1 BC	MAN
YM	6	164	110	9.25:1	2-1 BC	MAN
Z	6	164	95	8.25:1	2-1 BC	AUTO
ZH	6	164	95	8.25:1	2-1 BC	AUTO
ZD	6	164	95	8.25:1	2-1 BC	AUTO
ZF	6	164	110	9.25:1	2-1 BC	AUTO
ZG	6	164	110	9.25:1	2-1 BC	AUTO
YR	6	164	150	8.25:1	TURBO	MAN

CORVETTE

ENGINE CODE	NO. CYL.	CID	HORSE-POWER	COMP. RATIO	CARB	TRANS
RC	8	327	250	10.5:1	4 BC	MAN
RD	8	327	300	10.5:1	4 BC	MAN
RE	8	327	365	11.25:1	4 BC	MAN
RF	8	327	375	11.25:1	F.I.	MAN
RP	8	327	250	10.5:1	4 BC	MAN
RQ	8	327	300	10.5:1	4 BC	MAN
RR	8	327	365	11.25:1	4 BC	MAN
RT	8	327	365	11.25:1	4 BC	MAN
RU	8	327	365	11.25:1	4 BC	MAN
RX	8	327	375	11.25:1	F.I.	MAN
SC	8	327	250	10.5:1	4 BC	AUTO
SD	8	327	300	10.5:1	4 BC	AUTO
SK	8	327	250	10.5:1	4 BC	AUTO
SL	8	327	300	10.5:1	4 BC	AUTO

1964 CHEVROLET

CHEVY II

ENGINE CODE	NO. CYL.	CID	HORSE-POWER	COMP. RATIO	CARB	TRANS
EK	4	153	90	8.5:1	1 BC	MAN
EL	4	153	90	8.5:1	1 BC	AUTO
EQ	4	153	90	8.5:1	1 BC	AUTO
EP	4	153	90	8.5:1	1 BC	MAN
ER	4	153	90	8.5:1	1 BC	MAN
ES	4	153	90	8.5:1	1 BC	MAN
ET	4	153	90	8.5:1	1 BC	AUTO
E	4	153	90	8.5:1	1 BC	MAN
EB	4	153	90	8.5:1	1 BC	MAN
EG	4	153	90	8.5:1	1 BC	AUTO
HL	6	194	120	8.5:1	1 BC	MAN
HM	6	194	120	8.5:1	1 BC	AUTO
HT	6	194	120	8.5:1	1 BC	MAN
HU	6	194	120	8.5:1	1 BC	AUTO
H	6	194	120	8.5:1	1 BC	MAN
HB	6	194	120	8.5:1	1 BC	MAN
HF	6	194	120	8.5:1	1 BC	AUTO
BT	6	230	155	8.5:1	1 BC	AUTO
BU	6	230	155	8.5:1	1 BC	AUTO
LP	6	230	155	8.5:1	1 BC	MAN
LR	6	230	155	8.5:1	1 BC	MAN
CH	8	283	195	9.25:1	2 BC	MAN
CJ	8	283	195	9.25:1	2 BC	MAN
CF	8	283	195	9.25:1	2 BC	4-SP
CG	8	283	195	9.25:1	2 BC	4-SP
DE	8	283	195	9.25:1	2 BC	AUTO
DF	8	283	195	9.25:1	2 BC	AUTO

CHEVELLE

ENGINE CODE	NO. CYL.	CID	HORSE-POWER	COMP. RATIO	CARB	TRANS
GH	6	194	120	8.5:1	1 BC	MAN
GJ	6	194	120	8.5:1	1 BC	MAN
KC	6	194	120	8.5:1	1 BC	AUTO
KD	6	194	120	8.5:1	1 BC	AUTO
G	6	194	120	8.5:1	1 BC	MAN
GB	6	194	120	8.5:1	1 BC	MAN
GF	6	194	120	8.5:1	1 BC	MAN
GG	6	194	120	8.5:1	1 BC	MAN
GK	6	194	120	8.5:1	1 BC	MAN
GL	6	194	120	8.5:1	1 BC	MAN
GM	6	194	120	8.5:1	1 BC	MAN
GN	6	194	120	8.5:1	1 BC	MAN
K	6	194	120	8.5:1	1 BC	AUTO
KB	6	194	120	8.5:1	1 BC	AUTO
KJ	6	194	120	8.5:1	1 BC	AUTO
KH	6	194	120	8.5:1	1 BC	AUTO
BL	6	230	155	8.5:1	1 BC	AUTO
BM	6	230	155	8.5:1	1 BC	AUTO
BN	6	230	155	8.5:1	1 BC	AUTO
BP	6	230	155	8.5:1	1 BC	AUTO
LL	6	230	155	8.5:1	1 BC	MAN
LK	6	230	155	8.5:1	1 BC	MAN
LM	6	230	155	8.5:1	1 BC	MAN
LN	6	230	155	8.5:1	1 BC	MAN
J	8	283	195	9.25:1	2 BC	MAN
JA	8	283	195	9.25:1	2 BC	4-SP
JD	8	283	195	9.25:1	2 BC	AUTO
JG	8	283	220	9.25:1	4 BC	AUTO
JH	8	283	220	9.25:1	4 BC	MAN
JQ	8	327	250	10.5:1	4 BC	MAN
JR	8	327	300	10.5:1	4 BC	MAN
JS	8	327	NA	10.5:1	4 BC	MAN
JT	8	327	250	10.5:1	4 BC	MAN
SR	8	327	250	10.5:1	4 BC	AUTO
SS	8	327	300	10.5:1	4 BC	AUTO

CHEVROLET

ENGINE CODE	NO. CYL.	CID	HORSE-POWER	COMP. RATIO	CARB	TRANS
A	6	230	155	8.5:1	1 BC	MAN
AE	6	230	155	8.5:1	1 BC	MAN
AF	6	230	155	8.5:1	1 BC	MAN
AG	6	230	155	8.5:1	1 BC	MAN
B	6	230	155	8.5:1	1 BC	PG
BB	6	230	155	8.5:1	1 BC	PG
BQ	6	230	155	8.5:1	1 BC	PG
AQ	6	230	155	8.5:1	1 BC	PG
C	8	283	195	9.25:1	2 BC	PG
CB	8	283	195	9.25:1	2 BC	PG
D	8	283	195	9.25:1	2 BC	PG
R	8	327	250	10.5;1	4 BC	MAN
RB	8	327	300	10.5:1	4 BC	MAN
S	8	327	250	10.5:1	4 BC	PG
SB	8	327	300	10.5:1	4 BC	PG
QA	8	409	400	11.0;1	4 BC	MAN
QB	8	409	425	11.0:1	2-4 BC	MAN
QC	8	409	340	10.0:1	4 BC	MAN
QG	8	409	340	10.0:1	4 BC	PG
QQ	8	409	340	10.0:1	4 BC	MAN
QN	8	409	400	11.0:1	4 BC	MAN
QP	8	409	425	11.0:1	2-4 BC	MAN
QR	8	409	340	10.0:1	4 BC	PG

1965 CHEVROLET

1965 CHEVROLET

1965 CHEVELLE

1965 CHEVELLE

1965 CHEVY II

1965 CHEVY II

1965 CORVAIR

1965 CORVAIR

1965 CORVETTE

1965 CORVETTE

VEHICLE IDENTIFICATION NUMBER

CHEVROLET
164375T101555

Commonly referred to as the VIN NUMBER, this series of numbers and letters is stamped on a plate attached to the left front door hinge pillar.

CHEVROLET, CHEVELLE, and CHEVY II VINS are embossed on a stainless steel plate riveted to the left front door hinge post facing.

CORVAIR VIN is embossed on a stainless steel plate riveted to the left side-rail near the battery in the engine compartment.

CORVETTE VIN is embossed on a stainless steel plate riveted to the right side dash pillar brace under the glove box.

FIRST DIGIT: Identifies the Chevrolet division

NEXT FOUR DIGITS: Identify the model number

MODEL	CODE
Biscayne/Bel-Air	5000
Impala	6000
Chevelle, Malibu	3000
Chevy II, Nova	1000
Corvair	0000
Corvette	9000

SIXTH DIGIT: Identifies the model year (1965)

SEVENTH DIGIT: Identifies the assembly plant

ASSEMBLY PLANT	CODE
Atlanta, GA	A
Baltimore, MD	B
Southgate, CA	C
Flint, MI	F
Framingham, MA	G
Janesville, WI	J
Kansas City, MO	K
Los Angeles, CA	L
Norwood, OH	N
Arlington, TX GMAD	R
St. Louis, MO	S
Tarrytown, NY	T
Willow Run, MI	W
Wilmington, DE	Y
Fremont, CA	Z
Oshawa, Ont., CAN	1
St. Therese, Que., CAN	2
Pontiac, MI	P

LAST SIX DIGITS: Represent the basic production numbers

BODY NUMBER PLATE

Complete identification of each body is provided by a plate riveted to the top of the cowl. Exception: Corvair body tag is located on the left rear wheel housing inside the engine compartment.

CHEVROLET DIVISION
GENERAL MOTORS CORP.

ST 65 15411
BODY FL1 101555
TR 852
PAINT AA

BODY BY FISHER

EXAMPLE:

65	Model Year (1965)
15411	Body Series (Biscayne)
FL1	Assembly Plant (Flint, MI)
101555	Production Sequence
852	Trim
A	Lower Body Color
A	Upper Body Color

THE STYLE NUMBER is a combination of the year, series, and body style.

CORVAIR 500	CODE
2-Dr. Sport Coupe	10137
4-Dr. Sport Sedan	10139

CORVAIR MONZA	CODE
2-Dr. Sport Coupe	10537
2-Dr. Convertible	10567
4-Dr. Sport Sedan	10539

CORSA	CODE
2-Dr. Sport Coupe	10737
2-Dr. Convertible	10767

CHEVY II	L4	6 CYL	8 CYL
2-Dr. Sedan	11111	11311	11411
4-Dr. Sedan	11169	11369	11469
4-Dr. Sta. Wagon, 2-Seat	-	11335	11435

NOVA	6 CYL	8 CYL
4-Dr. Sedan	11569	11669
2-Dr. Sport Coupe	11537	11637
4-Dr. Sta. Wagon,2-Seat	11535	11635

NOVA SS	6 CYL	8 CYL
2-Dr. Sport Coupe	11737	11837

CORVETTE	CODE
2-Dr. Sport Coupe	19437
2-Dr. Convertible	19467

BISCAYNE	6 CYL	8 CYL
2-Dr. Sedan	15311	15411
4-Dr. Sedan	15369	15469
4-Dr. Sta. Wagon,2-Seat	15335	15435

BEL-AIR	6 CYL	8 CYL
2-Dr. Sedan	15511	15611
4-Dr. Sedan	15569	15669
4-Dr. Sta. Wagon,2-Seat	15535	15635
4-Dr. Sta. Wagon,3-Seat	15545	16645

IMPALA	6 CYL	8 CYL
4-Dr. Sedan	16369	16469
4-Dr. Sport Sedan	16339	16439*
2-Dr. Sport Coupe	16337	16437
2-Dr. Convertible	16367	16467
4-Dr. Sta. Wagon,2-Seat	16335	16435
4-Dr. Sta. Wagon,3-Seat	16345	16445

*Option Caprice

IMPALA SS	6 CYL	8 CYL
2-Dr. Sport Coupe	16537	16637
2-Dr. Converible	16567	16667

CHEVELLE 300	6 CYL	8 CYL
2-Dr. Sedan	13111	13211
4-Dr. Sedan	13169	13269
2-Dr. Sta. Wagon,2-Seat	13115	13215

CHEVELLE 300	6 CYL	8 CYL
2-Dr. Sedan	13311	13411
4-Dr. Sedan	13369	13469
4-Dr. Sta. Wagon,2-Seat	13335	13435

MALIBU	6 CYL	8 CYL
4-Dr. Sedan	13569	13669
2-Dr. Sport Coupe	13537	13637
2-Dr. Convertible	13567	13667
4-Dr. Sta. Wagon,2-Seat	13535	13635

MALIBU SS	6 CYL	8 CYL
2-Dr. Sport Coupe	13737	13837*
2-Dr. Convertible	13767	13867

* Option SS 396

THE BODY NUMBER is the production serial number of the body. The prefix letter denotes the plant in which the body was built.

ASSEMBLY PLANT	CODE
Atlanta, GA	A
Baltimore, MD	B
Southgate, CA	C
Flint, MI	F
Framingham, MA	G
Janesville, WI	J
Kansas City, MO	K
Los Angeles, CA	L
Norwood, OH	N
Arlington, TX GMAD	R
St. Louis, MO	S
Tarrytown, NY	T
Willow Run, MI	W
Wilmington, DE	Y
Fremont, CA	Z
Oshawa, Ont., CAN	1
St. Therese, Que., CAN	2
Pontiac, MI	P

THE TRIM NUMBER furnishes the key to trim color and material for each model series.

CORVAIR TRIM

COLOR	CLOTH	VINYL	LEATHER	CODE
Turquoise		•		723
Fawn		•		771
Red		•		782

CORVAIR MONZA TRIM

COLOR	CLOTH	VINYL	LEATHER	CODE
Saddle		•		706
Black		•		713
Blue		•		733
Fawn		•		773
Red		•		785
Slate		•		795
Ivory		•		797,798

CORSA TRIM

COLOR	CLOTH	VINYL	LEATHER	CODE
Saddle		•		706
Black		•		713
Blue		•		733
Fawn		•		773
Red		•		785
Slate		•		795
Ivory		•		797

CHEVY II TRIM

COLOR	CLOTH	VINYL	LEATHER	CODE
Turquoise	•	•		752
Turquoise		•		754
Fawn		•		758,761
Fawn	•	•		760
Red	•	•		776
Red		•		777

NOVA TRIM

COLOR	CLOTH	VINYL	LEATHER	CODE
Saddle	•	•		710
Saddle		•		703
Blue		•		734,736
Turquoise	•	•		745
Turquoise		•		747
Fawn	•	•		768
Fawn		•		769
Red	•	•		791
Red		•		793

NOVA SS TRIM

COLOR	CLOTH	VINYL	LEATHER	CODE
Saddle		•		702
Black		•		712
Fawn		•		718
Blue		•		732
Turquoise		•		744
Red		•		787

CHEVELLE 300 TRIM

COLOR	CLOTH	VINYL	LEATHER	CODE
Turquoise	•	•		751
Turquoise		•		755
Fawn	•	•		764
Fawn		•		765,759
Red	•	•		780
Red		•		781

CHEVELLE DELUXE TRIM

COLOR	CLOTH	VINYL	LEATHER	CODE
Turquoise	•	•		749
Fawn	•	•		762
Red	•	•		778

MALIBU TRIM

COLOR	CLOTH	VINYL	LEATHER	CODE
Saddle	•	•		707
Saddle		•		709
Blue	•	•		739
Turquoise	•	•		750
Turquoise		•		753
Fawn	•	•		763
Fawn		•		766
Red	•	•		772
Red		•		774

MALIBU SS TRIM

COLOR	CLOTH	VINYL	LEATHER	CODE
Saddle		•		710
Black		•		714
Blue		•		741
Fawn		•		770
Red		•		786
Ivory		•		792,796

BISCAYNE TRIM

COLOR	CLOTH	VINYL	LEATHER	CODE
Turquoise	•	•		852
Turquoise		•		855
Fawn	•	•		860
Fawn		•		861,865
Red	•	•		876
Red		•		877

BEL-AIR TRIM

COLOR	CLOTH	VINYL	LEATHER	CODE
Green	•	•		823
Blue	•	•		839
Turquoise	•	•		850
Fawn	•	•		863
Red	•	•		872

IMPALA TRIM

COLOR	CLOTH	VINYL	LEATHER	CODE
Black	•	•		811,817
Black		•		814
Green	•	•		826
Green		•		829
Blue	•	•		842,843
Blue		•		836
Turquoise		•		847
Saddle	•	•		857
Saddle		•		859
Fawn	•	•		866,858
Fawn		•		870
Red	•	•		874
Red		•		886

IMPALA SS TRIM

COLOR	CLOTH	VINYL	LEATHER	CODE
Ivory		•		802
Slate		•		805
Black		•		815
Blue		•		831
Ivory		•		845
Fawn		•		856
Saddle		•		862
Red		•		879

CORVETTE TRIM

COLOR	CLOTH	VINYL	LEATHER	CODE
Black			•	402
Red		•		407
Red			•	408
Blue		•		414
Blue			•	415
Saddle		•		420
Saddle			•	427
Silver		•		426
Silver			•	427
Green		•		430
Green			•	431
White		•		437,443,450
White			•	438,444,451
Maroon		•		435
Maroon			•	436

THE PAINT CODE furnishes the key to the exterior paint color. A two-letter code indicates the bottom and top colors respectively.

COLOR	CODE
Tuxedo Black	A
Ermine White	C
Mist Blue	D
Danube Blue	E
Nassau Blue	F
Glen Green	G
Willow Green	H
Cypress Green	J
Artesian Turquoise	K
Tahitian Turquoise	L
Milano Maroon	M
Madeira Maroon	N
Evening Orchid	P
Silver Pearl	Q
Regal Red	R
Sierra Tan	S
Rally Red	U
Cameo Beige	V
Glacier Gray	W
Goldwood Yellow	X
Crocus Yellow	Y

ENGINE NUMBER

All Chevrolet engines are stamped with a plant code, production date, and engine type code.

Note:

1. Corvette engines have the last six digits of the VIN stamped on the block next to the engine number.

2. Corvair engines are stamped on the top of the block forward of the generator.

3. 8 cylinder engines are stamped on the right front of the engine block.

4. 6 cylinder engines are stamped on the right side of the block at the rear of the distributor.

EXAMPLE:

T	01	01	RA
PLANT	MONTH	DAY	CODE

ENGINE PLANTS	CODE
Tonawanda	T
Flint	F

CORVAIR ENGINE

ENGINE CODE	NO. CYL.	CID	HORSE-POWER	COMP. RATIO	CARB	TRANS
RA	6	164	95	8.5:1	2-1 BC	MAN
RB	6	164	140	9.25:1	4-1 BC	MAN
RD	6	164	110	9.25:1	2-1 BC	MAN
RE	6	164	95	8.5:1	2-1 BC	MAN
RF	6	164	110	9.25:1	2-1 BC	MAN
RG	6	164	95	8.5:1	2-1 BC	AUTO
RH	6	164	110	9.25:1	2-1 BC	AUTO

1965 CHEVROLET

CORVAIR ENGINE

ENGINE CODE	NO. CYL.	CID	HORSE-POWER	COMP. RATIO	CARB	TRANS
RJ	6	164	95	8.5:1	2-1 BC	AUTO
RK	6	164	110	9.25:1	2-1 BC	AUTO
RL	6	164	180	8.25:1	TURBO	MAN
RM	6	164	140	9.25:1	4-1 BC	MAN
RN	6	164	140	9.25:1	4-1 BC	AUTO

CORVETTE

ENGINE CODE	NO. CYL.	CID	HORSE-POWER	COMP. RATIO	CARB	TRANS
HE	8	327	250	10.5:1	4 BC	MAN
HF	8	327	300	10.5:1	4 BC	MAN
HG	8	327	375	11.0:1	F.I.	MAN
HH	8	327	365	11.0:1	4 BC	MAN
HI	8	327	250	10.5:1	4 BC	MAN
HJ	8	327	300	10.5:1	4 BC	MAN
HK	8	327	365	11.0:1	4 BC	MAN
HL	8	327	365	11.0:1	4 BC	MAN
HM	8	327	365	11.0:1	4 BC	MAN
HN	8	327	375	11.0:1	F.I.	MAN
HO	8	327	250	10.5:1	F.I.	AUTO
HP	8	327	300	10.5:1	F.I.	AUTO
HQ	8	327	250	10.5:1	F.I.	AUTO
HR	8	327	300	10.5:1	F.I.	AUTO
HT	8	327	350	11.0:1	F.I.	MAN
HU	8	327	350	11.0:1	F.I.	MAN
HV	8	327	350	11.0:1	F.I.	MAN
HW	8	327	350	11.0:1	F.I.	MAN
IF	8	327	425	11.0:1	F.I.	MAN

CHEVY II

ENGINE CODE	NO. CYL.	CID	HORSE-POWER	COMP. RATIO	CARB	TRANS
OA	4	153	90	8.5:1	1 BC	MAN
OC	4	153	90	8.5:1	1 BC	MAN
OG	4	153	90	8.5:1	1 BC	MAN
OH	4	153	90	8.5:1	1 BC	AUTO
OJ	4	153	90	8.5:1	1 BC	AUTO
OK	6	194	120	8.5:1	1 BC	MAN
OM	6	194	120	8.5:1	1 BC	MAN
OQ	6	194	120	8.5:1	1 BC	MAN
OR	6	194	120	8.5:1	1 BC	AUTO
OT	6	194	120	8.5:1	1 BC	AUTO
PA	6	230	140	8.5:1	1 BC	MAN
PC	6	230	140	8.5:1	1 BC	AUTO
PV	6	230	140	8.5:1	1 BC	MAN
PX	6	230	140	8.5:1	1 BC	AUTO
PI	6	230	140	8.5:1	1 BC	AUTO
PD	8	283	195	9.25:1	2 BC	MAN
PE	8	283	220	9.25:1	4 BC	MAN
PF	8	283	195	9.25:1	2 BC	MAN
PG	8	283	220	9.25:1	4 BC	MAN
PL	8	283	195	9.25:1	2 BC	4-SP
PM	8	283	195	9.25:1	2 BC	4-SP
PN	8	283	195	9.25:1	2 BC	AUTO
PO	8	283	220	9.25:1	4 BC	AUTO
PP	8	283	195	9.25:1	2 BC	AUTO
PQ	8	283	220	9.25:1	4 BC	AUTO
PK	8	283	220	9.25:1	4 BC	AUTO
PB	8	283	220	9.25:1	4 BC	AUTO
ZA	8	327	250	10.5:1	4 BC	MAN
ZE	8	327	250	10.5:1	4 BC	MAN
ZK	8	327	250	10.5:1	4 BC	AUTO
ZM	8	327	250	10.5:1	4 BC	AUTO
ZB	8	327	300	10.5:1	4 BC	MAN
ZF	8	327	300	10.5:1	4 BC	MAN
ZL	8	327	300	10.5:1	4 BC	AUTO
ZN	8	327	300	10.5:1	4 BC	AUTO

CHEVELLE

ENGINE CODE	NO. CYL.	CID	HORSE-POWER	COMP. RATIO	CARB	TRANS
AA	6	194	120	8.5:1	1 BC	MAN
AC	6	194	120	8.5:1	1 BC	MAN
AG	6	194	120	8.5:1	1 BC	MAN
AG	6	194	120	8.5:1	1 BC	MAN
AH	6	194	120	8.5:1	1 BC	MAN
AK	6	194	120	8.5:1	1 BC	MAN
AL	6	194	120	8.5:1	1 BC	AUTO
AN	6	194	120	8.5:1	1 BC	AUTO
AR	6	194	120	8.5:1	1 BC	AUTO
BK	6	230	140	8.5:1	1 BC	MAN
BN	6	230	140	8.5:1	1 BC	MAN
BY	6	230	140	8.5:1	1 BC	AUTO
BZ	6	230	140	8.5:1	1 BC	AUTO
CA	6	230	140	8.5:1	1 BC	MAN
CB	6	230	140	8.5:1	1 BC	MAN
CC	6	230	140	8.5:1	1 BC	AUTO
CD	6	230	140	8.5:1	1 BC	AUTO
DA	8	283	195	9.25:1	2 BC	MAN
DB	8	283	195	9.25:1	2 BC	4-SP
DE	8	283	195	9.25:1	2 BC	AUTO
DG	8	283	220	9.25:1	4 BC	MAN
DH	8	283	220	9.25:1	4 BC	AUTO
EA	8	327	250	10.5:1	4 BC	MAN
EB	8	327	300	10.5:1	4 BC	MAN
EC	8	327	350	11.0:1	4 BC	MAN
ED	8	327	350	11.0:1	4 BC	MAN
EE	8	327	250	10.5:1	4 BC	AUTO
EF	8	327	300	10.5:1	4 BC	AUTO
IX	8	396	375	11.0;1	4 BC	MAN

CHEVROLET

ENGINE CODE	NO. CYL.	CID	HORSE-POWER	COMP. RATIO	CARB	TRANS
FA	6	230	140	8.5:1	1 BC	MAN
FE	6	230	140	8.5:1	1 BC	MAN
FF	6	230	140	8.5:1	1 BC	MAN
FK	6	230	140	8.5:1	1 BC	MAN
FL	6	230	140	8.5:1	1 BC	MAN
FM	6	230	140	8.5:1	1 BC	PG
FP	6	230	140	8.5:1	1 BC	PG
FR	6	230	140	8.5:1	1 BC	PG
N/A	6	250	150	8.5:1	1 BC	MAN
N/A	6	250	150	8.5:1	1 BC	PG
GA	8	283	195	9.25:1	2 BC	MAN
GC	8	283	195	9.25:1	2 BC	MAN
GF	8	283	195	9.25:1	2 BC	PG
GK	8	283	220	9.25:1	4 BC	MAN
GL	8	283	220	9.25:1	4 BC	PG
HA	8	327	250	10.5:1	4 BC	MAN
HB	8	327	300	10.5:1	4 BC	MAN
HC	8	327	250	10.5:1	4 BC	PG
HD	8	327	300	10.5:1	4 BC	PG
IA	8	396	325	10.25:1	4 BC	MAN
LF	8	396	325	10.25:1	4 BC	MAN
IE	8	396	425	11.0:1	4 BC	MAN
IC	8	396	325	10.25:1	4 BC	MAN
IG	8	396	325	10.25:1	4 BC	PG
LB	8	396	325	10.25:1	4 BC	PG
II	8	396	325	10.25:1	4 BC	PG
IV	8	396	325	10.25:1	4 BC	T.H.
LC	8	396	325	10.25:1	4 BC	T.H.
IW	8	396	325	10.25:1	4 BC	T.H.
IB	8	396	325	10.25:1	4 BC	N/A
JA	8	409	400	11.0;1	4 BC	MAN
JB	8	409	340	10.0:1	4 BC	MAN
JC	8	409	340	10.0:1	4 BC	MAN
JD	8	409	400	11.0:1	4 BC	MAN
JE	8	409	340	10.0:1	4 BC	PG
JF	8	409	340	10.0:1	4 BC	PG

1966 CHEVROLET

1966 CHEVROLET

1966 CHEVELLE

1966 CHEVELLE

1966 CHEVY II

1966 CHEVY II

1966 CORVAIR

1966 CORVAIR

1966 CORVETTE

1966 CORVETTE

VEHICLE IDENTIFICATION NUMBER

CHEVROLET
15411 T101555

Commonly referred to as the VIN NUMBER, this series of numbers and letters is stamped on a plate attached to the left front door hinge pillar.

CHEVROLET, CHEVELLE, and CHEVY II VINS are embossed on a stainless steel plate riveted to athe left front door hinge post facing.

CORVAIR VIN is embossed on a stainless steel plate riveted to the left side-rail near the battery in the engine compartment.

CORVETTE VIN is embossed on a stainless steel plate riveted to the right side dash pillar brace under the glove box.

FIRST DIGIT: Identifies the Chevrolet division

NEXT FOUR DIGITS: Identify the model number

MODEL	CODE
Biscayne/Bel-Air	5000
Impala, Caprice	6000
Chevelle	3000
Chevy II	1000
Corvair	0000
Corvette	9000

SIXTH DIGIT: Identifies the model year (1966)

SEVENTH DIGIT: Identifies the assembly plant

ASSEMBLY PLANT	CODE
Atlanta, GA	A
Baltimore, MD	B
Southgate, CA	C
Flint, MI	F
Framingham, MA	G
Janesville, WI	J
Kansas City, MO	K
Lordstown, OH	U
Los Angeles, CA	L
Norwood, OH	N
Arlington, TX GMAD	R
St. Louis, MO	S
Tarrytown, NY	T
Willow Run, MI	W
Wilmington, DE	Y
Fremont, CA	Z
Oshawa, Ont., CAN	1
St. Therese, Que., CAN	2
Pontiac, MI	P

LAST SIX DIGITS: Represent the basic production numbers

BODY NUMBER PLATE

Complete identification of each body is provided by a plate riveted to the top of the cowl. Exception: Corvair body tag is located on the left rear wheel housing inside the engine compartment.

CHEVROLET DIVISION
GENERAL MOTORS CORP.

ST 66-15411
FBD 101555 BODY
TR 840
AA PAINT

BODY BY FISHER

EXAMPLE:

66	Model Year (1966)
15411	Body Series (Biscayne)
FL1	Assembly Plant (Flint, MI)
101555	Production Sequence
840	Trim
A	Lower Body Color
A	Upper Body Color

THE STYLE NUMBER is a combination of the year, series and body style.

CORVAIR 500	CODE
2-Dr. Sport Coupe	10137
4-Dr. Sport Sedan	10139

CORVAIR MONZA	CODE
2-Dr. Sport Coupe	10537
2-Dr. Convertible	10567
4-Dr. Sport Sedan	10539

CORSA	CODE
2-Dr. Sport Coupe	10737
2-Dr. Convertible	10767

CHEVY II 100	L4	6 CYL.	8 CYL.
2-Dr. Sedan	11111	11311	11411
4-Dr. Sedan	11169	11369	11469
4-Dr. Sta. Wagon, 2-Seat		11335	11435

NOVA	6 CYL	8 CYL
4-Dr. Sedan	11569	11669
2-Dr. Sport Coupe	11537	11637
4-Dr. Sta. Wagon, 2-Seat	11535	11635

NOVA SS	6 CYL	8 CYL
2-Dr. Sport Coupe	11737	11837

CORVETTE	CODE
2-Dr. Sport Coupe	19437
2-Dr. Convertible	19467

BISCAYNE	6 CYL	8 CYL
2-Dr. Sedan	15311	15411
4-Dr. Sedan	15369	15469
4-Dr. Sta. Wagon, 2-Seat	15335	15435

BEL-AIR	6 CYL	8 CYL
2-Dr. Sedan	15511	15611
4-Dr. Sedan	15569	15669
4-Dr. Sta. Wagon, 2-Seat	15535	15635
4-Dr. Sta. Wagon, 3-Seat	15545	16645

IMPALA	6 CYL	8 CYL
4-Dr. Sedan	16369	16469
4-Dr. Sport Sedan	16339	16439
2-Dr. Sport Coupe	16337	16437
2-Dr. Convertible	16367	16467
4-Dr. Sta. Wagon, 2-Seat	16335	16435
4-Dr. Sta. Wagon, 3-Seat	16345	16445

IMPALA SS	6 CYL	8 CYL
2-Dr. Sport Coupe	16737	16837
2-Dr. Convertible	16767	16867

CAPRICE	CODE
4-Dr. Sedan	16639
2-Dr. Coupe	16647
4-Dr. Sta. Wagon, 3-Seat	16645
4-Dr. Sta. Wagon, 2-Seat	16635

CHEVELLE 300	6 CYL	8 CYL
2-Dr. Sedan	13111	13211
4-Dr. Sedan	13169	13269

CHEVELLE 300 (DLX.)	6 CYL	8 CYL
2-Dr. Sedan	13311	13411
4-Dr. Sedan	13369	13469
4-Dr. Sta. Wagon, 2-Seat	13335	13435

MALIBU	6 CYL	8 CYL
4-Dr. Sedan	13569	13669
2-Dr. Sport Coupe	13517	13617
2-Dr. Convertible	13567	13667
4-Dr. Sta. Wagon, 2-Seat	13535	13635
4-Dr. Sedan	13539	13639

CHEVELLE 396 SS	CODE
2-Dr. Sport Coupe	13817
2-Dr. Convertible	13867

THE BODY NUMBER is the production serial number of the body. The prefix letter denotes the plant in which the body was built.

ASSEMBLY PLANT	CODE
Atlanta, GA	A
Baltimore, MD	B
Southgate, CA	C
Flint, MI	F
Framingham, MA	G
Janesville, WI	J
Kansas City, MO	K
Los Angeles, CA	L
Norwood, OH	N
Arlington, TX GMAD	R
St. Louis, MO	S
Tarrytown, NY	T
Willow Run, MI	W
Wilmington, DE	Y
Fremont, CA	Z
Oshawa, Ont., CAN	1
St. Therese, Que., CAN	2
Pontiac, MI	P
Lordstown, OH	U

THE TRIM NUMBER furnishes the key to trim color and material for each model series.

CORVAIR TRIM

COLOR	CLOTH	VINYL	LEATHER	CODE
Fawn		•		701
Blue		•		721
Red		•		739

CORVAIR MONZA/CORSA TRIM

COLOR	CLOTH	VINYL	LEATHER	CODE
Fawn		•		702
Blue		•		722,792
Red		•		740
Black		•		758
Bronze		•		788
Ivory		•		795

CHEVY II 100

COLOR	CLOTH	VINYL	LEATHER	CODE
Fawn	•	•		714
Fawn		•		715
Blue	•	•		733
Blue		•		734
Red	•	•		752
Red		•		753

NOVA TRIM

COLOR	CLOTH	VINYL	LEATHER	CODE
Fawn	•	•		716
Fawn		•		717
Blue	•	•		735
Blue		•		736
Red	•	•		754
Red		•		755
Turquoise	•	•		779
Turquoise		•		780

NOVA SS TRIM

COLOR	CLOTH	VINYL	LEATHER	CODE
Fawn		•		718
Blue		•		737
Red		•		756
Black		•		765

CHEVELLE 300 TRIM

COLOR	CLOTH	VINYL	LEATHER	CODE
Fawn	•	•		704
Blue	•	•		724
Red	•	•		742

CHEVELLE 300 DELUXE TRIM

COLOR	CLOTH	VINYL	LEATHER	CODE
Fawn	•	•		706
Fawn		•		707
Blue	•	•		726
Blue		•		727
Red	•	•		744
Red		•		745

1966 CHEVROLET

MALIBU TRIM

COLOR	CLOTH	VINYL	LEATHER	CODE
Fawn	•	•		708
Fawn		•		709,712
Blue	•	•		728
Blue		•		729,731
Red	•	•		746
Red		•		747,750
Black		•		761,763
Turquoise	•	•		775
Turquoise		•		776
Bronze		•		790

CHEVELLE 396 SS TRIM

COLOR	CLOTH	VINYL	LEATHER	CODE
Fawn		•		709,712
Blue		•		729,732,731
Red		•		747,750
Black		•		761,763
Turquoise		•		776,777
Bronze		•		790
Ivory		•		797

BISCAYNE TRIM

COLOR	CLOTH	VINYL	LEATHER	CODE
Blue	•	•		840
Blue		•		832
Fawn	•	•		860
Fawn		•		861
Red	•	•		876
Red		•		877

BEL-AIR TRIM

COLOR	CLOTH	VINYL	LEATHER	CODE
Blue	•	•		839
Blue		•		833
Turquoise	•	•		850
Turquoise		•		854
Fawn	•	•		863
Fawn		•		867
Red	•	•		872
Red		•		878

IMPALA TRIM

COLOR	CLOTH	VINYL	LEATHER	CODE
Black	•	•		811
Black		•		814
Green	•	•		826
Green		•		829
Blue	•	•		842
Blue		•		836
Turquoise		•		847,853
Fawn	•	•		866
Fawn		•		870
Red	•	•		874
Red		•		871

IMPALA SS TRIM

COLOR	CLOTH	VINYL	LEATHER	CODE
Black		•		813
Green		•		830
Blue		•		837,844
Turquoise		•		846
Fawn		•		869
Red		•		873
Ivory		•		855

CAPRICE TRIM

COLOR	CLOTH	VINYL	LEATHER	CODE
Black	•	•		817,818,816
Black		•		814,815
Green		•		829
Blue	•	•		834,843,841
Blue		•		836,831
Turquoise		•		847,848
Fawn	•	•		857,868,864
Fawn		•		870,856
Red		•		879
Bronze		•		891

CORVETTE TRIM

COLOR	CLOTH	VINYL	LEATHER	CODE
Red				407
Blue				414,418
Saddle				420
Silver				426
White/Blue				450
Green				430

THE PAINT CODE furnishes the key to the exterior paint color. A two-letter code indicates the bottom and top colors respectively.

COLOR	CODE
Tuxedo Black	A
Tuxedo Black	*900
Ermine White	C
Ermine White	*972
Mist Blue	D
Danube Blue	E
Marina Blue	F
Willow Green	H
Artesian Turquoise	K
Tropic Turquoise	L
Aztec Bronze	M
Madeira Maroon	N
Regal Red	R
Sandalwood Tan	T
Cameo Beige	V
Chateau Slate	W
Lemonwood Yellow	Y
Rally Red	*974
Nassau Blue	*976
Laguna Blue	*978
Trophy Blue	*980
Mosport Green	*982
Sunfire Yellow	*984
Silver Pearl	*986
Milano Maroon	*988

*Corvette only

ENGINE NUMBER

All Chevrolet engines are stamped with a plant code, production date, and engine type code.

Note:

1. Corvette engines have the last six digits of the VIN stamped on the block next to the engine number.

2. Corvair engines are stamped on the top of the block forward of the generator.

3. 8 cylinder engines are stamped on the right front of the engine block.

4. 6 cylinder engines are stamped on the right side of the block at the rear of the distributor.

EXAMPLE:

T	01	01	RA
PLANT	MONTH	DAY	CODE

ENGINE PLANTS **CODE**

Tonawanda .... T
Flint .... F

CORVAIR

ENGINE CODE	NO. CYL.	CID	HORSE-POWER	COMP. RATIO	CARB	TRANS
RA	6	164	95	8.25:1	2-1 BC	MAN
RB	6	164	140	9.25:1	4-1 BC	MAN
RD	6	164	110	9.25:1	2-1 BC	MAN
RL	6	164	180	8.25:1	TURBO	MAN
RM	6	164	140	9.25:1	4-1 BC	MAN
RE	6	164	95	8.25:1	2-1 BC	MAN
RZ	6	164	140	9.25:1	4-1 BC	MAN
RR	6	164	140	9.25:1	4-1 BC	MAN
RF	6	164	110	9.25:1	4-1 BC	MAN
RS	6	164	95	8.25:1	4-1 BC	MAN
RT	6	164	140	9.25:1	4-1 BC	MAN
RU	6	164	110	9.25:1	2-1 BC	MAN
RQ	6	164	140	9.25:1	4-1 BC	MAN
RG	6	164	95	8.25:1	2-1 BC	AUTO
RH	6	164	110	9.25:1	2-1 BC	AUTO
RN	6	164	140	9.25:1	4-1 BC	AUTO
RJ	6	164	95	8.25:1	2-1 BC	AUTO
RK	6	164	110	9.25:1	2-1 BC	AUTO
RY	6	164	140	9.25:1	4-1 BC	AUTO
RX	6	164	140	9.25:1	4-1 BC	AUTO
RV	6	164	95	8.25:1	2-1 BC	AUTO
RW	6	164	110	9.25:1	2-1 BC	AUTO

CORVETTE

ENGINE CODE	NO. CYL.	CID	HORSE-POWER	COMP. RATIO	CARB	TRANS
HE	8	327	300	10.5:1	4 BC	MAN
HH	8	327	300	10.5:1	4 BC	MAN
HR	8	327	300	10.5:1	4 BC	AUTO
HD	8	327	350	11.0:1	4 BC	MAN
HO	8	327	300	10.5:1	4 BC	AUTO
HT	8	327	350	11.0:1	4 BC	MAN
HP	8	327	300	10.5:1	4 BC	MAN
HK	8	327	350	11.0:1	4 BC	MAN
IK	8	427	425	11.0:1	4 BC	MAN
IL	8	427	390	10.25:1	4 BC	MAN
IM	8	427	390	10.25:1	4 BC	MAN
IP	8	427	425	11.0:1	4 BC	MAN
IQ	8	427	390	10.25:1	4 BC	AUTO
IR	8	427	390	10.25:1	4 BC	AUTO

CHEVY II

ENGINE CODE	NO. CYL.	CID	HORSE-POWER	COMP. RATIO	CARB	TRANS
OA	4	153	90	8.5:1	1 BC	MAN
OC	4	153	90	8.5:1	1 BC	MAN
OG	4	153	90	8.5:1	1 BC	MAN
OH	4	153	90	8.5:1	1 BC	AUTO
OJ	4	153	90	8.5:1	1 BC	AUTO
OK	6	194	120	8.5:1	1 BC	MAN
OQ	6	194	120	8.5:1	1 BC	MAN
ZY	6	194	120	8.5:1	1 BC	MAN
ZV	6	194	120	8.5:1	1 BC	MAN
ZW	6	194	120	8.5:1	1 BC	MAN
OR	6	194	120	8.5:1	1 BC	AUTO
ZX	6	194	120	8.5:1	1 BC	AUTO
OS	6	194	120	8.5:1	1 BC	AUTO
OT	6	194	120	8.5:1	1 BC	AUTO
PV	6	230	140	8.5:1	1 BC	MAN
PC	6	230	140	8.5:1	1 BC	MAN
PX	6	230	140	8.5:1	1 BC	AUTO
PI	6	230	140	8.5:1	1 BC	AUTO
PO	8	283	195	9.25:1	2 BC	MAN
PF	8	283	195	9.25:1	2 BC	MAN
PL	8	283	195	9.25:1	2 BC	4-SP
PM	8	283	195	9.25:1	2 BC	4-SP
PE	8	283	195	9.25:1	2 BC	MAN
PG	8	283	195	9.25:1	2 BC	MAN
PQ	8	283	195	9.25:1	2 BC	4-SP
PS	8	283	195	9.25:1	2 BC	4-SP
PN	8	283	195	9.25:1	2 BC	AUTO
PP	8	283	195	9.25:1	2 BC	AUTO
PV	8	283	195	9.25:1	2 BC	AUTO
PO	8	283	195	9.25:1	2 BC	AUTO
QA	8	283	220	9.25:1	4 BC	MAN
QB	8	283	220	9.25:1	4 BC	MAN
QC	8	283	220	9.25:1	4 BC	MAN
QF	8	283	220	9.25:1	4 BC	MAN
PK	8	283	220	9.25:1	4 BC	AUTO
PP	8	283	220	9.25:1	4 BC	AUTO
QD	8	283	220	9.25:1	4 BC	AUTO
QE	8	283	220	9.25:1	4 BC	AUTO
ZA	8	327	275	10.5:1	4 BC	MAN
ZI	8	327	350	11.0:1	4 BC	MAN
ZE	8	327	275	10.5:1	4 BC	MAN
ZJ	8	327	350	11.0:1	4 BC	MAN
ZB	8	327	275	10.5:1	4 BC	MAN
ZC	8	327	275	10.5:1	4 BC	MAN
ZG	8	327	350	11.0:1	4 BC	MAN
ZH	8	327	350	11.0:1	4 BC	MAN
ZK	8	327	275	10.5:1	4 BC	AUTO
ZM	8	327	275	10.5:1	4 BC	AUTO
ZD	8	327	275	10.5:1	4 BC	AUTO
ZF	8	327	275	10.5:1	4 BC	AUTO

CHEVELLE

ENGINE CODE	NO. CYL.	CID	HORSE-POWER	COMP. RATIO	CARB	TRANS
AA	6	194	120	8.5:1	1 BC	MAN
AC	6	194	120	8.5:1	1 BC	MAN
AH	6	194	120	8.5:1	1 BC	MAN
AG	6	194	120	8.5:1	1 BC	MAN
AK	6	194	120	8.5:1	1 BC	MAN
AS	6	194	120	8.5:1	1 BC	MAN
AT	6	194	120	8.5:1	1 BC	MAN
AU	6	194	120	8.5:1	1 BC	MAN
AV	6	194	120	8.5:1	1 BC	MAN
AW	6	194	120	8.5:1	1 BC	MAN
AL	6	194	120	8.5:1	1 BC	MAN
AN	6	194	120	8.5:1	1 BC	MAN
AR	6	194	120	8.5:1	1 BC	AUTO
AX	6	194	120	8.5:1	1 BC	AUTO
AY	6	194	120	8.5:1	1 BC	AUTO
AZ	6	194	120	8.5:1	1 BC	AUTO
CA	6	230	140	8.5:1	1 BC	MAN
CB	6	230	140	8.5:1	1 BC	MAN
BN	6	230	140	8.5:1	1 BC	MAN
BO	6	230	140	8.5:1	1 BC	MAN
CC	6	230	140	8.5:1	1 BC	MAN
CD	6	230	140	8.5:1	1 BC	MAN
BL	6	230	140	8.5:1	1 BC	MAN
BM	6	230	140	8.5:1	1 BC	MAN
DA	8	283	195	9.25:1	2 BC	MAN
DB	8	283	195	9.25:1	2 BC	4-SP
DI	8	283	195	9.25:1	2 BC	MAN
DJ	8	283	195	9.25:1	2 BC	AUTO
DK	8	283	195	9.25:1	2 BC	4-SP
DF	8	283	195	9.25:1	2 BC	AUTO
DE	8	283	195	9.25:1	2 BC	N/A
DG	8	283	220	9.25:1	4 BC	MAN
DL	8	283	220	9.25:1	4 BC	MAN
DM	8	283	220	9.25:1	4 BC	AUTO
DH	8	283	220	9.25:1	4 BC	AUTO
EA	8	327	250	10.5:1	4 BC	MAN
EB	8	327	250	10.5:1	4 BC	MAN
EE	8	327	250	10.5:1	4 BC	AUTO
EC	8	327	250	10.5:1	4 BC	AUTO
ED	8	396	325	10.25:1	4 BC	MAN
EF	8	396	360	10.25:1	4 BC	MAN
EH	8	396	325	10.25:1	4 BC	MAN
EJ	8	396	360	10.25:1	4 BC	MAN
EK	8	396	325	10.25:1	4 BC	AUTO
EL	8	396	360	10.25:1	4 BC	AUTO
EM	8	396	325	10.25:1	4 BC	AUTO
EN	8	396	360	10.25:1	4 BC	AUTO
EG	8	396	375	11.0:1	4 BC	MAN

CHEVROLET

ENGINE CODE	NO. CYL.	CID	HORSE-POWER	COMP. RATIO	CARB	TRANS
FA	6	250	155	8.5:1	1 BC	MAN
FE	6	250	155	8.5:1	1 BC	MAN
FF	6	250	155	8.5:1	1 BC	MAN
FV	6	250	155	8.5:1	1 BC	MAN
FW	6	250	155	8.5:1	1 BC	MAN
FX	6	250	155	8.5:1	1 BC	MAN
FK	6	250	155	8.5:1	1 BC	MAN
FL	6	250	155	8.5:1	1 BC	MAN
FP	6	250	155	8.5:1	1 BC	PG
FR	6	250	155	8.5:1	1 BC	PG
FY	6	250	155	8.5:1	1 BC	PG
FM	6	250	155	8.5:1	1 BC	PG
FZ	6	250	155	8.5:1	1 BC	MAN
GP	6	250	155	8.5:1	1 BC	PG
GQ	6	250	155	8.5:1	1 BC	PG
GR	6	250	155	8.5:1	1 BC	PG
GA	8	283	195	9.25:1	2 BC	MAN
GC	8	283	195	9.25:1	2 BC	4-SP
GK	8	283	195	9.25:1	2 BC	MAN
GS	8	283	195	9.25:1	2 BC	4-SP
GF	8	283	195	9.25:1	2 BC	PG
GT	8	283	195	9.25:1	2 BC	PG
GW	8	283	220	9.25:1	4 BC	MAN
GX	8	283	220	9.25:1	4 BC	MAN
GL	8	283	220	9.25:1	4 BC	PG
GZ	8	283	220	9.25:1	4 BC	PG
HA	8	327	275	10.5:1	4 BC	MAN
HB	8	327	275	10.5:1	4 BC	MAN
HC	8	327	275	10.5:1	4 BC	PG
HF	8	327	275	10.5:1	4 BC	PG
ID	8	327	230	N/A	N/A	N/A
IA	8	396	325	10.5:1	4 BC	MAN
IB	8	396	325	10.5:1	4 BC	MAN
IG	8	396	325	10.5:1	4 BC	PG
IV	8	396	325	10.5:1	4 BC	T.H.
IC	8	396	325	10.5:1	4 BC	PG
IN	8	396	325	10.5:1	4 BC	T.H.
IH	8	427	390	10.5:1	4 BC	MAN
ID	8	427	425	11.0:1	4 BC	MAN
IJ	8	427	390	10.5:1	4 BC	T.H.
II	8	427	390	10.5:1	4 BC	MAN
IO	8	427	425	11.0:1	4 BC	T.H.

1967 CHEVROLET CAPRICE

1967 CAMARO

1967 CHEVELLE

1967 CHEVELLE

1967 CHEVY II NOVA

1967 CORVAIR

1967 CORVETTE

1967 CORVETTE

VEHICLE IDENTIFICATION NUMBER

CHEVROLET
154117T101555

Commonly referred to as the VIN NUMBER, this series of numbers and letters is stamped on a plate attached to the left front door hinge pillar.

CHEVROLET, CHEVELLE, CAMARO, and CHEVY II VINS are embossed on a stainless steel plate riveted to the left front door hinge post facing.

CORVAIR VIN is embossed on a stainless steel plate riveted to the left side-rail near the battery in the engine compartment.

CORVETTE VIN is embossed on a stainless steel plate riveted to the right side dash pillar brace under the glove box.

FIRST DIGIT: Identifies the Chevrolet division

NEXT FOUR DIGITS: Identify the model number

MODEL	CODE
Biscayne/Bel-Air	5000
Impala	6000
Chevelle, Malibu	3000
Chevy II, Nova	1000
Camaro	2000
Corvair	0000
Corvette	9000

SIXTH DIGIT: Identifies the model year (1967)

SEVENTH DIGIT: Identifies the assembly plant

ASSEMBLY PLANT	CODE
Atlanta, GA	A
Baltimore, MD	B
Southgate, CA	C
Doraville, GA	D
Flint, MI	F
Framingham, MA	G
Janesville, WI	J
Kansas City, MO	K
Lordstown, OH	U
Los Angeles, CA	L
Norwood, OH	N
Arlington, TX GMAD	R
St. Louis, MO	S
Tarrytown, NY	T
Willow Run, MI	W
Wilmington, DE	Y
Fremont, CA	Z
Oshawa, Ont., CAN	1
St. Therese, Que., CAN	2
Pontiac, MI	P

LAST SIX DIGITS: Represent the basic production numbers

BODY NUMBER PLATE

Complete identification of each body is provided by a plate riveted to the top of the cowl. Exception: Corvair body tag is located on the left rear wheel housing inside the engine compartment.

CHEVROLET DIVISION
GENERAL MOTORS CORP.

ST 67 15411
FL1 101555 BODY
TR 812
AA PAINT

BODY BY FISHER

EXAMPLE:

67	Model Year (1967)
15411	Body Series (Biscayne)
FL1	Assembly Plant (Flint, MI)
101555	Production Sequence
812	Trim
A	Lower Body Color
A	Upper Body Color

THE STYLE NUMBER is a combination of the year, series and body style.

CORVAIR 500	CODE
4-Dr. Sport Sedan	10139
2-Dr. Sport Coupe	10137

CORVAIR MONZA	CODE
4-Dr. Sport Sedan	10539
2-Dr. Sport Coupe	10537
2-Dr. Convertible	10567

CHEVY II 100	L4	6 CYL	8 CYL
2-Dr. Sedan	11111	11311	11411
4-Dr. Sedan	11169	11369	11469
4-Dr. Sta. Wagon	-	11335	11435

NOVA	6 CYL	8 CYL
4-Dr. Sedan	11569	11669
2-Dr. Sport Coupe	11537	11637
4-Dr. Sta. Wagon, 2-Seat	11535	11635

NOVA SS	6 CYL	8 CYL
2-Dr. Sport Coupe	11737	11837

CHEVELLE 300	6 CYL	8 CYL
2-Dr. Sedan	13111	13211
4-Dr. Sedan	13169	13269

CHEVELLE 300 (DLX)	6 CYL	8 CYL
2-Dr. Sedan	13311	13411
4-Dr. Sedan	13369	13469
4-Dr. Sta. Wagon, 2-Seat	13335	13435

MALIBU	6 CYL	8 CYL
4-Dr. Sedan	13569	13669
4-Dr. Sport Sedan	13539	13639
2-Dr. Coupe	13517	13617
2-Dr. Convertible	13567	13667
4-Dr. Sta. Wagon, 2-Seat	13535	13635

SUPER SPORT 396	6 CYL	8 CYL
2-Dr. Sport Coupe	-	13817
2-Dr. Convertible	-	13867

CONCOURS	6 CYL	8 CYL
4-Dr. Sta. Wagon, 2-Seat	13735	13835

CAMARO	6 CYL	8 CYL
2-Dr. Sport Coupe	12337	12437
2-Dr. Convertible	12367	12467

BISCAYNE	6 CYL	8 CYL
2-Dr. Sedan	15311	15411
4-Dr. Sedan	15369	15469
4-Dr. Sta. Wagon, 2-Seat	15335	15435

BEL-AIR	6 CYL	8 CYL
2-Dr. Sedan	15511	15611
4-Dr. Sedan	15569	15669
4-Dr. Sta. Wagon, 2-Seat	15535	15635
4-Dr. Sta. Wagon, 3-Seat	15545	15645

IMPALA	6 CYL	8 CYL
2-Dr. Sport Coupe	16387	16487
2-Dr. Convertible	16367	16467
4-Dr. Sedan	16369	16469
4-Dr. Sport Sedan	16339	16439
4-Dr. Sta. Wagon, 2-Seat	16335	16435
4-Dr. Sta. Wagon, 3-Seat	16345	16445

IMPALA SS	6 CYL	8 CYL
2-Dr. Sport Coupe	16787	16887
2-Dr. Convertible	16767	16867

CAPRICE	6 CYL	8 CYL
2-Dr. Custom Coupe	-	16647
4-Dr. Custom Sedan	-	16639
4-Dr. Custom Wagon, 2-Seat	-	16635
4-Dr. Custom Wagon, 3-Seat	-	16645

CORVETTE	CODE
2-Dr. Sport Coupe	19437
2-Dr. Convertible	19467

THE BODY NUMBER is the production serial number of the body. The prefix letter denotes the plant in which the body was built.

ASSEMBLY PLANT	CODE
Atlanta, GA	ATL
Baltimore, MD	BAL
Southgate, CA	BC
Doraville, GA	BA
Flint, MI	FL1
Framingham, MA	FM
Janesville, WI	JAN
Kansas City, MO	BK
Kansas City, KS	KAN
Los Angeles, CA	LOS
Norwood, OH	NOR
Arlington, TX GMAD	BT
St. Louis, MO	STL
Tarrytown, NY	TAR
Lordstown, OH	LOR
Willow Run, MI	WRN
Wilmington, DE	BW
Fremont, CA	BF
Oshawa, Ont., CAN	OS
St. Therese, Que., CAN	ST
Pontiac, MI	PON

THE TRIM NUMBER furnishes the key to trim color and material for each model series.

CORVAIR TRIM

COLOR	CLOTH	VINYL	LEATHER	CODE
Fawn		•		703
Blue		•		721
Black		•		751

CORVAIR MONZA TRIM

COLOR	CLOTH	VINYL	LEATHER	CODE
Gold		•		713
Blue		•		716,722
Black		•		758

CHEVY II 100 TRIM

COLOR	CLOTH	VINYL	LEATHER	CODE
Fawn		•		719
Blue	•	•		733
Blue		•		734
Fawn	•	•		771
Black		•		791

NOVA TRIM

COLOR	CLOTH	VINYL	LEATHER	CODE
Blue	•	•		735
Blue		•		736
Maroon	•	•		754
Fawn		•		774
Black		•		785
Black	•	•		786

NOVA SS TRIM

COLOR	CLOTH	VINYL	LEATHER	CODE
Blue		•		737
Red		•		749
Black		•		780
Gold		•		781

CAMARO TRIM

COLOR	CLOTH	VINYL	LEATHER	CODE
Yellow		•		707
Gold		•		709,711,712
Blue		•		717,732
Red		•		741,742
Black		•		760,765,767
Turquoise		•		778,779
Parchment		•		797

CHEVELLE 300 TRIM

COLOR	CLOTH	VINYL	LEATHER	CODE
Fawn	•	•		768
Fawn		•		720
Blue	•	•		724
Black		•		757

CHEVELLE 300 DELUXE TRIM

COLOR	CLOTH	VINYL	LEATHER	CODE
Blue	•	•		726
Blue		•		727
Black	•	•		764
Black		•		766
Fawn	•	•		769
Fawn		•		770

MALIBU TRIM

COLOR	CLOTH	VINYL	LEATHER	CODE
Plum	•	•		705
Blue	•	•		728,730
Blue		•		723,729
Blue		•		731,738
Maroon	•	•		746
Red		•		747,750
Black	•	•		759,762
Black		•		761,763
Turquoise	•	•		775
Turquoise		•		776
Gold	•	•		782,794
Gold		•		783,784

MALIBU SS/CONCOURS TRIM

COLOR	CLOTH	VINYL	LEATHER	CODE
Blue		•		723,729
Blue		•		731,738
Red		•		747,750
Black		•		761,763
Turquoise		•		776,778
Gold		•		783,784

BISCAYNE TRIM

COLOR	CLOTH	VINYL	LEATHER	CODE
Fawn	•	•		801
Fawn		•		802,865
Black		•		812
Blue	•	•		840
Blue		•		832

BEL-AIR TRIM

COLOR	CLOTH	VINYL	LEATHER	CODE
Fawn	•	•		803
Fawn		•		804
Black	•	•		819
Black		•		820
Blue	•	•		839
Blue		•		833
Turquoise	•	•		850
Turquoise		•		854

IMPALA TRIM

COLOR	CLOTH	VINYL	LEATHER	CODE
Black	•	•		811
Black		•		814
Blue	•	•		842
Blue		•		836,845
Turquoise	•	•		853
Turquoise		•		847
Red		•		871
Maroon	•	•		874
Gold	•	•		888
Gold		•		889
Parchment		•		894

IMPALA SS TRIM

COLOR	CLOTH	VINYL	LEATHER	CODE
Black		•		810,813
Blue		•		844,848
Red		•		870,873
Gold		•		885,890
Parchment		•		895,898

CAPRICE TRIM

COLOR	CLOTH	VINYL	LEATHER	CODE
Black	•	•		818
Black		•		814,815,821
Blue	•	•		843,834
Blue		•		836,835,837
Turquoise		•		847
Plum	•	•		860
Red		•		871
Gold	•	•		887,886
Gold		•		889,884,891

CORVETTE TRIM

COLOR	CLOTH	VINYL	LEATHER	CODE
Red				407
Red			•	408
Blue				414,450,418
Blue			•	415,419
Saddle				420
Saddle			•	421
Green				430
White/Black				455
Black			•	402

THE PAINT CODE furnishes the key to the exterior paint color. A two-letter code indicates the bottom and top colors respectively.

COLOR	CODE
Tuxedo Black	A
Tuxedo Black	*900
Ermine White	C
Ermine White	*972
Nantucket Blue	D
Deepwater Blue	E
Marina Blue	F
Granada Gold	G
Mountain Green	H
Emerald Turquoise	K
Tahoe Turquoise	L
Royal Plum	M
Madeira Maroon	N
Bolero Red	R
Sierra Fawn	S
Capri Cream	T
Butternut Yellow	Y
Rally Red*	974
Marina Blue*	976
Lynndale Blue*	977
Elkhart Blue*	980
Goodwood Green*	983
Sunfire Yellow*	984
Silver Pearl*	986
Marlboro Maroon*	988

* Corvette only

ENGINE NUMBER

All Chevrolet engines are stamped with a plant code, production date, and engine type code.

Note:

1. Corvette engines have the last six digits of the VIN stamped on the block next to the engine number.

2. Corvair engines are stamped on the top of the block forward of the generator.

3. 8 cylinder engines are stamped on the right front of the engine block.

4. 6 cylinder engines are stamped on the right side of the block at the rear of the distributor.

EXAMPLE:

T	01	01	RA
PLANT	MONTH	DAY	CODE

ENGINE PLANTS	CODE
Tonawanda	T
Flint	F

CORVAIR

ENGINE CODE	NO. CYL.	CID	HORSE-POWER	COMP. RATIO	CARB	TRANS
RA	6	164	95	8.25:1	2-1 BC	M/A
RD	6	164	110	9.0:1	2-1 BC	MAN
RE	6	164	95	8.25:1	2-1 BC	MAN
RF	6	164	110	9.0:1	2-1 BC	MAN
RS	6	164	95	8.25:1	2-1 BC	MAN
QM	6	164	95	8.25:1	2-1 BC	MAN
RU	6	164	110	9.0:1	2-1 BC	MAN
QS	6	164	110	9.0:1	2-1 BC	MAN
RG	6	164	95	8.25:1	2-1 BC	AUTO
RH	6	164	110	9.0:1	2-1 BC	AUTO
RJ	6	164	95	8.25:1	2-1 BC	AUTO
RK	6	164	110	9.0:1	2-1 BC	AUTO
RV	6	164	95	8.25:1	2-1 BC	AUTO
QO	6	164	95	8.25:1	2-1 BC	AUTO
RW	6	164	110	9.0:1	2-1 BC	AUTO
QP	6	164	110	9.0:1	2-1 BC	AUTO

CORVETTE

ENGINE CODE	NO. CYL.	CID	HORSE-POWER	COMP. RATIO	CARB	TRANS
HE	8	327	300	10.0:1	4 BC	MAN
HH	8	327	300	10.0:1	4 BC	MAN
HR	8	327	300	10.0:1	4 BC	PG
HD	8	327	350	11.0:1	4 BC	MAN
HO	8	327	300	10.0:1	4 BC	PG
HT	8	327	350	11.0:1	4 BC	MAN
HP	8	327	350	11.0:1	4 BC	MAN
KH	8	327	350	11.0:1	4 BC	MAN
IL	8	427	390	10.25:1	4 BC	MAN/PG
JC	8	427	400	10.25:1	3-2 BC	MAN
JE	8	427	435	11.0:1	3-2 BC	MAN
IT	8	427	425	12.5:1	4 BC	MAN
IU	8	427	435	11.0:1	3-2 BC	MAN
IM	8	427	390	10.25:1	4 BC	MAN
JF	8	427	400	10.25:1	3-2 BC	MAN
JH	8	427	435	11.0:1	3-2 BC	MAN
IQ	8	427	390	10.25:1	4 BC	PG
JD	8	427	400	10.25:1	3-2 BC	PG
IR	8	427	390	10.25:1	4 BC	PG
JG	8	427	400	10.25:1	3-2 BC	PG
JA	8	427	435	11.0:1	3-2 BC	MAN

CHEVY II

ENGINE CODE	NO. CYL.	CID	HORSE POWER	COMP. RATIO	CARB	TRANS
OA	4	153	90	8.5:1	1 BC	MAN
OC	4	153	90	8.5:1	1 BC	MAN
OH	4	153	90	8.5:1	1 BC	PG
OK	6	194	120	8.5:1	1 BC	MAN
OM	6	194	120	8.5:1	1 BC	MAN
ZY	6	194	120	8.5:1	1 BC	MAN
OR	6	194	120	8.5:1	1 BC	PG
ZX	6	194	120	8.5:1	1 BC	PG
PV	6	250	155	8.5:1	1 BC	MAN
PC	6	250	155	8.5:1	1 BC	MAN
PX	6	250	155	8.5:1	1 BC	PG
PI	6	250	155	8.5:1	1 BC	PG
PD	8	283	195	9.25:1	2 BC	MAN
PF	8	283	195	9.25:1	2 BC	MAN
PM	8	283	195	9.25:1	2 BC	4-SP
PE	8	283	195	9.25:1	2 BC	MAN
PQ	8	283	195	9.25:1	2 BC	4-SP
PL	8	283	195	9.25:1	2 BC	4-SP
PN	8	283	195	9.25:1	2 BC	PG
PP	8	283	195	9.25:1	2 BC	PG
PU	8	283	195	9.25:1	2 BC	PG
ZA	8	327	275	10.0:1	4 BC	MAN
ZB	8	327	275	10.0:1	4 BC	MAN
ZD	8	327	275	10.0:1	4 BC	PG
ZE	8	327	275	10.0:1	4 BC	MAN
ZK	8	327	275	10.0:1	4 BC	PG
ZM	8	327	275	10.0:1	4 BC	PG
ZG	8	327	350	11.0:1	4 BC	MAN
ZI	8	327	350	11.0:1	4 BC	MAN
ZJ	8	327	350	11.0:1	4 BC	MAN

CHEVELLE

ENGINE CODE	NO. CYL.	CID	HORSE-POWER	COMP. RATIO	CARB	TRANS
CA	6	230	140	8.5:1	1 BC	MAN
BC	6	230	140	8.5:1	1 BC	MAN
BB	6	230	140	8.5:1	1 BC	MAN
CB	6	230	140	8.5:1	1 BC	MAN
BN	6	230	140	8.5:1	1 BC	MAN
BO	6	230	140	8.5:1	1 BC	MAN
CC	6	230	140	8.5:1	1 BC	PG
CD	6	230	140	8.5:1	1 BC	PG
BL	6	230	140	8.5:1	1 BC	PG
BM	6	230	140	8.5:1	1 BC	PG
CM	6	250	155	8.5:1	1 BC	MAN
CN	6	250	155	8.5:1	1 BC	MAN
CO	6	250	155	8.5:1	1 BC	MAN
CP	6	250	155	8.5:1	1 BC	MAN
CQ	6	250	155	8.5:1	1 BC	PG
CR	6	250	155	8.5:1	1 BC	PG
CS	6	250	155	8.5:1	1 BC	PG
CT	6	250	155	8.5:1	1 BC	PG
DA	8	283	195	9.25:1	2 BC	MAN
DB	8	283	195	9.25:1	2 BC	4-SP
DI	8	283	195	9.25:1	2 BC	MAN
DJ	8	283	195	9.25:1	2 BC	PG
DK	8	283	195	9.25:1	2 BC	4-SP
DN	8	283	195	9.25:1	2 BC	MAN
DE	8	283	195	9.25:1	2 BC	AUTO
EA	8	327	275	10.0:1	4 BC	MAN
EP	8	327	325	11.0:1	4 BC	MAN
EB	8	327	275	10.0:1	4 BC	MAN
ER	8	327	325	11.0:1	4 BC	MAN
ES	8	327	325	11.0:1	4 BC	MAN
EQ	8	327	275	10.0:1	4 BC	MAN
EE	8	327	275	10.0:1	4 BC	PG
EC	8	327	275	10.0:1	4 BC	PG
ED	8	396	325	10.25:1	4 BC	PG/MAN
EF	8	396	325	10.25:1	4 BC	MAN

CHEVELLE

ENGINE CODE	NO. CYL.	CID	HORSE-POWER	COMP. RATIO	CARB	TRANS
EG	8	396	375	11.0:1	4 BC	MAN
EH	8	396	325	10.25:1	4 BC	MAN
EK	8	396	350	10.25:1	4 BC	PG
EL	8	396	350	10.25:1	4 BC	PG
EM	8	396	325	10.25:1	4 BC	PG
EN	8	396	350	10.25:1	4 BC	PG
ET	8	396	325	10.25:1	4 BC	TH
EU	8	396	350	10.25:1	4 BC	TH
EV	8	396	325	10.25:1	4 BC	TH
EW	8	396	350	10.25:1	4 BC	TH
EX	8	396	375	11.0:1	4 BC	MAN

CAMARO

ENGINE CODE	NO. CYL.	CID	HORSE-POWER	COMP. RATIO	CARB	TRANS
LA	6	230	140	8.5:1	1 BC	MAN
LB	6	230	140	8.5:1	1 BC	MAN
LC	6	230	140	8.5:1	1 BC	MAN
LD	6	230	140	8.5:1	1 BC	MAN
LE	6	230	140	8.5:1	1 BC	PG
LF	6	230	140	8.5:1	1 BC	PG
LG	6	230	140	8.5:1	1 BC	PG
LH	6	230	140	8.5:1	1 BC	PG
LN	6	250	155	8.5:1	1 BC	MAN
LO	6	250	155	8.5:1	1 BC	MAN
LP	6	250	155	8.5:1	1 BC	MAN
LQ	6	250	155	8.5:1	1 BC	MAN
FM	6	250	155	8.5:1	1 BC	PG
FR	6	250	155	8.5:1	1 BC	PG
GP	6	250	155	8.5:1	1 BC	PG
GQ	6	250	155	8.5:1	1 BC	PG
LT	6	250	155	8.5:1	1 BC	MAN
LI	6	250	155	8.5:1	1 BC	PG
LR	6	250	155	8.5:1	1 BC	MAN
LS	6	250	155	8.5:1	1 BC	MAN
MD	8	283	195	9.25:1	2 BC	4-SP
MJ	8	283	195	9.25:1	2 BD	PG
MO	8	302	290	11.0:1	4 BC	4-SP
MP	8	302	290	11.0:1	4 BC	4-SP
MA	8	327	210	8.75:1	2 BC	MAN
MB	8	327	210	8.75:1	2 BC	MAN
ME	8	327	210	8.75:1	2 BC	PG
MF	8	327	210	8.75:1	2 BC	PG
MK	8	327	275	10.0:1	4 BC	MAN
ML	8	327	275	10.0:1	4 BC	MAN
MM	8	327	275	10.0:1	4 BC	PG
MN	8	327	275	10.0:1	4 BC	PG
MS	8	350	295	10.25:1	4 BC	MAN
MT	8	350	295	10.25:1	4 BC	MAN
MU	8	350	295	10.25:1	4 BC	PG
MV	8	350	295	10.25:1	4 BC	PG
EI	8	396	350	10.25:1	4 BC	MAN
EQ	8	396	350	10.25:1	4 BC	TH

CAMARO

ENGINE CODE	NO. CYL.	CID	HORSE-POWER	COMP. RATIO	CARB	TRANS
EY	8	396	350	10.25:1	4 BC	MAN
MQ	8	396	375	10.25:1	4 BC	MAN
MR	8	396	375	10.25:1	4 BC	MAN
MW	8	396	325	10.25:1	4 BC	MAN/TH
MX	8	396	325	10.25:1	4 BC	MAN
MY	8	396	325	10.25:1	4 BC	TH
MZ	8	396	325	10.25:1	4 BC	TH

CHEVROLET

ENGINE CODE	NO. CYL.	CID	HORSE-POWER	COMP. RATIO	CARB	TRANS
FA	6	250	155	8.5:1	1 BC	MAN
FE	6	250	155	8.5:1	1 BC	MAN
FF	6	250	155	8.5:1	1 BC	MAN
FV	6	250	155	8.5:1	1 BC	MAN
FK	6	250	155	8.5:1	1 BC	MAN
FL	6	250	155	8.5:1	1 BC	MAN
FM	6	250	155	8.5:1	1 BC	PG
FP	6	250	155	8.5:1	1 BC	PG
FR	6	250	155	8.5:1	1 BC	PG
FY	6	250	155	8.5:1	1 BC	MAN
FZ	6	250	155	8.5:1	1 BC	MAN
GP	6	250	155	8.5:1	1 BC	PG
GQ	6	250	155	8.5:1	1 BC	PG
GR	6	250	155	8.5:1	1 BC	PG
GA	8	283	195	9.25:1	2 BC	MAN
GC	8	283	195	9.25:1	2 BC	4-SP
GK	8	283	195	9.25:1	2 BC	MAN
GS	8	283	195	9.25:1	2 BC	4-SP
GU	8	283	195	9.25:1	2 BC	MAN
GF	8	283	195	9.25:1	2 BC	PG
GO	8	283	195	9.25:1	2 BC	PG
GT	8	283	195	9.25:1	2 BC	PG
HA	8	327	275	10.5:1	4 BC	MAN
HB	8	327	275	10.5:1	4 BC	MAN
HC	8	327	275	10.5:1	4 BC	PG
HF	8	327	275	10.5:1	4 BC	PG
KE	8	327	275	10.5:1	4 BC	2-SP
KL	8	327	275	10.5:1	4 BC	TH
KM	8	327	275	10.5:1	4 BC	TH
IA	8	396	325	10.25:1	4 BC	MAN
IB	8	396	325	10.25:1	4 BC	MAN
IG	8	396	325	10.25:1	4 BC	PG
IV	8	396	325	10.25:1	4 BC	TH
IC	8	396	325	10.25:1	4 BC	PG
IN	8	396	325	10.25:1	4 BC	TH
IE	8	427	385	10.25:1	4 BC	MAN
IH	8	427	385	10.25:1	4 BC	MAN
ID	8	427	425	11.0:1	4 BC	MAN
IJ	8	427	385	10.25:1	4 BC	TH
IS	8	427	385	10.25:1	4 BC	TH
II	8	427	385	10.25:1	4 BC	MAN
IX	8	427	385	10.25:1	4 BC	MAN
IK	8	427	425	11.0:1	4 BC	MAN
IF	8	427	385	10.25:1	4 BC	TH
IO	8	427	385	10.25:1	4 BC	TH

1968 CAMARO

1968 CHEVROLET CAPRICE

1968 CHEVROLET IMPALA

1968 CHEVROLET IMPALA

1968 CHEVY II

1968 CHEVY II

1968 CORVAIR

1968 CORVAIR

1968 CHEVELLE

1968 CORVETTE

VEHICLE IDENTIFICATION NUMBER

CHEVROLET
154118T101555

Commonly referred to as the VIN NUMBER, this series of numbers and letters is stamped on a plate attached to the left front door hinge pillar.

CHEVROLET, CHEVELLE, CHEVY II, CAMARO and CORVAIR VINS are stamped on a plate on top of the instrument panel visible through the windshield near the left door.

CORVETTE VIN is stamped on a plate on the inner vertical surface of the left windshield pillar visible through the windshield.

FIRST DIGIT: Identifies the Chevrolet division

NEXT FOUR DIGITS: Identify the model number

MODEL	CODE
Biscayne/Bel-Air	5000
Impala/Caprice	6000
Chevelle, Malibu	3000
Chevy II, Nova	1000
Camaro	2000
Corvair	0000
Corvette	9000

SIXTH DIGIT: Identifies the model year (1968)

SEVENTH DIGIT: Identifies the assembly plant

ASSEMBLY PLANT	CODE
Atlanta, GA	A
Baltimore, MD	B
Southgate, CA	C
Doraville, GA	D
Flint, MI	F
Framingham, MA	G
Janesville, WI	J
Kansas City, MO	K
Lordstown, OH	U
Los Angeles, CA	L
Norwood, OH	N
Arlington, TX GMAD	R
St. Louis, MO	S
Tarrytown, NY	T
Willow Run, MI	W
Wilmington, DE	Y
Fremont, CA	Z
Oshawa, Ont., CAN	1
St. Therese, Que., CAN	2
Pontiac, MI	P

LAST SIX DIGITS: Represent the basic production numbers

BODY NUMBER PLATE

Complete identification of each body is provided by a plate riveted to the top of the cowl. Exception: Corvair body tag is located on the left rear wheel housing inside the engine compartment.

CHEVROLET DIVISION
GENERAL MOTORS CORP.

ST 68 15411
FL1 101555 BODY
TR 802
AA PAINT

BODY BY FISHER

EXAMPLE:

68	Model Year (1968)
15411	Body Series (Biscayne)
FL1	Assembly Plant (Flint, MI)
101555	Production Sequence
802	Trim
A	Lower Body Color
A	Upper Body Color

THE STYLE NUMBER is a combination of the year, series and body style.

CORVAIR 500	CODE
2-Dr. Sport Coupe	10137

CORVAIR MONZA	CODE
2-Dr. Sport Coupe	10537
2-Dr. Convertible	10567

CHEVY II	4L	6 CYL	8 CYL
2-Dr. Sport Coupe	11127	11327	*11427
4-Dr. Sedan	11169	11369	11469

*Option Super Sport

CAMARO	6 CYL	8 CYL
2-Dr. Sport Coupe	12337	12437
2-Dr. Convertible	12367	12467

*Option Z-28
*Option Rally Sport
*Option Super Sport

CHEVELLE 300	6 CYL	8 CYL
2-Dr. Pillar Coupe	13127	13227

NOMAD	6 CYL	8 CYL
4-Dr. Sta. Wagon, 2-Seat	13135	13235

CHEVELLE 300 (DLX)	6 CYL	8 CYL
2-Dr. Pillar Coupe	13327	13427
4-Dr. Sedan	13369	13469
2-Dr. Sport Coupe	13337	13437

CUSTOM NOMAD	6 CYL	8 CYL
4-Dr. Sta. Wagon, 2-Seat	13335	13435
4-Dr. Sta. Wagon, 3-Seat	-	13445

MALIBU	6 CYL	8 CYL
4-Dr. Sedan	13569	13669
4-Dr. Sport Sedan	13539	*13639
2-Dr. Sport Coupe	13537	13637
2-Dr. Convertible	13567	13667
4-Dr. Sta. Wagon, 2-Seat	13535	13635
4-Dr. Sta. Wagon, 3-Seat	-	13645

*Option Concours

SS 396	6 CYL	8 CYL
2-Dr. Sport Coupe	-	13837
2-Dr. Convertible	-	13867
4-Dr. Sta. Wagon, 3-Seat	-	13845

CONCOURS	6 CYL	8 CYL
4-Dr. Sta. Wagon, 2-Seat	13735	13835

CORVETTE	CODE
2-Dr. Sport Coupe	19437
2-Dr. Convertible	19467

BISCAYNE	6 CYL	8 CYL
2-Dr. Sedan	15311	15411
4-Dr. Sedan	15369	15469
4-Dr. Sta. Wagon, 2-Seat	15335	15435

BEL-AIR	6 CYL	8 CYL
2-Dr. Sedan	15511	15611
4-Dr. Sedan	15569	15669
4-Dr. Sta. Wagon, 2-Seat	15535	15635
4-Dr. Sta. Wagon, 3-Seat	15545	15645

IMPALA	6 CYL	8 CYL
2-Dr. Sport Coupe	16387	*16487
2-Dr. Convertible	-	*16467
4-Dr. Sedan	16369	16469
4-Dr. Sport Sedan	16339	16439
4-Dr. Sta. Wagon, 2-Seat	-	16435
4-Dr. Sta. Wagon, 3-Seat	-	16445

IMPALA CUSTOM	6 CYL	8 CYL
2-Dr. Sport Coupe	-	*16447

*Option Super Sport
*Option SS 427

CAPRICE	6 CYL	8 CYL
2-Dr. Sport Coupe	-	16647
4-Dr. Sport Sedan	-	16639
4-Dr. Custom Wagon, 2-Seat		16635
4-Dr. Custom Wagon, 3-Seat		16645

THE BODY NUMBER is the production serial number of the body. The prefix letter denotes the plant in which the body was built.

ASSEMBLY PLANT	CODE
Atlanta, GA	ATL
Baltimore, MD	BAL
Southgate, CA	BC
Doraville, GA	BA
Flint, MI	FL1
Framingham, MA	FM
Janesville, WI	JAN
Kansas City, MO	BK
Kansas City, KS	KAN
Los Angeles, CA	LOS
Norwood, OH	NOR
Arlington, TX GMAD	BT
St. Louis, MO	STL
Tarrytown, NY	TAR
Lordstown, OH	LOR
Willow Run, MI	WRN
Wilmington, DE	BW
Fremont, CA	BF
Oshawa, Ont., CAN	OS
St. Therese, Que., CAN	ST
Pontiac, MI	PON

THE TRIM NUMBER furnishes the key to trim color and material for each model series.

CORVAIR TRIM

COLOR	CLOTH	VINYL	LEATHER	CODE
Black		•		703
Blue		•		706
Gold		•		709

CORVAIR MONZA TRIM

COLOR	CLOTH	VINYL	LEATHER	CODE
Black		•		704
Blue		•		707
Gold		•		710

CHEVY II TRIM

COLOR	CLOTH	VINYL	LEATHER	CODE
Black		•		731,733,735
Black	•	•		734
Blue	•	•		737
Blue		•		739,740
Gold	•	•		741,742
Gold		•		745

CAMARO TRIM

COLOR	CLOTH	VINYL	LEATHER	CODE
Black		•		713,715
Black		•		704,707
Blue		•		718,720
Blue		•		717,719
Gold		•		723,721,722
Red		•		724,725
Turquoise		•		727,726
Parchment		•		730

CHEVELLE 300/DELUXE/NOMAD TRIM

COLOR	CLOTH	VINYL	LEATHER	CODE
Gold	•	•		788
Gold		•		752
Saddle		•		758,781,799
Blue	•	•		770
Blue		•		759,771,777
Black		•		760,761,763
Black	•	•		762

MALIBU TRIM

COLOR	CLOTH	VINYL	LEATHER	CODE
Green	•	•		753,791
Gold		•		754
Teal		•		755,757
Black	•	•		764,768
Black		•		765,766
Blue	•	•		772,776
Blue		•		773
Gold	•	•		779,780
Gold		•		756
Saddle		•		782
Turquoise		•		786
Red		•		795
Parchment		•		794

SS 396/CONCOURS TRIM

COLOR	CLOTH	VINYL	LEATHER	CODE
Gold		•		754,756
Teal		•		755,757
Black		•		765,766
Parchment		•		794

BISCAYNE TRIM

COLOR	CLOTH	VINYL	LEATHER	CODE
Black		•		802
Blue	•	•		816
Blue		•		817
Gold	•	•		831
Saddle		•		837

BEL-AIR TRIM

COLOR	CLOTH	VINYL	LEATHER	CODE
Black	•	•		803
Black		•		804,811
Blue	•	•		818
Blue		•		819
Gold	•	•		832
Saddle		•		838
Turquoise	•	•		843
Turquoise		•		844

IMPALA TRIM

COLOR	CLOTH	VINYL	LEATHER	CODE
Black	•	•		805
Black		•		806,813,812
Blue	•	•		820
Blue		•		821
Gold	•	•		833
Gold		•		830,836
Saddle		•		839,841
Turquoise		•		842,845
Green	•	•		853
Parchment		•		858,859
Teal		•		861,864,862
Red		•		866,868

CAPRICE TRIM

COLOR	CLOTH	VINYL	LEATHER	CODE
Black	•	•		807,808
Black		•		806,814,809
Blue	•	•		820
Blue 815,821,822,823,824		•		
Gold	•	•		834,835
Gold		•		840
Saddle		•		839
Turquoise		•		845
Green	•	•		852,856
Green		•		857

CORVETTE TRIM

COLOR	CLOTH	VINYL	LEATHER	CODE
Black			•	402
Red		•		407
Red			•	408
Blue		•		414,411
Blue			•	415
Orange		•		425
Orange			•	426
Tobacco		•		435
Tobacco			•	436
Gunmetal		•		442

THE PAINT CODE furnishes the key to the exterior color. A two-letter code indicates the bottom and top colors respectively.

COLOR	CODE
Tuxedo Black	A
Tuxedo Black	*900
Ermine White	C
Grotto Blue	D
Fathom Blue	E
Island Teal	F
Ash Gold	G
Grecian Green	H
Tripoli Turquoise	K
Teal Blue	L
Cordovan Maroon	N
Seafrost Green	P
Matador Red	R
Palomino Ivory	T
Sequoia Green	V
Butternut Yellow	Y
Polar White	*972
Rally Red	*974
LeMans Blue	*976
International Blue	*978
British Green	*983
Safari Yellow	*984
Silverstone Silver	*986
Cordovan Maroon	*988
Corvette Bronze	*992

*Corvette only

1968 CHEVROLET

ENGINE NUMBER

All Chevrolet engines are stamped with a plant code, production date, and engine type code.

Note:

1. Corvette engines have the last six digits of the VIN stamped on the block next to the engine number.

2. Corvair engines are stamped on the top of the block forward of the generator.

3. 8 cylinder engines are stamped on the right front of the engine block.

4. 6 cylinder engines are stamped on the right side of the block at the rear of the distributor.

EXAMPLE:

T	01	01	A
PLANT	MONTH	DAY	CODE

ENGINE PLANTS	CODE
Tonawanda	T
Flint	F

CORVAIR

ENGINE CODE	NO. CYL.	CID	HORSE-POWER	COMP. RATIO	CARB	TRANS
RS	6	164	95	8.25:1	2-1 BC	MAN
RU	6	164	110	9.25:1	2-1 BC	MAN
RV	6	164	95	8.25:1	2-1 BC	PG
RW	6	164	110	9.25:1	2-1 BC	PG
RY	6	164	140	9.25:1	4-1 BC	MAN
RZ	6	164	140	9.25:1	4-1 BC	PG
RE	6	164	95	8.25:1	2-1 BC	MAN
RF	6	164	110	9.25:1	2-1 BC	MAN
RJ	6	164	95	8.25:1	2-1 BC	PG
RK	6	164	110	9.25:1	2-1 BC	PG

CORVETTE

ENGINE CODE	NO. CYL.	CID	HORSE-POWER	COMP. RATIO	CARB	TRANS
HE	8	327	300	10.0:1	4 BC	MAN
HO	8	327	300	10.0:1	4 BC	TH
HP	8	327	300	10.0:1	4 BC	MAN
HT	8	327	350	11.0:1	4 BC	MAN
IL	8	427	390	10.25:1	4 BC	MAN
IM	8	427	400	10.25:1	3-2 BC	MAN
IO	8	427	400	10.25:1	3-2 BC	TH
IQ	8	427	390	10.25:1	4 BC	TH
IR	8	427	435	11.0:1	3-2 BC	MAN
IT	8	427	430	12.5:1	4 BC	MAN
IU	8	427	435	11.0:1	3-2 BC	MAN

CHEVY II

ENGINE CODE	NO. CYL.	CID	HORSE-POWER	COMP. RATIO	CARB	TRANS
OA	4	153	90	8.5:1	1 BC	MAN
OC	4	153	90	8.5:1	1 BC	MAN
OH	4	153	90	8.5:1	1 BC	PG
BA	6	230	140	8.5:1	1 BC	MAN
BB	6	230	140	8.5:1	1 BC	MAN
BC	6	230	140	8.5:1	1 BC	MAN
BD	6	230	140	8.5:1	1 BC	MAN
BF	6	230	140	8.5:1	1 BC	PG
BH	6	230	140	8.5:1	1 BC	PG
CM	6	250	155	8.5:1	1 BC	MAN
CN	6	250	155	8.5:1	1 BC	MAN
CQ	6	250	155	8.5:1	1 BC	PG
CR	6	250	155	8.5:1	1 BC	PG
DA	8	307	200	9.0:1	2 BC	MAN
DB	8	307	200	9.0:1	2 BC	4-SP
DE	8	307	200	9.0:1	2 BC	PG
MB	8	307	200	9.0:1	2 BC	MAN
MC	8	307	200	9.0:1	2 BC	4-SP
MD	8	307	200	9.0:1	2 BC	PG
EA	8	327	275	10.0:1	4 BC	MAN
MK	8	327	275	10.0:1	4 BC	MAN
ML	8	327	325	11.0:1	4 BC	MAN
EP	8	327	325	11.0:1	4 BC	MAN
EE	8	327	275	10.0:1	4 BC	PG
MM	8	327	275	10.0:1	4 BC	PG
EC	8	327	275	10.0:1	4 BC	PG
MS	8	350	295	10.25:1	4 BC	MAN
MU	8	350	295	10.25:1	4 BC	PG
MX	8	396	350	10.25:1	4 BC	MAN
MQ	8	396	375	11.0:1	4 BC	MAN
MR	8	396	375	11.0:1	4 BC	MAN

CHEVELLE

ENGINE CODE	NO. CYL.	CID	HORSE-POWER	COMP. RATIO	CARB	TRANS
BA	6	230	140	8.5:1	1 BC	MAN
BB	6	230	140	8.5:1	1 BC	MAN
BC	6	230	140	8.5:1	1 BC	MAN
BD	6	230	140	8.5:1	1 BC	MAN
BF	6	230	140	8.5:1	1 BC	PG
BH	6	230	140	8.5:1	1 BC	PG
CM	6	250	155	8.5:1	1 BC	MAN
CN	6	250	155	8.5:1	1 BC	MAN
CQ	6	250	155	8.5:1	1 BC	PG
CR	6	250	155	8.5:1	1 BC	PG
DA	8	307	200	9.0:1	2 BC	MAN
DB	8	307	200	9.0:1	2 BC	4-SP
DE	8	307	200	9.0:1	2 BC	PG
DF	8	307	200	9.0:1	2 BC	PG
DN	8	307	200	9.0:1	2 BC	MAN
EA	8	327	250	8.75:1	4 BC	MAN
EC	8	327	250	8.75:1	4 BC	PG
EE	8	327	250	8.75:1	4 BC	PG

1968 CHEVROLET

CHEVELLE

ENGINE CODE	NO. CYL.	CID	HORSE-POWER	COMP. RATIO	CARB	TRANS
EO	8	327	250	8.75:1	4 BC	MAN
EP	8	327	325	11.0:1	4 BC	MAN
ES	8	327	325	11.0:1	4 BC	MAN
EH	8	327	275	10.0:1	4 BC	MAN
EI	8	327	275	10.0:1	4 BC	PG
EJ	8	327	275	10.0:1	4 BC	MAN
EO	8	396	325	10.25:1	4 BC	MAN
EF	8	396	350	10.25:1	4 BC	MAN
EG	8	396	375	11.0:1	4 BC	MAN
EK	8	396	325	10.25:1	4 BC	PG
EL	8	396	350	10.25:1	4 BC	PG
ET	8	396	325	10.25:1	4 BC	TH
EU	8	396	350	10.25:1	4 BC	TH

CAMARO

ENGINE CODE	NO. CYL.	CID	HORSE-POWER	COMP. RATIO	CARB	TRANS
BA	6	230	140	8.5:1	1 BC	MAN
BB	6	230	140	8.5:1	1 BC	MAN
BC	6	230	140	8.5:1	1 BC	MAN
BD	6	230	140	8.5:1	1 BC	MAN
BF	6	230	140	8.5:1	1 BC	PG
BH	6	230	140	8.5:1	1 BC	PG
CM	6	250	155	8.5:1	1 BC	MAN
CN	6	250	155	8.5:1	1 BC	MAN
CQ	6	250	155	8.5:1	1 BC	PG
CR	6	250	155	8.5:1	1 BC	PG
MO	8	302	290	11.0:1	4 BC*	MAN
MA	8	327	210	8.75:1	2 BC	MAN
ME	8	327	210	8.75:1	2 BC	PG
EE	8	327	275	10.0:1	4 BC	PG
EA	8	327	275	10.0:1	4 BC	MAN
EC	8	327	275	10.0:1	4 BC	PG
MS	8	350	295	10.25:1	4 BC	MAN
MU	8	350	295	10.25:1	4 BC	PG
MQ	8	396	375	11.0:1	4 BC	MAN
MR	8	396	350	10.25:1	4 BC	TH
MT	8	396	375	11.0:1	4 BC	MAN
MW	8	396	375	10.25:1	4 BC	MAN/TH
MX	8	396	350	10.25:1	4 BC	MAN
MY	8	396	325	10.25:1	4 BC	TH

* 2-4 BC option

CHEVROLET

ENGINE CODE	NO. CYL.	CID	HORSE-POWER	COMP. RATIO	CARB	TRANS
CA	6	250	155	8.5:1	1 BC	MAN
CB	6	250	155	8.5:1	1 BC	MAN
CC	6	250	155	8.5:1	1 BC	MAN
CJ	6	250	155	8.5:1	1 BC	MAN
CK	6	250	155	8.5:1	1 BC	MAN
CL	6	250	155	8.5:1	1 BC	PG
CM	6	250	155	8.5:1	1 BC	MAN
CN	6	250	155	8.5:1	1 BC	MAN
CQ	6	250	155	8.5:1	1 BC	PG
CR	6	250	155	8.5:1	1 BC	PG
CS	6	250	155	8.5:1	1 BC	MAN
CT	6	250	155	8.5:1	1 BC	PG
DH	8	307	200	9.0:1	2 BC	PG
DK	8	307	200	9.0:1	2 BC	TH
DO	8	307	200	9.0:1	2 BC	MAN
DP	8	307	200	9.0:1	2 BC	4-SP
DS	8	307	200	9.0:1	2 BC	TH
DQ	8	307	200	9.0:1	2 BC	MAN
DR	8	307	200	9.0:1	2 BC	PG
HA	8	327	250	8.75:1	4 BC	MAN
HB	8	327	250	8.75:1	4 BC	MAN
HC	8	327	250	8.75:1	4 BC	PG
HF	8	327	250	8.75:1	4 BC	TH
HG	8	327	250	8.75:1	4 BC	PG
HH	8	327	250	8.75:1	4 BC	PG
HI	8	327	275	10.0:1	4 BC	MAN
HJ	8	327	275	10.0:1	4 BC	PG
HK	8	327	250	8.75:1	4 BC	PG
HL	8	327	250	8.75:1	4 BC	MAN
HM	8	327	250	8.75:1	4 BC	TH
HN	8	327	250	8.75:1	4 BC	PG
IA	8	396	325	10.25:1	4 BC	MAN
IG	8	396	325	10.25:1	4 BC	PG
IV	8	396	325	10.25:1	4 BC	TH
IK	8	396	325	10.25:1	4 BC	MAN
IN	8	396	325	10.25:1	4 BC	PG
IF	8	396	325	10.25:1	4 BC	MAN
IB	8	427	385	10.25:1	4 BC	TH
IE	8	427	385	10.25:1	4 BC	MAN
IH	8	427	385	10.25:1	4 BC	MAN
ID	8	427	425	11.0:1	4 BC	MAN
IJ	8	427	385	10.25:1	4 BC	TH
IS	8	427	385	10.25:1	4 BC	TH
IC	8	427	385	10.25:1	4 BC	MAN

1969 CAMARO

1969 CAMARO

1969 CHEVROLET CAPRICE

1969 CHEVROLET CHEVELLE

1969 CHEVROLET IMPALA

1969 CHEVROLET IMPALA

1969 CHEVY NOVA

1969 CHEVY NOVA

1969 CORVAIR

1969 CORVAIR

1969 CORVETTE STINGRAY

1969 CORVETTE STINGRAY

VEHICLE IDENTIFICATION NUMBER

CHEVROLET
154119T101555

Commonly referred to as the VIN NUMBER, this series of numbers and letters is stamped on a plate attached to the left front door hinge pillar.

CHEVROLET, CHEVELLE, CHEVY II, CAMARO and CORVAIR VINS are stamped on a plate on top of the instrument panel visible through the windshield near the left door.

CORVETTE VIN is stamped on a plate on the inner vertical surface of the left windshield pillar visible through the windshield.

FIRST DIGIT: Identifies the Chevrolet division

NEXT FOUR DIGITS: Identify the model number

MODEL	CODE
Corvair	0000
Nova	1000
Camaro	2000
Chevelle	3000
Biscayne, Bel-Air	5000
Impala/Caprice	6000
Corvette	9000

SIXTH DIGIT: Identifies the model year (1969)

SEVENTH DIGIT: Identifies the assembly plant

ASSEMBLY PLANT	CODE
Atlanta, GA	A
Baltimore, MD	B
Southgate, CA	C
Doraville, GA	D
Flint, MI	F
Framingham, MA GMAD	G
Janesville, WI	J
Kansas City, MO	K
Lordstown, OH	U
Los Angeles, CA	L
Norwood, OH	N
Arlington, TX GMAD	R
St. Louis, MO	S
Tarrytown, NY	T
Willow Run, MI	W
Wilmington, DE	Y
Fremont, CA	Z
St. Therese, Que., CAN	2

LAST SIX DIGITS: Represent the basic production numbers

BODY NUMBER PLATE

Complete identification of each body is provided by a plate riveted to the top of the cowl. Exception: Corvair body tag is located on the left rear wheel housing inside the engine compartment.

CHEVROLET DIVISION
GENERAL MOTORS CORP.

ST 69 15411
FL1 101555 BODY
TR 802
AA PAINT

BODY BY FISHER

EXAMPLE:

69	Model Year (1969)
15411	Body Series (Biscayne)
FL1	Assembly Plant (Flint, MI)
101555	Production Sequence
802	Trim
A	Lower Body Color
A	Upper Body Color

THE STYLE NUMBER is a combination of the year, series and body style.

CORVAIR 500	CODE
2-Dr. Sport Coupe	10137

CORVAIR MONZA	CODE
2-Dr. Sport Coupe	10537
2-Dr. Convertible	10567

NOVA	4 CYL	6 CYL	8 CYL
2-Dr. Sport Coupe	11127	11327	*11427
4-Dr. Sedan	11169	11369	11469

* Option Super Sport

CAMARO	6 CYL	8 CYL
2-Dr. Sport Coupe	12337	12437
2-Dr. Convertible	12367	12467

* Option Z-28, Rally Sport, Super Sport, Pace Car

CHEVELLE NOMAD	6 CYL	8 CYL
4-Dr. Sta. Wagon, 2-Seat	13135	13235
4-Dr. Sta. Wagon, Dual Tailgate	13136	13236

CHEVELLE 300 (DLX)	6 CYL	8 CYL
4-Dr. Sedan	13369	13469
2-Dr. Pillar Coupe	13327	*13427
2-Dr. Sport Coupe	13337	*13437
4-Dr. Sta. Wagon, 2-Seat (Greenbrier)	13335	13435
4-Dr. Sta. Wagon, 2-Seat Dual Tailgate (Greenbrier)	13336	13436
4-Dr. Sta. Wagon, 3-Seat (Greenbrier)	-	13446

1969 CHEVROLET

MALIBU	6 CYL	8 CYL
4-Dr. Sedan	13569	13669
4-Dr. Sport Sedan	+13539	+13639
2-Dr. Sport Coupe	13537	*13637
2-Dr. Convertible	13567	*13667
4-Dr. Sta. Wagon, 2-Seat (Concours)	13536	13636
4-Dr. Sta. Wagon, 3-Seat (Concours)	-	13646

* Option SS 396
\+ Option Concours

CONCOURS	6 CYL	8 CYL
4-Dr. Sta. Wagon, 2-Seat	-	13836

ESTATE WAGON	6 CYL	8 CYL
4-Dr. Sta. Wagon, 3-Seat	-	13846

CORVETTE	CODE
2-Dr. Sport Coupe	19437
2-Dr. Convertible	19467

BISCAYNE	6 CYL	8 CYL
2-Dr. Sedan	15311	15411
4-Dr. Sedan	15369	15469
4 Dr. Sta. Wagon, 2-Seat (Brookwood)	15336	15436

BEL-AIR	6 CYL	8 CYL
2-Dr. Sedan	15511	15611
4-Dr. Sedan	15569	15669
4-Dr. Sta. Wagon, 2-Seat (Townsman)	15536	15639
4-Dr. Sta. Wagon, 3-Seat (Townsman)	15546	15646

IMPALA	6 CYL	8 CYL
4-Dr. Sedan	16369	16469
4-Dr. Sport Sedan	16339	16439
2-Dr. Sport Coupe	16337	*16437
2-Dr. Convertible	-	*16467
4-Dr. Sta. Wagon, 2-Seat (Kingswood)	-	16436
4-Dr. Sta. Wagon, 3-Seat (Kingswood)	-	16446

IMPALA CUSTOM	6 CYL	8 CYL
2-Dr. Sport Coupe	-	*16447

* Option SS 427

CAPRICE	6 CYL	8 CYL
4-Dr. Sport Sedan	-	16639
2-Dr. Sport Coupe	-	16647
4-Dr. Sta. Wagon, 2-Seat (Estate Wagon)	-	16636
4-Dr. Sta. Wagon, 3-Seat (Estate Wagon)	-	16646

THE BODY NUMBER is the production serial number of the body. The prefix letter denotes the plant in which the body was built.

ASSEMBLY PLANT	CODE
Atlanta, GA	ATL
Baltimore, MD	BAL
Southgate, CA	BC
Doraville, GA	BA
Flint, MI	FL1
Framingham, MA	FM
Janesville, WI	JAN
Kansas City, MO	BK
Kansas City, KS	KAN
Los Angeles, CA	LOS
Norwood, OH	NOR
Arlington, TX GMAD	BT
St. Louis, MO	STL
Tarrytown, NY	TAR
Lordstown, OH	LOR
Willow Run, MI	WRN
Wilmington, DE	BW
Fremont, CA	BF
St. Therese, Que., CAN	ST

THE TRIM NUMBER furnishes the key to trim color and material for each model series.

CORVAIR TRIM

COLOR	CLOTH	VINYL	LEATHER	CODE
Black	•			700
Blue	•			703
Green	•			708

CORVAIR MONZA TRIM

COLOR	CLOTH	VINYL	LEATHER	CODE
Black	•			701
Blue	•			704
Green	•			707

NOVA TRIM

COLOR	CLOTH	VINYL	LEATHER	CODE
Black	•			731,732,733
Blue	•			735,736,737
Green	•			742,743
Green	•			744,745
Red	•			746

CAMARO TRIM

COLOR	CLOTH	VINYL	LEATHER	CODE
Black	•			711,712,713
Blue	•			715,716
Red	•			718,719
Green	•			721,722
Green	•			723,725
Ivory	•			727
Black/Ivory	•			729

1969 CHEVROLET

CHEVELLE NOMAD TRIM

COLOR	CLOTH	VINYL	LEATHER	CODE
Black	•			750
Blue	•			759
Saddle	•			772

CHEVELLE 300 DELUXE TRIM

COLOR	CLOTH	VINYL	LEATHER	CODE
Black	•			751,752
Blue	•			760,761
Saddle	•			773
Green	•			786

MALIBU TRIM

COLOR	CLOTH	VINYL	LEATHER	CODE
Black	•			753,754,755,756
Blue	•			762,763,765
Saddle	•			770
Turquoise	•			773,779
Green	•			782,783,784
Green	•			786,794,795
Green	•			785,796
Red	•			787,788
Parchment	•			790,791

BISCAYNE TRIM

COLOR	CLOTH	VINYL	LEATHER	CODE
Black	•			802
Blue	•			815,816
Saddle	•			831
Green	•			849

BEL-AIR TRIM

COLOR	CLOTH	VINYL	LEATHER	CODE
Black	•			803,804
Blue	•			818,819
Saddle	•			838
Green	•			848,850,851

IMPALA/CUSTOM TRIM

COLOR	CLOTH	VINYL	LEATHER	CODE
Black	•			805,806,812
Blue	•			820,821
Saddle	•			830
Gold	•			837
Turquoise	•			844
Green	•			852,853
Parchment	•			858,859
Parchment	•			860,861
Red	•			866,867

CAPRICE TRIM

COLOR	CLOTH	VINYL	LEATHER	CODE
Black	•			806,807,808
Black	•			809,812,813
Blue	•			821,822
Blue	•			824,826
Saddle	•			830
Gold	•			840
Turquoise	•			846
Green	•			854,855,856
Green	•			857,861,862
Red	•			866,867

CORVETTE TRIM

COLOR	CLOTH	VINYL	LEATHER	CODE
Black			•	402
Red		•		407
Red			•	408
Blue		•		411
Blue			•	412
Green		•		427
Green			•	428
Saddle		•		420
Saddle			•	421
Gunmetal		•		416
Gunmetal			•	417

THE PAINT CODE furnishes the key to the exterior paint color. A two-letter code indicates the bottom and top colors respectively.

COLOR	CODE
Tuxedo Black	10
Tuxedo Black	*900
Butternut Yellow	40
Dover White	50
Dusk Blue	51
Garnet Red	52
Glacier Blue	53
Azure Turquoise	55
Fathom Green	57
Fathom Green	*983
Frost Green	59
Burnished Brown	61
Champagne	63
Olympic Gold	65
Burgundy	67
Burgundy	*988
Cortez Silver	69
Cortez Silver	*986
LeMans Blue	71
LeMans Blue	*976
Hugger Orange	72
Hugger Orange	*990
Daytona Yellow	76
Daytona Yellow	*984
Rallye Green	79
Can-Am White	*972
Monza Red	*974
Riverside Gold	*980

*Corvette only

ENGINE NUMBER

All Chevrolet engines are stamped with a plant code, production date, and engine type code.

Note:

1. Corvette engines have the last six digits of the VIN stamped on the block next to the engine number.

2. Corvair engines are stamped on the top of the block forward of the generator.

3. 8 cylinder engines are stamped on the right front of the engine block.

4. 6 cylinder engines are stamped on the right side of the block at the rear of the distributor.

EXAMPLE:

T	01	01	A
PLANT	MONTH	DAY	CODE

ENGINE PLANTS	CODE
Tonawanda	T
Flint	F

CORVAIR

ENGINE CODE	NO. CYL.	CID	HORSE-POWER	COMP. RATIO	CARB	TRANS
AC	6	164	95	8.25:1	2-1 BC	MAN
AD	6	164	110	9.25:1	2-1 BC	MAN
AE	6	164	95	8.25:1	2-1 BC	PG
AF	6	164	110	9.25:1	2-1 BC	PG
AG	6	164	140	9.25:1	4-1 BC	MAN
AH	6	164	140	9.25:1	4-1 BC	PG

CORVETTE

ENGINE CODE	NO. CYL.	CID	HORSE-POWER	COMP. RATIO	CARB	TRANS
HY	8	350	300	10.0:1	4 BC	MAN
HZ	8	350	300	10.0:1	4 BC	TH
HW	8	350	350	11.0;1	4 BC	MAN
HX	8	350	350	11.0:1	4 BC	MAN
GD	8	350	350	11.0:1	4 BC	N/A
LM	8	427	390	10.25:1	4 BC	MAN
LL	8	427	390	10.25:1	4 BC	TH
LQ	8	427	400	10.25:1	3-2 BC	MAN
LN	8	427	400	10.25:1	3-2 BC	TH
LO	8	427	430	12.0:1	4 BC	MAN
LV	8	427	430	12.0:1	4 BC	TH
LR	8	427	435	11.0:1	3-2 BC	MAN
LX	8	427	435	11.0:1	3-2 BC	TH
LP	8	427	435	11.0:1	3-2 BC	MAN
LW	8	427	435	11.0:1	3-2 BC	TH
LT	8	427	435	11.0:1	3-2 BC	MAN
LU	8	427	435	11.0:1	3-2 BC	MAN
ME	8	427	430	12.0:1	4 BC	MAN
MG	8	427	430	12.0:1	4 BC	TH
MH	8	427	390	10.25:1	4 BC	MAN
MI	8	427	390	10.25:1	4 BC	TH
MJ	8	427	400	10.25:1	4 BC	TH
MK	8	427	400	10.25:1	4 BC	MAN
MS	8	427	N/A	N/A	N/A	N/A
MR	8	427	430	12.0:1	4 BC	MAN

NOVA

ENGINE CODE	NO. CYL.	CID	HORSE-POWER	COMP. RATIO	CARB	TRANS
AA	4	153	90	8.5:1	1 BC	MAN
AB	4	153	90	8.5:1	1 BC	TD/PG
AM	6	230	140	8.5:1	1 BC	MAN
AN	6	230	140	8.5:1	1 BC	TD/PG
AO	6	230	140	8.5:1	1 BC	TH
AP	6	230	140	8.5:1	1 BC	MAN
AQ	6	230	140	8.5:1	1 BC	TD/PG
AR	6	230	140	8.5:1	1 BC	TH
AU	6	230	N/A	L/C	1 BC	MAN
AT	6	230	N/A	L/C	1 BC	PG
AV	6	230	N/A	L/C	1 BC	PG
AS	6	230	N/A	L/C	1 BC	MAN
BB	6	250	155	L/C	1 BC	TD/PG
BC	6	250	155	L/C	1 BC	TD/PG
BD	6	250	155	L/C	1 BC	TH
BE	6	250	155	L/C	1 BC	MAN
BF	6	250	155	L/C	1 BC	MAN
BH	6	250	155	L/C	1 BC	TH
BK	6	250	N/A	L/C	1 BC	MAN
BI	6	250	N/A	L/C	1 BC	PG
DA	8	307	200	9.0:1	2 BC	MAN
DC	8	307	200	9.0:1	2 BC	PG
DD	8	307	200	9.0:1	2 BC	TH
DE	8	307	200	9.0:1	2 BC	4-SP
HA	8	350	300	10.25:1	4 BC	MAN
HB	8	350	300	10.25:1	4 BC	TH
HC	8	350	250	9.0:1	2 BC	MAN
HD	8	350	250	9.0:1	2 BC	TH
HE	8	350	300	10.25:1	4 BC	PG
HF	8	350	250	9.0:1	2 BC	PG
HQ	8	350	255	9.0:1	4 BC	MAN
HR	8	350	255	9.0:1	4 BC	PG
HS	8	350	255	9.0:1	4 BC	TH
JF	8	396	350	10.25:1	4 BC	MAN
JH	8	396	375	11.0:1	4 BC	MAN
JI	8	396	350	10.25:1	4 BC	TH
JL	8	396	375	11.0:1	4 BC	TH
JM	8	396	350	10.25:1	4 BC	TH
JU	8	396	350	10.25:1	4 BC	PG
KA	8	396	350	10.25:1	4 BC	MAN
KC	8	396	375	11.0:1	4 BC	MAN
KE	8	396	350	10.25:1	4 BC	MAN

CHEVELLE

ENGINE CODE	NO. CYL.	CID	HORSE-POWER	COMP. RATIO	CARB	TRANS
AM	6	230	140	8.5:1	1 BC	MAN
AN	6	230	140	8.5:1	1 BC	TD/PG
AO	6	230	140	8.5:1	1 BC	TH
AP	6	230	140	8.5:1	1 BC	MAN
AQ	6	230	140	8.5:1	1 BC	TD/PG
AR	6	230	140	8.5:1	1 BC	TH
AS	6	230	N/A	L/C	1 BC	MAN
AU	6	230	N/A	L/C	1 BC	MAN
AT	6	230	N/A	L/C	1 BC	PG
AV	6	230	N/A	L/C	1 BC	PG
BB	6	250	155	L/C	1 BC	TD/PG
BC	6	250	155	L/C	1 BC	TD/PG
BD	6	250	155	L/C	1 BC	TH
BE	6	250	155	L/C	1 BC	MAN
BF	6	250	155	L/C	1 BC	MAN
BH	6	250	155	L/C	1 BC	TH
BK	6	250	N/A	L/C	1 BC	MAN
BW	6	250	N/A	L/C	1 BC	MAN
BI	6	250	N/A	L/C	1 BC	PG
BJ	6	250	N/A	L/C	1 BC	PG
DA	8	307	200	9.0:1	2 BC	MAN
DC	8	307	200	9.0:1	2 BC	PG
DD	8	307	200	9.0:1	2 BC	TH
DE	8	307	200	9.0:1	2 BC	4-SP
HA	8	350	300	10.25:1	4 BC	MAN
HB	8	350	300	10.25:1	4 BC	TH
HC	8	350	250	9.0:1	2 BC	MAN
HD	8	350	250	9.0:1	2 BC	TH
HE	8	350	300	10.25:1	4 BC	PG
HF	8	350	250	9.0:1	2 BC	PG
HQ	8	350	255	9.0:1	4 BC	MAN
HR	8	350	255	9.0:1	4 BC	MAN/PG
HS	8	350	255	9.0:1	4 BC	TH
JA	8	396	325	9.0:1	4 BC	MAN

JC	8	396	350	9.0:1	4 BC	MAN
JD	8	396	375	11.0:1	4 BC	MAN
JE	8	396	350	10.25:1	4 BC	TH
JK	8	396	325	10.25:1	4 BC	TH
KF	8	396	375	11.0:1	4 BC	TH
KG	8	396	325	10.25:1	4 BC	MAN
KH	8	396	325	10.25:1	4 BC	TH
KB	8	396	350	10.25:1	4 BC	MAN
JV	8	396	325	10.25:1	4 BC	MAN
KD	8	396	375	11.0:1	4 BC	MAN
KI	8	396	325	10.25:1	4 BC	MAN

CAMARO ENGINE CODE	NO. CYL.	CID	HORSE-POWER	COMP. RATIO	CARB	TRANS
AM	6	230	140	8.5:1	1 BC	MAN
AN	6	230	140	8.5:1	1 BC	TD/PG
AO	6	230	140	8.5:1	1 BC	TH
AP	6	230	140	8.5:1	1 BC	MAN
AW	6	230	140	8.5:1	1 BC	PG
AR	6	230	140	8.5:1	1 BC	TH
AS	6	230	N/A	L/C	1 BC	MAN
AU	6	230	N/A	L/C	1 BC	MAN
AT	6	230	N/A	L/C	1 BC	PG
AV	6	230	N/A	L/C	1 BC	PG
BE	6	250	155	8.5:1	1 BC	MAN
BB	6	250	155	8.5:1	1 BC	TD/PG
BD	6	250	155	8.5:1	1 BC	TH
BF	6	250	155	8.5:1	1 BC	MAN
BC	6	250	155	8.5:1	1 BC	PG
BH	6	250	155	8.5:1	1 BC	TH
DZ	8	302	290	11.0:1	4 BC*	MAN
DA	8	307	200	9.0:1	2 BC	MAN
DE	8	307	200	9.0:1	2 BC	4-SP
DC	8	307	200	9.0:1	2 BC	PG
DD	8	307	200	9.0:1	2 BC	TH
FJ	8	327	210	9.0:1	2 BC	MAN
FK	8	327	210	9.0:1	2 BC	PG
FL	8	327	210	9.0:1	2 BC	TH
FS	8	327	N/A	L/C	2 BC	MAN
FT	8	327	N/A	L/C	2 BC	PG
HC	8	350	250	9.0:1	2 BC	MAN
HF	8	350	250	9.0:1	2 BC	PG
HD	8	350	250	9.0:1	2 BC	TH
HQ	8	350	255	9.0:1	4 BC	MAN
HR	8	350	255	9.0:1	4 BC	PG
HS	8	350	255	9.0:1	4 BC	TH
HA	8	350	300	10.25:1	4 BC	MAN
HE	8	350	300	10.25:1	4 BC	PG
HB	8	350	300	10.25:1	4 BC	TH
HP	8	350	300	10.25:1	4 BC	MAN
JB	8	396	325	10.25:1	4 BC	MAN
JG	8	396	325	10.25:1	4 BC	TH
JU	8	396	325	10.25:1	4 BC	MAN
JF	8	396	350	10.25:1	4 BC	MAN
JI	8	396	350	10.25:1	4 BC	TH
KA	8	396	350	10.25:1	4 BC	MAN
JH	8	396	375	11.0:1	4 BC	MAN
KL	8	396	375	11.0:1	4 BC	4-SP
JL	8	396	375	11.0:1	4 BC	TH
KC	8	396	375	11.0:1	4 BC	MAN
JJ	8	396	375	11.0:1	4 BC	MAN
JM	8	396	375	11.0:1	4 BC	TH
KE	8	396	375	11.0:1	4 BC	MAN
ME	8	427	430	12.0:1	4 BC	MAN
MG	8	427	430	12.0:1	4 BC	TH

* 2-4 BC option

CHEVROLET ENGINE CODE	NO. CYL.	CID	HORSE-POWER	COMP. RATIO	CARB	TRANS
BA	6	250	155	8.5:1	1 BC	MAN
BB	6	250	155	8.5:1	1 BC	PG
BD	6	250	155	8.5:1	1 BC	TH
BG	6	250	155	8.5:1	1 BC	MAN
BC	6	250	155	8.5:1	1 BC	PG
BH	6	250	155	8.5:1	1 BC	TH
BM	6	250	N/A	L/C	1 BC	MAN
BN	6	250	N/A	L/C	1 BC	MAN
BI	6	250	N/A	L/C	1 BC	PG
BJ	6	250	N/A	L/C	1 BC	PG
BO	6	250	N/A	L/C	1 BC	PG
BP	6	250	N/A	L/C	1 BC	MAN
BL	6	250	N/A	L/C	1 BC	PG
BQ	6	250	N/A	L/C	1 BC	MAN
FA	8	327	235	9.0:1	2 BC	MAN
FB	8	327	235	9.0:1	2 BC	PG
FH	8	327	235	9.0:1	2 BC	TH
FC	8	327	235	9.0:1	2 BC	TH
FM	8	327	N/A	L/C	2 BC	MAN
FN	8	327	N/A	L/C	2 BC	PG
FG	8	327	235	9.0:1	2 BC	MAN
FZ	8	327	235	9.0:1	2 BC	PG
GA	8	327	235	9.0:1	2 BC	TH
FY	8	327	235	9.0:1	2 BC	MAN
FJ	8	327	235	9.0:1	2 BC	MAN
FK	8	327	235	9.0:1	2 BC	PG
FL	8	327	235	9.0:1	2 BC	TH
GB	8	327	235	9.0:1	2 BC	TH
HI	8	350	250	9.0:1	2 BC	MAN
HL	8	350	250	9.0:1	2 BC	PG
HF	8	350	250	9.0:1	2 BC	PG
HD	8	350	250	9.0:1	2 BC	TH
HJ	8	350	250	9.0:1	2 BC	TH
HM	8	350	250	9.0:1	2 BC	TH
IL	8	350	250	9.0:1	2 BC	MAN
IM	8	350	250	9.0:1	2 BC	PG
IN	8	350	250	9.0:1	2 BC	TH
HT	8	350	255	9.0:1	4 BC	MAN
HU	8	350	255	9.0:1	4 BC	PG
IA	8	350	255	9.0:1	4 BC	TH
HV	8	350	255	9.0:1	4 BC	TH
IW	8	350	255	9.0:1	4 BC	MAN
IX	8	350	255	9.0:1	4 BC	PG
IY	8	350	255	9.0:1	4 BC	TH
IZ	8	350	255	9.0:1	4 BC	TH
HG	8	350	300	10.25:1	4 BC	MAN
HK	8	350	300	10.25:1	4 BC	PG
HH	8	350	300	10.25:1	4 BC	TH
HN	8	350	300	10.25:1	4 BC	TH
IR	8	350	300	10.25:1	4 BC	MAN
IS	8	350	300	10.25:1	4 BC	PG
IT	8	350	300	10.25:1	4 BC	TH
IQ	8	350	300	10.25:1	4 BC	MAN
HO	8	350	300	10.25:1	4 BC	MAN
IV	8	350	300	10.25:1	4 BC	TH
JN	8	396	265	9.0:1	2 BC	MAN
JQ	8	396	265	9.0:1	2 BC	TH
JP	8	396	265	9.0:1	2 BC	MAN
JO	8	396	265	9.0:1	2 BC	TH
JR	8	396	265	9.0:1	2 BC	MAN
JT	8	396	265	9.0:1	2 BC	MAN
LB	8	427	335	10.25:1	4 BC	MAN
LE	8	427	335	10.25:1	4 BC	TH
LK	8	427	335	10.25:1	4 BC	MAN
LJ	8	427	335	10.25:1	4 BC	TH
LY	8	427	335	10.25:1	4 BC	MAN
MA	8	427	335	10.25:1	4 BC	
LA	8	427	390	10.25:1	4 BC	MAN
LC	8	427	390	10.25:1	4 BC	TH
LG	8	427	390	10.25:1	4 BC	MAN
LF	8	427	390	10.25:1	4 BC	TH
LZ	8	427	390	10.25:1	4 BC	MAN
MB	8	427	390	10.25:1	4 BC	MAN
LH	8	427	390	10.25:1	4 BC	MAN
MC	8	427	390	10.25:1	4 BC	MAN
LI	8	427	390	10.25:1	4 BC	TH
LD	8	427	425	11.0:1	4 BC	MAN
LS	8	427	425	11.0:1	4 BC	TH
MD	8	427	425	11.0:1	4 BC	MAN

1960 OLDSMOBILE

1960 OLDSMOBILE

VEHICLE IDENTIFICATION NUMBER

OLDSMOBILE
608A001555

Commonly referred to as the VIN NUMBER, this series of numbers and letters is stamped on a plate attached to the left front door hinge pillar.

FIRST AND SECOND DIGITS: Identify the model year (1960)

THIRD DIGIT: Identifies the series

MODEL	CODE
Dynamic 88	7
Super 88	8
98	9

FOURTH DIGIT: Identifies the assembly plant

ASSEMBLY PLANT	CODE
Atlanta, GA	A
Framingham, MA	B
South Gate, CA	C
Kansas City, KS	K
Linden, NJ	L
Lansing, MI	M
Arlington, TX	T
Wilmington, DE	W

LAST SIX DIGITS: Represent the basic production numbers

BODY NUMBER PLATE

Complete identification of each body is provided by a plate under the hood below the left windshield wiper transmission.

OLDSMOBILE DIV. GENERAL
MOTORS CORP.
LANSING MICHIGAN

STYLE 60-3539 BODY BA 001555
TRIM 345 PAINT AC
*ACC.00

BODY BY FISHER

EXAMPLE:

60	Model Year (1960)
35	Super 88
39	Holiday Sedan
BA	Assembly Plant (Doraville, GA)
001555	Production Sequence
345	Trim Code
A	Lower Body Color
C	Upper Body Color

* Is unavailable at the time of printing

THE STYLE NUMBER is a combination of the year, series (35 for 3500, Super 88), and body style (39 for Holiday Sedan).

DYNAMIC "88"	CODE
2-Dr. Sedan	3211
4-Dr. Sedan	3219
Fiesta Station Wagon	3235
Fiesta Station Wagon, 3-Seat	3245
Holiday Coupe	3237
Holiday Sedan	3239
Convertible Coupe	3267

1960 OLDSMOBILE

SUPER "88"	CODE
4-Dr. Sedan	3519
Fiesta Station Wagon	3535
Fiesta Station Wagon, 3-Seat	3545
Holiday Coupe	3537
Holiday Sedan	3539
Convertible Coupe	3567

"98"	CODE
4-Dr. Sedan	3819
Holiday Coupe	3837
Holiday Sedan	3839
Convertible Coupe	3867

THE BODY NUMBER is the production serial number of the body. The prefix letter denotes the plant in which the body was assembled.

ASSEMBLY PLANT	CODE
Lansing	LA
Doraville	BA
Framingham	BF
Kansas City	BK
Linden	BL
South Gate	BC
Wilmington	BW
Arlington	BT

THE TRIM NUMBER furnishes the key to trim color and material for each model series.

DYNAMIC 88 TRIM

COLOR	CLOTH	VINYL	LEATHER	CODE
Gray		•		311,321
Gray		•		391
Green		•		312,322
Green		•		392
Blue		•		313,323
Blue		•		393
Fawn		•		314,394
Turquoise		•		316
Red		•		325,395

SUPER 88 TRIM

COLOR	CLOTH	VINYL	LEATHER	CODE
Gray	•			331,390
Gray		•		341
Gray			•	351
Green	•			332,397
Green		•		342
Green			•	352
Blue	•			333,398
Blue		•		343
Blue			•	353
Fawn	•			334,396
Fawn		•		344
Turquoise	•			336
Red	•			399
Red		•		345
Red			•	355

NINETY-EIGHT TRIM

COLOR	CLOTH	VINYL	LEATHER	CODE
Gray	•			361
Gray			•	371
Gray		•		381
Green	•			362
Green			•	372
Green		•		382
Blue	•			363
Blue			•	373
Blue		•		383
Fawn	•			364
Fawn			•	374
Fawn		•		384
Turquoise	•			366
Red			•	375
Red		•		385

THE PAINT CODE furnishes the key to the paint colors used on the car. A two-letter code indicates the bottom and top colors respectively.

COLOR	CODE
Ebony Black	A
Charcoal Mist	B
Provincial White	C
Platinum Mist	D
Gulf Blue	F
Resden Blue	H
Palmetto Mist	J
Fern Mist	K
Garnet Mist	L
Citron	M
Cordovan	N
Golden Mist	P
Shell Beige	R
Copper Mist	S
Turquoise	T

ENGINE NUMBER

The engine unit number is stamped on the left cylinder head. A prefix letter code identifies the engine followed by a production sequence number.

DYNAMIC 88

ENGINE CODE	NO. CYL.	CID	HORSE-POWER	COMP. RATIO	CARB
C	8	371	240	8.75:1	2 BC
CE	8	371	NA	7.9:1	2 BC
CH	8	371	260	9.75:1	4 BC

SUPER 88 & 98

ENGINE CODE	NO. CYL.	CID	HORSE-POWER	COMP. RATIO	CARB
D	8	394	315	9.75:1	4 BC
DE	8	394	NA	7.8:1	4 BC

1961 OLDSMOBILE

1961 OLDSMOBILE

1961 OLDSMOBILE F-85

1961 OLDSMOBILE F-85

VEHICLE IDENTIFICATION NUMBER

OLDSMOBILE
618A001555

Commonly referred to as the VIN NUMBER, this series of numbers and letters is stamped on a plate attached to the left front door hinge pillar.

FIRST AND SECOND DIGITS: Identify the model year (1961)

THIRD DIGIT: Identifies the series

MODEL	CODE
F85	0
F85 Deluxe	1
88	2
Super 88	5
Starfire	6
98	8

FOURTH DIGIT: Identifies the assembly plant

ASSEMBLY PLANT	CODE
Atlanta, GA	A
Framingham, MA	B
South Gate, CA	C
Kansas City, KS	K
Linden, NJ	L
Lansing, MI	M
Arlington, TX	T
Wilmington, DE	W

LAST SIX DIGITS: Represent the basic production numbers

BODY NUMBER PLATE

Complete identification of each body is provided by a plate under the hood below the left windshield wiper transmission.

OLDSMOBILE DIV. GENERAL
MOTORS CORP.
LANSING MICHIGAN

STYLE 61-3539 BODY BA 001555
TRIM 345 PAINT AC
*ACC.00

BODY BY FISHER

EXAMPLE:

61	Model Year (1961)
35	Super 88
39	Holiday Sedan
BA	Assembly Plant (Doraville, GA)
001555	Production Sequence
345	Trim Code
A	Lower Body Color
C	Upper Body Color

* Is unavailable at the time of printing

THE STYLE NUMBER is a combination of the year, series and body style.

F85	CODE
4-Dr. Sedan	3019
Club Coupe	3027
Station Wagon, 2-Seat	3035
Station Wagon, 3-Seat	3045

F85 DELUXE	CODE
Sport Coupe Cutlass	3117
4-Dr. Sedan	3119
Station Wagon, 2-Seat	3135
Station Wagon, 3-Seat	3145

DYNAMIC "88"	CODE
2-Dr. Sedan	3211
4-Dr. Sedan	3269
Fiesta Station Wagon	3235
Fiesta Station Wagon, 3-Seat	3245
Holiday Coupe	3237
Holiday Sedan	3239
Convertible Coupe	3267

SUPER "88"	CODE
4-Dr. Sedan	3569
Fiesta Station Wagon	3535
Fiesta Station Wagon, 3-Seat	3545
Holiday Coupe	3537
Holiday Sedan	3539
Convertible Coupe	3567

STARFIRE	CODE
Convertible Coupe	3667

"98"	CODE
4-Dr. Sedan	3819
Holiday Coupe	3837
Holiday Sedan	3829
Convertible Coupe	3867
Sport Sedan	3839

THE BODY NUMBER is the production serial number of the body. The prefix letter denotes the plant in which the body was assembled.

ASSEMBLY PLANT	CODE
Lansing	LA
Doraville	BA
Kansas City	BK
Linden	BL
South Gate	BC

THE TRIM NUMBER furnishes the key to interior color and material for each model series.

DYNAMIC 88 TRIM

COLOR	CLOTH	VINYL	LEATHER	CODE
Gray	•			311
White		•		310,921,391
Green	•			312
Green		•		317,922,392
Blue	•			313
Blue		•		318,923,393
Fawn	•			314
Fawn		•		319,924,394
Red	•			305*,925
Red		•		395
Turquoise		•		387

* Not available on Dynamic 88 2-Door Sedan.

SUPER 88 TRIM

COLOR	CLOTH	VINYL	LEATHER	CODE
White		•		331,390
Green		•		332,342
Green				352,397
Blue		•		333,343
Blue		•		353,398
Fawn		•		334,344
Fawn		•		354,396
Red		•		335,345
Red		•		355,399
Gray		•		341,351
Turquoise		•		388

NINETY-EIGHT TRIM

COLOR	CLOTH	VINYL	LEATHER	CODE
Gray		•		361,301
Gray		•		371,381
Green		•		362,302
Green		•		372,382
Blue		•		363,303
Blue		•		373,383
Fawn		•		364,304
Fawn		•		374,384
Turquoise		•		366,306
Red		•		375,385

F85 TRIM

COLOR	CLOTH	VINYL	LEATHER	CODE
Gray				901*,911
Gray				971,951
Green				902,912
Green				972,952
Blue				903*,913
Blue				973,953
Fawn				904*,904
Fawn				974,954,964
Red				905,975,965

*Available only on Club Coupe.

THE PAINT CODE furnishes the key to the paint colors used on the car. A two-letter code indicates the bottom and top colors respectively.

COLOR	CODE
Ebony Black	A
Twilight Mist	B
Provincial White	C
Platinum Mist	D
Azure Mist	F
Glacier Blue	H
Tropic Mist	J
Alpine Green	K
Garnet Mist	L
Cordovan Mist	N
Turquoise Mist	P
Aqua	Q
Sandalwood	R
Autumn Mist	S
Fawn Mist	T

ENGINE NUMBER

The engine unit number is stamped on the left cylinder head. A prefix letter code identifies the engine followed by a production sequence number.

DYNAMIC 88

ENGINE CODE	NO. CYL.	CID	HORSE-POWER	COMP. RATIO	CARB
F	8	394	250	8.5:1	2 BC
G	8	394	275	10.00:1	2 BC
G	8	394	325	10.0:1	4 BC

SUPER 88 & 98

ENGINE CODE	NO. CYL.	CID	HORSE-POWER	COMP. RATIO	CARB
G	8	395	325	10.00:1	4 BC

STARFIRE

ENGINE CODE	NO. CYL.	CID	HORSE-POWER	COMP. RATIO	CARB
G	8	394	330	10.25:1	4 BC

F85

ENGINE CODE	NO. CYL.	CID	HORSE-POWER	COMP. RATIO	CARB
S	8	215	155	8.75:1	2 BC
S*	8	215	185	10.25:1	4 BC

* Standard on Cutlass

1) If no Suffix code exists, it is a standard engine.
2) E,H Suffix indicates an export engine
3) G, Hi-Comp. L, Low-Comp. F85 series is stamped on the right cylinder head.

1962 OLDSMOBILE

1962 OLDSMOBILE

1962 OLDSMOBILE F-85

1962 OLDSMOBILE F-85

VEHICLE IDENTIFICATION NUMBER

OLDSMOBILE
628A001555

Commonly referred to as the VIN NUMBER, this series of numbers and letters is stamped on a plate attached to the left front door hinge pillar.

FIRST AND SECOND DIGITS: Identify the model year (1962)

THIRD DIGIT: Identifies the series

MODEL	CODE
F85	0
F85 Deluxe	1
88	2
Super 88	5
Starfire	6
98	8

FOURTH DIGIT: Identifies the assembly plant

ASSEMBLY PLANT	CODE
Atlanta, GA	A
South Gate, CA	C
Kansas City, KS	K
Linden, NJ	L
Lansing, MI	M
Arlington, TX	T
Wilmington, DE	W

LAST SIX DIGITS: Represent the basic production numbers

BODY NUMBER PLATE

Complete identification of each body is provided by a plate under the hood below the left windshield wiper transmission.

OLDSMOBILE DIV. GENERAL
MOTORS CORP.
LANSING MICHIGAN

STYLE 62-3539 BODY BA 001555
TRIM 345 PAINT AC
*ACC.00

BODY BY FISHER

EXAMPLE:

62	Model Year (1962)
35	Super 88
39	Holiday Sedan
BA	Assembly Plant (Doraville, GA)
001555	Production Sequence
345	Trim Code
A	Lower Body Color
C	Upper Body Color

* Is unavailable at the time of printing

THE STYLE NUMBER is a combination of the series and body style.

F85	CODE
4-Dr. Sedan	3019
Club Coupe	3027
Station Wagon, 2-Seat	3035
Station Wagon, 3-Seat	3045
Sports Convertible	3067

F85 DELUXE	CODE
Cutlass Coupe	3127
4-Dr. Sedan	3119
Station Wagon, 2-Seat	3135
Cutlass Convertible	3167
2-Dr. Cutlass Coupe	3117

DYNAMIC "88"	CODE
4-Dr. Sedan Celebrity	3269
Fiesta Station Wagon	3235
Fiesta Station Wagon, 3-Seat	3245
Holiday Coupe	3247
Holiday Sedan	3239
Convertible Coupe	3267

SUPER "88"	CODE
4-Dr. Sedan Celebrity	3569
Fiesta Station Wagon	3535
Holiday Coupe	3547
Holiday Sedan	3539

STARFIRE	CODE
Coupe	3647
Convertible	3667

"98"	CODE
4-Dr. Sedan	3819
Holiday Coupe	3847
Holiday Sedan	3829
Convertible Coupe	3867
Sports Sedan	3839

JETFIRE	CODE
2-Dr. Hardtop Coupe	3147

THE BODY NUMBER is the production serial number of the body. The prefix letter denotes the plant in which the body was assembled.

ASSEMBLY PLANT	CODE
Lansing	LA
Doraville	BA
Framingham	BF
Kansas City	BK
Linden	BL
South Gate	BC
Wilmington	BW
Arlington	BT

THE TRIM NUMBER furnishes the key to interior color and material for each model series.

F85 TRIM

COLOR	CLOTH	VINYL	LEATHER	CODE
Gray		•		900,911,981
Gray			•	971,991,951
Gray		•		950
Blue		•		908,903,983
Blue			•	913,973,993
Blue		•		953,958
Fawn		•		904,984,974
Fawn		•		994,954,964
Green		•		902,952
Red		•		905,985
Red		•		975,995
White		•		965

DYNAMIC 88 TRIM

COLOR	CLOTH	VINYL	LEATHER	CODE
Gray		•		300,310,311
Gray		•		321,391
Green		•		312,317
Green		•		322,392
Blue		•		313,318,923
Blue		•		323,393
Fawn		•		314,319,924
Fawn		•		324,394
Red		•		305,315,925
Red		•		325,395
Aqua		•		387

SUPER 88 TRIM

COLOR	CLOTH	VINYL	LEATHER	CODE
Gray		•		331,341,390
Green		•		332,342,397
Blue		•		333,343,398
Fawn		•		334,344,396
Red		•		335,345,399
Aqua		•		388

STARFIRE TRIM

COLOR	CLOTH	VINYL	LEATHER	CODE
Gray		•		931
Blue		•		933
Fawn		•		934
Red		•		935

NINETY-EIGHT TRIM

COLOR	CLOTH	VINYL	LEATHER	CODE
Gray		•		361,301
Gray		•		371,381
Green		•		362,302,372
Blue		•		363,303
Blue		•		373,383
Fawn		•		364,304
Fawn		•		374,384
Red		•		365,945
Red		•		375,385

THE PAINT CODE furnishes the key to the paint colors used on the car. A two-letter code indicates the bottom and top colors respectively.

COLOR	CODE
Ebony Black	A
Heather Mist	B
Provincial White	C
Sheffield Mist	D
Wedgewood Mist	E
Cirrus Blue	H
Willow Mist	J
Surf Green	K
Garnet Mist	L
Cameo Cream	M
Royal Mist	N
Pacific Mist	P
Sand Beige	R
Sahara Mist	T
Sunset Mist	X

ENGINE NUMBER

The engine unit number is stamped on the left cylinder head (a production number only). Each engine is stamped with a prefix letter code for identification. F85 series is stamped on the front of the right cylinder head.

F85 & DELUXE

ENGINE CODE	NO. CYL.	CID	HORSE-POWER	COMP. RATIO	CARB
S	8	215	155	8.75:1	2 BC
SE	8	215	NA	8.25:1	2 BC
SG	8	215	185	10.25:1	4 BC
SH	8	215	NA	8.5:1	4 BC

JETFIRE

ENGINE CODE	NO. CYL.	CID	HORSE-POWER	COMP. RATIO	CARB
ST	8	215	215	10.25:1	Turbo Charged

DYNAMIC 88

ENGINE CODE	NO. CYL.	CID	HORSE-POWER	COMP. RATIO	CARB
F	8	394	280	10.25:1	2 BC
FL	8	394	260	8.75:1	2 BC
FE	8	394	NA	8.3:1	2 BC
G	8	394	330	10.25:1	4 BC

SUPER 88 & 89

ENGINE CODE	NO. CYL.	CID	HORSE-POWER	COMP. RATIO	CARB
G	8	394	330	10.25:1	4 BC
GE	8	394	NA	8.3:1	4 BC

STARFIRE

ENGINE CODE	NO. CYL.	CID	HORSE-POWER	COMP. RATIO	CARB
GS	8	394	345	10.5:1	4 BC
GE	8	394	NA	8.3:1	4 BC

1) If no Suffix code exists, it is a standard engine
2) E,H Suffix indicates an export engine
3) G, Hi-Comp. L, Low-Comp.

1963 OLDSMOBILE

1963 OLDSMOBILE

1963 OLDSMOBILE F-85

1963 OLDSMOBILE F-85

VEHICLE IDENTIFICATION NUMBER

OLDSMOBILE
638A001555

Commonly referred to as the VIN NUMBER, this series of numbers and letters is stamped on a plate attached to the left front door hinge pillar.

FIRST AND SECOND DIGITS: Identify the model year (1963)

THIRD DIGIT: Identifies the series

MODEL	CODE
F85 Standard	0
F85 Deluxe	1
Dynamic 88	2
Super 88	5
Starfire	6
98	8
Custom 98	9

FOURTH DIGIT: Identifies the assembly plant

ASSEMBLY PLANT	CODE
Atlanta, GA	A
South Gate, CA	C
Kansas City, KS	K
Linden, NJ	L
Lansing, MI	M
Arlington, TX	T
Wilmington, DE	W

LAST SIX DIGITS: Represent the basic production numbers

BODY NUMBER PLATE

Complete identification of each body is provided by a plate under the hood below the left windshield wiper transmission. F85 located on cowl.

OLDSMOBILE DIV. GENERAL
MOTORS CORP.
LANSING MICHIGAN

STYLE 63-3539 BODY BA 001555
TRIM 345 PAINT AC
*ACC.00

BODY BY FISHER

EXAMPLE:

63	Model Year (1963)
35	Super 88
39	Holiday Sedan
BA	Assembly Plant (Doraville, GA)
001555	Production Sequence
345	Trim Code
A	Lower Body Color
C	Upper Body Color

* Is unavailable at the time of printing

THE STYLE NUMBER is a combination of the series and body style.

F85 STANDARD	CODE
4-Dr. Sedan	3019
Club Coupe	3027
Station Wagon	3035

F85 DELUXE	CODE
Cutlass Coupe	3117
4-Dr. Sedan	3119
Station Wagon	3135
Cutlass Convertible	3167

JETFIRE	CODE
2-Dr. Hardtop Coupe	3147

DYNAMIC 88	CODE
Fiesta Station Wagon, 2-Seat	3235
Holiday Sedan	3239
Fiesta Station Wagon, 3-Seat	3245
Holiday Coupe	3247
Convertible Coupe	3267
4-Dr. Celebrity Sedan	3269

SUPER 88	CODE
Fiesta Station Wagon, 2-Seat	3535
Holiday Sedan	3539
Holiday Coupe	3547
4-Dr. Celebrity Sedan	3569

STARFIRE	CODE
Coupe	3657
Convertible	3667

"98"	CODE
4-Dr. Town Sedan	3819
Luxury Sedan	3829
Sports Sedan	3839
Holiday Coupe	3847
Convertible Coupe	3867
Custom Sports Coupe	3947

THE BODY NUMBER is the production serial number of the body. The prefix letter denotes the plant in which the body was assembled.

ASSEMBLY PLANT	CODE
Lansing	LA
Doraville	BA
Kansas City	BK
Linden	BL
South Gate	BC
Wilmington	BW
Arlington	BT

THE TRIM NUMBER furnishes the key to interior color and material for each model series.

NINETY-EIGHT TRIM

COLOR	CLOTH	VINYL	LEATHER	CODE
Silver	•			391
Silver		•		361
Gray		•		371
Green	•			392
Green		•		362
Green		•		372
Blue	•			393
Blue		•		363
Blue		•		373,383,963
Fawn	•			394
Fawn		•		364
Fawn		•		374
Aqua	•			396
Aqua		•		366
Red		•		375,385,965
White		•		387,967
Saddle		•		388,968
Rose		•		969

SUPER 88 TRIM

COLOR	CLOTH	VINYL	LEATHER	CODE
Silver		•		341,351
Green		•		342,352,872
Blue		•		343,353,983
Fawn		•		344,354
Red		•		345,355,985
White		•		987
Saddle		•		988

DYNAMIC 88 TRIM

COLOR	CLOTH	VINYL	LEATHER	CODE
Gray		•		311
Blue		•		313,323,303
Blue		•		973,333
Fawn		•		314,324,304
Red		•		315,325,305
Red		•		975,335
Green		•		302,312
Green		•		972,332
Charcoal		•		300,311
Charcoal		•		971,331
White		•		327
Saddle		•		978,338

STARFIRE TRIM

COLOR	CLOTH	VINYL	LEATHER	CODE
Black		•		990
Blue		•		993
Red		•		995
White		•		997
Saddle		•		998
Rose		•		999

1963 OLDSMOBILE

F85 TRIM

COLOR	CLOTH	VINYL	LEATHER	CODE
Platinum		•		931,901,911
Green		•		932,922,912
Blue		•		933,923
Blue		•		953,913
Fawn		•		934,924,944
Fawn		•		904,914
Red		•		945,955,915
White		•		957
Saddle		•		958

JETFIRE TRIM

COLOR	CLOTH	VINYL	LEATHER	CODE
Black		•		950
Blue		•		953
Red		•		955
White		•		957
Saddle		•		958

THE PAINT CODE furnishes the key to the paint colors used on the car. A two-letter code indicates the bottom and top colors respectively.

COLOR	CODE
Ebony Black	A
Provincial White	C
Sheffield Mist	D
Wedgewood Mist	F
Cirrus Blue	H
Willow Mist	J
Barktone Mist	K
Regal Mist	L
Pacific Mist	P
Sand Beige	R
Saddle Mist	S
Sahara Mist	T
Holiday Red	V
Midnight Mist	W
Antique Rose	X

ENGINE NUMBER

The engine unit number is stamped on the left cylinder head (a production number only). Each engine is stamped with a prefix letter code for identification. F85 series is stamped on the front of the right cylinder head.

F85 STANDARD & DELUXE

ENGINE CODE	NO. CYL.	CID	HORSE-POWER	COMP. RATIO	CARB	TRANS.
S	8	215	155	8.75:1	2 BC	
SE	8	215	NA	8.25:1	2 BC	
SG	8	215	195	10.75:1	4 BC	AUTO
SG	8	215	185	10.25:1	4 BC	MAN
SH	8	215	NA	8.5:1	4 BC	

JETFIRE

ENGINE CODE	NO. CYL.	CID	HORSE-POWER	COMP. RATIO	CARB	TRANS.
ST	8	215	215	10.25:1Turbo Charged		

DYNAMIC 88

ENGINE	NO.	HORSE-	COMP.			
CODE	CYL.	CID	POWER	RATIO	CARB	TRANS.
H	8	394	280	10.25:1	2 BC	
HE	8	394	NA	8.3:1	2 BC	
HL	8	394	260	8.75:1	2 BC	
J	8	394	330	10.25:1	4 BC	

SUPER 88 & 98

ENGINE	NO.	HORSE-	COMP.			
CODE	CYL.	CID	POWER	RATIO	CARB	TRANS.
J	8	394	330	10.25:1	4 BC	
JE	8	394	NA	8.3:1	4 BC	

STARFIRE & 98 CUSTOM

ENGINE	NO.	HORSE-	COMP.			
CODE	CYL.	CID	POWER	RATIO	CARB	TRANS.
JS	8	394	345	10.5:1	4 BC	

1964 OLDSMOBILE

1964 OLDSMOBILE

1964 OLDSMOBILE F-85

1964 OLDSMOBILE F-85

VEHICLE IDENTIFICATION NUMBER

OLDSMOBILE
834M001002

Commonly referred to as the VIN NUMBER, this series of numbers and letters is stamped on a plate attached to the left front door hinge pillar.

THE FIRST DIGIT: Identifies the engine type: 6 (6 cyl.), 8 (8 cyl.)

THE SECOND DIGIT: Identifies the series

MODEL	CODE
F85 Standard	0
F85 Deluxe	1
F85 Cutlass	2
88 Jetstar	3
Dynamic 88	4
Super 88	5
Starfire	6
Jetstar I	7
98	8
98 Custom	9

THE THIRD DIGIT: Identifies the model year (1964)

THE FOURTH DIGIT: Identifies the assembly plant

ASSEMBLY PLANT	CODE
Atlanta, GA	A
Baltimore, MD	B
Southgate, CA	C
Kansas City, MO	D
Fremont, CA	F
Kansas City, KS	K
Linden, NJ	L
Lansing, MI	M
Arlington, TX	T

LAST SIX DIGITS: Represent the basic production numbers

BODY NUMBER PLATE

Complete identification of each body is provided by a plate on the cowl under the hood.

OLDSMOBILE DIV. GENERAL
MOTORS CORP.
LANSING MICHIGAN

STYLE 64-3539 BODY BA 001555
TRIM 321 PAINT AC
*ACC.00

BODY BY FISHER

EXAMPLE:

64	Model Year (1964)
35	Super 88
39	Holiday Sedan
BA	Assembly Plant (Baltimore, MD)
001555	Production Sequence
321	Trim Code
A	Lower Body Color
C	Upper Body Color

* Is unavailable at the time of printing

THE STYLE NUMBER is a combination of the series and body style.

F85 STANDARD	CODE
Club Coupe	3027
Station Wagon	3035
4-Dr. Sedan	3069

* Option 442

1964 OLDSMOBILE

F85 DELUXE	CODE
V6 Sport Coupe	3127
Station Wagon	3135
4-Dr. Sdan	3169
* Optic 442	

CUTASS	CODE
Sp s Coupe	3227
Ho ay Coupe	3237
Co ertible	3267
* tion 442	

V A-CRUISER STANDARD	
S on Wagon, 2-Seat	3055
S on Wagon, 3-Seat	3065

A-CRUISER CUSTOM	
on Wagon, 2-Seat	3255
on Wagon, 3-Seat	3265

TAR 88	CODE
ay Sedan	3339
ay Coupe	3347
ertible	3367
Celebrity Sedan	3369

TAR I	CODE
s Coupe	3457

MIC 88	CODE
Station Wagon, at	3435
y Sedan	3439
Station Wagon, at	3445
Coupe	3447
tible	3467
elebrity Sedan	3469

88	CODE
Sedan	3539
elebrity Sedan	3569

FIRE	CODE
	3657
rtible	3667

Y EIGHT	CODE
Town Sedan	3819
y Sedan	3829
ay Sports Sedan	3839
ay Sports Coupe	3847
ertible	3867
om Sports Coupe	3947

THE BODY NUMBER is the production serial number of the body. The prefix letter denotes the plant in which the body was assembled.

ASSEMBLY PLANT	CODE
Lansing	LA
Baltimore	BA
Fremont	BF
Kansas City, MO	KC
Atlanta	BA
Kansas City, KS	BK
Linden	BL
South Gate	BC
Arlington	BT

THE TRIM NUMBER furnishes the key to interior color and material for each model series.

NINETY EIGHT TRIM

COLOR	CLOTH	VINYL	LEATHER	CODE
Black				360,370L
Silver				351,341,381
Med. Green				342,362
Dk. Green				352,372L, 382
Blue				353,343,363
Blue				373L,383
Maroon				365,385
Red				375L
Aqua				356,346
Aqua				366,386
White				377L
Saddle				358,348,368

JETSTAR I TRIM

COLOR	CLOTH	VINYL	LEATHER	CODE
Silver				302V
Blue				303V
Red				305V
White				307V
Saddle				308V

F85 DELUXE TRIM

COLOR	CLOTH	VINYL	LEATHER	CODE
Black				960V,940
Black				920,930V
Green				922
Green				962V,942
Blue				963V,943,923
Maroon				935V
Red				965V,945v
Aqua				926
White				967V,947V
Saddle				968V,948
Saddle				928,938V

F85 TRIM

COLOR	CLOTH	VINYL	LEATHER	CODE
Silver				901,911V
Green				902,912V
Blue				903,913V
Maroon				915V
Aqua				906
Saddle				918V

JETSTAR 88 TRIM

COLOR	CLOTH	VINYL	LEATHER	CODE
Black				970V,990V
Silver				981,971
Green				982,972
Green				992V
Blue				983,993V,973
Maroon				995V
Red				994V
Aqua				986,976
White				997V,977V
Saddle				988,978,998V

STARFIRE TRIM

COLOR	CLOTH	VINYL	LEATHER	CODE
Black				330L
Green				332L
Blue				333L
Red				335L
White				337L
Saddle				338L

SUPER 88 TRIM

COLOR	CLOTH	VINYL	LEATHER	CODE
Silver				321,311
Green				322,312
Green				323,313
Aqua				326,316
Saddle				328,318

DYNAMIC 88 TRIM

COLOR	CLOTH	VINYL	LEATHER	CODE
Black				970V,990V
Silver				981,971
Green				982,972
Green				982V,312,992V
Blue				983,993V
Blue				973,993V,313
Maroon				995V,315V
Red				994V
Aqua				986,976
Aqua				996V,316
White				997V,977V
White				997V,317V
Saddle				988,978
Saddle				998V,318V

THE PAINT CODE furnishes the key to the paint colors used on the car. A two-letter code indicates the bottom and top colors respectively.

COLOR	CODE
Ebony Black	A
Provincial White	C
Sheffield Mist	D
Jade Mist	E
Wedgewood Mist	F
Bermuda Blue	H
Fern Mist	J
Tahitian Yellow	K
Regal Mist	L
Pacific Mist	P
Aqua Mist	Q
Cashmere Beige	R
Saddle Mist	S
Holiday Red	V
Midnight Mist	W

ENGINE NUMBER

The engine unit number is stamped with a production sequence number on a machined pad located on top of the center exhaust port on the left cylinder head (394 engine), which follows the engine identification code letter. 330 engine is stamped on the right cylinder head. V-6 engine is stamped on the right front cylinder head, year (K, 1964), compression (H, standard, J, low), and production date code.

F85 STANDARD & DELUXE VISTA CRUISER (V8 ONLY)

ENGINE CODE	NO. CYL.	CID	HORSE-POWER	COMP. RATIO	CARB
KH	6	225	155	9.0:1	1 BC
KJ	6	225	NA	8.3:1	1 BC
T	8	330	230	8.75:1	2 BC
TE	8	330	NA	8.3:1	2 BC
TG	8	330	290	10.25:1	4 BC
TH	8	330	NA	8.3:1	4 BC
*	8	330	310	10.25:1	4 BC

* 442 Option

CUTLASS

ENGINE CODE	NO. CYL.	CID	HORSE-POWER	COMP. RATIO	CARB
TG	8	330	290	10.25:1	4 BC
TH	8	330	NA	8.3:1	4 BC
*	8	330	310	10.25:1	4 BC

* 442 Option

JETSTAR 88

ENGINE CODE	NO. CYL.	CID	HORSE-POWER	COMP. RATIO	CARB
TK	8	330	245	10.25:1	2 BC
TE	8	330	NA	8.3:1	2 BC
TG	8	330	290	10.25:1	4 BC
TH	8	330	NA	8.3:1	4 BC

DYNAMIC 88

ENGINE CODE	NO. CYL.	CID	HORSE-POWER	COMP. RATIO	CARB
H	8	394	280	10.25:1	2 BC
HE	8	394	NA	8.3:1	2 BC
HL	8	394	260	8.75:1	2 BC
J	8	394	330	10.25:1	4 BC

SUPER 88 & 98

ENGINE CODE	NO. CYL.	CID	HORSE-POWER	COMP. RATIO	CARB
J	8	394	330	10.25:1	4 BC
JE	8	394	NA	8.3:1	4 BC
JS	8	394	345	10.5:1	4 BC

JETSTAR 1, STARFIRE

ENGINE CODE	NO. CYL.	CID	HORSE-POWER	COMP. RATIO	CARB
JS	8	394	345	10.5:1	4 BC

1965 OLDSMOBILE

1965 OLDSMOBILE

1965 OLDSMOBILE

1965 OLDSMOBILE F-85

1965 OLDSMOBILE F-85

VEHICLE IDENTIFICATION NUMBER

OLDSMOBILE
333275M600819

Commonly referred to as the VIN NUMBER, this series of numbers and letters is stamped on a plate attached to the left front door hinge pillar.

FIRST DIGIT: Manufacturer's Symbol (3 is Oldsmobile)

SECOND THRU FIFTH DIGITS: Identify the series and body style. Refer to the Fisher Body Plate, same as style number.

SIXTH DIGIT: Identifies the model year (1965)

SEVENTH DIGIT: Identifies the assembly plant

ASSEMBLY PLANT	CODE
Lansing, MI	M
Arlington, TX	R
Atlanta, GA	D
Baltimore, MD	B
South Gate, CA	C
Fremont, CA	Z
Kansas City, MO	K
Kansas City, KS	X
Linden, NJ	E

LAST SIX DIGITS: Represent the basic production numbers

BODY NUMBER PLATE

Complete identification of each body is provided by a plate on the cowl under the hood.

OLDSMOBILE DIV. GENERAL
MOTORS CORP.
LANSING MICHIGAN

STYLE 65-33327 BODY BA 001555
TRIM 310V PAINT AC
*ACC.00

BODY BY FISHER

EXAMPLE:

65	Model Year (1965)
3	GM Division (Oldsmobile)
33	Standard F-85
27	Club Coupe
BA	Assembly Plant (Baltimore, MD)
310V	Trim Code
A	Lower Body Color
C	Upper Body Color

* Is unavailable at the time of printing

THE STYLE NUMBER follows the year code; it is a combination of the series and body style. Third digit indicates engine type, odd number is a 6-cyl., even number is an 8-cyl.

F85 STANDARD	V-6	V-8
Club Coupe	3327	*3427
Station Wagon, 2-Seat	3335	3435
4-Dr. Sedan	3369	3469
Station Wagon, 2-Seat	—	3435
Vista-Cruiser, Sta. Wgn., 2 Seat	—	3455
Vista-Cruiser, Sta. Wgn., 3 Seat	—	3465

*442 option

F85 DELUXE	V-6	V-8
Sports Coupe	3527	—
Station Wagon, 2-Seat	3535	3635
4-Dr. Sedan	3569	3669

CUTLASS V-8	CODE
Sports Coupe*	3827
Holiday Coupe*	3837
Vista-Cruiser, 2-Seat	3855
Vista-Cruiser, 3-Seat	3865
Convertible*	3867

*442 option

JETSTAR 88	CODE
Holiday Coupe	5237
Holiday Sedan	5239
Convertible	5267
Celebrity Sedan	5269

JETSTAR I	CODE
Sports Coupe	5457

DYNAMIC 88	CODE
Holiday Coupe	5637
Holiday Sedan	5639
Convertible	5667
Celebrity Sedan	5669

DELTA 88	CODE
Holiday Coupe	5837
Holiday Sedan	5839
Celebrity Sedan	5869

STARFIRE	CODE
Coupe	6657
Convertible	6667

98	CODE
Holiday Sports Coupe	8437
Holiday Sports Sedan	8439
Convertible	8467
Town Sedan	8469
Luxury Sedan	8669

THE BODY NUMBER is the production serial number of the body. The prefix letter denotes the plant in which the body was assembled.

ASSEMBLY PLANTS	CODE
F85 Bodies	
Lansing	LA
Baltimore	BA
Fremont	BF
Kansas City	KC
88 and 98 Bodies	
Lansing	LA
Doraville	BA
Kansas City	BK
Linden	BL
South Gate	BC
Arlington	BT

All 98 series were assembled at Lansing.

THE TRIM NUMBER furnishes the key to the trim color and material for each model series.

NINETY-EIGHT TRIM

COLOR	CLOTH	VINYL	LEATHER	CODE
Black				360,370L
Silver				351,361,381
Green				272L,382
Green				362,352
Blue				353, 363
Blue				373L,383
Fawn				384,354,364
Red				365,375L
Turquoise				356,366,386
White				377L

STARFIRE TRIM

COLOR	CLOTH	VINYL	LEATHER	CODE
Black				340L
Silver				341L
Blue				343L
Fawn				344L
Red				345L
White				347L

DELTA 88 TRIM

COLOR	CLOTH	VINYL	LEATHER	CODE
Black				320
Silver				321V
Green				322
Blue				323
Fawn				324
Red				325
Turquoise				326

DYNAMIC 88/JETSTAR 88 TRIM

COLOR	CLOTH	VINYL	LEATHER	CODE
Silver				971V,981
Green				992V,972
Blue				973,983,993V
Fawn				974,984,994V
Red				975V,985V,995V
Turquoise				976,986
White				977V

JETSTAR I TRIM

COLOR	CLOTH	VINYL	LEATHER	CODE
Black				310V
Blue				313V
Fawn				314V
Red				315V
White				317V

VISTA CRUISER TRIM

COLOR	CLOTH	VINYL	LEATHER	CODE
Black				360
Green				962
Blue				963,913
Fawn				964V,914
Red				965V,915
White				967V

F85 CUTLASS TRIM

COLOR	CLOTH	VINYL	LEATHER	CODE
Black				300V,940V,950V
Silver				951V
Fawn				924V
Green				302
Blue				303,943V,953V
Fawn				304,944V,954V
Red				945V,955V
White				307V,947V,957V

F85 DELUXE TRIM

COLOR	CLOTH	VINYL	LEATHER	CODE
Black				300V,940V
Green				942V,302

THE PAINT CODE furnishes the key to the paint colors used on the car. A two-letter code indicates the bottom and top colors respectively.

COLOR	CODE
Ebony Black	A
Nocturne Mist	B
Provincial White	C
Lucerne Mist	D
Royal Mist	E
Laurel Mist	H
Forest Mist	J
Ocean Mist	K
Turquoise Mist	L
Burgundy Mist	N
Target Red	R
Mohave Mist	T
Almond Beige	V
Sterling Mist	W
Saffron Yellow	Y

ENGINE NUMBER

The engine unit number on the V-6 is stamped on the right cylinder block; deck face consists of two letters (L, 1965: plus H for standard or J for low comp.) and three-number date code. V-8 engines are stamped with a production sequence code and a prefix letter to identify the engine on the front of the right cylinder head.

F85, STANDARD & DELUXE

ENGINE CODE	NO. CYL.	CID	HORSE-POWER	COMP. RATIO	CARB
LH	6	225	155	9.0:1	1 BC
LJ	6	225	NA	7.6:1	1 BC

F85, STANDARD, DELUXE & CUTLASS

ENGINE CODE	NO. CYL.	CID	HORSE-POWER	COMP. RATIO	CARB
T	8	330	250	9.0:1	2 BC
TE	8	330	NA		2 BC
TG	8	330	315	10.25:1	4 BC
TH	8	330	NA	8.3:1	4 BC
V*	8	400	345	10.25:1	4 BC

*442 option

JETSTAR 88

ENGINE CODE	NO. CYL.	CID	HORSE-POWER	COMP. RATIO	CARB
U	8	330	260	10.25:1	2 BC
UL	8	330	250	9.0:1	2 BC
UE	8	330	NA	8.3:1	2 BC
UG	8	330	315	10.25:1	4 BC
UH	8	330	NA	8.3:1	4 BC

DYNAMIC 88 & DELTA 88

ENGINE CODE	NO. CYL.	CID	HORSE-POWER	COMP. RATIO	CARB
M	8	425	310	10.25:1	2 BC
ML	8	425	300	9.0:1	2 BC
ME	8	425	NA	8.3:1	2 BC
N	8	425	360	10.25:1	4 BC
NS	8	425	370	10.5:1	4 BC

NINETY-EIGHT

ENGINE CODE	NO. CYL.	CID	HORSE-POWER	COMP. RATIO	CARB
N	8	425	360	10.25:1	4 BC
NE	8	425	NA	8.3:1	4 BC
NS	8	425	370	10.5:1	4 BC

JETSTAR 8 & STARFIRE

ENGINE CODE	NO. CYL.	CID	HORSE-POWER	COMP. RATIO	CARB
NS	8	425	370	10.5:1	4 BC

1966 OLDSMOBILE DELTA 88

1966 OLDSMOBILE F-85

1966 OLDSMOBILE JETSTAR 88

1966 OLDSMOBILE NINETY-EIGHT

1966 OLDSMOBILE STARFIRE

1966 OLDSMOBILE STARFIRE

1966 OLDSMOBILE TORONADO

1966 OLDSMOBILE TORONADO

1966 OLDSMOBILE

VEHICLE IDENTIFICATION NUMBER

OLDSMOBILE
333076M600819

Commonly referred to as the VIN NUMBER, this series of numbers and letters is stamped on a plate attached to the left front door hinge pillar.

FIRST DIGIT: Manufacturer's Symbol (3 is Oldsmobile)

SECOND THRU FIFTH DIGITS: Identify the series & body style. Refer to the Fisher Body Plate, same as style number.

SIXTH DIGIT: Identifies the model year (1966)

SEVENTH DIGIT: Identifies the assembly plant

ASSEMBLY PLANT	CODE
Lansing, MI	M
Atlanta, GA	D
South Gate, CA	C
Fremont, CA	Z
Linden, NJ	E
Kansas City, KS	X

LAST SIX DIGITS: Represent the basic production numbers

BODY NUMBER PLATE

Complete identification of each body is provided by a plate on the cowl under the hood.

OLDSMOBILE DIV. GENERAL
MOTORS CORP.
LANSING MICHIGAN

STYLE 66-38469 LAN BODY
TRIM 390 TT PAINT
*ACC.00

BODY BY FISHER

EXAMPLE:

66	Model Year (1966)
3	Division (Oldsmobile)
84	Ninety-Eight
69	Town Sedan
LAN	Assembly Plant (Lansing, MI)
390	Trim Code
A	Seat Type
T	Lower Body Color
T	Upper Body Color

* Is unavailable at the time of printing

THE STYLE NUMBER is a combination of the series and body style. Third digit indicates engine type, odd number is a 6-cyl., even number is an 8-cyl.

F85 STANDARD	V-6	V-8
Club Coupe	3307	*3407
Station Wgn., 2-Seat	3335	3435
4-Dr. Sedan	3369	3469
Vista Cruiser, Sta. Wgn., 2-Seat	—	3455
Vista Cruiser Sta. Wgn., 3-Seat	—	3465

*442 option

F85 DELUXE	V-6	V-8
Holiday Coupe	3517	*3617
Station Wagon, 2-Seat	3535	3635
Holiday Sedan	3539	3639
4-Dr. Sedan	3569	3669

*442 option

CUTLASS V-8	CODE
Sports Coupe*	3807
Holiday Coupe*	3817
Supreme	3839
Convertible*	3867
Celebrity Sedan	3869
Custom Vista Cruiser, Sta. Wgn., 2-Seat	3855
V-8 Custom Vista Cruiser Sta. Wgn., 3-Seat	3865

*442 option

JETSTAR 88	CODE
Holiday Coupe	5237
Holiday Sedan	5239
Celebrity Sedan	5269

STARFIRE	CODE
Coupe	5457

DYNAMIC 88	CODE
Holiday Coupe	5637
Holiday Sedan	5639
Celebrity Sedan	5669
Convertible	5667

DELTA 88	CODE
Holiday Coupe	5837
Holiday Sedan	5839
Convertible	5867
Celebrity Sedan	5869

98	CODE
Holiday Coupe	8437
Holiday Sedan	8439
Convertible	8467
Town Sedan	8469
Luxury Sedan	8669

TORONADO	CODE
Sport Coupe	9487
Sport Coupe Custom	9687

THE BODY NUMBER is the production serial number of the body. The prefix letter denotes the plant in which the body was assembled.

ASSEMBLY PLANTS	CODE
F85 Bodies	
Lansing	LAN
Fremont	BF
88 and 98 Bodies	
Lansing	LAN
Doraville	BA
Kansas City	BK
Linden	BL
South Gate	BC

All 98 series were assembled at Lansing.

THE TRIM NUMBER furnishes the key to interior color and material for each model series.

TORONADO TRIM

COLOR	CLOTH	VINYL	LEATHER	CODE
Black		•		50,10
Green	•	•		52
Green		•		12
Blue	•	•		53
Blue		•		13
Fawn		•		54,14
Turquoise	•	•		56
Turquoise		•		16
Bronze		•		58,18
Plum	•	•		59
Plum		•		19

NINETY-EIGHT TRIM

COLOR	CLOTH	VINYL	LEATHER	CODE
Black	•	•		390,370
Black		•		380
Silver	•	•		391,361
Green	•	•		362
Blue	•	•		393,363,373
Blue		•		383
Fawn	•	•		394,364,374
Red	•	•		395
Red		•		385
Turquoise	•	•		396,366,376
White		•		387
Bronze	•	•		378

STARFIRE TRIM

COLOR	CLOTH	VINYL	LEATHER	CODE
Black		•		330,30
Blue		•		333
Red		•		335
White		•		337
Bronze		•		38

DELTA 88 TRIM

COLOR	CLOTH	VINYL	LEATHER	CODE
Black		•		350,910
Silver	•	•		341
Green	•	•		342,352
Blue	•	•		343,353
Blue		•		913
Fawn		•		344
Fawn	•	•		354
Red	•			355,915
Turquoise	•	•		346
Turquoise		•		356
White		•		917
Bronze	•			358,918

JETSTAR 88 & DYNAMIC 88 TRIM

COLOR	CLOTH	VINYL	LEATHER	CODE
Black	•			320
Silver		•		301
Green	•	•		302,312
Blue	•	•		303
Blue	•			313,323
Fawn	•	•		304,314
Red		•		325
Turquoise	•	•		306,316
White		•		327
Bronze		•		328

VISTA CRUISER TRIM

COLOR	CLOTH	VINYL	LEATHER	CODE
Black		•		970
Blue	•	•		973
Blue		•		933
Fawn		•		974,934
Red		•		935
Turquoise	•	•		976
Turquoise		•		936
Bronze		•		978

CUTLASS TRIM

COLOR	CLOTH	VINYL	LEATHER	CODE
Black		•		980,80
Black		•		960,990
Green	•	•		972
Blue	•	•		973,903
Blue		•		983,963,993
Fawn		•		974
Fawn	•	•		944
Red		•		905,985
Red		•		965,995
Turquoise	•	•		976,906,946
White		•		987,967
Bronze		•		978,88
Bronze	•	•		908

F85 DELUXE TRIM

COLOR	CLOTH	VINYL	LEATHER	CODE
Black		•		950,990
Green		•		952
Blue		•		953,993
Fawn	•	•		944
Fawn		•		954
Red		•		955,995
Turquoise	•	•		946

F85 STANDARD TRIM

COLOR	CLOTH	VINYL	LEATHER	CODE
Blue	•	•		923
Blue		•		933
Fawn	•	•		924
Fawn		•		934
Red		•		935
Turquoise		•		936

THE PAINT CODE furnishes the key to the paint colors used on the car. A two-letter code indicates the bottom and top colors respectively.

COLOR	CODE
Ebony Black	A
Nocturne Mist	B
Provincial White	C
Lucerne Mist	D
Royal Mist	E
Trumpet Gold	G
Laurel Mist	H
Forest Mist	J
Ocean Mist	K

1966 OLDSMOBILE

Tropic Turquoise L
Autumn Bronze .... M
Burgundy Mist .... N
Target Red .... R
Champagne Mist .... S
Sierra Mist .... T
Dubonnet .... U
Almond Beige V
Silver Mist .... W
Porcelain White X
Frost Green .... Z

ENGINE NUMBER

The L-6 engine has a DATE CODE stamped on the right side of the engine block, directly to the rear of the distributor.

The date code consists of a letter, four digits and two letters. The first letter stands for source identification. The first two digits show the month and the second two digits show the day the unit was built. The last two letters show transmission or option usage.

EXAMPLE:
F Source Code (Flint) or T Source Code (Tonawanda)

07 - July - Month
12 - Day of Month
VE - Jetaway equipped

V-8 engines have the engine unit number stamped on a machined pad at the front of the right cylinder head.

V-8 engines used in F85 Series (33400, 33600 and 33800) have a "W" prefix and the starting unit number is 001001.

Engines in the Jetstar 88 Series (35200) have an "X" prefix and also have a starting number of 001001.

Engines in "442" series have a "V" prefix and have a starting unit number of 100001.

Engines used in all other series (35400 through 38600) have an "M" prefix for 2-bbl. and an "N" prefix for 4-bbl. carburetor equipped engines with a starting unit number of 500001.

F85 & F85 DELUXE

ENGINE CODE	NO. CYL.	CID	HORSE-POWER	COMP. RATIO	CARB	TRANS.
VA,VB						
VC,VC	6	250	155	8.5:1	1 BC	MAN.
VJ	6	250	NA	7.25:1	1 BC	MAN.
VE,VF,VG	6	250	155	8.5:1	1 BC	AUTO
VK	6	250	NA	7.25:1	1 BC	AUTO

F85, F85 DELUXE & VISTA CRUISER

ENGINE CODE	NO. CYL.	CID	HORSE-POWER	COMP. RATIO	CARB	TRANS.
W	8	330	250	9.0:1	2 BC	*M&A
WE	8	330	NA	8.3:1	2 BC	*M&A
WL	8	330	310	9.0:1	4 BC	*M&A
WG	8	330	320	10.25:1	4 BC	*M&A
WH	8	330	NA	8.3:1	4 BC	*M&A

CUTLASS

ENGINE CODE	NO. CYL.	CID	HORSE-POWER	COMP. RATIO	CARB	TRANS.
WG	8	330	320	10.25:1	4 BC	*M&A
WL	8	330	310	9.0:1	4 BC	*M&A
WH	8	330	NA	8.3:1	4 BC	*M&A

442

ENGINE CODE	NO. CYL.	CID	HORSE-POWER	COMP. RATIO	CARB	TRANS.
V	8	400	350	10.25:1	4 BC	*M&A
V	8	400	360	10.25:1	3/2 BC	*M&A

JETSTAR 88

ENGINE CODE	NO. CYL.	CID	HORSE-POWER	COMP. RATIO	CARB	TRANS.
X	8	330	260	10.25:1	2 BC	*M&A
XE	8	330	NA	8.3:1	2 BC	*M&A
XG	8	330	320	10.25:1	4 BC	*M&A
XH	8	330	NA	8.3:1	4 BC	*M&A
XL	8	330	250	9.0:1	2 BC	*M&A

DYNAMIC 88 & DELTA 88

ENGINE CODE	NO. CYL.	CID	HORSE-POWER	COMP. RATIO	CARB	TRANS.
M	8	425	310	10.25:1	2 BC	*M&A
ME	8	425	NA	8.3:1	2 BC	*M&A
ML	8	425	300	9.0:1	2 BC	*M&A
N	8	425	365	10.25:1	4 BC	*M&A
NS	8	425	375	10.5:1	4 BC	*M&A

NINETY EIGHT

ENGINE CODE	NO. CYL.	CID	HORSE-POWER	COMP. RATIO	CARB	TRANS.
N	8	425	365	10.25:1	4 BC	AUTO
NE	8	425	NA	8.3:1	4 BC	AUTO
NS	8	425	375	10.5:1	4 BC	AUTO

STARFIRE

ENGINE CODE	NO. CYL.	CID	HORSE-POWER	COMP. RATIO	CARB	TRANS.
NS	8	425	375	10.5:1	4 BC	*M&A

TORONADO

ENGINE CODE	NO. CYL.	CID	HORSE-POWER	COMP. RATIO	CARB	TRANS.
NT	8	425	385	10.5:1	4 BC	AUTO

* MANUAL & AUTO

1967 OLDSMOBILE

1967 OLDSMOBILE CUTLASS SUPREME

1967 OLDSMOBILE CUTLASS SUPREME

1967 OLDSMOBILE DELTA CUSTOM

1967 OLDSMOBILE DELTA 88

1967 OLDSMOBILE TORONADO

1967 OLDSMOBILE TORONADO

1967 OLDSMOBILE 4-4-2

1967 OLDSMOBILE 4-4-2

1967 OLDSMOBILE 98

1967 OLDSMOBILE DELMONT 88

1967 OLDSMOBILE

VEHICLE IDENTIFICATION NUMBER

OLDSMOBILE
333077M100001

Commonly referred to as the VIN NUMBER, this series of numbers and letters is stamped on a plate attached to the left front door hinge pillar.

FIRST DIGIT: Identifies GM Division (3 is Oldsmobile)

SECOND THRU FIFTH DIGITS: Identify the series & body style. Refer to the Fisher Body Plate, same as style number.

SIXTH DIGIT: Identifies the model year (1967)

SEVENTH DIGIT: Identifies the assembly plant

ASSEMBLY PLANT	CODE
Lansing, MI	M
Atlanta, GA	D
South Gate, CA	C
Fremont, CA	Z
Linden, NJ	E
Kansas City, KS	X

LAST SIX DIGITS: Represent the basic production numbers

BODY NUMBER PLATE

Complete identification of each body is provided by a plate on the cowl under the hood.

OLDSMOBILE DIV. GENERAL
MOTORS CORP.
LANSING MICHIGAN

STYLE 67 33307 001555 LAN
BODY
TRIM 910 AC PAINT
*ACC.00

BODY BY FISHER

EXAMPLE:

67	Model Year (1967)
3	GM Division (Oldsmobile)
33	F-85
07	Coupe
LAN	Assembly Plant (Lansing, MI)
001555	Production Sequence
910	Trim Code
A	Lower Body Color
C	Upper Body Color

* Is unavailable at the time of printing

THE STYLE NUMBER follows the year code; it is a combination of the series and body style. First digit 3, indicates Oldsmobile Division. Third digit indicates engine type, odd number is a 6-cyl., even number is an 8-cyl.

F85 STANDARD	V-6	V-8
Club Coupe	3307	3407
Station Wagon	3335	3435
Town Sedan	3369	3469
Vista Cruiser, 3-Seat	—	3465

CUTLASS	V-6	V-8
Holiday Coupe	3517	3617
Station Wagon	3535	3635
Holiday Sedan	3539	3639
Convertible	3567	3667
Town Sedan	3569	3669

CUTLASS SUPREME	CODE
Sports Coupe*+	3807
Holiday Coupe*+	3817
Holiday Sedan	3839
Vista Cruiser, Cust. 2-Seat	3855
Vista Cruiser, Cust. 3-Seat	3865
Convertible*+	3867
Town Sedan	3869

+Turnpike Cruiser option
*442 option

DELMONT 88 "330"	CODE
Holiday Sedan	5239
Town Sedan	5269
Holiday Coupe	5287

DELTA 88 CUSTOM	CODE
Holiday Sedan	5439
Holiday Coupe	5487

DELMONT 88 "425"	CODE
Holiday Sedan	5639
Convertible	5667
Town Sedan	5669
Holiday Coupe	5687

DELTA 88	CODE
Holiday Sedan	5839
Convertible	5867
Town Sedan	5869
Holiday Coupe	5887

"98"	CODE
Holiday Sedan	8439
Holiday Coupe	8457
Convertible	8467
Town Sedan	8469
Luxury Sedan*	8669

* Royale option

TORONADO	CODE
Toronado Std.	9487
Toronado Deluxe	9687

1967 OLDSMOBILE

THE BODY NUMBER is the production serial number of the body. The prefix letter denotes the plant in which the body was assembled.

ASSEMBLY PLANTS	CODE
F85 Bodies	
Lansing	LAN
Fremont	BF
Framingham	FRA
88 and 98 Bodies	
Lansing	LAN
Doraville	BA
Kansas City	BK
Linden	BL
South Gate	BC

All 98 series were assembled at Lansing.

All 94 and 96 series were built at Lansing, Michigan and have code letters "EUC" for Body Unit Number(s) prefix.

THE TRIM NUMBER furnishes the key to trim color and material for each model series.

TORONADO TRIM

COLOR	CLOTH	VINYL	LEATHER	CODE
Black	•	•		090,080
Black		•		060
Blue	•	•		063,083,043
Champagne		•		094,084,064
Garnet		•		095,085
Turquoise	•	•		086,066,046
Dubonnet	•	•		089

NINETY-EIGHT TRIM

COLOR	CLOTH	VINYL	LEATHER	CODE
Black	•	•		040,020
Black		•		030
Black	•		•	050
Pewter	•	•		041,011,021
Blue	•	•		043,013,023
Blue		•		033
Gold	•	•		045,014
Burgundy	•	•		045,025
Burgundy		•		035
Turquoise	•	•		016,046,026
Yellow		•		038

DELTA CUSTOM TRIM

COLOR	CLOTH	VINYL	LEATHER	CODE
Black	•	•		340,380
Black		•		330
Pewter	•	•		341,381
Green	•	•		382
Blue		•		343
Blue	•	•		383
Champagne		•		344,384
Burgundy		•		345
Turquoise		•		386

DELTA 88 TRIM

COLOR	CLOTH	VINYL	LEATHER	CODE
Black		•		360,370
Black	•	•		350
Pewter	•	•		361,351
Green	•	•		352,362
Blue	•	•		363,353
Blue		•		373
Champagne		•		364,354,374
Red		•		365,375
Turquoise	•	•		366,356
Yellow		•		378

DELMONT 88 TRIM

COLOR	CLOTH	VINYL	LEATHER	CODE
Black		•		310,300
Black	•	•		320
Pewter	•	•		311
Green	•	•		302
Blue	•	•		313,303
Blue		•		323
Champagne		•		304,314,324
Red		•		325
Burgundy	•	•		305,315
Turquoise	•	•		306,316
Yellow		•		328

VISTA CRUISER TRIM

COLOR	CLOTH	VINYL	LEATHER	CODE
Black		•		910
Black	•	•		990
Blue		•		993,913
Champagne		•		914,994
Burgundy		•		995
Turquoise		•		995

STATION WAGON TRIM

COLOR	CLOTH	VINYL	LEATHER	CODE
Black		•		930,910
Blue		•		933,913
Champagne		•		934,914
Red		•		935

CUTLASS SUPREME TRIM

COLOR	CLOTH	VINYL	LEATHER	CODE
Black	•	•		940,950,920
Black		•		980,970,390
Blue	•	•		943,953,923
Blue		•		973,393
Champagne		•		984,934
Gold	•	•		954
Red		•		975
Burgundy		•		945,955
Turquoise	•	•		946
Turquoise		•		956,936
Yellow		•		978

CUTLASS TRIM

COLOR	CLOTH	VINYL	LEATHER	CODE
Black	•	•		920
Black		•		930
Blue	•	•		923
Blue		•		933
Champagne		•		934
Red		•		935,965
Turquoise		•		936
Yellow		•		938

1967 OLDSMOBILE

F85 TRIM

COLOR	CLOTH	VINYL	LEATHER	CODE
Black		•		910
Blue	•	•		903
Champagne		•		914
Red	•	•		905
Red		•		915

THE PAINT CODE furnishes the key to the paint colors used on the car. A two-letter code indicates the bottom and top colors respectively.

COLOR	CODE
Ebony Black	A
Turquoise Frost	B
Provincial White	C
Crystal Blue	D
Midnight Blue	E
Bimini Blue	F
Gold	G
Aspen Green	H
Emerald Green	J
Aquamarine	K
Tahoe Turquoise	L
Burgundy Mist	N
Pewter	P
Spanish Red	R
Champagne	S
Cameo Ivory	T
Dubonnet	U
Antique Pewter	V
Sauterne	W
Garnet Red	X
Saffron	Y
Florentine Gold	Z

ENGINE NUMBER

The L-6 Engine has a DATE CODE stamped on the right side of the engine block, directly to the rear of the distributor. The date code consists of a letter, four digits and two letters. The first letter stands for source identification. The first two digits show the month and the second two digits show the day the unit was built. The last two letters show transmission or option.

V-8 engines have the engine unit number stamped on a machined pad at the front of the right cylinder head.

F85 & CUTLASS

ENGINE CODE	NO. CYL.	CID	HORSE-POWER	COMP. RATIO	CARB
FVA	6	250	155	8.5:1	1 BC
FVB	6	250	155	8.5:1	1 BC
FVD	6	250	155	8.5:1	1 BC
FVC	6	250	155	8.5:1	1 BC
FVJ	6	250	NA	7.25:1	1 BC
FVE	6	250	155	8.5:1	1 BC
FVF	6	250	155	8.5:1	1 BC
FVG	6	250	155	8.5:1	1 BC
FVH	6	250	155	8.5:1	1 BC

F85, CUTLASS & VISTA CRUISER

ENGINE CODE	NO. CYL.	CID	HORSE-POWER	COMP. RATIO	CARB
W	8	330	260	10.25:1	2 BC
WE	8	330	250	9.0:1	2 BC

F85, CUTLASS & CUTLASS SUPREME

ENGINE CODE	NO. CYL.	CID	HORSE-POWER	COMP. RATIO	CARB
WG	8	350	320	10.25:1	4 BC
WH	8	350	320	8.3:1	4 BC

4-4-2

ENGINE CODE	NO. CYL.	CID	HORSE-POWER	COMP. RATIO	CARB
VG	8	400	350	10.5:1	4 BC
*	8	400	360	10.5:1	3/2 BC

* Option

TURNPIKE CRUISER

ENGINE CODE	NO. CYL.	CID	HORSE-POWER	COMP. RATIO	CARB
V	8	400	300	10.5:1	2 BC

DELMONT 88

ENGINE CODE	NO. CYL.	CID	HORSE-POWER	COMP. RATIO	CARB
X	8	330	260	10.25:1	2 BC
XG	8	330	320	10.25:1	4 BC
XE	8	330	250	9.0:1	2 BC

DELMONT 88, DELTA 88 & DELTA 88 CUSTOM

ENGINE CODE	NO. CYL.	CID	HORSE-POWER	COMP. RATIO	CARB
P	8	425	310	10.25:1	2 BC
PL	8	425	300	9.0:1	2 BC
PE	8	425	NA	8.3:1	2 BC
R	8	425	365	10.25:1	4 BC
RS	8	425	375	10.5:1	4 BC
RE	8	425	NA	8.3:1	4 BC

NINETY-EIGHT

ENGINE CODE	NO. CYL.	CID	HORSE-POWER	COMP. RATIO	CARB
R	8	425	365	10.25:1	4 BC
RS	8	425	375	10.5:1	4 BC
RE	8	425	NA	8.3:1	4 BC

TORONADO

ENGINE CODE	NO. CYL.	CID	HORSE-POWER	COMP. RATIO	CARB
RT	8	425	385	10.5:1	4 BC

1968 OLDSMOBILE CUTLASS SUPREME

1968 OLDSMOBILE DELMONT 88

1968 OLDSMOBILE DELTA CUSTOM

1968 OLDSMOBILE DELTA 88

1968 OLDSMOBILE TORONADO

1968 OLDSMOBILE TORONADO

1968 OLDSMOBILE 4-4-2

1968 OLDSMOBILE 4-4-2

1968 OLDSMOBILE 98

1968 OLDSMOBILE 98

1968 OLDSMOBILE

VEHICLE IDENTIFICATION NUMBER

OLDSMOBILE
336778M100001

Commonly referred to as the VIN NUMBER, this series of numbers and letters is stamped on a plate riveted to the top of the instrument panel visible through the windshied.

FIRST DIGIT: Identifies GM Division (3 is Oldsmobile)

SECOND THRU FIFTH DIGITS: Identify the series & body style. Refer to the Fisher Body Plate, same as style number.

SIXTH DIGIT: Identifies the model year (1968)

SEVENTH DIGIT: Identifies the assembly plant

ASSEMBLY PLANT	CODE
Lansing, MI	M
Fremont, CA	Z
Framingham, MA	G
Kansas City, KS	X
Atlanta, GA	D
Linden, NJ	E
South Gate, CA	C
Oshawa, CAN	1

LAST SIX DIGITS: Represent the basic production numbers

BODY NUMBER PLATE

Complete identification of each body is provided by a plate on the cowl under the hood.

OLDSMOBILE DIV. GENERAL
MOTORS CORP.
LANSING MICHIGAN

STYLE 68-3277 001555 LAN
BODY
TRIM 910 AC PAINT
*ACC.00

BODY BY FISHER

EXAMPLE:

68	Model Year (1968)
3	GM Division (Oldsmobile)
32	F-85
77	Sports Coupe
LAN	Assembly Plant (Lansing, MI)
001555	Production Sequence
910	Trim Code
A	Lower Body Color
C	Upper Body Color

* Is unavailable at the time of printing

THE STYLE NUMBER follows the year code, it is a combination of the series and body style. First digit 3, indicates Oldsmobile Division. Third digit indicates engine type, odd number is a 6-cyl., even number is an 8-cyl.

F85	V-6	V-8
Town Sedan	3169	3269
Club Coupe	3177	3277

CUTLASS	V-6	V-8
Station Wagon, 2-Seat	3535	3635
Holiday Sedan	3539	3639
Convertible S	3567	3667
Town Sedan	3569	3669
Sports Coupe S	3577	3677
Holiday Coupe S	3587	3687

CUTLASS SUPREME	CODE
Holiday Sedan	4239
Town Sedan	4269
Holiday Coupe	4287

4-4-2	CODE
Convertible	4467
Sports Coupe	4477
Holiday Coupe	4487

VISTA CRUISER	CODE
2-Seat	4855
3-Seat	4865

DELMONT 88	CODE
Holiday Sedan	5439
Convertible	5467
Town Sedan	5469
Holiday Coupe	5487

DELTA 88	CODE
Holiday Sedan	6439
Town Sedan	6469
Holiday Coupe	6487

DELTA 88 CUSTOM	CODE
Custom Holiday Sedan	6639
Custom Holiday Coupe	6687

NINETY-EIGHT	CODE
Holiday Sedan	8439
Holiday Coupe	8457
Convertible	8467
Town Sedan	8469
Luxury Sedan	8669

TORONADO	CODE
Holiday Coupe	9487

1968 OLDSMOBILE

THE BODY NUMBER is the production serial number of the body. The prefix letter denotes the plant in which the body was assembled.

ASSEMBLY PLANTS	CODE
F85 Bodies	
Lansing	LAN
Fremont	BF
Framingham	FRA
Oshawa, Ontario, Can.	OS
88 and 98 Bodies	
Lansing	LAN
Atlanta	ATL
Doraville	BA
Kansas City	BK
Linden	BL
South Gate	BC

All 98 series were assembled at Lansing.

All 94 series built at Lansing, Michigan have code letters "EUC" for Body Unit Number(s) prefix.

THE TRIM NUMBER furnishes the key to trim color and material for each model series.

F85 TRIM

COLOR	CLOTH	VINYL	LEATHER	CODE
Black		•		910
Gold		•		914
Blue	•	•		903
White		•		917
Turquoise		•		916

CUTLASS TRIM

COLOR	CLOTH	VINYL	LEATHER	CODE
Gold		•		934
Gold		•		944
Blue		•		923,943
Blue	•	•		953
White				947
Parchment		•		957
Garnet		•		945
Teal		•		939,949
Turquoise	•	•		926

VISTA CRUISER, STATION WAGON & CUSTOM TRIM

COLOR	CLOTH	VINYL	LEATHER	CODE
Black		•		930,990,390
Black		•		960,970
Gold		•		934,994
Gold				394,964,974
Blue	•	•		993,393
Blue	•	•		963,973
Garnet		•		995,395
Garnet		•		975,965
Teal		•		939,999
Teal		•		399,969
Parchment		•		977
Turquoise	•	•		396,966

CUTLASS SUPREME TRIM

COLOR	CLOTH	VINYL	LEATHER	CODE
Black		•		390,960
Black		•		970,980
Gold				394
Gold				964,974
Blue				393
Blue				963,973
Parchment		•		977,987
Garnet		•		395,965,975
Teal		•		399,969,989
Turquoise	•	•		396,966

4-4-2 TRIM

COLOR	CLOTH	VINYL	LEATHER	CODE
Black		•		940,950
Gold		•		944
Blue		•		943,953
Parchment		•		947,957
Garnet		•		945
Teal		•		949

DELMONT TRIM

COLOR	CLOTH	VINYL	LEATHER	CODE
Black		•		300,320
Gold		•		304,324
Gold	•	•		344,354
Blue				302,312,323
Blue				343,353
Parchment		•		327
Parchment	•	•		357
Garnet		•		305
Garnet	•	•		315,325
Teal				309,329
Teal				349,359
Turquoise				306,316
Turquoise				346,356

DELTA TRIM

COLOR	CLOTH	VINYL	LEATHER	CODE
Black		•		340,350
Gold	•	•		344,354
Blue		•		343,353
Parchment		•		357
Teal	•	•		349,359
Turquoise	•	•		346,356

DELTA CUSTOM TRIM

COLOR	CLOTH	VINYL	LEATHER	CODE
Black		•		360,370
Gold	•	•		362
Blue	•	•		363
Parchment		•		367,377
Teal	•	•		369
Turquoise	•	•		366

NINETY-EIGHT TRIM

COLOR	CLOTH	VINYL	LEATHER	CODE
Black				010,020,030
Black				040,050,070
Gold				012,022,024
Gold				032,042,044
Blue				013,023
Blue				033,043
Parchment		•		027,037
Teal	•	•		019,029,049
Turquoise	•	•		016,026,046

1968 OLDSMOBILE

TORONADO TRIM COLOR	CLOTH	VINYL	LEATHER	CODE
Black		•		030,060
Black	•	•		080,090
Gold	•	•		062,082
Parchment		•		067
Parchment	•	•		087
Garnet	•	•		085
Teal	•	•		069,089
Turquoise	•	•		086
Buckskin				068,088,098

THE PAINT CODE furnishes the key to the paint colors used on the car. A two-letter code indicates the bottom and top colors respectively.

COLOR	CODE
Ebony Black	A
Twilight Teal	B
Provincial White	C
Sapphire Blue	D
Nocturne Blue	E
Teal Frost	F
Willow Gold	G
Ocean Turquoise	K
Teal Blue	L
Cinnamon Bronze	M
Burgundy	N
Silver Green	P
Scarlet	R
Jade Gold	S
Ivory	T
Juneau Gray	V
Silver Beige	W
Buckskin	X
Saffron	Y
Peruvian Silver	Z

ENGINE NUMBER

The L-6 Engine has a DATE CODE stamped on the right side of the engine block, directly to the rear of the distributor. The date code consists of four digits and two letters. The last two letters identify the engine.

V-8 engines have the engine unit number stamped on a machined pad at the front of the right cylinder head.

F85 & CUTLASS

ENGINE CODE	NO. CYL.	CID	HORSE-POWER	COMP. RATIO	CARB	TRANS.
VB,VA	6	250	155	8.5:1	1 BC	MAN
VF,VE	6	250	155	8.5:1	1 BC	AUTO

F85, CUTLASS & CUTLASS SUPREME

ENGINE CODE	NO. CYL.	CID	HORSE-POWER	COMP. RATIO	CARB	TRANS.
QI,QJ	8	350	250	9.0:1	2 BC	MAN
QA,QB	8	350	250	9.0:1	2 BC	AUTO
QV,QX	8	350	310	10.25:1	4 BC	MAN
QN,QP	8	350	310	10.25:1	4 BC	AUTO

4-4-2

ENGINE CODE	NO. CYL.	CID	HORSE-POWER	COMP. RATIO	CARB	TRANS.
QW,QU	8	400	350	10.5:1	4 BC	MAN
QR,QS,QT	8	400	325	10.5:1	4 BC	AUTO
QL	8	400	290	9.0:1	2 BC	AUTO
*	8	400	360	10.5:1	4 BC	*M/A

* Option W-30

VISTA-CRUISER

ENGINE CODE	NO. CYL.	CID	HORSE-POWER	COMP. RATIO	CARB	TRANS.
QI,QJ	8	350	250	9.0:1	2 BC	MAN
QV,QX	8	350	310	10.25:1	4 BC	*M/A
QL	8	400	290	9.0:1	2 BC	AUTO
QR,QS	8	400	325	10.5:1	4 BC	AUTO

DELMONT 88

ENGINE CODE	NO. CYL.	CID	HORSE-POWER	COMP. RATIO	CARB	TRANS.
TL	8	350	250	9.0:1	2 BC	MAN
TB,TD	8	350	250	9.0:1	2 BC	AUTO
TN	8	350	310	10.25:1	4 BC	AUTO
UJ	8	455	310	9.0:1	2 BC	MAN
UC,UD	8	455	310	9.0:1	2 BC	AUTO
UN,UO	8	455	365	10.25:1	4 BC	AUTO
UA,UB	8	455	320	10.25:1	2 BC	AUTO

DELTA 88 & DELTA 88 CUSTOM

ENGINE CODE	NO. CYL.	CID	HORSE-POWER	COMP. RATIO	CARB	TRANS.
UJ	8	455	310	9.0:1	2 BC	MAN
UC,UD	8	455	310	9.0:1	2 BC	AUTO
UA,UB	8	455	320	9.0:1	2 BC	AUTO
UN,UO	8	455	365	10.25:1	4 BC	AUTO

NINETY-EIGHT

ENGINE CODE	NO. CYL.	CID	HORSE-POWER	COMP. RATIO	CARB	TRANS.
UN,UO	8	455	365	10.25:1	4 BC	AUTO

TORONADO

ENGINE CODE	NO. CYL.	CID	HORSE-POWER	COMP. RATIO	CARB	TRANS.
US,UT	8	455	375	10.25:1	4 BC	AUTO
UV,UW	8	455	375	10.25:1	4 BC	AUTO
*	8	455	400	10.25:1	4 BC	AUTO

* Option

HURST/OLDS

ENGINE CODE	NO. CYL.	CID	HORSE-POWER	COMP. RATIO	CARB	TRANS.
	8	455	390	10.5:1	4 BC	

* MANUAL & AUTO

1969 OLDSMOBILE CUTLASS SUPREME

1969 OLDSMOBILE CUTLASS SUPREME

1969 OLDSMOBILE DELTA 88 CUSTOM

1969 OLDSMOBILE DELTA 88 CUSTOM

1969 OLDSMOBILE DELTA 88 ROYALE

1969 OLDSMOBILE DELTA 88 ROYALE

1969 OLDSMOBILE TORONADO

1969 OLDSMOBILE TORONADO

1969 OLDSMOBILE 4-4-2

1969 OLDSMOBILE 4-4-2

1969 OLDSMOBILE 98

1969 OLDSMOBILE 98

1969 OLDSMOBILE

VEHICLE IDENTIFICATION NUMBER

OLDSMOBILE
332779M100001

Commonly referred to as the VIN NUMBER, this series of numbers and letters is stamped on a plate riveted to top of instrument panel visible through windshied.

FIRST DIGIT: Identifies the GM Division (3 is Oldsmobile)

SECOND THRU FIFTH DIGITS: Identify the series & body style. Refer to the Fisher Body Plate, same as style number.

SIXTH DIGIT: Identifies the model year (1969)

SEVENTH DIGIT: Identifies the assembly plant

ASSEMBLY PLANT	CODE
South Gate, CA	C
Atlanta, GA	D
Linden, NJ	E
Lansing, MI	M
Kansas City, KS	X
Fremont, CA	Z
Oshawa, CAN	1

LAST SIX DIGITS: Represent the basic production numbers

BODY NUMBER PLATE

Complete identification of each body is provided by a plate on the cowl under the hood.

OLDSMOBILE DIV. GENERAL
MOTORS CORP.
LANSING MICHIGAN

STYLE 69-33277 001555 LAN
BODY

TRIM 900 10 PAINT
*ACC.00

BODY BY FISHER

EXAMPLE:

69	Model Year (1969)
3	GM Division (Oldsmobile)
32	F-85 V8
77	Sports Coupe
LAN	Assembly Plant (Lansing, MI)
001555	Production Sequence
900	Trim Code
10	Color

* Is unavailable at the time of printing

THE STYLE NUMBER follows the year code; it is a combination of the series and body style. First digit 3, indicates Oldsmobile Division. Third digit indicates engine type, odd number is a 6-cyl., even number is an 8-cyl.

F85	V-6	V-8
Sports Coupe	3177	3277

CUTLASS	V-6	V-8
Station Wagon	3535	3635
Holiday Sedan	3539	3639
Convertible S	3567	3667
Town Sedan	3569	3669
Sports Coupe S	3577	3677
Holiday Coupe S	3587	3687

CUTLASS SUPREME	CODE
Holiday Sedan	4239
Town Sedan	4269
Holiday Coupe	4287

4-4-2	CODE
Convertible	4467
Sports Coupe	4477
Holiday Coupe	4487

VISTA CRUISER	CODE
2-Seat	4855
3-Seat	4865

DELTA 88	CODE
Holiday Coupe	5437
Holiday Sedan	5439
Convertible	5467
Town Sedan	5469

DELTA 88 CUSTOM	CODE
Holiday Coupe	6437
Holiday Sedan	6439
Town Sedan	6469

DELTA 88 ROYALE	CODE
Holiday Coupe	6647

NINETY EIGHT	CODE
Holiday Sedan	8439
Holiday Coupe	8457
Convertible	8467
Town Sedan	8469
Luxury Sedan	8639
Luxury Sedan	8669

TORONADO	CODE
Deluxe Coupe	9487

THE BODY NUMBER is the production serial number of the body. The prefix letter denotes the plant in which the body was assembled.

ASSEMBLY PLANTS	CODE
F85 Bodies	
Lansing	LAN
Fremont	BF
Linden	BL
Oshawa, Ontario, CAN	OS
88 and 98 Bodies	
Lansing	LAN
Atlanta	ATL
Kansas City	BK
Linden	BL
South Gate	BC

All 98 series were assembled at Lansing.

All 94 and 96 Series were built at Lansing, Michigan and have code letters "EUC" for Body Unit Number(s) prefix.

THE TRIM NUMBER furnishes the key to trim color and material for each model series.

F85 TRIM

COLOR	CLOTH	VINYL	LEATHER	CODE
Black		•		900
Green		•		902
Blue	•	•		903
Gold		•		904
Parchment		•		907

CUTLASS TRIM

COLOR	CLOTH	VINYL	LEATHER	CODE
Black		•		910,930,942
Green				912,942
Blue		•		333,923
Blue		•		933,943
Gold		•		334,924,934
Gold	•	•		944
Red		•		935
Parchment		•		937,947

CUSTOM-VISTA CRUISER SW TRIM

COLOR	CLOTH	VINYL	LEATHER	CODE
Black		•		910,990
Green		•		912,992
Blue		•		913,993
Gold		•		914,994
Red		•		915,995

CUTLASS SUPREME TRIM

COLOR	CLOTH	VINYL	LEATHER	CODE
Black		•		950,960
Black		•		970,980
Green		•		952,962,982
Blue		•		953,963
Blue	•	•		973,983
Gold		•		954,964
Gold	•	•		974,984
Red		•		975
Parchment		•		967,977,987

4-4-2 TRIM

COLOR	CLOTH	VINYL	LEATHER	CODE
Black		•		930,940
Green		•		942
Blue		•		933,333
Blue	•	•		943
Gold		•		334,934
Gold	•	•		944
Red		•		935
Parchment		•		937,947

DELTA TRIM

COLOR	CLOTH	VINYL	LEATHER	CODE
Black		•		300,310
Black	•	•		350
Green		•		302,312
Green	•	•		342,352
Blue	•	•		303,353
Blue		•		313,323
Gold		•		304,314
Gold	•	•		324,354,344
Turquoise	•	•		306,326
Turquoise	•	•		356,346
Parchment		•		317
Parchment	•	•		357

DELTA CUSTOM TRIM

COLOR	CLOTH	VINYL	LEATHER	CODE
Black	•	•		340,350
Green	•	•		342,352
Blue		•		343,353
Gold		•		344,354
Turquoise	•	•		346,356
Parchment		•		357

DELTA ROYALE TRIM

COLOR	CLOTH	VINYL	LEATHER	CODE
Black		•		360
Black	•	•		370
Green	•	•		362
Blue	•	•		363
Gold		•		364
Gold	•	•		374
Parchment		•		367,377

NINETY-EIGHT TRIM

COLOR	CLOTH	VINYL	LEATHER	CODE
Black				030,070,380
Black				390,020,040
Black				050
Green				012,022,032
Green				042,052
Blue				013,023,033
Blue				043,053
Gold				014,024,034
Gold				044,054
Sandlewood	•	•		018,028
Sandlewood	•	•		048,058

TORONADO TRIM

COLOR	CLOTH	VINYL	LEATHER	CODE
Black		•		060
Black	•	•		080,090
Green	•	•		082
Blue	•	•		083
Gold		•		064
Gold	•	•		084
Parchment				067,087

THE PAINT CODE furnishes the key to the paint colors used on the car. A two-letter code indicates the bottom and top colors respectively.

COLOR	CODE
Ebony Black	10
Saffron	40
Cameo White	50
Trophy Blue	51
Crimson	52
Nassau Blue	53
Tahitian Turquoise	55
Glade Green	57
Meadow Green	59
Sable	61
Topaz	65
Burgundy Mist	67
Platinum	69
Aztec Gold	75
Autumn Gold	*77
Powder Blue	*80
Flamingo Silver	*81
Covert Beige	*82
Deauville Gray	*83
Chestnut Bronze	*85
Amethyst	**01
Caribbean Turquoise	**02
Nugget Gold	**03

*Exclusive Toronado colors
** Special order Toronado colors

CONVERTIBLE TOP COLOR	CODE
White	1
Black	2
Blue	3
Gold	6

VINYL ROOF COLOR	CODE
Black	2
Blue	3
Antique Parchment	5
Sable	8
Green	9
Burgundy	7

ENGINE NUMBER

The L-6 Engine has a DATE CODE stamped on the right side of the engine block, directly to the rear of the distributor. The date code consists of four digits and two letters. The last two letters identify the engine.

V-8 engines have the engine unit number stamped on a machined pad at the front of the right cylinder head.

F85, CUTLASS & CUTLASS SUPREME (V-8 ONLY)

ENGINE CODE	NO. CYL.	CID	HORSE-POWER	COMP. RATIO	CARB	TRANS.
VA,VB	6	250	155	8.5:1	1 BC	MAN
VD,VJ	6	250	NA	7.25:1	1 BC	MAN
VE,VF	6	250	155	8.5:1	1 BC	AUTO
VK,VL	6	250	NA	7.25:1	1 BC	AUTO
QI	8	350	250	9.0:1	2 BC	MAN
QA,QB	8	350	250	9.0:1	2 BC	AUTO
QJ*	8	350	250	9.0:1	2 BC	AUTO
QV	8	350	310	10.25:1	4 BC	MAN
QN,QP	8	350	310	10.25:1	4 BC	AUTO
QX**	8	350	325	10.5:1	4 BC	MAN

*Cutlass only **W-31

4-4-2

ENGINE CODE	NO. CYL.	CID	HORSE-POWER	COMP. RATIO	CARB	TRANS.
QW	8	400	350	10.5:1	4 BC	MAN
QR,QS	8	400	325	10.5:1	4 BC	AUTO
QU*	8	400	360	10.5:1	4 BC	MAN
QT*	8	400	360	10.5:1	4 BC	AUTO

*W-30

VISTA-CRUISER

ENGINE CODE	NO. CYL.	CID	HORSE-POWER	COMP. RATIO	CARB	TRANS.
QI	8	350	250	9.0:1	2 BC	MAN
QA,QB	8	350	250	9.0:1	2 BC	AUTO
QV	8	350	310	10.25:1	4 BC	MAN
QN,QP	8	350	310	10.25:1	4 BC	AUTO
QR,QS	8	400	325	10.5:1	4 BC	AUTO

DELTA 88

ENGINE CODE	NO. CYL.	CID	HORSE-POWER	COMP. RATIO	CARB	TRANS.
TL	8	350	250	9.0:1	2 BC	MAN
TB,TO,TC	8	350	250	9.0:1	2 BC	AUTO
UJ	8	455	310	9.0:1	2 BC	MAN
UC,UD	8	455	310	9.0:1	2 BC	AUTO
UN,UO	8	455	365	10.25:1	4 BC	AUTO
UL	8	455	390	10.25:1	4 BC	AUTO

DELTA 88 CUSTOM & ROYALE

ENGINE CODE	NO. CYL.	CID	HORSE-POWER	COMP. RATIO	CARB	TRANS.
UJ	8	455	310	9.0:1	2 BC	MAN
UC,UD	8	455	310	9.0:1	2BC	AUTO
UN, UO	8	455	365	10.25:1	4 BC	AUTO
UL	8	455	390	10.25:1	4 BC	AUTO

NINETY-EIGHT

ENGINE CODE	NO. CYL.	CID	HORSE-POWER	COMP. RATIO	CARB	TRANS.
UN, UO	8	455	365	10.25:1	4 BC	AUTO

TORONADO

ENGINE CODE	NO. CYL.	CID	HORSE-POWER	COMP. RATIO	CARB	TRANS.
US,UT,UV	8	455	375	10.25:1	4 BC	AUTO
UW	8	455	400	10.25:1	4 BC	AUTO

HURST/OLDS

ENGINE CODE	NO. CYL.	CID	HORSE-POWER	COMP. RATIO	CARB	TRANS.
	8	455	380	10.1:1	4 BC	

1960 PONTIAC

1960 PONTIAC

VEHICLE IDENTIFICATION NUMBER

PONTIAC
360 P1555

Commonly referred to as the VIN NUMBER, this series of numbers and letters is stamped on the plate attached to the left front door hinge pillar.

FIRST DIGIT: Identifies the series

SERIES	CODE
Catalina	21
Ventura	23
Star Chief	24
Bonneville Safari	27
Bonneville	28

SECOND AND THIRD DIGIT: Identify the model year (1960)

FOURTH DIGIT: Identifies the assembly plant

ASSEMBLY PLANT	CODE
Pontiac, MI	P
South Gate, CA	S
Linden, NJ	L
Wilmington, DE	W
Kansas City, KS	K
Doraville, GA	D
Arlington, TX	A
Euclid, OH	E

LAST FOUR DIGITS: Represent the basic production numbers

BODY NUMBER PLATE

Complete identification of each body is provided by a plate riveted to the cowl at the left of center under the hood.

PONTIAC DIV. GENERAL MOTORS CORP.
PONTIAC, MICHIGAN

STYLE 60-2337 BODY PO2337
TRIM 243 PAINT AA
*ACC. B-F-KX-JX

BODY BY FISHER

EXAMPLE:

60	Model Year (1960)
23	Series (Ventura)
37	2-Dr. Sport Coupe
P0	Assembly Plant (Pontiac, MI)
2337	Production Sequence
243	Trim
A	Lower Body Color
A	Upper Body Color

* Is unavailable at the time of printing

THE STYLE NUMBER is a combination of the year, division, series, and body style.

CATALINA	CODE
Coupe, Convertible	2167
2-Dr. Sport Coupe	2137
2-Dr. Sport Sedan, 4 Window	2111
4-Dr. Sedan, 6 Window	2119
4-Dr. Vista, 4 Window	2139
4-Dr. Safari Sta. Wgn., 2-Seat	2135
4-Dr. Safari Sta. Wgn., 3-Seat	2145

VENTURA	CODE
Sport Coupe	2337
4-Dr. Vista, 4 Window	2339

STAR CHIEF	CODE
2-Dr. Sport Sedan	2411
4-Dr. Sedan, 6 Window	2419
4-Dr. Vista, 4 Window	2439

BONNEVILLE	CODE
4-Dr. Safari Sta. Wgn., 2 Seat	2735
Coupe, Convertible	2867
2-Dr. Sport Coupe	2837
4-Dr. Vista, 4 Window	2839

THE BODY NUMBER is the production serial number of the body. The prefix letter denotes the plant in which the body was built.

ASSEMBLY PLANT	CODE
Pontiac, MI	PO
South Gate, CA	BC
Linden, NJ	BL
Wilmington, DE	BW
Kansas City, KS	BK
Doraville, GA	BA
Arlington, TX	BT
Euclid, OH	EP

THE TRIM NUMBER furnishes the key to trim color and material for each model series.

CATALINA TRIM

COLOR	CLOTH	VINYL	LEATHER	CODE
Gray	•	•		201,212,299
Gray	•	•		218
Blue	•	•		202,206,207
Green	•	•		203,208
Fawn	•	•		204,209
Maroon	•	•		210,216,222

VENTURA TRIM

COLOR	CLOTH	VINYL	LEATHER	CODE
Gray	•	•		241
Fawn	•	•		242
Maroon	•	•		243

STAR CHIEF TRIM

COLOR	CLOTH	VINYL	LEATHER	CODE
Gray	•	•		224,229
Blue	•	•		225,230,237
Green	•	•		226,231,238
Fawn	•	•		227,232,239

BONNEVILLE TRIM

COLOR	CLOTH	VINYL	LEATHER	CODE
Gray	•	•		245
Blue	•	•		246,252,260
Blue			•	266,276
Green	•	•		247,253,261
Fawn	•	•		248,254,262
Fawn			•	267,277
Maroon	•	•		249,255
Maroon			•	268,278

THE PAINT CODE furnishes the key to the paint colors used on the car. A two-letter code indicates the bottom and top colors respectively.

COLOR	CODE
Regent Black	AA
Black Pearl	BB
Shelltone Ivory	CC
Richmond Gray	DD
Newport Blue	FF
Skymist Blue	HH
Fairway Green	JJ
Berkshire Green	KK
Coronado Red	LL
Stardust Yellow	MM
Mahogany	NN
Shoreline Gold	PP
Palomino Beige	RR
Sierra Copper	SS
Caribe Turquoise	TT

ENGINE NUMBER

Along with the VIN number, the engine block is stamped with an engine production code. The code has a letter and number that identify the engine. The production code is stamped on the right front of the engine block directly below the VIN number.

CATALINA, VENTURA & STAR CHIEF

ENGINE CODE	NO. CYL.	CID	HORSE-POWER	COMP. RATIO	CARB	TRANS
A-2	8	389	215	8.6:1	2 BC	MAN
C-4	8	389	318	10.75:1	3-2 BC	MAN
P-4	8	389	NA	10.25:1	4 BC	MAN
F-4	8	389	330	10.75:1	4 BC	MAN
M-4	8	389	345	10.75:1	3-2 BC	MAN
R-2	8	389	NA	7.8:1	2 BC	MAN
G-4	8	389		8.6:1	2 BC	MAN
A-1	8	389	283	10.25:1	2 BC	AUTO
B-1	8	389	303	10.25:1	4 BC	AUTO
E-3	8	389	215	8.6:1	2 BC	AUTO
C-1	8	389	318	10.75:1	3-2 BC	AUTO
P-1	8	389	NA	10.25:1	4 BC	AUTO
F-1	8	389	330	10.75:1	4 BC	AUTO
M-1	8	389	345	10.75:1	3-2 BC	AUTO
J-1	8	389	NA	8.6:1	2 BC	AUTO
K-1	8	389	NA	7.8:1	2 BC	AUTO

BONNEVILLE

ENGINE CODE	NO. CYL.	CID	HORSE-POWER	COMP. RATIO	CARB	TRANS
B-2	8	389	281	8.6:1	4 BC	MAN
C-4	8	389	318	10.75:1	3-2 BC	MAN
P-4	8	389	NA	10.25:1	4 BC	MAN
F-4	8	389	330	10.75:1	4 BC	MAN
M-4	8	389	345	10.75:1	3-2 BC	MAN
H-4	8	389	NA	8.6:1	4 BC	MAN
B-1	8	389	303	10.25:1	4 BC	AUTO
E-3	8	389	215	8.6:1	2 BC	AUTO
C-1	8	389	318	10.75:1	3-2 BC	AUTO
P-1	8	389	NA	10.25:1	4 BC	AUTO
F-1	8	389	330	10.75:1	4 BC	AUTO
M-1	8	389	345	10.75:1	3-2 BC	AUTO
L-1	8	389	NA	8.6:1	4 BC	AUTO
N-1	8	389	NA	7.8:1	4 BC	AUTO

1961 PONTIAC

1961 PONTIAC

1961 PONTIAC TEMPEST

1961 PONTIAC TEMPEST

VEHICLE IDENTIFICATION NUMBER

PONTIAC
361P1555

Commonly referred to as the VIN NUMBER, this series of numbers and letters is stamped on the plate attached to the left front door hinge pillar.

FIRST DIGIT: Identifies the series

SERIES	CODE
Tempest	21
Catalina	23
Ventura	25
Star Chief	26
Bonneville Safari	27
Bonneville	28

SECOND AND THIRD DIGIT: Identify the model year (1961)

FOURTH DIGIT: Identifies the assembly plant

ASSEMBLY PLANT	CODE
Pontiac, MI	P
South Gate, CA	S
Linden, NJ	L
Wilmington, DE	W
Kansas City, KS	K
Doraville, GA	D
Arlington, TX	A
Euclid, OH	E

LAST FOUR DIGITS: Represent the basic production numbers

BODY NUMBER PLATE

Complete identification of each body is provided by a plate riveted to the cowl at the left of center under the hood.

PONTIAC DIV. GENERAL MOTORS CORP.
PONTIAC, MICHIGAN

STYLE 61-2337 BODY PO237
TRIM 201 PAINT AA
*ACC.B-F-KX-JX

BODY BY FISHER

EXAMPLE:

61	Model Year (1961)
23	Series (Catalina)
37	Sport Coupe
PO	Assembly Plant (Pontiac, MI)
237	Production Sequence
201	Trim Code
A	Lower Body Color
A	Upper Body Color

* Is unavailable at the time of printing

1961 PONTIAC

THE STYLE NUMBER is a combination of the year, division, series, and body style.

TEMPEST	CODE
2-Dr. Sport Coupe, Std.	2127
2-Dr. Sport Coupe, Cust.	2117
4-Dr. Sedan, 6 Window	2119
Sedan, 2 Seat	2135

CATALINA	CODE
Coupe, Convertible	2367
2-Dr. Sport Coupe	2337
2-Dr. Sport Sedan, 4 Window	2311
4-Dr. Sedan, 6 Window	2369
4-Dr. Vista, 4 Window	2339
4-Dr. Safari Sta. Wgn., 2 Seat	2335
4-Dr. Safari Sta. Wgn., 3 Seat	2345

VENTURA	CODE
Sport Coupe	2537
4-Dr. Vista, 4 Window	2539

STAR CHIEF	CODE
4-Dr. Sedan, 6 Window	2669
4-Dr. Vista, 4 Window	2639

BONNEVILLE	CODE
4-Dr. Safari Sta. Wgn., 2 Seat	2735
Coupe, Convertible	2867
2-Dr. Sport Coupe	2837
4-Dr. Vista, 4 Window	2839

THE BODY NUMBER is the production serial number of the body. The prefix letter denotes the plant in which the body was built.

ASSEMBLY PLANT	CODE
Pontiac, MI	PO
South Gate, CA	BC
Linden, NJ	BL
Wilmington, DE	BW
Kansas City, KS	BK
Doraville, GA	BA
Arlington, TX	BT
Euclid, OH	EP

THE TRIM NUMBER furnishes the key to trim color and material for each model series.

TEMPEST TRIM COLOR	CLOTH	VINYL	LEATHER	CODE
Gray		•		271,298
Blue	•	•		262
Blue		•		272
Green	•	•		263
Green		•		273
Fawn	•	•		264
Fawn		•		274
Maroon	•	•		265
Maroon		•		275

CATALINA TRIM COLOR	CLOTH	VINYL	LEATHER	CODE
Gray	•	•		201,207
Gray		•		299,218,212
Blue	•	•		202
Blue		•		219,213
Green	•	•		203,208
Green		•		220,214
Fawn	•	•		204,209
Fawn		•		221,215
Maroon	•	•		210
Maroon		•		222,216

VENTURA COLOR	CLOTH	VINYL	LEATHER	CODE
Gray		•		224
Blue		•		225
Green		•		226
Fawn		•		227
Maroon		•		228

STAR CHIEF TRIM COLOR	CLOTH	VINYL	LEATHER	CODE
Gray	•	•		229
Blue	•	•		230
Blue		•		239
Green	•	•		213
Green		•		240
Fawn		•		241
Maroon		•		242

BONNEVILLE TRIM COLOR	CLOTH	VINYL	LEATHER	CODE
Gray	•	•		243
Silver			•	253-283
Green	•	•		245
Green		•		291,250
Green			•	254-284
Fawn	•	•		246
Fawn		•		292,251
Fawn			•	255-285
Maroon	•	•		247
Maroon		•		293,252
Maroon			•	256-286
Blue	•	•		244
Blue		•		249

THE PAINT CODE furnishes the key to the paint colors used on the car. A two-letter code indicates the bottom and top colors respectively.

COLOR	CODE
Regent Black	AA
Shelltone Ivory	CC
Richmond Gray	DD
Bristol Blue	EE
Richelieu Blue	FF
Tradewind Blue	HH
Jadestone Green	JJ
Seacrest Green	KK
Coronado Red	LL
Bamboo Cream	MM
Cherrywood Bronze	NN
Rainier Turquoise	PP
Fernando Beige	RR
Dawnfire Mist	SS
Mayan Gold	TT

1961 PONTIAC

ENGINE NUMBER

Along with the VIN number, the engine block is stamped with an engine production code. The code has a letter and number that identify the engine. The production code is stamped on the right front of the engine block directly below the VIN number.

TEMPEST

ENGINE CODE	NO. CYL.	CID	HORSE-POWER	COMP. RATIO	CARB	TRANS
DS	4	195	110	8.6:1	1 BC	MAN
ZS	4	195	NA	7.6:1	1 BC	MAN
XS	4	195	155	10.25:1	4 BC	MAN
OS	4	195	120	10.25:1	1 BC	MAN
YS	8	215	155	8.8:1	2 BC	MAN
AYS	8	215	NA	7.6:1	2 BC	MAN
DA	4	195	110	8.6:1	1 BC	AUTO
ZA	4	195	NA	7.6:1	1 BC	AUTO
XA	4	195	155	10.25:1	4 BC	AUTO
OA	4	195	140	10.25:1	1 BC	AUTO
YA	8	215	155	8.8:1	2 BC	AUTO
AYA	8	215	NA	7.6:1	2 BC	AUTO

CATALINA & VENTURA

ENGINE CODE	NO. CYL.	CID	HORSE-POWER	COMP. RATIO	CARB	TRANS
A2	8	389	215	8.6:1	2 BC	MAN
C4	8	389	318	10.75:1	3-2 BC	MAN
P4	8	389	235	10.25:1	4 BC	MAN
F4	8	389	333	10.75:1	4 BC	MAN
M4	8	389	348	10.75:1	3-2 BC	MAN
R2	8	389	NA	7.8:1	2 BC	MAN
G4	8	389	215	8.6:1	2 BC	MAN
B4	8	389	235	8.6:1	4 BC	MAN
RC4	8	389	318	10.75:1	3-2 BC	MAN
RM4	8	389	348	10.75:1	3-2 BC	MAN
A1	8	389	287	10.25:1	2 BC	AUTO
B1	8	389	303	10.25:1	4 BC	AUTO
E3	8	389	230	8.6:1	2 BC	AUTO
S1	8	389	267	10.25:1	2 BC	AUTO
W3	8	389	230	8.6:1	2 BC	AUTO
T1	8	389	303	10.25:1	4 BC	AUTO
C0	8	389	318	10.175:1	3-2 BC	AUTO
P0	8	389	303	10.25:1	4 BC	AUTO
F0	8	389	333	10.75:1	4 BC	AUTO
M0	8	389	348	10.75:1	3-2 BC	AUTO
J1	8	389	NA	8.6:1	2 BC	AUTO
K1	8	389	NA	7.8:1	2 BC	AUTO
RCO	8	389	318	10.75:1	3-2 BC	AUTO
RMO	8	389	348	10.75:1	3-2 BC	AUTO
	8	389	363		3-2 BC	
	N	421	373		2-4 BC	

STAR CHIEF

ENGINE CODE	NO. CYL.	CID	HORSE-POWER	COMP. RATIO	CARB	TRANS
A2	8	389	215	8.6:1	2 BC	MAN
C4	8	389	318	10.75:1	3-2 BC	MAN
F4	8	389	333	10.75:1	4 BC	MAN
M4	8	389	348	10.75:1	3-2 BC	MAN
R2	8	389	NA	7.8:1	2 BC	MAN
G4	8	389	215	8.6:1	2 BC	MAN
B4	8	389	235	8.6:1	4 BC	MAN
RC4	8	389	318	10.75:1	3-2 BC	MAN
RM4	8	389	348	10.75:1	3-2 BC	MAN
A5	8	389	287	10.25:1	2 BC	AUTO
B5	8	389	303	10.25:1	4 BC	AUTO
E7	8	389	230	8.6:1	2 BC	AUTO
S5	8	389	267	10.25:1	2 BC	AUTO
T5	8	389	303	10.25:1	4 BC	AUTO
W7	8	389	230	8.6:1	2 BC	AUTO
I9	8	389	318	10.75:1	3-2 BC	AUTO
U9	8	389	333	10.75:1	4 BC	AUTO
V9	8	389	348	10.75:1	3-2 BC	AUTO
Q5	8	389	NA	8.6:1	2 BC	AUTO
K5	8	389	NA	7.8:1	2 BC	AUTO
R19	8	389	318	10.75:1	3-2 BC	AUTO
RV9	8	389	348	10.75:1	3-2 BC	AUTO

BONNEVILLE

ENGINE CODE	NO. CYL.	CID	HORSE-POWER	COMP. RATIO	CARB	TRANS
C4	8	389	318	10.75:1	3-2 BC	MAN
F4	8	389	333	10.75:1	4 BC	MAN
M4	8	389	348	10.75:1	3-2 BC	MAN
H4	8	389	235	8.6:1	4 BC	MAN
B4	8	389	235	8.6:1	4 BC	MAN
RC4	8	389	318	10.75:1	3-2 BC	MAN
RM4	8	389	348	10.75:1	3-2 BC	MAN
B5	8	389	303	10.25:1	4 BC	AUTO
E7	8	389	230	8.6:1	2 BC	AUTO
T5	8	389	303	10.25:1	4 BC	AUTO
W7	8	389	230	8.6:1	2 BC	AUTO
I9	8	389	318	10.75:1	3-2 BC	AUTO
U9	8	389	333	10.75:1	4 BC	AUTO
V9	8	389	348	10.75:1	3-2 BC	AUTO
L5	8	389	NA	8.6:1	4 BC	AUTO
N5	8	389	NA	7.8:1	4 BC	AUTO
R19	8	389	318	10.75:1	3-2 BC	AUTO
RV9	8	389	348	10.75:1	3-2 BC	AUTO

1962 PONTIAC

1962 PONTIAC

1962 PONTIAC TEMPEST

1962 PONTIAC TEMPEST

VEHICLE IDENTIFICATION NUMBER

PONTIAC
362P1555

Commonly referred to as the VIN NUMBER, this series of numbers and letters is stamped on the plate attached to the left front door hinge pillar.

FIRST DIGIT: Identifies the series

SERIES	CODE
Tempest	21
Catalina	23
Star Chief	26
Bonneville Safari	27
Bonneville	28
Grand Prix	29

SECOND AND THIRD DIGIT: Identify the model year (1962)

FOURTH DIGIT: Identifies the assembly plant

ASSEMBLY PLANT	CODE
Pontiac, MI	P
South Gate, CA	S
Linden, NJ	L
Wilmington, DE	W
Kansas City, KS	K
Doraville, GA	D
Arlington, TX	A

LAST FOUR DIGITS: Represent the basic production numbers

BODY NUMBER PLATE

Complete identification of each body is provided by a plate riveted to the cowl at the left of center under the hood.

PONTIAC DIV. GENERAL MOTORS CORP.
PONTIAC, MICHIGAN

STYLE 62-2347 BODY PO237
TRIM 243 PAINT AA
*ACC.B-F-KX-JX

BODY BY FISHER

EXAMPLE:

62	Model Year (1962)
23	Series (Catalina)
47	Sport Coupe
PO	Assembly Plant (Pontiac, MI)
237	Production Sequence
243	Trim
A	Lower Body Color
A	Upper Body Color

* Is unavailable at the time of printing

THE STYLE NUMBER is a combination of the year, division, series and body style.

TEMPEST	CODE
2-Dr. Sport Coupe, Std.	2127
2-Dr. Sport Coupe, Cust.*	2117
4-Dr. Sedan, 6 Window,	2119
2 Seat	2135
Convertible*	2167

* Option LeMans

CATALINA	CODE
Coupe, Convertible	2367
2-Dr. Sport Coupe	2347
2-Dr. Sport Sedan, 4 Window	2311
4-Dr. Sedan, 6 Window	2369
4-Dr. Vista, 4 Window	2339
4-Dr. Safari Sta. Wgn., 2 Seat	2335
4-Dr. Safari Sta. Wgn., 3 Seat	2345

* Option Ventura

STAR CHIEF	CODE
4-Dr. Sedan, 6 Window	2669
4-Dr. Vista, 4 Window	2639

BONNEVILLE	CODE
4-Dr. Safari Sta. Wgn., 2 Seat	2735
Coupe, Convertible	2867
2-Dr. Sport Coupe	2847
4-Dr. Vista, 4 Window	2839

GRAND PRIX	CODE
2-Dr. Sport Coupe	2947

THE BODY NUMBER is the production serial number of the body. The prefix letter denotes the plant in which the body was built.

ASSEMBLY PLANT	CODE
Pontiac, MI	PO
South Gate, CA	BC
Linden, NJ	BL
Wilmington, DE	BW
Kansas City, KS	BK
Doraville, GA	BA
Arlington, TX	BT
Euclid, OH	EP

THE TRIM NUMBER furnishes the key to trim color and material for each model series.

TEMPEST TRIM COLOR	CLOTH	VINYL	LEATHER	CODE
Blue	•	•		201
Blue		•		206,215
Fawn	•	•		204
Fawn		•		209,216
Maroon	•	•		205
Maroon		•		210,218
Aqua		•		207
Green		•		208
Black		•		211
Red		•		213
Saddle		•		214
Gray		•		217

CATALINA TRIM COLOR	CLOTH	VINYL	LEATHER	CODE
Blue	•	•		221,226
Blue		•		231,241,236
Aqua	•	•		222,227
Aqua		•		232,242,237
Green	•	•		223,228
Green		•		233,243
Fawn	•	•		224,229
Fawn		•		234,244,239
Maroon	•	•		230
Maroon		•		235,245,240
Gray		•		299

STAR CHIEF TRIM COLOR	CLOTH	VINYL	LEATHER	CODE
Blue	•	•		246
Blue		•		251
Aqua	•	•		247
Aqua		•		252
Fawn	•	•		249
Fawn		•		254
Maroon		•		255

BONNEVILLE TRIM COLOR	CLOTH	VINYL	LEATHER	CODE
Blue	•			256
Aqua	•			257
Aqua			•	267-277
Green	•			258
Fawn	•			259,260
Fawn			•	267-278
Silver			•	266-276
Maroon			•	269-279

GRAND PRIX TRIM COLOR	CLOTH	VINYL	LEATHER	CODE
Fawn		•		281
Black		•		289
Red		•		296
Saddle		•		297
Blue		•		298

THE PAINT CODE furnishes the key to the paint colors used on the car. A two-letter code indicates the bottom and top colors respectively. Two-Tone color combinations are made-up of the first letter of each basic color.

COLOR	CODE
Starlight Black	AA
Cameo Ivory	CC
Silvermist Gray	DD
Ensign Blue	EE
Yorktown Blue	FF
Kimberley Blue	HH
Silverleaf Green	JJ
Aquamarine	PP
Seafoam Aqua	QQ
Caravan Gold	TT
Yuma Beige	RR
Burgundy	NN
Belmar Red	LL
Mandalay Red	VV
Bamboo Cream	MM

1962 PONTIAC

ENGINE NUMBER

Along with the VIN number, the engine block is stamped with an engine production code. The production code is stamped on the right front of the engine block directly below the VIN number.

TEMPEST

ENGINE CODE	NO. CYL.	CID	HORSE-POWER	COMP. RATIO	CARB	TRANS
832	4	195	NA	9.93:1	1 BC	MAN
842	4	195	NA	9.95:1	4 BC	MAN
892	4	195	110	8.6:1	1 BC	MAN
88Z	4	195	NA	7.6:1	1 BC	MAN
87Z	4	195	166	10.25:1	4 BC	MAN
86Z	4	195	120	10.25:1	1 BC	MAN
85Z	4	195	110	8.6:1	1 BC	MAN
79Y	4	195	115	8.6:1	1 BC	AUTO
78Y	4	195	NA	7.6:1	1 BC	AUTO
77Y	4	195	166	10.25:1	4 BC	AUTO
76Y	4	195	140	10.25:1	1 BC	AUTO
97Y	8	215	185	10.25:1	4 BC	AUTO
91Z	8	215	185	10.25:1	4 BC	AUTO
96Y	8	215	NA	8.8:1	4 BC	AUTO

CATALINA

ENGINE CODE	NO. CYL.	CID	HORSE-POWER	COMP. RATIO	CARB	TRANS
O1A	8	389	215	8.6:1	2 BC	MAN
O2B	8	389	235	8.6:1	4 BC	MAN
O3B	8	389	215	8.6:1	2 BC	MAN
O5A	8	389	NA	7.8:1	2 BC	MAN
O8B	8	389	333	10.75:1	4 BC	MAN
10B	8	389	318	10.75:1	3-2 BC	MAN
11B	8	389	348	10.75:1	3-2 BC	MAN
15H	8	389	267	10.25:1	2 BC	MAN
16K	8	389	303	10.25:1	4 BC	AUTO
17H	8	389	267	10.25:1	2 BC	AUTO
18K	8	389	303	10.25:1	4 BC	AUTO
20L	8	389	230	8.6:1	2 BC	AUTO
21L	8	389	230	8.6:1	2 BC	AUTO
23H	8	389	NA	7.8:1	2 BC	AUTO
25J	8	389	333	10.75:1	4 BC	AUTO
27J	8	389	318	10.75:1	3-2 BC	AUTO
28J	8	389	348	10.75:1	3-2 BC	AUTO
39N	8	389	303	10.25:1	4 BC	AUTO
	8	421	405	11.0:1	2-4 BC	MAN

STARCHIEF

ENGINE CODE	NO. CYL.	CID	HORSE-POWER	COMP. RATIO	CARB	TRANS
O1A	8	389	215	8.6:1	2 BC	MAN
O2B	8	389	235	8.6:1	4 BC	MAN
O3B	8	389	215	8.6:1	2 BC	MAN
O5A	8	389	NA	7.8:1	2 BC	MAN
O8B	8	389	333	10.75:1	4 BC	MAN
10B	8	389	318	10.75:1	3-2 BC	MAN
11B	8	389	348	10.75:1	3-2 BC	MAN
35M	8	389	283	10.25:1	2 BC	AUTO
36P	8	389	303	10.25:1	4 BC	AUTO
37M	8	389	283	10.25:1	2 BC	AUTO
38P	8	389	303	10.25:1	4 BC	AUTO
39N	8	389	303	10.25:1	4 BC	AUTO
40R	8	389	230	8.6;1	2 BC	AUTO
41R	8	389	230	8.6:1	2 BC	AUTO
44M	8	389	NA	7.8:1	2 BC	AUTO
47N	8	389	333	10.75:1	4 BC	AUTO
49N	8	389	318	10.75:1	3-2 BC	AUTO
50N	8	389	348	10.75:1	3-2 BC	AUTO

BONNEVILLE

ENGINE CODE	NO. CYL.	CID	HORSE-POWER	COMP. RATIO	CARB	TRANS
O2B	8	389	235	8.6:1	4 BC	MAN
O4B	8	389	235	8.6:1	4 BC	MAN
O8B	8	389	333	10.75:1	4 BC	MAN
10B	8	389	318	10.75:1	3-2 BC	MAN
11B	8	389	348	10.75:1	3-2 BC	MAN
36P	8	389	303	10.25:1	4 BC	AUTO
38P	8	389	303	10.25:1	4 BC	AUTO
39N	8	389	303	10.25:1	4 BC	AUTO
40R	8	389	230	8.6:1	2 BC	AUTO
41R	8	389	230	8.6:1	2 BC	AUTO
45P	8	389	NA	7.8:1	4 BC	AUTO
47N	8	389	333	10.75:1	4 BC	AUTO
49N	8	389	318	10.75:1	3-2 BC	AUTO
50N	8	389	348	10.75:1	3-2 BC	AUTO

GRAND PRIX

ENGINE CODE	NO. CYL.	CID	HORSE-POWER	COMP. RATIO	CARB	TRANS
O6B	8	389	303	10.25:1	4 BC	MAN
O8B	8	389	333	10.75:1	4 BC	MAN
10B	8	389	318	10.75:1	3-2 BC	MAN
11B	8	389	348	10.75:1	3-2 BC	MAN
16KJ	8	389	303	10.25:1	4 BC	AUTO
18K	8	389	303	10.25:1	4 BC	AUTO
20L	8	389	230	8.6:1	2 BC	AUTO
21L	8	389	230	8.6:1	2 BC	AUTO
23H	8	389	NA	7.8:1	2 BC	AUTO
25J	8	389	333	10.75:1	4 BC	AUTO
27J	8	389	318	10.75:1	3-2 BC	AUTO
28J	8	389	348	10.75:1	3-2 BC	AUTO
	8	421	405	11.0:1	2-4 BC	MAN

1963 PONTIAC

1963 PONTIAC

1963 PONTIAC TEMPEST

1963 PONTIAC TEMPEST

VEHICLE IDENTIFICATION NUMBER

PONTIAC
363P1555

Commonly referred to as the VIN NUMBER, this series of numbers and letters is stamped on the plate attached to the left front door hinge pillar.

FIRST DIGIT: Identifies the series

SERIES	CODE
Tempest	21
Le Mans	22
Catalina	23
Star Chief	26
Bonneville	28
Grand Prix	29

SECOND AND THIRD DIGIT: Identify the model year (1963)

FOURTH DIGIT: Identifies the assembly plant

ASSEMBLY PLANT	CODE
Pontiac, MI	P
South Gate, CA	S
Linden, NJ	L
Wilmington, DE	W
Kansas City, KS	K
Doraville, GA	D
Arlington, TX	A

LAST FOUR DIGITS: Represent the basic production numbers

BODY NUMBER PLATE

Complete identification of each body is provided by a plate riveted to the cowl at the left of center under the hood.

PONTIAC DIV. GENERAL MOTORS CORP.
PONTIAC, MICHIGAN

STYLE 63-2347 BODY PO237
TRIM 243 PAINT AA
*ACC.B-F-KX-JX

BODY BY FISHER

EXAMPLE:

63	Model Year (1963)
23	Series (Catalina)
47	Sport Coupe
PO	Assembly Plant (Pontiac, MI)
237	Production Sequence
243	Trim
A	Lower Body Color
A	Upper Body Color

* Is unavailable at the time of printing

THE STYLE NUMBER is a combination of the year, division, series and body style.

TEMPEST	CODE
2-Dr. Sport Coupe, Std.	2127
2-Dr. Sport Coupe, Cust.	2117
4-Dr. Sedan, 6 Window,	2119
2 Seat	2135
Convertible	2167

LE MANS	CODE
2-Dr. Sport Coupe	2217
Convertible	2267

CATALINA	CODE
Coupe, Convertible	2367
2-Dr. Sport Coupe	2347
2-Dr. Sport Sedan, 4 Window	2311
4-Dr. Sedan, 6 Window	2369
4-Dr. Vista, 4 Window	2339
4-Dr. Safari Sta. Wgn., 2 Seat	2335
4-Dr. Safari Sta. Wgn., 3 Seat	2345

STAR CHIEF	CODE
4-Dr. Sedan, 6 Window	2669
4-Dr. Vista, 4 Window	2639

BONNEVILLE	CODE
4-Dr. Safari Sta. Wgn., 2 Seat	2835
Coupe, Convertible	2867
2-Dr. Sport Coupe	2847
4-Dr. Vista, 4 Window	2839

GRAND PRIX	CODE
2-Dr. Sport Coupe	2957

THE BODY NUMBER is the production serial number of the body. The prefix letter denotes the plant in which the body was built.

ASSEMBLY PLANT	CODE
Pontiac, MI	PO
South Gate, CA	BC
Linden, NJ	BL
Wilmington, DE	BW
Kansas City, KS	BK
Doraville, GA	BA
Arlington, TX	BT
Euclid, OH	EP

THE TRIM NUMBER furnishes the key to interior color and material.

TEMPEST TRIM COLOR	CLOTH	VINYL	LEATHER	CODE
Blue	•	•		201
Blue		•		208
Aqua	•	•		202
Aqua		•		209
Fawn	•	•		204
Fawn		•		211
Maroon	•	•		205
Maroon		•		212,207
Black		•		213
Silver		•		206
Green		•		210

CATALINA TRIM COLOR	CLOTH	VINYL	LEATHER	CODE
Blue	•	•		228,233
Blue		•		248,243
Blue		•		238-294
Aqua	•	•		229,234
Aqua		•		249,244
Aqua		•		239-295
Fawn	•	•		231,236
Fawn		•		241,246,251
Maroon	•	•		237,232
Maroon		•		252,247
Maroon		•		242-296
Green		•		230,245,240
Gray		•		299

STAR CHIEF TRIM COLOR	CLOTH	VINYL	LEATHER	CODE
Blue	•	•		253
Blue		•		257
Aqua	•	•		254
Aqua		•		258
Fawn	•	•		255
Fawn		•		259
Maroon	•	•		256
Maroon		•		260

BONNEVILLE TRIM COLOR	CLOTH	VINYL	LEATHER	CODE
Blue	•	•		261
Blue		•		279
Blue		•		219-267
Blue			•	272-276
Aqua	•	•		262
Aqua		•		220-268
Aqua			•	273-277
Fawn	•	•		264
Fawn		•		280
Fawn		•		221-269
Fawn		•		223-289
Fawn		•		224-290
Fawn		•		225-291
Fawn			•	292-293
Maroon	•	•		265
Maroon		•		281
Maroon		•		222-270
Maroon			•	274-278
Black			•	271-275
Black		•		218-266

GRAND PRIX TRIM COLOR	CLOTH	VINYL	LEATHER	CODE
Black		•		282
Fawn		•		283,284,285
Red		•		286
Aqua		•		287
Blue		•		288

THE PAINT CODE furnishes the key to the paint colors used on the car. A two letter code indicates the bottom and top colors respectively.

COLOR	CODE
Starlight Black	A
Cameo Ivory	C
Silvermist Gray	D
Yorktown Blue	F
Kimberley Blue	H
Silverleaf Green	J
Marimba Red	L
Cordovan	K
Aquamarine	P
Marlin Aqua	Q
Yuma Beige	R
Saddle Bronze	S
Caravan Gold	T
Grenadier Red	V
Nocturne Blue	W

ENGINE NUMBER

Along with the VIN number the engine block is stamped with an engine production code. The production code is stamped on the engine block directly below the VIN number.

TEMPEST

ENGINE CODE	NO. CYL.	CID	HORSE-POWER	COMP. RATIO	CARB	TRANS
89Z	4	195	115	8.6:1	1 BC	MAN
88Z	4	195	NA	7.6:1	1 BC	MAN
87Z	4	195	166	10.0:1	4 BC	MAN
86Z	4	195	120	10.0:1	1 BC	MAN
85Z	4	195	115	8.6:1	1 BC	MAN
84Z	4	195	166	10.0:1	4 BC	MAN
83Z	4	195	120	10.0:1	1 BC	MAN
82Z	4	195	NA	7.6:1	1 BC	MAN
79Y	4	195	115	8.6:1	1 BC	AUTO
78Y	4	195	NA	7.6:1	1 BC	AUTO
77Y	4	195	166	10.0:1	4 BC	AUTO
76Y	4	195	140	10.0:1	1 BC	AUTO
68X	8	326	260	8.6:1	2 BC	MAN
71X	8	326	260	10.25:1	2 BC	MAN
600	8	326	260	10.25:1	2 BC	AUTO
690	8	326	260	8.6:1	2 BC	AUTO
70X	8	326	280	10.25:1	4 BC	MAN
590	8	326	280	10.25:1	4 BC	AUTO

CATALINA

ENGINE CODE	NO. CYL.	CID	HORSE-POWER	COMP. RATIO	CARB	TRANS
O1A	8	389	215	8.6:1	2 BC	MAN
O2B	8	389	235	8.6:1	4 BC	MAN
O3B	8	389	215	8.6:1	2 BC	MAN
O4B	8	389	235	8.6:1	4 BC	MAN
O5A	8	389	NA	7.6:1	2 BC	MAN
O6B	8	389	303	10.25:1	4 BC	MAN
O8B	8	421	353	10.75:1	4 BC	MAN
11B	8	421	370	10.75:1	3-2 BC	MAN
12-5	8	421	405	11.5:1	4 BC	MAN
13-5	8	421	420	11.5:1	2-4 BC	MAN
O7B	8	389	313	10.25:1	2-3 BC	MAN
22B	8	421	320	10.25:1	4 BC	MAN
15H	8	389	267	10.25:1	2 BC	AUTO
16K	8	389	303	10.25:1	4 BC	AUTO
17H	8	389	267	10.25:1	2 BC	AUTO
18K	8	389	303	10.25:1	4 BC	AUTO
20L	8	389	230	8.6:1	2 BC	AUTO
21L	8	389	230	8.6:1	2 BC	AUTO
23H	8	389	NA	7.6:1	2 BC	AUTO
25G	8	421	353	10.75:1	4 BC	AUTO
28G	8	421	370	10.75:1	3-2 BC	AUTO
26-6	8	389	313	10.25:1	3-2 BC	AUTO
34J	8	421	320	10.25:1	4 BC	AUTO

STAR CHIEF

ENGINE CODE	NO. CYL.	CID	HORSE-POWER	COMP. RATIO	CARB	TRANS
O1A	8	389	215	8.6:1	2 BC	MAN
O2B	8	389	235	8.6:1	4 BC	MAN
O3B	8	389	215	8.6:1	2 BC	MAN
O4B	8	389	235	8.6:1	4 BC	MAN
O5A	8	389	NA	7.6:1	2 BC	MAN
O6B	8	389	303	10.25:1	4 BC	MAN
O8B	8	421	353	10.75:1	4 BC	MAN
11B	8	421		10.75:1	3-2 BC	MAN
O7B	8	389	313	10.25:1	3-2 BC	MAN
22B	8	421	320	10.25:1	4 BC	MAN
35M	8	389	283	10.25:1	2 BC	AUTO
36P	8	389	303	10.25:1	4 BC	AUTO
37M	8	389	283	10.25:1	2 BC	AUTO
38P	8	389	303	10.25:1	4 BC	AUTO
40R	8	389	230	8.6:1	2 BC	AUTO
41R	8	389	230	8.6:1	2 BC	AUTO
43N	8	421	320	8.6:1	4 BC	AUTO
44M	8	389	NA	7.6:1	2 BC	AUTO
47Q	8	421	353	10.75:1	4 BC	AUTO
50Q	8	421	370	10.75:1	3-2 BC	AUTO
48N	8	389	313	10.25:1	3-2 BC	AUTO

BONNEVILLE

ENGINE CODE	NO. CYL.	CID	HORSE-POWER	COMP. RATIO	CARB	TRANS
O2B	8	389	235	8.6:1	4 BC	MAN
O4B	8	389	235	8.6:1	4 BC	MAN
O6B	8	389	303	10.25:1	4 BC	MAN
O8B	8	421	353	10.75:1	4 BC	MAN
11B	8	421	370	10.75:1	3-2 BC	MAN
O7B	8	389	313	10.25:1	3-2 BC	MAN
22B	8	421	320	10.25:1	4 BC	MAN
36P	8	389	303	10.25:1	4 BC	AUTO
38P	8	389	303	10.25:1	4 BC	AUTO
40R	8	389	230	8.6:1	2 BC	AUTO
41R	8	389	230	8.6:1	2 BC	AUTO
43N	8	421	320	8.6:1	4 BC	AUTO
45P	8	389	NA	7.6:1	4 BC	AUTO
47Q	8	421	353	10.75:1	4 BC	AUTO
50Q	8	421	370	10.75:1	3-2 BC	AUTO
48N	8	389	313	10.25:1	3-2 BC	AUTO

GRAND PRIX

ENGINE CODE	NO. CYL.	CID	HORSE-POWER	COMP. RATIO	CARB	TRANS
O6B	8	389	303	10.25:1	4 BC	MAN
O8B	8	421	353	10.75:1	4 BC	MAN
11B	8	421	370	10.75:1	3-2 BC	MAN
12-5	8	421	405	11.5:1	4 BC	MAN
13-5	8	421	420	11.5:1	2-4 BC	MAN
O7B	8	389	313	10.25:1	3-2 BC	MAN
22B	8	421	320	10.25:1	4 BC	MAN
16K	8	389	303	10.25:1	4 BC	AUTO
18K	8	389	303	10.25:1	4 BC	AUTO
20L	8	389	230	8.6:1	2 BC	AUTO
25G	8	421	353	10.75:1	4 BC	AUTO
28G	8	421	370	10.75:1	3-2 BC	AUTO
26-6	8	389	313	10.25:1	3-2 BC	AUTO
34J	8	421	320	10.25:1	4 BC	AUTO

1964 PONTIAC

1964 PONTIAC

1964 PONTIAC GRAND PRIX

1964 PONTIAC GRAND PRIX

1964 PONTIAC TEMPEST

1964 PONTIAC TEMPEST

VEHICLE IDENTIFICATION NUMBER

PONTIAC
834P1001

Commonly referred to as the VIN NUMBER, this series of numbers and letters is stamped on the plate attached to the left front door hinge pillar.

THE FIRST DIGIT: Identifies the engine type: 6 - 6 cylinder; 8 - 8 cylinder

THE SECOND DIGIT: Identifies the series

SERIES	CODE
Tempest	0
Tempest Custom	1
Le Mans	2
Catalina	3
Star Chief	6
Bonneville	8
Grand Prix	9

THE THIRD DIGIT: Identifies the model year (1964)

THE FOURTH DIGIT: Identifies the assembly plant

ASSEMBLY PLANT	CODE
Pontiac, MI	P
Linden, NJ*	L
South Gate, CA*	S
Kansas City, KS*	K
Doraville, GA*	D
Fremont, OH*	F
Arlington, TX*	A
Baltimore, MD**	B
Kansas City, KS**	M

* Buick, Oldsmobile & Pontiac
** Chevrolet

LAST FOUR DIGITS: Represent the basic production numbers

BODY NUMBER PLATE

Complete identification of each body is provided by a plate riveted to the cowl at the left of center under the hood.

PONTIAC DIV. GENERAL MOTORS CORP.
PONTIAC, MICHIGAN

STYLE 64-2311 BODY PO237
TRIM 221 PAINT AA
*ACC. 0-0-00-00

BODY BY FISHER

EXAMPLE:

64	Model Year (1964)
23	Series (Catalina)
11	Sport Coupe
PO	Assembly Plant (Pontiac, MI)
237	Production Sequence
221	Trim
A	Lower Body Color
A	Upper Body Color

* Is unavailable at the time of printing

THE STYLE NUMBER is a combination of the year, division, series and body style.

TEMPEST	CODE
4-Dr. Sedan	2069
2-Dr. Sport Coupe	2027
Safari Sta. Wgn., 2-Seat	2035

TEMPEST CUSTOM	CODE
2-Dr. Sport Coupe, Std.	2127
4-Dr. Sedan	2169
Safari Sta. Wgn., 2-Seat	2135
Convertible	2167

LE MANS	CODE
2-Dr. Sport Coupe	2227
Hardtop Sports Coupe	2237
Convertible	2267

* Option GTO

CATALINA	CODE
Coupe, Convertible	2367
2-Dr. Sport Coupe	2347
2-Dr. Sport Sedan, 4 Window	2311
4-Dr. Sedan, 6 Window	2369
4-Dr. Vista, 4 Window	2339
4-Dr. Safari Sta. Wgn., 2 Seat	2335
4-Dr. Safari Sta. Wgn., 3 Seat	2345

* Option Ventura

STAR CHIEF	CODE
4-Dr. Sedan, 6 Window	2669
4-Dr. Vista, 4 Window	2639

BONNEVILLE	CODE
4-Dr. Safari Sta. Wgn., 2 Seat	2835
Coupe, Convertible	2867
2-Dr. Sport Coupe	2847
4-Dr. Vista, 4 Window	2839

* Option Brougham

GRAND PRIX	CODE
2-Dr. Sport Coupe	2957

THE BODY NUMBER is the production serial number of the body. The prefix letter denotes the plant in which the body was built.

ASSEMBLY PLANT	CODE
Pontiac, MI	PO
South Gate, CA	BC
Linden, NJ	BL
Wilmington, DE	BW
Kansas City, KS	BK
Doraville, GA	BA
Arlington, TX	BT
Euclid, OH	EP

THE TRIM NUMBER furnishes the key to interior color and material for each model series.

TEMPEST TRIM

COLOR	CLOTH	VINYL	LEATHER	CODE
Blue	•	•		201
Aqua	•	•		202
Saddle	•	•		203
Saddle		•		206
Red		•		207
Maroon	•	•		204
Gray		•		205

TEMPEST CUSTOM TRIM

COLOR	CLOTH	VINYL	LEATHER	CODE
Blue		•		208
Aqua		•		209
Maroon		•		212
Saddle		•		211
Olive		•		210

CATALINA TRIM

COLOR	CLOTH	VINYL	LEATHER	CODE
Blue	•	•		221,286
Blue		•		231,226
Blue		•		236,276
Aqua	•	•		222,288
Aqua		•		232,227,237
Maroon	•	•		225
Olive	•	•		291,223
Olive		•		233
Saddle	•	•		297,224
Saddle		•		234,229,238
Maroon	•	•		298
Maroon		•		235,230
Silver		•		299
Black		•		258-282,240
Red		•		280,239

STAR CHIEF TRIM

COLOR	CLOTH	VINYL	LEATHER	CODE
Blue	•	•		241
Blue		•		245
Aqua	•	•		242
Aqua		•		246
Fawn	•	•		243
Fawn		•		247
Maroon	•	•		244
Maroon		•		248

BONNEVILLE TRIM

COLOR	CLOTH	VINYL	LEATHER	CODE
Blue	•	•		249
Blue		•		289,254,284
Blue			•	261-289
Aqua	•	•		250
Aqua		•		255
Aqua			•	262
Black	•	•		251,293
Black		•		253,283
Black			•	260-290
Rose	•	•		252
Rose		•		281,257
Saddle		•		279,256
Saddle			•	266-295
Parchment		•		267,259-292
Parchment			•	264-265-294
Red		•		287
Red			•	296
Maroon			•	263

GRAND PRIX TRIM

COLOR	CLOTH	VINYL	LEATHER	CODE
Black		•		268
Blue		•		269
Saddle		•		270
Aqua		•		271
Red		•		272
Parchment		•		273-274-275

THE PAINT CODE furnishes the key to the paint colors used on the car. A two-letter code indicates the bottom and top colors respectively.

COLOR	CODE
Starlight Black	A
Cameo Ivory	C
Silvermist Gray	D
Yorktown Blue	F
Skyline Blue	H
Pinehurst Green	J
Marimba Red	L
Sunfire Red	N
Aquamarine	P
Gulfstream Aqua	Q
Alamo Beige	R
Saddle Bronze	S
Singapore Gold	T
Grenadier Red	V
Nocturne Blue	W

1964 PONTIAC

ENGINE NUMBER

Along with the VIN number, the engine block is stamped with an engine production code. The production code is stamped on the engine block directly below the VIN number.

TEMPEST, LE MANS

ENGINE CODE	NO. CYL.	CID	HORSE-POWER	COMP. RATIO	CARB	TRANS
80Z	6	215	140	8.6:1	1 BC	MAN
81Z	6	215	140	8.6:1	1 BC	MAN
82Z	6	215	NA	8.9:1	1 BC	MAN
84Z	6	215	140	8.9:1	1 BC	MAN
85Z	6	215	140	8.9:1	1 BC	MAN
87Z	6	215	NA	8.9:1	1 BC	AUTO
88Y	6	215	140	8.9:1	1 BC	AUTO
89Y	6	215	140	8.9:1	1 BC	AUTO
83Y	6	215	140	8.9:1	1 BC	AUTO
92X	8	326	250	8.6:1	2 BC	MAN
94X	8	326	280	10.5:1	4 BC	MAN
960	8	326	250	8.6:1	2 BC	AUTO
970	8	326	280	10.5:1	4 BC	AUTO
76X	8	389	348	10.75:1	3-2 BC	MAN
77J	8	389	348	10.75:1	3-2 BC	AUTO
78X	8	389	325	10.75:1	4 BC	MAN
79J	8	389	325	10.75:1	4 BC	AUTO

CATALINA

ENGINE CODE	NO. CYL.	CID	HORSE-POWER	COMP. RATIO	CARB	TRANS
O1A	8	389	215	8.6:1	2 BC	MAN
02B	8	389	215	8.6:1	2 BC	MAN
03A	8	389	239	7.9:1	2 BC	MAN
23B	8	389	306	10.5:1	4 BC	MAN
32B	8	389	330	10.75:1	3-2 BC	MAN
35B	8	421	320	10.5:1	4 BC	MAN
44B	8	421	350	10.75:1	3-2 BC	MAN
45B	8	421	370	10.75:1	3-2 BC	MAN
10A	8	389	283	10.5:1	2 BC	MAN
O4L	8	389	230	8.6:1	2 BC	AUTO
O5L	8	389	230	8.6:1	2 BC	AUTO
46G	8	421	370	10.75:1	3-2 BC	AUTO
47S	8	421	350	10.75:1	3-2 BC	AUTO
25K	8	389	303	10.5:1	4 BC	AUTO
26K	8	389	303	10.5:1	4 BC	AUTO
11H	8	389	267	10.5:1	2 BC	AUTO
12H	8	389	267	10.5:1	2 BC	AUTO
13H	8	389	240	7.9:1	2 BC	AUTO
38S	8	421	320	10.5:1	4 BC	AUTO
336	8	389	330	10.75:1	3-2 BC	AUTO

STARCHIEF

ENGINE CODE	NO. CYL.	CID	HORSE-POWER	COMP. RATIO	CARB	TRANS
O1A	8	389	215	8.6:1	2 BC	MAN
O2B	8	389	215	8.6:1	2 BC	MAN
O3A	8	389	239	7.9:1	2 BC	MAN
23B	8	289	306	10.5:1	4 BC	MAN
32B	8	389	330	10.75:1	3-2 BC	MAN
35B	8	421	320	10.5:1	4 BC	MAN
44B	8	421	350	10.75:1	3-2 BC	MAN
45B	8	421	370	10.75:1	3-2 BC	MAN
10A	8	389	283	10.5:1	2 BC	MAN
49N	8	421	350	10.75:1	3-2 BC	AUTO
50Q	8	421	370	10.75:1	3-2 BC	AUTO
34N	8	389	330	10.75:1	3=2 BC	AUTO
O8R	8	389	230	8.6:1	2 BC	AUTO
O9R	8	389	230	8.6:1	2 BC	AUTO
27P	8	389	303	10.5:1	4 BC	AUTO
28P	8	389	303	10.5:1	4 BC	AUTO
17M	8	389	283	10.5:1	2 BC	AUTO
18M	8	389	283	10.5:1	2 BC	AUTO
19M	8	389	257	7.9:1	2 BC	AUTO
43N	8	421	320	10.5:1	4 BC	AUTO

BONNEVILLE

ENGINE CODE	NO. CYL.	CID	HORSE-POWER	COMP. RATIO	CARB	TRANS
23B	8	389	306	10.5:1	4 BC	MAN
22B	8	389	235	8.6:1	4 BC	MAN
32B	8	389	330	10.75:1	3-2 BC	MAN
35B	8	421	320	10.5:1	4 BC	MAN
44B	8	421	350	10.75:1	3-2 BC	MAN
45B	8	421	370	10.75:1	3-2 BC	MAN
49N	8	421	350	10.75:1	3-2 BC	AUTO
50Q	8	421	370	10.75:1	3-2 BC	AUTO
34N	8	389	330	10.75:1	3-2 BC	AUTO
08R	8	389	230	8.6:1	2 BC	AUTO
09R	8	389	230	8.6:1	2 BC	AUTO
27P	8	389	303	10.5:1	4 BC	AUTO
28P	8	389	303	10.5:1	4 BC	AUTO
29N	8	389	306	10.5:1	4 BC	AUTO
30P	8	389	276	7.9:1	4 BC	AUTO
43N	8	421	320	10.5:1	4 BC	AUTO

GRAND PRIX

ENGINE CODE	NO. CYL.	CID	HORSE-POWER	COMP. RATIO	CARB	TRANS
23B	8	389	306	10.5:1	4 BC	AUTO
32B	8	389	330	10.75:1	3-2 BC	AUTO
35B	8	421	320	10.5:1	4 BC	AUTO
44B	8	421	350	10.75:1	3-2 BC	AUTO
45B	8	421	370	10.75:1	3-2 BC	AUTO
04L	8	389	230	8.6:1	2 BC	AUTO
05L	8	389	230	8.6:1	2 BC	AUTO
46G	8	421	370	10.75:1	3-2 BC	AUTO
47S	8	421	350	10.75:1	3-2 BC	AUTO
25K	8	389	303	10.5:1	4 BC	AUTO
26K	8	389	303	10.5:1	4 BC	AUTO
13H	8	389	240	7.9:1	2 BC	AUTO
38S	8	421	320	10.5;1	4 BC	AUTO
33G	8	389	330	10.75:1	3-2 BC	AUTO

1965 PONTIAC

1965 PONTIAC

1965 PONTIAC TEMPEST

1965 PONTIAC TEMPEST

VEHICLE IDENTIFICATION NUMBER

PONTIAC
252695P100001

Commonly referred to as the VIN NUMBER, this series of numbers and letters is stamped on the plate attached to the left front door hinge pillar.

FIRST DIGIT: Identifies the GM Division (2 is Pontiac)

SECOND AND THIRD DIGITS: Identify the series

SERIES	CODE
Tempest	33
Tempest Custom	35
Tempest Le Mans	37
Catalina	52
Star Chief	56
Bonneville	62
Grand Prix	66

FOURTH AND FIFTH DIGITS: Identify the body style in each series

THE SIXTH DIGIT: Identifies the model year (1965)

THE SEVENTH DIGIT: Identifies the assembly plant

ASSEMBLY PLANT	CODE
Pontiac, MI	P
Linden, NJ	E
Southgate, CA	C
Kansas City, KS	X
Doraville, GA	D
Fremont, CA	Z
Arlington, TX	R
Baltimore, MD	B
Kansas City, MO	K

LAST SIX DIGITS: Represent the basic production numbers

BODY NUMBER PLATE

Complete identification of each body is provided by a plate riveted to the cowl at the left of center under the hood.

PONTIAC DIV. GENERAL MOTORS CORP.
PONTIAC, MICHIGAN

STYLE 65-25211 P0 132545 BODY
TRIM 223 AA PAINT
*ACC. 0-0-00-00

BODY BY FISHER

EXAMPLE:

65	Model Year (1965)
2	GM Division (Pontiac)
52	Series (Catalina)
11	Sport Sedan, 4-Window
PO	Assembly Plant (Pontiac, MI)
132545	Production Sequence
223	Trim
A	Lower Body Color
A	Upper Body Color

* Is unavailable at the time of printing

THE STYLE NUMBER is a combination of the year, division, series and body style.

TEMPEST	CODE
2-Dr. Sport Coupe	3327
Safari Sta. Wgn., 2-Seat	3335

TEMPEST CUSTOM	CODE
2-Dr. Sport Coupe, Std.	3527
4-Dr. Sedan	3569
Safari Sta. Wgn., 2-Seat	3535
Convertible	3567
2-Dr. Hardtop Coupe	3537

LE MANS	CODE
2-Dr. Sport Coupe*	3727
Hardtop Sports Coupe*	3737
Convertible*	3767
4-Dr. Sedan*	3769

* Option GTO

CATALINA	CODE
Coupe, Convertible*	5267
2-Dr. Sport Coupe*	5237
2-Dr. Sport Sedan, 4 Window	5211
4-Dr. Sedan, 6 Window	5269
4-Dr. Vista, 4 Window	5239
4-Dr. Safari Sta. Wgn., 2 Seat	5235
4-Dr. Safari Sta. Wgn., 3 Seat	5245

* Option 2 + 2
* Option Ventura trim

STAR CHIEF	CODE
4-Dr. Sedan, 6 Window	5669
4-Dr. Vista, 4 Window	5639

BONNEVILLE	CODE
4-Dr. Safari Sta. Wgn., 2 Seat	6235
Coupe, Convertible	6267
2-Dr. Sport Coupe	6237
4-Dr. Vista, 4 Window	6239

* Option Brougham

GRAND PRIX	CODE
2-Dr. Sport Coupe	6657

THE BODY NUMBER is the production serial number of the body. The prefix letter denotes the plant in which the body was built.

ASSEMBLY PLANT	CODE
Pontiac, MI	PO
South Gate, CA	BC
Linden, NJ	BL
Wilmington, DE	BW
Kansas City, KS	BK
Doraville, GA	BA
Arlington, TX	BT
Euclid, OH	EP

THE TRIM NUMBER furnishes the key to the interior color and material for each model series.

TEMPEST TRIM COLOR	CLOTH	VINYL	LEATHER	CODE
Blue	•	•		201
Turquoise	•	•		202
Turquoise		•		205
Gold	•	•		203
Gold		•		206
Red	•	•		204
Red		•		207
Silver		•		208

TEMPEST CUSTOM TRIM COLOR	CLOTH	VINYL	LEATHER	CODE
Blue	•	•		209
Turquoise	•	•		210
Gold	•	•		211
Red	•	•		212

LE MANS TRIM COLOR	CLOTH	VINYL	LEATHER	CODE
Blue	•	•		265
Burgundy	•	•		298
Black		•		213
Turquoise		•		214
Gold		•		215
Red		•		216
Blue		•		217
Parchment		•		218

CATALINA TRIM COLOR	CLOTH	VINYL	LEATHER	CODE
Blue	•	•		219,292
Blue		•		224,235,237,229
Turquoise	•	•		220,293
Turquoise		•		225,238,230
Red	•	•		223,296
Red		•		228,234,240,232
Bronze	•	•		295,222
Green	•	•		294,221
Green		•		226
Silver		•		299
Gold		•		227,239,231
Black		•		233,241,297
Parchment		•		236

STAR CHIEF TRIM COLOR	CLOTH	VINYL	LEATHER	CODE
Blue	•	•		242
Blue		•		237
Turquoise	•	•		243
Turquoise		•		238
Gold	•	•		244
Gold		•		239
Red	•	•		245
Red		•		240

BONNEVILLE TRIM COLOR	CLOTH	VINYL	LEATHER	CODE
Blue	•	•		246,262
Blue		•		251,266-273
Gold	•	•		248,263
Gold		•		253,268
Black	•	•		249

Black		•		255-260
Black		•		270-276
Turquoise	•	•		247
Turquoise		•		278,252,267
Plum	•	•		250,264
Slate		•		279
Red		•		280,254
Red		•		269-275
Parchment		•		256-257-261
Parchment		•		271-272-277

GRAND PRIX TRIM COLOR	CLOTH	VINYL	LEATHER	CODE
Blue	•	•		259-290,286
Gold	•	•		291,284
Black		•		258-281
Turquoise		•		282
Slate		•		283
Red		•		285
Plum		•		287
Parchment		•		288-289

THE PAINT CODE furnishes the key to the paint colors used on the car. A two-letter code indicates the bottom and top colors respectively.

COLOR	CODE
Starlight Black	A
Blue Charcoal	B
Cameo Ivory	C
Fontaine Blue	D
Nightwatch Blue	E
Palmetto Green	H
Reef Turquoise	K
Teal Turquoise	L
Burgundy	N
Iris Mist	P
Montero Red	R
Capri Gold	T
Mission Beige	V
Bluemist Slate	W
Mayfair Maize	Y

ENGINE NUMBER

Along with the VIN number, the engine block is stamped with an engine production code. The production code is stamped on the engine block directly below the VIN number.

TEMPEST - LE MANS

ENGINE CODE	NO. CYL	CID	HORSE-POWER	COMP. RATIO	CARB	TRANS
ZK	6	215	140	8.6:1	1 BC	MAN
ZR	6	215	140	8.6:1	1 BC	MAN
ZD	6	215	125	7.2:1	1 BC	MAN
ZS	6	215	140	8.6:1	1 BC	MAN
ZN	6	215	140	8.6:1	1 BC	MAN
WS	8	389	360	10.75:1	3-2 BC	MAN
WT	8	389	335	10.75:1	4 BC	MAN
WP	8	326	250	9.2:1	2 BC	MAN
WR	8	326	285	10.5:1	4 BC	MAN
ZE	6	215	125	7.2:1	1 BC	AUTO
ZL	6	215	140	8.6:1	1 BC	AUTO
ZM	6	215	140	8.6:1	1 BC	AUTO
YR	8	389	360	10.75:1	3-2 BC	AUTO
YS	8	389	335	10.75:1	4 BC	AUTO
YN	8	326	250	9.2:1	2 BC	AUTO
YP	8	326	285	10.5:1	4 BC	AUTO

CATALINA - GRAND PRIX

ENGINE CODE	NO. CYL.	CID	HORSE-POWER	COMP. RATIO	CARB	TRANS
WA	8	389	256	8.6:1	2 BC	MAN
WB	8	389	256	8.6:1	2 BC	MAN
XA	8	390	260	7.9:1	2 BC	MAN
WC	8	389	290	10.5:1	2 BC	MAN
WE	8	389	333	10.5:1	4 BC	MAN
WF	8	389	338	10.75:1	3-2 BC	MAN
WG	8	421	338	10.5:1	4 BC	MAN
WH	8	421	356	10.75:1	3-2 BC	MAN
WJ	8	421	376	10.75:1	3-2 BC	MAN
YA	8	389	256	8.6:1	2 BC	AUTO
YB	8	389	256	8.6:1	2 BC	AUTO
YC	8	389	290	10.5:1	2 BC	AUTO
YD	8	389	290	10.5:1	2 BC	AUTO
YE	8	389	325	10.5:1	4 BC	AUTO
YF	8	389	325	10.5:1	4 BC	AUTO
XB	8	389	260	7.9:1	2 BC	AUTO
YG	8	389	338	10.75:1	3-2 BC	AUTO
YH	8	421	338	10.75:1	4 BC	AUTO
YJ	8	421	356	10.75:1	3-2 BC	AUTO
YK	8	421	376	10.75:1	3-2 BC	AUTO

STAR CHIEF

ENGINE CODE	NO. CYL.	CID	HORSE-POWER	COMP. RATIO	CARB	TRANS
WE	8	389	333	10.5:1	4 BC	MAN
WF	8	389	338	10.75:1	3-2 BC	MAN
WG	8	421	338	10.5:1	4 BC	MAN
WH	8	421	356	10.75:1	3-2 BC	MAN
WJ	8	421	376	10.75:1	3-2 BC	MAN
YA	8	389	256	8.6:1	2 BC	AUTO
YB	8	389	256	8.6:1	2 BC	AUTO
YE	8	389	325	10.5:1	4 BC	AUTO
YF	8	389	325	10.5:1	4 BC	AUTO
XC	8	389	293	7.9:1	4 BC	AUTO
YG	8	389	338	10.75:1	3-2 BC	AUTO
YG	8	421	338	10.75:1	4 BC	AUTO
YH	8	421	338	10.75:1	4 BC	AUTO
YJ	8	421	356	10.75:1	3-2 BC	AUTO
YK	8	421	376	10.75:1	3-2 BC	AUTO

BONNEVILLE

ENGINE CODE	NO. CYL.	CID	HORSE-POWER	COMP. RATIO	CARB	TRANS
WD	8	389	276	8.6:1	4 BC	MAN
WE	8	389	333	10.5:1	4 BC	MAN
WF	8	389	338	10.75:1	3-2 BC	MAN
WG	8	421	338	10.5:1	4 BC	MAN
WH	8	421	356	10.75:1	3-2 BC	MAN
WJ	8	421	376	10.75:1	3-2 BC	MAN
YA	8	389	256	8.6:1	2 BC	AUTO
YB	8	389	256	8.6:1	2 BC	AUTO
YE	8	389	325	10.5:1	4 BC	AUTO
YF	8	389	325	10.5:1	4 BC	AUTO
XC	8	389	293	7.9:1	4 BC	AUTO
YG	8	389	338	10.75:1	3-2 BC	AUTO
YH	8	421	338	10.75:1	4 BC	AUTO
YJ	8	421	356	10.75:1	3-2 BC	AUTO
YK	8	421	376	10.75:1	3-2 BC	AUTO

1966 PONTIAC

1966 PONTIAC BONNEVILLE

1966 PONTIAC BONNEVILLE

1966 PONTIAC GRAND PRIX

1966 PONTIAC GRAND PRIX

1966 PONTIAC GTO

1966 PONTIAC LE MANS

1966 PONTIAC TEMPEST

1966 PONTIAC TWO & TWO

1966 PONTIAC

VEHICLE IDENTIFICATION NUMBER

PONTIAC
252696P100001

Commonly referred to the VIN NUMBER, this series of numbers and letters is stamped on the plate attached to the left front door hinge pillar.

FIRST DIGIT: Identifies the GM Division (2 is Pontiac)

SECOND AND THIRD DIGITS: Identify the series

SERIES	CODE
Tempest	33
Tempest Custom	35
Tempest Le Mans	37
Catalina	52
Star Chief	56
Bonneville	62
Grand Prix	66

FOURTH AND FIFTH DIGITS: Identify the body style in each series

SIXTH DIGIT: Identifies the model year (1966)

SEVENTH DIGIT: Identifies the assembly plant

ASSEMBLY PLANT	CODE
Pontiac, MI	P
Linden, NJ	E
Southgate, CA	C
Kansas City, KS	X
Doraville, GA	D
Fremont, CA	Z
Arlington, TX	R
Baltimore, MD	B
Kansas City, MO	K
Lordstown, OH	U

LAST SIX DIGITS: Represent the basic production numbers

BODY NUMBER PLATE

Complete identification of each body is provided by a plate riveted to the cowl at the left of center under the hood.

PONTIAC DIV. GENERAL MOTORS CORP.
PONTIAC, MICHIGAN

STYLE 66-3307 BODY PO237
TRIM 201 PAINT AA
*ACC. B-F-KX-JX

BODY BY FISHER

EXAMPLE:

66	Model Year (1966)
33	Series (Tempest)
07	Sports Coupe
PO	Assembly Plant (Pontiac, MI)
237	Production Sequence
201	Trim
A	Lower Body Color
A	Upper Body Color

* Is unavailable at the time of printing

THE STYLE NUMBER is a combination of the year, division, series and body style.

TEMPEST	CODE
Sports Coupe	3307
4-Dr. Sedan	3369
Station Wagon	3335

TEMPEST CUSTOM	CODE
Sports Coupe	3507
4-Dr. Sedan	3569
Hardtop Coupe	3517
4-Dr. Hardtop	3539
Convertible	3567
Station Wagon	3535

TEMPEST LE MANS	CODE
Sports Coupe	3707
Hardtop Coupe	3717
4-Dr. Hardtop	3739
Convertible	3767

TEMPEST GTO	CODE
Sports Coupe	4207
Hardtop Coupe	4217
Convertible	4267

CATALINA	CODE
2-Dr. Sedan	5211
4-Dr. Sedan	5269
Hardtop Coupe	5237
4-Dr. Hardtop	5239
Convertible	5267
Station Wagon, 2 Seat	5235
Station Wagon, 3 Seat	5245

* Option Ventura

2+2	CODE
Hardtop Coupe	5437
Convertible	5467

STAR CHIEF	CODE
Hardtop Coupe	5637
4-Dr. Hardtop	5639
4-Dr. Sedan	5669

BONNEVILLE	CODE
Hardtop Coupe	6237
4-Dr. Hardtop	6239
Convertible	6267
Station Wagon, 3 Seat	6245

* Option Brougham

1966 PONTIAC

GRAND PRIX	CODE
Hardtop Coupe	6657

THE BODY NUMBER is the production serial number of the body. The prefix letter denotes the plant in which the body was built.

ASSEMBLY PLANT	CODE
Pontiac, MI	PO
South Gate, CA	BC
Linden, NJ	BL
Wilmington, DE	BW
Kansas City, KS	BK
Doraville, GA	BA
Arlington, TX	BT
Euclid, OH	EP

THE TRIM NUMBER furnishes the key to the interior color and material for each model series.

TEMPEST TRIM

COLOR	CLOTH	VINYL	LEATHER	CODE
Blue	•	•		201
Turquoise	•	•		202
Turquoise		•		207
Fawn	•	•		203
Fawn		•		208
Red	•	•		204
Red		•		209
Black		•		205
Slate		•		210

TEMPEST CUSTOM TRIM

COLOR	CLOTH	VINYL	LEATHER	CODE
Blue		•		213
Turquoise		•		214
Fawn		•		215
Red		•		216

TEMPEST LE MANS & GTO TRIM

COLOR	CLOTH	VINYL	LEATHER	CODE
Black	•	•		228
Black		•		223,231
Blue		•		219,232
Turquoise		•		220
Fawn		•		221,233
Red		•		222
Parchment		•		224

CATALINA TRIM

COLOR	CLOTH	VINYL	LEATHER	CODE
Blue	•	•		501,506,534
Blue		•		511,516,525
Turquoise	•	•		502,507,535
Turquoise		•		512,517,526
Red	•	•		503,509
Red		•		519,514,528
Fawn	•	•		505,508
Fawn		•		518,513,527
Black	•	•		539,540,538
Black		•		515,520,529
Slate		•		599

STAR CHIEF TRIM

COLOR	CLOTH	VINYL	LEATHER	CODE
Blue		•		525
Blue	•	•		534
Turquoise		•		526
Turquoise	•	•		535
Fawn		•		527
Red		•		528
Black		•		529
Black	•	•		538

2+2 TRIM

COLOR	CLOTH	VINYL	LEATHER	CODE
Black		•		521
Red		•		522
Blue		•		523
Parchment		•		524

BONNEVILLE TRIM

COLOR	CLOTH	VINYL	LEATHER	CODE
Blue	•	•		542
Blue		•		547,560
Blue		•	•	563,570
Blue			•	266-273
Fawn	•	•		543
Fawn	•			569,596,557
Fawn		•		549,562
Fawn		•	•	565
Fawn			•	268
Black	•	•		544
Black	•			593,597,559
Black		•		551,554,561
Black		•	•	567,572
Turquoise	•	•		545
Turquoise		•		564
Turquoise		•	•	564
Turquoise			•	267
Plum	•	•		546
Plum	•			586,558
Gunmetal	•			556
Red		•		550
Red		•	•	566,571
Red			•	269-275
Parchment		•		552,555
Parchment		•	•	568,573
Parchment			•	271-272-277

THE PAINT CODE furnishes the key to the paint colors used on the car. A two-letter code indicates the bottom and top colors respectively.

COLOR	CODE
Starlight Black*	A
Blue Charcoal	B
Cameo Ivory*	C
Fontaine Blue	D
Nightwatch Blue	E
Palmetto Green	H
Reef Turquoise	K
Marina Turquoise	L
Burgundy	N
Barrier Blue	P
Montero Red*	R
Martinique Bronze	T
Mission Beige	V
Platinum	W
Candlelite Cream	Y

* Pin stripe colors

ENGINE NUMBER

Along with the VIN number, the engine block is stamped with an engine production code. The code has a letter and number that identify the engine. The production code is stamped on the right front of the engine block directly below the VIN number.

TEMPEST - LE MANS

ENGINE CODE	NO. CYL	CID	HORSE-POWER	COMP. RATIO	CARB	TRANS
ZK	6	230	165	9.0:1	1 BC	MAN
ZD	6	230	207	10.5:1	4 BC	MAN
ZF	6	230	155	7.8:1	1 BC	MAN
ZS	6	230	165	9.0:1	1 BC	MAN
WP	8	326	250	9.2:1	2 BC	MAN
WX	8	326	250	9.2:1	2 BC	MAN
WR	8	326	285	10.5:1	4 BC	MAN
ZN	6	230	165	9.0:1	1 BC	AUTO
ZG	6	230	155	7.8:1	1 BC	AUTO
ZE	6	230	207	10.5:1	4 BC	AUTO
ZM	6	230	165	9.0:1	1 BC	AUTO
YN	8	326	250	9.2:1	2 BC	AUTO
YP	8	326	285	10.5:1	4 BC	AUTO
XF	8	326	250	9.2:1	2 BC	AUTO
XG	8	326	285	10.5:1	4 BC	AUTO

GTO

ENGINE CODE	NO. CYL.	CID	HORSE-POWER	COMP. RATIO	CARB	TRANS
WV	8	389	360	10.75:1	3-2 BC	MAN
WW	8	389	335	10.75:1	4 BC	MAN
WS	8	389	360	10.75:1	3-2 BC	MAN
WT	8	389	335	10.75:1	4 BC	MAN
XS	8	389	360	10.75:1	3-2 BC	MAN
YR	8	389	360	10.75:1	3-2 BC	AUTO
YS	8	389	335	10.75:1	4 BC	AUTO
XE	8	389	335	10.75:1	4 BC	AUTO

CATALINA - STAR CHIEF

ENGINE CODE	NO. CYL.	CID	HORSE-POWER	COMP. RATIO	CARB	TRANS
WA	8	389	256	8.6:1	2 BC	MAN
WB	8	389	256	8.6:1	2 BC	MAN
XA	8	389	260	7.9:1	2 BC	MAN
WC	8	389	290	10.5:1	2 BC	MAN
WE	8	389	333	10.5:1	4 BC	MAN
WH	8	421	356	10.75:1	3-2 BC	MAN
WJ	8	421	376	10.75:1	3-2 BC	MAN
WK	8	421	338	10.5:1	4 BC	MAN
YA	8	389	256	8.6:1	2 BC	AUTO
YU	8	389	290	10.5:1	2 BC	AUTO
YC	8	389	290	10.5:1	2 BC	AUTO
YD	8	389	290	10.5:1	2 BC	AUTO
XB	8	389	260	7.6:1	2 BC	AUTO
YV	8	389	290	10.5:1	2 BC	AUTO
YL	8	389	325	10.5:1	4 BC	AUTO
YW	8	389	325	10.5:1	4 BC	AUTO
YE	8	389	325	10.5:1	4 BC	AUTO
YF	8	389	325	10.5:1	4 BC	AUTO
YX	8	389	325	10.5:1	4 BC	AUTO
XC	8	389	293	7.6:1	4 BC	AUTO
YZ	8	421	338	10.5:1	4 BC	AUTO
YT	8	421	338	10.5:1	4 BC	AUTO
YM	8	421	356	10.75:1	3-2 BC	AUTO
YJ	8	421	356	10.75:1	3-2 BC	AUTO
YK	8	421	376	10.75:1	3-2 BC	AUTO

2 + 2

ENGINE CODE	NO. CYL.	CID	HORSE-POWER	COMP. RATIO	CARB	TRANS
WG	8	421	338	10.5:1	4 BC	MAN
WH	8	421	356	10.75:1	3-2 BC	MAN
WJ	8	421	376	10.75:1	3-2 BC	MAN
YH	8	421	338	10.5:1	4 BC	AUTO
YJ	8	421	356	10.75:1	3-2 BC	AUTO
YK	8	421	376	10.75:1	3-2 BC	AUTO

BONNEVILLE - GRAND PRIX

ENGINE CODE	NO. CYL.	CID	HORSE-POWER	COMP. RATIO	CARB	TRANS
WB	8	389	256	8.6:1	2 BC	MAN
WE	8	389	333	10.5:1	4 BC	MAN
WK	8	421	338	10.5:1	4 BC	MAN
WH	8	421	356	10.75:1	3-2 BC	MAN
WJ	8	421	376	10.75:1	3-2 BC	MAN
YA	8	389	256	8.6:1	2 BC	AUTO
YW	8	389	325	10.5:1	4 BC	AUTO
YE	8	389	325	10.5:1	4 BC	AUTO
YF	8	389	325	10.5:1	4 BC	AUTO
YX	8	389	325	10.5:1	4 BC	AUTO
XC	8	389	293	7.9:1	4 BC	AUTO
YT	8	421	338	10.5:1	4 BC	AUTO
YJ	8	421	356	10.75:1	3-2 BC	AUTO
YK	8	421	376	10.75:1	3-2 BC	AUTO

1967 PONTIAC BONNEVILLE

1967 PONTIAC CATALINA

1967 PONTIAC LE MANS

1967 PONTIAC GRAND PRIX

1967 PONTIAC GTO

1967 PONTIAC GTO

1967 PONTIAC TEMPEST

1967 PONTIAC TEMPEST

VEHICLE IDENTIFICATION NUMBER

PONTIAC
252697P109038

Commonly referred to as the VIN NUMBER, this series of numbers and letters is stamped on the plate attached to the left front door hinge pillar.

FIRST DIGIT: Identifies the GM Division (2 is Pontiac)

SECOND AND THIRD DIGITS: Identify the series

SERIES	CODE
Firebird	23
Tempest	33
Tempest Custom	35
Le Mans	37
Tempest Safari	39
GTO	42
Catalina	52
Executive	56
Bonneville	62
Grand Prix	66

FOURTH AND FIFTH DIGITS: Identify the body style in each series

SIXTH DIGIT: Identifies the model year (1967)

SEVENTH DIGIT: Identifies the assembly plant

ASSEMBLY PLANT	CODE
Pontiac, MI	P
Linden, NJ	E
Southgate, CA	C
Kansas City, KS	X
Framington, MA	U
Fremont, CA	Z
Arlington, TX	R
Baltimore, MD	B
Kansas City, MO	K
Lordstown, OH	V

LAST SIX DIGITS: Represent the basic production number

BODY NUMBER PLATE

Complete identification of each body is provided by a plate attached to the left side of cowl under the hood.

PONTIAC DIV. GENERAL MOTORS CORP.
PONTIAC, MICHIGAN

STYLE 67-4207 PO 12237 BODY
TRIM 219 AA PAINT
*ACC. B-F-KX-JX

BODY BY FISHER

EXAMPLE:

67	Model Year (1967)
42	Series (GTO)
07	Sports Coupe
PO	Assembly Plant (Pontiac, MI)
219	Trim
A	Lower Body Color
A	Upper Body Color

* Is unavailable at the time of printing

THE STYLE NUMBER is a combination of the year, series, and body style.

FIREBIRD	CODE
Sport Coupe	2337
Convertible	2367
* Option Sprint	

TEMPEST	CODE
Sports Coupe	3307
4-Dr. Sedan	3369
Station Wagon	3335
* Option Sprint	

TEMPEST CUSTOM	CODE
Sports Coupe	3507
Hardtop Coupe	3517
4-Dr. Hardtop	3539
4-Dr. Sedan	3569
Convertible	3567
Station Wagon	3535
* Option Sprint	

LE MANS	CODE
Sports Coupe	3707
Hardtop Coupe	3717
4-Dr. Hardtop	3739
Station Wagon	3767
* Option Sprint	

TEMPEST SAFARI	CODE
Station Wagon, 2-Seat	3935

G.T.O.	CODE
Sports Coupe	4207
Hardtop Coupe	4217
Convertible	4267

CATALINA	CODE
2-Dr. Sedan	5211
4-Dr. Sedan	5269
Hardtop Coupe	5287
4-Dr. Hardtop	5239
Convertible	5267
Station Wagon, 2-Seat	5235
Station Wagon, 3-Seat	5245
* Option 2 + 2	
* Option Ventura	

EXECUTIVE	CODE
Hardtop Coupe	5687
4-Dr. Sedan	5669
4-Dr. Hardtop	5639
Station Wagon, 2-Seat	5635
Station Wagon, 3-Seat	5645

BONNEVILLE	CODE
Hardtop Coupe	6287
4-Dr. Hardtop	6239
Convertible	6267
Station Wagon	6245
* Option Brougham	

1967 PONTIAC

GRAND PRIX	CODE
Hardtop Coupe	6657
Convertible	6667

THE BODY NUMBER is the production serial number of the body. The prefix letter denotes the plant in which the body was built.

ASSEMBLY PLANT	CODE
Pontiac, MI	P
Arlington, TX	R
Baltimore, MD	B
Fremont, CA	Z
Kansas City, KS	X
Kansas City, MO	K
Linden, NJ	E
Southgate, CA	C
Lordstown, OH	U
Framingham, MA	G

THE TRIM NUMBER furnishes the key to the interior color and material.

FIREBIRD TRIM

COLOR	CLOTH	VINYL	LEATHER	CODE
Blue		•		250,270
Blue		•		265,255
Gold		•		251,271
Gold		•		257,267
Red		•		252,258
Black		•		253,272
Black		•		259,269
Parchment		•		254,260
Turquoise		•		256

TEMPEST TRIM

COLOR	CLOTH	VINYL	LEATHER	CODE
Blue	•	•		201
Blue		•		213
Turquoise	•	•		202
Gold	•	•		203
Black	•	•		205
Black		•		210

TEMPEST CUSTOM & SAFARI TRIM

COLOR	CLOTH	VINYL	LEATHER	CODE
Blue		•		213
Turquoise		•		214
Gold		•		215
Black		•		217
Red		•		218

LE MANS TRIM

COLOR	CLOTH	VINYL	LEATHER	CODE
Blue		•		219,232
Turquoise		•		220
Gold		•		221,233
Black		•		223,231
Parchment		•		224
Red		•		225

GTO TRIM

COLOR	CLOTH	VINYL	LEATHER	CODE
Blue		•		219
Turquoise		•		220
Gold		•		221
Black		•		223
Parchment		•		224
Red		•		225

CATALINA & EXECUTIVE TRIM

COLOR	CLOTH	VINYL	LEATHER	CODE
Black		•		599,515,528
Black		•		529,520
Black		•		532,521
Black	•	•		503,510,538
Blue		•		511,525
Blue		•		516,523,524
Blue	•	•		501,506,534
Turquoise		•		525,512,526
Turquoise	•	•		502,507,535
Gold		•		513,527,530
Gold		•		518,526
Gold	•	•		505,508
Burgundy		•		514,528,527
Burgundy	•	•		504,509
Red		•		519,522
Parchment		•		524

BONNEVILLE TRIM

COLOR	CLOTH	VINYL	LEATHER	CODE
Blue	•	•		542,559
Blue		•		536,560
Blue		•		563,547
Gold	•	•		543,557,569
Gold		•		548,562,549
Black	•	•		544,556,593
Black		•		550,561,567
Black		•		572,551,554
Turquoise	•	•		545
Turquoise		•		547,564,548
Burgundy	•	•		546,558,586
Burgundy		•		549,550
Parchment		•		552,568,573
Parchment		•		552,555
Red		•		566

GRAND PRIX TRIM

COLOR	CLOTH	VINYL	LEATHER	CODE
Turquoise		•		579
Blue		•		580
Gold		•		581
Black		•		583,591
Burgundy		•		584
Parchment		•		585,592
Red		•		594

THE PAINT CODE furnishes the key to the paint colors used on the car. A two-letter code indicates the bottom and top colors respectively.

Starlight Black	A
Cameo Ivory	C
Montreux Blue	D
Fathom Blue	E
Tyrol Blue	F
Signet Gold	G
Linden Green	H
Gulf Turquoise	K
Mariner Turquoise	L
Plum Mist	M
Burgundy	N
Silverglaze	P
Regimental Red	R
Champagne	S
Montego Cream	T

1967 PONTIAC

ENGINE NUMBER

Along with the VIN number, the engine block is stamped with an engine production code.

TEMPEST, CUSTOM & LE MANS

ENGINE CODE	NO. CYL	CID	HORSE-POWER	COMP. RATIO	CARB	TRANS
ZK	6	230	165	9.0:1	1 BC	MAN
ZS	6	230	165	9.0:1	1 BC	MAN
ZD	6	230	215	10.5:1	4 BC	MAN
ZR	6	230	215	10.5:1	4 BC	MAN
WP	8	326	250	9.2:1	2 BC	MAN
WX	8	326	250	9.2:1	2 BC	MAN
WR	8	326	285	10.5:1	4 BC	MAN
XR	8	326	285	10.5:1	4 BC	MAN
ZN	6	230	165	9.0:1	1 BC	AUTO
ZM	6	230	165	9.0:1	1 BC	AUTO
ZE	6	230	215	10.5:1	4 BC	AUTO
ZL	6	230	215	10.5:1	4 BC	AUTO
YN	8	326	250	9.2:1	2 BC	AUTO
XF	8	326	250	9.2:1	2 BC	AUTO
YP	8	326	285	10.5:1	4 BC	AUTO
XG	8	326	285	10.5:1	4 BC	AUTO
ZF	6	230	155	7.9:1	1 BC	MAN
ZG	6	230	155	7.9:1	1 BC	MAN

GTO

ENGINE CODE	NO. CYL	CID	HORSE-POWER	COMP. RATIO	CARB	TRANS
WT	8	400	335	10.75:1	4 BC	MAN
WW	8	400	335	10.75:1	4 BC	MAN
WS	8	400	360	10.75:1	4 BC	MAN
WS	8	400	360	10.75:1	4 BC	MAN
WV	8	400	360	10.75:1	4 BC	MAN
XS	8	400	360	10.75:1	4 BC	MAN
YR	8	400	360	10.75:1	4 BC	MAN
YS	8	400	335	10.75:1	4 BC	AUTO
XM	8	400	255	8.6:1	2 BC	AUTO
XL	8	400	255	8.6:1	2 BC	AUTO
YZ	8	400	360	10.75:1	4 BC	AUTO
XP	8	400	360	10.75:1	4 BC	AUTO

CATALINA & EXECUTIVE

ENGINE CODE	NO. CYL	CID	HORSE-POWER	COMP. RATIO	CARB	TRANS
WA	8	400	265	8.6:1	2 BC	MAN
WE	8	400	333	10.5:1	4 BC	MAN
WD	8	400	333	10.5:1	4 BC	MAN
WG	8	428	360	10.5:1	4 BC	MAN
YY	8	428	360	10.5:1	4 BC	MAN
WJ	8	428	376	10.75:1	4 BC	MAN
XK	8	428	376	10.75:1	4 BC	MAN
WB	8	400	265	8.6:1	2 BC	MAN
YC	8	400	290	10.5:1	2 BC	AUTO
YD	8	400	290	10.5:1	2 BC	AUTO
YE	8	400	325	10.5:1	4 BC	AUTO
YF	8	400	325	10.5;1	4 BC	AUTO
YA	8	400	265	8.6:1	2 BC	AUTO
YB	8	400	265	8.6:1	2 BC	AUTO
YH	8	428	360	10.5:1	4 BC	AUTO
XD	8	428	360	10.5:1	4 BC	AUTO
YK	8	428	376	10.75:1	4 BC	AUTO
WL	8	400	376	10.75:1	4 BC	AUTO
XZ	8	400	333	10.5:1	4 BC	MAN
XY	8	400	333	10.5:1	4 BC	MAN
XH	8	400	333	10.5:1	4 BC	AUTO
Y2	8	428	360	10.5:1	4 BC	AUTO
Y3	8	428	376	10.5:1	4 BC	AUTO
XB	8	400	260	7.9:1	2 BC	AUTO
XC	8	400	293	7.9:1	4 BC	AUTO

BONNEVILLE

ENGINE CODE	NO. CYL	CID	HORSE-POWER	COMP. RATIO	CARB	TRANS
WE	8	400	333	10.5:1	4 BC	MAN
WD	8	400	333	10.5:1	4 BC	MAN
WG	8	428	360	10.5:1	4 BC	MAN
YY	8	428	360	10.5:1	4 BC	MAN
WJ	8	428	376	10.75:1	4 BC	MAN
XK	8	428	376	10.75:1	4 BC	MAN
YE	8	400	325	10.5:1	4 BC	AUTO
YF	8	400	325	10.5:1	4 BC	AUTO
YA	8	400	265	8.6:1	2 BC	AUTO
YB	8	400	265	8.6:1	2 BC	AUTO
YH	8	428	360	10.5:1	4 BC	AUTO
XD	8	428	360	10.5:1	4 BC	AUTO
YK	8	428	376	10.75;1	4 BC	AUTO
WL	8	428	376	10.75:1	4 BC	AUTO

GRAND PRIX

ENGINE CODE	NO. CYL	CID	HORSE-POWER	COMP. RATIO	CARB	TRANS
XZ	8	400	350	10.5:1	4 BC	MAN
XY	8	400	350	10.5:1	4 BC	MAN
WG	8	428	360	10.5:1	4 BC	MAN
YY	8	428	360	10.5:1	4 BC	MAN
WJ	8	428	376	10.75:1	4 BC	MAN
XK	8	428	376	10.75:1	4 BC	MAN
XJ	8	400	350	10.5:1	4 BC	AUTO
YA	8	400	265	8.6:1	2 BC	AUTO
YB	8	400	265	8.6:1	2 BC	AUTO
YH	8	428	360	10.5:1	4 BC	AUTO
XD	8	428	360	10.5:1	4 BC	AUTO
YK	8	428	376	10.75:1	4 BC	AUTO
WL	8	428	376	10.75:1	4 BC	AUTO

FIREBIRD

ENGINE CODE	NO. CYL	CID	HORSE-POWER	COMP. RATIO	CARB	TRANS
ZK	6	230	165	9.0:1	1 BC	MAN
ZS	6	230	165	9.0:1	1 BC	MAN
ZN	6	230	165	9.0:1	1 BC	AUTO
ZM	6	230	165	9.0:1	1 BC	AUTO
ZD	6	230	215	10.5:1	*Q-JET	MAN
ZR	6	230	215	10.5:1	*Q-JET	MAN
ZE	6	230	215	10.5:1	*Q-JET	AUTO
ZL	6	230	215	10.5:1	*Q-JET	AUTO
ZF	6	230	155	7.6:1	1 BC	MAN
ZG	6	230	155	7.6:1	1 BC	AUTO
WH	8	326	250	9.2:1	2 BC	MAN
WC	8	326	250	9.2:1	2 BC	MAN
WI	8	400	325	10.75:1	4 BC	MAN
WZ	8	400	325	10.75:1	4 BC	MAN
YJ	8	326	250	9.2:1	2 BC	AUTO
XL	8	326	250	9.2:1	2 BC	AUTO
WK	8	326	285	10.5:1	4 BC	MAN
WO	8	326	285	10.5:1	4 BC	MAN
YM	8	326	285	10.5:1	4 BC	AUTO
XO	8	326	285	10.5:1	4 BC	AUTO
WZ	8	400	325	10.75:1	*Q-JET	MAN
WU	8	400	325	10.75:1	*Q-JET	MAN
YT	8	400	325	10.75:1	*Q-JET	AUTO
WL	8	400	325	10.75:1	*Q-JET	MAN
WQ	8	400	325	10.75:1	*Q-JET	MAN
XN	8	400	325	10.75:1	*Q-JET	AUTO

1968 PONTIAC

1968 PONTIAC EXECUTIVE

1968 PONTIAC BONNEVILLE CATALINA, EXECUTIVE

1968 PONTIAC BONNEVILLE

1968 PONTIAC CATALINA

1968 PONTIAC FIREBIRD

1968 PONTIAC FIREBIRD

1968 PONTIAC GRAND PRIX

1968 PONTIAC GTO

1968 PONTIAC TEMPEST

1968 PONTIAC LE MANS

1968 PONTIAC

VEHICLE IDENTIFICATION NUMBER

PONTIAC
252698P109038

Commonly referred to as the VIN NUMBER, this series of numbers and letters is stamped on the plate attached to the left front door hinge pillar.

FIRST DIGIT: Identifies the GM Division (2 is Pontiac)

SECOND AND THIRD DIGITS: Identify the series

SERIES	CODE
Firebird	23
Tempest	33
Tempest	35
Le Mans	37
Tempest Safari	39
GTO	42
Catalina	52
Executive	56
Bonneville	62
Grand Prix	66

NOTE: Tempest Le Mans Spirit does not change VIN.

FOURTH AND FIFTH DIGITS: Identify the body style in each series

SIXTH DIGIT: Identifies the model year (1968)

SEVENTH DIGIT: Identifies the assembly plant

ASSEMBLY PLANT	CODE
Pontiac, MI	P
Linden, NJ	E
Southgate, CA	C
Kansas City, KS	X
Framington, MA	G
Fremont, CA	Z
Arlington, TX	R
Baltimore, MD	B
Kansas City, MO	K
Van Nuys, CA	L
Atlanta, GA	A
Lordstown, OH	U
Oshawa, Ont., CAN	1

LAST SIX DIGITS: Represent the basic production numbers

BODY NUMBER PLATE

Complete identification of each body is provided by a plate attached to the left side of the cowl under the hood.

PONTIAC DIV. GENERAL MOTORS CORP.
PONTIAC, MICHIGAN

STYLE 68-2337 BODY PO237
TRIM 252 PAINT AA
*ACC. B-F-KX-JX

BODY BY FISHER

EXAMPLE:

68	Model Year (1968)
23	Series (Firebird)
37	2-Door Sport Coupe
PO	Assembly Plant (Pontiac, MI)
237	Production Sequence
252	Trim
A	Lower Body Color
A	Upper Body Color

* Is unavailable at the time of printing

THE STYLE NUMBER is a combination of the year, series, and body code.

FIREBIRD	CODE
Coupe	2337
Convertible	2367

* Option Sprint

TEMPEST	CODE
Sports Coupe	3327
4-Dr. Sedan	3369

* Option Sprint

TEMPEST CUSTOM	CODE
Sports Coupe	3527
Hardtop Coupe	3537
4-Dr. Hardtop	3539
4-Dr. Sedan	3569
Convertible	3567
Station Wagon	3535

* Option Sprint

LE MANS	CODE
Sports Coupe	3727
Hardtop Coupe	3737
4-Dr. Sedan	3739
Convertible	3767

* Option Sprint

TEMPEST SAFARI	CODE
Station Wagon, 2-Seat	3935

GTO	CODE
Hardtop Coupe	4237
Convertible	4267

1968 PONTIAC

CATALINA	CODE
2-Dr. Sedan	5211
4-Dr. Sedan	5269
Hardtop Coupe	5287
4-Dr. Hardtop	5239
Convertible	5267
Station Wagon, 2-Seat	5235
Station Wagon, 3-Seat	5245

* Option Ventura

EXECUTIVE	CODE
Hardtop Coupe	5687
4-Dr. Sedan	5669
4-Dr. Hardtop	5639
Station Wagon, 2-Seat	5635
Station Wagon, 3-Seat	5645

BONNEVILLE	CODE
Hardtop Coupe	6287
4-Dr. Hardtop	6239
Convertible	6267
Station Wagon	6245
4-Dr. Sedan	6269

* Option Brougham

GRAND PRIX	CODE
Hardtop Coupe	6657

THE BODY NUMBER is the production serial number of the body. The prefix letter denotes the plant in which the body was built.

ASSEMBLY PLANT	CODE
Pontiac, MI	P
Arlington, TX	R
Baltimore, MD	B
Fremont, MI	Z
Kansas City, KS	X
Kansas City, MO	K
Linden, NJ	E
Southgate, CA	C
Lordstown, OH	U
Framingham, MA	G

THE TRIM NUMBER furnishes the key to the interior color and material for each model series.

FIREBIRD TRIM

COLOR	CLOTH	VINYL	LEATHER	CODE
Teal		•		250,255
Gold		•		251,257
Red		•		252,258
Black		•		253-272
Black		•		259-269
Turquoise		•		261,256
Parchment		•		262-273
Parchment		•		260-275

TEMPEST TRIM

COLOR	CLOTH	VINYL	LEATHER	CODE
Black		•		206
Blue	•	•		201
Turquoise	•	•		202
Gold	•	•		203

TEMPEST CUSTOM TRIM

COLOR	CLOTH	VINYL	LEATHER	CODE
Blue		•		213
Turquoise		•		214
Gold		•		215
Black		•		217
Red		•		218

LE MANS & GTO TRIM

COLOR	CLOTH	VINYL	LEATHER	CODE
Teal		•		219,232
Turquoise		•		220
Gold		•		221
Black		•		223
Black	•	•		228
Parchment		•		224,236,233
Red		•		225
Black		•		235,231

TEMPEST SAFARI TRIM

COLOR	CLOTH	VINYL	LEATHER	CODE
Blue		•		213
Turquoise		•		214
Gold		•		215
Black		•		217

CATALINA TRIM

COLOR	CLOTH	VINYL	LEATHER	CODE
Blue	•	•		501,506,534
Blue		•		511,525,516
Black	•	•		503,510,538
Black		•		599,515,529
Black		•		520,521
Black			•	570
Gold	•	•		505,508,539
Gold		•		513,527,518
Turquoise	•	•		507,535,502
Turquoise		•		512,526
Burgundy	•	•		509,504
Burgundy		•		514
Teal		•		533
Parchment		•		528,524
Red		•		519
Saddle			•	571

EXECUTIVE TRIM

COLOR	CLOTH	VINYL	LEATHER	CODE
Blue	•	•		534
Blue		•		525
Turquoise	•	•		535
Turquoise		•		526
Gold	•	•		539
Gold		•		527
Black	•	•		538
Black		•		529
Teal		•		533
Parchment		•		528

BONNEVILLE TRIM

COLOR	CLOTH	VINYL	LEATHER	CODE
Turquoise		•		547,563
Turquoise	•	•		542
Teal		•		548,560,564
Teal	•	•		545
Gold		•		549,562
Gold	•	•		543
Burgundy		•		550
Burgundy	•	•		546,558
Black	•	•		544,556
Black		•		551,561
Black		•		567-572
Black		•		551-554
Black			•	570
Parchment		•		552
Parchment		•		568-573
Parchment		•		552-555
Red		•		566,549
Blue	•	•		559
Saddle			•	571

1968 PONTIAC

GRAND PRIX TRIM

COLOR	CLOTH	VINYL	LEATHER	CODE
Black	•	•		587-589
Black	•	•		588-590
Black		•		583,591
Black			•	593
Teal		•		579
Turquoise		•		580
Gold		•		581
Burgundy		•		584
Parchment		•		585,592
Saddle			•	594

THE PAINT CODE furnishes the key to paint colors used on the car. A two-letter code indicates the bottom and top colors respectively.

COLOR	CODE
Starlight Black	A
Cameo Ivory	C
Alpine Blue	D
Aegena Blue	E
Nordic Blue	F
April Gold	G
Autumn Bronze	I
Meridian Turquoise	K
Aleutian Blue	L
Flambeau Burgundy	N
Springmist Green	P
Verdoro Green	Q
Solar Red	R
Primavera Beige	T
Nightshade Green	V
Mayfair Maize	Y

ENGINE NUMBER

The engine code is stamped along with the VIN on the right hand side of the block.

TEMPEST CUSTOM & LE MANS

ENGINE CODE	NO. CYL.	CID	HORSE-POWER	COMP. RATIO	CARB	TRANS
ZK	6	250	175	9.0:1	1 BC	MAN
ZD	6	250	215	10.5:1	4 BC	MAN
WP	8	350	265	9.2:1	2 BC	MAN
WR	8	350	320	10.5:1	4 BC	MAN
ZN	6	250	175	9.0:1	1 BC	AUTO
ZE	6	250	215	10.5:1	4 BC	AUTO
YN	8	350	265	9.2:1	2 BC	AUTO
YP	8	350	320	10.5:1	4 BC	AUTO
ZO	6	250	215	10.5:1	4 BC	MAN
WD	8	350	265	9.2:1	4 BC	MAN

GTO

ENGINE CODE	NO. CYL.	CID	HORSE-POWER	COMP. RATIO	CARB	TRANS
WT	8	400	350	10.75:1	4 BC	MAN
WS	8	400	360	10.75:1	4 BC	MAN
XS	8	400	360	10.75:1	4 BC	MAN
YS	8	400	335	10.75:1	4 BC	AUTO
XM	8	400	265	8.6:1	2 BC	AUTO
YZ	8	400	360	10.75:1	4 BC	AUTO
XP	8	400	360	10.75:1	4 BC	AUTO

CATALINA & EXECUTIVE

ENGINE CODE	NO. CYL.	CID	HORSE-POWER	COMP. RATIO	CARB	TRANS
WA	8	400	290	10.5:1	2 BC	MAN
WB	8	400	290	10.5:1	2 BC	MAN
WE	8	400	340	10.5:1	4 BC	MAN
WG	8	428	375	1'0.5:1	4 BC	MAN
WJ	8	428	390	10.75:1	4 BC	MAN
YC	8	400	290	10.5:1	2 BC	AUTO
YE	8	400	340	10.5:1	4 BC	AUTO
YA	8	400	265	8.6:1	2 BC	AUTO
YH	8	428	375	10.5:1	4 BC	AUTO
YK	8	428	390	10.75:1	4 BC	AUTO

BONNEVILLE

ENGINE CODE	NO. CYL.	CID	HORSE-POWER	COMP. RATIO	CARB	TRANS
WE	8	400	340	10.5:1	4 BC	MAN
WG	8	428	375	10.5:1	4 BC	MAN
WJ	8	428	390	10.75:1	4 BC	MAN
YE	8	400	340	10.5:1	4 BC	AUTO
YA	8	400	265	8.6:1	2 BC	AUTO
YH	8	428	375	10.5:1	4 BC	AUTO
YK	8	428	390	10.75:1	4 BC	AUTO

GRAND PRIX

ENGINE CODE	NO. CYL.	CID	HORSE-POWER	COMP. RATIO	CARB	TRANS
XZ	8	400	350	10.5:1	4 BC	MAN
WG	8	428	375	10.5:1	4 BC	MAN
WJ	8	428	390	10.75:1	4 BC	MAN
XH	8	400	350	10.5:1	4 BC	AUTO
YA	8	400	265	8.6:1	2 BC	AUTO
YH	8	428	375	10.5:1	4 BC	AUTO
YK	8	428	390	10.75:1	4 BC	AUTO

FIREBIRD

ENGINE CODE	NO. CYL.	CID	HORSE-POWER	COMP. RATIO	CARB	TRANS
ZK	6	250	175	9.0:1	1 BC	MAN
ZD	6	250	215	10.5:1	4 BC	MAN
WC	8	350	265	9.2:1	2 BC	MAN
WK	8	350	320	10.5:1	4 BC	MAN
WZ	8	400	330	10.75:1	4 BC	MAN
WQ	8	400	335	10.75:1	4 BC	MAN
WI	8	400	335	10.75:1	4 BC	MAN
ZN	6	250	175	9.0:1	1 BC	AUTO
ZE	6	250	215	10.5:1	4 BC	AUTO
YJ	8	350	265	9.2:1	2 BC	AUTO
YM	8	350	320	10.5:1	4 BC	AUTO
YT	8	400	330	10.75:1	4 BC	AUTO
YW	8	400	335	10.75:1	4 BC	AUTO
XN	8	400	335	10.75:1	4 BC	AUTO

1969 PONTIAC BONNEVILLE

1969 PONTIAC CATALINA

1969 PONTIAC EXECUTIVE SAFARI WAGON

1969 PONTIAC EXECUTIVE SAFARI WAGON

1969 PONTIAC FIREBIRD

1969 PONTIAC FIREBIRD

1969 PONTIAC LE MANS

1969 PONTIAC LE MANS

1969 PONTIAC GRAND PRIX

1969 PONTIAC GTO

VEHICLE IDENTIFICATION NUMBER

PONTIAC
252699P109038

Commonly referred to as the VIN NUMBER, this series of numbers and letters is stamped on the plate located on the left edge of the instrument panel, visible through the windshield. The VIN is also stamped on all transmissions and engines.

FIRST DIGIT: Identifies the GM Division (2 is Pontiac)

SECOND AND THIRD DIGITS: Identify the series

SERIES	CODE
Firebird	23
Tempest	33
Tempest Custom	35
Le Mans	37
Tempest Safari	39
GTO	42
Catalina	52
Executive	56
Bonneville	62
Grand Prix	76

FOURTH AND FIFTH DIGITS: Identify the body style in each series

SIXTH DIGIT: Identifies the model year (1969)

SEVENTH DIGIT: Identifies the assembly plant

ASSEMBLY PLANT	CODE
Pontiac, MI	P
Linden, NJ	E
Southgate, CA	C
Kansas City, KS	X
Framington, MA	G
Fremont, CA	Z
Arlington, TX	R
Baltimore, MD	B
Van Nuys, CA	L
Atlanta, GA	A
Lordstown, OH	U
Oshawa, Ont., CAN	1

LAST SIX DIGITS: Represent the basic production numbers

BODY NUMBER PLATE

Complete identification of each body is provided by a plate attached to the left side of the cowl under the hood.

PONTIAC DIV. GENERAL MOTORS CORP.
PONTIAC, MICHIGAN

STYLE 69-24237 BODY PO237
TRIM 208 PAINT AA
*ACC. B-F-KX-JX

BODY BY FISHER

EXAMPLE:

69	Model Year (1969)
2	GM Division (Pontiac)
42	Series (GTO)
37	Hardtop Coupe
PO	Assembly Plant (Pontiac, MI)
237	Production Sequence
208	Trim
A	Lower Body Color
A	Upper Body Color

* Is unavailable at the time of printing

THE STYLE NUMBER is a combination of the year, series, and body style.

FIREBIRD	CODE
Coupe	2337
Convertible	2367

* Option Trans Am

TEMPEST	CODE
Sports Coupe	3327
4-Dr. Sedan	3369

CUSTOM S	CODE
Sports Coupe	3527
Hardtop Coupe	3537
4-Dr. Hardtop	3539
4-Dr. Sedan	3569
Convertible	3567
Station Wagon	3535

LE MANS	CODE
Sports Coupe	3727
Hardtop Coupe	3737
4-Dr. Sedan	3739
Convertible	3767

LE MANS SAFARI	CODE
Station Wagon, 2-Seat	3936

GTO	CODE
Hardtop Coupe	4237
Convertible	4267

* Option The Judge

CATALINA	CODE
4-Dr. Sedan	5269
Hardtop Coupe	5237
4-Dr. Hardtop	5239
Convertible	5267
Station Wagon, 2-Seat	5236
Station Wagon, 3-Seat	5246

* Option Ventura

EXECUTIVE	CODE
Hardtop Coupe	5637
4-Dr. Sedan	5669
4-Dr. Hardtop	5639
Safari, 2-Seat	5636
Safari, 3-Seat	5646

BONNEVILLE	CODE
Hardtop Coupe	6237
4-Dr. Hardtop	6239
4-Dr. Sedan	6269
Convertible	6267
Station Wagon, 3-Seat	6246

* Option Brougham

1969 PONTIAC

GRAND PRIX **CODE**

Hardtop Coupe 7657

* Option SJ

THE BODY NUMBER is the production serial number of the body. The prefix letter denotes the plant in which the body was built.

ASSEMBLY PLANT	CODE
Atlanta, GA	A
Pontiac, MI	P
Arlington, TX	R
Baltimore, MD	B
Fremont, CA	Z
Kansas City, KS	X
Van Nuys, CA	L
Linden, NJ	E
Southgate, CA	C
Lordstown, OH	U
Framingham, MA	G
Oshawa, Ont. CAN	1

THE TRIM NUMBER furnishes the key to the interior color and material for each model series.

FIREBIRD TRIM

COLOR	CLOTH	VINYL	LEATHER	CODE
Blue		•		200,210
Gold		•		202,212
Gold			•	293
Green		•		206,216
Parchment		•		207
Parchment		•		217-227
Black		•		208,249
Black		•		218-228
Red		•		214

TEMPEST & CUSTOM TRIM

COLOR	CLOTH	VINYL	LEATHER	CODE
Black			•	249,248
Blue			•	241
Blue	•	•		231
Gold		•		242
Gold	•	•		232
Green		•		246
Green	•	•		236

LE MANS & GTO TRIM

COLOR	CLOTH	VINYL	LEATHER	CODE
Blue		•		250,260
Gold		•		252,262
Red		•		254
Green		•		256,266
Parchment		•		257,267
Black		•		258,268,238

CATALINA TRIM

COLOR	CLOTH	VINYL	LEATHER	CODE
Blue		•		531,550
Blue	•	•		511,540,501
Gold		•		532,552
Gold	•	•		512,542,502
Burgundy		•		535
Burgundy	•	•		515,505
Green		•		536,556
Green	•	•		516,546,506
Black		•		538,558
Black		•		239,599
Black	•	•		518,548,508
Parchment		•		557
Red		•		534

EXECUTIVE TRIM

COLOR	CLOTH	VINYL	LEATHER	CODE
Blue	•	•		540
Blue		•		550
Gold	•	•		542
Gold		•		552
Green	•	•		546
Green		•		556
Black	•	•		548
Black		•		558
Parchment		•		557

BONNEVILLE TRIM

COLOR	CLOTH	VINYL	LEATHER	CODE
Black		•		539,568,578
Black	•	•		519,588
Black	•	•		529,598
Black			•	563
Blue		•		560,570
Blue	•	•		510,580
Blue	•	•		520,590
Gold		•		562,572
Gold	•	•		513,523
Gold			•	569
Burgundy		•		565,575
Burgundy	•	•		595
Green		•		566
Green	•	•		586,526,596
Parchment		•		567,577
Red		•		564

GRAND PRIX TRIM

COLOR	CLOTH	VINYL	LEATHER	CODE
Blue		•		280
Blue	•	•		270
Gold		•		282
Gold	•	•		272
Gold			•	292
Burgundy		•		285
Green		•		286
Green	•	•		276
Green			•	296
Parchment		•		287
Black		•		288
Black	•	•		278
Black			•	298

THE PAINT CODE furnishes the key to paint colors used on the car. A two-letter code indicates the bottom and top colors respectively.

COLOR	CODE
Starlight Black	A
Expresso Brown	B
Cameo White	C
Warwick Blue	D
Liberty Blue	E
Antique Gold	G
Limelight Green	H
Crystal Turquoise	K
Midnight Green	M
Burgundy	N
Palladium Silver	P
Verdoro Green	Q
Matador Red	R
Champagne	S
Mayfair Maize	Y
Castilian Bronze	J
Claret Red	L
Nocturne Blue	V

ENGINE NUMBER

The engine code is stamped along with the VIN on the right hand side of the block.

TEMPEST, CUSTOMS & LE MANS

ENGINE CODE	NO. CYL.	CID	HORSE-POWER	COMP. RATIO	CARB	TRANS
ZC	6	250	175	9.0:1	1 BC	MAN
ZH	6	250	230	10.5:1	4 BC	MAN
WU	8	350	265	9.2:1	2 BC	MAN
WV	8	350	330	10.5:1	4 BC	MAN
ZF	6	250	175	9.0:1	1 BC	AUTO
ZL	6	250	215	10.5:1	4 BC	AUTO
YU	8	350	265	9.2:1	2 BC	AUTO
XS	8	350	265	9.2:1	2 BC	AUTO
XU	8	350	330	10.5:1	4 BC	AUTO
ZK	6	250	175	9.0:1	1 BC	MAN
ZN	6	250	175	9.0:1	1 BC	AUTO
ZD	6	250	230	10.5:1	4 BC	MAN
ZE	6	250	215	10.5:1	4 BC	AUTO
XR	8	350	265	9.2:1	2 BC	AUTO
YN	8	350	265	9.2:1	2 BC	AUTO
WP	8	350	265	9.2:1	2 BC	MAN

GTO

ENGINE CODE	NO. CYL.	CID	HORSE-POWER	COMP. RATIO	CARB	TRANS
WT	8	400	350	10.75:1	4 BC	MAN
WS	8	400	366	10.75:1	4 BC	MAN
WW	8	400	366	10.75:1	4 BC	MAN
YS	8	400	350	10.75:1	4 BC	AUTO
XX	8	400	265	8.6:1	2 BC	AUTO
YZ	8	400	366	10.75:1	4 BC	AUTO
XP	8	400	370	10.75:1	4 BC	AUTO
XM	8	400	265	8.6:1	2 BC	AUTO

CATALINA & EXECUTIVE

ENGINE CODE	NO. CYL.	CID	HORSE-POWER	COMP. RATIO	CARB	TRANS
WD	8	400	290	10.5:1	2 BC	MAN
WE	8	400	290	10.5:1	2 BC	MAN
WG	8	428	360	10.5:1	4 BC	MAN
WJ	8	428	390	10.75:1	4 BC	MAN
YD	8	400	290	10.5:1	2 BC	AUTO
YB	8	400	265	8.6:1	2 BC	AUTO
YH	8	428	360	10.5:1	4 BC	AUTO
YK	8	428	390	10.75:1	4 BC	AUTO
XJ	8	428	360	10.5:1	4 BC	AUTO
XK	8	428	370	10.75:1	4 BC	AUTO
WA	8	400	290	10.5:1	2 BC	MAN
YA	8	400	265	8.6:1	2 BC	AUTO
WB	8	400	290	10.5:1	2 BC	MAN
YL	8	428	360	10.5:1	4 BC	AUTO
XE	8	428	360	10.5:1	4 BC	AUTO

BONNEVILLE

ENGINE CODE	NO. CYL.	CID	HORSE-POWER	COMP. RATIO	CARB	TRANS
WG	8	428	340	10.5:1	4 BC	MAN
WJ	8	428	390	10.75:1	4 BC	MAN
YH	8	428	360	10.5:1	4 BC	AUTO
YB	8	400	265	8.6:1	2 BC	AUTO
YK	8	428	390	10.75:1	4 BC	AUTO

GRAND PRIX

ENGINE CODE	NO. CYL.	CID	HORSE-POWER	COMP. RATIO	CARB	TRANS
WX	8	400	350	10.5:1	4 BC	MAN
WF	8	428	370	10.5:1	4 BC	MAN
WL	8	428	390	10.75:1	4 BC	MAN
XH	8	400	350	10.5:1	4 BC	AUTO
XF	8	428	370	10.5:1	4 BC	AUTO
XG	8	428	390	10.75:1	4 BC	AUTO
YF	8	400	265	8.6:1	2 BC	AUTO

FIREBIRD

ENGINE CODE	NO. CYL.	CID	HORSE-POWER	COMP. RATIO	CARB	TRANS
ZC	6	250	175	9.0:1	1 BC	MAN
ZH	6	250	230	10.5:1	4 BC	MAN
WM	8	350	265	9.2:1	2 BC	MAN
WN	8	350	325	10.5:1	4 BC	MAN
WZ	8	400	330	10.75:1	4 BC	MAN
WQ	8	400	335	10.75:1	4 BC	MAN
WH	8	400	345	10.75:1	4 BC	MAN
ZF	6	250	175	9.0:1	1 BC	AUTO
ZL	6	250	215	10.5:1	4 BC	AUTO
YE	8	350	265	9.2:1	2 BC	AUTO
XB	8	350	265	9.2:1	2 BC	AUTO
XG	8	350	325	10.5:1	4 BC	AUTO
YT	8	400	330	10.75:1	4 BC	AUTO
YW	8	400	335	10.75:1	4 BC	AUTO
XN	8	400	345	10.75:1	4 BC	AUTO
ZK	6	250	175	9.0:1	1 BC	MAN
ZN	6	250	175	9.0:1	1 BC	AUTO
ZD	6	250	230	10.5:1	4 BC	MAN
ZE	6	250	215	10.5:1	4 BC	AUTO
WC	8	350	265	9.2:1	2 BC	MAN
XL	8	350	265	9.2:1	2 BC	MAN
YJ	8	350	265	9.2:1	2 BC	MAN

1960 FORD

1960 FORD

1960 FORD FALCON

1960 FORD FALCON

1960 FORD THUNDERBIRD

1960 FORD THUNDERBIRD

VEHICLE IDENTIFICATION NUMBER

FORD
0A71Y100551

VIN LOCATION

FULL SIZED FORD VIN die-stamped into top of right-hand side-rail of the frame forward of front suspension member.

THUNDERBIRD VIN die-stamped into top surface of the front fender cross-brace to the right of the hood lock plate.

FALCON VIN die-stamped into top surface of left-hand brace extending from the top of firewall to the left front wheelhouse.

FIRST DIGIT: Identifies the model year (1960)

SECOND DIGIT: Identifies the assembly plant

Atlanta, GA	A
Chester, PA	C
Chicago, IL	G
Lorain, OH	H
Los Angeles, CA	J
Louisville, KY	U
Mahwah, NJ	E
Dallas, TX	D
Dearborn, MI	F
Kansas City, KS	K
Norfolk, VA	N
Pilot Plant	S
San Jose, CA	R
Twin Cities, MN	P
Metuchen, NJ	T
Wixom, MI	Y

THIRD AND FOURTH DIGITS: Identify the body series

THE BODY SERIES number identifies the model and the particular body style.

FAIRLANE	CODE
2-Dr. Club Sedan	31
4-Dr. Town Sedan	32
2-Dr. Business Sedan	33

FAIRLANE 500	CODE
2-Dr. Club Sedan	41
4-Dr. Town Sedan	42

GALAXIE	CODE
2-Dr. Club Sedan	51
4-Dr. Town Sedan	52
4-Dr. Town Victoria	54
2-Dr. Starliner Club Victoria	53
Sunliner Convertible	55

STATION WAGONS	CODE
2-Dr. Ranch Wagon	61
4-Dr. Ranch Wagon	62
4-Dr. 6-Pass. Country Sedan	64
4-Dr. 9-Pass. Country Sedan	66
4-Dr. 9-Pass. Country Squire	68
2 Door Courier (Commercial Ranch Wagon)	69

THUNDERBIRD	CODE
Tudor Hardtop	71
Convertible	73

FALCON	CODE
2-Dr. Sedan	11
4-Dr. Sedan	12
2-Dr. Station Wagon	21
4-Dr. Station Wagon	22

FIFTH DIGIT: Identifies the engine code

ENGINE	CODE
6 Cyl. 223 C.I.	V
8 Cyl. 292 C.I. (Dual)	W
8 Cyl. 352 C.I. (Dual)	X
8 Cyl. 352 C.I. (4-V)	Y
8 Cyl. 292 C.I. (Dual-L.C. Export, 84 Octane)	T
8 Cyl. 352 C.I. (4-V L.C. Export, 84 Octane)	G

FALCON	CODE
6 Cyl. OHV 144 C.I.	S
6 Cyl. OHV 144 C.I. (L.C., 84 Octane)	D

THUNDERBIRD	CODE
352 C.I. V-8	Y
430 C.I. V-8	J

LAST SIX DIGITS: Represent the basic production sequence

BODY NUMBER PLATE

THE BODY PLATE is located on the front body pillar on all passenger and Thunderbird models, and on the lock face of the left front door on Falcon models. Indicated on the body plate is body type, exterior paint color, trim scheme, production date, transmission type and rear axle ratio.

FORD MOTOR CORPORATION

SERIAL NUMBER
0F32Y100001

58E	AM	31	20K	_	3	8
BDY	CLR	TRM	DT	DSO	AX	TR

EXAMPLE:
Serial Number

0	Model Year (1960)
F	Assembly Plant (Dearborn, MI)
32	Model (4-Dr. Sedan)
Y	Engine (8 Cyl. 352 C.I.)
100001	Production Sequence
58E	Style (Fairlane)
A	Lower Body Color
M	Upper Body Color
31	Trim
20K	Production Date Code
3	Fordomatic (2-Speed) Trans
8	2.9:1

BODY STYLE	CODE
Galaxie Town Sedan	54A
Fairlane 500 Town Sedan	58A
Falcon 4-Door Sedan	58A
Fairlane Town Sedan	58E
Falcon 2-Door Ranch Wagon	59A
2-Door Ranch Wagon	59C
2-Door Commercial Ranch Wagon	59E
Wagon Courier Galaxie, Club Sedan	62A
Starliner Club Victoria	63A
Thunderbird Hardtop	63A
Fairlane 500 Club Sedan	64A
Falcon Tudor Sedan	64A
Fairlane Club Sedan	64F
Fairlane Business Coupe	64G
Falcon 4-Dr. Station Wagon	71A
Station Wagon	71E
Country Sedan (9-Pass.), Station Wagon	71F
Country Sedan (6-Pass.), Station Wagon	71G
Country Squire 4-Dr., Ranch Wagon	71H
Galaxie Town Victoria	75A
Thunderbird Convertible	76A
Galaxie Convertible	76A
Sunliner Convertible	76B

THE DAY AND MONTH CODE furnishes the date the vehicle was manufactured. The number indicates the day of the month and the letter indicates the month.

MONTH	CODE	*CODE
January	A	N
February	B	P
March	C	Q
April	D	R
May	E	S
June	F	T
July	G	U
August	H	V
September	J	W
October	K	X
November	L	Y
December	M	Z

*Two year code letters to be used if 1960 models exceed 12 months.

THE REAR AXLE CODE indicates the ratio of the rear axle installed in the vehicle.

REAR AXLE RATIO	REGULAR	LOCKING
3.10:1	3	C
3.56:1	1	A
3.70:1	9	
3.89:1	2	B
2.91:1	8	
3.78:1	4	
3.22:1	6	

THE TRANSMISSION CODE indicates the type of transmission installed in the vehicle.

TRANSMISSION	CODE
Standard	1
Overdrive	2
Fordomatic (2-Speed)	3
Cruise-O-Matic	4

THE TRIM NUMBER furnishes the key to trim color and material for each model series.

FORD TRIM COLOR	CLOTH	VINYL	LEATHER	CODE
Gray		•		31
Blue	•	•		32
Blue		•		42,62
Green	•	•		33
Green		•		43,63
Beige	•	•		34
Beige		•		44
Red	•	•		35
White	•	•		36
Black	•	•		36
Black		•		46
Turquoise	•	•		37
Turquoise		•		47,67
Yellow	•	•		38
Orchid	•	•		39
Orchid		•		49
Black/Red		•		45
White/Red		•		45
Yellow/Black		•		48

THUNDERBIRD TRIM COLOR	CLOTH	VINYL	LEATHER	CODE
Blue		•		52
Blue	•	•		72
Green		•		53
Green	•	•		73
Beige		•		54
Beige	•	•		74
Beige			•	84
Red/White		•		55
Black/White		•		56
Black/Gray	•	•		76
Turquoise		•		57
Turquoise	•	•		72
Turquoise			•	87
Red			•	85
Black			•	86

FALCON TRIM COLOR	CLOTH	VINYL	LEATHER	CODE
Gray	•	•		11,21
Blue	•	•		22
Green	•	•		23

THE PAINT CODE furnishes the key to the paint colors used on the car. A letter indicates the color of the car. A two-tone car has two sets of letters. The first indicates the lower body color, the second the upper body color.

COLOR	CODE
Raven Black	A
Kingston Blue	B
Aquamarine	C
Acapulco Blue	*E
Belmont Blue	E
Skymist Blue	F
Yosemite Yellow	G
Beachwood Brown	H
Monte Carlo Red	J
Sultana Turquoise	K
Corinthian White	M
Diamond Blue	*N
Orchid Gray	Q
Moroccan Ivory	*R
Briarcliffe Green	*S
Meadowvale Green	T
Springdale Rose	*U
Palm Springs Rose	*V
Adriatic Green	W
Royal Burgandy	*X
Gunpowder Gray	*Y
Platinum	Z

* Thunderbird only

ENGINE NUMBER

6-cylinder engine number is stamped on the top of the block on the front left side near the crankcase breather pipe. This code designates the engine plant, year, month and day of manufacture, and the inspector's identification.

292 engine number is stamped on the front of the block at the pushrod cover-to-cylinder head mounting surface.

352 engine number is stamped on the machined boss on the left front of the engine below the cylinder head.

430 engine number is stamped on the block in the front of the left cylinder head.

FALCON

ENGINE CODE	NO. CYL.	CID	HORSE-POWER	COMP. RATIO	CARB	TRANS
S	6	144	90	8.7:1	1 BC	** M & A
D*	6	144	N/A	N/A	1 BC	** M & A

* Export

THUNDERBIRD

ENGINE CODE	NO. CYL.	CID	HORSE-POWER	COMP. RATIO	CARB	TRANS
Y	8	352	300	9.6:1	4 BC	** M & A
J	8	430	350	10.0:1	4 BC	AUTO

FORD FAIRLANE, FAIRLANE 500, GALAXIE

ENGINE CODE	NO. CYL.	CID	HORSE-POWER	COMP. RATIO	CARB	TRANS
V	6	223	145	8.4:1	1 BC	** M & A
W	8	292	185	8.8:1	2 BC	** M & A
T*	8	292	N/A	N/A	2 BC	** M & A
X	8	352	235	8.9:1	2 BC	** M & A
Y	8	352	300	9.6:1	4 BC	** M & A
G*	8	352	N/A	N/A	4 BC	** M & A
Y	8	352	360	10.6:1	4 BC	MAN

* Export
** MAN & AUTO

1961 FORD

1961 FORD

1961 FORD FALCON

1961 FORD FALCON

1961 FORD THUNDERBIRD

1961 FORD THUNDERBIRD

VEHICLE IDENTIFICATION NUMBER

FORD
1A71W0055

VIN LOCATIONS

FULL SIZED FORD VIN die-stamped into top of right-hand side-rail of the frame forward of the front suspension member.

THUNDERBIRD VIN die-stamped into top of the front fender cross-brace to the right of the hood lock plate.

FALCON VIN die-stamped into top surface of left-hand brace extending from the top of firewall to the left front wheelhouse.

FIRST DIGIT: Identifies the model year (1961)

SECOND DIGIT: Identifies the assembly plant

ASSEMBLY PLANT	CODE
Atlanta, GA	A
Chester, PA	C
Chicago, IL	G
Lorain, OH	H
Los Angeles, CA	J
Louisville, KY	U
Mahwah, NJ	E
Dallas, TX	D
Dearborn, MI	F
Kansas City, KS	K
Norfolk, VA	N
Pilot Plant	S
San Jose, CA	R
Twin Cities, MN	P
Metuchen, NJ	T
Wixom, MI	Y

THIRD AND FOURTH DIGITS: Identify the body series

BODY SERIES identifies the model and the particular body style.

FALCON	CODE
2-Dr. Sedan	11
4-Dr. Sedan	12
2-Dr. Futura	17
2-Dr. Wagon	21
4-Dr. Wagon	22
Country Squire Wagon	26
Falcon Sedan Delivery	29

FAIRLANE	CODE
2-Dr. Club Sedan	31
4-Dr. Town Sedan	32

FAIRLANE 500	CODE
2-Dr. Club Sedan	41
4-Dr. Town Sedan	42

GALAXIE	CODE
2-Dr. Club Sedan	51
4-Dr. Town Sedan	52
2-Dr. Club Victoria Starliner	53
4-Dr. Town Victoria	54
Sunliner Convertible	55
2-Dr. Club Victoria	57

STATION WAGONS	CODE
2-Dr. Ranch Wagon	61
4-Dr. Ranch Wagon	62
4-Dr. Country Sedan, 6-Pass.	64
4-Dr. Country Sedan, 9-Pass.	66
4-Dr. Country Squire, 6-Pass.	67
4-Dr. Country Squire, 9-Pass.	68
2-Dr. Commercial Ranch Wagon, Futura	69

THUNDERBIRD	CODE
Tudor Hardtop	71
Convertible	73

FIFTH DIGIT: Identifies the engine code

ENGINE	CODE
6 Cyl. 223 C.I.	V
8 Cyl. 292 C.I. (Dual)	W
8 Cyl. 352 C.I. (Dual)	X
8 Cyl. 390 C.I. (4-V)	Z
8 Cyl. 292 C.I. (Dual, LC Export, 84 Octane)	T
8 Cyl. 390 C.I. (4-V LC, Export, 84 Octane)	R
6 Cyl. OHV 170 C.I. (Low Comp.)	E
8 Cyl. 390 (4-V) HP	Z
8 Cyl. 390 (8-V) HP	Z
8 Cyl. 390 (4-V Police)	Z
6 Cyl. OHV 144 C.I.	S
6 Cyl. OHV 144 C.I., (LC 84 Octane)	D
6 Cyl. OHV 170 C.I.	U

LAST SIX DIGITS: Represent the basic production sequence

BODY NUMBER PLATE

THE BODY PLATE is located on the front body pillar on all passenger and Thunderbird models, and on the lock face of the left front door on Falcon models. Indicated on the body plate is body type, exterior paint color, trim scheme, production date, transmission type and rear axle ratio.

FORD MOTOR CORPORATION

SERIAL NUMBER
1F52W100001

54A	AM1	32	17K	_	8	3
BDY	CLR	TRM	DT	DSO	AX	TR

EXAMPLE:

Serial Number

1	Model Year (1961)
F	Assembly Plant (Dearborn, MI)
52	Model (4-Dr. Town Sedan)
W	Engine (8 Cyl. 292 C.I.)
100001	Production Sequence

54A	Style (Galaxie Town Sedan)
A	Lower Body Color
M	Upper Body Color
32	Trim
17K	Production Date Code
8	2.91:1
3	Fordomatic (2-Speed)

BODY STYLE	CODE
Galaxie Town Sedan	54A
Fairlane 500 Town Sedan	58A
Falcon 4-Dr. Sedan	58A
Fairlane Town Sedan	58E
2-Dr. Ranch Wagon (Falcon)	59A
2-Dr. Ranch Wagon	59C
2-Dr. Courier Ranch Wagon	59E
Galaxie Club Sedan	62A
Galaxie Club Victoria, (Starliner)	63A
Thunderbird Hardtop	63A
Fairlane 500 Club Sedan	64A
Falcon Tudor Sedan	64A
2-Dr. Falcon Futura Sedan	64A
Fairlane Club Sedan	64F
Galaxie Club Victoria	65A
4-Dr. Ranch Wagon (Falcon)	71A
4-Dr. Falcon Country Squire Wagon	71B
Station Wagon Country Squire, (6-Pass.)	71J
Station Wagon Country Sedan, (9-Pass.)	71E
Station Wagon Country Sedan, (6-Pass.)	71F
Station Wagon Country Squire	71G
4-Dr. Ranch Wagon	71H
Galaxie Town Victoria	75A
Thunderbird Convertible	76A
Galaxie Convertible Sunliner	76B
Falcon Sedan Delivery	78A

THE DAY AND MONTH CODE furnishes the date the vehicle was manufactured. The number indicates the day of the month and the letter indicates the month.

MONTH	CODE	*CODE
January	A	N
February	B	P
March	C	Q
April	D	R
May	E	S
June	F	T
July	G	U
August	H	V
September	J	W
October	K	X
November	L	Y
December	M	Z

*Two year code letters to be used if 1961 models exceed 12 months.

THE REAR AXLE CODE indicates the ratio of the rear axle installed in the vehicle.

REAR AXLE RATIO	REGULAR	LOCKING
3.00:1	6	
3.10:1	3	C
3.56:1	1	A
3.50:1		J
3.89:1	2	B
2.91:1	8	H
4.00:1	4	
3.20:1	5	

THE TRANSMISSION CODE indicates the type of transmission installed in the vehicle.

TRANSMISSION	CODE
3-Speed Manual	1
Overdrive	2
Fordomatic (2-Speed)	3
Cruise-O-Matic	4
4-Speed Manual	5

THE TRIM NUMBER furnishes the key to trim color and material for each model series.

FORD TRIM COLOR	CLOTH	VINYL	LEATHER	CODE
Brown		•		4,84,94
Brown	•	•		24,34
Gray	•	•		11,21
Blue	•	•		12,22
Blue	•	•		32,72
Blue		•		62,92
Green	•	•		13,23
Green	•	•		33,73
Green		•		63
Turquoise	•	•		27,37,77
Turquoise		•		97
White/Black	•	•		30,96
White/Red	•	•		35
White/Red		•		85,95
Yellow/Black	•	•		38,98
Black/Gray		•		51

FALCON TRIM COLOR	CLOTH	VINYL	LEATHER	CODE
Gray	•	•		11,41
Brown	•	•		24
Blue	•	•		42
Blue		•		72
Green	•	•		23,43
Turquoise	•	•		47
Beige/Brown		•		54
White/Red		•		75
White/Black		•		76

THUNDERBIRD TRIM

COLOR	CLOTH	VINYL	LEATHER	CODE
Blue		•		52
Blue	•	•		72
Blue			•	82
Green		•		53
Green	•	•		73
White		•		54
Red		•		55
Red			•	85
Black		•		56
Black			•	86
Turquoise		•		57
Turquoise	•	•		77
Turquoise			•	87
Beige	•	•		74
Beige			•	84
Black/Gray	•	•		76

THE PAINT CODE furnishes the key to the paint colors used on the car. A letter indicates the color of the car. A two-tone car has two sets of letters. The first indicates the lower body color, the second the upper body color.

COLOR	CODE
Raven Black	A
Aquamarine	C
Starlight Blue	D
Laurel Green	E
Desert Gold	F
Chesapeake Blue	H
Monte Carlo Red	J
Algiers Bronze	K
Corinthian White	M
Diamond Blue	*N
Nautilis Gray	*P
Silver Gray	Q
Cambridge Blue	R
Mint Green	S
Honey Beige	*T
Palm Springs Rose	*V
Garden Turquoise	W
Heritage Burgundy	*X
Mahogany	*Y
Fieldstone Tan	*Z

* Thunderbird only

ENGINE NUMBER

The engine number is stamped on top of the block on the front left side near the crankcase breather pipe. The code designates the engine plant, year, month and day of manufacture, and inspector's identification.

FALCON

ENGINE CODE	NO. CYL.	CID	HORSE-POWER	COMP. RATIO	CARB	TRANS
S	6	144	85	8.7:1	1 BC	** M & A
D*	6	144	N/A	N/A	1 BC	** M & A
U	6	170	101	8.7:1	1 BC	** M & A

* Export

THUNDERBIRD

ENGINE CODE	NO. CYL.	CID	HORSE-POWER	COMP. RATIO	CARB	TRANS
Z	8	390	300	9.6:1	4 BC	AUTO

FORD FAIRLANE, FAIRLANE 500, GALAXIE

ENGINE CODE	NO. CYL.	CID	HORSE-POWER	COMP. RATIO	CARB	TRANS
V	6	223	135	8.4:1	1 BC	** M & A
W	8	292	175	8.8:1	2 BC	** M & A
T*	8	292	N/A	N/A	2 BC	** M & A
X	8	352	220	8.9:1	2 BC	** M & A
Z	8	390	300	9.6:1	4 BC	** M & A
R*	8	390	N/A	N/A	4 BC	** M & A
Z,P+	8	390	330	9.6:1	4 BC	** M & A
Z,Q	8	390	375	10.6:1	4 BC	MAN
Z	8	390	401	10.6:1	3-2 BC	MAN

* Export
+ Police
** MAN & AUTO

1962 FORD FAIRLANE

1962 FORD FAIRLANE

1962 FORD FALCON

1962 FORD FALCON

1962 FORD GALAXIE

1962 FORD GALAXIE

1962 FORD THUNDERBIRD

1962 FORD THUNDERBIRD

VEHICLE IDENTIFICATION NUMBER

FORD
2A83X100551

VIN LOCATION

FULL SIZED FORD VIN die-stamped into top of right-hand side-rail of the frame forward of front suspension member.

FAIRLANE VIN die-stamped into the side of the left front inner fender apron near the top.

THUNDERBIRD VIN die-stamped into top of the front fender cross-brace to the right of the hood lock plate.

FALCON VIN die-stamped into top of the left-hand brace extending from the top of firewall to the left front wheelhouse.

FIRST DIGIT: Identifies the model year (1962)

SECOND DIGIT: Identifies the assembly plant

ASSEMBLY PLANT	CODE
Atlanta, GA	A
Dallas, TX	D
Mahwah, NJ	E
Dearborn, MI	F
Chicago, IL	G
Lorain, OH	H
Los Angeles, CA	J
Kansas City, KS	K
Norfolk, VA	N
Twin Cities, MN	P
San Jose, CA	R
Pilot Plant	S
Metuchen, NJ	T
Louisville, KY	U
Wayne, MI	W
Wixom, MI	Y
St. Louis, MO	Z

THIRD AND FOURTH DIGITS: Identify the body series

THE BODY SERIES CODE identifies the model and the particular body style.

FALCON	CODE
2-Dr.	11
4-Dr.	12
Tudor Futura	17
2-Dr. Station Wagon	21
4-Dr. Station Wagon	22
Fordor Squire Station Wagon	26
Sedan Delivery Wagon	29

FAIRLANE	CODE
2-Dr. Club Sedan	31
4-Dr. Town Sedan	32

FAIRLANE 500	CODE
2-Dr. Club Sedan	41
4-Dr. Town Sedan	42
Sports Coupe	47

GALAXIE	CODE
2-Dr. Club Sedan	51
4-Dr. Town Sedan	52

GALAXIE	CODE
2-Dr. Club Sedan	61
4-Dr. Town Sedan	62
2-Dr. Club Victoria	63
4-Dr. Town Victoria	64
2-Dr. Convertible	65

GALAXIE STATION WAGONS	CODE
4-Dr. Ranch Wagon	71
4-Dr. 6-Pass. Country Sedan	72
4-Dr. 9-Pass. Country Sedan	74
4-Dr. 6-Pass. Country Squire	76

THUNDERBIRD	CODE
Tudor Hardtop	83
Convertible	85

FIFTH DIGIT: Identifies the engine

ENGINE	CODE
GALAXIE	
6 Cyl. 223 C.I	V
8 Cyl. 292 C.I. (2-V)	W
8 Cyl. 352 C.I. (2-V)	X
8 Cyl. 390 C.I. (4-V)	Z
8 Cyl. 292 C.I. (2-V, L.C., Export, 84 Octane)	T
8 Cyl. 390 C.I. (4-V, L.C., Export, 84 Octane)	R
8 Cyl. 390 C.I. (6-V, High Performance)	M
8 Cyl. 390 C.I. (4-V, High Performance)	Q
390 4-V Police	P
406 4-V High Performance	B
406 6-V High Performance	G
FALCON	
6 Cyl. 170 C.I. Export	E
6 Cyl. OHV 144 C.I.	S
6 Cyl.OHV 144 C.I., (L.C., 84 Octane)	D
6 Cyl. OHV 170 C.I.	U
FAIRLANE	
6 Cyl. 170 C.I.	U
8 Cyl. 221 C.I. (L.C. Export)	C
6 Cyl. 170 C.I. (L.C. Export)	E
8 Cyl. 221 C.I.	L
8 Cyl. 260 C.I.	F
THUNDERBIRD	
8 Cyl. 390 C.I. 4-V	Z
8 Cyl. 390 C.I. 6-V	M

BODY NUMBER PLATE

THE BODY PLATE is located on the front body pillar on Galaxie and Thunderbird models, and on the lock face of left front door on Fairlane and Falcon models. The rating for the Falcon Bus models is attached to the left front door hinge pillar. Indicated on the body plate is body type, exterior paint color, trim scheme, production date, transmission type and rear axle ratio.

FORD MOTOR CORPORATION

SERIAL NUMBER
2S63X100001

54A	AM	35	17K	33	1	1
BDY	CLR	TRM	DT	DSO	AX	TR

EXAMPLE:

Serial Number

2	Model Year (1962)
S	Assembly Plant (Pilot Plant)
63	Model (2-Dr. Club Victoria)
X	Engine (8-Cyl. 352 C.I.
100001	Production Sequence

54A	Body (Fairlane Town Sedan)
A	Lower Body Color
M	Upper Body Color
35	Trim
17K	Production Date Code
33	DSO (Detroit)
1	3.00:1
1	3-Speed Manual

BODY STYLE	CODE
Fairlane Town Sedan	54A
Galaxie 500 Town Sedan	54A
Fairlane 500 Town Sedan	54B
Galaxie Town Sedan	54B
Falcon 4-Dr. Sedan	58A
Falcon 4-Dr. Ranch Wagon	59A
Fairlane Club Sedan	62A
Galaxie 500 Club Sedan	62A
Fairlane 500 Club Sedan	62B
Galaxie Club Sedan	62B
Fairlane 500 Sports Coupe	62C
Falcon Tudor Futura	62C
Thunderbird Hardtop	63A
Thunderbird Hardtop (Landau)	63B
Falcon Tudor Sedan	64A
Falcon Tudor Sedan (Futura)	64C
Galaxie 500XL Tudor Hardtop	65B
Galaxie 500 Club Victoria	65A
4-Dr. Ranch Wagon (Falcon)	71A
Station Wagon Country Squire, (9-Pass.)	71A
Station Wagon Country Sedan	71B
4-Dr. Falcon Super Deluxe Wagon	71B
Station Wagon Country Sedan, (9-Pass.)	71C
4-Dr. Falcon	71B
4-Dr. Super Deluxe Ranch Wagon	71D
Station Wagon Country Squire	71E
Galaxie 500 Town Victoria, (6-Pass.)	75A
Thunderbird Convertible	S(76A)
Thunderbird Convertible	S(76B)
Sports Roadster Galaxie 500 Sunliner	76A
Falcon Sedan Delivery	78A
Galaxie 500XL Tudor Convertible	76B

THE DAY AND MONTH CODE furnishes the date the vehicle was manufactured. The number indicates the day of the month and the letter indicates the month.

MONTH	CODE	*CODE
January	A	N
February	B	P
March	C	Q
April	D	R
May	E	S
June	F	T
July	G	U
August	H	V
September	J	W
October	K	X
November	L	Y
December	M	Z

*Two year code letters to be used if 1962 models exceed 12 months.

DOMESTIC SPECIAL ORDERS

DSO units built to a Domestic Special Order, Foreign Special Order, or Pre-Approved Order have the complete order number recorded in this space. Also appearing in this space is the two digit code number of the District which ordered the unit. If the unit is regular production, only the District code number will appear.

DISTRICT	CODE
Boston	11
Buffalo	12
New York	13
Pittsburgh	14
Newark	15
Atlanta	21
Charlotte	22
Philadelphia	23
Jacksonville	24
Richmond	25
Washington	26
Cincinnati	31
Cleveland	32
Detroit	33
Inidanapolis	34
Lansing	35
Louisville	36
Chicago	41
Fargo	42
Rockford	43
Twin Cities	44
Davenport	45
Denver	51
Des Moines	52
Kansas City	53
Omaha	54
St. Louis	55
Dallas	61
Houston	62
Memphis	63
New Orleans	64
Oklahoma City	65
Los Angeles	71
San Jose	72
Salt Lake City	73
Seattle	74
Phoenix	75
Ford of Canada	81

Government	83
Home Office Reserve	84
American Red Cross	85
Transportation Services	89
Export	90-99

FORD OF CANADA

Central	B1
Eastern	B2
Atlantic	B3
Midwestern	B4
Western	B6
Pacific	B7

THE REAR AXLE CODE indicates the ratio of the rear axle installed in the vehicle.

REAR AXLE RATIO	REGULAR	LOCKING
3.00:1	1	A
3.20:1	3	B
3.50:1	5	E
3.56:1	6	F
3.80:1	7	G
3.89:1	8	H
4.00:1	9	Falcon
4.11:1	9	Galaxie

THE TRANSMISSION CODE indicates the type of transmission installed in the vehicle.

TRANSMISSION	CODE
3-Speed Manual	1
Overdrive	2
Fordomatic (2-Speed)	3
Cruise-O-Matic	4
4-Speed Manual	5

THE TRIM NUMBER furnishes the key to trim color and material for each model series.

FORD TRIM COLOR	CLOTH	VINYL	LEATHER	CODE
Blue	•	•		12,22
Blue	•	•		32,62
Blue		•		72,82
Green	•	•		13,23,63
Green		•		73
Beige	•	•		14,24,54
Beige	•	•		34,64
Beige		•		74,84
Red	•	•		15,25
Red	•	•		35,45
Red		•		55,75,85
Black	•	•		16
Black		•		56,86
Turquoise	•	•		17,27
Turquoise	•	•		37,67
Turquoise		•		77,87
Chestnut	•	•		19,39
Chestnut		•		59
Gray	•	•		11,21,61
Red/White		•		75
Black/White		•		76

THE PAINT CODE furnishes the key to the paint colors used on the car. A letter indicates the color of the car. A two-tone car has two sets of letters. The first indicates the lower body color, the second the upper body color.

COLOR	CODE
Raven Black	A
Ming Green	D
Viking Blue	E
Baffin Blue	F
Silver Mink	G
Oxford Blue	H
Rangoon Red	J
Chalfonte Blue	K
Sahara Rose	L
Corinthian White	M
Diamond Blue	N
Silver Moss	P
Silver Gray	Q
Tucson Yellow	R
Sandshell Beige	T
Deep Sea Turquoise	U
Chestnut	V
Heritage Maroon	X
Fieldstone Tan	Z

ENGINE NUMBER

6-cylinder engine number code is stamped on the crankcase outlet ventilation pipe boss on the crankcase just forward of the distributor. The code indicates place, day, and month of engine manufacture.

V-8 engine number code is stamped on the front face of the cylinder block above and to the left of the water pump mounting.

FALCON

ENGINE CODE	NO. CYL.	CID	HORSE-POWER	COMP. RATIO	CARB	TRANS
S	6	144	85	8.7:1	1 BC	** M & A
D*	6	144	N/A	N/A	1 BC	** M & A
U	6	170	101	8.7:1	1 BC	** M & A
E*	6	170	N/A	N/A	1 BC	** M & A

* Export

FAIRLANE

ENGINE CODE	NO. CYL.	CID	HORSE-POWER	COMP. RATIO	CARB	TRANS
U	6	170	101	8.7:1	1 BC	** M & A
E*	6	170	N/A	N/A	1 BC	** M & A
L	8	221	145	8.7:1	2 BC	** M & A
C*	8	221	N/A	N/A	2 BC	** M & A
F	8	260	164	8.7:1	2 BC	** M & A

* Export

THUNDERBIRD

ENGINE CODE	NO. CYL.	CID	HORSE-POWER	COMP. RATIO	CARB	TRANS
Z	8	390	300	9.6:1	4 BC	AUTO
M	8	390	340	10.5:1	2-3 BC	AUTO

FORD GALAXIE, GALAXIE 500

ENGINE CODE	NO. CYL.	CID	HORSE-POWER	COMP. RATIO	CARB	TRANS
V	6	223	138	8.4:1	1 BC	** M & A
W	8	292	170	8.8:1	2 BC	** M & A
T*	8	292	N/A	N/A	2 BC	** M & A
X	8	352	220	8.9:1	2 BC	** M & A
Z	8	390	300 9.6:1	4 BC	** M & A	
R*	8	390	N/A	N/A	4 BC	** M & A
P+	8	390	330	9.6:1	4 BC	** M & A
Q	8	390	375	10.6:1	4 BC	MAN
M	8	390	401	11.1:1	2-3 BC	MAN
B	8	406	385	11.4:1	4 BC	MAN
G	8	406	405	11.4:1	2-3 BC	MAN

* Export
+ Police
** MAN & AUTO

1963 FORD FAIRLANE

1963 FORD FAIRLANE

1963 FORD FALCON

1963 FORD FALCON

1963 FORD GALAXIE

1963 FORD GALAXIE

1963 FORD THUNDERBIRD

1963 FORD THUNDERBIRD

VEHICLE IDENTIFICATION NUMBER

FORD
3A83X 100551

VIN LOCATION

FULL SIZED FORD VIN die-stamped on the right-hand top of the cowl under the hood.

FAIRLANE VIN die-stamped into the side of the left front inner fender apron near the top.

THUNDERBIRD VIN die-stamped into top of the front fender cross-brace to the right of the hood lock plate.

FALCON VIN die-stamped into top of the left-hand brace extending from the top of firewall to the left front wheelhouse.

FIRST DIGIT: Identifies the model year (1963)

SECOND DIGIT: Identifies the assembly plant

ASSEMBLY PLANT	CODE
Atlanta, GA	A
Chicago, IL	G
Los Angeles, CA	J
Louisville, KY	U
Mahwah, NJ	E
Dallas, TX	D
Dearborn, MI	F
Lorain, OH	H
Kansas City, KS	K
Norfolk, VA	N
Pilot Plant	S
Metuchen, NJ	T
San Jose, CA	R
Twin Cities, MN	P
Wayne, MI	W
Wixom, MI	Y
St. Louis, MO	Z

THIRD AND FOURTH DIGITS: Identify the body series

THE BODY SERIES code identifies the model and the particular body style.

FALCON STANDARD	CODE
2-Dr. Sedan	01
4-Dr. Sedan	02

FALCON FUTURA	CODE
2-Dr. Convertible	15
4-Dr. Sedan	16
2-Dr. Hardtop	17
2-Dr. Sedan	19

STATION WAGONS	CODE
2-Dr. Wagon	21
4-Dr. Wagon	22
2-Dr. Deluxe Wagon	23
4-Dr. Deluxe Wagon	24
4-Dr. Country Squire	26

SEDAN DELIVERY	CODE
2-Dr. Sedan Delivery	29

FAIRLANE	CODE
2-Dr. Sedan	31
4-Dr. Sedan	32

FAIRLANE 500	CODE
2-Dr. Sedan	41
4-Dr. Sedan	42
2-Dr. Hardtop	43
2-Dr. Hardtop Sport Coupe	47

GALAXIE	CODE
2-Dr. Sedan	51
4-Dr. Sedan	52

FORD 300	CODE
2-Dr. Sedan	53
4-Dr. Sedan	54

GALAXIE 500	CODE
2 Dr. Sedan	61
4 Dr. Sedan	62
2 Dr. Hardtop	63
4 Dr. Hardtop	64
2 Dr. Convertible	65
4-Dr. Hardtop - Fastback	66

GALAXIE 500XL	CODE
2-Dr. Hardtop	67
4-Dr. Hardtop	60
2-Dr. Hardtop Fastback	68
2-Dr. Convertible	69

STATION WAGON	CODE
4-Dr. 6-Pass.	38
4-Dr. Custom 6-Pass.	48
4-Dr. Country Squire	49
4-Dr. Wagon	72
4-Dr. Wagon	74
4-Dr. Wagon	76
4-Dr. Wagon	78

THUNDERBIRD	CODE
2-Dr. Hardtop	83
2-Dr. Convertible	85
2-Dr. Landau	87
2-Dr. Roadster	89

FIFTH DIGIT: Identifies the engine

ENGINE	CODE
6 Cyl. 223 C.I.	V
8 Cyl. 352 C.I. (2-V)	X
8 Cyl. 390 C.I. (4-V)	Z
8 Cyl. 406 C.I. (4-V H.P.)	B
6 Cyl. 223 C.I. (Taxi)	E
8 Cyl. 260 C.I. (2-V)	F
8 Cyl. 406 C.I. (6-V H.P.)	G
8 Cyl. 390 C.I. (4-V Interceptor)	P
6 Cyl. OHV 144 C.I.	S
6 Cyl. OHV 144 C.I.(Low Comp. 84 Octane)	2
6 Cyl. OHV 170 C.I.	U
289 V-8 (2-V)	C
221 V-8	L
221 V-8 (Low Comp.)	3
170 Six (Low Comp.)	4
260 V-8 (Low Comp.)	8
223 Six (Low Comp.)	5
390 V-8 (4-V) (Low Comp.)	9
289 V-8 (4-V) HP	K
390 V-8 (6-V) HP	M
427 V-8 (4-V) HP	Q
427 V-8 (8-V) HP	R
200 I-6	T

BODY NUMBER PLATE

THE BODY PLATE is located on the front body pillar on Galaxie and Thunderbird models, and on the lock face of the left front door on Fairlane and Falcon models. Indicated on the body plate is body type, exterior paint color, trim scheme, production date, transmission type and rear axle ratio.

FORD MOTOR CORPORATION

SERIAL NUMBER
3A83X100551

63A	AA	56	17K	21	1	3
BDY	CLR	TRM	DT	DSO	AX	TR

EXAMPLE:

Serial Number

3	Model Year (1963)
A	Assembly Plant (Atlanta, GA)
83	Model (2-Dr. Hardtop)
X	Engine (8-Cyl. 352 C.I.)
100551	Production Sequence
63A	Style (Thunderbird HT)
A	Lower Body Color
A	Upper Body Color
56	Trim
17K	Production Date Code
21	DSO (Atlanta)
1	3.00:1
3	Fordomatic (2-Speed)

BODY STYLE	CODE
Falcon 2-Dr. Sedan	62A
Falcon 4-Dr. Sedan	54A
Falcon Futura 2-Dr. Sedan	62B
Falcon Futura 4-Dr. Sedan	54B
Falcon Futura Sports Sedan	62C
Falcon Futura 2-Dr., Hardtop, Bench Seat	62B
Falcon Futura 2-Dr., Hardtop, Bucket Seat	62C
Falcon 2-Dr. Super Deluxe Squire, Bucket Seat	71D
Falcon Futura Convertible	76A
Falcon Futura Sports Convertible	76B
Falcon 2-Dr. Station Wagon	59A
Falcon 4-Dr. Station Wagon	71A
Falcon Deluxe 2-Dr. Station Wagon	59B
Falcon Deluxe 4-Dr. Station Wagon	71B
Falcon Squire	71C
Falcon 2-Dr. Sedan Delivery	78A
Falcon 2-Dr. Sedan Deluxe Delivery	78B
Fairlane 2-Dr. Sedan	62A
Fairlane 4-Dr. Sedan	54A
Fairlane 500 2-Dr. Sedan	62B
Fairlane 500 4-Dr. Sedan	54B
Fairlane 500 Hardtop	65A
Fairlane 500 Sports Coupe	65B
Fairlane Ranch Wagon	71D
Fairlane 4-Dr. Squire, Bucket Seat	71G
Custom Ranch Wagon	71B
Fairlane Squire	71E
Ford 300 2-Dr. Sedan	62E
Ford 300 4-Dr. Sedan	54E
Galaxie 2-Dr. Sedan	62B
Galaxie 4-Dr. Sedan	54B
Galaxie 500 2-Dr. Sedan	62A
Galaxie 500 4-Dr. Sedan	54A
Galaxie 500 2-Dr. Hardtop Fastback	63B
Galaxie 500 2-Dr. Hardtop	65A
Galaxie 500 4-Dr. Hardtop	75A
Galaxie 500 Convertible	76A
Galaxie 500 XL 2-Dr. Hardtop Fastback	63C
Galaxie 500 XL 2-Dr. Hardtop	65B
Galaxie 500 XL 4-Dr. Hardtop	75C
Galaxie 500 XL Convertible	76B
Galaxie Country Squire, 6-Pass., Bucket Seat	71G
Galaxie Country Squire, 9-Pass., Bucket Seat	71H
Galaxie Country Sedan, 6-Pass.	71B
Galaxie Country Sedan, 9-Pass.	71C
Galaxie Country Squire, 6-Pass.	71E
Galaxie Country Squire, (9-Pass)	71A
Thunderbird Hardtop	63A
Thunderbird Landau	63B
Thunderbird Convertible	76A
Thunderbird Convertible, Sport Roadster	76B

THE DAY AND MONTH CODE furnishes the date the vehicle was manufactured. The number indicates the day of the month and the letter indicates the month.

MONTH	CODE	*CODE
January	A	N
February	B	P
March	C	Q
April	D	R
May	E	S
June	F	T
July	G	U
August	H	V
September	J	W
October	K	X
November	L	Y
December	M	Z

*Two year code letters to e used if 1963 models exceed 12 months.

DISTRICT CODE

DSO units built to a Domestic Special Order, Foreign Special Order, or Pre-Approved Order have the complete order number recorded in this space. Also appearing in this space is the two digit code number of the District which ordered the unit. If the unit is regular production, only the District code number will appear.

DISTRICT	CODE
Boston	11
Buffalo	12
New York	13
Pittsburgh	14
Newark	15
Atlanta	21
Charlotte	22
Philadelphia	23

Jacksonville	24
Richmond	25
Washington	26
Cincinnati	31
Cleveland	32
Detroit	33
Indianapolis	34
Lansing	35
Louisville	36
Chicago	41
Fargo	42
Rockford	43
Twin Cities	44
Davenport	45
Denver	51
Des Moines	52
Kansas City	53
Omaha	54
St. Louis	55
Dallas	61
Houston	62
Memphis	63
New Orleans	64
Oklahoma City	65
Los Angeles	71
San Jose	72
Salt Lake City	73
Seattle	74
Phoenix	75
Ford of Canada	81
Government	83
Home Office Reserve	84
American Red Cross	85
Transportation Services	89
Export	90-99
Spec. Lightweight Vehicle Package	AS-225-39D

FORD OF CANADA

Central	B1
Eastern	B2
Atlantic	B3
Midwestern	B4
Western	B6
Pacific	B7

THE REAR AXLE CODE indicates the ratio of the rear axle installed in the vehicle.

REAR AXLE RATIO	REGULAR	LOCKING
3.00:1	1	A
3.20:1	3	C
3.50:1	5	E
3.80:1	7	G
4.00:1	9*	I
3.10:1	2*	B
3.25:1	4	D
3.89:1	8	H
4.11:1	9**	I

* Falcon
** Galaxie & Fairlane

THE TRANSMISSION CODE indicates the type of transmission installed in the vehicle.

TRANSMISSION	CODE
Standard	1
Overdrive	2
Fordomatic (2-Speed)	3
Cruise-O-Matic	4
4 Speed	5

THE TRIM NUMBER furnishes the key to trim color and material for each model series.

FORD TRIM COLOR	CLOTH	VINYL	LEATHER	CODE
Blue	•	•		12,22,32
Blue		•		42,52,72,92
Beige	•	•		14,24
Beige		•		34,44,54
Beige				74,94
Red	•	•		15,25,35
Red		•		45,55,75
Red				85,95
Turquoise	•	•		17,27
Turquoise		•		57,77
Turquoise				87,97
Gold	•	•		18,28,38
Gold		•		58,78
Gold				88,98
Black	•	•		26
Black		•		56,66,86
Chestnut	•	•		29
Chestnut		•		39,69,89
Rose		•		80

GALAXIE TRIM COLOR	CLOTH	VINYL	LEATHER	CODE
Green		•		3
Beige		•		4,44,94
Beige	•	•		14,24
Red		•		5,45
Red				85,95
Red	•	•		15,25,35
Blue		•		42,82,92
Blue	•	•		12,22,32
Turquoise		•		87,97
Turquoise	•	•		17,27
Gold		•		88,98
Gold	•	•		18,28,38
Black		•		66,86
Black	•	•		26
Chestnut		•		69,89
Chestnut	•	•		29
Rose		•		80

FAIRLANE TRIM COLOR	CLOTH	VINYL	LEATHER	CODE
Green		•		3
Beige		•		4,34,44
Beige	•	•		24
Red		•		5,35,85
Red	•	•		15,25
Blue	•	•		12,22
Blue		•		32,42,82
Gold	•	•		18,28
Gold		•		38,88
Turquoise	•	•		27
Chestnut		•		39,89
Black		•		86

FALCON TRIM COLOR	CLOTH	VINYL	LEATHER	CODE
Gold	•	•		18,28,98
Gold		•		58,78,88
Blue	•	•		22,92
Blue		•		52,72,82
Beige	•	•		24
Beige		•		54,74
Red	•	•		25,95
Red		•		55,75,85
Turquoise	•	•		27
Turquoise		•		57,77,87
Black		•		56,86

THUNDERBIRD TRIM

COLOR	CLOTH	VINYL	LEATHER	CODE
Black				76
Black				56
Black				86
Beige				74
Beige				54
Beige				84
Blue				72
Blue				52
Blue				82
Turquoise				77
Turquoise				57
Red				55
Red				85
Chestnut				59
Rose				51
Gold				58

VINYL ROOF COLORS

White .... B
Black .... A
Dark Blue .... D
Dark Brown C

CONVERTIBLE ROOF COLORS

White 2
Black 1
Blue 4

THE PAINT CODE furnishes the key to the paint colors used on the car. A letter indicates the color of the car. A two-tone car has two sets of letters. The first indicates the lower body color, the second the upper body color.

COLOR	CODE
Raven Black	A
Patrician Green	*D
Acapulco Blue	*E
Viking Blue	E
Silver Mink	*G
Oxford Blue	H
Caspian Blue	*H
Champagne	I
Rangoon Red	J
Chalfonte Blue	*K
Sahara Rose	*L
Corinthian White	M
Diamond Blue	*N
Green Mist	O
Silver Moss	P
Green Mist	*Q
Tucson Yellow	*R
Cascade Green	*S
Sandshell Beige	T
Deep Sea Blue	*U
Chestnut	*V
Rose Beige	W
Heritage Burgundy	X
Glacier Blue	Y
Fieldstone Tan	Z

* Thunderbird

ENGINE NUMBER

144, 170, 200 engine numbers are stamped above the crankcase vent outlet pipe.

221, 260, 289 engine numbers are stamped on the distributor mounting boss.

352, 390 engine numbers are stamped near the engine dipstick.

406, 427 engine numbers are stamped on the right front corner of the block.

FALCON

ENGINE CODE	NO. CYL.	CID	HORSE-POWER	COMP. RATIO	CARB	TRANS
S	6	144	85	8.7:1	1 BC	** M & A
2*	6	144	N/A	N/A	1 BC	** M & A
U	6	170	101	8.7:1	1 BC	** M & A
4*	6	170	N/A	N/A	1 BC	** M & A
F	8	260	164	8.7:1	2 BC	** M & A
8*	8	260	N/A	N/A	2 BC	** M & A

* Export

FAIRLANE

ENGINE CODE	NO. CYL.	CID	HORSE-POWER	COMP. RATIO	CARB	TRANS
U	6	170	101	8.7:1	1 BC	MAN
R*	6	170	N/A	N/A	1 BC	MAN
T	6	200	116	8.9:1	1 BC	AUTO
L	8	221	145	8.7:1	2 BC	** M & A
3*	8	221	N/A	8.7:1	2 BC	** M & A
F	8	260	164	8.7:1	2 BC	** M & A
8*	8	260	N/A	N/A	2 BC	** M & A
K	8	289	271	11.0:1	4 BC	MAN

* Export

THUNDERBIRD

ENGINE CODE	NO. CYL.	CID	HORSE-POWER	COMP. RATIO	CARB	TRANS
Z	8	390	300	10.8:1+	4 BC	AUTO
9*	8	390	N/A	N/A	4 BC	AUTO
M	8	390	340	10.8:1+	2-3 BC	AUTO

* Export
+ Early engines had 10.5:1

FORD GALAXIE, GALAXIE 500, GALAXIE 500XL

ENGINE CODE	NO. CYL.	CID	HORSE-POWER	COMP. RATIO	CARB	TRANS
V	6	223	138	8.4:1	1 BC	AUTO
5*	6	223	N/A	N/A	1 BC	AUTO
E+	6	223	138	8.4:1	1 BC	AUTO
F	8	260	164	8.7:1	2 BC	AUTO
8*	8	260	N/A	N/A	2 BC	AUTO
C	8	289	195	8.7:1	2 BC	AUTO
X	8	352	220	8.9:1	2 BC	AUTO
Z	8	390	300	10.8:1#	4 BC	AUTO
9*	8	390	N/A	N/A	4 BC	AUTO
P	8	390	330	10.8:1#	4 BC	AUTO
B	8	406	385	11.5:1	4 BC	MAN
G	8	406	405	11.5:1	2-3 BC	MAN
Q	8	427	410	11.5:1	4 BC	MAN
R	8	427	425	11.5:1	2-3 BC	MAN

* Export
+ Taxi
# Early engines had 10.5:1
Galaxie 500XL did not come with 6-cylinder
** MAN & AUTO

1964 FORD FAIRLANE

1964 FORD FAIRLANE

1964 FORD FALCON

1964 FORD FALCON

1964 FORD GALAXIE

1964 FORD GALAXIE

1964 FORD THUNDERBIRD

1964 FORD THUNDERBIRD

1964 FORD

VEHICLE IDENTIFICATION NUMBER

FORD
4A83X100551

VIN LOCATION

FULL SIZED FORD VIN die-stamped into extension tab on top of cowl, on the right-hand side under the hood.

FAIRLANE VIN die-stamped into the side of the left front inner fender apron near the top.

THUNDERBIRD VIN die-stamped into top of the front fender cross-brace to the right of the hood lock plate.

MUSTANG VIN die-stamped the top of the front inner fender apron.

FALCON VIN die-stamped into top of the left front inner fender apron.

FIRST DIGIT: Identifies the model year (1964)

SECOND DIGIT: Identifies the assembly plant

ASSEMBLY PLANT	CODE
Atlanta, GA	A
Chicago, IL	G
Los Angeles, CA	J
Louisville, KY	U
Mahwah, NJ	E
Dallas, TX	D
Dearborn, MI	F
Lorain, OH	H
Kansas City, KS	K
Norfolk, VA	N
Pilot Plant	S
Metuchen, NJ	T
San Jose, CA	R
Twin Cities, MN	P
Wayne, MI	W
Wixom, MI	Y
St. Louis, MO	Z

THIRD AND FOURTH DIGITS: Identify the body series

THE BODY SERIES number identifies the model and the particular body style.

FALCON	CODE
2-Dr. Sedan	01
4-Dr. Sedan	02

MUSTANG	CODE
2-Dr. Hardtop	07
2-Dr. Convertible	08

FALCON FUTURA	CODE
2-Dr. Hardtop (Bucket Seat)	11
Convertible (Bucket Seat)	12
2-Dr. Hardtop Sprint	13
Convertible Sprint	14
2-Dr. Convertible (Bench seat)	15
4-Dr. Sedan (Bench Seat)	16
2-Dr. Hardtop (Bench Seat)	17
2-Dr. Sedan (Bench Seat)	19

STATION WAGONS	CODE
2-Dr. Wagon	21
4-Dr. Wagon	22
4-Dr. Deluxe Wagon	24
4-Dr. Squire	26

SEDAN DELIVERY	CODE
2-Dr. Sedan Delivery	29
2-Dr. Deluxe Sedan Delivery	29

FAIRLANE	CODE
2-Dr. Sedan	31
4-Dr. Sedan	32

FAIRLANE 500	CODE
2-Dr. Sedan	41
4-Dr. Sedan	42
2-Dr. Hardtop	43
2-Dr. Hardtop Sport Coupe	47

STATION WAGON	CODE
4-Dr. 6-Pass.	38
4-Dr. Custom 6-Pass.	48

FORD CUSTOM 500	CODE
2-Dr. Sedan	51
4-Dr. Sedan	52

FORD CUSTOM	CODE
2-Dr. Sedan	53
4-Dr. Sedan	54

GALAXIE 500	CODE
2-Dr. Sedan	61
4-Dr. Sedan	62
4-Dr. Hardtop	64
2-Dr. Convertible	65
2-Dr. Fastback	66

GALAXIE 500XL	CODE
4-Dr. Fastback	60
2-Dr. Fastback	68
2-Dr. Convertible	69

STATION WAGONS	CODE
4-Dr. 6-Pass. Country Sedan	72
4-Dr. 9-Pass. Country Sedan	74
4-Dr. 6-Pass. Country Squire	76
4-Dr. 9-Pass. Country Squire	78

THUNDERBIRD	CODE
2-Dr. Hardtop	83
2-Dr. Convertible	85
2-Dr. Landau	87

FIFTH DIGIT: Identifes the engine

ENGINE	CODE
6 Cyl. 223 C.I.	V
8 Cyl. 289 C.I. (2-V)	C
8 Cyl. 260 C.I. (2-V)	F
8 Cyl. 289 C.I. (4-V)	D
8 Cyl. 289 C.I. HP (4-V)	K
6 Cyl. 200 C.I. (1-V)	T
6 Cyl. 170 C.I. (1-V)	U
8 Cyl. 427 C.I. (4-V, H.P.)	Q
8 Cyl. 427 C.I. (8-V, H.P.)	R
6 Cyl. 144 C.I.	S
8 Cyl. 352 C.I. (4-V)	X
8 Cyl. 390 C.I. (4-V)	Z
6 Cyl. 223 C.I. (Police)	B
6 Cyl. 223 C.I. (Taxi)	E
8 Cyl. 390 C.I., (4-V, Interceptor)	P
6 Cyl. 289 C.I. (L.C.)	3
6 Cyl. 223 C.I. (L.C.)	5
8 Cyl. 390 V-8 (4-V, L.C.)	9
6 Cyl. 170 C.I. (1-V, L.C.)	4
8 Cyl. 260 C.I. (2-V, L.C.)	6

THE LAST SIX DIGITS: Represent the basic production numbers

1964 FORD

BODY NUMBER PLATE

THE BODY PLATE is located on the front body pillar on Galaxie and Thunderbird models, and on the lock face of left front door on Fairlane and Falcon models. Indicated on the body plate is body type, exterior paint color, trim scheme, production date, transmission type and rear axle ratio.

FORD MOTOR
CORPORATION

SERIAL NUMBER
4A83X1005511

63A	AA	56	11G	21	1	3
BDY	CLR	TRM	DT	DSO	AX	TR

EXAMPLE:

Serial Number

4	Model Year (1964)
A	Assembly Plant (Atlanta, GA)
83	Model (2-Dr. Hardtop)
X	Engine (8-Cyl. 352 C.I., 4-V)
100551	Production Sequence
63A	Style (Thunderbird Hardtop)
A	Lower Body Color
A	Upper Body Color
56	Trim
11G	Production Date Code
21	DSO (Atlanta)
1	3.00:1
3	Fordomatic (2-Speed)

BODY STYLE	CODE
Falcon 2-Dr. Sedan	62A
Falcon 4-Dr. Sedan	54A
Falcon Futura 2-Dr. Sedan	62B
Falcon Futura 4-Dr. Sedan	54B
Falcon Futura Convertible (Bench Seat)	76A
Falcon Futura Sports Convertible (Bucket Seat)	76B
Falcon 2-Dr. Station Wagon	59A
Falcon 4-Dr. Station Wagon	71A
Falcon 2-Dr. Sedan	62D
Falcon 4-Dr. Sedan	54D
Falcon 2-Dr. Hardtop, Futura (Bench Seat)	63B
Falcon 2-Dr. Hardtop (Bucket Seat)	63C
Falcon 2-Dr. Hardtop Sprint (Bucket Seat)	63D
Falcon 2-Dr. Hardtop Sprint (Bench Seat)	63E
Falcon Convertible Sprint (Bucket Seat)	76D
Falcon Convertible Sprint (Bench Seat)	76E
Falcon 4-Dr. Deluxe Ranch Wagon	71B
Falcon Squire	71C
Falcon Sedan Delivery	78A
Falcon Deluxe Sedan Delivery	78B
Fairlane Club Sedan	62A
Fairlane Town Sedan	54A
Fairlane 500 Club Sedan	62B
Fairlane 500 Town Sedan	54B
Fairlane 500 Hardtop	65A
Fairlane 500 Sports Coupe	65B
Fairlane Ranch Wagon	71D
Fairlane Custom Ranch Wagon	71B
Ford Custom 2-Dr. Sedan	62E
Custom 500 4-Dr. Sedan	54B
Ford Custom 4-Dr. Sedan	54E
Ford Custom 2-Dr. Sedan	62B
Galaxie 500 Club Sedan	62A
Galaxie 500 4-Dr. Town Sedan	54A
Galaxie 500 4-Dr. Hardtop	57B
Galaxie 500 Convertible	76A
Galaxie 500 Sportroof (Fastback)	63B
Galaxie 500 XL Sportroof Fastback (Bucket Seat)	63C
Galaxie 500 XL 4-Dr. Hardtop (Bucket Seat)	57C
Galaxie 500 XL Convertible	76B
Galaxie Country Sedan, 6-Pass.	71B
Galaxie Country Sedan, 9-Pass.	71C
Galaxie Country Squire, 6-Pass.	71E
Galaxie Country Squire, 9-Pass.	71A
Mustang 2-Dr. Hardtop	65A
Mustang 2-Dr. Convertible	76A
Thunderbird Hardtop	63A
Thunderbird Hardtop Landau	63B
Thunderbird Convertible	76A

THE DAY AND MONTH CODE furnishes the date the vehicle was manufactured. The number indicates the day of the month and the letter indicates the month.

MONTH	CODE	*CODE
January	A	N
February	B	P
March	C	Q
April	D	R
May	E	S
June	F	T
July	G	U
August	H	V
September	J	W
October	K	X
November	L	Y
December	M	Z

*Two year code letters to be used if 1964 models exceed 12 months.

DISTRICT CODE

DSO units built to a Domestic Special Order, Foreign Special Order, or Pre-Approved Order have the complete order number recorded in this space. Also appearing in this space is the two digit code number of the District which ordered the unit. If the unit is regular production, only the District code number will appear.

DISTRICT	CODE
Boston	11
Buffalo	12
New York	13
Pittsburgh	14
Newark	15
Atlanta	21
Charlotte	22
Philadelphia	23
Jacksonville	24
Richmond	25
Washington	26
Cincinnati	31
Cleveland	32
Detroit	33
Indianapolis	34
Lansing	35

1964 FORD

District	Code
Louisville	36
Chicago	41
Fargo	42
Rockford	43
Twin Cities	44
Davenport	45
Denver	51
Des Moines	52
Kansas City	53
Omaha	54
St. Louis	55
Dallas	61
Houston	62
Memphis	63
New Orleans	64
Oklahoma City	65
Los Angeles	71
San Jose	72
Salt Lake City	73
Seattle	74
Phoenix	75
Ford of Canada	81
Government	83
Home Office Reserve	84
American Red Cross	85
Transportation Services	89
Export	90-99
Spec. Lightweight Vehicle With Automatic	84-0007
Spec. Lightweight Vehicle With 4-Speed	84-0018

FORD OF CANADA

District	Code
Central	B1
Eastern	B2
Atlantic	B3
Midwestern	B4
Western	B6
Pacific	B7

THE REAR AXLE CODE indicates the ratio of the rear axle installed in the vehicle.

REAR AXLE RATIO	REGULAR	LOCKING
3.00:1	1	A
3.10:1	2*	B
3.20:1	3	C
3.25:1	4**	E
3.50:1	5**	F
3.80:1	7	G
4.00:1	9*	I
3.10:1	2	B
3.25:1	4	D
3.89:1	8	H
4.11:1	9**	I
2.80:1	6	F

* Falcon
** Galaxie

THE TRANSMISSION CODE indicates the type of transmission installed in the vehicle.

TRANSMISSION	CODE
Standard	1
Overdrive	2
Fordomatic (2-Speed)	3
Cruise-O-Matic	4
4 Speed	5
C4 Dual Range Automatic	6

THE TRIM NUMBER furnishes the key to trim color and material for each model series.

FORD TRIM COLOR	CLOTH	VINYL	LEATHER	CODE
Blue	•	•		12,22,32
Blue		•		42,52,72
Blue		•		82,92
Beige	•	•		14,24,34
Beige		•		44,54
Beige		•		74,94
Red	•	•		15,25,35
Red		•		45,55,75
Red		•		85,95
Turquoise	•	•		17,27
Turquoise		•		57,77
Turquoise		•		87,97
Gold	•	•		18,28,38
Gold		•		58,78
Gold		•		88,98
Black	•	•		26
Black		•		56,66,86
Chestnut	•	•		29
Chestnut		•		39,69,89
Rose		•		80

GALAXIE TRIM COLOR	CLOTH	VINYL	LEATHER	CODE
Green		•		3
Beige		•		4,42,64
Beige		•		74,84
Beige	•	•		14,24,34
Blue	•	•		12,22,32
Blue		•		42,72
Blue		•		63,82
Silver		•		71,81
Red	•	•		15,25,35
Red		•		42,75,85
Black	•	•		16
Black		•		76,86
Turquoise	•	•		17,27
Turquoise		•		42,77,87
Palomino		•		79,89
White		•		80

FAIRLANE TRIM COLOR	CLOTH	VINYL	LEATHER	CODE
Beige	•	•		14,24,44
Beige		•		4,64
Blue	•	•		12,22
Blue	•	•		42,62
Blue		•		82
Red	•	•		15,25
Red		•		65,85
Turquoise	•	•		27
Black		•		66,86
Palomino		•		69,89
White		•		80
Silver		•		81

FALCON TRIM COLOR	CLOTH	VINYL	LEATHER	CODE
Blue	•	•		12,22
Blue		•		62,82
Beige	•	•		14,24
Beige		•		44,64
Red	•	•		15,25
Red		•		65,85
Turquoise	•	•		27,67
Turquoise		•		87
Black		•		66,86
Palomino		•		69,89

THUNDERBIRD TRIM

COLOR	CLOTH	VINYL	LEATHER	CODE
Rose		•		50
Silver	•	•		71
Silver		•		51
Blue	•	•		72
Blue		•		52
Blue			•	82
Beige	•	•		74
Beige		•		54
Red		•		55
Red			•	85
Black	•	•		76
Black		•		56
Black			•	86
Turquoise		•		57
Gold		•		58
Palomino		•		59
Palomino			•	89
White			•	83

VINYL ROOF COLORS

Black .... A
White .... B
Brown C
Blue .... D

CONVERTIBLE ROOF COLORS

Black 1
White 2
Blue 4

THE PAINT CODE furnishes the key to the paint colors used on the car. A letter indicates the color of the car. A two-tone car has two sets of letters. The first indicates the lower body color, the second the upper body color.

COLOR	CODE
Raven Black	A
Pagoda Green	B
Ming Green	D
Dynasty Green	*D
Silver Mink	**E
Arcadian Blue	**F
Guardsman Blue	F
Prairie Tan	G
Caspian Blue	**H
Rangoon Red	J
Silver Smoke Gray	K
Samoan Coral	**L
Wimbledon White	M
Diamond Blue	**N
Prairie Bronze	+P
Brittany Blue	**Q
Phoenician Yellow	R
Cascade Green	**S
Navaho Beige	T
Sunlight Yellow	V
Rose Beige	**W
Vintage Burgundy	X
Skylight Blue	Y
Chantilly Beige	Z
Poppy Red	+3

* Falcon
** Thunderbird
+ Mustang

ENGINE NUMBER

144, 170, 200 engine numbers are stamped above the crankcase vent outlet pipe.

260, 289 engine numbers are stamped on the distributor mounting boss.

352, 390, 427 engine numbers are stamped near the engine dipstick.

After early January, 1964, an identification tag is attached under the coil-to-engine attaching bolt.

FALCON

ENGINE CODE	NO. CYL.	CID	HORSE-POWER	COMP. RATIO	CARB	TRANS
S	6	144	85	8.7:1	1 BC	** M & A
U	6	170	101	8.7:1	1 BC	** M & A
4*	6	170	N/A	N/A	1 BC	** M & A
T	6	200	116	8.7:1	1 BC	** M & A
F	8	260	164	8.8:1	2 BC	** M & A
G*	8	260	N/A	N/A	2 BC	** M & A
K	8	289	271	10.5:1	4 BC	MAN

* Export

MUSTANG

ENGINE CODE	NO. CYL.	CID	HORSE-POWER	COMP. RATIO	CARB	TRANS
U	6	170	101	8.7:1	1 BC	MAN
4*	6	170	N/A	N/A	1 BC	MAN
F	8	260	164	8.8:1	2 BC	MAN
G*	8	260	N/A	N/A	2 BC	MAN
D	8	289	210	9.0:1	4 BC	MAN
K	8	289	271	10.5:1	4 BC	MAN

* Export

FAIRLANE

ENGINE CODE	NO. CYL.	CID	HORSE-POWER	COMP. RATIO	CARB	TRANS
U	6	170	101	8.7:1	1 BC	MAN
4*	6	170	N/A	N/A	1 BC	MAN
T	6	200	116	8.7:1	1 BC	AUTO
F	8	260	164	8.8:1	2 BC	** M & A
6*	8	260	N/A	N/A	2 BC	** M & A
C	8	289	195	9.0:1	2 BC	** M & A
3*	8	289	N/A	N/A	2 BC	** M & A
K	8	289	271	10.5:1	4 BC	MAN
R	8	427	425	11.2:1	2-4 BC	** M & A

* Export

THUNDERBIRD

ENGINE CODE	NO. CYL.	CID	HORSE-POWER	COMP. RATIO	CARB	TRANS
Z	8	390	300	10.1:1	4 BC	AUTO
9*	8	390	N/A	N/A	4 BC	AUTO

* Export

FORD CUSTOM, CUSTOM 500, GALAXIE 500 AND GALAXIE 500XL

ENGINE CODE	NO. CYL.	CID	HORSE-POWER	COMP. RATIO	CARB	TRANS
V	6	223	138	8.4:1	1 BC	** M & A
5*	6	223	N/A	N/A	1 BC	** M & A
B**	6	223	138	N/A	1 BC	** M & A
E+	6	223	138	N/A	1 BC	** M & A
C	8	289	195	9.0:1	2 BC	** M & A
3*	8	289	N/A	N/A	2 BC	** M & A
X	8	352	250	9.3:1	4 BC	** M & A
Z	8	390	300	10.1:1	4 BC	** M & A
9*	8	390	N/A	N/A	4 BC	** M & A
P**	8	390	330	10.1:1	4 BC	** M & A
Q	8	427	410	11.5:1	4 BC	MAN
R	8	427	425	11.2:1	2-4 BC	MAN

* Export ** Police + Taxi ** MAN & AUTO
Galaxie 500XL not offered with 6-cylinder

1965 FORD

1965 FORD FAIRLANE

1965 FORD FAIRLANE

1965 FORD FALCON

1965 FORD FALCON

1965 FORD GALAXIE

1965 FORD GALAXIE

1965 FORD MUSTANG

1965 FORD MUSTANG

1965 FORD THUNDERBIRD

1965 FORD THUNDERBIRD

1965 FORD

VEHICLE IDENTIFICATION NUMBER

FORD
5A83X100551

VIN LOCATION

FULL SIZED FORD VIN die-stamped into extension tab on top of cowl, on the right-hand side under the hood.

FAIRLANE VIN die-stamped into the side of the left front inner fender apron near the top.

THUNDERBIRD VIN die-stamped into top of the front fender cross-brace to the right of the hood lock plate.

MUSTANG VIN die-stamped into the top of the front inner fender apron.

FALCON VIN die-stamped into top of the left front inner fender apron.

FIRST DIGIT: Identifies the model year (1965)

SECOND DIGIT: Identifies the assembly plant

ASSEMBLY PLANT	CODE
Atlanta, GA	A
Oakville, Ont., CAN	B
Dallas, TX	D
Mahwah, NJ	E
Dearborn, MI	F
Chicago, IL	G
Lorain, OH	H
Los Angeles, CA	J
Kansas City, KS	K
Long Beach, CA	L
Norfolk, VA	N
Twin Cities, MN	P
San Jose, CA	R
Pilot Plant	S
Metuchen, NJ	T
Louisville, KY	U
Wayne, MI	W
Wixom, MI	Y
St. Louis, MO	Z

THIRD AND FOURTH DIGIT: Identifies the body series

THE BODY SERIES identifies the model and the particular body style.

FORD CUSTOM	CODE
2-Dr. Sedan	53
4-Dr. Sedan	54

FORD CUSTOM 500	CODE
2-Dr. Sedan	51
4-Dr. Sedan	52

GALAXIE 500	CODE
4-Dr. Sedan	62
4-Dr. Hardtop	64
2-Dr. Convertible	65
2-Dr. Fastback	66

GALAXIE 500XL	CODE
2-Dr. Fastback (Bucket Seat)	68
2-Dr. Convertible (Bucket Seat)	69

GALAXIE 500 LTD	CODE
4-Dr. Hardtop	60
2-Dr. Fastback	67

FAIRLANE	CODE
2-Dr. Sedan	31
4-Dr. Sedan	32

FAIRLANE 500	CODE
2-Dr. Sedan	41
4-Dr. Sedan	42
2-Dr. Hardtop	43
2-Dr. Hardtop (Bucket Seat)	47
4-Dr. Ranch Wagon	38
4-Dr. Custom Ranch Wagon	48

STATION WAGONS	CODE
4-Dr. Custom 9-Pass.	72
4-Dr. 9-Pass.	74

COUNTRY SQUIRE	CODE
4-Dr. 6-Pass.	76
4-Dr. 9-Pass.	78

THUNDERBIRD	CODE
2-Dr. Landau Special	81
2-Dr. Hardtop	83
2-Dr. Convertible	85
2-Dr. Landau	87

FALCON STANDARD	CODE
2-Dr. Sedan	01
4-Dr. Sedan	02

FALCON FUTURA	CODE
2-Dr. Sedan (2)	19
2-Dr. Convertible (2)	15
4-Dr. Sedan (2)	16
2-Dr. Hardtop (1)	11
Convertible (1)	12
Deluxe	27

(1) RPO Bucket Seat
(2) Bench Seat

STATION WAGONS	CODE
2-Dr. Wagon	21
4-Dr. Wagon	22
4-Dr. Deluxe Wagon	24
4-Dr. Squire	26

SEDAN DELIVERY	CODE
2-Dr. Sedan Delivery	29
2-Dr. Deluxe Sedan Delivery	29

MUSTANG	CODE
2-Dr. Fastback*	09
2-Dr. Hardtop*	07
2-Dr. Convertible*	08
2-Dr. Fastback (Luxury Trim)	09
2-Dr. Hardtop (Luxury Trim)	07
2-Dr. Convertible (Luxury Trim)	08
2-Dr. Hardtop (Bench Seat)	07
2-Dr. Convertible (Bench Seat)	08

* Option: GT

1965 FORD

FIFTH DIGIT: Identifies the engine

ENGINE	CODE
6 Cyl. 240 C.I.	V
8 Cyl. 289 C.I. (4-V) Prem.	A
8 Cyl. 289 C.I. (2-V)	C
8 Cyl. 289 C.I. (4-V) H.P.	K
6 Cyl. 200 C.I. (1-V)	T
6 Cyl. 170 C.I. (1-V)	U
8 Cyl. 427 C.I. (8-V, H.P.)	R
8 Cyl. 427 C.I. (4-V OH Cam)	L
8 Cyl. 427 C.I. (8-V OH Cam)	M
8 Cyl. 352 C.I. (4-V)	X
8 Cyl. 390 C.I. (4-V)	Z
8 Cyl. 390 C.I.(4-V, Interceptor)	P
8 Cyl. 260 C.I. (2-V)	F
8 Cyl. 289 C.I. (4-V) Reg.	D
6 Cyl. 240 C.I. Police	B
6-Cyl. 240 C.I. Taxi	E
8 Cyl. 289 C.I. (Low Comp.)	3
6 Cyl. 240 C.I. (Low Comp.)	5
8 Cyl. 390 V-8 (4-V, Low Comp.)	9
6 Cyl. 170 C.I. (1-V, Low Comp.)	4
6 Cyl. 200 C.I. (1-V, Low Comp.)	2

BODY NUMBER PLATE

THE BODY PLATE is located on the left front door lock face panel on all models. Indicated on the body plate is the body type, exterior paint color, trim scheme, production date, district code and D.S.O. numbers, rear axle ratio and transmission type.

FORD MOTOR CORPORATION

SERIAL NUMBER 5A83X100551

63A	AA	36	11G	21	1	1
BDY	CLR	TRM	DT	DSO	AX	TR

EXAMPLE:

Serial Number

5	Model Year (1965)
A	Assembly Plant (Atlanta, GA)
83	Model (2-Dr. Hardtop)
X	Engine (8-Cyl. 352 C.I., 4-V)
100551	Production Sequence
63A	Style (Thunderbird, HT)
A	Lower Body Color
A	Upper Body Color
36	Trim
11G	Production Date Code
21	DSO (Atlanta)
1	3.00:1
1	Standard

BODY STYLE	CODE
Falcon 2-Dr. Sedan	62A
Falcon 2-Dr. Hardtop (Bucket Seat)	63C
Falcon 4-Dr. Sedan	54A
Falcon Futura 2-Dr. Sedan	62B
Falcon Futura 4-Dr. Sedan	54B
Falcon Futura 2-Dr. Hardtop (Bucket Seat Less Console)	63H
Falcon Futura Convertible	76A
Falcon Futura Convertible (Bucket Seat)	76B
Falcon 2-Dr. Station Wagon	59A
Falcon 4-Dr. Station Wagon	71A
Falcon 2-Dr. Sedan	62D
Falcon 4-Dr. Sedan	54D
Falcon 2-Dr. Hardtop Futura (Bench Seat)	63B
Falcon 4-Dr. Ranch Wagon	71B
Falcon 4-Dr. Country Squire Wagon	71C
Falcon Sedan Delivery	78A
Falcon Deluxe Sedan Delivery	78B
Fairlane 2-Dr. Sedan	62A
Fairlane 4-Dr. Sedan	54A
Fairlane 500 2-Dr. Sedan	62B
Fairlane 500 4-Dr. Sedan	54B
Fairlane 500 2-Dr. Hardtop	65A
Fairlane 500 2-Dr. Sports Coupe (Bucket Seat)	65B
Fairlane Ranch Wagon	71D
Fairlane Custom Ranch Wagon	71B
Ford Custom 500 2-Dr. Sedan	62B
Ford Custom 2-Dr. Sedan	62E
Ford Custom 500 4-Dr. Sedan	54B
Ford Custom 4-Dr. Sedan	54E
Galaxie 500 LTD 4-Dr. Hardtop	57F
Galaxie 500 LTD 2-Dr. Fastback	63F
Galaxie 500 4-Dr. Sedan	54A
Galaxie 500 4-Dr. Hardtop	57B
Galaxie 500 Convertible	76A
Galaxie 500 2-Dr. Fastback	63B
Galaxie 500XL 2-Dr. Fastback	63C
Galaxie 500XL Convertible	76B
Galaxie Country Sedan (6-Pass.)	71B
Galaxie Country Sedan (9-Pass.)	71C
Galaxie Country Squire (6-Pass.)	71E
Galaxie Country Squire (9-Pass.)	71A
Mustang 2-Dr. Fastback	63A
Mustang 2-Dr. Hardtop	65A
Mustang 2-Dr. Convertible	76A
Mustang 2-Dr. Fastback (Luxury Trim)	63B
Mustang 2-Dr. Hardtop (Luxury Trim)	65B
Mustang 2-Dr. Convertible (Luxury Trim)	76B
Mustang 2-Dr. Hardtop (Bench Seat)	65C
Mustang 2-Dr. Convertible (Bench Seat)	76C
Thunderbird 2-Dr. Landau Special	63D
Thunderbird 2-Dr. Hardtop	63A
Thunderbird Convertible	76A
Thunderbird 2-Dr. Landau	63B

THE DAY AND MONTH CODE furnishes the date the vehicle was manufactured. The number indicates the day of the month and the letter indicates the month.

MONTH	CODE	*CODE
January	A	N
February	B	P
March	C	Q
April	D	R
May	E	S
June	F	T
July	G	U
August	H	V
September	J	W
October	K	X
November	L	Y
December	M	Z

*Two year code letters to be used if 1965 models exceed 12 months.

DISTRICT CODE

DSO units built to a Domestic Special Order, Foreign Special Order, or Pre-Approved Order have the complete order number recorded in this space. Also appearing in this space is the two digit code number of the District which ordered the unit. If the unit is regular production, only the District code number will appear.

DISTRICT	CODE
Boston	11
Buffalo	12
New York	13
Pittsburgh	14
Newark	15
Atlanta	21
Charlotte	22
Philadelphia	23
Jacksonville	24
Richmond	25
Washington	26
Cincinnati	31
Cleveland	32
Detroit	33
Indianapolis	34
Lansing	35
Louisville	36
Chicago	41
Fargo	42
Rockford	43
Twin Cities	44
Davenport	45
Denver	51
Des Moines	52
Kansas City	53
Omaha	54
St. Louis	55
Dallas	61
Houston	62
Memphis	63
New Orleans	64
Oklahoma City	65
Los Angeles	71
San Jose	72
Salt Lake City	73
Seattle	74
Phoenix	75
Ford of Canada	81
Government	83
Home Office Reserve	84
American Red Cross	85
Transportation Services	89
Export	90-99

THE REAR AXLE CODE indicates the ratio of the rear axle installed in the vehicle.

REAR AXLE RATIO	REGULAR	LOCKING
2.80:1	6	F
2.83:1	2	B
3.00:1	1	A
3.20:1	3	C
3.50:1	5	E
3.80:1	7	G
3.25:1	4	D
3.89:1	8	H
4.11:1	9*	I

* Ford, Fairlane, Mustang

THE TRANSMISSION CODE indicates the type of transmission installed in the vehicle.

TRANSMISSION	CODE
Standard	1
Overdrive	2
Cruise-O-Matic	4
4-Speed	5
C4 Dual Range Automatic	6

THE TRIM NUMBER furnishes the key to trim color and material for each model series.

FORD TRIM

COLOR	CLOTH	VINYL	LEATHER	CODE
Green		•		1
Beige		•		4
Blue		•		12,62
Blue		•		72,N2
Blue	•	•		32,52
Red	•	•		15,35,55
Red		•		65,75
Red		•		N5,Y5
Palomino	•	•		19,29
Palomino	•	•		39,59
Palomino		•		69,K9,N9
Palomino		•		P9,Y9,Z9
Turquoise	•	•		37,57
Turquoise		•		67
Black	•	•		56
Black		•		66,76,Z6
Gold	•	•		58
Gold		•		68
White/Blue		•		L2
White/Red		•		L5
White/Black		•		L6
White/Turquoise		•		L7
White/Gold		•		L8
White/Palomino		•		L9

FAIRLANE TRIM

COLOR	CLOTH	VINYL	LEATHER	CODE
Beige		•		4
Blue	•	•		12,22
Blue		•		32,36,42
Blue		•		52,82
Red	•	•		15,25
Red		•		35,55,85
Palomino	•	•		19,29
Palomino	•	•		79,99
Palomino		•		39,49
Palomino		•		59,89
Turquoise	•	•		27
Gold	•	•		28
Gold		•		88

 1965 FORD

COLOR	CLOTH	VINYL	LEATHER	CODE
Black		•		56,86
Black	•	•		96
White/Blue		•		C2,H2
White/Red		•		C5,H5
White/Black		•		C6,H6
White/Turquoise		•		C7,H7
White/Gold		•		C8,H8
White/Palomino		•		C9,H9

FALCON TRIM

COLOR	CLOTH	VINYL	LEATHER	CODE
Blue	•	•		12,22
Blue		•		32,52
Blue		•		62,82
Red	•	•		15,25
Red		•		35,55
Red		•		65,85
Turquoise	•	•		17
Turquoise		•		37
Palomino	•	•		19,29
Palomino		•		39,49,59
Palomino		•		69,89
Turquoise	•	•		27
Turquoise		•		57,87
Gold	•	•		28
Gold		•		38,58,88
Black		•		36,56
Black		•		66,86

MUSTANG TRIM

COLOR	CLOTH	VINYL	LEATHER	CODE
Blue		•		22,32,62
Blue		•		82,C2
Red		•		25,35,65
Red		•		85,C5
Black		•		26,36,66
Black		•		86,C6
Black	•	•		56,76,96
Gold		•		28,38
Gold		•		68,C8
Palomino		•		29,39,69
Palomino		•		89,C9
Palomino	•	•		79,99
White/Blue		•		42,D2,F2
White/Red		•		45,D5,F5
White/Black		•		46,D6,F6
White/Palomino		•		49,D9,F9
White/Gold		•		D8,68,F8
White/Turquoise		•		67,F7
Turquoise		•		67

THUNDERBIRD TRIM

COLOR	CLOTH	VINYL	LEATHER	CODE
Silver		•		21
Blue	•			12
Blue		•		22
Blue			•	32
Burgundy		•		23
Burgundy			•	33
Beige		•		24
Red		•		25
Red			•	35
Black	•			16
Black		•		26
Black			•	36
Turquoise		•		27
Gold		•		28
Palomino	•			19
Palomino		•		29
Palomino			•	39
White/Blue		•		G-2
White/Blue			•	H-2
White/Burgundy		•		G-3
White/Burgundy			•	H-3
White/Beige		•		G-4
White/Beige			•	H-4
White/Red		•		G-5
White/Red			•	H-5
White/Black		•		G-6
White/Black			•	H-6
White/Turquoise		•		G-7
White/Turquoise			•	H-7
White/Gold		•		G-8
White/Gold			•	H-8
White/Palomino		•		G-9
White/Palomino			•	H-9

THE PAINT CODE furnishes the key to the paint colors used on the car. A letter indicates the color of the car. A two-tone car has two sets of letters. The first indicates the lower body color, the second the upper body color.

COLOR	CODE
Light Peacock	0
Poppy Red (Mustang)	3
Frost Blue	4
Twilight Turquoise	5
Raven Black	A
Pagoda Green	B
White Mustang (Pace Car)	*C
Honey Gold	**C
Dynasty Green	D
Silver Mink	**E
Arcadian Blue	F
Guardsman Blue	F
Lemontree Yellow	**G
Caspian Blue	H
Champagne Beige	I
Rangoon Red	J
Silver Smoke Gray	K
Wimbledon White	M
Diamond Blue Platinum	**N
Prairie Bronze	P
Brittany Blue	**Q
Charcoal Green	R
Cascade Green	**S
Navaho Beige	T
Patrician Green	**U
Sunlight Yellow	V
Rose Beige	**W
Vintage Burgundy	X
Silver Blue	Y
Skylight Blue	Y
Chantilly Beige	**Z
Springtime Yellow	*8

* Mustang
** Thunderbird

ENGINE NUMBER

6-cylinder engine number tag is located on the ignition coil mounting bracket bolt.

289 engine number tag is located under the electric heat bulb indicator.

352, 390, 427 engine number tag is located under the coil attaching bolt.

FALCON

ENGINE CODE	NO. CYL.	CID	HORSE-POWER	COMP. RATIO	CARB	TRANS
U	6	170	105	9.1:1	1 BC	** M & A
4*	6	170	N/A	7.7:1	1 BC	** M & A
T	6	200	120	9.2:1	1 BC	** M & A
2*	6	200	N/A	N/A	1 BC	** M & A
C	8	289	200	9.3:1	2 BC	** M & A
3*	8	289	N/A	N/A	2 BC	** M & A
A	8	289	225	10.0:1	4 BC	** M & A

* Export

MUSTANG

ENGINE CODE	NO. CYL.	CID	HORSE-POWER	COMP. RATIO	CARB	TRANS
T	6	200	120	9.2:1	1 BC	** M & A
2*	6	200	N/A	N/A	1 BC	** M & A
C	8	289	200	9.3:1	2 BC	** M & A
3*	8	289	N/A	N/A	2 BC	** M & A
A	8	289	225	10.0;1	4 BC	** M & A
K	8	289	271	10.0;1	4 BC	MAN

* Export

FAIRLANE

ENGINE CODE	NO. CYL.	CID	HORSE-POWER	COMP. RATIO	CARB	TRANS
T	6	200	120	9.2:1	1 BC	** M & A
2*	6	200	N/A	N/A	1 BC	** M & A
C	8	289	200	9.3:1	2 BC	** M & A
3*	8	289	N/A	N/A	2 BC	** M & A
A	8	289	225	10.0:1	4 BC	** M & A
K	8	289	271	10.0:1	4 BC	** M & A

* Export

THUNDERBIRD

ENGINE CODE	NO. CYL.	CID	HORSE-POWER	COMP. RATIO	CARB	TRANS
Z	8	390	300	10.1:1	4 BC	AUTO
9*	8	390	N/A	N/A	4 BC	AUTO

* Export

FORD CUSTOM, CUSTOM 500 AND GALAXIE 500

ENGINE CODE	NO. CYL.	CID	HORSE-POWER	COMP. RATIO	CARB	TRANS
V	6	240	150	9.2:1	1 BC	** M & A
5*	6	240	N/A	N/A	1 BC	** M & A
B**	6	240	150	9.2:1	1 BC	** M & A
E+	6	240	150	9.2:1	1 BC	** M & A
C	8	289	200	9.3:1	2 BC	** M & A
3*	8	289	N/A	N/A	2 BC	** M & A
X	8	352	250	9.3:1	4 BC	AUTO
Z	8	390	300	10.1:1	4 BC	** M & A
9*	8	390	N/A	N/A	4 BC	** M & A
P	8	390	330	10.1:1	4 BC	** M & A
R	8	427	425	11.1:1	2-4 BC	MAN

* Export

FORD GALAXIE 500XL, GALAXIE 500 LTD

ENGINE CODE	NO. CYL.	CID	HORSE-POWER	COMP. RATIO	CARB	TRANS
C	8	289	200	9.3:1	2 BC	AUTO
3*	8	289	N/A	N/A	2 BC	AUTO
X	8	352	250	9.3:1	4 BC	AUTO
Z	8	390	300	10.1:1	4 BC	** M & A
9*	8	390	N/A	N/A	4 BC	** M & A
P	8	390	330	N/A	4 BC	** M & A
R	8	427	425	11.1:1	2-4 BC	MAN

* Export

ENGINES USED IN RACING

ENGINE CODE	NO. CYL.	CID	HORSE-POWER	COMP. RATIO	CARB	TRANS
L*	8	427	N/A	12:1	4 BC	MAN
M*	8	427	N/A	12:1	2-4 BC	MAN

* O.H. Cam
** MAN & AUTO

1966 FORD

1966 FORD

1966 FORD FAIRLANE

1966 FORD FAIRLANE

1966 FORD FALCON

1966 FORD FALCON

1966 FORD MUSTANG

1966 FORD MUSTANG

1966 FORD THUNDERBIRD

1966 FORD THUNDERBIRD

1966 FORD

VEHICLE IDENTIFICATION NUMBER

FORD
6A83X100551

VIN LOCATION

FULL SIZED FORD VIN die-stamped into extension tab on top of cowl, right-hand side of the car under the hood.

FAIRLANE VIN die-stamped into top of the inner fender panel & radiator support at the left-hand side under the hood.

THUNDERBIRD VIN die-stamped into top of the front fender cross-brace to the right of the hood lock plate under the hood.

MUSTANG VIN die-stamped into top of the left front fender apron.

FALCON VIN die-stamped into top of the inner fender panel & radiator support at the left-hand side under the hood.

FIRST DIGIT: Identifies the model year (1966)

SECOND DIGIT: Identifies the assembly plant

ASSEMBLY PLANT	CODE
Atlanta, GA	A
Oakville, Ont, CAN	B
Ontario, CAN	C
Dallas, TX	D
Mahwah, NJ	E
Dearborn, MI	F
Chicago, IL	G
Lorain, OH	H
Los Angeles, CA	J
Kansas City, KS	K
Michigan Truck	L
Norfolk, VA	N
Twin Cities, MN	P
San Jose, CA	R
Pilot Plant	S
Metuchen, NJ	T
Louisville, KY	U
Wayne, MI	W
Wixom, MI	Y
St. Louis, MO	Z

THIRD AND FOURTH DIGIT: Identify the body series

THE BODY SERIES identifies the model and the particular body style.

FALCON STANDARD	CODE
2-Dr. Sedan	01
4-Dr. Sedan	02

FALCON FUTURA	CODE
2-Dr. Sedan (Bench Seat)	11
4-Dr. Sedan (Bench Seat)	12
2-Dr. Sport Coupe (Bucket Seat)	14

STATION WAGONS	CODE
4-Dr. Wagon	22
4-Dr. Deluxe Wagon	24

FAIRLANE	CODE
2-Dr. Sedan	31
4-Dr. Sedan	32

FAIRLANE 500 GT	CODE
2-Dr. Hardtop (Bucket Seat)	40
2-Dr. Convertible (Bucket Seat)	44

FAIRLANE 500	CODE
2-Dr. Sedan	41
4-Dr. Sedan	42
2-Dr. Hardtop	43
2-Dr. Convertible	45

FAIRLANE 500 XL	CODE
2-Dr. Convertible (Bucket Seat)	46
2-Dr. Hardtop (Bucket Seat)	47

FAIRLANE WAGONS	CODE
2-Dr. Ranch Wagon	38
4-Dr. Custom Ranch Wagon	48
4-Dr. Squire	49

FORD CUSTOM	CODE
2-Dr. Sedan	53
4-Dr. Sedan	54

FORD CUSTOM 500	CODE
2-Dr. Sedan	51
4-Dr. Sedan	52

GALAXIE 500	CODE
4-Dr. Sedan	62
4-Dr. Fastback	64
2-Dr. Convertible	65
2-Dr. Fastback	66

GALAXIE 500XL	CODE
2-Dr. Fastback (Bucket Seat)	68
2-Dr. Convertible (Bucket Seat)	69

GALAXIE 500 LTD	CODE
4-Dr. Hardtop	60
2-Dr. Fastback	67

GALAXIE 500 7.0 Liter	CODE
2-Dr. Fastback	61
2-Dr. Convertible	63

RANCH WAGON	CODE
4-Dr., 6-Pass.	71

COUNTRY SEDAN	CODE
4-Dr., 6-Pass.	72
4-Dr. Custom, 9-Pass.	74

COUNTRY SQUIRE	CODE
4-Dr., 6-Pass.	76
4-Dr. Custom, 9-Pass.	78

THUNDERBIRD	CODE
2-Dr. Town Hardtop (Blind quarter roof-painted)	81
2-Dr. Hardtop	83
2-Dr. Convertible	85
2-Dr. Town Landau (Blind quarter roof-vinyl)	87

MUSTANG **CODE**

2-Dr. Fastback* (Std. Bucket Seat) 09
2-Dr. Hardtop* (Std. Bucket Seat) 07
2-Dr. Convertible* (Std. Bucket Seat) 08
2-Dr. Fastback (Luxury Bucket Seat) 09
2-Dr. Hardtop (Luxury Bucket Seat) 07
2-Dr. Convertible (Luxury Bucket Seat) 08
2-Dr. Hardtop (Std. Bench Seat) 07
2-Dr. Convertible (Std. Bench Seat) 08

* Option: GT

FIFTH DIGIT: Identifies the engine

ENGINE **CODE**

6 Cyl. 240 C.I. V
6 Cyl. 240 C.I. Police ....B
6 Cyl. 240 C.I.(Taxi) ....E
8 Cyl. 289 C.I. (4-V) Prem. ....A
8 Cyl. 289 C.I. (2-V) C
8 Cyl. 289 C.I. (4-V, H.P.) ....K
6 Cyl. 200 C.I. (1-V) ....T
8 Cyl. 427 C.I. (8-V, H.P.) ....R
8 Cyl. 410 C.I. (4-V) ....M
8 Cyl. 352 C.I. (4-V) X
8 Cyl. 390 C.I. (4-V) ....Z
8 Cyl. 390 C.I. (2-V) ....Y
8 Cyl. 390 C.I. (2-V, Special) ....H
8 Cyl. 428 C.I. (4-V, Police) ....P
8 Cyl. 428 C.I. (4-V) ....Q
8 Cyl. 390 C.I. (4-V) GT ....S
6 Cyl. 200 C.I. (1-V) ....U
8 Cyl. 427 (4-V HP) ....W
6 Cyl. 170 (1-V Low Comp.) 4

8 Cyl. 289 (Low Comp.) 3
6 Cyl. 240 (Low Comp.) 5
8 Cyl. 428 C.I.(4-V, Low Comp.) 8
6 Cyl. 200 C.I.(1-V, Low Comp.) 2

LAST SIX DIGITS: Represent the basic production numbers

BODY NUMBER PLATE

THE BODY PLATE is located on the left front door lock face panel on all models. Indicated on the body plate is the body type, exterior paint color, trim scheme, production date, district code and D.S.O. numbers, rear axle ratio and transmission type.

FORD MOTOR CORPORATION

SERIAL NUMBER
6A83Z100551

63A	AA	56	26H	33	1	4
BDY	CLR	TRM	DT	DSO	AX	TR

EXAMPLE:

Serial Number	
6	Model Year (1966)
A	Assembly Plant (Atlanta, GA)
83	Model (2-Dr. Hardtop)
Z	Engine (8 Cyl. 390 C.I.)
100001	Production Sequence
63A	Style (Thunderbird, Hardtop)
A	Lower Body Color
A	Uppper Body Color
56	Trim
26H	Production Date Code
33	DSO (Detroit)
1	Axle (3.00:1)
4	C-6 Automatic

BODY STYLE

FORD **CODE**

2-Dr. Custom Sedan 62E
4-Dr. Custom Sedan 54E
4-Dr. Custom 500 Sedan 54B
2-Dr. Custom 500 Sedan 62B
Galaxie 500 Sedan 54A
4-Dr. Galaxie 500 Fastback 57B
2-Dr. Galaxie 500 Fastback 63B
Galaxie 500 Convertible 76A
Galaxie 500 XL Fastback 63C
Galaxie 500 XL Convertible 76B
Galaxie 500 7.0 Fastback 63D
Galaxie 500 7.0 Convertible 76D
4-Dr. Galaxie 500 LTD Fastback 57F
2-Dr. Galaxie 500 LTD Fastback 63F
4-Dr. Ranch Wagon, 6-Pass. 71D
4-Dr. Country Sedan, 6-Pass. 71B
4-Dr. Country Sedan, 9-Pass. 71C
4-Dr. Country Squire, 6-Pass. 71E
4-Dr. Country Squire, 9-Pass. 71A

THUNDERBIRD **CODE**

2-Dr. Hardtop, (Conventional roof) 63A
2-Dr. Hardtop, (Blind quarter roof-paint) 63C
2-Dr. Landau, (Blind quarter roof-vinyl) 63D
Convertible 76A

FALCON **CODE**

4-Dr. Sedan (Standard) 54A
2-Dr. Sedan 62A
4-Dr. Sedan Futura (Bench) 54B
2-Dr. Sedan Futura (Bench) 62B
2-Dr. Sport Coupe Futura (Bucket) 62C
4-Dr. Station Wagon 71A
4-Dr. Deluxe Wagon 71B

FAIRLANE **CODE**

2-Dr. Coupe 62A
4-Dr. Club Coupe 54A
2-Dr. 500 ....62B
4-Dr. 500 ....54B
2-Dr. 500 Hardtop 63B
Convertible 500 ....76B
2-Dr. 500 XL Hardtop 63C
Convertible 500 XL 76C
2-Dr. 500 GT Hardtop 63D
Convertible 500 GT 76D
4-Dr. Ranch Wagon 71D
4-Dr. Custom Ranch Wagon 71B
4-Dr. Squire 71E

MUSTANG	CODE
2-Dr. Fastback	63A
2-Dr. Hardtop	65A
Convertible	76A
2-Dr. Fastback	63B
2-Dr. Hardtop	65B
Convertible	76B
2-Dr. Hardtop	65C
Convertible	76C

THE DAY AND MONTH CODE furnishes the date the vehicle was manufactured. The number indicates the day of the month and the letter indicates the month.

MONTH	CODE	*CODE
January	A	N
February	B	P
March	C	Q
April	D	R
May	E	S
June	F	T
July	G	U
August	H	V
September	J	W
October	K	X
November	L	Y
December	M	Z

*Two year code letters to be used if 1966 models exceed 12 months.

DISTRICT CODE

DSO units built to a Domestic Special Order, Foreign Special Order, or Pre-Approved Order have the complete order number recorded in this space. Also appearing in this space is the two digit code number of the district which ordered the unit. If the unit is regular production, only the district code number will appear.

DISTRICT	CODE
Boston	11
Buffalo	12
New York	13
Pittsburgh	14
Newark	15
Atlanta	21
Charlotte	22
Philadelphia	23
Jacksonville	24
Richmond	25
Washington	26
Cincinnati	31
Cleveland	32
Detroit	33
Indianapolis	34
Lansing	35
Louisville	36
Chicago	41
Fargo	42
Rockford	43
Twin Cities	44
Davenport	45
Denver	51
Des Moines	52
Kansas City	53
Omaha	54
St. Louis	55
Dallas	61
Houston	62
Memphis	63
New Orleans	64
Oklahoma City	65
Los Angeles	71
San Jose	72
Salt Lake City	73
Seattle	74
Phoenix	75
Ford of Canada	81
Government	83
Home Office Reserve	84
American Red Cross	85
Transportation Services	89
Export	90

THE REAR AXLE CODE indicates the ratio of the rear axle installed in the vehicle. A number designates a conventional axle, while a letter designates an Equa-Lock axle.

REAR AXLE RATIO	CODE
3.00:1	1
2.83:1	2
3.20:1	3
3.25:1	4
3.50:1	5
2.80:1	6
3.89:1	8
4.11:1	9
3.00:1	A
3.20:1	C
3.25:1	D
3.25:1	*D
3.25:1	E
3.50:1	F
2.80:1	*F
3.89:1	H
2.83:1	L
4.11:1	I

* Falcon, Fairlane, Mustang

THE TRANSMISSION CODE indicates the type of transmission installed in the vehicle.

TRANSMISSION	CODE
3-Speed Manual (2.77)	1
Overdrive	2
3-Speed Manual (3.03)	3
C-6 Automatic (XPL)	4
4 Speed Manual-Shift	5
C-4 Automatic (XP)	6
Cruise-o-matic (FX)	7
Cruise-o-matic (MX)	8

THE TRIM NUMBER furnishes the key to trim color and material for each model series.

FORD TRIM COLOR	CLOTH	VINYL	LEATHER	CODE
Blue	•	•		12,32,52
Blue		•		22,42,62
Blue		•		82,92,K2
Blue		•		N2,72
Red	•	•		15,35,55
Red		•		25,45,65
Red		•		75,85,95
Red		•		N5,X5,Y5
Black	•	•		16,36,56
Black		•		26,46,66
Black		•		76,86,96
Black		•		K6,Z6
Aqua	•	•		17,37,57
Aqua		•		47,67,77
Palomino	•	•		19,39
Silver	•	•		31,51
Gold	•	•		38,58
Gold		•		48,68
Green		•		O3

Beige		•		O4
Burgundy	•	•		53,93
Burgundy			•	A3
Emberglo		•		64,84,94
Parchment		•		XD,ZD
Blue/Parchment		•		B2,S2
Black/Parchment		•		B6
Aqua/Parchment		•		B7
Gold/Parchment		•		B8
Palomino/Parchment		•		B9
White/Black		•		D6,E6
Blue/White		•		F2,G2
Burgundy/White		•		F3,G3
Emberglo/White		•		F4,G4
Black/White		•		F6,G6
Aqua/White		•		F7,G7
Gold/White		•		F8,G8
Palomino/White		•		F9,G9

FAIRLANE, FALCON, MUSTANG TRIM

COLOR	CLOTH	VINYL	LEATHER	CODE
Silver	•	•		11
Blue	•	•		12,32,52
Blue		•		22,42
Blue		•		62,82
Red	•	•		15,35,55
Red		•		25,45
Red		•		65,85
Aqua	•	•		17,37,57
Aqua		•		27,47
Aqua		•		67,87
Black		•		26,36,46
Black		•		66,86
Gold		•		38,48
Gold		•		68,88
Emberglo		•		44,64,84
Parchment	•	•		1D,3D,5D
Parchment		•		2D,4D,0D
Parchment/Silver		•		B1
Parchment/Blue		•		B2,C2
Parchment/Blue		•		D2,F2
Parchment/Emberglo		•		B4,C4
Parchment/Emberglo		•		D4,F4
Parchment/Red		•		B5
Parchment/Black		•		B6,C6
Parchment/Black		•		D6,F6
Parchment/Aqua		•		B7,C7
Parchment/Aqua		•		D7,F7
Parchment/Gold		•		B8,C8
Parchment/Gold		•		D8,F8
Parchment/Palomino		•		B9,C9
Parchment/Palomino		•		D9,F9
Parchment/Burgundy		•		C3,D3,F3
White/Silver		•		H1
White/Blue		•		H2
White/Emberglo		•		H4

THUNDERBIRD COLOR	TRIM CLOTH	VINYL	LEATHER	CODE
Blue	•	•		12,42
Blue		•		22,52
Blue			•	62
Black	•	•		16,46
Black		•		26,56
Black			•	66
Silver		•		21,51
Burgundy		•		23,53
Emberglo		•		24,54
Red		•		25,55
Red			•	65
Aqua		•		27,57
Gold		•		28,58
Parchment	•	•		1D,4D
Blue/Parchment		•		B2,K2
Blue/Parchment			•	LB2
Burgundy/Parchment		•		B3,K3
Burgundy/Parchment			•	L3
Emberglo/Parchment		•		B4,K4
Emberglo/Parchment			•	L4
Black/Parchment		•		B6,K6
Black/Parchment			•	L6
Turquoise/Parchment		•		B7,K7
Turquoise/Parchment			•	L7
Gold/Parchment		•		B8,K8
Gold/Parchment			•	L8
Palomino/Parchment		•		B9,K9
Palomino/Parchment			•	L9
Silver/White		•		G1,P1
Blue/White		•		G2,P2
Burgundy/White		•		G3,P3
Emberglo/White		•		G4,P4
Black/White		•		G6,P6
Turquoise/White		•		G7,P7
Gold/White		•		G8,P8
Palomino/White		•		G9,P9

THE PAINT CODE furnishes the key to the paint colors used on the car. A letter indicates the color of the car. A two-tone car has two sets of letters. The first indicates the lower body color, the second the upper body color.

THUNDERBIRD

COLOR	CODE
Black	A
Light Beige (Metallic)	B
Med. Silver Mink (Metallic)	E
Light Blue	F
Brite Blue (Metallic)	G
Light Beige	H
Dark Blue (Metallic)	K
Ivy Yellow	L
White	M
Platinum	N
Med. Palomino (Metallic)	P
Med. Blue (Metallic)	Q
Dk. Green (Metallic)	R
Cascade Green	S
Red	T
Med. Turquoise (Metallic)	U
Emberglo (Metallic)	V
Maroon (Metallic)	X
Med. Sage Gold (Metallic)	Z
Rose (Metallic)	1
Dk. Turquoise (Metallic)	2

FORD

COLOR	CODE
Black	A
Dk. Executive Gray (Metallic)	C
Med. Silver Mink (Metallic)	E
Light Blue	F
Light Beige	H
Dark Blue (Metallic)	K
White	M
Med. Palomino (Metallic)	P
Dk. Green (Metallic)	R
Red	T
Med. Turquoise (Metallic)	U
Emberglo (Metallic)	V
Maroon (Metallic)	X
Med. Sage Gold (Metallic)	Z
Dk. Turquoise (Metallic)	2
Med. Silver (Metallic)	4
Yellow	8

FAIRLANE, FALCON, MUSTANG

COLOR	CODE
Black	A
Light Blue	F
Light Beige	H
Dark Blue (Metallic)	K
White	M
Med. Palomino (Metallic)	P
Dk. Green (Metallic)	R
Red	T
Med. Turquoise (Metallic)	U
Emberglo (Metallic)	V
Maroon (Metallic)	X
Lt. Blue (Metallic)	Y
Med. Sage Gold (Metallic)	Z
Med. Silver (Metallic)	4
Red	5
Yellow	8

ENGINE NUMBER

6-cylinder engine tag is located on the ignition coil mounting bracket bolt.

289 engine tag is located under the electric heat bulb indicator.

All other engine tags are located under the coil attaching bolt.

FALCON

ENGINE CODE	NO. CYL.	CID	HORSE-POWER	COMP. RATIO	CARB	TRANS
U	6	170	105	9.1:1	1 BC	** M & A
4*	6	170	N/A	N/A	1 BC	** M & A
T	6	200	120	9.2:1	1 BC	** M & A
2*	6	200	N/A	N/A	1 BC	** M & A
C	8	289	200	9.3:1	2 BC	** M & A
3*	8	289	N/A	N/A	2 BC	** M & A

* Export

MUSTANG

ENGINE CODE	NO. CYL.	CID	HORSE-POWER	COMP. RATIO	CARB	TRANS
T	6	200	120	9.2:1	1 BC	** M & A
2*	6	200	N/A	N/A	1 BC	** M & A
C	8	289	200	9.3:1	2 BC	** M & A
3*	8	289	N/A	N/A	2 BC	** M & A
A	8	289	225	10.0:1	4 BC	** M & A
K	8	289	271	10.5:1	4 BC	** M & A

* Export

FAIRLANE

ENGINE CODE	NO. CYL.	CID	HORSE-POWER	COMP. RATIO	CARB	TRANS
T	6	200	120	9.2:1	1 BC	** M & A
2*	6	200	N/A	N/A	1 BC	** M & A
C	8	289	200	9.3:1	2 BC	** M & A
3*	8	289	200	9.3:1	2 BC	** M & A
Y	8	390	265	9.5:1	2 BC	MAN
H	8	390	275	9.5:1	2 BC	AUTO
S	8	390	335	10.5:1	4 BC	** M & A

* Export

FAIRLANE GT AND GTA

ENGINE CODE	NO. CYL.	CID	HORSE-POWER	COMP. RATIO	CARB	TRANS
S	8	390	335	10.5;1	4 BC	** M & A

THUNDERBIRD

ENGINE CODE	NO. CYL.	CID	HORSE-POWER	COMP. RATIO	CARB	TRANS
Z	8	390	315	10.5:1	4 BC	AUTO
Q	8	428	345	10.5:1	4 BC	AUTO
8*	8	428	N/A	N/A	4 BC	AUTO

* Export

FORD CUSTOM, CUSTOM 500 AND GALAXIE 500

ENGINE CODE	NO. CYL.	CID	HORSE-POWER	COMP. RATIO	CARB	TRANS
V	6	240	150	9.2:1	1 BC	** M & A
5*	6	240	N/A	N/A	1 BC	** M & A
B**	6	240	150	9.2:1	1 BC	** M & A
E+	6	240	150	9.2:1	1 BC	** M & A
C	8	289	200	9.3:1	2 BC	** M & A
3*	8	289	N/A	N/A	2 BC	** M & A
X	8	352	250	9.3:1	4 BC	AUTO
H	8	390	275	9.5:1	2 BC	AUTO
Z	8	390	315	10.5:1	4 BC	** M & A
Q	8	428	345	10.5:1	4 BC	** M & A
8*	8	428	N/A	N/A	4 BC	** M & A
P**	8	428	360	10.5:1	4 BC	** M & A
W	8	427	410	11.1:1	4 BC	MAN
4	8	427	425	11.1:1	2-4 BC	MAN

* Export
** Police
\+ Taxi

FORD LTD AND 500 XL

ENGINE CODE	NO. CYL.	CID	HORSE-POWER	COMP. RATIO	CARB	TRANS
C	8	289	200	9.3:1	2 BC	** M & A
3*	8	289	N/A	N/A	2 BC	** M & A
X	8	352	250	9.3:1	4 BC	AUTO
H	8	390	275	9.5:1	2 BC	AUTO
Z	8	390	315	10.5:1	4 BC	** M & A
Q	8	428	345	10.5:1	4 BC	** M & A
8*	8	428	N/A	N/A	4 BC	** M & A
W	8	427	410	11.1:1	4 BC	MAN
R	8	427	425	11.1:1	2-4 BC	MAN

* Export

FORD 7-LITRE

ENGINE CODE	NO. CYL.	CID	HORSE-POWER	COMP. RATIO	CARB	TRANS
Q	8	428	345	10.5:1	4 BC	** M & A
8*	8	428	N/A	N/A	4 BC	** M & A

 1967 FORD

1967 FORD FAIRLANE

1967 FORD FAIRLANE

1967 FORD FALCON

1967 FORD GALAXIE

1967 FORD MUSTANG

1967 FORD MUSTANG

1967 FORD THUNDERBIRD

1967 FORD THUNDERBIRD

1967 FORD LTD

1967 FORD XL

VEHICLE IDENTIFICATION NUMBER

FORD
7A81C100551

VIN LOCATION

FAIRLANE, FALCON VIN die-stamped on the top surface of the radiator and front fender apron support.

THUNDERBIRD VIN die-stamped on the cowl top panel tab on the right-hand side.

MUSTANG VIN die-stamped on the top upper flange of the left front fender apron.

FIRST DIGIT: Identifies the model year (1967)

SECOND DIGIT: Identifies the assembly plant

ASSEMBLY PLANT	CODE
Atlanta, GA	A
Oakville, Ont., CAN	B
Ontario, CAN	C
Dallas, TX	D
Mahwah, NJ	E
Dearborn, MI	F
Chicago, IL	G
Lorain, OH	H
Los Angeles, CA	J
Kansas City, KS	K
Michigan Truck	L
Norfolk, VA	N
Twin Cities, MN	P
San Jose, CA	R
Pilot Plant	S
Metuchen, NJ	T
Louisville, KY	U
Wayne, MI	W
Wixom, MI	Y
St. Louis, MO	Z

THIRD AND FOURTH DIGITS: Identify the body series

THE BODY SERIES number identifies the model and the particular body style.

FORD CUSTOM	CODE
2-Dr. Sedan (1)	50
4-Dr. Sedan (1)	51

FORD CUSTOM 500	CODE
2-Dr. Sedan (1)	52
4-Dr. Sedan (1)	53

GALAXIE 500	CODE
4-Dr. Sedan (1)	54
4-Dr. Hardtop (1)	56
2-Dr. Convertible (1)	57
2-Dr. Fastback (1)	55

GALAXIE 500XL	CODE
2-Dr. Hardtop (2)	58
2-Dr. Convertible (2)	59

LTD	CODE
4-Dr. Hardtop (1)	66
2-Dr. Hardtop (1,3)	62
4-Dr. Sedan	64
2-Dr. Convertible (1,3)	3
2-Dr. Hardtop (2)	1
2-Dr. Convertible (2)	3

RANCH WAGON	CODE
4-Dr., 6-Pass.	70

COUNTRY SEDAN	CODE
4-Dr., 6-Pass.	71
4-Dr., 6+4-Pass.	72

COUNTRY SQUIRE	CODE
4-Dr., 6-Pass.	73
4-Dr., 6+4-Pass.	74

FAIRLANE	CODE
2-Dr. Sedan (1)	30
4-Dr. Sedan (1)	31

FAIRLANE 500	CODE
2-Dr. Sedan (1)	33
4-Dr. Sedan (1)	34
2-Dr. Hardtop (1)	35
2-Dr. Convertible (1)	36

FAIRLANE 500 XL	CODE
2-Dr. Hardtop (2)	40
2-Dr. Convertible (2)	41

FAIRLANE 500 GT	CODE
2-Dr. Hardtop (2)	42
2-Dr. Convertible (2)	43

STATION WAGONS	CODE
4-Dr. Wagon	32
4-Dr. Wagon	37
4-Dr. Wagon	38

THUNDERBIRD	CODE
2-Dr. Hardtop (Painted Roof)	81
2-Dr. Hardtop Landau (Vinyl Roof)	82
4-Dr. Sedan (Vinyl Roof)	84

FALCON STANDARD	CODE
2-Dr. Club Coupe (1)	10
4-Dr. Sedan (1)	11

FUTURA	CODE
2-Dr. Club Coupe (1)	20
4-Dr. Sedan (1)	21

SPORT COUPE	CODE
2-Door (2)	22

STATION WAGONS	CODE
4-Dr. Wagon	12
4-Dr. Deluxe Wagon	23

MUSTANG	CODE
2-Dr. Fastback (1)	02
2-Dr. Hardtop (1)	01
2-Dr. Convertible (1)	03
2-Dr. Fastback (1,3)	02
2-Dr. Hardtop (1,3)	01

(1) Bench Seat
(2) Bucket Seat
(3) Formal Roof

FIFTH DIGIT: Identifies the engine

ENGINE	CODE
6 Cyl. 240 C.I.	V
6 Cyl. 240 C.I. (Police)	B
6 Cyl. 240 C.I.(Taxi)	E
8 Cyl. 289 C.I. (4-V) Prem.	A
8 Cyl. 289 C.I. (2-V)	C
8 Cyl. 289 C.I. (4-V, H.P.)	K
6 Cyl. 200 C.I. (1-V)	T
8 Cyl. 427 C.I. (8-V, H.P.)	R
8 Cyl. 427 C.I. (4-V, H.P.)	W
8 Cyl. 390 C.I. (2-V)	Y
8 Cyl. 390 C.I. (4-V)	Z
8 Cyl. 390 C.I. (4-V) GT	S
8 Cyl. 390 C.I. (2-V)	H
8 Cyl. 428 C.I. (4-V, Police)	P
8 Cyl. 428 C.I. (4-V)	Q
8 Cyl. 289 (Low Comp.)	3
6 Cyl. 240 (Low Comp.)	5
8 Cyl. 428 C.I. (4-V, Low Comp.)	8
6 Cyl. 200 C.I. (1-V, Low Comp.)	2
6 Cyl. 170 C.I. (1-V)	U

LAST SIX DIGITS: Represent the basic production numbers

BODY NUMBER PLATE

THE BODY PLATE is located on the left front door lock face panel on all models. Indicated on the body plate is the body type, exterior paint color, trim scheme, production date, district code and D.S.O. numbers, rear axle ratio and transmission type.

FORD MOTOR CORPORATION

SERIAL NUMBER
7A81C100551

65A	AA	2A	11G	21	1	W
BDY	CLR	TRM	DT	DSO	AX	TR

EXAMPLE:

Serial Number

7	Model Year (1967)
A	Assembly Plant (Atlanta, GA)
81	Model (Thunderbird)
C	Engine (8-Cyl. 289 C.I.)
100551	Production Sequence
65A	Body Type (2-Dr. Hardtop)
A	Lower Body Color
A	Upper Body Color
2A	Trim
11G	Production Date Code
21	DSO (Atlanta)
1	Axle (3.00:1)
W	Transmission (Automatic C-4)

BODY STYLE

FORD	CODE
4-Dr. Custom	54E
2-Dr. Custom	62E
4-Dr. Custom 500	54B
2-Dr. Custom 500	62B
4-Dr. Galaxie 500	54A
4-Dr. Galaxie 500 Hardtop	57B
2-Dr. Galaxie 500 Hardtop	63B
Galaxie Convertible	76A
2-Dr. Galaxie 500 XL Hardtop	63C
Galaxie 500 XL Convertible	76B
4-Dr. LTD Hardtop	67F
2-Dr. LTD Hardtop	63J
4-Dr. LTD Sedan	54C
4-Dr. Ranch Wagon, 6-Pass.	71D
4-Dr. Country Sedan, 6-Pass.	71B
4-Dr. Country Sedan, 6+4-Pass.	71C
4-Dr. Country Squire, 6-Pass.	71E
4-Dr. Country Squire, 6+4-Pass.	71A

THUNDERBIRD	CODE
2-Dr. Hardtop (Painted Roof)	65A
2-Dr. Hardtop Landau (Vinyl Roof)	65B
4-Dr. Sedan (Vinyl Roof)	57B

MUSTANG	CODE
2-Dr. Fastback (Bucket Seat)	63A
2-Dr. Hardtop (Bucket Seat)	65A
2-Dr. Convertible, (Bucket Seat)	76A
2-Dr. Fastback, (Bucket Seat, Luxury)	63B
2-Dr. Hardtop, (Bucket Seat, Luxury)	65B
2-Dr. Convertible, (Bucket Seat, Luxury)	76B
2-Dr. Hardtop (Bench Seat)	65C
2-Dr. Convertible, (Bench Seat)	76C

FAIRLANE	CODE
4-Dr. Fairlane	54A
2-Dr. Fairlane	62A
4-Dr. Fairlane 500	54B
2-Dr. Fairlane 500	62B
2-Dr. Fairlane 500 Hardtop	63B
Fairlane 500 Convertible	76B
2-Dr. Fairlane 500 XL Hardtop	63C
Fairlane 500 XL Convertible	76C
2-Dr. Fairlane 500 GT Hardtop	63D
Fairlane 500 GT Convertible	76D
4-Dr. Station Wagon	71D
4-Dr. Station Wagon	71B
4-Dr. Station Wagon	71E

FALCON	CODE
2-Dr. Standard Club Coupe	62A
4-Dr. Standard Sedan	54A
2-Dr. Futura Club Coupe	62B
4-Dr. Futura Sedan	54B
2-Dr. Sport Coupe	62C
4-Dr. Wagon Standard	71A
4-Dr. Wagon Deluxe	71B

THE DAY AND MONTH CODE furnishes the date the vehicle was manufactured. The number indicates the day of the month and the letter indicates the month.

MONTH	CODE	*CODE
January	A	N
February	B	P
March	C	Q
April	D	R
May	E	S
June	F	T
July	G	U
August	H	V
September	J	W
October	K	X
November	L	Y
December	M	Z

*Two year code letters to be used if 1967 models exceed 12 months.

DISTRICT CODE

DSO units built to a Domestic Special Order, Foreign Special Order, or other Special Orders will have the complete order number in this space. Also appearing in this space is the two digit code number of the District which ordered the unit. If the unit is regular production, only the District Code will appear.

DISTRICT	CODE
Boston	11
New York	13
Newark	15
Philadelphia	16
Washington	17
Atlanta	21
Charlotte	22
Jacksonville	24
Richmond	25
Cincinnati	27
Louisville	28
Cleveland	32
Detroit	33
Indianapolis	34
Lansing	35
Buffalo	37
Pittsburgh	38
Chicago	41
Fargo	42
Milwaukee	43
Twin Cities	44
Davenport	45
Denver	51
Des Moines	52
Kansas City	53
Omaha	54
St. Louis	55
Dallas	61
Houston	62
Memphis	63
New Orleans	64
Oklahoma City	65
Los Angeles	71
San Jose	72
Salt Lake City	73
Seattle	74
Phoenix	75
Ford of Canada	81
Government	83
Home Office Reserve	84
American Red Cross	85
Transportation Services	89
Export	90-99

THE REAR AXLE CODE indicates the ratio of the rear axle installed in the vehicle. A number designates a conventional axle, while a letter designates an Equa-Lock axle.

REAR AXLE RATIO	CODE
3.00:1	1
2.83:1	2
3.20:1	3
3.25:1	4
3.50:1	5
2.80:1	6
3.36:1	7
2.75:1	8
4.11:1	9
3.10:1	0
3.00:1	A
2.83:1	B
3.20:1	C
3.25:1	D
2.80:1	F
3.50:1	E
3.36:1	G
2.75:1	H
4.11:1	I

THE TRANSMISSION CODE indicates the type of transmission installed in the vehicle.

TRANSMISSION	CODE
Standard 3-Speed	1
Overdrive	2
3-Speed Manual	3
4 Speed Manual-Shift	5
Automatic (C-4)	W
Automatic (C-6)	U
Automatic (MX)	Y
Automatic (FX)	X
Automatic (XPL Special, C-6)	Z

THE TRIM NUMBER furnishes the key to trim color and material for each model series.

FORD TRIM COLOR	CLOTH	VINYL	LEATHER	CODE
Blue	•	•		3B,5B
Blue	•	•		1B,9B
Blue	•	•		E2,G2,ZB
Blue		•		2B,4B,6B
Blue		•		7B,NB,8B
Blue		•		CB,DB,JB
Blue		•		RB
Red	•	•		1D,9D,ZD
Red		•		2D,4D
Red		•		6D,7D
Red		•		8D,BD,RD
Parchment	•	•		1U,3U,5U
Parchment	•	•		9U,E9,G9
Parchment	•	•		PU,VU,ZU
Parchment		•		6U,7U,CU
Parchment		•		DU,JU,NU
Parchment		•		OU,RU,UU
Parchment		•		WU
Black		•		2A,4A,6A
Black		•		7A,RA,8A
Black		•		F1,H1,KA
Black		•		SA,UA,WA
Black	•	•		5A,9A,E1
Black	•	•		G1,LA,PA
Black	•	•		ZA
Black			•	HA

COLOR	CLOTH	VINYL	LEATHER	CODE
Saddle		•		2F,6F
Saddle		•		8F,RF
Gold		•		2G,4G
Gold		•		6G,8G
Gold	•	•		3G,5G
Gold	•	•		9G,ZG
Aqua		•		2K,4K,6K
Aqua		•		7K,8J
Aqua	•	•		3K,5K
Aqua	•	•		9K,ZK
Parchment/Black		•		2U,4U,8U
Silver	•	•		4L,8L
Silver	•	•		9L,ZL
Beige		•		OE

FAIRLANE, FALCON, MUSTANG TRIM

COLOR	CLOTH	VINYL	LEATHER	CODE
Blue	•	•		1B,3B,5B
Blue	•	•		9B,ZB
Blue		•		2B,4B,6B
Blue		•		7B,8B,LD
Blue/Parchment		•		GB
Red	•	•		1D,ZD,9D
Red		•		2D,4D,6D
Red		•		8D,LB
Red/Parchment		•		GD
Aqua	•	•		1K,3K,5K
Aqua	•	•		ZK,9K
Aqua		•		2K,4K
Aqua		•		6K,8K
Aqua/Parchment		•		GK
Parchment	•	•		1U,3U,5U
Parchment	•	•		7U,ZU,9U
Parchment	•	•		LU
Parchment		•		6U,OU
Parchment/Black		•		2U,4U,8U
Parchment/Black		•		FA,UA
Parchment/Blue		•		FB,UB
Parchment/Red		•		FD,UD
Parchment/Gold		•		FG,UG
Parchment/Aqua		•		FA,UK
Parchment/Saddle		•		UF
Black		•		2A,4A,6A
Black		•		7A,8A
Black	•	•		5A,9A,ZA
Black/Parchment		•		GA
Saddle		•		2F,6F,8F
Saddle/Parchment		•		GF
Gold		•		2G,4G
Gold		•		6G,8G
Gold	•	•		3G,ZG
Gold/Parchment		•		GG
Silver	•	•		4L,ZL

THUNDERBIRD TRIM

COLOR	CLOTH	VINYL	LEATHER	CODE
Black		•		2A,4A,8A
Black	•	•		5A
Black			•	HA,LA
Blue		•		2B,4B,8B
Red		•		2D,4D,8D
Saddle		•		2F
Gold		•		2G,4G,8G
Aqua		•		2K,4K,8K
Parchment	•	•		5U
Parchment		•		8U
Parchment/Black		•		2U,4U
Silver	•	•		4L,8L

THE PAINT CODE furnishes the key to the paint colors used on the car. A letter indicates the color of the car. A two-tone car has two sets of letters. The first indicates the lower body color, the second the upper body color.

COLOR	CODE
Black	A
Lt. Aqua	B
Dk. Gray (Metallic)	*C
Med. Beige (Metallic)	E
Light Blue	F
Diamond Green	*H
Lime (Metallic)	I
Dark Blue (Metallic)	K
White	M
Platinum	*N
Pewter (Metallic)	*P
Med. Blue (Metallic)	Q
Dk. Green (Metallic)	*R
Red	T
Med. Turquoise (Metallic)	*U
Bronze (Metallic)	V
Med. Aqua (Metallic)	W
Maroon (Metallic)	X
Dk. Green (Metallic)	Y
Med. Gold (Metallic)	Z
Yellow	2
Med. Gray (Metallic)	4
Lt. Beige	6
Yellow	8

* Thunderbird

1967 FORD

ENGINE NUMBER

6-cylinder engine number tag is attached with the ignition coil mounting bracket bolt.

289 engine number tag is located under the electric heat bulb indicator.

All other engine number tags are located under the coil attaching bolt.

FALCON

ENGINE CODE	NO. CYL.	CID	HORSE-POWER	COMP. RATIO	CARB	TRANS
U	6	170	105	9.1:1	1 BC	** M & A
T	6	200	120	9.2:1	1 BC	** M & A
2*	6	200	N/A	N/A	1 BC	** M & A
C	8	289	200	9.3:1	2 BC	** M & A
3*	8	289	N/A	N/A	2 BC	** M & A
A	8	289	225	9.8;1	4 BC	** M & A

* Export

MUSTANG

ENGINE CODE	NO. CYL.	CID	HORSE-POWER	COMP. RATIO	CARB	TRANS
T	6	200	120	9.2:1	1 BC	** M & A
2*	6	200	N/A	N/A	1 BC	** M & A
C	8	289	200	9.3:1	2 BC	** M & A
3*	8	289	N/A	N/A	2 BC	** M & A
A	8	289	225	9.8:1	4 BC	** M & A
K	8	289	271	10.5:1	4 BC	** M & A
S	8	390	320	10.5:1	4 BC	** M & A

* Export

FAIRLANE

ENGINE CODE	NO. CYL.	CID	HORSE-POWER	COMP. RATIO	CARB	TRANS
T	6	200	120	9.2:1	1 BC	** M & A
2*	6	200	N/A	N/A	1 BC	** M & A
C	8	289	200	9.3:1	2 BC	** M & A
3*	8	289	N/A	N/A	2 BC	** M & A
Y	8	390	270	9.5:1	2 BC	MAN
H	8	390	270	9.5:1	2 BC	AUTO
S	8	390	320	10.5:1	4 BC	** M & A
W	8	427	410	11.1:1	4 BC	MAN
R	8	427	425	11.1:1	2-4 BC	MAN

* Export

THUNDERBIRD

ENGINE CODE	NO. CYL.	CID	HORSE-POWER	COMP. RATIO	CARB	TRANS
Z	8	390	315	10.5:1	4 BC	AUTO
8*	8	428			4 BC	AUTO
Q	8	428	345	10.5:1	4 BC	AUTO

* Export

FORD CUSTOM, CUSTOM 500, GALAXIE 500

ENGINE CODE	NO. CYL.	CID	HORSE-POWER	COMP. RATIO	CARB	TRANS
V	6	240	150	9.2:1	1 BC	** M & A
5*	6	240	N/A	N/A	1 BC	** M & A
B**	6	240	150	9.2:1	1 BC	** M & A
E+	6	240	150	9.2:1	1 BC	** M & A
C	8	289	200	9.3:1	2 BC	** M & A
3*	8	289	N/A	N/A	2 BC	** M & A
Y	8	390	270	9.5:1	2 BC	MAN
H	8	390	270	9.5:1	2 BC	AUTO
Z	8	390	315	10.5:1	4 BC	** M & A
Q	8	428	345	10.5:1	4 BC	** M & A
8*	8	428	N/A	N/A	4 BC	** M & A
P**	8	428	360	10.5:1	4 BC	** M & A
W	8	427	410	11.1:1	4 BC	MAN
R	8	427	425	11.1:1	2-4 BC	MAN

FORD XL, LTD

ENGINE CODE	NO. CYL.	CID	HORSE-POWER	COMP. RATIO	CARB	TRANS
C	8	289	200	9.3:1	2 BC	** M & A
3*	8	289	N/A	N/A	2 BC	** M & A
Y	8	390	270	9.5:1	2 BC	MAN
H	8	390	270	9.5:1	2 BC	AUTO
Z	8	390	315	10.5:1	4 BC	** M & A
Q	8	428	345	10.5:1	4 BC	** M & A
8*	8	428	N/A	N/A	4 BC	** M & A
W	8	427	410	11.1:1	4 BC	MAN
R	8	427	425	11.1:1	2-4 BC	MAN

** MAN & AUTO

1968 FORD FAIRLANE

1968 FORD FALCON

1968 FORD GALAXIE

1968 FORD LTD

1968 FORD MUSTANG

1968 FORD MUSTANG

1968 FORD THUNDERBIRD

1968 FORD TORINO

1968 FORD XL

1968 FORD XL

VEHICLE IDENTIFICATION NUMBER

FORD
8A83Z100551

VIN LOCATION

The official Vehicle Identification Number (VIN) for title and registration purposes will be stamped on an aluminum tab that will be riveted to the instrument panel close to the windshield on the passenger side of the car and will be visible from the outside.

FIRST DIGIT: Identifies the model year (1968)

SECOND DIGIT: Identifies the assembly plant

ASSEMBLY PLANT	CODE
Atlanta, GA	A
Oakville, Ont., CAN	B
Ontario, CAN	C
Dallas, TX	D
Mahwah, NJ	E
Dearborn, MI	F
Chicago, IL	G
Lorain, OH	H
Los Angeles, CA	J
Kansas City, KS	K
Michigan Truck	L
Norfolk, VA	N
Twin Cities, MN	P
San Jose, CA	R
Pilot Plant	S
Metuchen, NJ	T
Louisville, KY	U
Wayne, MI	W
St. Thomas, Ont., CAN	X
Wixom, MI	Y
St. Louis, MO	Z

THIRD AND FOURTH DIGITS: Identify the body series

BODY SERIES

THE BODY SERIES number identifies the model and the particular body style.

FORD CUSTOM	CODE
2-Dr. Sedan (1)	50
4-Dr. Sedan (1)	51

FORD CUSTOM 500	CODE
2-Dr. Sedan (1)	52
4-Dr. Sedan (1)	53

GALAXIE 500	CODE
4-Dr. Sedan (1)	54
4-Dr. Hardtop (1)	56
2-Dr. Convertible (1)	57
2-Dr. Hardtop (1)	55
2-Dr. Hardtop (3)	58

FORD XL	CODE
4-Dr. Hardtop (2)	60
2-Dr. Convertible (2)	61

LTD	CODE
4-Dr. Hardtop (1)	66
2-Dr. Hardtop (1,3)	62
4-Dr. Sedan	64

RANCH WAGON	CODE
4-Dr., 6-Pass.	70

CUSTOM RANCH WAGON	CODE
4-Dr., 6-Pass.	71
4-Dr., 10-Pass.	72

COUNTRY SEDAN	CODE
4-Dr., 6-Pass.	73
4-Dr., 10-Pass.	74

COUNTRY SQUIRE	CODE
4-Dr., 6-Pass.	75
4-Dr., 10-Pass.	76

FAIRLANE	CODE
2-Dr. Hardtop (1)	30
4-Dr. Sedan (1,3)	31

FAIRLANE 500	CODE
2-Dr. Hardtop (1,3)	33
4-Dr. Sedan (1)	34
2-Dr. Hardtop (2)	35
2-Dr. Convertible (1)	36
2-Dr. Hardtop (2,3)	33
2-Dr. Hardtop (1)	35
2-Dr. Convertible (2)	36

TORINO	CODE
2-Dr. Hardtop (1,3)	40
4-Dr. Sedan (1)	41

TORINO GT	CODE
2-Dr. Hardtop (2)	42
2-Dr. Hardtop (2,3)	44
2-Dr. Convertible (2)	43

STATION WAGONS	CODE
4-Dr. Fairlane (1)	32
4-Dr. Fairlane 500 (1)	37
4-Dr. Torino Squire (1)	38

THUNDERBIRD	CODE
2-Dr. Hardtop (2)	83
2-Dr. Landau Hardtop (2)	84
2-Dr. Hardtop (1)	83
2-Dr. Landau Hardtop (1)	84
4-Dr. Landau (2)	87
4-Dr. Landau (1)	87

FALCON STANDARD	CODE
2-Dr. Club Coupe (1)	10
4-Dr. Sedan (1)	11

FUTURA	CODE
2-Dr. Club Coupe (1)	20
4-Dr. Sedan (1)	21

SPORT COUPE	CODE
2-Door (2)	22

STATION WAGONS	CODE
4-Dr. Wagon	12
4-Dr. Deluxe Wagon	23

MUSTANG

	CODE
2-Dr. Fastback (2,4)	02
2-Dr. Hardtop (2,4)	01
2-Dr. Convertible (2,4)	03
2-Dr. Fastback (2)	02
2-Dr. Hardtop (2)	01
2-Dr. Convertible (2)	03
2-Door Hardtop (1)	01
2-Door Fastback (1)	02
2-Door Hardtop (1,4)	01
2-Door Fastback (1,4)	02

(1) Bench Seat
(2) Bucket Seat
(3) Formal Roof
(4) Luxury model

FIFTH DIGIT: Identifies the engine

ENGINE	CODE
6 Cyl. 240 C.I.	V
6 Cyl. 240 C.I. (Police)	B
6 Cyl. 240 C.I. (Taxi)	E
8 Cyl. 289 C.I. (2-V)	C
6 Cyl. 200 C.I. (1-V)	T
8 Cyl. 427 C.I. (4-V, H.P.)	W
8 Cyl. 390 C.I. (4-V)	Z
8 Cyl. 390 C.I. (4-V GT)	S
8 Cyl. 390 C.I. (2-V)	Y
8 Cyl. 390 C.I. (2-V, Prem. Fuel)	X
8 Cyl. 428 C.I. (4-V, Police)	P
8 Cyl. 428 C.I. (4-V)	Q
8 Cyl. 428 C.I. (4-V CJ)	R
6 Cyl. 240 (Low Comp.)	5
8 Cyl. 428 C.I. (4-V, Low Comp.)	8
6 Cyl. 200 C.I. (1-V, Low Comp.)	2
6 Cyl. 170 C.I. (1-V)	U
8 Cyl. 302 C.I. (2-V)	F
8 Cyl. 302 C.I. (2-V, Low Comp.)	6
8 Cyl. 302 C.I. (4-V)	J
8 Cyl. 429 C.I. (4-V)	N

LAST SIX DIGITS: Represent the basic production numbers

BODY NUMBER PLATE

THE BODY PLATE is located on the front door hinge pillar. Indicated on the body plate is: the body type, exterior paint color, trim scheme, production date, district code and D.S.O. numbers, rear axle ratio and transmission type.

FORD MOTOR
CORPORATION

SERIAL NUMBER
8A83Z100551

65C	AA	3A	11G	21	5	1
BDY	CLR	TRM	DT	DSO	AX	TR

EXAMPLE:

Serial Number

8	Model Year (1968)
A	Assembly Plant (Atlanta, GA)
83	Model (Thunderbird)
Z	Engine (8 Cyl. 390 C.I.)
100551	Production Sequence
65C	Body Type (2-Dr. Hardtop)
A	Lower Body Color
A	Upper Body Color
3A	Trim
11G	Production Date Code
21	DSO (Atlanta)
5	Axle (3.00:1)
U	Transmission (C6 Automatic XPL)

BODY STYLE

FORD	CODE
4-Dr. Custom (1)	54E
2-Dr. Custom (1)	62E
4-Dr. Custom 500 (1)	54B
4-Dr. Custom 500 (1)	62B
4-Dr. Galaxie 500 (1)	54A
4-Dr. Galaxie 500 Hardtop (1)	57B
2-Dr. Galaxie 500 Hardtop (1)	63B
Galaxie 500 Convertible (1)	76A
2-Dr. Galaxie 500 Hardtop (3)	65C
2-Dr. Ford XL Hardtop (2)	63C
Ford XL Convertible (2)	76B
4-Dr. LTD Hardtop (1)	57F
2-Dr. LTD Hardtop (1,3)	65A
4-Dr. LTD Sedan	54C
4-Dr. Ranch Wagon, 6-Pass.	71D
4-Dr. Custom Ranch Wagon, 6-Pass.	71H
4-Dr. Custom Ranch Wagon, 10-Pass.	71J
4-Dr. Country Sedan, 6-Pass.	71B
4-Dr. Country Sedan, 10-Pass.	71C
4-Dr. Country Squire, 6-Pass.	71E
4-Dr. Country Squire, 10-Pass.	71A

(1) Bench Seat
(2) Bucket Seat
(3) Formal Roof

THUNDERBIRD	CODE
2-Dr. Hardtop	65C
2-Dr. Landau	65D
4-Dr. Landau	57C

MUSTANG	CODE
2-Dr. Fastback (2)	63A
2-Dr. Hardtop (2)	65A
Convertible (2)	76A
2-Dr. Fastback (1,2)	63B
2-Dr. Hardtop (2,3)	65B
Convertible (1,2)	76B
2-Dr. Hardtop (1)	65C
2-Dr. Fastback (1)	63C
2-Dr. Hardtop (1,3)	65D
2-Dr. Fastback (1,3)	63D

(1) Bench Seat
(2) Bucket Seat
(3) Luxury Model

FALCON	CODE
2-Dr. Standard Club Coupe (1)	62A
4-Dr. Standard Sedan (1)	54A
2-Dr. Futura Club Coupe (1)	62B
4-Dr. Futura Sedan (1)	54B
2-Dr. Futura Sports Coupe (2)	62C
4-Dr. Wagon (Standard)	71A
4-Dr. Wagon (Deluxe)	71B

(1) Bench Seat
(2) Bucket Seat

FAIRLANE	CODE
4-Dr. Sedan (1)	54A
2-Dr. Hardtop (1,3)	65A
4-Dr. 500 Sedan (1)	54B
2-Dr. 500 Hardtop (1,3)	65B
2-Dr. 500 Hardtop (1)	63B
500 Convertible (1)	76B
2-Dr. 500 Hardtop (2)	63E
2-Dr. 500 Hardtop (2,3)	65E
500 Convertible (2)	76E
2-Dr. Torino Hardtop (1,3)	65D
4-Dr. Torino Sedan (1)	54C
2-Dr. Torino GT Hardtop (2)	63D
2-Dr. Torino GT Hardtop (2,3)	65D
Torino GT Convertible (2)	76D
4-Dr. Fairlane Wagon (1)	71D
4-Dr. Fairlane 500 Wagon (1)	71B
4-Dr. Torino Squire Wagon (1)	71E

(1) Bench Seat
(2) Bucket Seat
(3) Formal Roof

THE DAY AND MONTH CODE furnishes the date the vehicle was manufactured. The number indicates the day of the month and the letter indicates the month.

MONTH	CODE	*CODE
January	A	N
February	B	P
March	C	Q
April	D	R
May	E	S
June	F	T
July	G	U
August	H	V
September	J	W
October	K	X
November	L	Y
December	M	Z

*Two year code letters to be used if 1968 models exceed 12 months.

DISTRICT CODE

DSO units built to a Domestic Special Order, Foreign Special Order, or other Special Orders will have the complete order number in this space. Also appearing in this space is the two digit code number of the District which ordered the unit. If the unit is regular production, only the District code number will appear.

DISTRICT	CODE
Boston	11
New York	13
Newark	15
Philadelphia	16
Washington	17
Atlanta	21
Charlotte	22
Jacksonville	24
Richmond	25
Cincinnati	27
Louisville	28
Cleveland	32
Detroit	33
Indianapolis	34
Lansing	35
Buffalo	37
Pittsburgh	38
Chicago	41
Fargo	42
Milwaukee	43
Twin Cities	44
Davenport	45
Denver	51
Des Moines	52
Kansas City	53
Omaha	54
St. Louis	55
Dallas	61
Houston	62
Memphis	63
New Orleans	64
Oklahoma City	65
Los Angeles	71
San Jose	72
Salt Lake City	73
Seattle	74
Phoenix	75
Ford of Canada	81
Government	83
Home Office Reserve	84
American Red Cross	85
Transportation Services	89
Export	90-99

THE REAR AXLE CODE indicates the ratio of the rear axle installed in the vehicle. A number designates a conventional axle, while a letter designates an Equa-Lock axle.

REAR AXLE RATIO	CODE
2.75:1	1
2.79:1	2
2.80:1	3
2.83:1	4
3.00:1	5
3.20:1	6
3.25:1	7
3.50:1	8
3.10:1	9
2.50:1	0
2.80:1	C
2.83:1	D
3.20:1	F
3.00:1	E
3.25:1	G
3.50:1	H
2.75:1	A
3.91:1	*V
4.30:1	*W

* Mustang, Fairlane

THE TRANSMISSION CODE indicates the type of transmission installed in the vehicle.

TRANSMISSION	CODE
3-Speed Manual	1
4-Speed Manual-Shift Wide Ratio 2.78 1st Gear	5
4-Speed Manual Shift Close Ratio 2.32 1st Gear	6
C4 Automatic (XP3)	W
C6 Automatic (XPL)	U
Automatic (MX)	Y
Automatic (FMX)	X
C6 Automatic (XPL Special)	Z

THE TRIM NUMBER furnishes the key to trim color and material for each model series.

FORD TRIM

COLOR	CLOTH	VINYL	LEATHER	CODE
Black	•	•		1A,3A,5A
Black	•	•		BA,EA,KA
Black	•	•		9A,SA,SY
Black		•		2A,4A,6A
Black		•		CA,DA,FA
Black		•		NA,PA,RA
Black		•		7A,HA
Blue	•	•		1B,3B,5B
Blue	•	•		BB,EB,KB
Blue	•	•		ZB,9B,SB
Blue		•		2B,4B,6B
Blue		•		CB,BD,FB
Blue		•		NB,PB,RB
Blue		•		7B,HB
Red	•	•		1D,3D,9D
Red	•	•		ED,KD,BD
Red		•		2D,4D,6D
Red		•		CD,DD,FD
Red		•		ND,PD,RD
Red		•		7D,HD
Gold	•	•		1G,1Y,2G
Gold	•	•		3Y,5G,5Y
Gold	•	•		9Y,BG,BY
Gold	•	•		SG,KG,KY
Gold	•	•		ZY,3G,9G
Gold	•	•		EF,SG
Gold		•		2Y,4Y,6G
Gold		•		7G,CY,EG
Gold		•		FY,HG,PG
Gold		•		RY,ZA,6Y
Gold		•		FG,RG
Aqua	•	•		1K,3K,5K
Aqua	•	•		EK,SK,9K
Aqua		•		4K,6K,RK
Parchment	•	•		1U,2U
Parchment		•		4U,6U,7U
Parchment		•		FU,HU,NU
Parchment		•		RU,DU,PU
Parchment/Black		•		CU
Beige		•		LE

FAIRLANE, FALCON, MUSTANG TRIM

COLOR	CLOTH	VINYL	LEATHER	CODE
Black	•	•		1A,3A
Black		•		2A,3A,4A
Black		•		6A,8A,9A
Black		•		LA,MA,QA
Black		•		5A,HA,RA
Blue	•	•		1B,3B
Blue	•	•		7B,KB
Blue		•		2B,4B,5B
Blue		•		7B,8B,9B
Blue		•		LB,MB,QB
Blue		•		6B,HB,RB
Gold	•	•		1G,3G,3Y
Gold	•	•		7G,7Y,KG
Gold	•	•		5G
Gold		•		1Y,2G,2Y
Gold		•		4Y,5Y,6G
Gold		•		8G,8Y,9Y
Gold		•		HY,4G,6Y
Gold		•		HG
Aqua	•	•		3K,7K
Aqua		•		1K,2K,4K
Aqua		•		8K,9K,HK
Aqua		•		6K
Parchment	•	•		1U,3U
Parchment		•		2U,4U,5U
Parchment		•		8U,9U,BU
Parchment		•		DU,EU,FU
Parchment		•		JU,KU,LU
Parchment		•		OU,QU,RU
Parchment		•		UU,6U,CU
Parchment		•		HU,MU,TU
Parchment/Black		•		AA,FA,UA
Parchment/Black		•		ZU,YU
Parchment/Blue		•		AB,FB,UB
Parchment/Red		•		AD,FD,UD
Parchment/Saddle		•		AF,FF,UF
Parchment/Gold		•		AG,AY,FG
Parchment/Gold		•		UG,UY,FY
Parchment/Aqua		•		AK,FK,UK
Saddle		•		2F,6F
Saddle/Black		•		8F
Red	•	•		7D,3D
Red		•		2D,3D,4D
Red		•		6D,8D,9D
Red		•		LD,MD,RD
Red		•		5D,HD

THUNDERBIRD TRIM

COLOR	CLOTH	VINYL	LEATHER	CODE
Black	•	•		1A,3A
Black		•		2A
Blue	•	•		1B,3B
Blue		•		2B
Red	•	•		1D
Red		•		2D
Gold	•	•		1G,1Y
Gold		•		2G,2Y
Aqua	•	•		1K
Aqua		•		2K
Saddle	•	•		2F
Parchment		•		2U

THE PAINT CODE furnishes the key to the paint colors used on the car. A letter indicates the color of the car. A two-tone car has two sets of lettes. The first indicates the lower body color, the second the upper body color.

COLOR	CODE
Black	A
Maroon	B
Med. Beige (Metallic)	**E
Diamond Green	**H
Dk. Aqua (Metallic)	**J
Dk. Green	**L
White	M
Diamond Blue	N
Light Green	O
Pewter (Metallic)	P
Med. Blue (Metallic)	Q
Dk. Green (Metallic)	R
Red	T
Med. Aqua (Metallic)	U
Lt. Blue	**V
Yellow	W
Dark Blue (Metallic)	X
Gold (Metallic)	Y
Dk. Gray (Metallic)	**Z
Rose (Metallic)	**2
Vermillion	*3
Low Gloss Black	*5
Lt. Beige	6

* Mustang, Fairlane, Falcon

** Thunderbird

ENGINE NUMBER

6-cylinder engine number tag is located under the coil attaching bolt.

289 engine number tag is located under the electric heat bulb indicator.

All other engine number tags are located under the coil attaching bolt.

FALCON

ENGINE NO.	NO. CYL.	CID	HORSE-POWER	COMP. RATIO	CARB	TRANS
U	6	170	100	8.7:1	1 BC	*** M & A
T	6	200	115	8.8:1	1 BC	*** M & A
2*	6	200	N/A	N/A	1 BC	*** M & A
C	8	289	195	8.7:1	2 BC	*** M & A
J	8	302	230	10.0:1	4 BC	*** M & A

* Export
*** MAN & AUTO

MUSTANG

ENGINE NO.	NO. CYL.	CID	HORSE-POWER	COMP. RATIO	CARB	TRANS
T	6	200	115	8.8:1	1 BC	*** M & A
2*	6	200	N/A	N/A	1 BC	*** M & A
C	8	289	195	8.7:1	2 BC	*** M & A
J	8	302	230	10.0:1	4 BC	*** M & A
X	8	390	280	10.5:1	2 BC	AUTO
S	8	390	325	10.5:1	4 BC	*** M & A
W	8	427	390	10.9:1	4 BC	AUTO
N/A	8	302	306	11.0:1	2-4 BC	MAN
R**	8	428	335	10.7:1	4 BC	*** M & A

* Export
** Cobra Jet
*** MAN & AUTO

FAIRLANE/TORINO

ENGINE NO.	NO. CYL.	CID	HORSE-POWER	COMP. RATIO	CARB	TRANS
T	6	200	115	8.8:1	1 BC	*** M & A
2 *	6	2 0 0	N / A	N/A	1 BC	*** M&A
F	8	302	210	9.0:1	2 BC	*** M&A
6*	8	302	N/A	N/A	2 BC	*** M&A
Y	8	390	265	9.5:1	2 BC	*** M&A
S	8	390	325	10.5:1	4 BC	*** M&A
W	8	427	390	10.9:1	4 BC	AUTO
R**	8	428	335	10.7:1	4 BC	AUTO

* Export
** Cobra Jet
*** MAN & AUTO

THUNDERBIRD

ENGINE NO.	NO. CYL.	CID	HORSE-POWER	COMP. RATIO	CARB	TRANS
Z	8	390	315	10.5:1	4 BC	AUTO
N	8	429	360	10.5:1	4 BC	AUTO

FORD CUSTOM, CUSTOM 500, GALAXIE 500 AND XL

ENGINE NO.	NO. CYL.	CID	HORSE-POWER	COMP. RATIO	CARB	TRANS
V	6	240	150	8.75:1	1 BC	*** M & A
5*	6	240	N/A	N/A	1 BC	*** M & A
E+	6	240	155	9.2:1	1 BC	*** M & A
B**	6	240	155	9.2:1	1 BC	*** M & A
F	8	302	210	9.0:1	2 BC	*** M & A
6*	8	302	N/A	N/A	2 BC	*** M & A
Y	8	390	265	9.5:1	2 BC	*** M & A
Z	8	390	315	10.5:1	4 BC	*** M & A
P**	8	428	360	10.5:1	4 BC	*** M & A
Q	8	428	340	10.5:1	4 BC	*** M & A
8*	8	428	N/A	N/A	4 BC	*** M & A
W	8	427	390	10.9:1	4 BC	AUTO

* Export
** Police
+ Taxi
*** MAN & AUTO

FORD LTD

ENGINE CODE	NO. CYL.	CID	HORSE-POWER	COMP. RATIO	CARB	TRANS
F	8	302	210	9.0:1	2 BC	*** M & A
6*	8	302	N/A	N/A	2 BC	*** M & A
Y	8	390	265	9.5:1	2 BC	*** M & A
Z	8	390	315	10.5:1	4 BC	*** M & A
Q	8	428	340	10.5:1	4 BC	*** M & A
8*	8	428	N/A	N/A	4 BC	*** M & A
W	8	427	390	10.9:1	4 BC	AUTO

* Export
*** MAN & AUTO

1969 FORD FALCON

1969 FORD GALAXIE

1969 FORD LTD

1969 FORD LTD

1969 FORD MUSTANG

1969 FORD MUSTANG

1969 FORD THUNDERBIRD

1969 FORD THUNDERBIRD

1969 FORD TORINO

1969 FORD TORINO

VEHICLE IDENTIFICATION NUMBER

FORD
9A83S100551

VIN LOCATION

The official Vehicle Identification Number (VIN) for title and registration purposes will be stamped on an aluminum tab that will be riveted to the instrument panel close to the windshield on the passenger side of the car and will be visible from outside.

FIRST DIGIT: Identifies the model year (1969)

SECOND DIGIT: Identifies the assembly plant

ASSEMBLY PLANT	CODE
Atlanta, GA	A
Oakville, Ont., CAN	B
Ontario, CAN	C
Dallas, TX	D
Mahwah, NJ	E
Dearborn, MI	F
Chicago, IL	G
Lorain, OH	H
Los Angeles, CA	J
Kansas City, KS	K
Michigan Truck	L
Norfolk, VA	N
Twin Cities, MN	P
San Jose, CA	R
Allen Park (Pilot Plant)	S
Metuchen, NJ	T
Louisville, KY	U
Wayne, MI	W
St. Thomas, Ont., CAN	X
Wixom, MI	Y
St. Louis, MO	Z

THIRD AND FOURTH DIGITS: Identify the body series

THE BODY SERIES number identifies the model and the particular body style.

FORD CUSTOM	CODE
2-Dr. Sedan (1)	50
4-Dr. Sedan (1)	51

FORD CUSTOM 500	CODE
2-Dr. Sedan (1)	52
4-Dr. Sedan (1)	53

FORD XL	CODE
4-Dr. Hardtop-Fastback (1,3)	60
2-Dr. Convertible (1,3)	61

Galaxie 500	CODE
4-Dr. Sedan (1)	54
4-Dr. Hardtop (1)	56
2-Dr. Convertible (1)	57
2-Dr. Hardtop Fastback (1)	55
2-Dr. Hardtop (1)	58

LTD	CODE
4-Dr. Hardtop (1,2)	66
2-Dr. Hardtop (1,2)	62
4-Dr. Sedan (1,2)	64

RANCH WAGON	CODE
4-Dr., 6-Pass. (1)	70

CUSTOM 500 RANCH WAGON	CODE
4-Dr., 6-Pass. (1)	71
4-Dr. Dual Face Rear (1)	72

COUNTRY SEDAN	CODE
4-Dr., 6-Pass. (1)	73
4-Dr. Dual Face Rear (1)	74

COUNTRY SQUIRE	CODE
4-Dr., 6-Pass. (1)	75
4-Dr. Dual Face Rear (1)	76

FAIRLANE	CODE
2-Dr. Hardtop Formal (1)	30
4-Dr. Sedan (1)	31

FAIRLANE 500	CODE
2-Dr. Hardtop Formal (1)	33
4-Dr. Sedan (1)	34
2-Dr. Hardtop Fastback (1)	35
2-Dr. Convertible (1)	36
2-Dr. Hardtop Formal (3)	33
2-Dr. Hardtop Fastback (3)	35
2-Dr. Convertible (3)	36

TORINO	CODE
2-Dr. Hardtop Formal (1)	40
4-Dr. Sedan (1)	41

TORINO GT	CODE
2-Dr. Hardtop Fastback (1)	42
2-Dr. Hardtop Formal (1)	44
Convertible (1)	43
2-Dr. Hardtop Fastback (3)	42
2-Dr. Hardtop Formal (3)	44
Convertible (3)	43

COBRA	CODE
2-Dr. Hardtop Fastback (1)	46
2-Dr. Hardtop Fastback (3)	46
2-Dr. Hardtop Formal (1)	45
2-Dr. Hardtop Formal (3)	45

STATION WAGONS	CODE
4-Dr. Fairlane (1)	32
4-Dr. Fairlane 500 (1)	37
4-Dr. Torino Squire (1)	38

THUNDERBIRD	CODE
2-Dr. Hardtop (3)	83
2-Dr. Hardtop (1)	83
2-Dr. Landau (3,4)	84
2-Dr. Landau (1,4)	84
4-Dr. Landau (3)	87
4-Dr. Landau (1)	87

(1) Bench Seat
(2) Split Bench Seat
(3) Bucket Seat
(4) Blind Quarter Roof

FALCON STANDARD	CODE
2-Dr. Sedan (1)	10
4-Dr. Sedan (1)	11

FUTURA	CODE
2-Dr. Sedan (1)	20
4-Dr. Sedan (1)	21
2-Dr. Sports Coupe (3)	22

STATION WAGONS	CODE
Standard (1)	12
Futura (1)	23

MUSTANG	CODE
2-Dr. Hardtop Standard (3,4)	01
2-Dr. Fastback Standard (3,4)	02
2-Dr. Convertible Standard (3,4)	03
2-Dr. Hardtop Luxury (3,4)	01
2-Dr. Fastback Luxury (3,4)	02
2-Dr. Convertible Luxury (3,4)	03
2-Dr. Hardtop Standard (1)	01
2-Dr. Hardtop Luxury (1)	01
2-Dr. Hardtop Grande (3)	01
2-Dr. Fastback Mach 1 (4)	02

(1) Bench Seat
(2) Split Bench Seat
(3) Bucket Seat
(4) Hi-Back Bucket Seat

FIFTH DIGIT: Identifies the engine

ENGINE	CODE
6 Cyl. 170 C.I.	U
6 Cyl. 240 C.I.	V
6 Cyl. 240 C.I. (Police)	B
6 Cyl. 240 C.I. (Taxi)	E
6 Cyl. 240 (Low Comp.)	5
6 Cyl. 250 C.I.	L
6 Cyl. 250 C.I. (Low Comp.)	3
6 Cyl. 200 C.I. (1-V)	T
6 Cyl. 200 C.I. (1-V, Low Comp.)	2
8 Cyl. 302 C.I. (4-V) Boss	G
8 Cyl. 390 C.I. (2-V)	Y
8 Cyl. 390 C.I. (4-V, Improved Perf.)	S
8 Cyl. 428 C.I. (4 -V, Police, Prem. Fuel)	P
8 Cyl. 428 C.I. (4-V) CJ	Q
8 Cyl. 428 C.I. (4-V, Ram Air Induction) CJ	R
8 Cyl. 302 C.I. (2-V)	F
8 Cyl. 302 C.I. (4-V, Low Comp.)	6
8 Cyl. 302 C.I. (2-V) (Police & Taxi)	D
8 Cyl. 351 C.I. (2-V)	H
8 Cyl. 351 C.I. (4-V)	M
8 Cyl. 429 C.I. (2-V)	K
8 Cyl. 429 C.I. (4-V)	N
8 Cyl. 429 C.I. (4-V) Boss	Z

LAST SIX DIGITS: Represent the basic production numbers

BODY NUMBER PLATE

THE BODY PLATE is located on the lock face of the left front door on all passenger cars. Indicated on the body plate is: the body type, exterior paint color, trim scheme, production date, district code and D.S.O. numbers, rear axle ratio and transmission type.

FORD MOTOR
CORPORATION

SERIAL NUMBER
9A83S100551

65A	AA	6Y	11G	21	1	1
BDY	CLR	TRM	DT	DSO	AX	TR

EXAMPLE:

Serial Number	
9	Model Year (1969)
A	Assembly Plant (Atlanta, GA)
83	Model (Thunderbird)
S	Engine (8 Cyl. 390 C.I. 4-V)
100551	Production Sequence
65A	Body Type (2-Dr. Hardtop)
A	Lower Body Color
A	Upper Body Color
6Y	Trim
11G	Production Date Code
21	DSO (Atlanta)
1	Axle (2.50:1)
1	Transmission (3-Speed Manual)

BODY TYPE

FORD	CODE
2-Dr. Custom Sedan (1)	62E
4-Dr. Custom Sedan (1)	54E
2-Dr. Custom 500 (1)	62B
4-Dr. Custom 500 (1)	54B
4-Dr. Galaxie 500 (1)	54A
2-Dr. Galaxie 500 Hardtop, Fastback (1)	63B
2-Dr. Galaxie 500 Hardtop, Formal (1)	65C
4-Dr. Galaxie 500 Hardtop (1)	57B
Galaxie 500 Convertible (1)	76A
2-Dr. Ford XL Hardtop, Fastback (1,3)	63C
Ford XL Convertible (1,3)	76B
4-Dr. LTD Sedan (1,2)	54C
2-Dr. LTD Hardtop, Formal (1,2)	65A
4-Dr. LTD Hardtop (1,2)	57F
4-Dr. Ranchwagon, 6-Pass. (1)	71D
Custom 500 Ranchwagon, 6-Pass. (1)	71H
Custom 500 Ranchwagon, Dual Face Rear (1)	71J
Country Sedan, 6-Pass. (1)	71B
Country Sedan, Dual Face Rear (1)	71C
Country Squire, 6-Pass. (1)	71E
Country Squire, Dual Face Rear (1)	71A

(1) Bench Seat
(2) Split Bench
(3) Bucket Seat

THUNDERBIRD	CODE
2-Dr. Hardtop (3)	65A
2-Dr. Hardtop (1)	65C
2-Dr. Landau (3,4)	65B
2-Dr. Landau (1,4)	65D
4-Dr. Landau (3)	57B
4-Dr. Landau (1)	57C

(1) Bench Seat
(2) Split Bench Seat
(3) Bucket Seat
(4) Blind Quarter Roof

MUSTANG	CODE
2-Dr. Standard Hardtop (3,4)	65A
2-Dr. Standard Fastback (3,4)	63A
Standard Convertible (3,4)	76A
2-Dr. Luxury Hardtop (3,4)	65B
2-Dr. Luxury Fastback (3,4)	63B
Luxury Convertible (3,4)	76B
2-Dr. Standard Hardtop (1)	65C
2-Dr. Luxury Hardtop (1)	65D
2-Dr. Grand Hardtop (3)	65E
2-Dr. Mach 1 Fastback (4)	63C

(1) Bench Seat
(2) Split Bench Seat
(3) Bucket Seat
(4) Hi-Back Bucket Seat

FAIRLANE	CODE
2-Dr. Hardtop Formal (1)	65A
4-Dr. Sedan (1)	54A
4-Dr. 500 Sedan (10)	54B
2-Dr. 500 Hardtop, Fastback (1)	63B
2-Dr. 500 Hardtop Formal (1)	65B
500 Convertible (1)	76B
2-Dr. 500 Hardtop Fastback (3)	63E
2-Dr. 500 Hardtop Formal (3)	65E
500 Convertible (3)	76E
2-Dr. Torino Hardtop Formal (1)	65C
4-Dr. Torino Sedan (1)	54C
2-Dr. Torino GT Hardtop, Fastback (1)	63F
2-Dr. Torino GT Hardtop Formal (1)	65F
Torino GT Convertible (1)	76F
2-Dr. Torino GT Hardtop, Fastback (3)	63D
2-Dr. Torino GT Hardtop, Formal (3)	65D
Torino GT Convertible (3)	76D
2-Dr. Cobra Hardtop Fastback (1)	63B
2-Dr. Cobra Hardtop, Fastback (3)	63E
2-Dr. Cobra Hardtop, Formal (1)	65A
2-Dr. Cobra Hardtop, Formal (3)	65E
4-Dr. Fairlane Wagon (1)	71D
4-Dr. Fairlane 500 Wagon (1)	71B
4-Dr. Fairlane Torino Squire Wagon (1)	71E

(1) Bench Seat
(2) Split Bench Seat
(3) Bucket Seat

FALCON	CODE
2-Dr. Standard (1)	62A
4-Dr. Standard (1)	54A
2-Dr. Futura (1)	62B
2-Dr. Futura Sports Coupe (3)	62B
4-Dr. Futura Sedan (1)	54B
4-Dr. Standard Wagon (1)	71A
4-Dr. Standard Wagon Futura (1)	71B

(1) Bench Seat
(2) Split Bench Seat
(3) Bucket Seat

THE DAY AND MONTH CODE furnishes the date the vehicle was manufactured. The number indicates the day of the month and the letter indicates the month.

MONTH	CODE	*CODE
January	A	N
February	B	P
March	C	Q
April	D	R
May	E	S
June	F	T
July	G	U
August	H	V
September	J	W
October	K	X
November	L	Y
December	M	Z

*Two year code letters to be used if 1969 models exceed 12 months.

DISTRICT CODE

DSO units built to a Domestic Special Order, Foreign Special Order, or other Special Orders will have the complete order number in this space. Also appearing in this space is the two digit code number of the District which ordered the unit. If the unit is regular production, only the District code number will appear.

DISTRICT	CODE
Boston	11
New York	13
Newark	15
Philadelphia	16
Washington	17
Atlanta	21
Charlotte	22
Jacksonville	24
Richmond	25
Cincinnati	27
Louisville	28
Detroit	33
Indianapolis	34
Lansing	35
Buffalo	37
Pittsburgh	38
Chicago	41
Fargo	42
Milwaukee	43
Twin Cities	44
Davenport	45
Denver	51
Des Moines	52
Kansas City	53
Omaha	54
St. Louis	55
Dallas	61
Houston	62
Memphis	63
New Orleans	64
Oklahoma City	65
Los Angeles	71
San Jose	72
Salt Lake City	73
Seattle	74
Phoenix	75
Government	83
Home Office Reserve	84
American Red Cross	85
Transportation Services	89
Export	90-99

1969 FORD

FORD OF CANADA

Central	B1
Eastern	B2
Atlantic	B3
Midwestern	B4
Pacific	B7
Export	I1-I7

THE REAR AXLE CODE indicates the ratio of the rear axle installed in the vehicle.

REAR AXLE RATIO	LIMITED SLIP	CONVENTIONAL
2.50:1	J	1
2.75:1	K	2
2.79:1	L	3
2.80:1	M	4
2.83:1	N	5
3.00:1	O	6
3.10:1	P	7
3.20:1	Q	8
3.25:1	R	9
3.50:1	S	A
3.07:1	T	B
3.08:1	U	C
3.91:1	V	D
4.30:1	W	E

THE TRANSMISSION CODE indicates the type of transmission installed in the vehicle.

TRANSMISSION	CODE
3-Speed Manual (3.03)	1
4-Speed Manual Shift, Wide Ratio 2.78 1st Gear	5
4-Speed Manual Shift, Close Ratio 2.32 1st Gear	6
C4 Automatic (XP3)	W
C6 Automatic (XPL)	U
Cruise-O-matic (FMX)	X
Automatic (MX)	Y
C6 Automatic (XPL Special)	Z

THE TRIM NUMBER furnishes the key to trim color and material for each model series.

FORD TRIM

COLOR	CLOTH	VINYL	LEATHER	CODE
Black	•	•		3A,5A,7A
Black	•	•		CA,DA,EA
Black		•		6A,8A,9A
Black		•		GA,HA,JA
Black		•		NA,PA,WA
Black		•		FA,KA,YA
Blue	•	•		3B,5B,EB
Blue	•	•		DB,CB
Blue		•		6B,7B,8B
Blue		•		FB,GB,NB
Blue		•		YB,9B,PB
Gold	•	•		3G,3Y,5G
Gold	•	•		EG,EY,CG
Gold	•	•		DG,DY,5Y
Gold	•	•		CY
Gold		•		6G,6Y,7G
Gold		•		8G,8Y,9G
Gold		•		FG,FY,GG
Gold		•		HY,JY,KY
Gold		•		PY,WY,YG
Gold		•		7Y,9Y,GY
Gold		•		YY
Aqua	•	•		5K,EK
Aqua	•	•		CK,DK
Aqua		•		9K,YK
Red	•	•		ED,CD,DD
Red		•		6D,8D,9D
Red		•		GD,YD,FD
White		•		6W,8W
White		•		JW,WW
Parchment		•		LE

FAIRLANE, TORINO TRIM

COLOR	CLOTH	VINYL	LEATHER	CODE
Black	•	•		1A,3A
Black	•	•		7A,EA
Black		•		2A,4A,5A
Black		•		8A,9A,HA
Black		•		QA,VA,WA
Black		•		6A,MA
Blue	•	•		1B,3B,7B
Blue		•		2B,5B,6B
Blue		•		9B,HB,8B
Gold	•	•		1Y,3G,3Y
Gold	•	•		7Y,7G
Gold		•		2Y,4Y,5G
Gold		•		6G,6Y,7G
Gold		•		8G,8Y,9G
Gold		•		HG,HY,NY
Gold		•		5Y,7Y,9Y
Aqua	•	•		3K,7K
Aqua		•		5K,6K
Aqua		•		9K,HK
Red	•	•		7D
Red		•		5D,6D,8D
Red		•		HD,9D
White	•	•		7W
White		•		5W,6W,8W
White		•		HW,QW,VW
White		•		WW,EW

FALCON TRIM

COLOR	CLOTH	VINYL	LEATHER	CODE
Black		•		1A,2A
Black		•		4A,8A
Black	•	•		3A
Blue		•		1B,2B
Blue		•		4B,8B
Blue	•	•		3B
Gold		•		1Y,2Y
Gold		•		4Y,8Y
Gold	•	•		3Y
Red		•		4D,8D

THUNDERBIRD TRIM

COLOR	CLOTH	VINYL	LEATHER	CODE
Black	•	•		1A,3A
Black		•		4A,2A
Black			•	8A
Blue	•	•		1B,3B
Blue		•		4B,2B
Red	•	•		1D,3D
Red		•		4D,2D
Gold	•	•		3G
Gold		•		2G
White		•		4W,2W
White			•	8W
Nugget	•	•		1Y,3Y
Nugget		•		4Y,2Y

THE PAINT CODE furnishes the key to the paint colors used on the car. A letter indicates the color of the car. A two-tone car has two sets of letters. The first indicates the lower body color, the second the upper body color.

COLOR	CODE
Black	A
Maroon	B
Dk. Ivy Green (Met.) (Mustang)	C
Bright Blue (Met.) (Mustang)	D
Lt. Aqua	E
Dk. Aqua (Metallic) (Exc. Bronco)	F
Med. Orchid	G
Diamond Green	H
Lime (Metallic)	I
Dk. Aqua (Metallic) (T-Bird)	J
Med. Gray (Metallic) (T-Bird)	L
White	M
Platinum Diamond Blue	N
Pewter (Metallic)	P
Med. Blue (Metallic)	Q
Lt. Gold	R
Red	T
Med. Aqua (Metallic)	U
Lt. Aurora Copper (Metallic)	V
Yellow	W
Dark Blue (Metallic)	X
Burnt Orange (Metallic)	Y
Dk. Gray (Metallic) (T-Bird)	Z
Lt. Ivy Yellow	2
Calypso Coral	3
Med. Emerald (Metallic)	4
Med. Blue (Metallic)	6
Lt. Emerald Green (Metallic	7
Lt. Blue	8
Primer (Red or Gray), DSO Option	9

ENGINE NUMBER

The engine number tag is located under coil attaching bolt.

FALCON

ENGINE CODE	NO. CYL.	CID	HORSE-POWER	COMP. RATIO	CARB	TRANS
U	6	170	105	9.1:1	1 BC	*** M & A
T	6	200	115	8.8:1	1 BC	*** M & A
2*	6	200	N/A	N/A	1 BC	*** M & A
F	8	302	220	9.5:1	2 BC	*** M & A
6*	8	302	N/A	N/A	2 BC	*** M & A

* Export
*** MAN & AUTO

MUSTANG

ENGINE CODE	NO. CYL.	CID	HORSE-POWER	COMP. RATIO	CARB	TRANS
T	6	200	119	8.8:1	1 BC	*** M & A
2*	6	200	N/A	N/A	1 BC	*** M & A
F	8	30	220	9.5:1	2 BC	*** M & A
6*	8	302	N/A	N/A	2 BC	*** M & A
H	8	351	250	9.5:1	2 BC	*** M & A
M	8	351	290	10.7:1	4 BC	*** M & A
S	8	390	320	10.5:1	4 BC	*** M & A
Q	8	428	335	10.6:1	4 BC	*** M & A
R**	8	428	335	10.6:1	4 BC	*** M & A
G+	8	302	290	10.5:1	4 BC	MAN
Z	8	429	370	10.5:1	4 BC	MAN

* Export
** Ram Air
+ Boss 302
*** MAN & AUTO

FAIRLANE/TORINO

ENGINE CODE	NO. CYL.	CID	HORSE-POWER	COMP. RATIO	CARB	TRANS
L	6	250	155	9.0:1	1 BC	*** M & A
3*	6	250	N/A	N/A	1 BC	*** M & A
F	8	302	220	9.5:1	2 BC	*** M & A
6*	8	302	N/A	N/A	2 BC	*** M & A
H	8	351	250	9.5:1	2 BC	*** M & A
M	8	351	290	10.7:1	4 BC	*** M & A
S	8	390	320	10.5:1	4 BC	*** M & A
Q	8	428	335	10.6:1	4 BC	*** M & A
R**	8	428	335	10.6:1	4 BC	*** M & A

* Export
** Ram Air
*** MAN & AUTO

THUNDERBIRD

ENGINE CODE	NO. CYL.	CID	HORSE-POWER	COMP. RATIO	CARB	TRANS
N	8	429	360	10.5:1	4 BC	AUTO

FORD CUSTOM, CUSTOM 500, GALAXIE 500, XL

ENGINE CODE	NO. CYL.	CID	HORSE-POWER	COMP. RATIO	CARB	TRANS
V	6	240	150	9.2:1	1 BC	*** M & A
5*	6	240	N/A	N/A	1 BC	*** M & A
B**	6	240	155	N/A	1 BC	*** M & A
E+	6	240	155	N/A	1 BC	*** M & A
F	8	302	220	9.5:1	2 BC	*** M & A
6*	8	302	N/A	N/A	2 BC	*** M & A
D**+	8	302	220	9.5:1	2 BC	*** M & A
H	8	351	250	9.5:1	2 BC	*** M & A
Y	8	390	265	9.5:1	2 BC	*** M & A
K	8	429	320	10.5:1	2 BC	AUTO
N	8	429	360	10.5:1	4 BC	*** M & A

* Export
** Police
+ Taxi
*** MAN & AUTO

FORD LTD

ENGINE CODE	NO. CYL.	CID	HORSE-POWER	COMP. RATIO	CARB	TRANS
F	8	302	220	9.5:1	2 BC	*** M & A
6*	8	302	N/A	N/A	2 BC	*** M & A
H	8	351	250	N/A	2 BC	*** M & A
Y	8	390	265	N/A	2 BC	*** M & A
K	8	429	320	10.5:1	2 BC	AUTO
N	8	429	360	10.5:1	4 BC	*** M & A
P**	8	428	360	10.5:1	4 BC	*** M & A

* Export
** Police
*** MAN & AUTO

1960 LINCOLN / MERCURY

1960 LINCOLN

1960 LINCOLN

1960 LINCOLN CONTINENTAL

1960 LINCOLN CONTINENTAL

1960 MERCURY

1960 MERCURY

1960 MERCURY COMET

1960 MERCURY COMET

1960 LINCOLN / MERCURY

VEHICLE IDENTIFICATION NUMBER

LINCOLN / MERCURY
0H34N500551

VIN LOCATION

COMET VIN is die-stamped into top surface of left-hand brace extending from top of firewall to left front wheel base.

MERCURY VIN is die-stamped into top of right-hand frame side rail forward of cowl under the hood.

LINCOLN VIN is die-stamped into top face of front compartment lock flange near right-hand side.

FIRST DIGIT: Identifies the model year (1960)

SECOND DIGIT: Identifies the assembly plant

ASSEMBLY PLANT	CODE
Lorain, OH	H
Los Angeles, CA	J
Kansas City, KS	K
Metuchen, NJ	T
Wayne, MI	W
Wixom, MI	Y
St. Louis, MO	Z
San Jose, CA	R

THIRD AND FOURTH DIGITS: Identify the body series

COMET	CODE
2-Dr. Sedan	01
4-Dr. Sedan	02
2-Dr. Station Wagon	06
4-Dr. Station Wagon	07

MONTEREY	CODE
2-Dr. Sedan	31
4-Dr. Sedan	32
2-Dr. Hardtop	33
4-Dr. Hardtop	34
2-Dr. Convertible	35
4-Dr. Commuter Wagon, 6-8 Pass.	37

MONTCLAIR	CODE
4-Dr. Sedan	42
2-Dr. Hardtop	43
4-Dr. Hardtop	44

PARKLANE	CODE
2-Dr. Hardtop	53
4-Dr. Hardtop	54
2-Dr. Convertible	55

COLONY PARK	CODE
4-Dr. Wagon, 6-8 Pass.	57

LINCOLN	CODE
4-Dr. Sedan	62
2-Dr. Hardtop	63
4-Dr. Hardtop	64
4-Dr. Premiere Sedan	72
2-Dr. Premiere Hardtop	73
4-Dr. Premiere Hardtop	74
4-Dr. Continental Sedan	82
2-Dr. Continental Hardtop	83
4-Dr. Continental Hardtop	84
2-Dr. Continental Convertible	85
Formal Sedan	92
Limousine	99

FIFTH DIGIT: Identifies the engine code

MERCURY ENGINE	CODE
430 C.I.D. 8 Cyl. 2-V Carb.	M
383 C.I.D. 8 Cyl. 2-V Carb.	N
312 C.I.D. 8 Cyl. 2-V Carb.	P
383 C.I.D. 2-V Low Comp.	E
430 C.I.D. 2-V Low Comp.	F

COMET ENGINE	CODE
6 Cyl. OHV 144 Cubic Inch	S
6 Cyl. OHV 144 Cubic Inch Low Comp. (84 Octane)	D

LINCOLN ENGINE	CODE
430 C.I.D. 8 Cyl. 2-V	H
430 C.I.D. 2-V (Export)	K

LAST SIX DIGITS: Represent the basic production numbers

BODY NUMBER PLATE

THE BODY PLATE is riveted to the front body pillar between the front door hinges on the Lincoln and Mercury. The Comet Body Plate is riveted to the left front door below the door lock. The Body Plate includes information relative to the type of engine, axle, transmission, trim (exterior and interior), and body style of the vehicle. It also includes the date (day, month and year) and place of manufacture.

FORD MOTOR CORPORATION

SERIAL NUMBER
0H34N100551

57A	AA	50	11G	5	5
BDY	CLR	TRM	DT	TR	AX

EXAMPLE:

Serial Number

0	Model Year (1960)
H	Assembly Plant (Lorain, OH)
34	Body Series (4-Dr. Hardtop)
N	Engine (383 8 Cyl. 2-V)
100551	Production Sequence
57A	Body Style (Monterey 4-Dr.)
A	Lower Body Color
A	Upper Body Color
50	Trim
11G	Date Production Code
5	Transmission (Auto. Single)
5	Axle (2.71)

BODY STYLE

COMET	CODE
4-Dr. Sedan	54A
2-Dr. Station Wagon	59A
2-Dr. Sedan	62A
4-Dr. Station Wagon	71A

 1960 LINCOLN / MERCURY

MERCURY	CODE
4-Dr. Monterey Sedan	57A
4-Dr. Montclair Sedan	57B
4-Dr. Parklane Sedan	57F
4-Dr. Monterey Sedan	58A
4-Dr. Montclair Sedan	58B
2-Dr. Monterey Hardtop	63A
2-Dr. Montclair Hardtop	63B
2-Dr. Parklane Hardtop	63F
2-Dr. Monterey Sedan	64A
2-Dr. Monterey Convertible	76A
2-Dr. Parklane Convertible	76D
4-Dr. Commuter Wagon, 6-8 Pass.	77A
4-Dr. Colony Park Wagon, 6-8 Pass.	77B

LINCOLN	CODE
4-Dr. Lincoln Sedan	53A
4-Dr. Premiere Sedan	53B
4-Dr. Continental Sedan	54A
4-Dr. Lincoln Landau	57A
4-Dr. Premiere Landau	57B
2-Dr. Lincoln Coupe	63A
2-Dr. Premiere Coupe	63B
2-Dr. Continental Coupe	65A
2-Dr. Continental Convertible	68A
4-Dr. Continental Landau	75A
Lincoln Formal Sedan	23B
Lincoln Limousine	23A

THE DAY AND MONTH CODE furnishes the date the vehicle was manufactured. The number indicates the day of the month and the letter indicates the month.

MONTH	CODE	*CODE
January	A	N
February	B	P
March	C	Q
April	D	R
May	E	S
June	F	T
July	G	U
August	H	V
September	J	W
October	K	X
November	L	Y
December	M	Z

*Two year code letters to be used if 1960 models exceed 12 months.

THE TRANSMISSION CODE indicates the type of transmission installed in the vehicle.

TRANSMISSION	CODE
3-Speed Standard	1
Comet Drive 2-Speed Auto.	3
Automatic Dual Range	4
Automatic Single Range	5
Automatic Dual Range	6
Automatic Single Range	7

THE REAR AXLE CODE indicates the ratio of the rear axle installed in the vehicle.

REAR AXLE RATIO	CODE
3.56	1
3.10	3
2.71	5
2.91	6
2.71	7
2.91	8

THE TRIM NUMBER furnishes the key to trim color and material for each model series.

LINCOLN TRIM

COLOR	CLOTH	VINYL	LEATHER	CODE
Gray	•			01,04,07,11
Blue	•			02,05,08,12
Blue	•		•	22,44
Blue			•	29
Green	•			03,06,09,13
Green	•		•	23,45
Green			•	30
Brown	•			10
White/ Champagne	•		•	24,46
White/Red			•	31
White/ Turquoise			•	32
White/Gold			•	33
White/Black			•	34
White/Black	•		•	49
Sand/Black	•		•	26
Red/Black	•		•	27
Coral/Black	•		•	47
Flamingo/ Black	•		•	48
Black	•		•	28
Black			•	36
Sand/Buff			•	35
Red/White/ Black*			•	37
Coral/White/ Black*			•	38
Flamingo/White/ Black*			•	39
Turquoise/White/ Black*			•	40
Gold/White/ Black*			•	42

* Optional

COMET TRIM

COLOR	CLOTH	VINYL	LEATHER	CODE
White	•	•		01
Green	•	•		02
Red	•	•		03
Turquoise	•	•		04,*07
Green	•	•		*05
Red/Black	•	•		*06
White/Black		•		*08
Red/Black		•		09

* Deluxe RPO Trim

MONTEREY TRIM

COLOR	CLOTH	VINYL	LEATHER	CODE
Silver	•	•		21
Blue	•	•		22
Bronze	•	•		24
Red	•	•		25
Turquoise	•	•		27

MONTEREY TRIM

COLOR	CLOTH	VINYL	LEATHER	CODE
Blue		•		42
Bronze		•		44
Turquoise		•		47
Black/Silver		•		50
Red/Silver		•		55

1960 LINCOLN / MERCURY

MONTCLAIR TRIM

COLOR	CLOTH	VINYL	LEATHER	CODE
Silver/ Gray	•	•		11
Blue	•	•		12
Bronze	•	•		14
Bronze		•		44
Red	•	•		15
Red		•		45
Turquoise	•	•		17
Turquoise		•		47
Black/Silver		•		50

PARKLANE TRIM

COLOR	CLOTH	VINYL	LEATHER	CODE
Silver/Gray		•		51
Silver/Gray	•	•		31
Blue	•	•		31
Blue	•	•		32
Bronze	•	•		34
Turquoise	•	•		37
Rose	•	•		39

PARKLANE CONVERTIBLE TRIM

COLOR	CLOTH	VINYL	LEATHER	CODE
Blue		•		42
Bronze		•		44
Red		•		45
Turquoise		•		47
Gray/Silver		•		70

COMMUTER COUNTRY WAGON

COLOR	CLOTH	VINYL	LEATHER	CODE
Silver/Gray	•	•		61
Blue	•	•		62
Bronze	•	•		64
Bronze		•		44
Red/Gray	•	•		65
Turquoise		•		47
Black/Silver		•		50
Red/Silver		•		55

THE PAINT CODE furnishes the key to the paint colors used on the car. A letter indicates the color of the car. A two-tone car has two sets of letters. The first indicates the lower body color, the second the upper body color.

LINCOLN

COLOR	CODE
Presidential Black	A
Marine Blue Poly	B
Sapphire Poly	D
Electric Blue Poly	E
Blue Crystal	F
Tawny Beige	G
Pale Turquoise	I
Cherokee Red	J
Gold Dust Poly	L
Polaris White	M
Platinum	N
Copper Poly	Q
Pastel Yellow	R
Deerfield Green Poly	S
Terre Veree Green Poly	T
Metallic Rose Glow Poly	U
Twilight Pink	V
Killarney Green	W
Maple Leaf Poly	X
Spartan Gray Poly	Y
Silver Poly	Z

MERCURY/COMET

COLOR	CODE
Tuxedo Black	A
Sultana White	M
Med. Valley Green Met.	T
Lt. Innlet Blue	F
Med. Cote D'Azur Blue Met.	E
Signal Red	J
Cloud Silver Metallic	Z
Sun Haze Yellow	R
Polynesian Beige	N
Med. Javelin Bronze Met.	H
Mountain Rose Metallic	U
Summer Rose (Light)	V
Lt. Tucson Turquoise Met.	X
Med. Aztec Turquoise Met.	D
Marine Blue Metallic (Dark)	B
Crystal Turquoise	C
Twilight Turquoise	K
Cameo Green	W

CONVERTIBLE TOP COLORS

COLOR	CODE
Black	1
White	2
Tan	3
Lt. Blue	4
Lt. Green	5

ENGINE NUMBER

Comet engine number is die-stamped on the top surface of the block on the front left side near the crankcase breather pipe. This designates the engine plant, year, month and day of manufacture and inspector's identification.

Lincoln engine number is die-stamped on the cylinder block directly in front of the left hand cylinder head.

Mercury 312 early engine number is die-stamped on the front of the cylinder block at pushrod valley cover. The later is die-stamped on the left front corner of cylinder block just below the cylinder head.

Mercury 383 and 430 engine number is die-stamped on the cylinder block in front of the left cylinder head.

COMET

ENGINE NO.	NO. CYL.	CID	HORSE-POWER	COMP. RATIO	CARB	TRANS
S	6	144	90	8.7:1	1 BC	** M & A
D*	6	144	N/A	N/A	1 BC	** M & A

* Export

MERCURY MONTEREY AND COMMUTER

ENGINE NO.	NO. CYL.	CID	HORSE-POWER	COMP. RATIO	CARB	TRANS
P	8	312	205	8.9:1	2 BC	** M & A
N	8	383	280	8.5:1	2 BC	AUTO
E*	8	383	N/A	N/A	2 BC	AUTO

* Export

MONTCLAIR, COLONY PARK AND PARKLANE

ENGINE NO.	NO. CYL.	CID	HORSE-POWER	COMP. RATIO	CARB	TRANS
M	8	430	310	10.0:1	2 BC	AUTO
F*	8	430	N/A	N/A	2 BC	AUTO

LINCOLN AND CONTINENTAL

ENGINE NO.	NO. CYL.	CID	HORSE-POWER	COMP. RATIO	CARB	TRANS
H	8	430	315	10.0:1	2 BC	AUTO
K*	8	430	N/A	N/A	2 BC	AUTO

* Export
** MAN & AUTO

1961 LINCOLN / MERCURY

1961 LINCOLN CONTINENTAL

1961 LINCOLN CONTINENTAL

1961 MERCURY

1961 MERCURY

1961 MERCURY COMET

1961 MERCURY COMET

VEHICLE IDENTIFICATION NUMBER

LINCOLN / MERCURY
1H62X500551

VIN LOCATION

LINCOLN VIN is die-stamped into the right front inner fender apron under the hood.

MERCURY VIN is die-stamped into the top of right-hand frame siderail forward of cowl under the hood.

COMET VIN is die-stamped into the top surface of the left-hand brace.

FIRST DIGIT: Identifies the model year (1961)

SECOND DIGIT: Identifies the assembly plant

ASSEMBLY PLANT	CODE
Mahwah, NJ	E
Lorain, OH	H
Los Angeles, CA	J
Kansas City, KS	K
San Jose, CA	R
Wayne, MI	W
Wixom, MI	Y
St. Louis, MO	Z

THIRD AND FOURTH DIGITS: Identify the body series

COMET	CODE
2-Dr. Sedan	11
4-Dr. Sedan	12
2-Dr. Sedan (S-22)	17
2-Dr. Station Wagon	21
4-Dr. Station Wagon	22

LINCOLN	CODE
4-Dr. Continental Sedan	82
4-Dr. Continental Convertible	86

MERCURY	CODE
4-Dr. Meteor Sedan (800)	52
4-Dr. Meteor Sedan (600)	42
2-Dr. Meteor Sedan (800)	51
2-Dr. Meteor Sedan (600)	41
2-Dr. Meteor Hardtop (800)	57
4-Dr. Meteor Hardtop (800)	54
4-Dr. Monterey Sedan	62
2-Dr. Monterey Hardtop	67
4-Dr. Monterey Hardtop	64
Monterey Convertible	65
4-Dr. Commuter Wagon, 6-9 Pass.	74
4-Dr. Colony Park Wagon, 6-9 Pass.	76

FIFTH DIGIT: Identifies the engine code

ENGINE	CODE
223 C.I.D. 6 Cyl., 1 BC	V
292 C.I.D. 8 Cyl., 2 BC	W
352 C.I.D. 8 Cyl., 2 BC	X
390 C.I.D. 8 Cyl., 4 BC	Z
390 C.I.D. 4 BC (Low Comp.), Before January 1961	T
292 C.I.D. 8 Cyl., 2 BC (Low Comp. 84 Oct.)	T
292 C.I.D. 2 BC (Low Comp.), Before January 1961	R
390 C.I.D. 8 Cyl., 4 BC (Low Comp. 84 Oct.)	R
430 C.I.D. 8 Cyl. 2 BC	H
430 C.I.D. 8 Cyl. 2 BC (Low Comp. 84 Oct.)	K
144 C.I.D. 6 Cyl. OHV	S
144 C.I.D. 6 Cyl. OHV (Low Comp. 84 Oct.)	D
170 C.I.D. 6 Cyl. (Low Comp. 84 Oct.)	E
170 C.I.D. 6 Cyl. OHV	U

LAST SIX DIGITS: Identify the basic production numbers

BODY NUMBER PLATE

THE BODY PLATE is riveted to the front body pillar between the front door hinges on the Lincoln and Mercury. The Comet Body Plate is riveted to the left front door below the door lock. The Body Plate includes information relative to the type of engine, axle, transmission, trim (exterior and interior), and body style of the vehicle. It also includes the date (day, month and year) and place of manufacture.

FORD MOTOR
CORPORATION

SERIAL NUMBER
1H62X500551

54B	AA	33	11G	4	3
BDY	CLR	TRM	DT	TR	AX

EXAMPLE:

Serial Number

1	Model Year (1961)
H	Assembly Plant (Lorain, OH)
62	Body Series (4-Dr. Sedan)
X	Engine (352 CID 8 Cyl.)
500551	Production Sequence
54B	Body Style (Meteor 4-Dr.)
A	Lower Body Color
A	Upper Body Color
33	Trim
11G	Date Production Code
4	Transmission (Auto. S/R)
3	Axle (3.10:1)

BODY STYLE

COMET	CODE
4-Dr. Sedan	54A
2-Dr. Sedan	62A
4-Dr. Commuter Station Wagon, 6-9 Pass.	71A
2-Dr. Sedan	62A

LINCOLN	
4-Dr. Continental Sedan	53A
4-Dr. Continental Convertible	74A

LINCOLN/MERCURY	CODE
4-Dr. Sedan	54A
4-Dr. Meteor (800) Sedan	54A
4-Dr. Monterey Sedan	54B
4-Dr. Meteor (600) Sedan	58A
2-Dr. Meteor (800) Sedan	62A
2-Dr. Meteor (600) Sedan	64A
2-Dr. Meteor (800) Hardtop	65A
2-Dr. Monterey Hardtop	65B
4-Dr. Meteor (800) Hardtop	75A
4-Dr. Monterey Hardtop	75B
2-Dr. Monterey Convertible	76A
4-Dr. Commuter Station Wagon, 6-9 Pass.	71A
4-Dr. Colony Park Station Wagon, 6-9 Pass.	71B
4-Dr. Colony Park Station Wagon, 6-9 Pass.	71B

THE DAY AND MONTH CODE furnishes the date the vehicle was manufactured. The number indicates the day of the month and the letter indicates the month.

MONTH	CODE	*CODE
January	A	N
February	B	P
March	C	Q
April	D	R
May	E	S
June	F	T
July	G	U
August	H	V
September	J	W
October	K	X
November	L	Y
December	M	Z

*2 year code letters to be used if 1961 models exceed 12 months.

THE REAR AXLE RATIO CODE indicates the ratio of the rear axle installed in the vehicle.

REAR AXLE RATIO	REGULAR	LOCKING
3.56:1	1	A
3.89:1	2	B
3.10:1	3	C
4.00:1	4	
3.20:1	5	
3.00:1	6	F
3.50:1		J
2.89:1	7	G
2.91:1	8	
3.11:1	13	

THE TRANSMISSION CODE indicates the type of transmission installed in the vehicle.

TRANSMISSION	CODE
Standard (S/T)	1
Overdrive (O/D)	2
Two Speed Automatic (2/S)	3
Dual Range (or D/R) Automatic	4
Automatic Single Range 3-Spd.	5

THE TRIM NUMBER furnishes the key to trim color and material for each model series.

LINCOLN TRIM

COLOR	CLOTH	VINYL	LEATHER	CODE
Gray	•		•	11
Gray	•			31
Blue	•		•	12,22
Blue			•	14,82
Green	•		•	23
Green			•	83
White/Black	•		•	20
Black	•		•	26
Black			•	86
Turquoise	•		•	27
Turquoise			•	87
Rose	•		•	29
Fawn	•			34
Beige			•	84
Red			•	85
White/Red			•	95
White/Black			•	96

COMET TRIM

COLOR	CLOTH	VINYL	LEATHER	CODE
White/ Black	•	•		*10
Blue	•	•		*12
Green	•	•		*13
Red/Black	•	•		*15
White/ Blue-Green	•	•		40
Blue/ Blue-Green	•	•		42
Green/ Blue-Green	•	•		43
Red/ Red-Gray	•	•		45
White/Red		•		*75
White/Black		•		*76

* Deluxe RPO trim

MERCURY TRIM

COLOR	CLOTH	VINYL	LEATHER	CODE
Blue	•			01
Blue		•		11,24
Blue	•	•		05,34
Gold	•	•		03,08,27
Red		•		32,45
Red	•	•		36
Black		•		33
White/Black	•	•		02,06,25
White/Black		•		12
White/Red		•		13
White/Gold		•		14
Turquoise	•	•		09,29,30
Green	•	•		10
Green		•		44
Turquoise		•		15
Blue/ Turquoise	•	•		37
White/Gray	•	•		35
Turquoise/ Brown	•	•		43

1961 LINCOLN / MERCURY

THE PAINT CODE furnishes the key to the paint colors used on the car. A letter indicates the color of the car. A two-tone car has two sets of letters. The first indicates the lower body color, the second the upper body color.

COLOR	CODE
Presidential Black	A
Royal Red Metallic	B
Turquoise Metallic	C
Blue Haze	D
Saxon Green	E
Sunburst Yellow	F
Tawny Beige	G
Empress Blue	H
Green Velvet	I
Signal Red	J
Crystal Green	K
Gold Dust Metallic	L
Sultana White	M
Platinum	N
Executive Gray	P
Sheffield Gray Metallic	Q
Columbia Blue Metallic	R
Green Frost	S
Honey Beige	T
Rose Glow Metallic	U
Summer Rose	V
Regency Turquoise Metallic	W
Black Cherry Metallic	X
Briar Brown Metallic	Y
Desert Frost	Z

ENGINE NUMBER

Comet engine number is stamped on the top of the block on the front left side near the crankcase breather pipe. This designates the engine plant, year, month and day of manufacture and inspector's identification.

Lincoln engine number is stamped on the cylinder block directly in front of the left hand cylinder head.

COMET

ENGINE NO.	NO. CYL.	CID	HORSE-POWER	COMP. RATIO	CARB	TRANS
S	6	144	90	8.7:1	1 BC	** M & A
D*	6	144	N/A	N/A	1 BC	** M & A
E	6	170	101	8.7:1	1 BC	** M & A
U*	6	170	N/A	N/A	1 BC	** M & A

* Export

MERCURY METEOR 600, METEOR 800 AND COMMUTER

ENGINE NO.	NO. CYL.	CID	HORSE-POWER	COMP. RATIO	CARB	TRANS
V	6	223	135	8.4:1	1 BC	** M & A
W	8	292	175	8.8:1	2 BC	** M & A
T*	8	292	N/A	N/A	2 BC	** M & A
X	8	352	220	8.9:1	2 BC	** M & A

* Export

MERCURY METEOR 800, MONTEREY AND WAGONS

ENGINE NO.	NO. CYL.	CID	HORSE-POWER	COMP. RATIO	CARB	TRANS
W	8	292	175	8.8:1	2 BC	** M & A
T*	8	292	N/A	N/A	2 BC	** M & A
X	8	352	220	8.9:1	2 BC	** M & A
Z	8	390	300	9.6:1	4 BC	AUTO
R*	8	390	N/A	N/A	4 BC	AUTO

* Export

LINCOLN

ENGINE NO.	NO. CYL.	CID	HORSE-POWER	COMP. RATIO	CARB	TRANS
H	8	430	300	10:01	2 BC	AUTO
K*	8	430	N/A	N/A	2 BC	AUTO

* Export
** MAN & AUTO

 1962 LINCOLN / MERCURY

1962 LINCOLN CONTINENTAL

1962 LINCOLN CONTINENTAL

1962 MERCURY COMET

1962 MERCURY COMET

1962 MERCURY METEOR

1962 MERCURY METEOR

1962 MERCURY MONTEREY

1962 MERCURY MONTEREY

1962 LINCOLN / MERCURY

VEHICLE IDENTIFICATION NUMBER

LINCOLN / MERCURY
2H54X500551

LINCOLN VIN is die-stamped into the right front inner fender apron under the hood.

MERCURY VIN is die-stamped into the top of the right-hand frame side rail forward of cowl under the hood.

COMET VIN is die-stamped into the top surface of left-hand brace.

METEOR VIN is die-stamped on the left front inner fender apron under the hood.

FIRST DIGIT: Identifies the model year (1962)

SECOND DIGIT: Identifies the assembly plant

ASSEMBLY PLANT	CODE
Mahwah, NJ	E
Dearborn, MI	F
Lorain, OH	H
Los Angeles, CA	J
Kansas City, KS	K
San Jose, CA	R
Pilot Plant	S
Metuchen, NJ	T
Wayne, MI	W
Wixom, MI	Y
St. Louis, MO	Z

THIRD AND FOURTH DIGITS: Identify the body series

METEOR	CODE
4-Dr. Sedan	32
4-Dr. Sedan - Custom	42
2-Dr. Sedan	31
2-Dr. Sedan - Custom	41
2-Dr. Sedan - (S-33)	47

COMET	CODE
4-Dr. Sedan - C/P	02
4-Dr. Sedan - Custom - C/P	12
2-Dr. Sedan - C/P	01
2-Dr. Sedan - Custom - C/P	11
2-Dr. Sedan - Special (S-22)	17
2-Dr. Station Wagon	21
2-Dr. Station Wagon - Custom	23
4-Dr. Station Wagon	22
4-Dr. Station Wagon - Custom	24
4-Dr. Station Wagon - Villager	26
4-Dr. Station Wagon - Villager (Bucket Seat)	26

MERCURY	CODE
4-Dr. Sedan - C/P	52
4-Dr. Sedan - Custom - C/P	62
2-Dr. Sedan	51
2-Dr. Hardtop	53
2-Dr. Hardtop - Custom	63
2-Dr. "S-55" Hardtop	67
4-Dr. Hardtop	54
4-Dr. Hardtop - Custom	64
2-Dr. Convertible	65
2-Dr. "S-55" Convertible	69
4-Dr. Commuter Station Wagon, 6-Pass.	72
4-Dr. Colony Park Station Wagon - Custom, 6-Pass.	76
4-Dr. Commuter Station Wagon, 9-Pass.	72
4-Dr. Colony Park Station Wagon - Custom, 9-Pass.	76

LINCOLN	CODE
4-Dr. Continental Sedan	82
4-Dr. Continental Hardtop	84
4-Dr. Continental Convertible	86

FIFTH DIGIT: Identifies the engine code

ENGINE	CODE
223 C.I.D. 6 Cyl., 1 BC	V
292 C.I.D. 8 Cyl., 2 BC	W
352 C.I.D. 8 Cyl., 2 BC	X
390 C.I.D. 8 Cyl., 4 BC	Z
390 C.I.D. 8 Cyl., 4 BC Interceptor RPO	P
292 C.I.D. 8 Cyl., 2 BC (Low Comp. 84 Oct.)	T
390 C.I.D. 8 Cyl., 4 BC (Low Comp. 84 Oct.)	R
406 C.I.D. 8 Cyl., 4 BC	B
406 C.I.D. 8 Cyl., 2-3 BC	G
170 C.I.D. 6 Cyl. OHV 1 BC	U
170 C.I.D. 6 Cyl. OHV 1 BC (Low Comp.)	E
221 C.I.D. 8 Cyl. OHV 2 BC	L
221 C.I.D. 8 Cyl. OHV 2 BC (Low Comp.)	C
260 C.I.D. 8 Cyl. OHV 2 BC	F
430 C.I.D. 8 Cyl. 2 BC	H
430 C.I.D. 8 Cyl. 2 BC (Low Comp. 84 Oct.)	K
144 C.I.D. 6 Cyl. OHV	S
144 C.I.D. 6 Cyl. OHV (Low Comp.)	D

LAST SIX DIGITS: Represent the basic production numbers

BODY NUMBER PLATE

THE BODY PLATE is riveted to the front body pillar between the front door hinges on the Lincoln and Mercury. The Comet Body Plate is riveted to the left front door below the door lock. The Body Plate includes information relative to the type of engine, axle, transmission, trim (exterior and interior), and body style of the vehicle. It also includes the date (day, month and year), place manufactured, and the code number of the district ordering the unit.

FORD MOTOR CORPORATION

SERIAL NUMBER
2H54X500551

75A	AA	26	11G	32-0551	1	3
BDY	CLR	TRM	DT	DSO	AX	TR

1962 LINCOLN / MERCURY

EXAMPLE:

Serial Number

2	Model Year (1962)
H	Assembly Plant (Lorain, OH)
54	Body Series (4-Dr. Hardtop)
X	Engine (352 8 Cyl. 2 BC)
500551	Production Sequence
75A	Body Style (Mercury 4-Dr.)
A	Lower Body Color
A	Upper Body Color
26	Trim
11G	Date Production Code
32	District Code
0551	DSO Number
1	Axle ((3.00:1)
3	Transmission (2-Spd. Automatic)

BODY STYLE

MERCURY	CODE
4-Dr. Sedan	54A
4-Dr. Sedan - Custom	54B
2-Dr. Sedan	62A
2-Dr. Hardtop	65A
2-Dr. Hardtop - Custom	65B
2-Dr. "S-55" Hardtop	65C
4-Dr. Hardtop	75A
4-Dr. Hardtop - Custom	75B
2-Dr. Convertible	76A
2-Dr. "S-55" Convertible	76B
4-Dr. Commuter Station Wagon, 6-Pass.	71A
4-Dr. Colony Park Station Wagon, 6-Pass.	71B
4-Dr. Commuter Station Wagon, 9-Pass.	71C
4-Dr. Colony Park Station Wagon, 9-Pass.	71D

COMET	CODE
4-Dr. Sedan	54A
4-Dr. Sedan - Custom	54B
2-Dr. Sedan	62A
2-Dr. Sedan - Custom	62B
2-Dr. Sedan - (S-22)	62C
2-Dr. Station Wagon	59A
2-Dr. Station Wagon Custom	59B
4-Dr. Station Wagon	71A
4-Dr. Station Wagon Custom	71B
4-Dr. Station Wagon - Villager	71C
4-Dr. Station Wagon - Villager (Bucket Seat)	71D

METEOR	CODE
4-Dr. Sedan	54A
4-Dr. Sedan - Custom	54B
2-Dr. Sedan	62A
2-Dr. Sedan - Custom	62B
2-Dr. Sedan - (S-33)	62C

LINCOLN	CODE
4-Dr. Sedan	53A
4-Dr. Hardtop	57C
4-Dr. Convertible	74A

THE DAY AND MONTH CODE furnishes the date the vehicle was manufactured. The number indicates the day of the month and the letter indicates the month.

MONTH	CODE	*CODE
January	A	N
February	B	P
March	C	Q
April	D	R
May	E	S
June	F	T
July	G	U
August	H	V
September	J	W
October	K	X
November	L	Y
December	M	Z

*2 year code letters to be used if 1962 models exceed 12 months.

DISTRICT CODE

DISTRICT	CODE
Boston	11
Philadelphia	12
New York	13
Washington	14
Atlanta	21
Dallas	22
Jacksonville	24
Memphis	25
Buffalo	31
Cincinnati	32
Cleveland	33
Detroit	34
Pittsburgh	35
Chicago	41
Kansas City	43
St. Louis	44
Twin Cities	45
Denver	51
Los Angeles	52
Oakland	53
Seattle	54
Phoenix	75
Ford of Canada	81
Home Office Reserve	84
Export	90-99

THE REAR AXLE RATIO CODE indicates the ratio of the rear axle installed in the vehicle.

REAR AXLE RATIO	REGULAR	LOCKING
2.89:1	1	A
3.00:1	1	A
3.20:1	3	-
3.25:1	4	-
3.50:1	5	-
3.56:1	6	F
3.80:1	7	B
3.89:1	8	H
4.00:1	9	-

THE TRANSMISSION CODE indicates the type of transmission installed in the vehicle.

TRANSMISSION	CODE
Standard (3-Speed) (S/T)	1
Overdrive (O/D)	2
Two Speed Automatic (2/S)	3
Dual Range Automatic (D/R)	4
Standard (4-Speed) (4/S)	5

THE TRIM NUMBER furnishes the key to trim color and material for each model series.

COMET TRIM

COLOR	CLOTH	VINYL	LEATHER	CODE
Beige	•	•		14
Beige		•		54,84,74
Blue	•	•		12,42
Blue		•		52,82,72
Red		•		55,85
Black		•		56,86
Turquoise	•	•		17,47
Turquoise		•		57
White/Red		•		75
White/Black	•	•		40
White/Black		•		76
Red/Black	•	•		45,15

LINCOLN TRIM

COLOR	CLOTH	VINYL	LEATHER	CODE
Blue	•			30
Blue	•		•	60,72
Blue			•	82
Beige	•			34
Beige	•		•	64,74
Beige			•	84
White	•		•	71
Green	•		•	73
Green			•	83
Black	•		•	76
Turquoise	•		•	77
Turquoise			•	87
Chestnut	•		•	79
Chestnut			•	89
Red			•	85
Black			•	86
White/Black			•	96

MERCURY TRIM

COLOR	CLOTH	VINYL	LEATHER	CODE
White/Black	•	•		26,16
White/Black		•		96
Blue	•	•		22,12
Blue		•		92
Turquoise	•	•		27,17
Turquoise		•		97
Green	•	•		23,13
Beige	•	•		24,14
Beige		•		94
White/Red		•		95

METEOR TRIM

COLOR	CLOTH	VINYL	LEATHER	CODE
Red/Black	•	•		15
Blue	•	•		12
Beige			•	84
Beige	•			34
Green	•		•	73
White/Black	•		•	71
Black	•		•	76
Chestnut	•		•	79
Chestnut			•	89

THE PAINT CODE furnishes the key to the paint colors used on the car. A letter indicates the color of the car. A two-tone car has two sets of letters. The first indicates the lower body color, the second the upper body color.

LINCOLN

COLOR	CODE
Presidential Black	A
Royal Red	B
Oxford Gray	C
Riviera Turquoise	D
Bermuda Blue	E
Powder Blue	F
Silver Mink	G
Nocturne Blue	H
Castilian Gold	I
Teaberry	L
Sultana White	M
Platinum	N
Scotch Green	P
Jamaica Yellow	R
Highlander Green	S
Champagne	T
Velvet Turquoise	U
Chestnut	V
Black Cherry	X
Desert Frost	Z

MERCURY

COLOR	CODE
Presidential Black	A
Ocean Turquoise Metallic	D
Pacific Blue Metallic	E
Sea Blue	F
Blue Satin Metallic	H
Castilian Gold	I
Carnival Red	J
Sultana White	M
Scotch Green	P
Sheffield Gray Metallic	Q
Jamaica Yellow	R
Champagne	T
Chestnut	V
Black Cherry Metallic	X
Desert Frost Metallic	Z

1962 LINCOLN / MERCURY

ENGINE NUMBER

Comet engine number is stamped on the crankcase outlet ventilation pipe boss on the crankcase just forward of the distributor. This indicates the place, day and month of engine manufacture.

Lincoln engine number is stamped on the cylinder block directly in front of the left hand cylinder head.

Meteor 6-cylinder engine number is stamped on the crankcase outlet ventilation pipe boss on the crankcase just forward of the distributor. The V8 is stamped on the front face of the cylinder block above and to the left of the water pump mounting.

COMET

ENGINE NO.	NO. CYL.	CID	HORSE-POWER	COMP. RATIO	CARB	TRANS
S	6	144	85	8.7:1	1 BC	** M & A
D	6	144	N/A	N/A	1 BC	** M & A
U	6	170	101	8.7:1	1 BC	** M & A
E*	6	170	N/A	N/A	1 BC	** M & A

* Export

METEOR

ENGINE NO.	NO. CYL.	CID	HORSE-POWER	COMP. RATIO	CARB	TRANS
U	6	170	101	8.7:1	1 BC	** M & A
E*	6	170	N/A	N/A	1 BC	** M & A
L	8	221	145	8.7:1	2 BC	** M & A
C*	8	221	N/A	N/A	2 BC	** M & A
F	8	260	164	8.7:1	2 BC	** M & A

* Export

MONTEREY

ENGINE NO.	NO. CYL.	CID	HORSE-POWER	COMP. RATIO	CARB	TRANS
V	6	223	138	8.4:1	1 BC	** M & A
W	8	292	170	8.8:1	2 BC	** M & A
T*	8	292	170	8.8:1	2 BC	** M & A
X	8	352	220	8.9:1	2 BC	** M & A
Z	8	390	300	9.6:1	4 BC	** M & A
R*	8	390	N/A	N/A	4 BC	** M & A
P	8	390	330	9.6:1	4 BC	** M & A
B	8	406	385	9.6:1	4 BC	MAN
G	8	406	405	10.9:1	3-2 BC	MAN

* Export

LINCOLN

ENGINE NO.	NO. CYL.	CID	HORSE-POWER	COMP. RATIO	CARB	TRANS
H	8	430	300	10.0:1	2 BC	AUTO
K*	8	430	N/A	N/A	2 BC	AUTO

* Export
** MAN & AUTO

1963 LINCOLN / MERCURY

1963 LINCOLN CONTINENTAL

1963 LINCOLN CONTINENTAL

1963 MERCURY COMET

1963 MERCURY COMET

1963 MERCURY METEOR

1963 MERCURY METEOR

1963 MERCURY MONTEREY

1963 MERCURY MONTEREY

VEHICLE IDENTIFICATION NUMBER

LINCOLN / MERCURY
• 3H54Y500551 •

LINCOLN VIN is die-stamped into the right front inner fender apron under the hood.

MERCURY VIN is die-stamped into the extension tab of top of right cowl under the hood.

COMET VIN is die-stamped into the top of the left front inner fender apron under the hood.

METEOR VIN is die-stamped into the left front inner fender apron under the hood.

FIRST DIGIT: Identifies the model year (1963)

SECOND DIGIT: Identifies the assembly plant

ASSEMBLY PLANT	CODE
Mahwah, NJ	E
Dearborn, MI	F
Lorain, OH	H
Los Angeles, CA	J
Kansas City, KS	K
San Jose, CA	R
Pilot Plant	S
Metuchen, NJ	T
Wayne, MI	W
Wixom, MI	Y
St. Louis, MO	Z

THIRD AND FOURTH DIGITS: Identify the body series

MERCURY	CODE
4-Dr. Sedan - C/P	52
4-Dr. Sedan - Custom-C/P	62
2-Dr. Sedan	51
2-Dr. Fastback Hardtop - Custom	66
2-Dr. "S-55" Fastback Hardtop	68
4-Dr. Hardtop	53
2-Dr. Fastback	57
2-Dr. Hardtop - Custom	63
2-Dr. "S-55" Hardtop	67
4-Dr. Hardtop	54
4-Dr. Hardtop - Custom	64
4-Dr. "S-55" Hardtop	60
2-Dr. Convertible	65
2-Dr. "S-55" Convertible	69
4-Dr. Colony Park Station Wagon - Custom, 6-Pass.	76
4-Dr. Colony Park Station Wagon - Custom, 9-Pass.	76

METEOR	CODE
4-Dr. Sedan	32
4-Dr. Sedan - Custom	42
2-Dr. Sedan	31
2-Dr. Sedan - Custom	41
2-Dr. Hardtop - Custom	43
2-Dr. "S-33" Hardtop - Custom	47
4-Dr. Station Wagon - Custom, 8-Pass.	48
4-Dr. Station Wagon, 6-Pass.	38
4-Dr. Station Wagon, 8-Pass.	38
4-Dr. Station Wagon - Country Cruiser, 6-Pass.	49
4-Dr. Station Wagon - Custom 6-Pass.	48
4-Dr. Station Wagon - Country Cruiser, 8-Pass.	49

COMET	CODE
4-Dr. Sedan	02
4-Dr. Sedan - Custom	12
2-Dr. Station Wagon	21
2-Dr. Station Wagon - Custom	23
2-Dr. Sedan	01
2-Dr. Sedan - Custom	11
2-Dr. "S-22" Sedan	17
2-Dr. Hardtop	17
2-Dr. "S-22" Sedan	19
4-Dr. Station Wagon	22
4-Dr. Station Wagon - Custom	24
4-Dr. Station Wagon-Villager	26
4-Dr. Station Wagon-Villager (Bucket Seat)	26
2-Dr. Convertible	15
2-Dr. "S-22" Convertible	15

LINCOLN	CODE
4-Dr. Continental	82
4-Dr. Continental Hardtop	84
4-Dr. Continental Convertible	86

FIFTH DIGIT: Identifies the engine code

ENGINE	CODE
8 Cyl. - 390 C.I.D., 2-V Carb	Y
8 Cyl. - 390 C.I.D., 4-V Carb	Z
8 Cyl. - 390 C.I.D., 4-V Carb Interceptor	P
8 Cyl. - 390 C.I.D., 4-V Carb (Low Comp.)	9
8 Cyl. - 406 C.I.D., 4-V Carb	B
8 Cyl. - 406 C.I.D., 6-V Carb	G
8 Cyl. - 427 C.I.D., 4-V Carb	Q
8 Cyl. - 427 C.I.D., 8-V Carb	R
6 Cyl. - 170 C.I.D., 1-V Carb	U
6 Cyl. - 170 C.I.D., 1-V Carb (Low Comp.)	4
6 Cyl. - 200 C.I.D., 1-V Carb	T
8 Cyl. - 221 C.I.D., 2-V Carb	L
8 Cyl. - 221 C.I.D., 2-V Carb (Low Comp.)	3
6 Cyl. 223 C.I.D. 1-V	E
6 Cyl. 223 C.I.D. 1-V (Low Comp.)	5
8 Cyl. - 260 C.I.D., 2-V Carb	F
8 Cyl. - 260 C.I.D., 2-V Carb (Low Comp.)	8
8 Cyl. 430 C.I.D., 4-V Carb	N
8 Cyl. 430 C.I.D., 4-V Carb (Low Comp.)	7
6 Cyl. - 144 C.I.D., 1-V Carb	S
6 Cyl. - 144 C.I.D., 1-V Carb (Low Comp.)	2

LAST SIX DIGITS: Represent the basic production numbers

BODY NUMBER PLATE

THE BODY PLATE is riveted to the left front door below the door lock. The Body Plate includes information relative to the type of engine, axle, transmission, trim (exterior and interior), and body style of the vehicle. It also includes the date (day, month and year) and place of manufacture.

FORD MOTOR
CORPORATION

SERIAL NUMBER
3H54Y500551

75A	AA	26	11G	32-0551	1	5
BDY	CLR	TRM	DT	DSO	AX	TR

EXAMPLE:

Serial Number

3	Model Year (1963)
H	Assembly Plant (Lorain, OH)
54	Body Series (4-Dr. Hardtop)
Y	Engine (390 8 Cyl. 2 BC)
500551	Production Sequence
75A	Body Style (Mercury 4 Dr.)
A	Lower Body Color
A	Upper Body Color
26	Trim
11G	Date Production Code
32	District Code
0551	DSO Number
1	Axle (2.00:1)
5	Transmission (Standard 4-Spd.)

BODY STYLE

MERCURY	CODE
4-Dr. Sedan	54A
4-Dr. Sedan - Custom	54B
2-Dr. Sedan	62A
2-Dr. Fastback Hardtop - Custom	63B
2-Dr. "S-55" Fastback Hardtop	63C
2-Dr. Hardtop	65A
2-Dr. Hardtop - Custom	65B
2-Dr. "S-55" Hardtop	65C
4-Dr. Colony Park Station Wagon, 6-Pass.	71B
4-Dr. Colony Park Station Wagon, 9-Pass.	71D
4-Dr. Hardtop	75A
4-Dr. Hardtop - Custom	75B
4-Dr. "S-55" Hardtop	75C
2-Dr. Convertible	76A
2-Dr. "S-55" Convertible	76B

LINCOLN	CODE
4-Dr. Sedan	54A
4-Dr. Hardtop	57C
4-Dr. Convertible	74A

COMET	CODE
4-Dr. Sedan	54A
4-Dr. Sedan - Custom	54B
2-Dr. Sedan	62A
2-Dr. Sedan - Custom	62B
2-Dr. "S-22" Sedan	62C
2-Dr. Hardtop	63B
2-Dr. "S-22" Hardtop	63C
2-Dr. Convertible	76A
2-Dr. "S-22" Convertible	76B
2-Dr. Station Wagon	59A
2-Dr. Station Wagon - Custom	59B
4-Dr. Station Wagon	71A
4-Dr. Station Wagon - Custom	71B
4-Dr. Station Wagon - Villager	71C
4-Dr. Station Wagon - Villager	71C
4-Dr. Station Wagon - Villager (Bucket Seat)	71D

METEOR	CODE
4-Dr. Sedan	54A
4-Dr. Sedan - Custom	54B
2-Dr. Sedan	62A
2-Dr. Sedan - Custom	62B
2-Dr. Hardtop - Custom	65A
2-Dr. "S-33" Hardtop - Custom	65B
4-Dr. Station Wagon - Custom, 8-Pass.	71A
4-Dr. Station Wagon, 6-Pass.	71B
4-Dr. Station Wagon, 8-Pass.	71C
4-Dr. Station Wagon - Country Cruiser, 6-Pass.	71D
4-Dr. Station Wagon - Custom, 6-Pass.	71E
4-Dr. Station Wagon - Country Cruiser, 8-Pass.	71F

THE DAY AND MONTH CODE furnishes the date the vehicle was manufactured. The number indicates the day of the month and the letter indicates the month.

MONTH	CODE	*CODE
January	A	N
February	B	P
March	C	Q
April	D	R
May	E	S
June	F	T
July	G	U
August	H	V
September	J	W
October	K	X
November	L	Y
December	M	Z

*2 year code letters to be used if 1963 models exceed 12 months.

1963 LINCOLN / MERCURY

DSO AND DISTRICT CODES

Units built on a Domestic Special Order, Foreign Special Order, or other special orders will have the complete order number in this space. Also to appear in this space is the two-digit code number of the District which ordered the unit. If the unit is a regular production unit, only the District code number will appear.

DISTRICT	CODE
Boston	11
Philadelphia	12
New York	13
Washington	14
Atlanta	21
Dallas	22
Jacksonville	24
Memphis	25
Buffalo	31
Cincinnati	32
Cleveland	33
Detroit	34
Pittsburgh	35
Chicago	41
Kansas City	43
St. Louis	44
Twin Cities	45
Denver	51
Los Angeles	52
Oakland	53
Seattle	54
Phoenix	75
Ford of Canada	81
Home Office Reserve	84
Export	90-99

THE REAR AXLE RATIO CODE indicates the ratio of the rear axle installed in the vehicle.

REAR AXLE RATIO	REGULAR	LOCKING
3.00:1	1	A
3.10:1	2	B
3.20:1	3	C
3.25:1	4	D
3.50:1	5	E
3.80:1	7	G
3.89:1	8	H
4.00:1	9-Comet	I
4.11:1	9	I
2.89:1	1-Lincoln	
2.89:1		A-Lincoln

THE TRANSMISSION CODE indicates the type of transmission installed in the vehicle.

TRANSMISSION	CODE
Standard 3-Speed (3/S)	1
Overdrive (O/D)	2
Automatic 2-Speed (2/S)	3
Dual Range Automatic (D/R)	4
Standard 4-Speed (4/S)	5

THE TRIM NUMBER furnishes the key to trim color and material for each model series.

COMET TRIM COLOR	CLOTH	VINYL	LEATHER	CODE
Blue	•	•		12,42
Blue		•		52,72,82
Beige	•	•		14,44
Beige		•		54,74,84
Red		•		55,85
White/Red		•		75
White/Black		•		76,86
Black/Red	•	•		15,45
Black/White	•	•		16,46
Black/Beige		•		56
Turquoise	•	•		17,47
Turquoise		•		57,77
Gold		•		58,78

METEOR TRIM COLOR	CLOTH	VINYL	LEATHER	CODE
Green		•		03
Beige		•		04,36,54
Beige	•	•		14,44
Red		•		05,35,55
Blue	•	•		12,42
Blue		•		52
Black/Red	•	•		15,45
Black	•	•		16,46
Black		•		34,56
Turquoise	•	•		17,47
Turquoise		•		57
Gold		•		58

MERCURY TRIM COLOR	CLOTH	VINYL	LEATHER	CODE
Rose	•	•		10
Rose		•		50
Blue	•	•		12,22
Blue		•		52
Beige	•	•		14,24
Beige		•		54,04
Black	•	•		16,26
Black		•		56
Turquoise	•	•		17,27
Turquoise		•		57
Gold	•	•		18
Gold		•		58
Red		•		55,05
Green		•		03

LINCOLN TRIM COLOR	CLOTH	VINYL	LEATHER	CODE
Blue	•			30
Blue	•		•	72
Blue			•	82
Beige	•		•	64
Beige			•	84
Black	•		•	66
Black			•	86
Turquoise	•		•	67
Turquoise			•	87
Silver Blue	•		•	70
Rose Beige	•		•	71
Rose Beige			•	81
Black/White	•		•	76
Gold	•		•	78
Gold			•	88
Red			•	85
White/Black			•	96

1963 LINCOLN / MERCURY

THE PAINT CODE furnishes the key to the paint colors used on the car. A letter indicates the color of the car. A two-tone car has two sets of letters. The first indicates the lower body color, the second the upper body color.

LINCOLN

COLOR	CODE
Black Satin	A
Oxford Gray	C
Riviera Turquoise	D
Bermuda Blue	E
Silver Mink	G
Nocturne Blue	H
Polynesian Gold	I
Teaberry	L
Ermine White	M
Platinum	N
Inverness Green	O
Scotch Green	P
Spanish Red	Q
Premier Yellow	R
Highlander Green	S
Nassau Beige	T
Chestnut	V
Rose Metallic	W
Burgundy Frost	X
Autumn Frost	Z

MERCURY

COLOR	CODE
Presidential Black	A
Peacock Turquoise	B
Ocean Turquoise Metallic	D
Pacific Blue Metallic	E
Sea Blue	F
Carnival Red	J
Light Aqua	K
Blue Satin Metallic	H
Castilian Gold	I
Sultana White	M
Scotch Green	P
Sheffield Gray Metallic	Q
Jamaica Yellow	R
Champagne	T
Pink Frost	W
Black Cherry Metallic	X
Cascade Blue	Y
Desert Frost Metallic	Z

ENGINE NUMBERS

6-cylinder 144, 170 and 200 engine number is stamped above the crankcase vent outlet pipe. 223 engine number is stamped above the generator on the left side. This indicates place, year, month, day of month and plant inspector.

221, 260 and 289 engine numbers are stamped on the distributor mounting boss.

390 engine number is stamped near the engine dipstick.

406 and 427 engine numbers are stamped on the right front corner of the block.

Lincoln engine number is stamped on the cylinder block in front of the left cylinder head.

COMET

ENGINE NO.	NO. CYL.	CID	HORSE-POWER	COMP. RATIO	CARB	TRANS
S	6	144	85	8.7:1	1 BC	** M & A
2*	6	144	N/A	N/A	1 BC	** M & A
U	6	170	101	8.7:1	1 BC	** M & A
4	6	170	N/A	N/A	1 BC	** M & A
F	8	260	164	8.7:1	2 BC	** M & A
8*	8	260	N/A	N/A	2 BC	** M & A

* Export

METEOR

ENGINE NO.	NO. CYL.	CID	HORSE-POWER	COMP. RATIO	CARB	TRANS
U	6	170	101	8.7:1	1 BC	** M & A
4*	6	170	N/A	N/A	1 BC	** M & A
T	6	200	116	8.7:1	1 BC	** M & A
L	8	221	145	8.7:1	2 BC	** M & A
3*	8	221	N/A	N/A	2 BC	** M & A
F	8	260	164	8.7:1	2 BC	** M & A
8*	8	260	N/A	N/A	2 BC	** M & A
K	8	289	271	10.5:1	4 BC	MAN

* Export

MONTEREY AND MARAUDER

ENGINE NO.	NO. CYL.	CID	HORSE-POWER	COMP. RATIO	CARB	TRANS
Y	8	390	250	8.9:1	2 BC	** M & A
Z	8	390	300	10.8:1+	4 BC	** M & A
9*	8	390	N/A	N/A		** M & A
P	8	390	330	10.8:1+	4 BC	** M & A
B	8	406	385	11.5:1	4 BC	MAN
G	8	406	405	11.5:1	3-2 BC	MAN
Q	8	427	410	11.5:1	4 BC	MAN
R	8	427	425	11.5:1	2-4 BC	MAN

* Export
+ Early engines 10.5:1

LINCOLN

ENGINE NO.	NO. CYL.	CID	HORSE-POWER	COMP. RATIO	CARB	TRANS
N	8	430	320	10.0:1	4 BC	AUTO
7*	8	430	N/A	N/A	4 BC	AUTO

* Export
** MAN & AUTO

1964 LINCOLN CONTINENTAL

1964 LINCOLN CONTINENTAL

1964 MERCURY

1964 MERCURY

1964 MERCURY COMET

1964 MERCURY COMET

VEHICLE IDENTIFICATION NUMBER

LINCOLN / MERCURY
4H64Y500551

LINCOLN VIN is die-stamped into the right front inner fender apron under the hood.

COMET VIN is die-stamped into the top of the left front inner fender apron under the hood.

MERCURY VIN is die-stamped into the extension tap of the top of the right cowl under the hood.

FIRST DIGIT: Identifies the model year (1964)

SECOND DIGIT: Identifies the assembly plant

ASSEMBLY PLANT	CODE
Mahwah, NJ	E
Dearborn, MI	F
Lorain, OH	H
Los Angeles, CA	J
Kansas City, KS	K
San Jose, CA	R
Pilot Plant	S
Metuchen, NJ	T
Wayne, MI	W
Wixom, MI	Y
St. Louis, MO	Z

THIRD AND FOURTH DIGITS: Identify the body series

COMET	CODE
4-Dr. Sedan - 202	02
4-Dr. Sedan - 404	12
4-Dr. Sedan - Caliente	22
2-Dr. Sedan - 202	01
2-Dr. Sedan - 404	11
2-Dr. Hardtop - Caliente	23
2-Dr. Hardtop - Cyclone	27
4-Dr. Station Wagon - 202	32
4-Dr. Station Wagon - 404	34
4-Dr. Station Wagon - 404	36
2-Dr. Convertible - Caliente	25

MERCURY MONTEREY	CODE
2-Dr. Sedan	41
4-Dr. Sedan	42
2-Dr. Hardtop	43
2-Dr. Convertible	45
2-Dr. Hardtop-Fastback	47
4-Dr. Hardtop-Fastback	48

MERCURY MONTCLAIR	CODE
4-Dr. Sedan	52
2-Dr. Hardtop	53

MERCURY PARKLANE	CODE
4-Dr. Sedan	62
2-Dr. Hardtop	63
4-Dr. Hardtop	64
2-Dr. Convertible	65

MERCURY MARAUDER	CODE
2-Dr. Hardtop Montclair, Fastback	57
4-Dr. Hardtop Montclair, Fastback	58
2-Dr. Hardtop Parklane Fastback	67
4-Dr. Hardtop Parklane, Fastback	68

COMMUTER	CODE
4-Dr. Station Wagon, 6-Pass.	72
4-Dr. Station Wagon, 9-Pass.	72

COLONY PARK	CODE
4-Dr. Station Wagon, 6-Pass.	76
4-Dr. Station Wagon, 9-Pass.	76

LINCOLN	CODE
4-Dr. Sedan	82
4-Dr. Convertible	86

FIFTH DIGIT: Identifies the engine code

ENGINE	CODE
6 Cyl. - 170 C.I.D., 1-V	U
6 Cyl. - 170 C.I.D., 1-V (Low Comp.)	4
6 Cyl. - 200 C.I.D., 1-V	T
8 Cyl. - 260 C.I.D., 2-V	F
8 Cyl. - 260 C.I.D., 2-V (Low Comp.)	6
8 Cyl. - 289 C.I.D., 4-V HP	D
8 Cyl. - 289 C.I.D., 4-V	K
8 Cyl. - 390 C.I.D., 2-V (Reg.)	Y
8 Cyl. - 390 C.I.D., 2-V (Spec.)	H
8 Cyl. - 390 C.I.D., 4-V	Z
8 Cyl. - 390 C.I.D., 4-V (Low Comp.)	9
8 Cyl. - 427 C.I.D., 4-V	Q
8 Cyl. - 427 C.I.D., 8-V	R
8 Cyl. - 430 C.I.D., 4-V	N
8 Cyl. - 430 C.I.D., 4-V (Low Comp.)	7

LAST SIX DIGITS: Represent the basic production numbers

BODY NUMBER PLATE

THE BODY PLATE is riveted to the left front door below the door lock. The Body Plate includes information relative to the type of engine, axle, transmission, trim (exterior and interior), and body style of the vehicle. It also includes the date (day, month and year) and place of manufacture.

FORD MOTOR CORPORATION

SERIAL NUMBER
4H64Y 500551

75F	AA	16	11G	32	0551	1	5
BDY	CLR	TRM	DT	DIST	DSO	TR	AX

EXAMPLE:

Serial Number

4	Model Year (1964)
H	Assembly Plant (Lorain, OH)
64	Body Series (4-Dr. Hardtop)
Y	Engine (390 8 Cyl. 2 BC)
500551	Production Sequence
75F	Body Style (Mercury Parklane)
A	Lower Body Color
A	Upper Body Color
16	Trim
11G	Date Production Code
32	District Code
0551	DSO Number
1	Transmission (Manual 3-Spd.)
5	Axle (3.50:1)

LINCOLN	CODE
4-Dr. Sedan	53A
4-Dr. Convertible	74A

MERCURY	CODE
4-Dr. Sedan (Monterey)	54A
4-Dr. Sedan (Montclair)	54B
4-Dr. Sedan (Parklane)	54F
4-Dr. Hardtop-Fastback (Monterey)	57A
4-Dr. Hardtop-Fastback (Parklane)	57C
4-Dr. Hardtop-Fastback (Montclair Marauder)	57D
4-Dr. Hardtop-Fastback (Parklane Marauder)	57F
2-Dr. Sedan (Monterey)	62A
2-Dr. Hardtop-Fastback (Monterey)	63A
2-Dr. Hardtop-Fastback (Parklane Marauder)	63C
2-Dr. Hardtop-Fastback (Montclair Marauder)	63D
2-Dr. Hardtop-Fastback (Parklane Marauder)	63F
2-Dr. Hardtop (Monterey)	65A
2-Dr. Hardtop (Montclair)	65B
2-Dr. Hardtop (Parklane)	65C
2-Dr. Hardtop (Parklane)	65F
4-Dr. Commuter Station Wagon, 6-Pass.	71A
4-Dr. Colony Park Station Wagon, 6-Pass.	71B
4-Dr. Commuter Station Wagon, 9-Pass.	71C
4-Dr. Colony Park Station Wagon, 9-Pass.	71D
4-Dr. Hardtop (Parklane)	75F
2-Dr. Convertible (Monterey)	76A
2-Dr. Convertible (Parklane)	76C
2-Dr. Convertible (Parklane)	76F

COMET	CODE
4-Dr. Sedan - 202	54A
4-Dr. Sedan - 404	54B
4-Dr. Sedan (Caliente)	54C
4-Dr. Sedan (Caliente)	54D
2-Dr. Sedan - 202	62A
2-Dr. Sedan - 404	62B
2-Dr. Sedan - 404	62C
2-Dr. Hardtop (Caliente)	63C
2-Dr. Hardtop (Caliente)	63D
2-Dr. Hardtop (Cyclone)	63E
4-Dr. Station Wagon - 202	71A
4-Dr. Station Wagon - 404	71B
4-Dr. Station Wagon - 404	71C
2-Dr. Convertible (Caliente)	76B
2-Dr. Convertible (Caliente)	76D

THE DAY AND MONTH CODE furnishes the date the vehicle was manufactued. The number indicates the day of the month and the letter indicates the month.

MONTH	CODE	*CODE
January	A	N
February	B	P
March	C	Q
April	D	R
May	E	S
June	F	T
July	G	U
August	H	V
September	J	W
October	K	X
November	L	Y
December	M	Z

*2 year code letters to be used if 1964 models exceed 12 months.

1964 LINCOLN / MERCURY

DSO AND DISTRICT CODES

Units built on a Domestic Special Order, Foreign Special Order, or other special orders will have the complete order number in this space. Also to appear in this space is the two-digit code number of the District which ordered the unit. If the unit is a regular production unit, only the District code number will appear.

DISTRICT	CODE
Boston	11
New York	15
Philadelphia	16
Washington	17
Atlanta	21
Dallas	22
Jacksonville	23
Memphis	26
Buffalo	31
Cincinnati	32
Cleveland	33
Detroit	34
Chicago	41
St. Louis	42
Denver	51
Los Angeles	52
Oakland	53
Seattle	54
Phoenix	75
Ford of Canada	81
Home office Reserve	84
Export	90-99

THE REAR AXLE RATIO CODE indicates the ratio of the rear axle installed in the vehicle.

MERCURY AXLE RATIO	REGULAR	LOCKING
3.00:1	A	1
3.20:1	C	3
3.25:1	D	4
3.50:1	F	5
2.80:1	E	6
3.89:1	H	8
3.10:1	B	2
3.80:1	G	7
4.00:1	Comet I	9
4.11:1	I	9

LINCOLN AXLE RATIO	REGULAR	LOCKING
2.89:1	A	1
3.11:1	C	3

THE TRANSMISSION CODE indicates the type of transmission installed in the vehicle.

TRANSMISSION	CODE
Manual 3-Speed (3/S)	1
Overdrive 3-Speed (O/D	2
Automatic 2-Speed (2/S)	3
Dual Range Automatic (D/R)	4
Manual 4-Speed (4/S)	5
C4 Dual Range Automatic 3-Speed (Dir) (XP)	6

THE TRIM NUMBER furnishes the key to trim color and material for each model series.

COMET TRIM COLOR	CLOTH	VINYL	LEATHER	CODE
White	•	•		40
White		•		55
Blue	•	•		42,12,21
Blue	•	•		22
Blue		•		72,32,62
Beige	•	•		44,14,24
Black	•	•		26
Black		•		56,16,76
Black		•		36,66
Red	•	•		15
Red		•		75,35,65
Red/Black	•	•		D6
Palomino		•		59,79,89
Palomino		•		39,69
Turquoise	•	•		47,17,27
Turquoise		•		37,67
White/Blue		•		92
White/Red		•		95
White/Black		•		96
White/ Turquoise		•		97
White/ Palomino		•		99

MERCURY TRIM COLOR	CLOTH	VINYL	LEATHER	CODE
Silver	•	•		11,61
Blue	•	•		12,22,62
Blue		•		32,52,72,92
Beige	•	•		14,24,64
Black	•	•		16,26,66,96
Red		•		35,55,75,95
Black		•		36,56,76
Palomino		•		39,59,79,99
Turquoise	•	•		67
Turquoise		•		97
White		•		82
White/Red		•		85
White/Black		•		86
White/ Turquoise		•		87
White/ Palomino		•		89

LINCOLN TRIM COLOR	CLOTH	VINYL	LEATHER	CODE
Rose	•	•		20,70
Blue	•	•		22,71
Turquoise	•	•		27

CONVERTIBLE TOP COLOR	CODE
Black	1
White	2
Blue	4

 1964 LINCOLN / MERCURY

THE PAINT CODE furnishes the key to the paint colors used on the car. A letter indicates the color of the car. A two-tone car has two sets of letters. The first indicates the lower body color, the second the upper body color.

LINCOLN

COLOR	CODE
Black Satin	A
Princetone Gray	C
Silver Blue	E
Powder Blue	F
Buckskin	G
Nocturne Blue	H
Fiesta Red	J
Arctic White	M
Platinum	N
Silver Green	O
Burnish Bronze	P
Huron Blue	Q
Encino Yellow	R
Highlander Green	S
Desert Sand	T
Regal Turquoise	U
Rose	W
Royal Maroon	X
Silver Sand	Z

MERCURY

COLOR	CODE
Onyx	A
Peacock	B
Silver Turquoise	D
Pacific Blue	F
Palomino	G
Aztec Gold	I
Carnival Red	J
Anniversary Silver	K
Bittersweet	L
Polar White	M
Pecan Frost	P
Yellow Mist	R
Fawn	T
Maize	V
Pink Frost	W
Burgundy	X
Glacier Blue	Y
Platinum Beige	Z

ENGINE NUMBER

COMET

ENGINE NO.	NO. CYL.	CID	HORSE-POWER	COMP. RATIO	CARB	TRANS
U	6	170	101	8.7:1	1 BC	** M & A
4*	6	170	N/A	N/A	1 BC	** M & A
T	6	200	116	8.7:1	1 BC	** M & A
F	8	260	164	8.8:1	2 BC	** M & A
6*	8	260	N/A	N/A	2 BC	** M & A
D	8	289	210	9.0:1	4 BC	** M & A
K	8	289	271	10.5:1	4 BC	MAN
R	8	427	425	11.2:1	2-4 BC	MAN

* Export

MERCURY

ENGINE NO.	NO. CYL.	CID	HORSE-POWER	COMP. RATIO	CARB	TRANS
Y	8	390	250	9.4:1	2 BC	** M & A
H	8	390	266	9.4:1	2 BC	AUTO
Z	8	390	300	10.1:1	4 BC	** M & A
P	8	390	330	10.1:1	4 BC	** M & A
9*	8	390	N/A	N/A	4 BC	** M & A
Q	8	427	410	11.5:1	4 BC	MAN
R	8	427	425	11.2:1	2-4 BC	MAN

* Export

LINCOLN

ENGINE NO.	NO. CYL.	CID	HORSE-POWER	COMP. RATIO	CARB	TRANS
N	8	430	320	10.0:1	4 BC	AUTO
7*	8	430	N/A	N/A	4 BC	AUTO

* Export
** MAN & AUTO

1965 LINCOLN / MERCURY

1965 LINCOLN CONTINENTAL

1965 LINCOLN CONTINENTAL

1965 MERCURY

1965 MERCURY

1965 MERCURY COMET

1965 MERCURY COMET

1965 LINCOLN / MERCURY

VEHICLE IDENTIFICATION NUMBER

LINCOLN / MERCURY
• 5H62Z500551 •

LINCOLN VIN is die-stamped into the right front inner fender apron under the hood.

COMET VIN is die-stamped into the top of the left front inner fender apron under the hood.

MERCURY VIN is die-stamped into the extension tab of the top of the right cowl under the hood.

FIRST DIGIT: Identifies the model year (1965)

SECOND DIGIT: Identifies the assembly plant

ASSEMBLY PLANT	CODE
Atlanta, GA	A
Dallas, TX	D
Mahwah, NJ	E
Dearborn, MI	F
Chicago, IL	G
Lorain, OH	H
Los Angeles, CA	J
Kansas City, KS	K
Michigan Truck	L
Norfolk, VA	N
Twin Cities, MN	P
San Jose, CA	R
Pilot Plant	S
Metuchen, NJ	T
Louisville, KY	U
Wayne, MI	W
Wixom, MI	Y
St. Louis, MO	Z

THIRD AND FOURTH DIGITS: Identify the body series

LINCOLN CONTINENTAL	CODE
4-Dr. Sedan	82
4-Dr. Convertible	86

COMET 202	CODE
4-Dr. Sedan	02
2-Dr. Sedan	01
4-Dr. Wagon	32

COMET 404	CODE
4-Dr. Sedan	12
2-Dr. Sedan	11
2-Dr. Sedan	11
4-Dr. Wagon	34
4-Dr. Station Wagon Villager	36

COMET CALIENTE	CODE
4-Dr. Sedan	22
4-Dr. Sedan	22
2-Dr. Hardtop, Fastback	23
2-Dr. Hardtop, Fastback	23
2-Dr. Convertible	25
2-Dr. Convertible	25

CYCLONE	CODE
2-Dr. Hardtop, Fastback	23

MERCURY MONTEREY	CODE
4-Dr. Sedan	42
2-Dr. Sedan	43
4-Dr. Sedan	44
2-Dr. Convertible	45
2-Dr. Hardtop	47
4-Dr. Hardtop	68

MERCURY COMMUTER	CODE
4-Dr. Station Wagon, 6-Pass.	72
4-Dr. Station Wagon, 9-Pass.	72

MERCURY COLONY PARK	CODE
4-Dr. Station Wagon, 6-Pass.	76
4-Dr. Station Wagon, 9-Pass.	76

MERCURY PARKLANE	CODE
4-Dr. Sedan	62
2-Dr. Convertible	65
2-Dr. Convertible	65
2-Dr. Hardtop, Fastback	67
2-Dr. Hardtop, Fastback	67

FIFTH DIGIT: Identifies the engine code

ENGINE	CODE
6 Cyl. 170 Cu. In. (1-V)	4
8 Cyl. 390 Cu. In. (2-V Spec.)	H
8 Cyl. 390 Cu. In. (4-V Spec.)	P
8 Cyl. 427 Cu. In. (8-V H.P.)	R
8 Cyl. 390 Cu. In. (2-V)	Y
8 Cyl. 390 Cu. In. (4-V)	Z
6 Cyl. *240 Cu. In. (1-V)	5
8 Cyl. *390 Cu. In. (4-V)	9
8 cyl. 289 Cu. In. (4-V Prem.)	A
8 Cyl. 289 Cu. In. (2-V)	C
8 Cyl. 289 Cu. In. (4-V Hi-Perf.)	K
6 Cyl. 200 Cu. In. (1-V)	T
6 Cyl. *200 Cu. In. (1-V)	2
8 Cyl. *289 Cu. In. (2-V)	3
8-Cyl. 430 Cu. In. 4-V Carb	N
8-Cyl. *430 Cu. In. 4-V Carb	7

* Low Compression

LAST SIX DIGITS: Represent the basic production numbers

1965 LINCOLN / MERCURY

BODY NUMBER PLATE

The vehicle data appears in a line across the top of the Body Plate. The first two letters and a number identify the body style. The following one or two letters identify the exterior paint color. The next code consisting of two numbers, or a letter and a number, identifies the interior trim. The date code showing the date the car was manufactured, follows the trim code and consists of two numbers and a letter. The next code gives the District in which the car was ordered and consists of two numbers. The next to the last code is the axle ratio code and is designated by a number for a conventional axle or a letter for an Equa-Lock axle. The last code in the vehicle data is the transmission code and consists of one number.

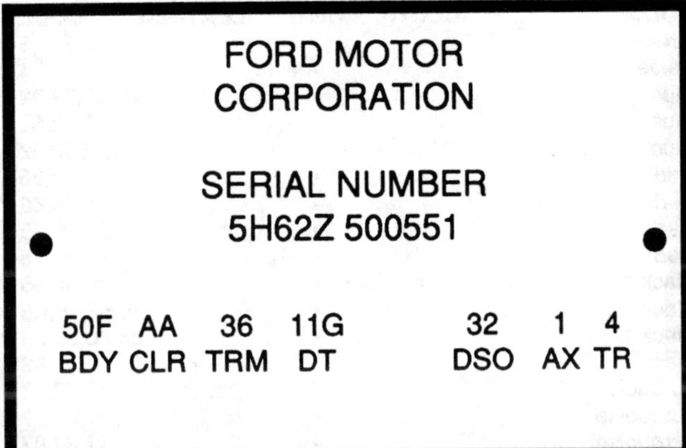

EXAMPLE:

Serial Number

5	Model Year (1965)
H	Assembly Plant (Lorain, OH)
62	Body Series (4-Dr. Sedan)
Z	Engine (8 Cyl. 390 Cu. In.)
500551	Production Sequence
50F	Body Type (Parklane)
A	Lower Body Color
A	Upper Body Color
36	Trim
11G	Date Production Code
32	DSO Number
1	Axle Ratio (3.00:1)
4	Transmission (Twin-Range Turbo Dr.)

BODY STYLE

LINCOLN CONTINENTAL	CODE
4-Dr. Sedan	53A
4-Dr. Convertible	74A

COMET 202	CODE
4-Dr. Sedan	54A
2-Dr. Sedan	62A
4-Dr. Wagon	71A

COMET 404	CODE
4-Dr. Sedan	54B
2-Dr. Sedan	62B
2-Dr. sedan	62C
4-Dr. Wagon	71B
4-Dr. Wagon, Villager	71C

COMET CALIENTE	CODE
4-Dr. Sedan	54D
2-Dr. Hardtop, Fastback	63C
2-Dr. Hardtop, Fastback	63D
2-Dr. Convertible	76B
2-Dr. Convertible	76D

CYCLONE	CODE
2-Dr. Hardtop, Fastback	63E

MERCURY MONTEREY	CODE
4-Dr. Sedan	50A
2-Dr. Sedan	62A
4-Dr. Sedan	54A
2-Dr. Convertible	76A
2-Dr. Hardtop	63A
4-Dr. Hardtop	57A
2-Dr. Convertible	76G
2-Dr. Hardtop, Fastback	63G

MERCURY MONTCLAIR	CODE
4-Dr. Sedan	60B
2-Dr. Hardtop	63B
4-Dr. Hardtop	57B

MERCURY PARKLANE	CODE
4-Dr. Sedan	50F
2-Dr. Convertible	76F
2-Dr. Convertible	76C
2-Dr. Hardtop, Fastback	63F
2-Dr. Hardtop, Fastback	63C
4-Dr. Hardtop	57F

MERCURY COMMUTER	CODE
4-Dr. Station Wagon, 6-Pass.	71B
4-Dr. Station Wagon, 9-Pass.	71C

MERCURY COLONY PARK	CODE
4-Dr. Station Wagon, 6-Pass.	71A
4-Dr. Station Wagon, 9-Pass.	71E

THE DAY AND MONTH CODE furnishes the date the vehicle was manufactured. The number indicates the day of the month and the letter indicates the month.

MONTH	CODE	*CODE
January	A	N
February	B	P
March	C	Q
April	D	R
May	E	S
June	F	T
July	G	U
August	H	V
September	J	W
October	K	X
November	L	Y
December	M	Z

*2 year code letters to be used if 1965 models exceed 12 months.

DSO AND DISTRICT CODES

Units built on a Domestic Special Order, Foreign Special Order, or other special orders will have the complete order number in this space. Also to appear in this space is the two-digit code number of the District which ordered the unit. If the unit is a regular production unit, only the District code number will appear.

DISTRICT	CODE
Boston	11
Philadelphia	*12
Philadelphia	16
New York	*13
New York	15
Washington	14
Washington	**17
Atlanta	21
Dallas	22
Jacksonville	23
Jacksonville	*24
Memphis	*25
Memphis	26
Buffalo	31

1965 LINCOLN / MERCURY

Cincinnati	32
Cleveland	33
Detroit	34
Chicago	41
St. Louis	42
St. Louis	*44
Twin Cities	45
Denver	51
Los Angeles	52
Oakland	53
Seattle	54
Ford of Canada	81
Home Office Reserve	84
Export	90-99

* Lincoln only
** Mercury only

THE REAR AXLE RATIO CODE indicates the ratio of the rear axle installed in the vehicles. A number designates a conventional axle, while a letter designates an Equa-Lock differential.

AXLE RATIO	CODE
3.00:1	1
3.20:1	3
3.25:1	4
3.50:1	5
2.80:1	6
2.89:1	*1
3.11:1	*3
3.89:1	8
4.11:1	9
3.00:1	*A
3.20:1	*C
2.89:1	A
3.11:1	C
3.25:1	D
3.50:1	E
2.80:1	F
3.89:1	H
4.11:1	I

* Lincoln

THE TRANSMISSION CODE indicates the type of transmission installed in the vehicle.

TRANSMISSION	CODE
3-Speed Manual-Shift	1
3-Speed Overdrive	2
Twin-Range Multi-Drive	4
4-Speed Manual-Shift	5
C-4 Automatic Dual Range	6
430 V-8 (4-V)	320

THE TRIM NUMBER furnishes the key to trim color and material for each model series.

COMET TRIM

COLOR	CLOTH	VINYL	LEATHER	CODE
Beige		•		4
Blue	•	•		12,22,32,52
Blue		•		62,72,82,92
Red	•	•		15,25,35,55
Red		•		65,75,85,95
Black	•	•		16,36,56,96
Black		•		26,66,76,86
Turquoise	•	•		17,27,37
Turquoise		•		67,77,87
Palomino	•	•		19,29,39
Palomino	•	•		59,99
Palomino		•		49,69,79,89
Gold	•	•		28,38
Gold		•		68,78,88
White/Blue		•		42,G2,H2
White/Red		•		45,G5,H5
White/Red	•	•		F2
White/Black		•		46,G6,H6
White/Black	•	•		F5
White/Gold		•		48,G8,H8
White/Gold	•	•		F8
White/ Turquoise	•	•		F6
White/ Turquoise		•		G7,H7
White/ Palomino	•	•		F9
White/ Palomino		•		G9,H9

MERCURY TRIM

COLOR	CLOTH	VINYL	LEATHER	CODE
Green		•		3
Beige		•		4
Blue	•	•		12,52,92
Blue		•		22,42,62
Blue		•		72,K2,32,82
Red	•	•		15,55
Red		•		25,45,65
Red		•		95,75,K5
Red		•		35,85,Y5
Black	•	•		16,56,96
Black		•		46,66,76,K6
Black		•		26,36,86,Z6
Black	•		•	66
Turquoise	•	•		17,57,97
Turquoise		•		47,67,77
Turquoise		•		K7,37,87
Palomino	•	•		19,59,99
Palomino	•	•		A9,P9
Palomino		•		39,49,69
Palomino		•		89,29,79
Palomino		•		K9,Y9,Z9
Palomino			•	B9,C9
Gold	•	•		58
Gold		•		38,48,68
Gold		•		78,K8
Gold	•		•	68
Burgundy	•	•		93
Burgundy		•		33
Burgundy			•	B3,C3
Aqua	•		•	67
Silver	•		•	71
White/Black		•		D6,E6,F6
White/Black		•		G6,L6,M6
White/Blue		•		E2,G2,L2
White/ Burgundy		•		E3,G3,L3
White/Red		•		E5,G5,L5
White/ Turquoise		•		E7,L7,G7
White/Gold		•		E8,G8,L8
White/ Palomino		•		E9,G9,L9

LINCOLN TRIM

COLOR	CLOTH	VINYL	LEATHER	CODE
White/Blue			•	12
White/Beige			•	14
White/Red			•	15
White/Black			•	16,26,83
White/Gold			•	18
Green			•	99
Silver	•			31
Silver			•	51,81
Silver	•		•	61,71
Blue	•		•	42,62,72
Blue			•	52,82
Beige	•		•	44,74
Beige			•	54,84
Black	•		•	46,66,73
Black			•	56,86

1965 LINCOLN / MERCURY

Burgundy		•	50,80
Red		•	55,85
Aqua		•	57,87
Aqua	•	•	67,77
Gold		•	58,88
Gold	•	•	68,78
Palomino		•	59,89

THE PAINT CODE furnishes the key to the paint colors used on the car. A letter indicates the color of the car. A two-tone car has two sets of letters. The first indicates the lower body color, the second the upper body color.

LINCOLN

COLOR	CODE
Black	A
Dk. Turquoise Metallic	B
Med. Ivy Gold Metallic	C
Med. Silver Mink Metallic	E
Lt. Blue	F
Lt. Ivy Gold	G
Dk. Blue Metallic	H
Red	J
Lilac Mist Metallic	L
White	M
Platinum	N
Palomino Metallic	P
Med. Blue Metallic	Q
Dk. Ivy Green Metallic	R
Dk. Gray Metallic	S
Lt. Beige	T
Med. Turquoise Metallic	U
Maroon Metallic	X
Med. Beige Metallic	Z
Lt. Aqua	4

COMET/MERCURY

COLOR	CODE
Black	A
Med. Ivy Gold Metallic	C
Med. Turquoise Metallic	D
Dk. Blue Metallic	H
Lt. Beige Metallic	I
Red	J
Med. Gray Metallic	K
White	M
Lt. Peacock	O
Palomino Metallic	P
Dk. Ivy Green Metallic	R
Yellow	V
Maroon Metallic	X
Med. Blue Metallic	Y
Dk. Turquoise Metallic	5
Med. Ivy Gold Metallic	F
Lt. Beige	T

ENGINE NUMBER

6-cylinder and Lincoln engine tag is attached to the engine with the ignition coil mounting bracket bolt.

289 engine tag is located under the electric heat bulb indicator.

390 and 427 engine tag is located under the coil attaching bolt.

COMET

ENGINE NO.	NO. CYL.	CID	HORSE-POWER	COMP. RATIO	CARB	TRANS
T	6	200	120	9.2:1	1 BC	** M & A
2*	6	200	N/A	7.7:1	1 BC	** M & A
C	8	289	200	9.3:1	2 BC	** M & A
3*	8	289	N/A	N/A	2 BC	** M & A
A	8	289	225	10.0:1	4 BC	** M & A
K	8	289	271	10.5:1	4 BC	MAN

* Export

MERCURY

ENGINE NO.	NO. CYL.	CID	HORSE-POWER	COMP. RATIO	CARB	TRANS
Y	8	390	250	9.4:1	2 BC	** M & A
H	8	390	266	9.4:1	2 BC	AUTO
Z	8	390	300	10.1:1	4 BC	** M & A
9*	8	390	N/A	N/A	4 BC	** M & A
P	8	390	330	10.1:1	4 BC	** M & A
Q	8	427	410	11.5:1	4 BC	MAN
R	8	427	425	11.1:1	2-4 BC	** M & A

* Export

LINCOLN

ENGINE NO.	NO. CYL.	CID	HORSE-POWER	COMP. RATIO	CARB	TRANS
N	8	430	320	10.1:1	4 BC	AUTO
7*	8	430	N/A	N/A	4 BC	AUTO

* Export

** MAN & AUTO

1966 LINCOLN / MERCURY

1966 LINCOLN CONTINENTAL

1966 LINCOLN CONTINENTAL

1966 MERCURY

1966 MERCURY

1966 MERCURY COMET

1966 MERCURY COMET

1966 LINCOLN / MERCURY

VEHICLE IDENTIFICATION NUMBER

LINCOLN / MERCURY
6H62Z500551

LINCOLN VIN is die-stamped into the right front inner fender apron under the hood.

MERCURY VIN is die-stamped into the extension tab of the top of the cowl under the hood.

COMET VIN is die-stamped into the top surface of the inner fender panel and radiator support at the left side of the car under the hood.

FIRST DIGIT: Identifies the model year (1966)

SECOND DIGIT: Identifies the assembly plant

ASSEMBLY PLANT	CODE
Atlanta, GA	A
Oakville Passenger	B
Ontario Truck	C
Dallas, TX	D
Mahwah, NJ	E
Dearborn, MI	F
Chicago, IL	G
Lorain, OH	H
Los Angeles, CA	J
Kansas City, KS	K
Michigan Truck	L
Norfolk, VA	N
Twin Cities, MN	P
San Jose, CA	R
Pilot Plant	S
Metuchen, NJ	T
Louisville, KY	U
Wayne, MI	W
Wixom, MI	Y
St. Louis, MO	Z

THIRD AND FOURTH DIGITS: Identify the body series

LINCOLN CONTINENTAL	CODE
4-Dr. Sedan	82
2-Dr. Hardtop	89
4-Dr. Convertible	86

COMET 202	CODE
4-Dr. Sedan*	02
2-Dr. Sedan*	01
4-Dr. Wagon*	06

CAPRI	CODE
4-Dr. Sedan*	12
2-Dr. Hardtop*	13

COMET CALIENTE	CODE
4-Dr. Wagon* - Villager	16
4-Dr. Sedan*	22
2-Dr. Hardtop**	23
2-Dr. Hardtop*	23
2-Dr. Convertible**	25
2-Dr. Convertible*	25

CYCLONE	CODE
2-Dr. Hardtop**	27
2-Dr. Hardtop** (GT)	27
2-Dr. Convertible	29
2-Dr. Convertible** (GT)	29

*Bench Seat
**Bucket Seat

MERCURY MONTEREY	CODE
4-Dr. Sedan**	42
2-Dr. Sedan	43
4-Dr. Sedan	44
4-Dr. Hardtop, Fastback	48
2-Dr. Convertible*	45
2-Dr. Hardtop, Fastback*	47

MERCURY MONTCLAIR	CODE
4-Dr. Sedan**	52
4-Dr. Sedan	54
4-Dr. Hardtop, Fastback	58
2-Dr. Hardtop, Fastback	57

MERCURY S-55	CODE
2-Dr. Convertible	45
2-Dr. Hardtop, Fastback	47

MERCURY PARKLANE	CODE
4-Dr. Sedan**	62
2-Dr. Convertible	65
2-Dr. Convertible*	65
2-Dr. Hardtop, Fastback	67
2-Dr. Hardtop, Fastback*	67
4-Dr. Hardtop, Fastback	68

MERCURY COMMUTER	CODE
4-Dr. Station Wagon, 6-Pass.	72
4-Dr. Station Wagon, 9-Pass.	72

MERCURY COLONY PARK	CODE
4-Dr. Sedan	54
4-Dr. Station Wagon, 6-Pass.	76
4-Dr. Station Wagon, 9-Pass.	76

* Bench seat
** Bucket seat

FIFTH DIGIT: Identifies the engine code

ENGINE	CODE
8 Cyl. 289 Cu. In. (4-V, Prem.)	A
8 Cyl. 289 Cu. In. (2-V)	C
8 Cyl. 390 Cu. In. (2-V, Spec.)	H
8 Cyl. 410 Cu. In. (4-V)	M
8 Cyl. 428 Cu. In. (4-V, Police)	P
8 Cyl. 428 Cu. In. (4-V)	Q
8 Cyl. 427 Cu. In. (8-V, Hi-Perf)	R
8 Cyl. 390 Cu. In. (2-V)	Y
8 Cyl. 289 Cu. In. (2-V)*	3
8 Cyl. 428 Cu. In. (4-V)*	8
6 Cyl. 200 Cu. In. (1-V)	T
6 Cyl. 200 Cu. In. (1-V)*	2
8 Cyl. 390 Cu. In. (4-V) GT	S
8 Cyl. 462 Cu. In. (4-V)	G

*Low Compression

LAST SIX DIGITS: Represent the basic production numbers

BODY NUMBER PLATE

The vehicle data appears in a line across the top of the Body Plate. The first two letters and a number identify the body style. The following one or two letters identify the exterior paint color. The next code consisting of two numbers, or a letter and a number, identifies the interior trim. The date code showing the date the car was manufactured, follows the trim code and consists of two numbers and a letter. The next code gives the District in which the car was ordered and consists of two numbers. The next to the last code is the axle ratio code and is designated by a number for a conventional axle or a letter for an Equa-Lock axle. The last code in the vehicle data is the transmission code and consists of one number.

FORD MOTOR
CORPORATION

SERIAL NUMBER
6H62Y500551

50F	AA	26	11G	32	1	4
BDY	CLR	TRM	DT	DSO	AX	TR

EXAMPLE:

Serial Number

6	Model Year (1966)
H	Assembly Plant (Lorain, OH)
62	Body Series (4-Dr. Sedan)
Y	Engine (8 Cyl. 390 C.I.)
500551	Production Sequence

50F	Body Style (4-Dr. Sedan)
A	Lower Body Color
A	Upper Body Color
26	Trim
11G	Date Production Code
32	DSO Number
1	Axle (3.00:1)
4	Transmission (C-6 Automatic)

BODY STYLE

LINCOLN CONTINENTAL	CODE
4-Dr. Sedan	53A
2-Dr. Hardtop	65A
4-Dr. Convertible	74A

COMET 202	CODE
4-Dr. Sedan*	54A
2-Dr. Sedan*	62A
4-Dr. Wagon	71A

CAPRI	CODE
4-Dr. Sedan*	54B
2-Dr. Hardtop*	63B

COMET CALIENTE	CODE
4-Dr. Wagon* - Villager	71C
4-Dr. Sedan*	54D
2-Dr. Hardtop**	63C
2-Dr. Hardtop*	63D
2-Dr. Convertible**	76B
2-Dr. Convertible*	76D

CYCLONE	CODE
2-Dr. Hardtop**	63E
2-Dr. Hardtop** (GT)	63H
2-Dr. Convertible	76C
2-Dr. Convertible** (GT)	76H

MERCURY MONTEREY	CODE
4-Dr. Sedan**	50A
2-Dr. Sedan	62A
4-Dr. Sedan	54A
4-Dr. Hardtop, Fastback	67A
2-Dr. Convertible*	76G
2-Dr. Hardtop, Fastback	63G

MERCURY MONTCLAIR	CODE
4-Dr. Sedan**	50B
4-Dr. Sedan	54B
2-Dr. Hardtop, Fastback	63B
4-Dr. Hardtop, Fastback	67B

MERCURY S-55	CODE
2-Dr. Convertible	76A
2-Dr. Hardtop, Fastback	63A

MERCURY PARKLANE	CODE
4-Dr. Sedan**	50F
2-Dr. Convertible	76F
2-Dr. Convertible*	76C
2-Dr. Hardtop, Fastback	76C
2-Dr. Hardtop, Fastback	63C
4-Dr. Hardtop, Fastback	57F

MERCURY COMMUTER	CODE
4-Dr. Station Wagon, 6-Pass.	71B
4-Dr. Station Wagon, 9-Pass.	57F

MERCURY COLONY PARK	CODE
4-Dr. Station Wagon, 6-Pass.	71A
4-Dr. Station Wagon, 9-Pass.	71E

*Bench seat
**Bucket seat

THE DAY AND MONTH CODE furnishes the date the vehicle was manufactured. The number indicates the day of the month and the letter indicates the month.

MONTH	CODE	*CODE
January	A	N
February	B	P
March	C	Q
April	D	R
May	E	S
June	F	T
July	G	U
August	H	V
September	J	W
October	K	X
November	L	Y
December	M	Z

*2 year code letters to be used if 1966 models exceed 12 months.

DSO AND DISTRICT CODES

Domestic Special Orders, Foreign Special Orders, Limited Production Option, and Pre-Approved Special Orders will have the complete order number recorded in this space. Also to appear in this space is the two-digit code number of the District which ordered the unit. If the unit is a regular production unit, only the District code number will appear.

DISTRICT	CODE
Boston	11
Philadelphia	16
New York	15
Washington	17
Atlanta	21

1966 LINCOLN / MERCURY

Dallas	22
Jacksonville	23
Memphis	26
Buffalo	31
Cincinnati	32
Cleveland	33
Detroit	34
Chicago	41
St. Louis	42
Twin Cities	46
Denver	51
Los Angeles	52
Oakland	53
Seattle	54
Ford of Canada	81
Home Office Reserve	84
Export	90-99

THE REAR AXLE RATIO CODE indicates the ratio of the rear axle installed in the vehicle. A number designates a conventional axle, while a letter designates an Equa-Lock differential.

AXLE RATIO	CODE
3.00:1	1
2.83:1	2
3.20:1	3
3.25:1	4
2.89:1 (Locking)	4
3.50:1	5
2.80:1	6
3.89:1	8
2.89:1	8
4.11:1	9
3.00:1	A
3.20:1	C
3.25:1	E
3.50:1	F
2.80:1	F
3.89:1	H
4.11:1	I

THE TRANSMISSION CODE indicates the type of transmission installed in the vehicle.

TRANSMISSION	CODE
3-Speed Manual Shift	1
Overdrive	2
3-Speed Manual (303)	3
C-6 Automatic (XPL)	4
4-Speed Manual-Shift	5
C-4 Automatic Dual Range	6
Cruise-o-matic (MX)	8
Multi-Drive (Mercury)	

THE TRIM NUMBER furnishes the key to trim color and material for each model series.

LINCOLN TRIM COLOR	CLOTH	VINYL	LEATHER	CODE
White/Black		•		16,26
White/Black			•	83
Black/White	•		•	73
Silver	•			31
Silver			•	81
Silver	•		•	61,71
Black	•		•	46,66
Black			•	56,86
Blue			•	52,82
Blue	•		•	62,72
Gold			•	58,88
Gold	•		•	68,78
Burgundy			•	80
Burgundy	•		•	60,70
Aqua	•		•	67,77
Aqua			•	87
Palomino	•		•	69,79
Palomino			•	89
Parchment			•	5D,8D
Parchment	•		•	6D
Emberglow			•	84
Red			•	85
Green	•		•	7G
Green			•	8G

MERCURY TRIM COLOR	CLOTH	VINYL	LEATHER	CODE
Blue	•	•		12,32,52
Blue		•		22,42,62,N2
Blue		•		72,82,92,K2
Red	•	•		15,35,55
Red		•		25,45,65
Red		•		N5,X5,Y5
Red		•		75,85,95
Black	•	•		16,36,56
Black		•		26,46,66,96
Black		•		76,86,K6,Z6
Aqua	•	•		17,37,57
Aqua		•		47,67,77
Palomino	•	•		19,39
Silver	•	•		31,51
Gold	•	•		38,58
Gold		•		48,68
Green		•		03
Beige		•		04
Burgundy	•	•		53,93
Burgundy			•	A3
Emberglo		•		64,84,94
Parchment		•		XD,ZD
Blue/ Parchment		•		B2,S2
Burgundy/ Parchment		•		B3
Black/ Parchment		•		B6
Aqua/ Parchment		•		B7
Gold/ Parchment		•		B8
Palomino/ Parchment		•		B9
White/Black		•		D6,E6
Black/White		•		F6,G6
Blue/White		•		F2,G2
Burgundy/White		•		F3,G3
Emberglo/White		•		F4,G4
Aqua/White		•		F7,G7
Gold/White		•		F8,G8
Palomino/White		•		F9,G9

COMET TRIM COLOR	CLOTH	VINYL	LEATHER	CODE
Silver/ Black	•	•		11
Black		•		26,36,46,66,86
Blue	•	•		12,32,52
Blue		•		22,42,62,82
Red	•	•		15,35,55
Red		•		25,45,65,85
Aqua	•	•		17,37,57
Aqua		•		27,47,67,87
Gold	•	•		38
Gold		•		48,68,88
Emberglo		•		44,64,84
Parchment	•	•		1D,3D,5D
Parchment		•		2D,4D,0D
Parchment/ Silver		•		B1
Parchment/ Blue		•		B2,C2,D2,F2
Parchment/				

1966 LINCOLN / MERCURY

Emberglow	•	B4,C4,D4,F4
Parchment/Red	•	B5
Parchment/ Black	•	B6,C6,D6,F6
Parchment/Aqua	•	B7,C7,D7,F7
Parchment/Gold	•	B8,C8,D8,F8
Parchment/ Palomino	•	B9,C9,D9,F9
Parchment/ Burgundy	•	C3,D3,F3
White/Silver	•	H1
White/Blue	•	H2
White/ Emberglo	•	H4
White/Red	•	H5
White/Black	•	H6
White/Aqua	•	H7
White/ Palomino	•	H8

THE PAINT CODE furnishes the key to the paint colors used on the car. A letter indicates the color of the car. A two-tone car has two sets of letters. The first indicates the lower body color, the second the upper body color.

LINCOLN

COLOR	CODE
Black	A
Lt. Beige Metallic	B
Med. Silver Mink Metallic	E
Lt. Blue	F
Lt. Beige	H
Dk. Blue Metallic	K
Ivy Yellow	L
White	M
Platinum	N
Med. Palomino Metallic	P
Med. Blue Metallic	Q
Dk. Green Metallic	R
Dk. Gray Metallic	S
Red	T
Med. Turquoise Metallic	U
Emberglo Metallic	V
Maroon Metallic	X
Med. Sage Gold Metallic	Z
Rose Metallic	1
Dk. Turquoise Metallic	2

COMET/MERCURY

COLOR	CODE
Black	A
Dk. Executive Gray Metallic	C
Lt. Blue	F
Lt. Beige	H
Dk. Blue Metallic	K
White	M
Med. Palomino Metallic	P
Dk. Green Metallic	R
Red	T
Med. Turquoise Metallic	U
Emberglo Metallic	V
Maroon Metallic	X
Lt. Blue Metallic	Y
Med. Sage Gold Metallic	Z
Dk. Turquoise Metallic	2
Med. Silver Metallic	4
Red	5
Yellow	8

ENGINE NUMBER

The engine tag is attached to the engine with the ignition coil mounting bracket bolt.

COMET

ENGINE NO.	NO. CYL.	CID	HORSE-POWER	COMP. RATIO	CARB	TRANS
T	6	200	120	9.2:1	1 BC	** M & A
2*	6	200	N/A	N/A	1 BC	** M & A
C	8	289	200	9.3:1	2 BC	** M & A
3*	8	289	N/A	N/A	2 BC	** M & A
Y	8	390	265	9.5:1	2 BC	MAN
H	8	390	275	9.5:1	2 BC	AUTO

CYCLONE GT

ENGINE NO.	NO. CYL.	CID	HORSE-POWER	COMP. RATIO	CARB	TRANS
S	8	390	335	10.5:1	4 BC	** M & A

MERCURY

ENGINE NO.	NO. CYL.	CID	HORSE-POWER	COMP. RATIO	CARB	TRANS
Y	8	390	265	9.5:1	2 BC	MAN
H	8	390	275	9.5:1	2 BC	AUTO
M	8	410	330	10.5:1	4 BC	** M & A
Q	8	428	345	10.5:1	4 BC	** M & A
8*	8	428	N/A	N/A	4 BC	** M & A
P	8	428	360	10.1:1	4 BC	** M & A
R	8	427	425	11.1:1	2-4 BC	** M & A

LINCOLN

ENGINE NO.	NO. CYL.	CID	HORSE-POWER	COMP. RATIO	CARB	TRANS
G	8	462	340	10.25:1	4 BC	AUTO

** MAN & AUTO

1967 LINCOLN / MERCURY

1967 LINCOLN CONTINENTAL

1967 MERCURY CALIENTE

1967 MERCURY COUGAR

1967 MERCURY COUGAR

1967 MERCURY CYCLONE GT

1967 MERCURY CYCLONE GT

1967 MERCURY MARQUIS

1967 MERCURY MARQUIS

1967 MERCURY PARK LANE

1967 MERCURY PARK LANE

1967 LINCOLN / MERCURY

VEHICLE IDENTIFICATION NUMBER

LINCOLN / MERCURY
7H64S500551

VIN LOCATION

LINCOLN VIN is die-stamped into the right front inner fender apron under the hood.

MERCURY VIN is die-stamped into the extension tab of the top of the cowl under the hood.

COMET VIN is die-stamped into the top surface of the inner fender panel and radiator support at the left side of the car under the hood.

COUGER VIN is die-stamped into the top surface of the inner fender panel and radiator support at the left side of the car under the hood.

FIRST DIGIT: Identifies the model year (1967)

SECOND DIGIT: Identifies the assembly plant

ASSEMBLY PLANT	CODE
Atlanta, GA	A
Oakville, CAN	B
Ontario Truck	C
Dallas, TX	D
Mahwah, NJ	E
Dearborn, MI	F
Chicago, IL	G
Lorain, OH	H
Los Angeles, CA	J
Kansas City, KS	K
Michigan Truck	L
Norfolk, VA	N
Twin Cities, MN	P
San Jose, CA	R
Metuchen, NJ	T
Louisville, KY	U
Wayne, MI	W
Wixom, MI	Y
St. Louis, MO	Z

THIRD AND FOURTH DIGITS: Identify the body series

MONTERY	CODE
4-Dr. Sedan	44
4-Dr. Hardtop	48
2-Dr. Hardtop	47
2-Dr. Convertible	45

MONTCLAIR	CODE
4-Dr. Sedan	54
2-Dr. Hardtop	57
4-Dr. Hardtop	58

PARKLANE	CODE
4-Dr. Sedan	64
4-Dr. Hardtop	68
2-Dr. Hardtop	67
2-Dr. Convertible	65

BROUGHAM	CODE
4-Dr. Sedan	61
4-Dr. Hardtop	62

MARQUIS	CODE
2-Dr. Hardtop	69

COMMUTER	CODE
4-Dr., 6-Pass.	72
4-Dr., 9-Pass.	72

COLONY PARK STATION WAGON	CODE
4-Dr., 6-Pass.	76

COMET 202	CODE
4-Dr. Sedan	02
2-Dr. Sedan	01

COMET CAPRI	CODE
4-Dr. Sedan	08
2-Dr. Hardtop	07

CALIENTE	CODE
4-Dr. Sedan	10
2-Dr. Hardtop	11
2-Dr. Convertible	12

CYCLONE	CODE
2-Dr. Hardtop	15
2-Dr. Convertible	16

GT	CODE
2-Dr. Hardtop	17
2-Dr. Convertible	18

COMET VOYAGER STATION WAGON	CODE
4-Dr., 6-Pass.	03

VILLAGER STATION WAGON	CODE
4-Dr., 6-Pass.	08

COUGAR	CODE
2-Dr. Hardtop	91
2-Dr. Hardtop XR-7	93

LINCOLN CONTINENTAL	CODE
4-Dr. Sedan	82
2-Dr. Hardtop	89
4-Dr. Convertible	86

FIFTH DIGIT: Identifies the engine code

ENGINE	CODE
6 Cyl. 200 Cu. In. (1-V)	T
6 Cyl. *200 Cu. In. (1-V)	2
8 Cyl. 289 Cu. In. (2-V)	C
8 Cyl. *289 Cu. In. (2-V)	3
8 Cyl. 289 Cu. In. (4-V) Prem. Fuel	A
8 Cyl. 390 Cu. In. (2-V)	H
8 Cyl. 390 Cu. In. (4-V)	S
8 Cyl. 410 Cu. In. (4-V)	M
8 Cyl. 428 Cu. In. (4-V)	Q
8 Cyl. *428 Cu. In. (4-V)	8
8 Cyl. 428 Cu. In. (4-V) Police	P
8 Cyl. 462 Cu. In. (4-V)	G
8 Cyl. *462 Cu. In. (4-V)	7
8 Cyl. 427 Cu. In. (4-V) Hi-Perf	W
8 Cyl. 427 Cu. In. (8-V) Hi-Perf	R

* Low compression

LAST SIX DIGITS: Represent the basic production numbers

1967 LINCOLN / MERCURY

BODY NUMBER PLATE

The vehicle data appears in a line across the top of the Body Plate. The first two letters and a number identify the body style. The following one or two letters identify the exterior paint color. The next code consisting of two numbers, or a letter and a number, identifies the interior trim. The date code showing the date the car was manufactured, follows the trim code and consists of two numbers and a letter. The next code gives the district in which the car was ordered and consists of two numbers. The next to the last code is the axle ratio code and is designated by a number for a conventional axle or a letter for an Equa-Lock axle. The last code in the vehicle data is the transmission code and consists of one number.

FORD MOTOR
CORPORATION

SERIAL NUMBER
7H64S500551

54E	AA	2A	11G	32	1	5
BDY	CLR	TRM	DT	DSO	AX	TR

EXAMPLE:

Serial Number

7	Model Year (1967)
H	Assembly Plant (Lorain, OH)
64	Body Series (4-Dr. Sedan)
S	Engine (8 Cyl. 390 C.I.)
500551	Production Sequence

54E	Body Style (4-Dr. Sedan)
A	Lower Body Color
A	Upper Body Color
2A	Trim
11G	Date Production Code
32	DSO Number
1	Axle (3.00:1)
5	Transmission (4-Spd. Manual)

MERCURY	CODE
4-Dr. Sedan	54A
4-Dr. Sedan	54B
4-Dr. Hardtop	57A
2-Dr. Hardtop	63A
2-Dr. Convertible	76A
2-Dr. Hardtop S-55	63G
2-Dr. Convertible S-55	76G

MERCURY MONTCLAIR	CODE
4-Dr. Sedan	54C
4-Dr. Sedan	54D
4-Dr. Hardtop	57B
2-Dr. Hardtop	63B

MERCURY PARKLANE	CODE
4-Dr. Sedan	54E
4-Dr. Hardtop	57F
2-Dr. Hardtop	63F
2-Dr. Convertible	76F

MERCURY BROUGHAM	CODE
4-Dr. Sedan	54J
4-Dr. Hardtop	57C

MERCURY MARQUIS	CODE
2-Dr. Hardtop	63D

MERCURY COMMUTER	CODE
4-Dr., 6-Pass.	71B
4-Dr., 9-Pass.	71C

COLONY PARK STATION WAGON	CODE
4-Dr., 6-Pass.	71E
4-Dr., 9-Pass.	71A

COMET 202	CODE
4-Dr. Sedan	54A
2-Dr. Sedan	62A

COMET CAPRI	CODE
4-Dr. Sedan	54B
2-Dr. Hardtop	63B

CALIENTE	CODE
4-Dr. Sedan	54D
2-Dr. Hardtop	63D
2-Dr. Convertible	76D

CYCLONE	CODE
2-Dr. Hardtop	63E
2-Dr. Convertible	76C

GT	CODE
2-Dr. Hardtop	63H
2-Dr. Convertible	76H

COMET VOYAGER STATION WAGON	CODE
4-Dr., 6-Pass.	71A

VILLAGER STATION WAGON	CODE
4-Dr., 6-Pass.	71C

COUGAR	CODE
2-Dr. Hardtop	65A
2-Dr. Hardtop XR-7	65B
2-Dr. Hardtop	65D
2-Dr. Hardtop (Bench Seat)	65C
Option - Dan Gurney Special	
Option - GT	

LINCOLN CONTINENTAL	CODE
4-Dr. Sedan	53A
2-Dr. Hardtop	65A
4-Dr. Convertible	74A

THE DAY AND MONTH CODE furnishes the date the vehicle was manufactured. The number indicates the day of the onth and the letter indicates the month.

MONTH	CODE	*CODE
January	A	N
February	B	P
March	C	Q
April	D	R
May	E	S
June	F	T
July	G	U
August	H	V
September	J	W
October	K	X
November	L	Y
December	M	Z

*2 year code letters to be used if the 1967 models exceed 12 months.

1967 LINCOLN / MERCURY

DSO AND DISTRICT CODES

Units built on a Domestic Special Order, Foreign Special Order or other special orders will have the complete order number in this space. Also to appear in this space is the two-digit code number of the District which ordered the unit. If the unit is a regular production unit, only the District code number will appear.

DISTRICT	CODE
Boston	11
Philadelphia	16
New York	15
Washington	17
Atlanta	21
Dallas	22
Jacksonville	23
Memphis	26
Buffalo	31
Cincinnati	32
Cleveland	33
Detroit	34
Chicago	41
St. Louis	42
Twin Cities	46
Denver	51
Los Angeles	52
Oakland	53
Seattle	54
Home Office Reserve	84
Export	90-99

REAR AXLE RATIO CODES

THE REAR AXLE RATIO CODE indicates the ratio of the rear axle installed in the vehicle. A number designates a conventional axle, while a letter designates an Equa-Lock differential.

AXLE RATIO	CODE
3.10:1	0
3.00:1	1
3.89:1	1
2.83:1	2
3.20:1	3
3.25:1	4
3.50:1	5
2.80:1	6
2.75:1	8
4.11:1	9
3.00:1	A
3.20:1	C
3.25:1	D
2.80:1	F
3.50:1	E
2.75:1	H

THE TRANSMISSION CODE indicates the type of transmission installed in the vehicle.

TRANSMISSION	CODE
3-Speed Manual	1
3-Speed Overdrive	2
C-6 Dual Range	
3-Speed Manual	3
4-Speed Manual	5
C-4 Automatic	W
C-6 Automatic	U
Automatic (MX)	Y
C-6 Automatic (XPL Special)	Z

THE TRIM NUMBER furnishes the key to trim color and material for each model series.

COLOR	CLOTH	VINYL	LEATHER	CODE
Black	•	•		1A,5A
Black	•	•		9A,KA
Black			•	5A*,2A*,7A*
Black		•		2A,4A,6A
Black		•		7A,8A,DA
Blue	•	•		1B,3B,5B
Blue	•	•		9B,KB
Blue	•		•	5B*,2B*
Blue		•		2B,4B
Blue		•		6B,7B
Blue		•		8B,DB,LD
Blue			•	7B*
Red	•	•		1D,KD
Red		•		2D,4D
Red		•		6D,7D
Red		•		8D,DD,LB
Red			•	2D*,5D
Red			•	JD,TD
Gold	•	•		1G,3G,5G
Gold	•	•		9G,AG,KG
Gold	•		•	5G*,GG
Gold		•		2G,6G
Gold		•		7G,DG
Gold			•	2G*,BG,EG
Aqua	•	•		1K,3K
Aqua	•	•		5K,9K
Aqua		•		2K,4G,6K
Aqua			•	BK,EK
Silver	•	•		1L,3L
Silver	•	•		5L,9L
Silver			•	2L
Parchment	•	•		1U,7U
Parchment	•		•	2U,5U,7U*
Parchment		•		4U,6U
Saddle		•		2F,6F
Saddle		•		7F,8F
Saddle			•	2F*,5F
Parchment/ Black	•	•		3U,9U
Parchment/ Black	•	•		LU,SU
Parchment/ Black		•		2U,8U
Parchment/ Black		•		BA,CA
Parchment/ Black		•		FA,MA,UA
Parchment/ Black			•	2U*
Parchment/ Blue		•		BB,CB,FB
Parchment/ Blue		•		MB,UB
Parchment/ Red		•		BD,CD,FD
Parchment/ Red		•		MD,UD
Parchment/ Saddle		•		BF,CF
Parchment/ Saddle		•		MF,UF
Parchment/ Saddle	•	•		5U,KU
Parchment/ Saddle	•		•	5U*

1967 LINCOLN / MERCURY

Parchment/ Gold	•		BG,FG
Parchment/ Gold	•		MG,UG
Parchment/ Gold		•	BG*
Parchment/ Aqua	•		BK,FK
Parchment/ Aqua	•		MK,UK
Parchment/ Aqua		•	BK*

* Leather on Lincoln Continental

THE PAINT CODE furnishes the key to the paint colors used on the car. A letter indicates the color of the car. A two-tone car has two sets of letters. The first indicates the lower body color, the second the upper body color.

COLOR	CODE
Black	A
Lt. Aqua	B
Dk. Gray Metallic	C
Med. Beige Metallic	E
Lt. Blue	F
Diamond Green	H
Lime Metallic	I
Dk. Blue Metallic	K
White	M
Platinum	N
Lt. Green	O
Pewter Metallic	P
Med. Blue Metallic	Q
Dk. Green Metallic	R
Red	T
Med. Turquoise Metallic	U
Bronze Metallic	V
Med. Aqua Metallic	W
Maroon Metallic	X
Dk. Green Metallic	Y
Med. Gold Metallic	Z
Yellow	2
Med. Gray Metallic	4
Lt. Beige	6
Yellow	8

ENGINE NUMBER

The engine tag is located under the coil attaching bolt.

COMET

ENGINE NO.	NO. CYL.	CID	HORSE-POWER	COMP. RATIO	CARB	TRANS
T	6	200	120	9.2:1	1 BC	*** M & A
2*	6	200	N/A	N/A	1 BC	*** M & A
C	8	289	200	9.3:1	2 BC	*** M & A
3*	8	289	N/A	N/A	2 BC	*** M & A
H	8	390	270	9.5:1	2 BC	*** M & A
W	8	427	410	11.1:1	4 BC	MAN
R	8	427	425	11.1:1	2-4 BC	MAN

* Export

CYCLONE GT

ENGINE NO.	NO. CYL.	CID	HORSE-POWER	COMP. RATIO	CARB	TRANS
S	8	390	320	10.5:1	4 BC	*** M & A

COUGAR

ENGINE NO.	NO. CYL.	CID	HORSE-POWER	COMP. RATIO	CARB	TRANS
C	8	289	200	9.3:1	2 BC	*** M & A
3*	8	289	N/A	N/A	2 BC	*** M & A
A	8	289	225	9.8:1	4 BC	*** M & A
S	8	390	320	10.5:1	4 BC	*** M & A
N/A	8	289	341	10.5:1	2-4 BC	MAN

* Export

MERCURY, MONTCLAIR, MONTEREY

ENGINE NO.	NO. CYL.	CID	HORSE-POWER	COMP. RATIO	CARB	TRANS
H	8	390	270	9.5:1	2 BC	*** M & A
M	8	410	330	10.5:1	4 BC	*** M & A
Q	8	428	345	11.1:1	4 BC	*** M & A
8*	8	428	N/A	N/A	4 BC	*** M & A
P**	8	428	360	10.5:1	4 BC	*** M & A

* Export
** Police

MERCURY MARQUIS, BROUGHAM AND PARKLANE

ENGINE NO.	NO. CYL.	CID	HORSE-POWER	COMP. RATIO	CARB	TRANS
M	8	410	330	10.5:1	4 BC	*** M & A
Q	8	428	345	10.5:1	4 BC	*** M & A
8*	8	428	N/A	N/A	4 BC	*** M & A

* Export

S-55

ENGINE NO.	NO. CYL.	CID	HORSE-POWER	COMP. RATIO	CARB	TRANS
Q	8	428	345	10.5:1	4 BC	*** M & A
8*	8	428	N/A	N/A	4 BC	*** M & A

* Export

LINCOLN

ENGINE NO.	NO. CYL.	CID	HORSE-POWER	COMP. RATIO	CARB	TRANS
G	8	462	340	10.5:1	4 BC	AUTO
7*	8	462	N/A	N/A	4 BC	AUTO

* Export
*** MAN & AUTO

1968 LINCOLN / MERCURY

1968 LINCOLN CONTINENTAL

1968 LINCOLN CONTINENTAL

1968 MERCURY COUGAR

1968 MERCURY COUGAR

1968 MERCURY CYCLONE

1968 MERCURY MONTEGO

1968 MERCURY MONTCLAIR

1968 MERCURY MONTCLAIR

1968 MERCURY PARK LANE

1968 MERCURY PARK LANE

1968 LINCOLN / MERCURY

VEHICLE IDENTIFICATION NUMBER

LINCOLN / MERCURY
8H64Z500551

VIN LOCATION

LINCOLN VIN is die-stamped on the metal tab riveted to the instrument panel on the right hand side. VIN is visible through the windshield.

MERCURY VIN is die-stamped on the metal tab aluminum riveted to the instrument panel on the right hand side. VIN is visible through the windshield.

FIRST DIGIT: Identifies the model year (1968)

SECOND DIGIT: Identifies the assembly plant

ASSEMBLY PLANT	CODE
Atlanta, GA	A
Oakville, CAN	B
Ontario Truck	C
Dallas, TX	D
Mahwah, NJ	E
Dearborn, MI	F
Chicago, IL	G
Lorain, OH	H
Los Angeles, CA	J
Kansas City, KS	K
Michigan Truck	L
Norfolk, VA	N
Twin Cities, MN	P
San Jose, CA	R
Pilot Plant	S
Metuchen, NJ	T
Louisville, KY	U
Wayne, MI	W
St. Thomas, Ont. CAN	X
Wixom, MI	Y
St. Louis, MO	Z

THIRD AND FOURTH DIGITS: Identify the body series

LINCOLN	CODE
4-Dr. Sedan	82
2-Dr. Hardtop	80

MONTEGO COMET	CODE
Sports Coupe	01

MONTEGO	CODE
4-Dr. Sedan	06
2-Dr. Hardtop	07

MONTEGO MX	CODE
4-Dr. Sedan	10
2-Dr. Hardtop	11
2-Dr. Convertible	12

BROUGHAM	CODE
4-Dr. Sedan	10
2-Dr. Hardtop	11

CYCLONE	CODE
2-Dr. Hardtop	15
2-Dr. Hardtop	17

MONTEGO MX	CODE
4-Dr. Station Wagon	03
4-Dr. Station Wagon	08

COUGAR	CODE
2-Dr. Hardtop	91
2-Dr. Hardtop XR-7	93

MONTEREY	CODE
4-Dr. Sedan	44
4-Dr. Hardtop	48
2-Dr. Hardtop	47
2-Dr. Convertible	45

MONTCLAIR	CODE
4-Dr. Sedan	54
4-Dr. Hardtop	58
2-Dr. Hardtop	57

PARKLANE	CODE
4-Dr. Sedan	64
4-Dr. Hardtop	68
2-Dr. Hardtop	67
2-Dr. Convertible	65

PARKLANE BROUGHAM	CODE
4-Dr. Sedan	64
4-Dr. Hardtop	68

MARQUIS	CODE
2-Dr. Hardtop	69

COMMUTER	CODE
4-Dr., 6-Pass.	72
4-Dr., 10-Pass.	72

COLONY PARK	CODE
4-Dr., 6-Pass.	76
4-Dr., 10-Pass.	76

FIFTH DIGIT: Identifies the engine code

ENGINE	CODE
8 Cyl. 302 Cu. In. (2-V)	F
8 Cyl. *302 Cu. In. (2-V)	6
8 Cyl. 390 Cu. In. (2-V)	Y
8 Cyl. 390 Cu. In. (2-V) Prem. Fuel	X
8 Cyl. 390 Cu. In. (4-V)	Z
8 Cyl. 428 Cu. In. (4-V)	Q
8 Cyl. *428 Cu. In. (4-V)	8
8 Cyl. 428 Cu. In. (4-V) Police	P
8 Cyl. 427 Cu. In. (4-V) Hi-Perf	W
6 Cyl. 200 Cu. In. (1-V)	T
6 Cyl. *200 Cu. In. (1-V)	2
8 Cyl. 302 Cu. In. (4-V)	J
8 Cyl. 390 Cu. In. (4-V) and GT	S
8 Cyl. 462 Cu. In. (4-V)	G
8 Cyl. *462 Cu. In. (4-V)	7
8 Cyl. 460 Cu. In. (4-V)	A
8 Cyl. *460 Cu. In. (4-V)	1

* Low Compression

LAST SIX DIGITS: Represent the basic production numbers

1968 LINCOLN / MERCURY

BODY NUMBER PLATE

The vehicle data appears on the second or lower line on the Body Plate. The first two numbers and a letter identify the body style. A letter or a number appears next indicating the exterior paint color followed by a number-letter combination designating the interior trim. To the right of this code appears the date code, indicating the date the car was manufactured. A two-digit number next designates the District in which the car was ordered and may appear in conjunction with a Domestic Special Order or Foreign Special Order number when applicable. The final two spaces indicate the rear axle ratio (numbers for regular axles, letters for locking-types) and the transmission type (numbers for manual, letters for automatic).

FORD MOTOR
CORPORATION

SERIAL NUMBER
8H64Z500551

54E	AA	2A	11G	32	5	U
BDY	CLR	TRM	DT	DSO	AX	TR

EXAMPLE:

Serial Number

8	Model Year (1968)
H	Assembly Plant (Lorain, OH)
64	Body Series (4-Dr. Sedan)
Z	Engine (8 Cyl. 390 C.I.)
500551	Production Sequence

54E	Body Style (Parklane)
A	Lower Body Color
A	Upper Body Color
2A	Trim
11G	Date Production Code
32	DSO Number
5	Axle (3.00:1)
U	Transmission (C6 Automatic)

BODY STYLE

LINCOLN	CODE
4-Dr. Sedan	53A
2-Dr. Hardtop	65A

MONTEGO COMET	CODE
Sports Coupe	65A

MONTEGO	CODE
4-Dr. Sedan	54B
2-Dr. Hardtop	65B

MONTEGO MX	CODE
4-Dr. Sedan	54D
2-Dr. Hardtop	65D
2-Dr. Convertible	76D
2-Dr. Hardtop	65E
2-Dr. Convertible	76B

BROUGHAM	CODE
4-Dr. Sedan	54C
2-Dr. Hardtop	65C

CYCLONE	CODE
2-Dr. Hardtop Fastback	63A
2-Dr. Hardtop	65F
2-Dr. HardtopFastback	63C
2-Dr. Hardtop	65G
2-Dr. Hardtop GT Fastback	63H
2-Dr. Hardtop GT	65H

MONTEGO MX	CODE
4-Dr. Station Wagon	71B
4-Dr. Station Wagon	71C

COUGAR	CODE
2-Dr. Hardtop	65A
2-Dr. Hardtop XR-7	65B
2-Dr. Hardtop (Bench Seat)	65C
Option - GT	
Option - GTE	
Option - Dan Gurney XR7-G	

MERCURY MONTEREY	CODE
4-Dr. Sedan	54A
4-Dr. Sedan	54B
4-Dr. Hardtop	57A
2-Dr. Hardtop	63A
2-Dr. Convertible	76A

MONTCLAIR	CODE
4-Dr. Sedan	54C
4-Dr. Sedan	54D
4-Dr. Hardtop	57B
2-Dr. Hardtop	63B

PARKLANE	CODE
4-Dr. Sedan	54E
4-Dr. Hardtop	57F
2-Dr. Hardtop	63F
4-Dr. Convertible	76F

PARKLANE BROUGHAM	CODE
4-Dr. Sedan	54J
4-Dr. Hardtop	57C

MARQUIS	CODE
2-Dr. Hardtop	63D

COMMUTER	CODE
4-Dr., 6-Pass.	71B
4-Dr., 10-Pass.	71C

COLONY PARK	CODE
4-Dr., 6-Pass.	71E
4-Dr., 10-Pass.	71A

THE DAY AND MONTH CODE the date the vehicle was manufactured. The number indicates the day of the month and the letter indicates the month.

MONTH	CODE	*CODE
January	A	N
February	B	P
March	C	Q
April	D	R
May	E	S
June	F	T
July	G	U
August	H	V
September	J	W
October	K	X
November	L	Y
December	M	Z

*2 year code letters to be used if 1968 models exceed 12 months.

1968 LINCOLN / MERCURY

DSO AND DISTRICT CODES

Domestic Special Orders, Foreign Special Orders, Limited Production Option, and Pre-Approved Special Orders have the complete order number recorded in this space. Also to appear in this space is the two-digit code number of the District which ordered the unit. If the unit is a regular production unit, only the District code number will appear.

DISTRICT	CODE
Boston	11
Philadelphia	16
New York	15
Washington	17
Atlanta	21
Dallas	22
Jacksonville	23
Memphis	26
Buffalo	31
Cincinnati	32
Cleveland	33
Detroit	34
Chicago	41
St. Louis	42
Twin Cities	46
Denver	51
Los Angeles	52
Oakland	53
Seattle	54
Home Office Reserve	84
Export	90-99

FORD OF CANADA

Central	B1
Eastern	B2
Atlantic	B3
Midwestern	B4
Western	B6
Pacific	B7

THE REAR AXLE RATIO CODE indicates the ratio of the rear axle installed in the vehicle. A number designates a conventional axle, while a letter designates an Equa-Lock differential.

AXLE RATIO	CODE
2.75:1	1
2.79:1	2
2.83:1	4
3.00:1	5
3.20:1	6
3.25:1	7
3.50:1	8
3.10:1	9
2.75:1	A
2.80:1	C
2.80:1	3
3.00:1	E
3.20:1	F
3.25:1	G
3.50:1	H

THE TRANSMISSION CODE indicates the type of transmission installed in the vehicle.

TRANSMISSION	CODE
3-Speed Manual	1
4-Speed Manual	5
C-4 Automatic (XP3)	W
C-6 Automatic (XPL)	U
MX Automatic	Y
FMX Automatic	X
C-6 Automatic (XPL Special)	Z

THE TRIM NUMBER furnishes the key to trim color and material for each model series.

MERCURY TRIM

COLOR	CLOTH	VINYL	LEATHER	CODE
Black	•	•		1A,3A,5A
Black	•	•		9A,BA,EA
Black	•	•		KA,SA,ZA
Black		•		2A,4A,6A,7A
Black		•		CA,DA,FA,HA
Black		•		NA,PA,RA
Blue	•	•		1B,2B,3B
Blue	•	•		5B,9B,BB
Blue	•	•		EB,SB,ZB
Blue		•		2B,4B,6B,7B
Blue		•		CB,DB,FB,HB
Blue		•		NB,PB,RB
Red	•	•		1D,3D,9D,BD
Red	•	•		ED,KD
Red		•		2D,4D,6D,7D
Red		•		CD,DD,FD,HD
Red		•		ND,PD,RD
Gold	•	•		1G,2G,3G,5G
Gold	•	•		9G,BG,EG,KG
Gold	•	•		SG,ZY
Gold		•		6G,7G,FG
Gold		•		PG,RG,HG
Aqua	•	•		1K,3K,5K
Aqua	•	•		EK,SK,9K
Aqua		•		4K,6K,RK
Parchment	•	•		1U,2U
Parchment		•		4U,7U,DU,FU
Parchment		•		HU,NU,PU,RU
Beige		•		LE
Nugget	•	•		1Y,3Y,5Y,9Y
Nugget	•	•		BY,EY,KY,SY
Nugget		•		2Y,4Y,6Y
Nugget		•		FY,RY,CY
Nugget/Black		•		4K
Parchment/ Black		•		CU
Blue/Red	•	•		KB

MONTEGO/COUGAR TRIM

COLOR	CLOTH	VINYL	LEATHER	CODE
Black	•	•		1A,5A,7A
Black		•		2A,3A,4A,6A
Black		•		8A,9A,HA,LA
Black		•		MA,QA,RA
Blue	•	•		1B,3B,5B
Blue	•	•		7B,KB
Blue		•		2B,3B,4B,6B
Blue	•	•		8B,9B,HB,LB
Blue	•	•		MB,QB,RB
Gold	•	•		1G,3G,5G
Gold	•	•		7G,KG
Gold		•		2G,4G,6G
Gold		•		8G,HG
Aqua		•		1K,2K,4K
Aqua		•		6K,8K,HK
Aqua	•	•		3K,5K,7K
Parchment	•	•		1U,3U,5U,KU
Parchment		•		2U,4U,6U,8U
Parchment		•		9U,BU,CU,HU
Parchment		•		DU,EU,FU,JU
Parchment		•		LU,MU,OU,QU
Parchment		•		RU,TU,YU,ZU
Nugget	•	•		3Y,5Y,7Y
Nugget		•		1Y,2Y,4Y,6Y
Nugget		•		8Y,9Y,AY,HY
Red	•	•		5D,7D
Red		•		2D,3D,4D,6D
Red		•		8D,9D,HD,LD
Red		•		MD,RD
Saddle		•		2F,6F
Saddle/Black		•		8F

1968 LINCOLN / MERCURY

Parchment/ Black	•	AA,FA,UA
Parchment/ Blue	•	AB,FB,UB
Parchment/ Red	•	AD,FD,UD
Parchment/ Saddle	•	AF,FF,UF
Parchment/ Gold	•	AG,FG,UG
Parchment/ Nugget	•	FY,UU,UY
Parchment/ Aqua	•	AK,FK,UK

LINCOLN TRIM

COLOR	CLOTH	VINYL	LEATHER	CODE
Black	•	•		1A,4A,6A
Black	•	•		AA,JA
Black			•	2A,5A,7A
Black			•	KA,RA
Blue	•	•		1B,AB,JB
Blue			•	2B,4B,5B,7B
Blue			•	BB,KB,RB,SB
Red	•	•		1D,4D
Red			•	2D,5D
Gold	•	•		1G,4G,AG,JG
Gold			•	2G,5G,7G,BG
Gold			•	KG,RG,SG
Saddle			•	2F,5F
Aqua	•	•		AK,JK
Aqua			•	2K,5K
Parchment			•	2U,5U,7U
Parchment			•	KU,RU
Nugget	•	•		AY,JY
Nugget			•	2Y,5Y
Silver	•	•		AL,JL
Silver			•	KL,RL

THE PAINT CODE furnishes the key to the paint colors used on the car. A letter indicates the color of the car. A two-tone car has two sets of letters. The first indicates the lower body color, the second the upper body color.

COLOR	CODE
Black	A
Maroon	B
Bright Blue Metallic	D
Med. Beige Metallic	E
Bright Aqua Metallic	F
Med. Green Metallic	G
Lt. Green	H
Lime Metallic	I
Dk. Aqua Metallic	J
Silver Metallic	L
White	M
Platinum	N
Light Green	O
Pewter Metallic	P
Med. Blue Metallic	Q
Dk. Green Metallic	R
Iris Metallic	S
Red	T
Med. Aqua Metallic	U
Lt. Blue	V
Yellow	W
Dk. Blue Metallic	X
Nugget Bold Metallic	Y
Dk. Gray Metallic	Z
Rose Metallic	2
Vermillion	3
Low Gloss Black	5
Lt. Beige	6

ENGINE NUMBER

The engine tag is located under the coil attaching bolt.

MONTEGO

ENGINE NO.	NO. CYL.	CID	HORSE-POWER	COMP. RATIO	CARB	TRANS
T	6	200	115	8.8:1	1 BC	** M & A
2*	6	200	N/A	N/A	1 BC	** M & A
F	8	302	210	9.0:1	2 BC	** M & A
6*	8	302	N/A	N/A	2 BC	** M & A
J	8	302	230	10.0:1	4 BC	** M & A
Y	8	390	265	9.5:1	2 BC	** M & A
S	8	390	325	10.5:1	4 BC	** M & A
W	8	427	390	10.9:1	4 BC	AUTO
Q	8	428	335	10.6:1	4 BC	** M & A

* Export

COUGAR

ENGINE NO.	NO. CYL.	CID	HORSE-POWER	COMP. RATIO	CARB	TRANS
C+	8	289	200	9.3:1	2 BC	** M & A
3*	8	289	N/A	N/A	2 BC	** M & A
F+	8	302	210	9.0:1	2 BC	** M & A
6*	8	302	N/A	N/A	2 BC	** M & A
J	8	302	230	10.0:1	4 BC	** M & A
X	8	390	280	10.5:1	2 BC	** M & A
S	8	390	325	10.5:1	4 BC	** M & A
W	8	427	390	10.9:1	4 BC	AUTO
Q	8	428	335	10.6:1	4 BC	** M & A

* Export
+ As of 1-68

MERCURY MONTEREY, MONTCLAIR

ENGINE NO.	NO. CYL.	CID	HORSE-POWER	COMP. RATIO	CARB	TRANS
Y	8	390	265	9.5:1	2 BC	** M & A
X	8	390	280	10.5:1	2 BC	AUTO
Z	8	390	315	10.5:1	4 BC	** M & A
Q	8	428	340	10.5:1	4 BC	AUTO
8*	8	428	N/A	N/A	4 BC	AUTO
P	8	428	360	10.5:1	4 BC	AUTO

* Export

MERCURY PARKLANE, MARQUIS, BROUGHAM

ENGINE NO.	NO. CYL.	CID	HORSE-POWER	COMP. RATIO	CARB	TRANS
Z	8	390	315	10.5:1	4 BC	** M & A
Q	8	428	340	10.5:1	4 BC	AUTO
8*	8	428	N/A	N/A	4 BC	AUTO
P	8	428	360	10.5:1	4 BC	AUTO

* Export

LINCOLN

ENGINE NO.	NO. CYL.	CID	HORSE-POWER	COMP. RATIO	CARB	TRANS
G	8	462	340	10.25:1	4 BC	AUTO
7*	8	462	N/A	N/A	4 BC	AUTO
A	8	460	265	10-5:1	4 BC	AUTO
1*	8	460	N/A	N/A	4 BC	AUTO

* Export
** MAN & AUTO

1969 LINCOLN / MERCURY

1969 LINCOLN CONTINENTAL

1969 LINCOLN CONTINENTAL MARK III

1969 MERCURY COUGAR

1969 MERCURY COUGAR

1969 MERCURY COMET

1969 MERCURY CYCLONE

1969 MERCURY MARAUDER

1969 MERCURY MARQUIS

1969 MERCURY MONTEGO

1969 MERCURY MONTEREY

VEHICLE IDENTIFICATION NUMBER

LINCOLN / MERCURY
9H82A800551

VIN LOCATION

LINCOLN VIN is die-stamped on the metal tab aluminum riveted to the instrument panel on the left hand side. The VIN is visible through the windshield.

MERCURY VIN is die-stamped on the metal tab aluminum riveted to the instrument panel on the left hand side. The VIN is visible through the windshield.

FIRST DIGIT: Identifies the model year (1969)

SECOND DIGIT: Identifies the assembly plant

ASSEMBLY PLANT	CODE
Atlanta, GA	A
Oakville, CAN	B
Ontario Truck	C
Dallas, TX	D
Mahwah, NJ	E
Dearborn, MI	F
Chicago, IL	G
Lorain, OH	H
Los Angeles, CA	J
Kansas City, KS	K
Michigan Truck	L
Norfolk, VA	N
Twin Cities, MN	P
San Jose, CA	R
Allen Park (Pilot Plant)	S
Metuchen, NJ	T
Louisville, KY	U
Wayne, MI	W
St. Thomas, Ont., CAN	X
Wixom, MI	Y
St. Louis, MO	Z

THIRD AND FOURTH DIGITS: Identify the body series

LINCOLN CONTINENTAL	CODE
4-Dr. Sedan	82
2-Dr. Hardtop	80

CONTINENTAL MARK II	CODE
2-Dr. Hardtop	89

COUGAR - STANDARD	CODE
2-Dr. Hardtop	91
Convertible	92

COUGAR - XR-7 Luxury	CODE
2-Dr. Hardtop	93
Convertible	94

MERCURY MONTEREY	CODE
4-Dr. Sedan	44
2-Dr. Hardtop	46
4-Dr. Hardtop	48
Convertible	45

MARQUIS (CANADA ONLY)	CODE
4-Dr. Hardtop Sedan	40
2-Dr. Hardtop	41
4-Dr. Hardtop	42

MONTEREY CUSTOM	CODE
4-Dr. Sedan	54
2-Dr. Hardtop	56
4-Dr. Hardtop	58

MARQUIS (U.S.)/BROUGHAM (CAN)	CODE
4-Dr. Hardtop Sedan	63
2-Dr. Hardtop	66
4-Dr. Hardtop	68
Convertible	65

MERCURY MARAUDER	CODE
2-Dr. Hardtop	60
2-Dr. Hardtop	61

MONTEREY WAGON	CODE
4-Dr., 2-Seat	72
4-Dr., 3-Seat (Side Facing)	72

MONTEREY CUSTOM WAGON	CODE
4-Dr., 2 Seat	74
4-Dr., 3- Seat (Side Facing)	74

MARQUIS COLONY PARK	CODE
4-Dr., 2-Seat	76
4-Dr., 3 Seat (Side Facing)	76

MONTEGO COMET	CODE
2-Dr. Hardtop	01
4-Dr. Sedan	02

MONTEGO	CODE
4-Dr. Sedan	06
2-Dr. Hardtop	07

MONTEGO MX/BROUGHAM	CODE
4-Dr. Sedan	10
2-Dr. Hardtop	11
Convertible	12

CYCLONE/CYCLONE CJ	CODE
2-Dr. Hardtop	15
2-Dr. Hardtop GT	16
Option - Spoiler	

STATION WAGONS	CODE
Montego	03
Montego MX	08

FIFTH DIGIT: Identifies the engine code

ENGINE	CODE
6 Cyl. 250 Cu. In. (1-V)	L
6 Cyl. *250 Cu. In. (1-V)	3
8 Cyl. 302 Cu. In. (2-V)	F
8 Cyl. 302 Cu. In. (2-V)	6
8 Cyl. 351 Cu. IN. (2-V)	H
8 Cyl. 351 Cu. In. (4-V)	M
8 Cyl. 390 Cu. In. (2-V)	Y
8 Cyl. 390 Cu. In. (2-V) Prem. Fuel	X
8 Cyl. 390 Cu. In. (4-V)	S
8 Cyl. 428 Cu. In. (4-V) CJ	Q
8 Cyl. 428 Cu. In. (4-V) CJ Ram Air	R
8 Cyl. 428 Cu. In. (4-V) Prem. Fuel (Police)	P
8 Cyl. 429 Cu. In. (2-V)	K
8 Cyl. 429 Cu. In. (4-V)	N
8 Cyl. 460 Cu. In. (4-V)	A

* Low compression

LAST SIX DIGITS: Represent the basic production numbers

BODY NUMBER PLATE

The vehicle data appears on the second or lower line on the Body Plate. The first two numbers and a letter identify the body style. A letter or a number appears next indicating the exterior paint color followed by a number-letter combination designating the interior trim. To the right of this code appears the date code indicating the date the car was manufactured. A two-digit number next designates the District in which the car was ordered and may appear in conjunction with a Domestic Special Order or Foreign Special Order number when applicable. The final two spaces indicate the rear axle ratio (numbers for regular axles, letters for locking-types) and the transmission type (numbers for manual, letters for automatic).

FORD MOTOR
CORPORATION

SERIAL NUMBER
9H82A500551

53A	A	3A	11G	32	4	U
BDY	CLR	TRM	DT	DSO	AX	TR

Serial Number

9	Model Year (1969)
H	Assembly Plant (Lorain, OH)
82	Body Series (Lincoln Cont.)
A	Engine (390 C.I. 8 Cyl.)
500551	Production Sequence

53A	Body Style (4-Dr. Sedan)
A	Body Color
3A	Trim
11G	Date Production Code
32	DSO Number
4	Axle (2.80:1)
U	Transmission (Automatic C6)

LINCOLN CONTINENTAL/MARK II	CODE
4-Dr. Sedan	53A
2-Dr. Hardtop	65A

COUGAR - STANDARD	CODE
2-Dr. Hardtop*	65C
2-Dr. Hardtop	65A
Convertible	76A

* Option: Eliminator
Option: Spoiler

COUGAR - XR-7 LUXURY	CODE
2-Dr. Hardtop	65B
Convertible	76B

MERCURY MONTEREY	CODE
4-Dr. Sedan	54A
2-Dr. Hardtop Formal	65A
4-Dr. Hardtop	57A
Convertible	76A

MARQUIS (CANADA ONLY)	CODE
4-Dr. Hardtop Sedan	53M
2-Dr. Hardtop Formal	65M
4-Dr. Hardtop	57M

MONTEREY - CUSTOM	CODE
4-Dr. Sedan	54C
2-Dr. Hardtop Formal	65B
4-Dr. Hardtop	57B

MARQUIS (U.S.)/BROUGHAM (CAN)	CODE
4-Dr. Hardtop Sedan	53F
2-Dr. Hardtop Formal	65F
4-Dr. Hardtop	57F
Convertible	76F

BROUGHAM (Option)	CODE
4-Dr. Hardtop Sedan	53C
2-Dr. Hardtop Formal	65C
4-Dr. Hardtop	57C

MERCURY MARAUDER	CODE
2-Dr. Hardtop	63G
2-Dr. Hardtop	63H

MONTEREY WAGON	CODE
4-Dr., 2-Seat	71B
4-Dr., 3-Seat	71C

MONTEREY CUSTOM WAGON	CODE
4-Dr., 2-Seat	71F
4-Dr., 3-Seat	71G

MARQUIS COLONY PARK	CODE
4-Dr., 2-Seat	71E
4-Dr., 3-Seat	71A

MONTEGO COMET	CODE
2-Dr. Hardtop	65A
4-Dr. Sedan	54A

MONTEGO	CODE
4-Dr. Sedan	54B
2-Dr. Hardtop	65B

MONTEGO MX	CODE
4-Dr. Sedan	54D
2-Dr. Hardtop	65D
Convertible	76D

MONTEGO MX	CODE
2-Dr. Hardtop	65E
Convertible	76B

MONTEGO MX BROUGHAM	CODE
4-Dr. Sedan	54C
2-Dr. Hardtop	65C

CYCLONE/CYCLONE CJ	CODE
2-Dr. Hardtop	63A
2-Dr. Hardtop	63C
2-Dr. Hardtop GT	63H

STATION WAGONS	CODE
Montego	71B
Montego MX	71C
Montego MX	71A

THE DAY AND MONTH CODE furnishes the date the vehicle was manufactued. The number indicates the day of the month and the letter indicates the month.

MONTH	CODE	CODE
January	A	N
February	B	P
March	C	Q
April	D	R
May	E	S
June	F	T
July	G	U
August	H	V
September	J	W
October	K	X
November	L	Y
December	M	Z

*2 year code letters to be used if 1969 models exceed 12 months.

DSO AND DISTRICT CODES

Units built on a Domestic Special Order, Foreign Special Order, or other special orders will have the complete order numer in this space. Also to appear in this space is the two-digit code number of the District which ordered the unit. If the unit is a regular production unit, only the District code number will appear.

LINCOLN/MERCURY

DISTRICT	CODE
Boston	11
New York	15
Philadelphia	16
Washington	17
Atlanta	21
Dallas	22
Jacksonville	23
Memphis	26
Buffalo	31
Cincinnati	32
Cleveland	33
Detroit	34
Chicago	41
St. Louis	42
Twin Cities	46
Denver	51
Los Angeles	52
Oakland	53
Seattle	54
Home Office Reserve	84
Export	90

THE REAR AXLE RATIO CODE indicates the ratio fo the rear axle installed in the vehicle. A number designates a conventional axle, while a letter designates an Equa-Lock differential.

AXLE RATIO	CONV.	LIMITED-SLIP
2.50:1	1	J
2.75:1	2	K
2.79:1	3	L
2.80:1	4	M
2.83:1	5	N
3.00:1	6	O
3.10:1	7	P
3.20:1	8	Q
3.25:1	9	R
3.50:1	A	S
3.07:1	3	T
3.08:1	C	U
3.91:1	D	V
4.30:1	E	W

THE TRANSMISSION CODE indicates the type of transmission installed in the vehicle.

TRANSMISSION	CODE
3-Speed Manual	1
4-Speed Manual - Wide Ratio	5
4-Speed Manual - Close Ratio	6
C-4 Automatic	W
C-6 Automatic	U
Automatic (FMX)	X
Automatic MX	Y
C-6 Automatic Special	Z

THE TRIM NUMBER furnishes the key to trim color and material for each model series.

CONTINENTAL/MARK II TRIM

COLOR	CLOTH	VINYL	LEATHER	CODE
Black	•	•		1A,4A,6A,AA
Black		•	•	2A,3A,5A
Black		•	•	7A,KA,LA
Blue	•	•		1B,AB,JB
Blue		•	•	2B,5B,KB
Blue		•	•	7B,BB,SB
Blue		•	•	3B,LB
Red	•	•		1D
Red		•	•	2D,5D
Saddle		•	•	2F,5F
Gold	•	•		1G,4G,AG,JG
Gold		•	•	2G,5G,KG
Gold		•	•	BG,SG,7G
Gold		•	•	3G,LG,CG,TG
Aqua	•	•		1K,AK
Aqua		•	•	2K,5K
Gray	•	•		1P
Gray		•	•	2P
White		•	•	2W,5W,KW
White		•	•	7W,3W,LW
Nugget	•	•		1Y,AY,JY
Nugget		•	•	2Y,5Y
Silver		•	•	KL,AL
Green		•	•	7G,3G,LG
Green		•	•	CG,TG

MONTEREY TRIM

COLOR	CLOTH	VINYL	LEATHER	CODE
Black	•	•		1A
Black		•		2A
Blue	•	•		1B
Blue		•		2B
Gold	•	•		1G
Gold		•		2G
Aqua	•	•		1K
Nugget	•	•		1Y
Nugget		•		2Y
Red		•		2D
White		•		2W

MONTEREY CUSTOM TRIM

COLOR	CLOTH	VINYL	LEATHE	CODE
Black	•	•		3A
Black		•		4A
Blue	•	•		3B
Blue		•		4B
Gold	•	•		3G
Gold		•		4G
Aqua	•	•		3K
Nugget	•	•		3Y
Nugget		•		4Y
Red		•		4D
White		•		4W

MONTEREY CUSTOM WAGON TRIM

COLOR	CLOTH	VINYL	LEATHER	CODE
Black		•		4A
Blue		•		4B
Red		•		4D
Gold		•		4G
Nugget		•		4Y
Nugget	•	•		3Y

MARAUDER TRIM

COLOR	CLOTH	VINYL	LEATHER	CODE
Black	•	•		1A
Black		•		2A,8A,VA
Black		•	•	RA
Blue	•	•		1B
Blue		•		2B,8B,VB
Gold	•	•		1G
Gold		•		2G,8G
Aqua	•	•		1K
Nugget	•	•		1Y
Nugget		•		VY
Red		•		2D,8D
Red		•	•	RD
White		•		2W,8W,VW
White		•	•	RW

MARQUIS TRIM

COLOR	CLOTH	VINYL	LEATHER	CODE
Black	•	•		5A,EA,ZA
Black		•		6A,FA,VA
Black		•	•	RA,HA
Blue	•	•		5B,EB,ZB
Blue		•		6B,FB,VB
Red		•		6D
Red	•	•		5D,ED
Red		•	•	RD,HD
Gold	•	•		5G,EG,ZG
Gold		•		6G,FG
Aqua	•	•		5K,EK
Aqua		•		6K
Nugget	•	•		5Y,EY
Nugget		•		6Y,VY
White		•		6W,FW,VW
White		•	•	RW,HW

MARQUIS BROUGHAM TRIM

COLOR	CLOTH	VINYL	LEATHER	CODE
Black	•	•		KA
Blue	•	•		KB
Red	•	•		KD
Gold	•	•		KG
Nugget	•	•		KY

MARQUIS COLONY PARK WAGON TRIM

COLOR	CLOTH	VINYL	LEATHER	CODE
Black		•		4A,DA,VA
Blue		•		4B,DB,VB
Red		•		4D,DD
Gold		•		4G,DG,VG
Nugget		•		4Y,DY,VY
Nugget	•	•		3Y,CY,7Y

MONTEGO COMET TRIM

COLOR	CLOTH	VINYL	LEATHER	CODE
Black	•	•		KA
Blue	•	•		KB
Nugget	•	•		KY

MONTEGO TRIM

COLOR	CLOTH	VINYL	LEATHER	CODE
Black	•	•		1A
Black		•		2A
Blue	•	•		1B
Blue		•		2B
Nugget	•	•		1Y
Red		•		2D
Nugget		•		2Y

MONTEGO MX TRIM

COLOR	CLOTH	VINYL	LEATHER	CODE
Black	•	•		5A
Black		•		3A,RA,6A
Black		•		MA*
Blue	•	•		5B
Blue		•		3B,RB,6B
Blue		•		MB*
Red		•		3D,RD,MD*
Red	•	•		5D,6D
Gold	•	•		5G
Gold	•	•		6G
Aqua	•	•		5K
Aqua	•	•		6K
Nugget	•	•		5Y
Nugget		•		3Y,RY,6Y
White		•		3W,RW,6W
White		•		MW*

* Convertible only

MONTEGO MX BROUGHAM TRIM

COLOR	CLOTH	VINYL	LEATHER	CODE
Black	•	•		7A
Blue	•	•		7B
Red	•	•		7D
Gold	•	•		7G
Nugget	•	•		7Y

1969 LINCOLN / MERCURY

MONTEGO MX WAGON TRIM

COLOR	CLOTH	VINYL	LEATHER	CODE
Black		•		9A
Blue		•		9B
Red		•		9D
Nugget		•		9Y

CYCLONE TRIM

COLOR	CLOTH	VINYL	LEATHER	CODE
Black		•		4A,LA,8A
Blue		•		4B,LB,8B
Red		•		4D,LD,8D
Gold		•		4G
Aqua		•		4K
White		•		4W,LW,8W
Nugget		•		4Y,LY,8Y

CYCLONE CJ TRIM

COLOR	CLOTH	VINYL	LEATHER	CODE
Black		•		2A,CA
Blue		•		2B,CB
Red		•		2D,CD
Nugget		•		2Y,CY

COUGAR TRIM

COLOR	CLOTH	VINYL	LEATHER	CODE
Black		•		1A
Blue		•		1B
Red		•		1D
Gold		•		1G
White/Black		•		AA
White/Blue		•		AB
White/Red		•		AD
White/Gold		•		AG

COUGAR CONVERTIBLE TRIM

COLOR	CLOTH	VINYL	LEATHER	CODE
Black		•		2A,4A
Blue		•		2B,4B
Red		•		2D,4D
Saddle		•		2F
Gold		•		2G
Aqua		•		2K
Nugget		•		2Y
White/Black		•		BA,DA
White/Blue		•		BB,DB
White/Red		•		BD,DD
White/Gold		•		BG
White/Aqua		•		BK
White/Nugget		•		BY

COUGAR XR-7 TRIM

COLOR	CLOTH	VINYL	LEATHER	CODE
Black		•	•	6A
Black		•		8A
Blue		•	•	6B
Blue		•		8B
Red		•	•	6D
Red		•		8D
Saddle		•	•	6F
Saddle		•		8F
Gold		•	•	6G
Aqua		•	•	6K
Nugget		•	•	6Y
White/Black		•	•	FA
White/Blue		•	•	FB
White/Red		•	•	FD
White/Gold		•	•	FG
White/Aqua		•	•	FK
White/Nugget		•	•	FY

VINYL/CONVERTIBLE ROOF COLORS

COLOR	CODE
Black	2
White	4
Blue	5

THE PAINT CODE furnishes the key to the paint colors used on the car. A letter indicates the color of the car. A two-tone car has two sets of letters. The first indicates the lower body color, the second the upper body color.

COLOR	CODE
Black	A
Maroon	B
Dk. Ivy Green Metallic	C
Pastel Gray	D
Lt. Aqua	E
Dk. Aqua Metallic	F
Med. Orchid Metallic	G
Lt. Green	H
Med. Lime Metallic	I
Dk. Aqua Metallic	J
Dk. Orchid Metallic	K
Lt. Gray Metallic	L
White	M
Platinum	N
Med. Blue Metallic	P
Med. Blue Metallic	Q
Lt. Gold	R
Med. Gold Metallic	S
Red	T
Med. Aqua Metallic	U
Lt. Aurora Copper Metallic	V
Yellow	W
Dk. Blue Metallic	X
Burnt Orange Metallic	Y
Dk. Gray Metallic	Z
Lt. Ivy Yellow	2
Calpyso Coral	3
Med. Emerald Metallic	4
Med. Blue Metallic	6
Lt. Emerald Green Metallic	7
Lt. Blue	8
Red Primer	9
Gray Primer	9

1969 LINCOLN / MERCURY

ENGINE NUMBER

The engine tag is located under the coil attaching bolt.

COMET, MONTEGO, MONTEGO MX

ENGINE NO.	NO. CYL.	CID	HORSE-POWER	COMP. RATIO	CARB	TRANS
L	6	250	250	9.5:1	1 BC	*** M & A
3*	6	250	N/A	N/A	1 BC	*** M & A
F	8	302	220	9.5:1	2 BC	*** M & A
6*	8	302	N/A	N/A	2 BC	*** M & A
H	8	351	250	9.5:1	2 BC	*** M & A
M	8	351	290	10.7:1	4 BC	*** M & A
S	8	390	320	10.5:1	4 BC	*** M & A
Q**	8	428	335	10.6:1	4 BC	*** M & A
R+	8	428	335	10.6:1	4 bc	*** M & A
P	8	428	360	10.5:1	4 BC	*** M & A

* Export
+ Ram Air
** Police

MONTEGO MX BROUGHAM

ENGINE NO.	NO. CYL.	CID	HORSE-POWER	COMP. RATIO	CARB	TRANS
L	6	250	155	9.0:1	1 BC	*** M & A
3*	6	250	N/A	N/A	1 BC	*** M & A
F	8	302	220	9.5:1	2 BC	*** M & A
G*	8	302	N/A	N/A	2 BC	*** M & A
H	8	351	250	9.5:1	2 BC	*** M & A
M	8	351	290	10.7:1	4 BC	*** M & A
S	8	390	320	10.5:1	4 BC	*** M & A

* Export

CYCLONE

ENGINE NO.	NO. CYL.	CID	HORSE-POWER	COMP. RATIO	CARB	TRANS
F	8	302	220	9.5:1	2 BC	*** M & A
6*	8	302	N/A	N/A	2 BC	*** M & A
H	8	351	250	9.5:1	2 BC	*** M & A
M	8	351	290	10.7:1	4 BC	MAN/AUOT
S	8	390	320	10.5:1	4 BC	*** M & A
Q	8	428	335	10.6:1	4 BC	*** M & A
K+	8	429	320	10.5:1	2 BC	

* Export
+ Ram Air

CYCLONE CJ

ENGINE NO.	NO. CYL.	CID	HORSE-POWER	COMP. RATIO	CARB	TRANS
Q	8	428	335	10.6:1	4 BC	*** M & A
R+	8	428	335	10.6:1	4 BC	*** M & A

CYCLONE SPOILER

ENGINE NO.	NO. CYL.	CID	HORSE-POWER	COMP. RATIO	CARB	TRANS
M	8	351	290	10.7:1	4 BC	*** M & A
R+	8	351	335	10.6:1	4 BC	*** M & A
Z	8	429	370	10.5:1	4 BC	*** M & A

+ Ram Air

COUGAR

ENGINE NO.	NO. CYL.	CID	HORSE-POWER	COMP. RATIO	CARB	TRANS
H	8	351	250	9.5:1	2 BC	*** M & A
M	8	351	290	10.7:1	4 BC	*** M & A
S	8	390	320	10.5:1	4 BC	*** M & A
Q	8	428	335	10.6:1	4 BC	*** M & A
R+	8	428	335	10.6:1	4 BC	*** M & A
G**	8	302	290	10.5:1	4 BC	MAN
G**	8	302	N/A	N/A	2-4 BC	MAN
Z	8	429	370	10.5:1	4 BC	*** M & A

MERCURY MONTEREY, MONTEREY CUSTOM AND MARAUDER

ENGINE NO.	NO. CYL.	CID	HORSE-POWER	COMP. RATIO	CARB	TRANS
Y	8	390	265	9.5:1	2 BC	*** M & A
X	8	390	280	10.5:1	2 BC	*** M & A
K	8	429	320	10.5:1	2 BC	AUTO
N	8	429	360	10.5:1	4 BC	AUTO

MARAUDER X-100

ENGINE NO.	NO. CYL.	CID	HORSE-POWER	COMP. RATIO	CARB	TRANS
N	8	429	360	10.5:1	4 BC	AUTO

MARQUIS, MARQUIS BROUGHAM

ENGINE NO.	NO. CYL.	CID	HORSE-POWER	COMP. RATIO	CARB	TRANS
K	8	429	320	10.5:1	2 BC	AUTO
N	8	429	360	10.5:1	4 BC	AUTO

LINCOLN

ENGINE NO.	NO. CYL.	CID	HORSE-POWER	COMP. RATIO	CARB	TRANS
A	8	460	365	10.5:1	4 BC	AUTO

*** MAN & AUTO

1960 EDSEL

1960 EDSEL

VEHICLE IDENTIFICATION NUMBER

EDSEL
0U13W-700001

The VIN is stamped into the top of the right side of the frame side-rail in front of the firewall.

FIRST DIGIT: Identifies the model year (1960)

SECOND DIGIT: Identifies the assembly plant

ASSEMBLY PLANT	CODE
Louisville, KY	U

THIRD AND FOURTH DIGITS: Identify the body type

BODY TYPE	CODE
2-Dr. Sedan (Ranger)	11
4-Dr. Sedan (Ranger)	12
2-Dr. Hardtop (Ranger)	13
4-Dr. Hardtop (Ranger)	14
Convertible (Ranger)	16
4-Dr. Sta. Wagon (Villager), 6-Pass.	17
4-Dr. Sta. Wagon (Villager), 9-Pass.	18

FIFTH DIGIT: Identifies the engine

ENGINE	CODE
223 CID 6-Cyl.	V
292 CID 2 BBL	W
292 CID Export	T
352 CID 4 BBL	Y
352 CID Export	G

LAST SIX DIGITS: Represent the basic production sequence

BODY NUMBER PLATE

The body code plate, which includes the serial number, body style, body color, trim code, date of assembly, transmission code, and axle ratio code, is riveted to the left front body pillar between the front door hinges.

SERIAL NUMBER 0U13W-700001	MADE IN U.S.A. BY EDSEL
BODY	63B
COLOR	AM
TRIM	11
DATE	15K
TRANS	3
AXLE	1

THE SERIAL NUMBER is a repeat of the VIN.

EXAMPLE:

63B	Body Style (Ranger, 2-Dr. HD)
A	Lower Body Color
M	Upper Body Color
11	Trim
15K	Production Date
3	Transmission (2-Spd)
1	Axle (3:56)

BODY STYLE

RANGER	CODE
2-Dr. Sedan	64A
4-Dr. Sedan	58A
	58B
2-Dr. Hardtop	63A
	63B
4-Dr. Hardtop	57A
	57B
2-Dr. Convertible	76B

VILLAGER	CODE
4-Dr. Sta. Wagon, 6-Pass.	71F
4-Dr. Sta. Wagon, 9-Pass.	71E

THE DAY/MONTH CODE number indicates the day of the month the vehicle was built and the letter indicates the month.

MONTH	CODE
January	A
February	B
March	C
April	D
May	E
June	F
July	G
August	H
September	J
October	K
November	L
December	M

THE TRANSMISSION CODE number indicates the type of transmission installed in the vehicle.

TRANSMISSION	CODE
Standard	1
Mile-O-Matic (2-speed)	3
Dual Power (3-speed)	4

THE REAR AXLE RATIO CODE indicates the ratio of the axle installed in the vehicle.

STD	EQUA-LOCK	AXLE RATIO
1	A	3:56
2	B	3:89
3	C	3:10
8		2:91

THE TRIM NUMBER furnishes the key to the interior color and material.

RANGER STANDARD TRIM

COLOR	CLOTH	VINYL	LEATHER	CODE
Silver/Black	•	•		20
Blue/Black	•	•		22
Green/Brown	•	•		23
Gold/Brown	•	•		24
Red/Black	•	•		25

RANGER CONVERTIBLE TRIM

COLOR	CLOTH	VINYL	LEATHER	CODE
Gold		•		54
Red/Silver		•		55
Black		•		56
Turquoise		•		57

RANGER DELUXE TRIM

COLOR	CLOTH	VINYL	LEATHER	CODE
Silver/Gray	•	•		11
Red/Gray	•	•		15
Turquoise/ Gray	•	•		17

THE PAINT CODE furnishes the key to the paint used on the car. A two-digit code indicates the top and bottom colors respectively. The first letter is the lower color and the second letter the upper color.

COLOR	CODE
Black Velvet	A
Turquoise	C
Cadet Blue Metallic	E
Hawaiian Blue	F
Alaskan Gold Metallic	H
Regal Red	J
Turquoise Metallic	K
Polar White	M
Sahara Beige	N
Lilac Metallic	Q
Buttercup Yellow	R
Sherwood Green Metallic	U
Sea Foam Green	W
Cloud Silver Metallic	Z

ENGINE NUMBER

The engine number is stamped on a boss behind the water pump. The number provides the code to identify the series, block, displacement, and month/day production date.

ENGINE NO.	NO. CYL.	CID	HORSE-POWER	COMP. RATIO	CARB	TRANS
R-22	6	223	145	8.4:1	1 BC	
R-29	8	292	185	8.8:1	2 BC	
R-35	8	352	300	9.6:1	4 BC	

1960 CHRYSLER / IMPERIAL

1960 CHRYSLER

1960 CHRYSLER

1960 CHRYSLER 300F

1960 IMPERIAL

1960 IMPERIAL

VEHICLE IDENTIFICATION NUMBER

CHRYSLER
8203100551

The vehicle number (serial number) is stamped and embossed on a stainless steel plate attached to the left front door hinge pillar. It consists of car make symbol, series code, model year code, assembly plant symbol, and a sequential production number.

FIRST DIGIT: Identifies the car make

Chrysler	8
Imperial	9

SECOND DIGIT: Identifies the series

SERIES	CODE
Windsor, Imperial Custom	1
Saratoga, Imperial Crown	2
New Yorker, Imperial LeBaron	3
300F	4
Windsor, Station Wagon	5
New Yorker, Town & Country Station Wagon	7
Taxi	8
Crown Limousine	9

THIRD DIGIT: Identifies the model year (1960)

FOURTH DIGIT: Identifes the assembly plant

ASSEMBLY PLANT	CODE
Jefferson Plant, Detroit, MI	3
Imperial Plant, Detroit, MI	4
Los Angeles, CA	5
Newark, DE	6
Windsor, Ont., CAN	9

LAST SIX DIGITS: Represent the basic production numbers

BODY NUMBER PLATE

THE BODY NUMBER PLATE is stamped and embossed on a stainless steel plate under the hood. It is attached to the right or left fender, cowl, or radiator cross member depending on the model and assembly plant. This plate will indicate schedule date, body production number, body series, trim, paint, and accessory code.

CHRYSLER MOTORS CORPORATION

SO	NUMBER	BDY	TRM	PNT
0224	0555	812	101	BB1

EXAMPLE:

0224	SO (February 24)
0555	Production Sequence
812	Body Style (Windsor 2-Dr.)
101	Trim
BB1	Color (Formal Black)

THE SHIPPING ORDER NUMBER is assigned prior to production. It consists of a four-digit planned delivery month/day date code, 0224 (February 24th). Then a plant production sequence number follows (0555).

THE BODY NUMBER is a three-digit number which indicates the model and body style.

WINDSOR	CODE
2-Dr. Hardtop	812
4-Dr. Sedan	813
4-Dr. Hardtop	814
2-Dr. Convertible	815
4-Dr. Town & Country Wagon, 2-Seat	858
4-Dr. Town & Country Wagon, 3-Seat	859

SARATOGA	CODE
2-Dr. Hardtop	822
4-Dr. Sedan	823
4-Dr. Hardtop	824

NEW YORKER	CODE
2-Dr. Hardtop	832
4-Dr. Sedan	833
4-Dr. Hardtop	834
2-Dr. Convertible	835
4-Dr. Town & Country Wagon, 2-Seat	878
4-Dr. Town & Country Wagon, 3-Seat	879

300F	CODE
2-Dr. Hardtop	842
4-Dr. Convertible	845

IMPERIAL CUSTOM	CODE
2-Dr. Southhampton	912
4-Dr. Sedan	913
4-Dr. Southhampton	914

IMPERIAL CROWN	CODE
2-Dr. Southhampton	922
4-Dr. Sedan	923
4-Dr. Southhampton	924
2-Dr. Convertible	925

IMPERIAL LEBARON	CODE
4-Dr. Sedan	933
4-Dr. Southhampton	934

CROWN IMPERIAL	CODE
4-Dr. Limousine, 8-Pass.	993

1960 CHRYSLER / IMPERIAL

THE TRIM NUMBER furnishes the key to the interior color and material.

WINDSOR TRIM

COLOR	CLOTH	VINYL	LEATHER	CODE
Blue				101
Tan				103,113
Silver				104
Turquoise				105
Mauve				106
Terra Cotta				107
Black				114,134
Red				118,138
White				119,139
Blue				131,141
Black/Tan				143
Black/Silver				144

SARATOGA TRIM

COLOR	CLOTH	VINYL	LEATHER	CODE
Blue				221,201,241
Tan				223,203
Silver				224,204
Turquoise				225,205
Mauve				226,206
Terra Cotta				227,207
Black				234
Red				238
White				239
Tan/Black				243
Silver/Black				244

NEW YORKER TRIM

COLOR	CLOTH	VINYL	LEATHER	CODE
Blue				361,321,301
Blue				331,341
Tan				363,323
Tan				303,313
Silver				364
Terra Cotta				367,327,307
Black				324,314,334
Turquoise				325,305
Mauve				326,306
Red				318,338
White				319,339
Silver/Black				304,344
Tan/Black				343

THE PAINT CODE furnishes the key to the paint used on the car. A two- digit code indicates the top and bottom colors respectively. A number follows which designates two-tone, sports-tone, convertible top, etc.

CODE	COLOR
Sunburst	A
Formal Black	B
Starlight Blue	C
Polar Blue	D
Surf Green	F
Ivy Green	G
Silverpine	H
Seaspray	J
Bluegrass	K
Sheffield Silver	L
Executive Gray	N
Toreador Red	P
Lilac	R
Iris	S
Daytona Sand	T
Autumn Haze	U
Alaskan White	W
Petal Pink	Y
Terra Cotta	Z

ENGINE NUMBER

The engine number is stamped on a boss behind the water pump. The number provides the code to identify the series, block, displacement, and month/day production date.

EXAMPLE:

P	38	____	2	24
YEAR	383	*	FEBRUARY	24th DAY

* Non-standard designation

WINDSOR

ENGINE NO.	NO. CYL.	CID	HORSE-POWER	COMP. RATIO	CARB	TRANS
PR-38	8	383	305	10.1:1	2 BC	MAN/AUTO

SARATOGA

ENGINE NO.	NO. CYL.	CID	HORSE-POWER	COMP. RATIO	CARB	TRANS
PR-38	8	383	325	10.1:1	4 BC	AUTO
P-41	8	413	350	10.1:1	4 BC	AUTO

NEW YORKER/IMPERIAL

ENGINE NO.	NO. CYL.	CID	HORSE-POWER	COMP. RATIO	CARB	TRANS
P-41	8	413	350	10.1:1	4 BC	AUTO

300F

ENGINE NO.	NO. CYL.	CID	HORSE-POWER	COMP. RATIO	CARB	TRANS
P-41	8	413	375	10.1:1	2-4 BC	AUTO
P-41	8	413	400	10.1:1	2-4 BC	MAN

*If it has code after 38 or 41:

A - .020" overbore
B - .010" undersize journals
AB - Both
* - .008" oversize valve lifters

 1961 CHRYSLER / IMPERIAL

1961 CHRYSLER

1961 CHRYSLER

1961 CHRYSLER 300G

1961 IMPERIAL

1961 IMPERIAL

1961 CHRYSLER / IMPERIAL

VEHICLE IDENTIFICATION NUMBER

CHRYSLER
8214100551

The vehicle number (serial number) is stamped and embossed on a stainless steel plate attached to the left front door hinge pillar. It consists of car make symbol, series code, model year code, assembly plant symbol, and a sequential production number.

FIRST DIGIT: Identifies the car make

Chrysler	8
Imperial	9

SECOND DIGIT: Identifies the series

Newport, Imperial Custom	1
Windsor, Imperial Crown	2
New Yorker, Imperial LeBaron	3
300G	4
Newport Station Wagon	5
New Yorker Station Wagon	7
Taxi	8
Police	9
Crown Limousine	10

THIRD DIGIT: Identifies the model year (1961)

FOURTH DIGIT: Identifies the assembly plant

ASSEMBLY PLANT	CODE
Jefferson Plant, Detroit, MI	3
Imperial Plant, Detroit, MI	4
Los Angeles, CA	5
Newark, DE	6
St. Louis, MO	7

LAST SIX DIGITS: Represent the basic production numbers

BODY NUMBER PLATE

THE BODY PLATE is stamped and embossed on a stainless steel plate under the hood. It is attached to the right or left fender, cowl, or radiator cross member depending on the model and assembly plant. This plate will indicate schedule date, body production number, body series, trim, paint, and accessory code.

CHRYSLER MOTORS CORPORATION

SO	NUMBER	BDY	TRM	PNT
0224	0555	812	701	BB1

EXAMPLE:

0224	SO (February 24)
0555	Production Sequence
812	Body Style (Windsor 2-Dr.)
701	Trim
B	Lower Body Color
B	Upper Body Color

THE SHIPPING ORDER NUMBER is assigned prior to production. It consists of a four-digit planned delivery month/day date code, 0224 (February 24th). Then a plant production sequence number follows (0555).

THE BODY NUMBER is a three-digit number which indicates the model and body style.

NEWPORT	CODE
2-Dr. Hardtop	812
4-Dr. Sedan	813
4-Dr. Hardtop	814
2-Dr. Convertible	815
4-Dr. Town & Country Wagon, 2-Seat	858
4-Dr. Town & Country Wagon, 3-Seat	859

WINDSOR	**CODE**
2-Dr. Hardtop	822
4-Dr. Sedan	823
4-Dr. Hardtop	824

NEW YORKER	**CODE**
2-Dr. Hardtop	832
4-Dr. Sedan	833
4-Dr. Hardtop	834
2-Dr. Convertible	835
4-Dr. Town & Country Wagon, 2-Seat	878
4-Dr. Town & Country Wagon, 3-Seat	879

300G	**CODE**
2-Dr. Hardtop	842
2-Dr. Convertible	845

IMPERIAL CUSTOM	**CODE**
2-Dr. Southhampton	912
4-Dr. Southhampton	914

IMPERIAL CROWN	**CODE**
2-Dr. Southhampton	922
4-Dr. Southhampton	924
2-Dr. Convertible	925

IMPERIAL LEBARON	**CODE**
4-Dr. Southhampton	934

1961 CHRYSLER / IMPERIAL

THE TRIM NUMBER furnishes the key to the interior color and material.

NEWPORT TRIM

COLOR	CLOTH	VINYL	LEATHER	CODE
Blue	•	•		701
Blue		•		801
Green	•	•		702
Brown	•	•		703
Black	•	•		704
Black		•		806
Cerise	•	•		709
Red		•		805
White		•		807
Tan		•		803

WINDSOR TRIM

COLOR	CLOTH	VINYL	LEATHER	CODE
Blue	•	•		711
Green	•	•		712
Brown	•	•		713
Black	•	•		714
Tan	•	•		719
Red		•		805
White		•		807

NEW YORKER TRIM

COLOR	CLOTH	VINYL	LEATHER	CODE
Green	•	•		732
Green	•			752
Tan	•	•		733
Tan	•			753
Tan		•		843
Black	•	•		734
Black	•			754
Black		•		826
Cerise	•	•		739
Cerise	•			759
Blue	•	•		731
Blue	•			721
Blue		•		821
Gray	•			724
Red		•		825,845
White		•		827

300G TRIM

COLOR	CLOTH	VINYL	LEATHER	CODE
Blue	•		•	921,971
Blue	•			931
Blue			•	951
Topaz	•		•	923,973
Topaz	•	•		903
Gray	•		•	924,974,923
Gray	•	•		904,906
Gray	•			934
Russet	•	•		908
Russet	•		•	978,924
Russet			•	958
Black	•		•	928
Black	•			966
Black			•	956
Green	•	•		902
Green	•		•	922
Red	•			965
Red		•		845
Red			•	955
White	•			967
White			•	957
Tan		•		803
Tan			•	833

THE PAINT CODE furnishes the key to the paint used on the car. A three-digit code indicates the top and bottom colors respectively. A number follows which designates two-tone, sports-tone, convertible top, etc.

COLOR	CODE
Formal Black	B
Parisian Blue	C
Capri Blue	D
Pinehurst Green	G
Tahitian Turquoise	J
Sheffield Silver	L
Dubonnet	O
Mardi Gras Red	P
Cinnamon	R
All Colors	W
Tuscan Bronze	Y
Alaskan White	Z

ENGINE NUMBER

The engine number is stamped on a boss behind the water pump. The number provides the code to identify the series, block, displacement, and month/day production date.

EXAMPLE:

R	38	___	2	24
YEAR	383	*	FEBRUARY	24th DAY

* Non-standard designation

NEWPORT

ENGINE NO.	NO. CYL.	CID	HORSE-POWER	COMP. RATIO	CARB	TRANS
R-36	8	361	265	9.0:1	2 BC	MAN/AUTO
R-41	8	413	350	10.1:1	4 BC	MAN/AUTO

WINDSOR

ENGINE NO.	NO. CYL.	CID	HORSE-POWER	COMP. RATIO	CARB	TRANS
R-38	8	383	305	10.0:1	2 BC	MAN/AUTO

NEW YORKER/IMPERIAL

ENGINE NO.	NO. CYL.	CID	HORSE-POWER	COMP. RATIO	CARB	TRANS
R-41	8	413	350	10.1:1	4 BC	AUTO

300G

ENGINE NO.	NO. CYL.	CID	HORSE-POWER	COMP. RATIO	CARB	TRANS
R-41	8	413	375	10.1:1	2-4 BC	MAN/AUTO
R-41	8	413	400	10.1:1	2-4 BC	MAN

*Non-standard designation
A - .020 overbore
Maltese Cross - .001" bearing undersize
X & Maltese Cross - .010" bearing undersize
* - .008" valve lifter oversize
HP - High performance engine

1962 CHRYSLER / IMPERIAL

1962 CHRYSLER

1962 CHRYSLER

1962 CHRYSLER 300

1962 CHRYSLER 300

1962 IMPERIAL

1962 IMPERIAL

 1962 CHRYSLER / IMPERIAL

VEHICLE IDENTIFICATION NUMBER

CHRYSLER
8323100551

The vehicle number (serial number) is stamped and embossed on a stainless steel plate attached to the left front door hinge pillar. It consists of car make symbol, series code, model year code, assembly plant symbol, and a sequential production number.

FIRST DIGIT: Identifies the car make

Chrysler	8
Imperial	9

SECOND DIGIT: Identifies the series

Newport, Imperial Custom	1
300, Imperial Crown	2
New Yorker, Imperial LeBaron	3
Newport Station Wagon	5
New Yorker Station Wagon	7
Taxi	8
Police	9
Commercial	10

THIRD DIGIT: Identifies the model year (1962)

FOURTH DIGIT: Identifies the assembly plant

ASSEMBLY PLANT	CODE
Jefferson Plant, Detroit, MI	3
Newark, DE	6

LAST SIX DIGITS: Represent the basic production numbers

BODY NUMBER PLATE

THE BODY PLATE is stamped and embossed on a stainless steel plate under the hood. It is attached to the right or left fender, cowl, or radiator cross member depending on the model and assembly plant. This plate will indicate schedule date, body production number, body series, trim, paint, and accessory code.

CHRYSLER MOTORS CORPORATION

SO	NUMBER	BDY	TRM	PNT
0224	0555	812	301	BB1

EXAMPLE:

0224	SO (February 24)
0555	Production Sequence
812	Body Style (Windsor 2-Dr.)
301	Trim
B	Lower Body Color
B	Upper Body Color

THE SHIPPING ORDER NUMBER is assigned prior to production. It consists of a four-digit planned delivery month/day date code, 0224 (February 24th). Then a plant production sequence number follows (0555).

THE BODY NUMBER is a three-digit number which indicates the model and body style.

NEWPORT	CODE
2-Dr. Hardtop	812
4-Dr. Sedan	813
4-Dr. Hardtop	814
2-Dr. Convertible	815
Suburban, 6-Pass.	858
Suburban, 9-Pass.	859

300	CODE
2-Dr. Hardtop	822
4-Dr. Hardtop	824
Convertible	825

NEW YORKER	CODE
4-Dr. Sedan	833
4-Dr. Hardtop	834
Suburban, 6-Pass.	878
Suburban, 9-Pass.	879

300-H	CODE
2-Dr. Hardtop	842
Convertible	845

IMPERIAL	CODE
2-Dr. Hardtop	912
4-Dr. Hardtop	914

CROWN IMPERIAL	CODE
2-Dr. Hardtop	922
4-Dr. Hardtop	924
2-Dr. Convertible	925

LEBARON	CODE
4-Dr. Hardtop	934

THE TRIM NUMBER furnishes the key to the interior color and material.

NEWPORT TRIM

COLOR	CLOTH	VINYL	LEATHER	CODE
Blue	•	•		301
Blue		•		401
Cocoa	•	•		303
Cocoa		•		403
Gray		•		444
Gray/Black	•	•		304
Red	•	•		305
Red		•		405
Black		•		404

NEWPORT 300 TRIM

COLOR	CLOTH	VINYL	LEATHER	CODE
Tan	•	•		313
Tan			•	463
Gray/Black	•	•		314
Red	•	•		315
Red		•		415
Red			•	455
Gold		•		413
Gold			•	453
Black		•		414
Black			•	454

1962 CHRYSLER / IMPERIAL

NEW YORKER TRIM

COLOR	CLOTH	VINYL	LEATHER	CODE
Blue	•			321
Blue	•	•		331
Cocoa	•			323
Cocoa	•	•		333
Cocoa		•		423
Gray	•			324
Gray	•	•		334
Gray		•		444
Red	•	•		335
Red		•		425,465
Black		•		424,464

IMPERIAL TRIM

COLOR	CLOTH	VINYL	LEATHER	CODE
Blue	•	•		501
Green	•	•		502
Cocoa	•	•		503
Gray	•	•		504

CROWN IMPERIAL TRIM

COLOR	CLOTH	VINYL	LEATHER	CODE
Blue	•		•	511
Green	•		•	512
Cocoa	•		•	513
Gray	•		•	514
Red	•		•	515
Red			•	555
Black	•		•	516
Black			•	556
Tan			•	553
Off White			•	557

LEBARON TRIM

COLOR	CLOTH	VINYL	LEATHER	CODE
Black	•			521
Green	•		•	522
Cocoa	•		•	523
Gray	•		•	524
Gray	•			534

THE PAINT CODE furnishes the key to the paint used on the car. A three-digit code indicates the top and bottom colors respectively. A number follows which designates two-tone, sports-tone, convertible top, etc.

CODE	COLOR
Formal Black	B
Dawn Blue	C
Sapphire Blue	D
Moonlight Blue	E
Willow Green	G
Sage Green	H
Bermuda Turquoise	J
Dove Gray	L
Alabaster	O
Festival Red	P
Embassy Red	Q
Silver Lilac	R
Coral Gray	S
Cordovan	T
Caramel	U
Rosewood	Y
Oyster White	Z

ENGINE NUMBER

The engine number is stamped on a boss behind the water pump. The number provides the code to identify the series, block, displacement, and month/day production date.

EXAMPLE:

S	38	___	2	24
YEAR	383	*	FEBRUARY	24th DAY

* Non-standard designation

NEWPORT

ENGINE NO.	NO. CYL.	CID	HORSE-POWER	COMP. RATIO	CARB	TRANS
S-36	8	361	265	9.1:1	2 BC	MAN/AUTO

300

ENGINE NO.	NO. CYL.	CID	HORSE-POWER	COMP. RATIO	CARB	TRANS
S-38	8	383	305	10.1:1	4 BC	MAN/AUTO
S-41	8	413	340	10.1:1	4 BC	MAN/AUTO
S-41	8	413	365	10.1:1	4 BC	MAN
S-41	8	413	380	10.1:1	2-4 BC	MAN/AUTO
S-41	8	413	405	11.0:1	2-4 BC	MAN/AUTO
S-42	8	426	373	11.0:1	4 BC	MAN
S-42	8	426	385	12.0:1	4 BC	MAN
S-42	8	426	413	11.0:1	2-4 BC	MAN/AUTO
S-42	8	426	421	12.0:1	2-4 BC	MAN/AUTO

NEW YORKER/IMPERIAL

ENGINE NO.	NO. CYL.	CID	HORSE-POWER	COMP. RATIO	CARB	TRANS
S-41	8	413	340	10.1:1	4 BC	AUTO

300 H

ENGINE NO.	NO. CYL.	CID	HORSE-POWER	COMP. RATIO	CARB	TRANS
S-41	8	413	380	10.1:1	2-4 BC	AUTO
S-41	8	413	405	11.0:1	2-4 BC	AUTO
S-42	8	4265	413	11.0:1	2-4 BC	AUTO
S-42	8	426	421	12.0:1	2-4 BC	AUTO

Non-standard designation
A - .020" overbore
Maltese Cross - .001" bearings undersize
X & Maltese Cross - .010" bearings undersize
* - .008" lifters oversize
HP - High performance

1963 CHRYSLER / IMPERIAL

1963 CHRYSLER

1963 CHRYSLER

1963 CHRYSLER 300

1963 CHRYSLER 300

1963 IMPERIAL

1963 IMPERIAL

1963 CHRYSLER / IMPERIAL

VEHICLE IDENTIFICATION NUMBER

CHRYSLER
8533100551

The vehicle number (serial number) is stamped and embossed on a stainless steel plate attached to the left front door hinge pillar. It consists of car make symbol, series code, model year code, assembly plant symbol, and a sequential production number.

FIRST DIGIT: Identifies the car make

Chrysler	8
Imperial	9

SECOND DIGIT: Identifies the series

SERIES	CODE
Newport, Imperial Custom	1
300, Imperial Crown	2
New Yorker, Imperial LeBaron	3
Chrysler 300J	4
Newport Station Wagon	5
New Yorker Station Wagon	7
Taxi	8
Police	9
Commercial	10

THIRD DIGIT: Identifies the model year (1963)

FOURTH DIGIT: Identifies the assembly plant

ASSEMBLY PLANT	CODE
Jefferson Plant, Detroit, MI	3
Newark, DE	6

LAST SIX DIGITS: Represent the basic production numbers

BODY NUMBER PLATE

THE BODY PLATE is stamped and embossed on a stainless steel plate under the hood. It is attached to the right or left fender, cowl, or radiator cross member depending on the model and assembly plant. This plate will indicate schedule date, body production number, body series, trim, paint, and accessory code.

CHRYSLER MOTORS
CORPORATION

SO	NUMBER	BDY	TRM	PNT
0224	0555	812	101	BB1

EXAMPLE:

0224	SON (Feb. 24)
0555	Production Sequence
812	Body Style (2-Dr. Hardtop)
101	Trim
B	Lower Body Color
B	Upper Body Color

THE SHIPPING ORDER NUMBER is assigned prior to production. It consists of a four-digit planned delivery month/day date code, 0224 (February 24th). Then a plant production sequence number follows (0555).

THE BODY NUMBER is a three-digit number which indicates the model and body style.

NEWPORT	CODE
2-Dr. Hardtop	812
4-Dr. Sedan	813
4-Dr. Hardtop	814
2-Dr. Convertible	815
Suburban, 6-Pass.	858
Suburban, 9-Pass.	859
4-Dr. Sedan (Police)	893
Suburban, 6-Pass. (Police)	898

300	CODE
2-Dr. Hardtop*	822
4-Dr. Hardtop	824
2-Dr. Convertible	825

*Option Pace Setter

NEW YORKER	CODE
4-Dr. Sedan	833
4-Dr. Hardtop*	834
Suburban, 6-Pass.	878
Suburban, 9-Pass.	879
4-Dr. Limousine, 6-Pass.	884

* Option Salon

300-J	CODE
2-Dr. Hardtop	842

IMPERIAL CUSTOM	CODE
2-Dr. Hardtop	912
4-Dr. Hardtop	914

IMPERIAL CROWN	CODE
2-Dr. Hardtop	922
4-Dr. Hardtop	924
2-Dr. Convertible	925

IMPERIAL LEBARON	CODE
4-Dr. Hardtop	934

THE TRIM NUMBER furnishes the key to the interior color and material.

NEWPORT TRIM COLOR	CLOTH	VINYL	LEATHER	CODE
Blue	•	•		101
Blue		•		111,201
Green	•	•		102
Green		•		112
Tan	•	•		103
Tan		•		113,203
Red	•	•		105
Red		•		115,205
Turquoise	•	•		108
Turquoise		•		208
Gray	•	•		104
Gray		•		204
Black		•		206

1963 CHRYSLER / IMPERIAL

300 TRIM

COLOR	CLOTH	VINYL	LEATHER	CODE
Blue	•	•		121
Blue		•		221
Tan	•	•		123
Tan		•		223
Red	•	•		125
Red		•		225,245
Black/ Alabaster	•	•		126
Alabaster		•		227
Turquoise		•		228

NEW YORKER TRIM

COLOR	CLOTH	VINYL	LEATHER	CODE
Blue	•	•		141
Blue		•		231
Green	•	•		142
Tan	•	•		143
Tan		•		233
Gray	•	•		144
Turquoise	•	•		148
Turquoise		•		236
Red		•		235

IMPERIAL TRIM

COLOR	CLOTH	VINYL	LEATHER	CODE
Blue	•	•		901
Tan	•	•		903
Gray	•	•		904
Turquoise	•	•		908
Gold	•	•		909

IMPERIAL CROWN TRIM

COLOR	CLOTH	VINYL	LEATHER	CODE
Blue	•		•	921,951
Tan	•		•	923
Gray	•		•	924
Red	•		•	925,955
Turquoise	•		•	928
Gold	•		•	929,939
Black	•		•	956
Alabaster	•		•	957

LEBARON TRIM

COLOR	CLOTH	VINYL	LEATHER	CODE
Blue	•		•	941
Tan	•		•	943
Gray	•		•	944
Gray	•			934
Gold	•		•	949
Red			•	975
Black			•	976
White			•	977

THE PAINT CODE furnishes the key to the paint used on the car. A three-digit code indicates the top and bottom colors respectively. A number follows which designates two-tone, sports-tone, convertible top, etc.

COLOR	CODE
Formal Black	B
Glacier Blue	C
Cord Blue	D
Navy Blue	E
Surf Green	G
Forest Green	H
Holiday Turquoise	J
Teal	K
Madison Gray	N
Dubonnet	O
Festival	P
Claret	Q
Fawn	T
Cypress Tan	U
Alabaster	W
Embassy Gold	Y
Oyster White	Z

ENGINE NUMBER

The engine number is stamped on a boss behind the water pump. The number provides the code to identify the series, block, displacement, and month/day production date.

EXAMPLE:

T	38	___	2	24
YEAR	383	*	FEBRUARY	24th DAY

* Non-standard designation

NEWPORT

ENGINE NO.	NO. CYL.	CID	HORSE-POWER	COMP. RATIO	CARB	TRANS
T-36	8	361	265	9.0:1	2 BC	MAN/AUTO

300

ENGINE NO.	NO. CYL.	CID	HORSE-POWER	COMP. RATIO	CARB	TRANS
T-38	8	383	305	10.1:1	2 BC	MAN/AUTO
T-41	8	413	360	10.1:1	4 BC	MAN/AUTO
T-41	8	413	365	11.0:1	4 BC	MAN/AUTO
T-42*	8	426	373	11.0:1	4 BC	N/A
T-42*	8	426	415	11.0:1	2-4 BC	N/A
T-42*	8	426	425	13.5:1	2-4 BC	N/A

* Before 12-19-62 — T-42
After 12-19-62 (11.0:1 - 426 TMP)
(13.5:1 - 426 TMP-HC)

NEW YORKER/IMPERIAL

ENGINE NO.	NO. CYL.	CID	HORSE-POWER	COMP. RATIO	CARB	TRANS
T-41	8	413	340	10.1:1	4 BC	AUTO

300J

ENGINE NO.	NO. CYL.	CID	HORSE-POWER	COMP. RATIO	CARB	TRANS
T-41 (early) C300J (later)	8	413	390	9.6:1	2-4 BC	AUTO

Note: Various marks as listed below may be found on the engine number pad and indicate variations in engine specifications which affect service procedures.

Engine Specifications:

LC - Low compression
HC - High compression
HP - High performance
MP - Maximum performance
Maltese Cross - .001" undersize crankshaft journals
Maltese Cross & X. - 010" undersize crankshaft journals (318")

A - .020" oversize cylinder bores
* - .008" oversize valve lifters

1964 CHRYSLER / IMPERIAL

1964 CHRYSLER NEW YORKER

1964 CHRYSLER NEW YORKER

1964 CHRYSLER 300

1964 CHRYSLER 300

1964 IMPERIAL

1964 IMPERIAL

1964 CHRYSLER / IMPERIAL

VEHICLE IDENTIFICATION NUMBER

CHRYSLER
8443100551

The vehicle number (serial number) is stamped and embossed on a stainless steel plate attached to the left front door hinge pillar. It consists of car make symbol, series code, model year code, assembly plant symbol, and a sequential production number.

FIRST DIGIT: Identifies the car make

Chrysler	8
Imperial	9

SECOND DIGIT: Identifies the series

Newport	1
300, Imperial Crown	2
New Yorker, Imperial LeBaron	3
Chrysler 300K	4
Newport Station Wagon	5
New Yorker Station Wagon	7
New Yorker Salon	8
Police	9

THIRD DIGIT: Identifies the model year (1964)

FOURTH DIGIT: Identifies the assembly plant

ASSEMBLY PLANT	CODE
Jefferson Plant, Detroit, MI	3
Newark, DE	6

LAST SIX DIGITS: Represent the basic production numbers

BODY NUMBER PLATE

THE BODY PLATE is stamped and embossed on a stainless steel plate under the hood. It is attached to the right or left fender, cowl, or radiator cross member depending on the model and assembly plant. This plate will indicate schedule date, body production number, body series, trim, paint, and accessory code.

CHRYSLER MOTORS CORPORATION

SO	NUMBER	BDY	TRM	PNT
0224	0555	812	L1B	BB1

EXAMPLE:

0224	SO (February 24)
0555	Production Sequence
812	Body Style (Newport 2-Dr.)
L1B	Trim
B	Lower Body Color
B	Upper Body Color

THE SHIPPING ORDER NUMBER is assigned prior to production. It consists of a four-digit planned delivery month/day date code, 0224 (February 24th). Then a plant production sequence number follows (0555).

THE BODY NUMBER is a three-digit number which indicates the model and body style.

NEWPORT	CODE
2-Dr. Hardtop	812
4-Dr. Sedan	813
4-Dr. Hardtop	814
2-Dr. Convertible	815
Suburban, 6-Pass.	858
Suburban, 9-Pass.	859
4-Dr. Sedan (Police)	893
4-Dr. Station Wagon (Police)	898

CHRYSLER 300	CODE
2-Dr. Hardtop*	822
4-Dr. Hardtop	824
2-Dr. Convertible	825

* Option Silver 300

300K	CODE
2-Dr. Hardtop	842
2-Dr. Convertible	845

NEW YORKER	CODE
4-Dr. Sedan	833
4-Dr. Hardtop	834
4-Dr. Town & Country Wagon, 6-Pass.	878
4-Dr. Town & Country Wagon, 9-Pass.	879

NEW YORKER SALON	CODE
4-Dr. Hardtop	884

CROWN IMPERIAL	CODE
2-Dr. Hardtop	922
4-Dr. Hardtop	924
2-Dr. Convertible	925

LEBARON	CODE
4-Dr. Hardtop	934

THE TRIM NUMBER furnishes the key to the interior color and material.

NEWPORT TRIM COLOR	CLOTH	VINYL	LEATHER	CODE
Blue	•	•		L1B,L2B,L4B
Blue	•	•		K1B,K4B
Green	•	•		L1F,L2F,K1F
Mauve	•	•		L1M,L2M,K1M
Black/White	•	•		L1N,L4N
Black/White	•	•		K1N,K4N
Turquoise	•	•		LIQ,L2Q,L4Q
Tan	•	•		L1T,L2T,L4T
Tan	•	•		K1T,K4T
Red		•		L4R,K4R
Gray	•	•		K5A,K8A

1964 CHRYSLER / IMPERIAL

NEWPORT 300 TRIM

COLOR	CLOTH	VINYL	LEATHER	CODE
Blue	•	•		M1B,M4B
Mauve	•	•		M1M
Black/White	•	•		M1N
Tan	•	•		M1T,M4T
Black	•	•		M4X,M8X
White	•	•		M4W,M8W
Red		•		M4R

NEW YORKER TRIM

COLOR	CLOTH	VINYL	LEATHER	CODE
Blue	•	•		H1B,H4B
Blue	•		•	H3B,H7B
Green	•	•		H1F
Gold	•		•	H3L,H7L
Mauve	•	•		H1M
Black/White	•	•		H1N,H2N
Turquoise	•	•		H1Q,H4Q
Red		•		H4R
Tan	•	•		H1T,H4T
White		•		H4W

CROWN IMPERIAL TRIM

COLOR	CLOTH	VINYL	LEATHER	CODE
Blue		•	•	M3B,M9B
Blue	•	•	•	M7B,M8B
Blue/White		•	•	M9C
Red		•	•	M3R,M9R
Tan		•	•	M3T,M9T
White		•	•	M3W,M9W
Black		•	•	M3X,M9X
Green		•	•	M3F,M9F
Red/White		•	•	M3V,M9V,M9W
Green/Tan	•	•	•	M7H,M8H
Mauve	•	•	•	M7M,M8M
Black/White	•	•	•	M7N,M8N
Turquoise	•	•	•	M7Q,M8Q
Black/Gray	•	•	•	M7P

LEBARON TRIM

COLOR	CLOTH	VINYL	LEATHER	CODE
Blue	•	•	•	H3B,H7B
Blue/White		•	•	H3C
Red		•	•	H3R
White		•	•	H3W
Black		•	•	H3X
Green		•	•	H3F
Red/White		•	•	H3V
Green/Tan	•	•	•	H7H
Mauve	•	•	•	H7M
Tan	•	•	•	H7T
Black/Gray	•	•	•	H7P

THE PAINT CODE furnishes the key to the paint used on the car. A three-digit code indicates the top and bottom colors respectively. A number follows which designates two-tone, sports-tone, convertible top, etc.

COLOR	CODE
Formal Black	B
Wegewood	C
Chrysler/Nassau Blue	D
Monarch Blue	E
Pine Mist	F
Sequoia Green	G
Silver Turquoise	K
Royal Turquoise	L
Madison Gray	M
Charcoal Gray	N
Rosewood	O
Royal Ruby	P
Royal Ruby	R
Ivory	S
Roman Red	T
Embassy Gold	U
Persian White	W
Dune Beige	X
Sable Tan	Y

ENGINE NUMBER

The engine number is stamped on a boss behind the water pump. The number provides the code to identify the series, block, displacement, and month/day production date.

EXAMPLE:

V	38	___	2	24
YEAR	383	*	FEBRUARY	24th DAY

* Non-standard designation

NEWPORT

ENGINE NO.	NO. CYL.	CID	HORSE-POWER	COMP. RATIO	CARB	TRANS
V-36	8	361	265	9.0:1	2 BC	MAN/AUTO

300

ENGINE NO.	NO. CYL.	CID	HORSE-POWER	COMP. RATIO	CARB	TRANS
V-38	8	383	305	10.0:1	2 BD	MAN/AUTO
V-41	8	413	360	10.1:1	4 BC	MAN/AUTO

NEW YORKER/IMPERIAL

ENGINE NO.	NO. CYL.	CID	HORSE-POWER	COMP. RATIO	CARB	TRANS
V-41	8	413	340	10.0:1	4 BC	AUTO

300K

ENGINE NO.	NO. CYL.	CID	HORSE-POWER	COMP. RATIO	CARB	TRANS
V-41	8	413	360	10.1:1	4 BC	MAN/AUTO
V-41	8	413	390	9.6;1	2-4 BC	MAN/AUTO

Note: Various marks as listed below may be found on the engine number pad and indicate variations in engine specifications which affect service procedures.

Engine Specifications:

Maltese Cross - .001" undersize crankshaft journals
B - .010" undersize crankshaft journals (273",318")
Maltese Cross & X - (Others)
A - .020" oversize cylinder bores
* - .008" oversize valve lifters

1965 CHRYSLER / IMPERIAL

1965 CHRYSLER

1965 CHRYSLER

1965 CHRYSLER 300

1965 CHRYSLER 300

1965 IMPERIAL

1965 IMPERIAL

1965 CHRYSLER / IMPERIAL

VEHICLE IDENTIFICATION NUMBER

CHRYSLER
C453100003

The vehicle number (serial number) is stamped and embossed on a stainless steel plate attached to the left front door hinge pillar. It consists of car make symbol, series code, model year code, assembly plant symbol, and a sequential production number.

FIRST DIGIT: Identifies the car make

Chrysler	C
Imperial	Y

SECOND DIGIT: Identifies the series

SERIES	CODE
Newport	1
300, Crown	2
New Yorker, LeBaron	3
300L	4
Newport Station Wagon	5
New Yorker Station Wagon	7
Police	9

THIRD DIGIT: Identifies the model year (1965)

FOURTH DIGIT: Identifies the assembly plant

Jefferson Plant, Detroit, MI	3
Newark, DE	6

LAST SIX DIGITS: Represent the basic production numbers

BODY NUMBER PLATE

THE BODY PLATE is stamped and embossed on a stainless steel plate under the hood. It is attached to the right or left fender, cowl, or radiator cross member depending on the model and assembly plant. This plate will indicate schedule date, body production number, body series, trim, paint, and accessory code.

CHRYSLER MOTORS CORPORATION

SO	NUMBER	BDY	TRM	PNT
0224	0555	C12	L1N	BB1

EXAMPLE:

0224	SON (Feb. 24)
0555	Production Sequence
C12	Body Style (2-Dr. Hardtop)
L1N	Trim
B	Lower Body Color
B	Upper Body Color

THE SHIPPING ORDER NUMBER is assigned prior to production. It consists of a four-digit planned delivery month/day date code, 0224 (February 24th). Then a plant production sequence number follows (0555).

THE BODY NUMBER is a three-digit number which indicates the model and body style.

NEWPORT	CODE
2-Dr. Hardtop	C12
4-Dr. Sedan	C13
4-Dr. Hardtop	C14
2-Dr. Convertible	C15
4-Dr. Town Sedan	C18
4-Dr. Town & Country Wagon, 6-Pass.	C56
4-Dr. Town & Country Wagon, 9-Pass.	C57

CHRYSLER 300	CODE
2-Dr. Hardtop	C22
4-Dr. Hardtop	C24
2-Dr. Convertible	C25
4-Dr. Town Sedan	C28

300L	CODE
2-Dr. Hardtop	C42
2-Dr. Convertible	C45

NEW YORKER	CODE
2-Dr. Hardtop	C32
4-Dr. Hardtop	C34
4-Dr. Sedan	C38
4-Dr. Town & Country Wagon, 6-Pass.	C76
4-Dr. Town & Country Wagon, 9-Pass.	C77

CROWN IMPERIAL	CODE
2-Dr. Hardtop	Y22
4-Dr. Hardtop	Y24
2-Dr. Convertible	Y25

LEBARON	CODE
4-Dr. Hardtop	Y34

THE TRIM NUMBER furnishes the key to the interior color and material.

NEWPORT TRIM

COLOR	CLOTH	VINYL	LEATHER	CODE
Blue	•	•		L1B,L2B,L4B
Blue	•	•		L5B,L8B,L9B
Gold/Black	•	•		L2L,L4L
Black/White	•	•		L1N,L2N,L4N
Turquoise	•	•		L1Q,L2Q,L8Q
Red	•	•		L1R,L2R,L4R
Red	•	•		L5R,L8R,L9R
Tan	•	•		L1T,L2T,L4T
Tan	•	•		L5T,L8T
Black		•		L4X,L9X

CHRYSLER 300 TRIM

COLOR	CLOTH	VINYL	LEATHER	CODE
Blue	•	•		M4B
Gold/Black		•		M4L
Red			•	M3R,M4R
Tan		•		M4T
White		•		M4W
Black		•	•	M3X,M4X

1965 CHRYSLER / IMPERIAL

NEW YORKER TRIM

COLOR	CLOTH	VINYL	LEATHER	CODE
Blue	•	•		H1B,H4B
Gold/Black	•	•		H1L,H4L
Black/White	•	•		H1N
Turquoise	•	•		H1Q
Red	•	•		H1R,H4R
Tan	•	•		H1T,H4T
Black		•		H4X

CHRYSLER 300 TRIM

COLOR	CLOTH	VINYL	LEATHER	CODE
Blue		•		P4B
Gold/Black		•		P4L
Red		•		P3R,P4R
Tan		•		P4T
White		•		· P4W
Black		•	•	P3X,P4X

IMPERIAL CROWN TRIM

COLOR	CLOTH	VINYL	LEATHER	CODE
Blue	•		•	M3B,M7B
Blue	•		•	M8B,M9B
Blue/White			•	M3C,M9C
Green/Gold	•		•	M7G,M8G
Purple			•	M3K,M9K
Black/White	•		•	M7N,M8N
Gray/Black	•		•	M7P
Turquoise	•		•	M7Q
Red	•		•	M3R,M5R
Red	•		•	M7R,M9R
Tan	•		•	M3T,M7T,M9T
Red/White			•	M3V,M9V
White			•	M3W,M5W,M9W

LEBARON TRIM

COLOR	CLOTH	VINYL	LEATHER	CODE
Black			•	M3X,M5X,M9X

THE PAINT CODE furnishes the key to the paint used on the car. A three-digit code indicates the top and bottom colors respectively. A number follows which designates two-tone, sports-tone, convertible top, etc.

COLOR	CODE
Royal Gold Metallic	A
Formal Black	B
Ice Blue	C
Nassau Blue Metallic	D
Navy Blue Metallic	E
Mist Blue Metallic	F
Sequoia Green Metallic	G
Moss Gold Metallic	4
Sage Green Metallic	2
Peacock Turquoise Metallic	K
Royal Turquoise Metallic	L
Silver Mist Metallic	N
Granite Gray Metallic	M
Pink Silver Metallic	3
French Ivory	S
Spanish Red Metallic	T
Cordovan Metallic	V
Persian White	W
Sand Dune Beige	X
Sable Tan Metallic	Y
Frost Turquoise Metallic	Z
Black Plum Metallic	5
Mauve Metallic	6
Patrician Gold Metallic	7
Sierra Sand	R

ENGINE NUMBER

The engine number is stamped on a boss behind the water pump. The number provides the code to identify the series, block, displacement, and month/day production date.

EXAMPLE:

V	38	2	24
YEAR	383	FEBRUARY	24th DAY

NEWPORT

ENGINE NO.	NO. CYL.	CID	HORSE-POWER	COMP. RATIO	CARB	TRANS
A-383	8	383	270	9.2:1	2 BC	MAN/AUTO
A-383	8	383	315	10.0;1	4 BC	MAN/AUTO

300

ENGINE NO.	NO. CYL.	CID	HORSE-POWER	COMP. RATIO	CARB	TRANS
A-383	8	383	315	10.0;1	4 BC	MAN/AUTO
A-413	8	413	360	10.0:1	4 BC	MAN/AUTO

NEW YORKER

ENGINE NO.	NO. CYL.	CID	HORSE-POWER	COMP. RATIO	CARB	TRANS
A-413	8	413	340	10.1:1	4 BC	AUTO
A-413	8	413	360	10.1:1	4 BC	AUTO

300L

ENGINE NO.	NO. CYL.	CID	HORSE-POWER	COMP. RATIO	CARB	TRANS
A-413	8	413	360	10.1:1	4 BC	MAN/AUTO

IMPERIAL

ENGINE NO.	NO. CYL.	CID	HORSE-POWER	COMP. RATIO	CARB	TRANS
A-413	8	413	340	10.1:1	4 BC	AUTO
A-413	8	413	350	10.1:1	4 BC	AUTO

Note: Various marks as listed below may be found on the engine number pad and indicate variations in engine specifications which affect service procedures.

Engine Specifications:

Maltese Cross - .001" undersize crankshaft journals
Maltese Cross & X - .010" undersize crankshaft
A - .020" oversize cylinder bores
* - .008" oversize valve lifters

1966 CHRYSLER / IMPERIAL

1966 CHRYSLER

1966 CHRYSLER

1966 IMPERIAL

1966 IMPERIAL

VEHICLE IDENTIFICATION NUMBER

CHRYSLER
CH42G63100551

The vehicle number (serial number) is stamped and embossed on a stainless steel plate attached to the left front door hinge pillar. It consists of car make symbol, series code, model year code, assembly plant symbol, and a sequential production number.

FIRST DIGIT: Identifies the car make

Chrysler	C
Imperial	Y

SECOND DIGIT: Identifies the class

CLASS	CODE
Economy	E
Low	L
High	H
Medium	M

THIRD AND FOURTH DIGIT: Identify the body style

BODY STYLE	CODE
2-Dr. Hardtop	23
Convertible	27
4-Dr. Sedan	41
4-Dr. Town Sedan	42
4-Dr. Hardtop	43
6-Ps. Station Wagon	45
9-Ps. Station Wagon	46

FIFTH DIGIT: Identifies the cubic inch displacement

CID	CODE
383	G
440 Cu. In.	J
Special Order 8 Cyl.	K

SIXTH DIGIT: Identifies the model year (1966)

SEVENTH DIGIT: Identifies the assembly plant

ASSEMBLY PLANT	CODE
Jefferson Plant, Detroit, MI	3
Newark, DE	6

LAST SIX DIGITS: Represent the basic production numbers

1966 CHRYSLER / IMPERIAL

BODY NUMBER PLATE

THE BODY PLATE is stamped and embossed on a plate which is attached on the engine side of the cowl just above the master cylinder on Imperial models. On Chrysler models, the plate is located above the top hinge of the driver's side door. The plate shows the body type, trim code, schedule date, paint code, and some accessory codes.

CHRYSLER MOTORS
CORPORATION

SO	NUMBER	BDY	TRM	PNT
0224	0555	CH42	H1R	BB1

EXAMPLE:

0224	SON (Feb. 24)
0555	Production Sequence
CH42	Body Style (4-Dr. Town Sedan)
H1R	Trim
B	Lower Body Color
B	Upper Body Color

THE SHIPPING ORDER NUMBER consists of a three-digit month and day scheduled production date, and a five-digit production order number.

MONTH	CODE
JAN	1
FEB	2
MAR	3
APR	4
MAY	5
JUN	6
JULY	7
AUG	8
SEPT	9
OCT	A
NOV	B
DEC	C

(O1 through 31 days)

THE BODY NUMBER is a four-digit number which indicates the car line, price class, and body style. Same first four digits of the VIN.

NEWPORT	CODE
2-Dr. Hardtop	CL23
4-Dr. Sedan	CL41
4-Dr. Hardtop	CL48
2-Dr. Convertible	CL27
4-Dr. Town Sedan	CL42
4-Dr. Town & Country Wagon, 6-Pass.	CL45
4-Dr. Town & Country Wagon, 9-Pass.	CL46

CHRYSLER 300	CODE
2-Dr. Hardtop	CM23
4-Dr. Hardtop	CM43
2-Dr. Convertible	CM27

NEW YORKER	CODE
2-Dr. Hardtop	CH23
4-Dr. Hardtop	CH43
4-Dr. Town Sedan	CH42

CROWN IMPERIAL	CODE
2-Dr. Hardtop	YM23
4-Dr. Hardtop	YM43
2-Dr. Convertible	YM27

IMPERIAL LEBARON	CODE
4-Dr. Hardtop	YH43

THE TRIM NUMBER furnishes the key to the interior color and material.

NEWPORT TRIM

COLOR	CLOTH	VINYL	LEATHER	CODE
Red	•	•		L1R,L2R,L8R
Red		•		L5R,L7R,L9R
Green	•	•		L1F,L2F,L8F
Blue	•	•		L1D,L2D,L8D
Blue		•		L7D,L5D
Blue		•		L9D,L0D
Tan	•	•		L1T,L2T,L8T
Tan		•		L7T
Turquoise	•	•		L1J,L2J,L8J
Black	•	•		L6X
Black		•		L5X,L7X
Black		•		L9X,L0X

300 TRIM

COLOR	CLOTH	VINYL	LEATHER	CODE
Blue	•	•		M1D
Blue		•		M4D
White/Black	•	•		M1N
Black		•		M4X
Black			•	M3X
Red		•		M4R
Red			•	M3R
Tan		•		M4T
White		•		M4W
Silver		•		M4A

NEW YORKER TRIM

COLOR	CLOTH	VINYL	LEATHER	CODE
Blue	•	•		H1D,H8D
Green	•	•		H1F
Red	•	•		H1R
Red		•		H4R
Tan	•	•		H1T
Turquoise	•	•		H1J
Black		•		H4X
White		•		H4W
White/Black	•	•		H8N

1966 CHRYSLER / IMPERIAL

IMPERIAL CROWN TRIM

COLOR	CLOTH	VINYL	LEATHER	CODE
Blue	•		•	M7D,M8B
Blue			•	M3B,M9B
Gold	•		•	M7L
Gold			•	M3L,M9L
Red	•		•	M7M
Red			•	M3M,M9M
Green			•	M3F,M9F
White/Black	•		•	M7N,M8W
White/Black			•	M3W,M9W
White/Blue			•	M3C,M9C
Turquoise	•		•	M7Q,M8Q
Green/Gold	•		•	M7G,M8G
Black/Silver	•		•	M7P,M9A
Black/Gold			•	M3E
Black			•	M3X,M9X

IMPERIAL LEBARON TRIM

COLOR	CLOTH	VINYL	LEATHER	CODE
Blue	•		•	H7D
Blue			•	H3B
Gold	•		•	H7L
Gold			•	H3L
Black			•	H3X
Red			•	H3M
Green			•	H3F
Green/Gold	•		•	H7G
Black/Silver	•		•	H7P
Black/Gold			•	H3E
White/Black			•	H3W
White/Blue			•	H3C
Silver/Black	•			H6A

THE PAINT CODE furnishes the key to the paint used on the car. A three-digit code indicates the top and bottom colors respectively. A number follows which designates two-tone, sports-tone, convertible top, etc.

COLOR	CODE
Silver Mist Metallic	A
Black	B
Blue (Powder)	C
Crystal Blue Metallic	D
Royal Blue Metallic	E
Haze Green Metallic	F
Sequoia Green Metallic	G
Frost Turquoise Metallic	K
Royal Turquoise Metallic	L
Scorch Red	P
Spanish Red Metallic	Q
Ruby Metallic	7
Daffodil Yellow	R
Ivory	S
Persian White	W
Desert Beige	X
Saddle Bronze	Y
Spice Gold Metallic	Z
Dove Tan	3
Moss Gold Metallic	4
Dusty Gold Metallic	5
Lilac	6
Deep Plum Metallic	8

ENGINE NUMBER

The 383 engine number is stamped on the right front of the block near the distributor. The number provides the code to identify the series, block, displacement, and month/day production date.

The 440 engine number is stamped on the left front of the block near the water pump.

EXAMPLE:

B	38	2	24
YEAR	383	FEBRUARY	24th DAY

NEWPORT

ENGINE NO.	NO. CYL.	CID	HORSE-POWER	COMP. RATIO	CARB	TRANS
B-383	8	383	270	9.2:1	2 BC	MAN/AUTO
B-383	8	383	325	10.0:1	4 BC	MAN/AUTO
B-440	8	440	350	10.1:1	4 BC	AUTO
B-440	8	440	365	10.1:1	4 BC	AUTO

300

ENGINE NO.	NO. CYL.	CID	HORSE-POWER	COMP. RATIO	CARB	TRANS
B-383	8	383	325	10.1:1	4 BC	MAN/AUTO
B-440	8	440	350	10.1:1	4 BC	AUTO
B-440	8	440	365	10.1:1	4 BC	AUTO

NEW YORKER

ENGINE NO.	NO. CYL.	CID	HORSE-POWER	COMP. RATIO	CARB	TRANS
B-440	8	440	350	10.1:1	4 BC	AUTO
B-440	8	440	365	10.1:1	4 BC	AUTO

IMPERIAL

ENGINE NO.	NO. CYL.	CID	HORSE-POWER	COMP. RATIO	CARB	TRANS
B-440	8	440	350	10.1:1	4 BC	AUTO

Note: Various marks as listed below may be found on the engine number pad and indicate variations in engine specifications which affect service procedures.

Engine Specification:

Maltese Cross - .001" undersize crankshaft journals
Maltese Cross & X - .010" undersize crankshaft
A - .020" oversize cylinder bores
* - .008" oversize valve lifters

1967 CHRYSLER / IMPERIAL

1967 CHRYSLER NEWPORT

1967 CHRYSLER NEWPORT

1967 CHRYSLER NEW YORKER

1967 CHRYSLER 300

1967 IMPERIAL

1967 IMPERIAL

1967 CHRYSLER / IMPERIAL

VEHICLE IDENTIFICATION NUMBER

CHRYSLER
CH41K73100551

The vehicle number (serial number) is stamped and embossed on a stainless steel plate attached to the left front door hinge pillar. It consists of car make symbol, series code, model year code, assembly plant symbol, and a sequential production number.

FIRST DIGIT: Identifies the car make

Chrysler	C
Imperial	Y

SECOND DIGIT: Identifies the class

CLASS	CODE
Economy	E
Low	L
High	H
Medium	M

THIRD AND FOURTH DIGITS: Identify the body style

BODY STYLE	CODE
2-Dr. Hardtop	23
Convertible	27
4-Dr. Sedan	41
4-Dr. Hardtop	43
4-Dr. Sta. Wagon, 6-Pass.	45
4-Dr. Sta. Wagon, 9-Pass.	46

FIFTH DIGIT: Identifies the cubic inch displacement

CID	CODE
383 CID	G
383 CID High Performance	H
440 CID	K
440 CID High Performance	L
Special Order 8 Cyl.	M

SIXTH DIGIT: Identifies the model year (1967)

SEVENTH DIGIT: Identifies the assembly plant

ASSEMBLY PLANT	CODE
Jefferson Plant, Detroit, MI	3
Newark, DE	6

LAST SIX DIGITS: Represent the basic production numbers

BODY NUMBER PLATE

THE BODY PLATE is stamped and embossed on a stainless steel plate attached to the fender shield under the hood. The plate indicates the code for the body type, engine, transmission, schedule date, paint, trim and some option codes. The plate is read left to right, bottom to top, starting with the bottom row of numbers.

CHRYSLER MOTORS
CORPORATION

AX TR PNT UBS
4 H1T BB1 S

CH41 61 5 635 224 055551

EXAMPLE:

C	Car Make (Chrysler)
H	Car Class (High)
41	Body Style (4-Dr. Sedan)
61	Engine CID (383 1 BC 8 CYL)
5	Transmission (3-Sp. Auto.)
635	Tire Size and Type
224	Production Date (2-24)
055551	Production Sequence
4	Axle
H1T	Trim
B	Lower Body Color
B	Upper Body Color
UBS	Accent Color

THE ENGINE CID CODE identifies the engine.

ENGINE CID	CODE
383 1 BBL 8 Cyl.	61
383 1-4 BBL 8 Cyl.	62

TRANSMISSION	CODE
3-Speed Automatic	5
3-Speed Automatic HD	6
Special Order	9

1967 CHRYSLER / IMPERIAL

THE BODY NUMBER is a four-digit number which indicates the car line, price class, and body style. Same first four digits of the VIN.

NEWPORT	CODE
4-Dr. Sedan	CE41
4-Dr. Hardtop	CE43
2-Dr. Hardtop	CE23
2-Dr. Convertible	CE27

NEWPORT CUSTOM	CODE
2-Dr. Hardtop	CL23
4-Dr. Sedan	CL41
4-Dr. Hardtop	CL43

CHRYSLER 300	CODE
2-Dr. Hardtop	CM23
4-Dr. Hardtop	CM43
Convertible	CM27

NEW YORKER	CODE
4-Dr. Sedan	CH41
2-Dr. Hardtop	CH23
4-Dr. Hardtop	CH43

TOWN & COUNTRY	CODE
4-Dr. Sta. Wagon, 6-Pass.	CE45
4-Dr. Sta. Wagon, 9-Pass.	CE46

CROWN IMPERIAL	CODE
4-Dr. Sedan	YM41
2-Dr. Hardtop	YM23
4-Dr. Hardtop	YM43
2-Dr. Convertible	YM27

LEBARON	CODE
4-Dr. Hardtop	YH43

The next three-digit code indicates the tire size and type; this option code is not included.

THE SHIPPING ORDER NUMBER consists of a three-digit month and day scheduled production date, and a five digit production order number.

THE AXLE CODE identifies the number of axles.

THE UBS CODE identifies the upper door frame color, and the accent stripe color.

THE TRIM CODE furnishes the key to the interior color and material.

NEWPORT TRIM

COLOR	CLOTH	VINYL	LEATHER	CODE
Blue	•	•		E1B
Blue		•		E5B,E6B
Turquoise	•	•		E1Q
Red	•	•		E1R
Red		•		E5R,E6R
Tan	•	•		E1T
Black	•	•		E1X
Black		•		E5X,E6X
Gold		•		E5Y
White		•		E6W

NEWPORT CUSTOM TRIM

COLOR	CLOTH	VINYL	LEATHER	CODE
Blue	•	•		L2B
Blue		•		L9B,L6B
Gold	•	•		L2Y
Green	•	•		L2F
Turquoise	•	•		L2Q
Black	•	•		L2X
Black		•		L9X,L6X
Red		•		L6R

300 TRIM

COLOR	CLOTH	VINYL	LEATHER	CODE
Blue	•	•		M2B
Blue		•		M6B,M5B
Red		•		M6R
Red			•	M3R,M5R
Black	•	•		M2X
Black		•		M6X,M5X
Black			•	M3X
White		•		M6W
Gold	•	•		M2Y
Gold		•		M5Y
Turquoise	•	•		M2Q

NEW YORKER TRIM

COLOR	CLOTH	VINYL	LEATHER	CODE
Blue	•	•		H1B,H2B,H8B
Blue		•		H6B
Tan	•	•		H1T,H2T
Turquoise	•	•		H1Q,H2Q
Black	•	•		H1X,H2X,H8X
Black		•		H9X,H6X
Black			•	H3X
Red	•	•		H1R
Red		•		H9R,H6R
Red			•	H3R
Gold	•	•		H8Y
Gold		•		H6Y

TOWN & COUNTRY WAGON TRIM

COLOR	CLOTH	VINYL	LEATHER	CODE
Blue		•		E5B,E9B
Red		•		E5R
Black	•	•		E8X
Black		•		E5X
Tan		•		E5T,E9T

THE PAINT CODE furnishes the key to the paint used on the car. A three-digit code indicates the top and bottom colors respectively. A number follows which designates two-tone, sports-tone, convertible top, etc.

COLOR	CODE
Silver Mist Metallic	A
Black	B
Blue (Powder)	C
Crystal Blue Metallic	D
Royal Blue Metallic	E
Haze Green Metallic	F
Sequoia Green Metallic	G
Frost Turquoise Metallic	K
Royal Turquoise Metallic	L
Scorch Red	P
Spanish Red Metallic	Q
Ruby Metallic	7
Daffodil Yellow	R
Ivory	S
Persian White	W
Desert Beige	X
Saddle Bronze	Y
Spice Gold Metallic	Z
Moss Gold Metallic	4
Lilac	6

ENGINE NUMBER

The 383 engine number is stamped on the right front of the block near the distributor. The number provides the code to identify the series, block, displacement, and month/day production date.

The 440 engine number is stamped on the left front of the block near the water pump.

EXAMPLE:

C	38	2	24
YEAR	383	FEBRUARY	24th DAY

NEWPORT, NEWPORT CUSTOM

ENGINE NO.	NO. CYL.	CID	HORSE-POWER	COMP. RATIO	CARB	TRANS
C-383	8	383	270	9.2:1	2 BC	MAN/AUTO
C-383	8	383	325	10.0:1	4 BC	MAN/AUTO
C-440	8	440	375	10.1:1	4 BC	MAN/AUTO

300

ENGINE NO.	NO. CYL.	CID	HORSE-POWER	COMP. RATIO	CARB	TRANS
C-440	8	440	350	10.1:1	4 BC	MAN/AUTO
C-440	8	440	375	10.1:1	4 BC	MAN/AUTO

NEW YORKER

ENGINE NO.	NO. CYL.	CID	HORSE-POWER	COMP. RATIO	CARB	TRANS
C-440	8	440	350	10.1:1	4 BC	AUTO
C-440	8	440	375	10.1:1	4 BC	AUTO

TOWN & COUNTRY

ENGINE NO.	NO. CYL.	CID	HORSE-POWER	COMP. RATIO	CARB	TRANS
C-383	8	383	270	9.2:1	2 BC	AUTO
C-383	8	383	325	10.0:1	4 BC	AUTO
C-440	8	440	350	10.1:1	4 BC	AUTO

IMPERIAL

ENGINE NO.	NO. CYL.	CID	HORSE-POWER	COMP. RATIO	CARB	TRANS
C-440	8	440	350	10.1:1	4 BC	AUTO

Note: Various marks as listed below may be found on the engine number pad and indicate variations in engine specifications which affect service procedures.

Engine Specification:

Maltese Cross - .001" undersize crankshaft journals
Maltese Cross & X - .010" undersize crankshaft
A - .020" oversize cylinder bores
* - .008" oversize valve lifters

1968 CHRYSLER / IMPERIAL

1968 CHRYSLER NEW YORKER

1968 CHRYSLER NEW YORKER

1968 CHRYSLER 300

1968 CHRYSLER 300

1968 IMPERIAL

1968 IMPERIAL

VEHICLE IDENTIFICATION NUMBER

CHRYSLER
CH41K8F100551

The vehicle number (serial number) is stamped and embossed on a stainless steel plate attached to the left front door hinge pillar. It consists of car make symbol, series code, model year code, assembly plant symbol, and a sequential production number.

FIRST DIGIT: Identifies the car make

Chrysler	C
Imperial	Y

SECOND DIGIT: Identifies the class

CLASS	CODE
Economy	E
Low	L
High	H
Medium	M

THIRD AND FOURTH DIGITS: Identify the body style

BODY STYLE	CODE
2-Dr. Hardtop	23
Convertible	27
4-Dr. Sedan	41
4-Dr. Hardtop	43
4-Dr. Station Wagon, 6-Pass.	45
4-Dr. Station Wagon, 9-Pass.	46

FIFTH DIGIT: Identifies the cubic inch displacement

CID	CODE
383 CID	G
383 CID High Performance	H
440 CID	K
440 CID High Performance	L
Special Order 8 Cyl.	M

SIXTH DIGIT: Identifies the model year (1968)

SEVENTH DIGIT: Identifies the assembly plant

ASSEMBLY PLANT	CODE
Jefferson Plant, Detroit, MI	E
Newark, DE	F

LAST SIX DIGITS: Represent the basic production numbers

BODY NUMBER PLATE

THE BODY PLATE is stamped and embossed on a stainless steel plate attached to the fender shield under the hood. The plate indicates the code for the body type, engine, transmission, schedule date, paint, trim and some option codes. The plate is read left to right, bottom to top, starting with the bottom row of numbers.

CHRYSLER MOTORS
CORPORATION

AX TR PNT UBS
4 H1T BB1 W

CH41 81 5 635 224 055551

EXAMPLE:

C	Car Make (Chrysler)
H	Car Class (High)
41	Body Style (4-Dr. Sedan)
81	Engine CID (440 4 BC 8 Cyl.)
5	Transmission (3-Sp. Auto.)
635	Tire Size and Type
224	Production Date (2-24)
055551	Production Sequence
4	Axle
H1T	Trim
B	Lower Body Color
B	Upper Body Color
UBS	Accent Color

THE ENGINE CID CODE identifies the engine.

ENGINE CID	CODE
383 2 BBL 8 Cyl.	61
383 4 BBL 8 Cyl.	62
440 4 BBL 8 Cyl.	81
440 4 BBL HP	83

TRANSMISSION	CODE
3-Speed Automatic	5
3-Speed Automatic HD	6
Special Order	9

THE BODY NUMBER is a four-digit number which indicates the car line, price class, and body style. Same first four digits of the VIN.

NEWPORT	CODE
2-Dr. Hardtop	CE23
4-Dr. Sedan	CE41
4-Dr. Hardtop	CE43
2-Dr. Convertible	CE27

NEWPORT CUSTOM	CODE
2-Dr. Hardtop	CL23
4-Dr. Sedan	CL41
4-Dr. Hardtop	CL43

CHRYSLER 300	CODE
2-Dr. Hardtop	CM23
4-Dr. Hardtop	CM43
Convertible	CM27

NEW YORKER	CODE
4-Dr. Sedan	CH41
2-Dr. Hardtop	CH23
4-Dr. Hardtop	CH43

TOWN & COUNTRY	CODE
4-Dr. Sta. Wagon, 6-Pass.	CE45
4-Dr. Sta. Wagon, 9-Pass.	CE46

CROWN IMPERIAL	CODE
4-Dr. Sedan	YM41
2-Dr. Hardtop	YM23
4-Dr. Hardtop	YM43
Convertible	YM27

LEBARON	CODE
4-Dr. Hardtop	YH43

The next three-digit code indicates the tire size and type; this option code is not included.

THE SHIPPING ORDER NUMBER consists of a three-digit month and day scheduled production date, and a five-digit production order number.

THE AXLE CODE identifies the number of axles.

THE UBS CODE identifies the upper door frame color, and the accent stripe color.

THE TRIM CODE furnishes the key to the interior color and material.

NEWPORT TRIM

COLOR	CLOTH	VINYL	LEATHER	CODE
Blue	•	•		E1B
Blue		•		E5B,E6B
Green	•	•		E1F
Green		•		E6F
Turquoise	•	•		E1Q
Tan	•	•		E1T
Black	•	•		E1X
Black		•		E5X,E6X
Gold		•		E5Y
Red		•		E6R
White/Black		•		E6W

NEWPORT CUSTOM TRIM

COLOR	CLOTH	VINYL	LEATHER	CODE
Blue	•	•		L2B
Blue		•		L9B,L6B
Green	•	•		L2F
Green		•		L6F
Turquoise	•	•		L2Q
Black	•	•		L2X
Black		•		L9X,L6X
Gold	•	•		L2Y
Red		•		L6R

300 TRIM

COLOR	CLOTH	VINYL	LEATHER	CODE
Blue	•	•		M2B
Blue		•		M6B,M5B
Green	•	•		M2F
Green		•		M6F
Red		•		M6R
White/Black		•		M6W
Black	•	•		M7X,M2X
Black		•		M6X,M5X
Black			•	M3X
Gold	•	•		M2Y
Gold		•		M5Y

NEW YORKER TRIM

COLOR	CLOTH	VINYL	LEATHER	CODE
Blue	•	•		H1B,H2B,H8B
Blue		•		H6B
Green	•	•		H1F
Green		•		H6F
Turquoise	•	•		H1Q,H2Q
Tan	•	•		H1T,H2T,H8T
Black	•	•		H1X,H2X,H8X
Black		•		H9X,H6X
Black			•	H3X
Red		•		H9R,H6R
Gold		•		H9Y
White/Black		•		H6W

TOWN & COUNTRY WAGON TRIM

COLOR	CLOTH	VINYL	LEATHER	CODE
Blue		•		E5B
Red		•		E5R
Tan		•		E5T
Black	•	•		E8X
Black		•		E5X

1968 CHRYSLER / IMPERIAL

IMPERIAL TRIM

COLOR	CLOTH	VINYL	LEATHER	CODE
Blue	•	•		M1D
Blue	•		•	M2D,M3D
Blue			•	M3B,M9B,M9D
Green	•	•		M1F
Green	•		•	M2F,M8F
Green			•	M3F,M9F
Turquoise	•	•		M1Q
Turquoise	•		•	M2Q,M8Q
Turquoise			•	M3Q,M9Q
Red	•	•		M1R
Red	•		•	M2R,M8R
Red			•	M3R,M9R
Tan	•	•		M1T
Tan	•		•	M2T,M8T
Black	•	•		M1X
Black	•		•	M2X,M8X
Black			•	M3X,M9X
Gold			•	M3E,M3Y
Gold			•	M9E,M9Y
White			•	M3W,M9W

IMPERIAL LEBARON TRIM

COLOR	CLOTH	VINYL	LEATHER	CODE
Gray	•		•	H8A
Blue	•		•	H8D
Blue			•	H9B,H9D
Tan	•		•	H8T
Gold			•	H9E,H9Y
Green			•	H9F
Turquoise			•	H9Q
Red			•	H9R
White			•	H9W
Black			•	H9X

THE PAINT CODE furnishes the key to the paint used on the car. A three-digit code indicates the top and bottom colors respectively. A number follows which designates two-tone, sports-tone, convertible top, etc.

COLOR	CODE
Silver Haze Metallic	A
Formal Black	B
Consort Blue Metallic	C
Sky Blue Metallic	D
Military Blue Metallic	E
Frost Green Metallic	F
Forest Green Metallic	G
Antique Ivory	H
Sovereign Gold Metallic	J
Mist Turquoise Metallic	K
Turbine Bronze Metallic	M
Red Flame	P
Burgundy Metallic	R
Meadow Green Metallic	T
Polar White	W
Sandalwood	X
Beige Mist Metallic	Y
Charcoal Gray Metallic	5

ENGINE NUMBER

The engine number is stamped on the pan rail at the rear corner under the starter opening. The number provides the code to identify the manufacturing plant, cubic inch displacement and the engine model.

EXAMPLE:

PM	440	P
ENG. PLANT	CID	ENGINE

ENGINE PLANTS	CODE
Mound Rd.	PM
Trenton	PT

ENGINE MODEL	CODE
Regular Fuel	R
Low Compression	L
Premium Fuel	P
Special Engine	S

NEWPORT/NEWPORT CUSTOM

ENGINE NO.	NO. CYL.	CID	HORSE-POWER	COMP. RATIO	CARB	TRANS
383	8	383	290	9.2:1	2 BC	MAN/AUTO
383	8	383	330	10.0:1	4 BC	MAN/AUTO
440	8	440	375	10.1:1	4 BC	AUTO

300/NEW YORKER

ENGINE NO.	NO. CYL.	CID	HORSE-POWER	COMP. RATIO	CARB	TRANS
440	8	440	350	10.1:1	4 BC	AUTO
440	8	440	375	10.1:1	4 BC	AUTO

TOWN & COUNTRY

ENGINE NO.	NO. CYL.	CID	HORSE-POWER	COMP. RATIO	CARB	TRANS
383	8	383	290	9.2:1	2 BC	AUTO
383	8	383	330	10.0:1	4 BC	AUTO
440	8	440	350	10.1:1	4 BC	AUTO

IMPERIAL

ENGINE NO.	NO. CYL.	CID	HORSE-POWER	COMP. RATIO	CARB	TRANS
440	8	440	350	10.1:1	4 BC	AUTO

Note: The following special marks may also be found on the engine number pad and indicate variations in engine specifications which affect service procedures.

Engine Specification:

L or LC - Low compression
A - .020" oversize cylinder bores
Maltese Cross - .001" undersize bearing shells
X - .010" undersize crankshaft
* - Oversize engine tappets

 1969 CHRYSLER / IMPERIAL

1969 CHRYSLER NEW YORKER

1969 CHRYSLER 300

1969 IMPERIAL

1969 IMPERIAL

VEHICLE IDENTIFICATION NUMBER

CHRYSLER
CH41K9F100551

The vehicle number (serial number) is located on a plate which is attached to the instrument panel between the left windshield wiper pivot and the left "A" post. It consists of car make symbol, price class, body type, engine displacement, model year code, assembly plant symbol, and a sequential production number.

FIRST DIGIT: Identifies the car make

Chrysler	C
Imperial	Y

SECOND DIGIT: Identifies the class

CLASS	CODE
Economy	E
Low	L
High	H
Medium	M
Premium	P

THIRD AND FOURTH DIGITS: Identify the body style

BODY STYLE	CODE
2-Dr. Hardtop	23
Convertible	27
4-Dr. Sedan	41
4-Dr. Hardtop	43
4-Dr. Station Wagon, 6-Pass.	45
4-Dr. Station Wagon, 9-Pass.	46

FIFTH DIGIT: Identifies the cubic inch displacement

CID	CODE
383 CID	G
383 High Performance CID	H
440 CID	K
440 High Performance CID	L
Special Order 8 Cyl.	M

SIXTH DIGIT: Identifies the model year (1969)

SEVENTH DIGIT: Identifies the assembly plant

ASSEMBLY PLANT	CODE
Jefferson Plant, Detroit, MI	C
Newark, DE	F

LAST SIX DIGITS: Represent the basic production numbers

BODY NUMBER PLATE

THE BODY PLATE is read left to right, bottom to top. For 1969, Chrysler Corp. started a new system on their body code plates. Each plate contains all the code numbers for every option on the car. If one plate didn't hold all the information, a second tag was used. Listed here will be the codes found (usually) on the bottom two rows.

CHRYSLER MOTORS
CORPORATION

TRM UBS
X9 X9 H3X W

CH41 E63 D32 K9F 055551

EXAMPLE:

C	Car Make (Chrysler)
H	Car Class (High)
41	Body Style (4-Dr. Sedan)
E63	Engine (383 4 BC 8 Cyl.)
D32	Transmission (3-Spd. Auto.)
100555	Production Sequence
X9	Upper Body Color
X9	Lower Body Color
H3X	Trim
W	Accent Color

First is a four-digit body model and style code, a three-digit engine code and a three-digit transmission code, and the last nine digits of the vin number. The next row is a four-digit plant code number, two-digit upper body or roof color, two-digit lower body color, a three-digit trim code number followed by special trim, stripping and door frame color codes, if any.

THE UBS CODE identifies the upper door frame color, and the accent stripe color.

THE ENGINE CID CODE identifies the engine.

ENGINE CID	CODE
383 1-2 BBL 8 Cyl.	E 61
383 1-4 BBL 8 Cyl.	E 63
440 1-4 BBl 8 Cyl.	E 85
440 1 BBl 8 Cyl. HP	E 86

TRANSMISSION	CODE
3-Spd. Automatic	D31
3-Spd. Automatic HD	D32
Special Order	D34

THE BODY NUMBER is a four-digit number which indicates the car line, price class, and body style. Same first four digits of the VIN.

NEWPORT	CODE
2-Dr. Hardtop	CE23
4-Dr. Sedan	CE41
4-Dr. Hardtop	CE43
2-Dr. Convertible	CE27

NEWPORT CUSTOM	CODE
4-Dr. Sedan	CL41
4-Dr. Hardtop	CL43
2-Dr. Hardtop	CL23

CHRYSLER 300	CODE
2-Dr. Hardtop	CM23
4-Dr. Hardtop	CM43
Convertible	CM27

NEW YORKER	CODE
4-Dr. Sedan	CH41
2-Dr. Hardtop	CH23
4-Dr. Hardtop	CH43

CROWN IMPERIAL	CODE
4-Dr. Sedan	YM41

LEBARON	CODE
4-Dr. Hardtop	YH43
2-Dr. Hardtop	YH23

TOWN & COUNTRY	CODE
4-Dr. Sta. Wagon, 6-Pass.	CP45
4-Dr. Sta. Wagon, 9-Pass.	CP46

THE TRIM NUMBER furnishes the key to the interior color and material.

NEWPORT TRIM

COLOR	CLOTH	VINYL	LEATHER	CODE
Green	•	•		E1G
Blue	•	•		E1D
Blue		•		E2D
Champagne	•	•		E1L
Turquoise	•	•		E1Q
Black	•	•		E1X
Black		•		E2X,E6X
Gold		•		E2Y
Saddle		•		E2T
Tan		•		E6T
White/Black		•		E6W

NEWPORT CUSTOM TRIM

COLOR	CLOTH	VINYL	LEATHER	CODE
Blue	•	•		L3D
Blue		•		L4D
Green	•	•		L3G
Turquoise	•	•		L3Q
Black	•	•		L3X
Black		•		L4X,L8X
Gold	•	•		L3Y
Briar	•	•		L7E
Briar		•		L4E
Champagne	•	•		L7L

300 TRIM

COLOR	CLOTH	VINYL	LEATHER	CODE
Green	•	•		M3G
Green		•		M6G
Black	•	•		M3X
Black		•		M4X,M6X
Gold	•	•		M3Y
Briar		•		M4E
Blue		•		M4D,M6D
Champagne	•	•		M5L
Saddle		•		M6T
White/Black		•		M6W

NEW YORKER TRIM

COLOR	CLOTH	VINYL	LEATHER	CODE
Turquoise	•	•		H1Q,H3Q
Blue	•	•		H1D,H3D,H7D
Blue		•		H6D
Green	•	•		H1G,H3G
Black	•	•		H1X,H3X
Black		•		H8X,H6X
Gold	•	•		H1Y,H3Y
Champagne	•	•		H7L
Champagne		•		H8L
Saddle		•		H6T
Saddle			•	HST
Briar	•	•		H7E
White/Black		•		H6W

1969 CHRYSLER / IMPERIAL

TOWN & COUNTRY WAGON TRIM

COLOR	CLOTH	VINYL	LEATHER	CODE
Blue		•		E4D
Briar		•		E4E
Green		•		E4G,E8G
Saddle		•		E4T
Black		•		E4X,E8X
Champagne	•	•		E7L

IMPERIAL CROWN TRIM

COLOR	CLOTH	VINYL	LEATHER	CODE
Green	•	•		M1G
Blue	•	•		M1D
Walnut/ Beige	•	•		M1K
Burgundy	•	•		M1M
Turquoise	•	•		M1Q
Black	•	•		M1X

IMPERIAL LEBARON TRIM

COLOR	CLOTH	VINYL	LEATHER	CODE
Burgundy	•		•	MDM,MBM
Blue	•		•	MDD,MBD
Blue			•	MSB,MSD,MRB
Green	•		•	MDG,MBG
Green			•	MSG,MRG
Walnut/ Beige	•		•	MDK,MBK
Turquoise	•		•	MDQ,MBQ
Black	•		•	MDX,MBX
Black			•	MSX,MRX
Gold			•	MSY,MSN
Red			•	MSR
Saddle			•	MST,MRT
White			•	MSW,MRW

THE PAINT CODE furnishes the key to the paint used on the car.

COLOR	CODE
Bahama Blue Metallic	B3
Jubilee Blue Metallic	B7
Dark Briar Metallic	E7
Surf Green Metallic	F3
Avocado Metallic	F5
Jade Green Metallic	F8
Sandalwood	L1
Aquamarine Metallic	Q4
Bronze Mist Metallic	T3
Burnished Bronze Metallic	T5
Tuscan Bronze Metallic	T7
Formal Black	X9
Antique Ivory	Y3
Classic Gold Metallic	Y4
Platinum Metallic	A4
Crimson	R6
Spinnaker White	W1
Charcoal Metallic	A9
Midnight Blue Metallic	B9
Dark Emerald Metallic	F9
Deep Plum	M9

ENGINE NUMBER

The engine number is stamped on the pan rail at the rear corner under the starter opening. The number provides the code to identify the series, block, displacement, and month/day production date.

EXAMPLE:

PM	383	P
ENG. PLANT	CID	ENGINE

ENGINE PLANTS	CODE
Mound Rd.	PM
Trenton	PT

ENGINE MODEL	CODE
Regular Fuel	R
Low Compression	L
Premium	P
Special Engine	S

NEWPORT/NEWPORT CUSTOM

ENGINE NO.	NO. CYL.	CID	HORSE-POWER	COMP. RATIO	CARB	TRANS
383	8	383	290	9.2:1	2 BC	MAN/AUTO
383	8	383	330	10.0:1	4 BC	MAN/AUTO
440	8	440	375	10.1:1	4 BC	AUTO

300/NEW YORKER

ENGINE NO.	NO. CYL.	CID	HORSE-POWER	COMP. RATIO	CARB	TRANS
440	8	440	350	10.1:1	4 BC	AUTO
440	8	440	375	10.1:1	4 BC	AUTO

TOWN & COUNTRY

ENGINE NO.	NO. CYL.	CID	HORSE-POWER	COMP. RATIO	CARB	TRANS
383	8	383	290	9.2:1	2 BC	AUTO
383	8	383	330	10.0:1	4 BC	AUTO
440	8	440	350	10.1:1	4 BC	AUTO

IMPERIAL

ENGINE NO.	NO. CYL.	CID	HORSE-POWER	COMP. RATIO	CARB	TRANS
440	8	440	350	10.1:1	4 BC	AUTO

Note: Various marks as listed below may be found on the engine number pad and indicate variations in engine specifications which affect service procedures.

Engine Specification:

Maltese Cross - .001" undersize crankshaft
Maltese Cross & X - .010" undersize crankshaft
M-2-3 - #2 & 3 main bearing journals undersize
R-1-4 - #1 & 4 connecting rod journals undersize
M-10 - .010" undersize main bearing journals
R-10 - .010" undersize connecting rod journals
A - .020" oversize cylinder bores
Diamond - .008" oversize tappets
O.S. - .005" oversize valve stems

1960 DODGE

1960 DODGE

1960 DODGE DART

1960 DODGE DART

VEHICLE IDENTIFICATION NUMBER

DODGE
6105100553

The vehicle number (serial number) is stamped and embossed on a stainless steel plate attached to the left front door hinge pillar. It consists of car make symbol, series code, model year code, assembly plant symbol and a sequential production number.

FIRST DIGIT: Identifies the car make

CAR MAKE	CODE
Dodge Dart (6 Cyl.)	4
Dodge Dart (8 Cyl.)	5
Dodge (8 Cyl.)	6

SECOND DIGIT: Identifies the series

SERIES	CODE
Seneca Matador	1
Pioneer	2
Phoenix, Polara	3
Seneca Matador Wagon	5
Pioneer Wagon	6
Polara Wagon	7
Taxi	8
Special, Police	9

THIRD DIGIT: Identifies the model year (1960)

FOURTH DIGIT: Identifies the assembly plant

ASSEMBLY PLANT	CODE
Detroit, MI	2-3
Los Angeles, CA	5
Newark, DE	6
St. Louis, MO	7
Clairpointe	8

LAST SIX DIGITS: Represent the basic production numbers

BODY NUMBER PLATE

THE BODY PLATE is stamped and embossed on a stainless steel plate under the hood. It is attached to the right or left fender, cowl, or radiator cross member depending on the model and assembly plant. This plate indicates schedule date, body production number, body series, trim, paint, and accessory code.

CHRYSLER MOTORS
CORPORATION

SO	NUMBER	BDY	TRM	PNT
0224	0555	643	-	BB1

1960 DODGE

EXAMPLE:

0224	SON (Feb. 24)
0555	Production Sequence
643	Body Style (4-Dr. Hardtop)
B	Lower Body Color
B	Upper Body Color

THE SHIPPING ORDER NUMBER is assigned prior to production. It consists of a 4-digit planned delivery month/day date code, 0224 (February 24th). Then a plant production sequence number follows (0555).

THE BODY NUMBER is a 3-digit number which indicates the model and body style.

DART SENECA	CODE 6 CYL	8 CYL
4-Dr. Sedan	411	511
4-Dr. Sedan	413	513
4-Dr. Wagon	456	556

DART PIONEER	CODE 6 CYL	8 CYL
2-Dr. Sedan	421	521
4-Dr. Sedan	423	523
4-Dr. Wagon	466	566
4-Dr. Wagon	467	567
2-Dr. Hardtop	422	522

DART PHOENIX	CODE 6 CYL	8 CYL
4-Dr. Sedan	433	533
4-Dr. Hardtop	434	534
2-Dr. Hardtop	432	532
Convertible	435	535

MATADOR	CODE
4-Dr. Sedan	643
2-Dr. Hardtop	642
4-Dr. Hardtop	644
4-Dr. Wagon	678
4-Dr. Wagon	679

POLARA	CODE
4-Dr. Sedan	543
2-Dr. Hardtop	542
4-Dr. Hardtop	544
Convertible	545
4-Dr. Wagon	578
4-Dr. Wagon	579

THE TRIM NUMBER
As of the print date, no trim codes were available for 1960 Dodge.

THE PAINT CODE furnishes the key to the paint used on the car. A two-digit code indicates the top and bottom colors respectively. A number follows which designates two-tone, sports-tone, convertible top, etc.

COLOR	CODE
Raven	B
Azure	C
Mediterranean	D
Spray	F
Spruce	G
Cactus	H
Frost Turquoise	J
Teal	K
Cloud	L
Charcoal	M
Vermilion	P
Deep Burgundy	R
Raw Sienna	S
Fawn	T
Satin	W
Pewter	X
Cocoa	Y

ENGINE NUMBER

6 cylinder engine number is stamped on the right side of the block below the cylinder head at the front or rear of the engine.

361-383 engine numbers are is stamped on the boss on the top right side of the cylinder block behind the water pump.

318 engine number is stamped on the front face of the left hand cylinder block.

EXAMPLE:

P	38	2	24
YEAR	383	FEBRUARY	DAY

DART SENECA AND PIONEER

ENGINE CODE	NO. CYL.	CID	HORSE-POWER	COMP. RATIO	CARB	TRANS
P-22	6	225	145	8.5:1	1 BC	* M & A
P-318	8	318	230	9.0:1	2 BC	* M & A
P-318	8	318	255	9.0:1	4 BC	* M & A

DART PHOENIX

ENGINE CODE	NO. CYL.	CID	HORSE-POWER	COMP. RATIO	CARB	TRANS
P-318	8	318	255	9.0:1	4 BC	* M & A
P-36	8	361	310	10.0:1	2-4 BC	* M & A
P-38	8	383	330	10.0:1	2-4 BC	* M & A

MATADOR

ENGINE CODE	NO. CYL.	CID	HORSE-POWER	COMP. RATIO	CARB	TRANS
P-36	8	361	295	10.0:1	2 BC	* M & A
P-38	8	383	330	10.0:1	2-4 BC	* M & A

POLARA

ENGINE CODE	NO. CYL.	CID	HORSE-POWER	COMP. RATIO	CARB	TRANS
P-38	8	383	325	10.0:1	4 BC	* M & A
P-38	8	383	330	10.0:1	2-4 BC	* M & A

* MAN & AUTO

Other identifying engine marks are as follows:

AF - Blank engine is standard
A - .020" oversize cylinder
B - .010" undersize crankshaft journals
AB - Both
Maltese Cross - .001" undersize crankshaft journals
Diamond - .08" oversize lifters

Note: Some early 361,383 were marked with engine displacement followed by a serial number, similar to the 318.

1961 DODGE DART

1961 DODGE DART

1961 DODGE LANCER

1961 DODGE LANCER

1961 DODGE POLARA

1961 DODGE POLARA

VEHICLE IDENTIFICATION NUMBER

DODGE
5212100553

The vehicle number (serial number) is stamped and embossed on a stainless steel plate attached to the left front door hinge pillar. It consists of car make symbol, series code, model year code, assembly plant symbol and a sequential production number.

FIRST DIGIT: Identifies the car make

CAR MAKE	CODE
Dodge Dart (6 Cyl.)	4
Dodge (8 Cyl.)	5
Lancer	7

SECOND DIGIT: Identifies the series

SERIES	CODE
Seneca, Lancer 170	1
Pioneer	2
Phoenix, Lancer 770	3
Polara	4
Seneca 170 Wagon	5
Pioneer Wagon	6
Polara Wagon	7
Taxi	8
Special, Police	9
Fleet	0

THIRD DIGIT: Identifies the model year (1961)

FOURTH DIGIT: Identifies the assembly plant

ASSEMBLY PLANT	CODE
Detroit, MI	2-3
Los Angeles, CA	5
Newark, DE	6
St. Louis, MO	7

LAST SIX DIGITS: Represent the basic production numbers

BODY NUMBER PLATE

THE BODY PLATE is stamped and embossed on a stainless steel plate under the hood. It is attached to the right or left fender, cowl, or radiator cross member depending on the model and assembly plant. This plate indicates schedule date, body production number, body series, trim, paint and accessory code.

CHRYSLER MOTORS CORPORATION

SO	NUMBER	BDY	TRM	PNT
0224	0555	523	201	BB1

EXAMPLE:

0224 SON (Feb. 24)
0555 Production Sequence
523 Body Style (4-Dr. Sedan)
201 Trim
B Lower Body Color
B Upper Body Color

THE SHIPPING ORDER NUMBER is assigned prior to production. It consists of a 4-digit planned delivery month/day date code, 0224 (February 24th). Then a plant production sequence number follows (0555).

THE BODY NUMBER is a 3-digit number which indicates the model and body style.

LANCER	CODE 6 CYL	8 CYL
	170	770
2-Dr. Sedan	711	—
4-Dr. Sedan	713	733
2-Dr. Hardtop	—	732
2-Dr. Sports Coupe	—	731
4-Dr. Wagon	756	776

DART SENECA	CODE 6 CYL	8 CYL
4-Dr. Sedan	411	511
4-Dr. Sedan	413	513
4-Dr. Wagon	456	556

DART PIONEER	CODE 6 CYL	8 CYL
2-Dr. Sedan	421	521
4-Dr. Sedan	423	523
4-Dr. Wagon	466	566
4-Dr. Wagon	467	567
2-Dr. Hardtop	422	522

DART PHOENIX	CODE 6 CYL	8 CYL
4-Dr. Sedan	433	533
4-Dr. Hardtop	434	534
2-Dr. Hardtop	432	532
Convertible	435	535

POLARA	CODE
4-Dr. Sedan	543
2-Dr. Hardtop	542
4-Dr. Hardtop	544
Convertible	545
4-Dr. Wagon	578
4-Dr. Wagon	579

THE TRIM NUMBER furnishes the key to the interior color and material.

COLOR	CLOTH	VINYL	LEATHER	CODE
Gray	•	•		201,202,203
Gray	•	•		204,205,314
Gray	•	•		334,304
Gray		•		434,251,252
Gray		•		254,255
Blue	•	•		231,311,321
Blue	•	•		331,301
Blue		•		431,411,421
Blue		•		401
Black	•	•		234
Black		•		404
Red	•	•		235,335
Red		•		435,425
Green	•	•		312,322,332
Green		•		432
Brown	•	•		313,333,303
Brown		•		423,423,404
Tan		•		433
Silver		•		414,424

THE PAINT CODE furnishes the key to the paint used on the car. A two-digit code indicates the top and bottom colors respectively. A number follows which designates two-tone, sports-tone, convertible top, etc.

COLOR	CODE
Bamboo	A
Midnight	B
Glacier Blue	C
Marlin Blue	D
Spring Green	F
Frosted Mint	G
Cactus	H
Turquoise	J
Nassau Green	K
Silver Gray	L
Vermilion	P
Rose Mist	S
Aztec Gold	U
Snow	W
Buckskin	Y
Roman Bronze	Z

ENGINE NUMBER

6 cylinder engine number is stamped on the right side of the block below the cylinder head opposite the no. 1 cylinder.

318 engine number is stamped on the front face of the left hand cylinder block.

Others are stamped on a boss on the top right side of the cylinder block just behind the water pump.

EXAMPLE:

R	38	2	24
YEAR	383	FEBRUARY	DAY

LANCER

ENGINE CODE	NO. CYL.	CID	HORSE-POWER	COMP. RATIO	CARB	TRANS
R-17	6	170	101	8.2:1	1 BC	* M & A
R-17	6	170	148	8.2:1	4 BC	* M & A
R-22*	6	225	145	8.2:1	1 BC	* M & A
R-22*	6	225	196	8.2:1	4 BC	* M & A

*If the 225 C.I. engine is aluminum, the code is AR-22

DART SENECA, PIONEER AND PHOENIX

ENGINE CODE	NO. CYL.	CID	HORSE-POWER	COMP. RATIO	CARB	TRANS
R-22	6	225	145	8.2:1	1 BC	* M & A
R-318	8	318	230	9.0:1	2 BC	* M & A
R-318	8	318	265	9.0:1	4 BC	AUTO
R-36	8	361	305	9.0:1	4 BC	* M & A
R-38	8	383	330	10.0:1	2-4 BC	* M & A
R-38	8	383	340	10.0:1	2-4 BC	* M & A
R-38	8	383	325	10.0:1	4 BC	* M & A
R-38*	8	383	330	10.0:1	2-4 BC	* M & A
R-41	8	413	350	10.0:1	4 BC	* M & A
R-41**	8	413	375	10.0:1	2-4 BC	* M & A
R-41	8	413	375	10.0:1	2-4 BC	* M & A

* Runner
** Short Ram

POLARA

ENGINE CODE	NO. CYL.	CID	HORSE-POWER	COMP. RATIO	CARB	TRANS
R-36	8	361	265	9.0:1	2 BC	* M & A
R-38	8	383	325	10.0:1	4 BC	* M & A
R-38	8	383	330	10.0:1	2-4 BC	AUTO
R-38	8	383	340	10.0:1	2-4 BC	AUTO

* MAN & AUTO

Other identifying engine marks are as follows:

A - .020" oversize cylinder bores
Maltese Cross - .001" undersize bearing journals
X and Maltese Cross - .010" undersize bearing journals
Diamond - .008" oversize valve lifters
SP - Special Police cars
HP - High performance

1962 DODGE DART

1962 DODGE DART

1962 DODGE LANCER

1962 DODGE LANCER

1962 DODGE POLARA

1962 DODGE POLARA

VEHICLE IDENTIFICATION NUMBER

DODGE
4222100553

The vehicle number (serial number) is stamped and embossed on a stainless steel plate attached to the left front door hinge pillar. It consists of car make symbol, series code, model year code, assembly plant symbol and a sequential production number.

FIRST DIGIT: Identifies the car make

CAR MAKE	CODE
Dart (6 Cyl.)	4
Dart (8 Cyl.), Polar 500	5
Custom 880	6
Lancer 170, 770, GT	7

SECOND DIGIT: Identifies the series

SERIES	CODE
Lancer 170, Dart, 880	1
Dart 330	2
Lancer 770, Dart 440	3
Lancer GT, Polara 500	4
Lancer 170, Dart Custom Wagon	5
Dart 330 Wagon	6
Lancer 770, Dart 440 Wagon	7
Taxi	8
Special	9
Fleet	10

THIRD DIGIT: Identifies the model year (1962)

FOURTH DIGIT: Identifies the assembly plant

ASSEMBLY PLANT	CODE
Detroit, MI	2-3
Los Angeles, CA	5
Newark, DE	6
St. Louis, MO	7

LAST SIX DIGITS: Represent the basic production numbers

BODY NUMBER PLATE

THE BODY PLATE is stamped and embossed on a stainless steel plate under the hood. It is attached to the right or left fender, cowl, or radiator cross member depending on the model and assembly plant. This plate indicates schedule date, body production number, body series, trim, paint, and accessory code.

CHRYSLER MOTORS
CORPORATION

SO	NUMBER	BDY	TRM	PNT
0224	0555	413	704	BB1

EXAMPLE:

0224	SON (Feb. 24)
0551	Production Sequence
413	Body Style (4-Dr. Sedan)
704	Trim
B	Lower Body Color
B	Upper Body Color

THE SHIPPING ORDER NUMBER is assigned prior to production. It consists of a 4 digit planned delivery month/day date code, 0224 (February 24th). Then a plant production sequence number follows (0555).

THE BODY NUMBER is a 3-digit number which indicates the model and body style.

LANCER 170	CODE
4-Dr. Sedan	713
2-Dr. Sedan	711
4-Dr. Wagon	756
Taxi	783

LANCER 770	CODE
2-Dr. Sedan	731
4-Dr. Sedan	733
4-Dr. Wagon	776

LANCER GT	CODE
2-Dr. Hardtop Coupe	742

DART	6 CYL	8 CYL
2-Dr. Sedan	411	511
4-Dr. Sedan	413	513
4-Dr. Wagon	456	556

DART 330	6 CYL	8 CYL
2-Dr. Sedan	421	521
4-Dr. Sedan	423	523
2-Dr. Hardtop	422	522
4-Dr. Wagon	466	566
4-Dr. Wagon	—	567

DART 440	6 CYL	8 CYL
4-Dr. Sedan	433	533
2-Dr. Hardtop	431	531
4-Dr. Hardtop	—	532
Convertible	—	535
4-Dr. Wagon	—	576
4-Dr. Wagon	—	577

FLEET	6 CYL	8 CYL
2-Dr. Sedan	401	501
4-Dr. Sedan	403	503

CUSTOM 880	CODE
4-Dr. Sedan	613
2-Dr. Hardtop	612
4-Dr. Hardtop	614
Convertible	615
4-Dr. Wagon	658
4-Dr. Wagon	659

POLARA 500	CODE
2-Dr. Hardtop	542
4-Dr. Hardtop	544
Convertible	545

THE TRIM NUMBER furnishes the key to the interior color and material.

COLOR	CLOTH	VINYL	LEATHER	CODE
Black/Gray w/Blue	•	•		611
Black/Gray w/Blue		•		641
Black/Gray	•	•		614
Black/Gray		•		644
Black/Gray w/Red	•	•		615
Black/Gray w/Red		•		645
Blue	•	•		631,701,711
Blue	•	•		721
Blue		•		651,671,801
Blue		•		811,821,831
Blue		•		841
Green	•	•		632,712,722
Green		•		652,812
Cocoa	•	•		633,703,713
Cocoa	•	•		723
Cocoa		•		653,803,813
Red	•	•		635,715,725
Red		•		655,675,815
Gray	•	•		704,714,724
Gray		•		694,804,814
Gray		•		824,834,844
Blue/Beige		•		851
Green/Beige		•		852
Cocoa/Beige		•		853
Red/Beige		•		855

THE PAINT CODE furnishes the key to the paint used on the car. A two-digit code indicates the top and bottom colors respectively. A number follows which designates two-tone, sports-tone, convertible top, etc.

COLOR	CODE
Flax	A
Onyx	B
Powder Blue	C
Medium Blue	D
Cobalt Blue	E
Light Green	F
Glade Green	G
Metallic Emerald	H
Pearl Gray	M
Vermilion	P
Dusty Rose	R
Deep Cordovan	S
Buff	T
Shell Beige	U
Polar	W
Nutmeg Brown	Y

ENGINE NUMBER

6-cylinder engine number is stamped on the right side of the cylinder block below cylinder head opposite the no. 1 cylinder. The number provides the code to identify the series, block displacement, and month/day production date.

318 engine number is stamped on the left front of the block under the cylinder head.

361 engine number is stamped on the right side of the block below the distributor.

EXAMPLE:

S	38	2	24
YEAR	383	FEBRUARY	24th DAY

LANCER

ENGINE CODE	NO. CYL.	CID	HORSE-POWER	COMP. RATIO	CARB	TRANS
S-17	6	170	101	8.2:1	1 BC	* M & A
S-22	6	225	145	8.2:1	1 BC	* M & A

DART

ENGINE CODE	NO. CYL.	CID	HORSE-POWER	COMP. RATIO	CARB	TRANS
S-22	6	225	145	8.2:1	1 BC	* M & A
S-318	8	318	230	9.0:1	2 BC	* M & A
S-318	8	318	260	9.0:1	4 BC	AUTO
S-36	8	361	305	9.0:1	4 BC	* M & A
S-36	8	361	310	9.0:1	2-4 BC	* M & A
S-38	8	383	330	10.0:1	4 BC	* M & A
S-38	8	383	335	10.0:1	2-4 BC	* M & A
S-41	8	413	365	11.0:1	2-4 BC	* M & A
S-41	8	413	385	11.0:1	2-4 BC	* M & A
S-41	8	413	410	11.0:1	2-4 BC	* M & A
S-41	8	413	N/A	13.5:1	2-4 BC	* M & A

POLARA

ENGINE CODE	NO. CYL.	CID	HORSE-POWER	COMP. RATIO	CARB	TRANS
S-36	8	361	305	9.0:1	4 BC	* M & A
S-36	8	361	310	9.0:1	2-4 BC	* M & A
S-38	8	383	330	10.0:1	4 BC	* M & A
S-38	8	383	335	10.0:1	2-4 BC	* M & A
S-41	8	413	365	11.0:1	2-4 BC	* M & A
S-41	8	413	385	11.0:1	2-4 BC	* M & A
2-41	8	413	410	11.0:1	2-4 BC	* M & A
S-41	8	413	N/A	13.5:1	2-4 BC	* M & A

CUSTOM 880

ENGINE CODE	NO. CYL.	CID	HORSE-POWER	COMP. RATIO	CARB	TRANS
S-36	8	361	265	9.0:1	2 BC	* M & A

* MAN & AUTO

Other identifying engine marks are as follows:

6-cylinder engine:
A - .020" oversize cylinder bore
Diamond - .008" oversize tappets
Maltese Cross - .001" undersize bearing shells
M - Main journal
R - Connecting rod journal
X - .010" undersize crankshaft and crankshaft counterweight will be stamped M-10 or R-10 to indicate main and/or connecting rod journals are .010" undersize.

361 engine:
Maltese Cross and X - .010" undersize bearings

318 engine:
B - .010" undersize bearings
HD - 10 1/2" clutch
Diamond - .008" oversize lifters
LC - Low compression
HP - High performance
SP - Special police

1963 DODGE

1963 DODGE

1963 DODGE CUSTOM 880

1963 DODGE CUSTOM 880

1963 DODGE DART

1963 DODGE DART

VEHICLE IDENTIFICATION NUMBER

DODGE
7432100553

The vehicle number (serial number) is stamped and embossed on a stainless steel plate attached to the left front door hinge pillar. It consists of car make symbol, series code, model year code, assembly plant symbol and a sequential production number.

FIRST DIGIT: Identifies the car make

CAR MAKE	CODE
Dodge (6 Cyl.)	4
Dodge 880	5
Dodge V-8	6
Dart 170, 270, GT	7

SECOND DIGIT: Identifies the series

SERIES	CODE
170, 330, Custom 880	1
440	2
270, Polara	3
Dart GT, Polara 500	4
170, 330, 880 Custom Wagons	5
440 Wagon	6
Polara 270 Wagon	7
Taxi	8
Police	9
880, Fleet	10

THIRD DIGIT: Identifies the model year (1963)

FOURTH DIGIT: Identifies the assembly plant

ASSEMBLY PLANT	CODE
Detroit, MI	2-3
Los Angeles, CA	5
Newark, DE	6
St. Louis, MO	7

LAST SIX DIGITS: Represent the basic production numbers

BODY NUMBER PLATE

THE BODY PLATE is stamped and embossed on a stainless steel plate under the hood. It is attached to the right or left fender, cowl, or radiator cross member depending on the model and assembly plant. This plate indicates schedule date, body production number, body series, trim, paint, and accessory code.

CHRYSLER MOTORS
CORPORATION

SO	NUMBER	BDY	TRM	PNT
0224	0551	742	655	BB1

EXAMPLE:

0224	SON (Feb. 24)
0551	Production Sequence
742	Body Style (2-Dr. Hardtop)
655	Trim
B	Lower Body Color
B	Upper Body Color

THE SHIPPING ORDER NUMBER is assigned prior to production. It consists of a 4-digit planned delivery month/day date code, 0224 (February 24th). Then a plant production sequence number follows (0555).

THE BODY NUMBER is a 3-digit number which indicates the model and body style.

DART 170	CODE
2-Dr. Sedan	711
2-Dr. Sedan	713
4-Dr. Wagon	756

DART 270	CODE
2-Dr. Sedan	731
Convertible	735
4-Dr. Sedan	733
4-Dr. Wagon	776

DART GT	CODE
2-Dr. Hardtop	742
Convertible	745

440	6 CYL	8 CYL
2-Dr. Sedan	421	621
2-Dr. Hardtop	422	622
4-Dr. Sedan	423	623
4-Dr. Wagon	—	666
4-Dr. Wagon	—	667

330	6 CYL	8 CYL
2-Dr. Sedan	411	611
4-Dr. Sedan	413	613
4-Dr. Wagon	456	656
4-Dr. Wagon	457	657

FLEET	6 CYL	8 CYL
2-Dr. Sedan	401	601
4-Dr. Sedan	403	603

880	CODE
4-Dr. Sedan	503
4-Dr. Wagon	556
4-Dr. Wagon	557

CUSTOM 880	CODE
4-Dr. Sedan	513
2-Dr. Hardtop	512
4-Dr. Hardtop	514
Convertible	515
4-Dr. Wagon	558
4-Dr. Wagon	559

POLARA	6 CYL	8 CYL
2-Dr. Hardtop	432	632
4-Dr. Sedan	433	633
4-Dr. Hardtop	—	634
Convertible	—	635

POLARA 500	CODE
2-Dr. Hardtop	642
Convertible	645
4-Dr. Wagon	559

THE TRIM NUMBER furnishes the key to the interior color and material.

COLOR	CLOTH	VINYL	LEATHER	CODE
Tan	•	•		503,523,543
Tan	•	•		573,803,833
Tan		•		603,613,623
Tan		•		643,653,673
Tan		•		853,873,893
Red	•	•		505,525,545
Red	•	•		575,805,835
Red		•		605,625,654
Red		•		655,675,855
Red		•		875,895
Turquoise	•	•		508,528,548
Turquoise	•	•		578,808,838
Turquoise		•		608,628,648
Turquoise		•		658,678,858
Turquoise		•		878,898
Blue	•	•		521,541,571
Blue	•	•		801,831,501
Blue		•		601,611,621
Blue		•		641,651,671
Blue		•		851,871,891
Gray	•	•		584
Gray		•		694,684,894
Alabaster/ Black	•	•		526,546
Alabaster/ Black		•		626,646,656
Green	•	•		572
Green		•		672

THE PAINT CODE furnishes the key to the paint used on the car. A two-digit code indicates the top and bottom colors respectively. A number follows which designates two-tone, sports-tone, convertible top, etc.

COLOR	CODE
Ivory	A
Onyx	B
Light Blue	C
Medium Blue	D
Dark Blue	E
Light Green	F
Forest Green	G
Slate Green	H
Aqua	J
Turquoise	K
Dark Turquoise	L
Steel Gray	N
Vermilion	P
Cordovan	S
Beige	U
Polar	W
Sandalwood	Y

ENGINE NUMBER

6-cylinder engine number is stamped on the right side of the block just behind the distributor or on a boss on the top side of the cylinder block behind the water pump. The number provides the code to identify the series, block displacement, and month/day production date.

318 engine number is stamped on the left front of the block under the cylinder head.

361, 383, 413, 426 engine numbers are stamped on the right side of the block below the distributor, or on the left front of the block behind the thermostat housing.

EXAMPLE:

R	38	2	24
YEAR	383	FEBRUARY	DAY

DART

ENGINE CODE	NO. CYL.	CID	HORSE-POWER	COMP. RATIO	CARB	TRANS
T-17	6	170	101	8.2:1	1 BC	* M & A
T-22	6	225	145	8.2:1	1 BC	* M & A

POLARA, 440, 330

ENGINE CODE	NO. CYL.	CID	HORSE-POWER	COMP. RATIO	CARB	TRANS
T-22	6	225	145	8.2:1	1 BC	* M & A
T-318	8	318	230	9.0:1	2 BC	* M & A
T-38	8	383	305	10.0:1	2 BC	* M & A
T-38	8	383	330	10.0:1	4 BC	* M & A
T-42	8	426	425	13.5:1	2-4 BC	* M & A

POLARA 500

ENGINE CODE	NO. CYL.	CID	HORSE-POWER	COMP. RATIO	CARB	TRANS
T-38	8	383	305	10.0:1	2 BC	* M & A
T-38	8	383	330	10.0:1	4 BC	* M & A
T-42	8	426	425	13.5;1	2-4 BC	* M & A
T-42	8	426	415	11.0:1	2-4 BC	* M & A

880, 880 CUSTOM

ENGINE CODE	NO. CYL.	CID	HORSE-POWER	COMP. RATIO	CARB	TRANS
T-36	8	361	265	9.0:1	2 BC	* M & A
T-38	8	383	305	10.0:1	2 BC	* M & A
5-41	8	413	360	10.1:1	4 BC	* M & A

* MAN & AUTO

Other identifying engine marks are as follows:

6-cylinder:
Maltese Cross - .001" undersize crankshaft journals (M and R plus a number stamped on crankshaft counterweight indicates which main and rod journals are undersize).
X - .010" undersize crankshaft journals (M-10 and R-10 stamped on crankshaft counterweight indicates all rod and main journals are undersize).
A - .020" oversize cylinder bores
Diamond plus a number - .008" oversize lifters (number indicates which lifter).
"o/s" - .005 oversize valves

318, 361, 383, 413, 426:
Maltese Cross - .001" undersize crankshaft journals
B - .010" undersize crankshaft journals (318 only)
Maltese Cross and X - .010" undersize crankshaft journals
A - 020" oversize cylinder bores
Diamond - .008" oversize valve lifters
o/s - valves with .005" oversize stems

LC - Low compression
HC - High compression
HP - High performance
MP - Maximum performance

1964 DODGE

1964 DODGE

1964 DODGE CUSTOM 880

1964 DODGE CUSTOM 880

1964 DODGE DART

1964 DODGE DART

1964 DODGE

VEHICLE IDENTIFICATION NUMBER

DODGE
7442100559

The vehicle number (serial number) is stamped and embossed on a stainless steel plate attached to the left front door hinge pillar. It consists of car make symbol, series code, model year code, assembly plant symbol and a sequential production number.

FIRST DIGIT: Identifies the car make

CAR MAKE	CODE
Dodge (6 Cyl.)	4
880	5
Dodge (8 Cyl.)	6
Dart	7

SECOND DIGIT: Identifies the series

SERIES	CODE
170, 330, 880	1
440, Custom 880	2
270, Polara	3
Dart GT, Polara	4
170, 330, 880 Wagon	5
440, Custom 880 Wagons	6
Dart 270 Wagon	7
Taxi	8
Special	9

THIRD DIGIT: Identifies the model year (1964)

FOURTH DIGIT: Identifies the assembly plant

ASSEMBLY PLANT	CODE
Detroit, MI	2-3
Los Angeles, CA	5
Newark, DE	6
St. Louis, MO	7

LAST SIX DIGITS: Represent the basic production numbers

BODY NUMBER PLATE

THE BODY PLATE is stamped and embossed on a stainless steel plate under the hood. It is attached to the right or left fender, cowl, or radiator cross member depending on the model and assembly plant. This plate indicates the schedule date, body production number, body series, trim, paint, and accessory code.

CHRYSLER MOTORS
CORPORATION

SO	NUMBER	BDY	TRM	PNT
0224	0551	742	H4R	BB1

EXAMPLE:

0224	SON (Feb. 24)
0551	Production Sequence
742	Body Style (2-Dr. Hardtop)
H4R	Trim
B	Lower Body Color
B	Upper Body Color

THE SHIPPING ORDER NUMBER is assigned prior to production. It consists of a 4-digit planned delivery month/day date code, 0224 (February 24th). Then a plant production sequence number follows (0555).

THE BODY NUMBER is a 3-digit number which indicates the model and body style.

DART 170	CODE
2-Dr. Sedan	711
2-Dr. Sedan	713
4-Dr. Wagon	756

1964 DODGE

DART 270	CODE
2-Dr. Sedan	731
4-Dr. Sedan	733
Convertible	735
4-Dr. Wagon	776

DART GT	CODE
2-Dr. Hardtop	742
Convertible	745

330	CODE	
	6 CYL	8 CYL
2-Dr. Sedan	411	611
4-Dr. Sedan	413	613
4-Dr. Wagon	456	656
4-Dr. Wagon	457	657

440	CODE	
	6 CYL	8 CYL
2-Dr. Sedan	421	621
2-Dr. Hardtop	422	622
4-Dr. Sedan	423	623
4-Dr. Wagon	—	666
4-Dr. Wagon	—	667

POLARA	CODE	
	6 CYL	8 CYL
2-Dr. Hardtop	432	632
4-Dr. Sedan	433	633
4-Dr. Hardtop	—	634
Convertible	—	635

880	CODE
4-Dr. Sedan	513
4-Dr. Wagon	556
4-Dr. Wagon	557

CUSTOM 880	CODE
2-Dr. Hardtop	522
Convertible	525
4-Dr. Sedan	523
4-Dr. Hardtop	524
4-Dr. Wagon	568
4-Dr. Wagon	569

THE TRIM NUMBER furnishes the key to the interior color and material.

COLOR	CLOTH	VINYL	LEATHER	CODE
Blue	•	•		L1B,L4B,K1B
Blue	•	•		H1B,H4B,E1B
Blue	•	•		M1B,M5B
Blue		•		L5B,H4B,P4B
Blue		•		M4B,L1B,L4B
Turquoise	•	•		L1Q,H1Q,K1Q
Turquoise	•	•		M1Q,E1Q
Turquoise		•		L5Q,H4Q,L4Q
Turquoise		•		K4Q,M4Q,P4Q
Turquoise		•		L1Q
Red	•	•		L1R,L4R,K1R
Red	•	•		H1R,H4R
Red	•	•		M1R,M5R
Red		•		L5R,H4R,P4R
Red		•		L4R,K4R,M4R
Red		•		L1R
Tan	•	•		L1T,L4T,K1T
Tan	•	•		H1T,H4T,E1T
Tan	•	•		M1T,M5T
Tan		•		L5T,H4T,P4T
Tan		•		L4T,K4T,M4T
Tan		•		L1T
Gold	•	•		M1Y,H1Y,E1Y
Gold	•	•		K1Y
Gold		•		P4Y,M4Y,H4Y
Gold		•		L1Y,L4Y
Black		•		P4X
Gray	•	•		L2A,K2A,L8A
Gray		•		K4A,K2A
Gray		•		M8A
Black/Gray	•	•		X1P

THE PAINT CODE furnishes the key to the paint used on the car. A two-digit code indicates the top and bottom colors respectively. A number follows which designates two-tone, sports-tone, convertible top, etc.

COLOR	CODE
Black	B
Light Blue	C
Medium Blue	D
Dark Blue	E
Light Turquoise/Aqua	J
Medium Turquoise Metallic	K
Dk. Green/Turquoise Metallic	L
Red	P
Ivory	S
White	W
Beige/Light Tan	X
Tan/Medium/Tan Metallic	Y
Anniversary Gold/Gold Metallic	Z

1964 DODGE

ENGINE NUMBER

6-cylinder engine number is stamped on the right side of the block on the top boss directly behind the ignition coil. The number provides the code to identify the series, block displacement, and month/day production date.

273 and 318 engine numbers are stamped on the left front of the block under the cylinder head.

361, 383, 413 and 426 engine numbers are stamped on the right side of the block below the distributor.

EXAMPLE:

V	38	2	24
YEAR	383	FEBRUARY	DAY

DART

ENGINE CODE	NO. CYL.	CID	HORSE-POWER	COMP. RATIO	CARB	TRANS
V-17	6	170	101	8.5:1	1 BC	* M & A
V-22	6	225	145	8.4:1	1 BC	* M & A
V-273	8	273	180	8.8:1	2 BC	* M & A

DODGE 330, 440, POLARA

ENGINE CODE	NO. CYL.	CID	HORSE-POWER	COMP. RATIO	CARB	TRANS
V-22	6	225	145	8.4:1	1 BC	* M & A
V-318	8	318	230	9.0:1	2 BC	* M & A
V-38	8	383	305	10.0:1	2 BC	* M & A
V-38	8	383	330	10.0:1	4 BC	* M & A
V-42	8	426	365	10.3:1	4 BC	* M & A
426VMP	8	426	415	11.0:1	2-4 BC	* M & A
426VMPHC	8	426	425	12.5:1	2-4 BC	* M & A

880, CUSTOM 880

ENGINE CODE	NO. CYL.	CID	HORSE-POWER	COMP. RATIO	CARB	TRANS
V-36	8	361	265	9.0:1	2 BC	* M & A
V-38	8	383	305	10.0;1	2 BC	* M & A

* MAN & AUTO

Other identifying engine marks are as follows:

6-cylinder:
Maltese Cross - .001" undersize crankshaft journals (M and R plus a number stamped on the crankshaft counterweight indicates which main and rod journals are undersize).
X - .010" undersize crankshaft journals (M-10 and R-10 stamped on the crankshaft counterweight indicates all rod and main journals are undersize).
A - .020" oversize cylinder bores
B - Main and connecting rod bearings .010" undersize
Diamond - .008" oversize lifters

All other engines:
Maltese Cross - .001" undersize crankshaft journals
B - .010" undersize crankshaft journals (273,318)
A - .020" oversize cylinder bores
Diamond - .008" oversize valve lifters
o/s - .005" oversize stems

1965 DODGE CORONET

1965 DODGE MONACO

1965 DODGE DART

1965 DODGE DART

1965 DODGE POLARA

1965 DODGE POLARA

VEHICLE IDENTIFICATION NUMBER

DODGE
W352100553

The vehicle number (serial number) is stamped and embossed on a stainless steel plate attached to the left front door hinge pillar. It consists of car make symbol, series code, model year code, assembly plant symbol and a sequential production number.

FIRST DIGIT: Identifies the car make

CAR MAKE	CODE
Dart (6 Cyl.)	2
Dart (8 Cyl.)	L
Coronet (6 Cyl.)	4
Coronet (8 Cyl.)	W
880, Polara, Monaco	D

SECOND DIGIT: Identifies the series

SERIES	CODE
170, Polara, Coronet Deluxe	1
270, Coronet 500, Custom 880	3
Dart GT, Coronet 440, Monaco	4
170, Coronet, Polara, Wagons	5
270, Coronet 440, Custom 880 Wagons	7
Police	9
Taxi	8
Super Stock	0

THIRD DIGIT: Identifies the model year (1965)

FOURTH DIGIT: Identifies the assembly plant

ASSEMBLY PLANT	CODE
Detroit, MI	2-3
Los Angeles, CA	5
Newark, DE	6
St. Louis, MO	7

LAST SIX DIGITS: Represent the basic production numbers

BODY NUMBER PLATE

THE BODY PLATE is stamped and embossed on a stainless steel plate under the hood. It is attached to the right or left fender, cowl, or radiator cross member depending on the model and assembly plant. This plate indicates the schedule date, body production number, body series, trim, paint, and accessory code.

CHRYSLER MOTORS
CORPORATION

SO	NUMBER	BDY	TRM	PNT
0224	0553	W32	H4R	BB1

EXAMPLE:

0224	SON (Feb. 24)
0553	Production Sequence
W32	Body Style (2-Dr. Sedan)
H4R	Trim
B	Lower Body Color
B	Upper Body Color

THE SHIPPING ORDER NUMBER is assigned prior to production. It consists of a 4-digit planned delivery month/day date code, 0224 (February 24th). Then a plant production sequence number follows (0555).

THE BODY NUMBER is a 3-digit number which indicates the model and body style.

DART 170		CODE
	6 CYL	**8 CYL**
2-Dr. Sedan	211	L11
2-Dr. Sedan	213	L13
4-Dr. Wagon	256	L56

DART 270

	6 CYL	8 CYL (CODE)
2-Dr. Sedan	231	L31
4-Dr. Sedan	233	L33
2-Dr. Hardtop	232	L32
Convertible	235	L35
4-Dr. Wagon	276	L76

DART GT

	6 CYL	8 CYL (CODE)
2-Dr. Hardtop	242	L42
Convertible	245	L45

CORONET

	6 CYL	8 CYL (CODE)
2-Dr. Sedan	421	W21
4-Dr. Sedan	423	W23

* Introduced in Feb. 1965

CORONET DELUXE

	6 CYL	8 CYL (CODE)
2-Dr. Sedan	411	W11
4-Dr. Sedan	413	W13
4-Dr. Wagon	456	W56

CORONET 440

	6 CYL	8 CYL (CODE)
2-Dr. Sedan	432	W32
2-Dr. Hardtop	433	W33
Convertible	435	W35
4-Dr. Wagon	476	W76
4-Dr. Wagon	477	W77

CORONET HEMI-CHARGER

	CODE
2-Dr. Hardtop	W01

CORONET 500

	CODE
2-Dr. Hardtop	W42
Convertible	W42

POLARA

	CODE
4-Dr. Sedan	D13
2-Dr. Hardtop	D12
4-Dr. Hardtop	D14
Convertible	D15
4-Dr. Wagon	D56
4-Dr. Wagon	D57

CUSTOM 880

	CODE
4-Dr. Sedan	D38
2-Dr. Hardtop	D32
4-Dr. Hardtop	D34
Convertible	D35
4-Dr. Wagon	D76
4-Dr. Wagon	D77

MONACO

	CODE
2-Dr. Hardtop	D42

THE TRIM NUMBER furnishes the key to the interior color and material.

COLOR	CLOTH	VINYL	LEATHER	CODE
Blue	•	•		L1B,K1B,H1B
Blue	•	•		L4B,L5B,H4B
Blue	•	•		H5B
Blue		•		L4B,K4B,L5B
Blue		•		P1B,L9B,H1B
Blue		•		H4B,H5B,P4B
Turquoise	•	•		L1Q,K1Q,H1Q
Turquoise	•	•		H4Q
Turquoise		•		L4Q,K4Q,P1Q
Turquoise		•		H1Q,H4Q,P4Q
Red	•	•		L1R,K1R,H1R
Red	•	•		L4R,L5R,H4R
Red	•	•		H5R
Red		•		L4R,K4R,L5R
Red		•		P4R,L9R,H1R
Red		•		H4R,H5R
Tan	•	•		L1T,K1T,H1T
Tan	•	•		L2T,K2T,L4T
Tan	•	•		L5T,H4T,H5T
Tan		•		L4T,K4T,L8T
Tan		•		K8T,T8T,L5T
Tan		•		P4T,H1T,H4T
Tan		•		H5T
Cordovan		•		P4U
Black		•		P4X,L9X,H4X
White		•		P4W
Gold	•	•		L1Y,K1Y
Gold		•		L4Y,H1Y,H4Y
Gold		•		P4Y

THE PAINT CODE furnishes the key to the paint used on the car. A two-digit code indicates the top and bottom colors respectively. A number follows which designates two-tone, sports-tone, convertible top, etc.

COLOR	CODE
Gold Metallic	A
Black	B
Light Blue	C
Medium Blue Metallic	D
Dark Blue Metallic	E
Pale Blue Metallic	F
Dark Green Metallic	G
Light Turquoise	J
Medium Turquoise Metallic	K
Dark Turquoise Metallic	L
Pale Silver Metallic	N
Bright Red	P
Beige	R
Ivory	S
Ruby Red	T
Cordovan Metallic	V
White	W
Light Tan	X
Medium Tan Metallic	Y
Pale Turquoise Metallic	Z
Medium Green Metallic	2
Pink Gold Metallic	3
Yellow	8

ENGINE NUMBER

6-cylinder engine number is stamped on the right side of the block on a machined boss directly behind the ignition coil. The number provides the code to identify the series, block displacement, and month/day production date.

273 and 318 engine numbers are stamped on the left front of the block under the cylinder head.

361, 383, 413 and 426 engine numbers are stamped on the right side of the block below the distributor.

Hemi engine numbers are stamped on the left side of the cylinder block behind the thermostat housing.

EXAMPLE:

A	38	2	24
YEAR	383	FEBRUARY	DAY

DART

ENGINE CODE	NO. CYL.	CID	HORSE-POWER	COMP. RATIO	CARB	TRANS
A-170	6	170	101	8.5:1	1 BC	* M & A
A-225	6	225	145	8.4:1	1 BC	* M & A
A-273	8	273	180	8.8:1	2 BC	* M & A
A-773	8	273	235	10.5:1	4 BC	* M & A

CORONET

ENGINE CODE	NO. CYL.	CID	HORSE-POWER	COMP. RATIO	CARB	TRANS
A-225	6	225	145	8.4:1	1 BC	* M & A
A-273	8	273	180	8.8:1	2 BC	* M & A
A-318	8	318	230	9.0:1	2 BC	* M & A
A-361	8	361	265	9.0:1	2 BC	* M & A
A-383	8	383	330	10.0:1	4 BC	* M & A
A-426	8	426	365	10.3:1	4 BC	* M & A
AH-426	8	426	400	11.0:1	2-4 BC	* M & A
AH-426HC	8	426	425	12.5:1	2-4 BC	* M & A

POLARA AND CUSTOM 880

ENGINE CODE	NO. CYL.	CID	HORSE-POWER	COMP. RATIO	CARB	TRANS
A-383	8	383	270	9.2:1	2 BC	* M & A
A-383	8	383	315	10.0:1	4 BC	* M & A
A-413	8	413	340	10.1:1	4 BC	AUTO
A-426	8	426	365	10.3:1	4 BC	* M & A

MONACO

ENGINE CODE	NO. CYL.	CID	HORSE-POWER	COMP. RATIO	CARB	TRANS
A-383	8	383	315	10.0:1	4 BC	* M & A
A-413	8	413	340	10.1:1	4 BC	AUTO
A-426	8	426	365	10.3:1	4 BC	* M & A

* MAN & AUTO

Other identifying engine marks are as follows:

6-cylinder engine:
Maltese Cross - .001" undersize crankshaft journals (M and R plus a number stamped on crankshaft counterweight indicates which main and rod journals are undersize).
X - .010" undersize crankshaft journals (M-10 and R-10 stamped on crankshaft counterweight indicates all rod and main journals are undersize).
A - .020" oversize cylinder bores
B - .010" undersize
Diamond - .008" oversize lifters

Other engines:
R - Regular fuel
LC - Low compression
HC - High compression
HP - High performance

1966 DODGE CORONET

1966 DODGE DART

1966 DODGE MONACO

1966 DODGE MONACO

1966 DODGE POLARA

1966 DODGE POLARA

VEHICLE IDENTIFICATION NUMBER

DODGE
DM21B65100551

The vehicle number (serial number) is stamped and embossed on a stainless steel plate attached to the left front door hinge pillar. It consists of car make symbol, series code, model year code, assembly plant symbol and a sequential production number.

FIRST DIGIT: Identifies the car make

CAR MAKE	CODE
Charger	X
Dart	L
Coronet	W
Polara, Monaco	D

SECOND DIGIT: Identifies the series

SERIES	CODE
Coronet, Polara 318	E
Dart, Coronet Deluxe, Polara	L
Dart 270, Coronet 440, Monaco	H
Dart GT, Coronet 500, Monaco 500, Charger	P
Polara 500	M
Police	K
Taxi	T

THIRD AND FOURTH DIGITS: Identify the body style

BODY STYLE	CODE
2-Dr. Sedan	21
2-Dr. Hardtop	23
Convertible	27
2-Dr. Sports Hardtop	29
4-Dr. Sedan	41
4-Dr. Hardtop	43
Station Wagon, 6-Pass.	45
Station Wagon, 9-Pass.	46

FIFTH DIGIT: Identifies the engine

ENGINE	CODE
170	A
225	B
Special Order 6 Cyl.	C
273	D
318	E
361	F
383	G
426 Hemi	H
440	J
Special Order 8 Cyl.	K

SIXTH DIGIT: Identifies the model year (1966)

SEVENTH DIGIT: Identifies the assembly plant

ASSEMBLY PLANT	CODE
Lynch Rd, Detroit, MI	1
Hamtramck, MI	2
Jefferson Ave., Detroit, MI	3
Belvidere, IL	4
Los Angeles, CA	5
Newark, DE	6
St. Louis, MO	7
Windsor, Ont., CAN	9

LAST SIX DIGITS: Represent the basic production numbers

BODY NUMBER PLATE

THE BODY PLATE is stamped and embossed on a plate which is attached on the engine side of the cowl just above the master cylinder on the driver's side door. The plate shows the body type, trim code, schedule date, paint code, and some accessory codes.

CHRYSLER MOTORS
CORPORATION

SO	NUMBER	BDY	TRM	PNT
0224	0555	LL21	L6R	BB1

EXAMPLE:

0224	SON (Feb. 24)
0555	Production Sequence
LL21	Body Style (2-Dr. Sedan)
L6R	Trim
B	Lower Body Color
B	Upper Body Color

THE SHIPPING ORDER NUMBER consists of a three-digit month and day based on 01 through 31 days production date, and a five digit production order number.

MONTH	CODE
JAN	1
FEB	2
MAR	3
APR	4
MAY	5
JUN	6
JULY	7
AUG	8
SEPT	9
OCT	A
NOV	B
DEC	C

THE BODY NUMBER is a 4-digit number which indicates the car line, price class, and body style. Same first four digits of the VIN.

DART	CODE
2-Dr. Sedan	LL21
4-Dr. Sedan	LL41
4-Dr. Wagon	LL45

DART 270	CODE
2-Dr. Sedan	LH21
4-Dr. Sedan	LH41
2-Dr. Hardtop	LH23
Convertible	LH27
4-Dr. Wagon	LH45

DART GT	CODE
2-Dr. Hardtop	LP23
Convertible	LP27

CORONET	CODE
2-Dr. Sedan	WE21
4-Dr. Sedan	WE41

CORONET DELUXE	CODE
2-Dr. Sedan	WL21
4-Dr. Sedan	WL41
4-Dr. Wagon, 2-seat	WL45

CORONET 440	CODE
4-Dr. Sedan	WH41
2-Dr. Hardtop Sedan	WH23
Convertible	WH27
4-Dr. Wagon	WH45
4-Dr. Wagon	WH46*

CORONET 500	CODE
2-Dr. Hardtop	WP23
4-Dr. Sedan	WP41
Convertible	WP27

DODGE CHARGER	CODE
2-Dr. Hardtop	XP29*

POLARA 318	CODE
4-Dr. Sedan	DE41*

POLARA	CODE
4-Dr. Sedan	DL41*
2-Dr. Hardtop	DL23*
4-Dr. Hardtop	DL43*
Convertible	DL27*
4-Dr. Wagon	DL45*
4-Dr. Wagon	DL46*

POLARA 500	CODE
2-Dr. Hardtop	DM23
Convertible	DM27

MONACO	CODE
2-Dr. Hardtop	DH23*
4-Dr. Sedan	DH41*
4-Dr. Hardtop	DH43*
4-Dr. Wagon, 2-seat	DH45*
4-Dr. Wagon, 3-seat	DH46*

MONACO 500	CODE
2-Dr. Hardtop	DP23*

* Indicates 8 cylinder only in these models

THE TRIM NUMBER furnishes the key to the interior color and material.

COLOR	CLOTH	VINYL	LEATHER	CODE
Blue	•	•		L1B,L6B,P1D
Blue	•	•		P4B,H1B,E1B
Blue		•		L4B,L5B,P4D
Blue		•		H4B,H4D
Turquoise	•	•		L1Q,L6Q,P1Q
Turquoise	•	•		H1Q,E1Q
Turquoise		•		L4Q,H4J
Tan	•	•		L1T,L6T,P1T
Tan	•	•		H1T,E1T
Tan		•		L4T,P4T,H4T
Red	•	•		L6R,L1R,H1H
Red	•	•		H1R
Red		•		L5R,L4R,P4H
Red		•		P4R,H4H,H4R
Black	•	•		L1X,P1X,H1X
Black		•		L5X,L4X,P4X
Black		•		H4X
White		•		L5W,L4W,P4W
White		•		H4W
Cordovan		•		P4U
Gold		•		P4Y,H4Y

THE PAINT CODE furnishes the key to the paint used on the car. A three-digit code indicates the top and bottom colors respectively. A number follows which designates two-tone, sports-tone, convertible top, etc.

COLOR	CODE
Silver Metallic	A
Black	B
Light Blue	C
Medium Blue Metallic	D
Dark Blue Metallic	E
Light Green Metallic	F
Dark Green Metallic	G
Medium Turquoise Metallic	K
Bright Red	P
Red Metallic	Q
Yellow	R
Cream	S
White	W
Beige	X
Bronze Metallic	Y
Gold Metallic	Z
Sandstone Metallic	4
Mauve Metallic	6
Maroon Metallic	7

ENGINE NUMBER

6-cylinder engine number is stamped on the right side of the block on the top boss directly behind the ignition coil. The number provides the code to identify the series, block displacement, and month/day production date.

273, 318, 440 engine numbers are stamped on the left front of the block under the cylinder head.

361 and 383 engine numbers are stamped on the right side of the block below the distributor.

426 engine number is stamped on the left side on the horizontal surface behind the thermostat housing.

EXAMPLE:

B	38	2	24
YEAR	383	FEBRUARY	DAY

DART

ENGINE CODE	NO. CYL.	CID	HORSE-POWER	COMP. RATIO	CARB	TRANS
B-170	6	170	101	8.5:1	1 BC	** M & A
B-225	6	225	145	8.4:1	1 BC	** M & A
B-273	8	273	180	8.8:1	2 BC	** M & A
B-273	8	273	235	10.5:1	4 BC	** M & A

CORONET

ENGINE CODE	NO. CYL.	CID	HORSE-POWER	COMP. RATIO	CARB	TRANS
B-225	6	225	145	8.4:1	1 BC	** M & A
B-273	8	273	180	8.8:1	2 BC	** M & A
B-318	8	318	230	9.0:1	2 BC	** M & A
B-361	8	361	265	9.0:1	2 BC	** M & A
B-383	8	383	325	10.0:1	4 BC	** M & A
B-426	8	426	425	10.3;1	2-4 BC	** M & A

CHARGER

ENGINE CODE	NO. CYL.	CID	HORSE-POWER	COMP. RATIO	CARB	TRANS
B-318	8	318	230	9.0:1	2 BC	** M & A
B-361	8	361	265	9.0:1	2 BC	** M & A
B-383	8	383	325	10.0:1	4 BC	** M & A
B-426	8	426	425	10.3:1	2-4 BC	** M & A

POLARA

ENGINE CODE	NO. CYL.	CID	HORSE-POWER	COMP. RATIO	CARB	TRANS
B-318	8	318	230	9.0:1	2 BC	** M & A

POLARA, POLARA 500, MONACO

ENGINE CODE	NO. CYL.	CID	HORSE-POWER	COMP. RATIO	CARB	TRANS
B-383	8	383	270	9.2:1	2 BC	** M & A
B-383	8	383	325	10.0:1	4 BC	** M & A
B-1440	8	440	350	10.0:1	4 BC	** M & A

MONACO 500

ENGINE CODE	NO. CYL.	CID	HORSE-POWER	COMP. RATIO	CARB	TRANS
B-383	8	383	325	10.0:1	4 BC	** M & A
B-440	8	440	350	10.0:1	4 BC	** M & A
B-383*	8	383	270	9.2:1	2 BC	** M & A

* Optional
** MAN & AUTO

Other identifying engine marks are as follows:

6-cylinder engine:
Maltese Cross - .001" undersize bearings
Maltese Cross and X - .010" undersize bearings
A - .020" oversize cylinder bores
Diamond - Oversize tappet

Other engines:
LC - Low compression
HC - High compression
HP - High performance
MP - Maximum performance
R - 383" engine with 2 BC
A - .020" oversize cylinder bores
B - .010" undersize bearings (273" & 318")

1967 DODGE CHARGER

1967 DODGE CHARGER

1967 DODGE CORONET

1967 DODGE CORONET

1967 DODGE DART

1967 DODGE DART

1967 DODGE MONACO

1967 DODGE MONACO

1967 DODGE POLARA

1967 DODGE POLARA

VEHICLE IDENTIFICATION NUMBER

DODGE
DP23K74100553

The vehicle number (serial number) is stamped and embossed on a stainless steel plate attached to the left front door hinge pillar. It consists of car make symbol, series code, model year code, assembly plant symbol and a sequential production number.

FIRST DIGIT: Identifies the car make

CAR MAKE	CODE
Charger	X
Dart	L
Coronet	W
Polara, Monaco	D

SECOND DIGIT: Identifies the series

SERIES	CODE
Coronet	E
Dart, Polara, Coronet Deluxe	L
Dart 270, Monaco, Coronet 440	H
Polara 500	M
Dart GT, Coronet 500, Monaco 500, Charger	P
Police	K
Taxi	T
R/T	S
Super Stock	0

THIRD AND FOURTH DIGITS: Identify the body style

BODY STYLE	CODE
2-Dr. Sedan	21
2-Dr. Hardtop	23
Convertible	27
2-Dr. Sports Hardtop	29
4-Dr. Sedan	41
4-Dr. Hardtop	43
Station Wagon, 6-Pass.	45
Station Wagon, 9-Pass.	46

FIFTH DIGIT: Identifies the engine

ENGINE	CODE
170	A
225	B
Special Order 6 Cyl.	C
273	D
273 Hi Per	E
318	F
383	G
383 Hi Per	H
426 Hemi	J
440	K
440 Hi Per	L
Special Order 8 Cyl.	M

SIXTH DIGIT: Identifies the model year (1967)

SEVENTH DIGIT: Identifies the assembly plant

ASSEMBLY PLANT	CODE
Lynch Rd., Detroit, MI	1
Hamtramck, MI	2
Jefferson Ave., Detroit, MI	3
Belvidere, IL	4
Los Angeles, CA	5
Newark, DE	6
St. Louis, MO	7
Windsor, Ont., CAN	9

BODY NUMBER PLATE

THE BODY PLATE is stamped and embossed on a stainless steel plate attached to the fender shield under the hood. The plate indicates the code for body type, engine, transmission, schedule date, paint, trim and some option codes. The plate is read left to right, bottom to top, starting with the bottom row of numbers.

CHRYSLER MOTORS
CORPORATION

AX TRM PNT UBS
4 H4R BB1 S

DP23 81 5 635 224 00551

EXAMPLE:

4	Axle
H4R	Trim
B	Lower Body Color
B	Upper Body Color
S	Accent Colors
DP23	Body Style (2-Dr. Hardtop)
81	Engine (440 4 BC)
5	Transmission (3-Spd. Auto)
635	Tire Size and Type
224	SON (Feb. 24)
00551	Production Sequence

THE SHIPPING ORDER NUMBER consists of a three-digit month and day scheduled production date, and a five-digit production order number.

THE UBS CODE identifies the upper door frame color, and the accent stripe color.

THE BODY NUMBER is a four-digit number which indicates the car line, price class, and body style. Same first 4 digits of the VIN.

DART	CODE
2-Dr. Sedan	LL21
4-Dr. Sedan	LL41

DART 270	CODE
4-Dr. Sedan	LH41
2-Dr. Hardtop	LH23

DART GT	CODE
2-Dr. Hardtop	LP23
Convertible	LP27

CORONET	CODE
4-Dr. Wagon	WE45

CORONET DELUXE	CODE
2-Dr. Sedan	WL21
4-Dr. Sedan	WL41
4-Dr. Wagon, 2-Seat	WL45

CORONET 440	CODE
2-Dr. Hardtop	WH23
4-Dr. Sedan	WH41
Convertible	WH27
4-Dr. Wagon	WH45
4-Dr. Wagon	WH46
Super Stock	WO23

CORONET 500	CODE
2-Dr. Hardtop	WP23
4-Dr. Sedan	WP41
Convertible	WP27

CORONET R/T	CODE
2-Dr. Hardtop	WS23
Convertible	WS27

CHARGER	CODE
2-Dr. Hardtop	XP29*

POLARA 318	CODE
4-Dr. Sedan	DE41*

POLARA	CODE
4-Dr. Sedan	DL41*
2-Dr. Hardtop	DL23*
4-Dr. Hardtop	DL43*
Convertible	DL27*
4-Dr. Wagon	DL45*
4-Dr. Wagon	DL46*

POLARA 500	CODE
2-Dr. Hardtop	DM43*
Convertible	DM27*

MONACO	CODE
2-Dr. Hardtop	DH23*
4-Dr. Sedan	DH41*
4-Dr. Hardtop	DH43*
4-Dr. Wagon, 2-Seat	DH45*
4-Dr. Wagon, 3-Seat	DH46*

MONACO 500	CODE
2-Dr. Hardtop	DP23*

* 8 cylinder only

THE ENGINE CODE identifies the engine.

ENGINE	CODE
170 1 BC	11
225 1 BC	21
273 2 BC	31
273 4 BC HP	32
318 2 BC	41
383 2 BC	61
383 4 BC	62
426 2-4 BC Hemi HP	73
440 4 BC	81
440 4 BC HP	83

TRANSMISSION	CODE
3-Speed Manual	1
3-Speed Manual HD	2
4-Speed Manual	3
3-Speed Automatic	5
3-Speed Automatic HD	6
Special Order Transmission	9

The tire size and type three-digit option code is not included.

THE TRIM NUMBER furnishes the key to the interior color and material.

COLOR	CLOTH	VINYL	LEATHER	CODE
Blue	•	•		E1B,L1B,H1B
Blue	•	•		X1B
Blue		•		E4B,L4B,H4B
Blue		•		P1B,P6B,S6B
Blue		•		L4B,M6B,H5B
Blue		•		H6B,P6B,P4B
Red	•	•		E1R,L1R,X1R
Red	•	•		H1R
Red		•		E4R,L4R,H4R
Red		•		P6R,S6R,M6R
Red		•		H5R,H6R,P4R
Tan	•	•		E1T,K1T,L1T
Tan	•	•		H1T,X1T
Tan		•		E4T,K4T,T4T
Tan		•		L4T,H4T,H5T
Tan		•		H6T
Turquoise	•	•		H1Q,E1Q,L1Q
Turquoise		•		P1Q,H5Q,P6Q
Turquoise		•		X5Q
Black	•	•		H1X,E1X,L1X
Black	•	•		P7X
Black		•		H4X,P1X,P6X
Black		•		S6X,L4X,M6X
Black		•		H5X,H6X,X5X
Black		•		P4X
Copper		•		H4K,P6K,S6K
Copper		•		P4K
White/Black		•		H4W,P6W,S6W
White/Black		•		L4W,M6W,P4W
Black/Gold		•		P1E,P6E,S6E
Gray	•	•		K1A
Gray		•		K4A,T4A
Gold	•	•		H1Y
Gold		•		P6Y
White/Blue		•		H4C,P4C,P6C
White/Red		•		H4V,P4V,P6V

THE PAINT CODE furnishes the key to the paint used on the car. A three-digit code indicates the top and bottom colors respectively. A number follows which designates two-tone, sports-tone, convertible top, etc.

COLOR	CODE
Silver Metallic	A
Black	B
Medium Blue Metallic	C
Light Blue Metallic	D
Dark Blue Metallic	E
Light Green Metallic	F
Dark Green Metallic	G
Dark Copper Metallic	H
Chestnut Metallic	J
Medium Turquoise Metallic	K
Dark Turquoise Metallic	L
Bronze Metallic	M
Bright Red	P
Dark Red Metallic	Q
Yellow	R
Cream	S
Medium Copper Metallic	T
White	W
Light Tan	X
Medium Tan Metallic	Y
Gold Metallic	Z
Mauve Metallic	6
Bright Blue Metallic	8

ENGINE NUMBER

6-cylinder engine number is stamped on the right side of the block on the top boss directly behind the ignition coil. The number provides the code to identify the series, block displacement, and month/day production date.

273, 318, 440 engine numbers are stamped on the left front of the block under the cylinder head.

383 engine number is stamped on the right side of the block below the distributor.

426 engine number is stamped on the left side on the horizontal surface behind the thermostat housing.

EXAMPLE:

C	38	2	24
YEAR	383	FEBRUARY	DAY

DART

ENGINE CODE	NO. CYL.	CID	HORSE-POWER	COMP. RATIO	CARB	TRANS
C-170	6	170	115	8.5:1	1 BC	* M & A
C-225	6	225	145	8.4:1	1 BC	* M & A
C-273	8	273	180	8.8:1	2 BC	* M & A
C-273	8	273	235	10.5:1	4 BC	* M & A

CORONET, DELUXE, 440, 500

ENGINE CODE	NO. CYL.	CID	HORSE-POWER	COMP. RATIO	CARB	TRANS
C-225	6	225	145	8.4:1	1 BC	* M & A
C-273	8	273	180	8.8:1	2 BC	* M & A
C-318	8	318	230	9.2:1	2 BC	* M & A
C-383	8	383	270	9.2:1	2 BC	* M & A
C-383	8	383	325	10.0:1	4 BC	* M & A
C-440	8	440	375	10.1:1	4 BC	* M & A
C-426	8	426	425	10.25:1	2-4 BC	* M & A

CORONET R/T

ENGINE CODE	NO. CYL.	CID	HORSE-POWER	COMP. RATIO	CARB	TRANS
C-440	8	440	375	10.1:1	4 BC	* M & A
C-426	8	426	425	10.25:1	2-4 BC	* M & A

POLARA 318

ENGINE CODE	NO. CYL.	CID	HORSE-POWER	COMP. RATIO	CARB	TRANS
C-318	8	318	230	9.2:1	2 BC	* M & A

POLARA, POLARA 500, MONACO, MONACO 500

ENGINE CODE	NO. CYL.	CID	HORSE-POWER	COMP. RATIO	CARB	TRANS
C-383	8	383	270	9.2:1	2 BC	* M & A
C-383	8	383	325	10.0:1	4 BC	* M & A
C-440	8	440	350	10.1:1	4 BC	* M & A
C-440	8	440	375	10.1:1	4 BC	* M & A

CHARGER

ENGINE CODE	NO. CYL.	CID	HORSE-POWER	COMP. RATIO	CARB	TRANS
C-318	8	318	230	9.2:1	2 BC	* M & A
C-383	8	383	270	9.2:1	2 BC	* M & A
C-383	8	383	325	10.0:1	4 BC	* M & A
C-440	8	440	375	10.1:1	4 BC	* M & A
C-426	8	426	425	10.25:1	2-4 BC	* M & A

* MAN & AUTO

Other identifying engine marks are as follows:

Maltese Cross - .001" undersize bearings
Maltese Cross and X - .010" undersize bearings
A - .020" oversize cylinder bores
Diamond - Oversize tappet
LC - Low compression
HC - High compression
HP - High performance
MP - Maximum performance
R - 383" engine with 2 BC (regular fuel may be used)
B - .010" undersize bearings (273 & 318)

1968 DODGE

1968 DODGE CHARGER

1968 DODGE CORONET

1968 DODGE DART

1968 DODGE MONACO

1968 DODGE POLARA

1968 DODGE CHARGER

1968 DODGE CORONET

1968 DODGE DART

1968 DODGE MONACO

1968 DODGE POLARA

VEHICLE IDENTIFICATION NUMBER

DODGE
WH23G8E100551

The vehicle number (serial number) is stamped and embossed on a stainless steel plate attached to the left front door hinge pillar. It consists of car make symbol, series code, model year code, assembly plant symbol and a sequential production number.

FIRST DIGIT: Identifies the car make

CAR MAKE	CODE
Charger	X
Dart	L
Coronet	W
Polara, Monaco	D

SECOND DIGIT: Identifies the series

SERIES	CODE
Dart, Coronet Deluxe, Polara	L
Dart 270, Coronet 440, Monaco	H
Polara 500, Super Bee	M
Dart GT, Coronet 500, Monaco 500, Charger	P
Police	K
Taxi	T
R/T, GTS	S
Super Stock	O
Sports Top	X
New York Taxi	N

THIRD AND FOURTH DIGITS: Identify the body style

BODY STYLE	CODE
2-Dr. Sedan	21
2-Dr. Hardtop	23
Convertible	27
2-Dr. Sports Hardtop	29
4-Dr. Sedan	41
4-Dr. Hardtop	43
Station Wagon, 6-Pass.	45
Station Wagon, 9-Pass.	46

FIFTH DIGIT: Identifies the engine

ENGINE	CODE
170	A
225	B
Special Order 6 Cyl.	C
273	D
318	F
383	G
383 Hi Per	H
426 Hemi	J
440	K
440 Hi Per	L
Special Order 8 Cyl.	M
340	P

SIXTH DIGIT: Identifies the model year (1968)

SEVENTH DIGIT: Identifies the assembly plant

ASSEMBLY PLANT	CODE
Lynch Rd., Detroit, MI	A
Hamtramck, MI	B
Jefferson Ave., Detroit, MI	C
Belvidere, IL	D
Los Angeles, CA	E
Newark, DE	F
St. Louis, MO	G
Windsor, Ont., CAN	R

BODY NUMBER PLATE

THE BODY PLATE is stamped and embossed on a stainless steel plate attached to the fender shield under the hood. The plate indicates the code for the body type, engine, transmission, schedule date, paint, trim and some option codes. The plate is read left to right, bottom to top, starting with the bottom row of numbers.

CHRYSLER MOTORS
CORPORATION

		AX	TRM	PNT	UBS
		4	H4R	BB1	S
WH23	61	5	650	224	00551

EXAMPLE:

4	Axle
H4R	Trim
B	Lower Body Color
B	Upper Body Color
S	Accent Colors
WH23	Body Style (2-Dr. Hardtop)
61	Engine (383 2BC)
5	Transmission (3-Spd. Auto)
650	Tire Size and Type
224	SON (Feb. 24)
00551	Production Sequence

THE SHIPPING ORDER NUMBER consists of a three-digit month and day scheduled production date, and a five-digit production order number.

THE AXLE CODE is found directly under the AX column.

THE UBS CODE identifies the upper door frame color and the accent stripe color.

THE BODY NUMBER is a four-digit number which indicates the car line, price class, and body style. Same first four digits of the VIN.

DART	CODE
2-Dr. Sedan	LL21
4-Dr. Sedan	LL41

DART 270	CODE
4-Dr. Sedan	LH41
2-Dr. Hardtop	LH23

DART GT	CODE
2-Dr. Hardtop	LP23
Convertible	LP27

DART GTS	CODE
2-Dr. Hardtop	LS23
Convertible	LS27
Super Stock	LO23

CORONET SUPER BEE	CODE
2-Dr. Coupe	WM21

CORONET DELUXE	CODE
2-Dr. Coupe	WL21
4-Dr. Sedan	WL41
4-Dr. Wagon, 2-seat	WL45

CORONET 440	CODE
2-Dr. Hardtop	WH23
4-Dr. Sedan	WH41
4-Dr. Wagon	WH45
4-Dr. Wagon	WH46

CORONET 500	CODE
2-Dr. Hardtop	WP23
4-Dr. Sedan	WP41
Convertible	WP27
4-Dr. Wagon	WP45
4-Dr. Wagon	WP46

CORONET R/T	CODE
2-Dr. Hardtop	WS23
Convertible	WS27

DODGE CHARGER	CODE
2-Dr. Hardtop	XP29

DODGE CHARGER RT*	CODE
2-Dr. Hardtop	XS29

POLARA*	CODE
4-Dr. Sedan	DL41
2-Dr. Hardtop	DL23
4-Dr. Hardtop	DL43
4-Dr. Wagon	DL45
4-Dr. Wagon	DL46
Convertible	DL27

POLARA 500*	CODE
2-Dr. Hardtop	DM23
Convertible	DM27

MONACO*	CODE
4-Dr. Sedan	DH41
2-Dr. Hardtop	DH23
4-Dr. Hardtop	DH43
4-Dr. Wagon	DH45
4-Dr. Wagon	DH46

MONACO 500*	CODE
2-Dr. Hardtop	DP23

* Indicates 8 cylinder only in these models.

THE ENGINE CODE identifies the engine.

ENGINE	CODE
170 1 BC	11
225 1 BC	21
273 2 BC	31
318 2 BC	41
340 4 BC	52
383 2 BC	61
383 4 BC	62
426 2-4 BC Hemi HP	73
440 4 BC	81
440 4 BC HP	83

TRANSMISSION	CODE
3-Spd. Manual	1
3-Spd. Manual HD	2
4-Spd. Manual	3
3-Spd. Automatic	5
3-Spd. Automatic HD	6
Special Order Transmission	9

The tire size and type option codes are not included.

THE TRIM NUMBER furnishes the key to the interior color and material.

COLOR	CLOTH	VINYL	LEATHER	CODE
Blue	•	•		E1B,L1B,H1B
Blue	•	•		X1B
Blue		•		E4B,L4B,H4B
Blue		•		P1B,P6B,S6B
Blue		•		M6B,H5B,H6B
Blue		•		P4B
Red	•	•		E1R,L1R,X1R
Red	•	•		H1R
Red		•		E4R,L4R,H4R
Red		•		P6R,S6R,M6R
Red		•		H5R,H6R,P4R
Tan	•	•		E1T,K1T,L1T
Tan	•	•		H1T,X1T
Tan		•		E4T,K4T,T4T
Tan		•		L4T,H4T,H5T
Tan		•		H6T
Turquoise	•	•		H1Q,E1Q,L1Q
Turquoise		•		P1Q,H5Q,P6Q
Turquoise				X5Q
Black	•	•		H1X,E1X,L1X
Black		•		H4X,P1X,P6X
Black		•		S6X,L4X,M6X
Black		•		H5X,H6X,P7X
Black		•		P4X
Black				X5X
Copper		•		H4K,P6K,S6K
Copper		•		P4K
White/Black		•		H4W,P6W,S6W
White/Black		•		L4W,M6W,P4W
White/Blue		•		H4C,P6C,P4C
White/Red		•		H4V,P6V,P4V
Black/Gold		•		P1E,P6E,S6E
Gray	•	•		K1A
Gray		•		K4A,T4A
Gold	•	•		H1Y,P6Y

THE PAINT CODE furnishes the key to the paint used on the car. A three-digit code indicates the top and bottom colors respectively. A number follows which designates two-tone, sports-tone, convertible top, etc.

COLOR	CODE
Silver Metallic	A
Black	B
Medium Blue Metallic	C
Pale Blue Metallic	D
Dark Blue Metallic	E
Light Green Metallic	F
Racing Green Metallic	G
Light Gold	H
Medium Gold Metallic	J
Light Turquoise Metallic	K
Dark Turquoise Metallic	L
Bronze Metallic	M
Red	P
Bright Blue Metallic	Q
Burgundy Metallic	R
Yellow	S
Medium Green Metallic	T
Light Blue Metallic	U
White	W
Beige	X
Medium Tan Metallic	Y

ENGINE NUMBER

6-cylinder engine number is stamped on the right side of the block below the number one spark plug.

273, 318, and 340 engine numbers are stamped on the left front of the block below the cylinder head.

383, 426, and 440 engine numbers are stamped on the pan rail at the rear corner under the starter opening.

EXAMPLE:

PM	383	2187	2401
PLANT CODE	CID	JULIAN DATE	DAILY SEQUENTIAL NUMBER

ENGINE PLANTS
PM - Mound Road
PT - Trenton

DART, DART 270, DART GT

ENGINE CODE	NO. CYL.	CID	HORSE-POWER	COMP. RATIO	CARB	TRANS
PT-170	6	170	115	8.5:1	1 BC	* M & A
PT-225	6	225	145	8.4:1	1 BC	* M & A
PT-273	8	273	190	9.0:1	2 BC	* M & A
PT-318	8	318	230	9.2:1	2 BC	* M & A

DART GTS

ENGINE CODE	NO. CYL.	CID	HORSE-POWER	COMP. RATIO	CARB	TRANS
PT-340	8	340	275	10.5:1	4 BC	* M & A
PT-383	8	383	300	10.0:1	4 BC	* M & A
PT-426	8	426	425	10.25:1	2-4 BC	* M & A

CORONET DELUXE, CORONET 400

ENGINE CODE	NO. CYL.	CID	HORSE-POWER	COMP. RATIO	CARB	TRANS
PT-225	6	225	145	8.4;1	1 BC	* M & A
PT-273	8	273	190	9.0:1	2 BC	* M & A
PT-318	8	318	230	9.2:1	2 BC	* M & A
PT-383	8	383	290	9.2:1	2 BC	* M & A
PT-383	8	383	330	10.0:1	4 BC	* M & A
PT-440	8	440	375	10.1:1	4 BC	* M & A
PT-426	8	426	425	10.25:1	2-4 BC	* M & A

SUPER BEE

ENGINE CODE	NO. CYL.	CID	HORSE-POWER	COMP. RATIO	CARB	TRANS
PT-383	8	383	335	10.0:1	4 BC	* M & A
PT-426	8	426	425	10.25:1	2-4 BC	* M & A

CORONET R/T AND CHARGER R/T

ENGINE CODE	NO. CYL.	CID	HORSE-POWER	COMP. RATIO	CARB	TRANS
PT-440	8	440	375	10.1:1	4 BC	* M & A
PT-426	8	426	425	10.25:1	2-4 BC	* M & A

CHARGER

ENGINE CODE	NO. CYL.	CID	HORSE-POWER	COMP. RATIO	CARB	TRANS
PT-318	8	318	230	9.2:1	2 BC	* M & A
PT-383	8	383	290	9.2:1	2 BC	* M & A
PT-383	8	383	330	10.0:1	4 BC	* M & A
PT-440	8	440	375	10.1:1	4 BD	* M & A
PT-426	8	426	425	10.25:1	2-4 BC	* M & A

POLARA AND POLARA 500

ENGINE CODE	NO. CYL.	CID	HORSE-POWER	COMP. RATIO	CARB	TRANS
PT-318	8	318	230	9.2:1	2 BC	* M & A
PT-383	8	383	290	9.2:1	2 BC	* M & A
PT-383	8	383	330	10.0:1	4 BC	* M & A
PT-440	8	440	350	10.1:1	4 BC	* M & A
PT-440	8	440	375	10.1:1	4 BC	* M & A

MONACO AND MONACO 500

ENGINE CODE	NO. CYL.	CID	HORSE-POWER	COMP. RATIO	CARB	TRANS
PT-383	8	383	290	9.2:1	2 BC	* M & A
PT-383	8	383	330	10.0:1	4 BC	* M & A
PT-440	8	440	350	10.1:1	4 BC	* M & A
PT-440	8	440	375	10.1:1	4 BC	* M & A

* MAN & AUTO

Other identifying engine marks are as follows:

L or LC - Low compression
HP - High performance
R - Regular fuel
A - .020" oversize cylinder bores
Maltese Cross - .001" undersize bearing shells (except 273 and 318). They are marked with .001" undersize crankshafts on the number eight counterweight.
X - .010" undersize crankshaft. On 273 and 318, indicates one or more .005" oversize valve stems.
B - .010" undersize crankshaft
Diamond - Oversize tappets

1969 DODGE CHARGER

1969 DODGE CHARGER

1969 DODGE CORONET

1969 DODGE CORONET

1969 DODGE DART

1969 DODGE DART

1969 DODGE MONACO

1969 DODGE MONACO

1969 DODGE POLARA

1969 DODGE POLARA

VEHICLE IDENTIFICATION NUMBER

DODGE
WH23F9F100551

The vehicle number (serial number) is stamped and embossed on a stainless steel plate attached to the left front door hinge pillar. It consists of car make symbol, series code, model year code, assembly plant symbol and a sequential production number.

FIRST DIGIT: Identifies the car make

CAR MAKE	CODE
Charger	X
Dart	L
Coronet	W
Polara, Monaco	D

SECOND DIGIT: Identifies the series

SERIES	CODE
Dart, Polara, Coronet Deluxe, Dart Swinger	L
Dart Dustom, Coronet 440, Monaco	H
Polara 500, Super Bee, Swinger 340	M
Dart GT, Coronet 500, Charger	P
Police	K
Taxi	T
Dart GTS, Coronet R/T, Charger R/T	S
Super Stock	O
Charger 500, Daytona	X
New York Taxi	N

THIRD AND FOURTH DIGITS: Identify the body style

BODY STYLE	CODE
2-Dr. Sedan	21
2-Dr. Hardtop	23
Convertible	27
2-Dr. Sports Hardtop	29
4-Dr. Sedan	41
4-Dr. Hardtop	43
Station Wagon, 6-Pass.	45
Station Wagon, 9-Pass.	46

FIFTH DIGIT: Identifies the engine

ENGINE	CODE
170	A
225	B
Special Order 6 Cyl.	C
273	D
318	F
383	G
383 Hi Per	H
426 Hemi	J
440	K
440 Hi Per	L
440-6	M
340 Hi Per	P

SIXTH DIGIT: Identifies the model year (1969)

SEVENTH DIGIT: Identifies the assembly plant

ASSEMBLY PLANT	CODE
Lynch Road, Detroit, MI	A
Hamtramck, MI	B
Jefferson Ave., Detroit, MI	C
Belvidere, IL	D
Los Angeles, CA	E
Newark, DE	F
St. Louis, MO	G
Windsor, Ont., CAN	R
Wyoming	P

BODY NUMBER PLATE

THE BODY PLATE is stamped and embossed on a stainless steel plate attached to the fender shield under the hood. The plate indicates the code for the body type, engine, transmission, schedule date, paint, trim and some option codes. The plate is read left to right, bottom to top, starting with the bottom row of numbers.

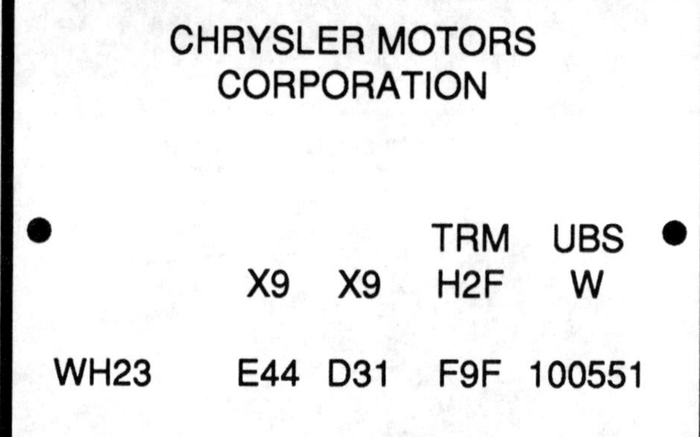

EXAMPLE:

H2F	Trim
X9	Upper Body Color
X9	Lower Body Color
W	Accent Colors
WH23	Body Style (2-Dr. Hardtop)
E44	Engine (318 2-BC)
D31	Transmission (3-Spd. Auto.)
F	Engine (318)
9	Model Year (1969)
F	Assembly Plant (Newark, DE)
100551	Production Sequence

THE UBS CODE identifies the upper door frame color and the accent stripe color.

THE BODY NUMBER is a four-digit number which indicates the car line, price class, and body style. Same first four digits of the VIN.

DART SWINGER	CODE
2-Dr. Hardtop	LL23

DART	CODE
4-Dr. Sedan	LL41

DART CUSTOM	CODE
4-Dr. Sedan	LH41
2-Dr. Hardtop	LH23

DART GT	CODE
2-Dr. Hardtop	LP23
Convertible	LP27

DART SWINGER 340*	CODE
2-Dr. Hardtop	LM23

DART GTS*	CODE
2-Dr. Hardtop	LS23
Convertible	LS27

CORONET DELUXE	CODE
2-Dr. Coupe	WL21
4-Dr. Sedan	WL41
4-Dr. Wagon, 2-Seat	WL45

CORONET 440	CODE
2-Dr. Coupe	WH21
2-Dr. Hardtop	WH23
4-Dr. Sedan	WH41
4-Dr. Wagon	WH45
4-Dr. Wagon	WH46

CORONET 500	CODE
2-Dr. Hardtop	WP23
4-Dr. Sedan	WP41
Convertible	WP27
4-Dr. Wagon	WP45
4-Dr. Wagon	WP46

CORONET SUPER BEE*	CODE
2-Dr. Coupe	WM21
2-Dr. Hardtop	WM23

CORONET R/T*	CODE
2-Dr. Hardtop	WS23
Convertible	WS27

CHARGER	CODE
2-Dr. Hardtop+	XP29
+ Option SE	

CHARGER R/T*	CODE
2-Dr. Hardtop	XS29

CHARGER 500 AND DAYTONA*	CODE
2-Dr. Hardtop	XX29

POLARA*	CODE
4-Dr. Sedan	DL41
2-Dr. Hardtop	DL23
4-Dr. Hardtop	DL43
Convertible	DL27
4-Dr. Wagon	DL45
4-Dr. Wagon	DL46

POLARA 500*	CODE
2-Dr. Hardtop	DM23
Convertible	DM27

MONACO*	CODE
4-Dr. Sedan+	DH41
2-Dr. Hardtop++	DH23
4-Dr. Hardtop+	DH43
4-Dr. Wagon	DH45
4-Dr. Wagon	DH46

+ Option Brougham
++ Option 500
* Indicates 8-cylinder only

THE ENGINE CODE identifies the engine.

ENGINE	CODE
Special 6 Cyl.	E06
Special 8 Cyl.	E08
170 1 BC	E11
225 1 BC	E24
225 1 BC	E25
273 2 BC	E31
318 2 BC	E44
340 4 BC	E55
383 2 BC	E61
383 4 BC	E62
426 2-4 BC Hemi Hi Per	E74
440 4 BC	E85
440 4 BC Hi Per	E86

TRANSMISSION	CODE
3-Spd. Manual	D11
3-Spd. Manual	D12
3-Spd. Manual HD	D13
4-Spd. Manual	D21
3-Spd. Automatic	D31
3-Spd. Automatic	D32
3-Spd. Automatic HD	D34
Clutch HD	D41
Special Order Transmission	D49

THE TRIM NUMBER furnishes the key to the interior color and material.

COLOR	CLOTH	VINYL	LEATHER	CODE
Blue	•	•		H1B,H7B,L1B
Blue		•		P6B,P2B,H2B
Blue		•		H4D,M6B,L2B
Blue		•		C6D,P6D,P3D
Blue		•		P2D,D2D,M2B
Blue		•	•	CRD
Blue/White		•		P6C,H2C,M6C
Green	•	•		H1G,H7G,L1G
Green		•		P6G,H2G,H4G
Green		•		H6G,M6G,L2G
Green		•		C6G,P3G,P2G
Green		•		D2G
Green		•	•	CRG
Green/White		•		P6F,M6F,H2F
Red		•		P6R,P2R,H2R
Red		•		C6R,P6R,M6R
Red/White		•		P6V
Black	•	•		H1X,H7X,H8X
Black	•	•		L1X,C5X,L1L
Black		•		P6X,P2X,H2X
Black		•		C6X,L2X,D2X
Black		•		H4X,H6X,M6X
Black		•		P3X,M2X
Black		•	•	CRX
Black/White		•		P6W,P2W,H2W
Black/White		•		H6W,M6X,L2W
Black/White		•		C6W,M6W
Black/ Champagne	•	•		H1L
Black/Tan		•		L2T,D2T
Black/Blue		•		D2B
Gold	•	•		H1Y,H6Y,L1Y
Gold		•		P3Y,P6Y
Gold/White		•		P6E
Gold/ Champagne	•	•		H1L
Tan	•	•		H8T
Tan		•		H2T,H4T,M6T
Tan		•		L2T,C6T,P6T
Tan		•		P2T,D2T,M2T
Tan		•	•	CRT
Tan/White		•		H4H

THE PAINT CODE furnishes the key to the paint used on the car.

COLOR	CODE
Medium Blue Metallic	B7
Bright Blue Metallic	B5
Light Blue Metallic	B3
Dark Green Metallic	F8
Medium Green Metallic	F5
Light Green Metallic	F3
Bright Turquoise Metallic	Q5
Cream	Y3
Gold Metallic	Y4
Yellow	Y2
Dark Bronze Metallic	T7
Copper Metallic	T5
Light Bronze Metallic	T3
Beige	L1
Red	R6
Silver Metallic	A4
White	W1
Black	X9

ENGINE NUMBER

All engine serial numbers contain fourteen characters and digits. The first two designate the engine plant; the next three are the cubic inch displacement, the next one designates low compression, the next four are based on a Julian calendar and the production sequence number of engines built that day.

6-cylinder engine numbers are stamped on the right side of the block below the number one spark plug.

273, 318, and 340 engine numbers are stamped on the the left front on the block below the cylinder head.

383, 426, and 440 engine numbers are stamped on the pan rail at the rear corner under the starter opening.

EXAMPLE:

PM	383	2187	2401
PLANT CODE	CID DATE	JULIAN	DAILY SEQUENTIAL

ENGINE PLANT
PM-Mound Rd.
PT-Trenton

DART SWINGER, CUSTOM GT

ENGINE CODE	NO. CYL.	CID	HORSE-POWER	COMP. RATIO	CARB	TRANS
PT-170	6	170	115	8.5:1	1 BC	* M & A
PT-225	6	225	145	8.4:1	1 BC	* M & A
PT-273	8	273	190	9.0:1	2 BC	* M & A
PT-318	8	318	230	9.2:1	2 BC	* M & A

SWINGER 340

ENGINE CODE	NO. CYL.	CID	HORSE-POWER	COMP. RATIO	CARB	TRANS
PT-340	8	340	275	10.5:1	4 BC	* M & A

DART GTS

ENGINE CODE	NO. CYL.	CID	HORSE-POWER	COMP. RATIO	CARB	TRANS
PT-340	8	340	275	10.5:1	4 BC	* M & A
PT-383	8	383	330	10.0:1	4 BC	* M & A

CORONET DELUXE, 440

ENGINE CODE	NO. CYL.	CID	HORSE-POWER	COMP. RATIO	CARB	TRANS
PT-225	6	225	145	8.4:1	1 BC	* M & A
PT-318	8	318	230	9.2:1	2 BC	* M & A
PT-383	8	383	290	9.2:1	2 BC	* M & A
PT-383	8	383	330	10.0:1	4 BC	* M & A

SUPER BEE

ENGINE CODE	NO. CYL.	CID	HORSE-POWER	COMP. RATIO	CARB	TRANS
PT-383	8	383	335	10.0:1	4 BC	* M & A
PT-426	8	426	425	10.25:1	2-4 BC	* M & A
PT-440	8	440	390	10.1:1	3-2 BC	* M & A

CORONET 500

ENGINE CODE	NO. CYL.	CID	HORSE-POWER	COMP. RATIO	CARB	TRANS
PT-318	8	318	230	9.2:1	2 BC	* M & A
PT-383	8	383	290	9.2:1	2 BC	* M & A
PT-3838	8	383	330	10.0:1	4 BC	* M & A

CORONET R/T, CHARGER R/T, CHARGER 500

ENGINE CODE	NO. CYL.	CID	HORSE-POWER	COMP. RATIO	CARB	TRANS
PT-440	8	440	375	10.1:1	4 BC	* M & A
PT-426	8	426	425	10.25:1	2-4 BC	* M & A

CHARGER

ENGINE CODE	NO. CYL.	CID	HORSE-POWER	COMP. RATIO	CARB	TRANS
PT-225	6	225	145	8.4;1	1 BC	* M & A
PT-318	8	318	230	9.2:1	2 BC	* M & A
PT-383	8	383	290	9.2:1	2 BC	* M & A
PT-383	8	383	330	10.0:1	4 BC	* M & A

POLARA, POLARA 500

ENGINE CODE	NO. CYL.	CID	HORSE-POWER	COMP. RATIO	CARB	TRANS
PT-318	8	318	230	9.2:1	2 BC	* M & A
PT-383	8	383	290	9.2:1	2 BC	* M & A
PT-383	8	383	330	10.0:1	4 BC	* M & A
PT-440	8	440	350	10.1:1	4 BC	* M & A
PT-440	8	440	375	10.1:1	4 BC	* M & A

MONACO

ENGINE CODE	NO. CYL.	CID	HORSE-POWER	COMP. RATIO	CARB	TRANS
PT-383	8	383	290	9.2:1	2 BC	* M & A
PT-383	8	383	330	10.0:1	4 BC	* M & A
PT-440	8	440	350	10.1:1	4 BC	* M & A
PT-440	8	440	375	10.1:1	4 BC	* M & A

* MAN & AUTO

Other identifying engine marks are as follows:

Maltese Cross - .001" undersize crankshaft
Maltese Cross and X - .010" undersize crankshaft
M or R - Main or rod journals undersize
M-10 - All main journals .010" undersize
R-10 - All rod journals .010" undersize
A - .020" oversize cylinder bores
Diamond - .008" oversize tappets

1960 PLYMOUTH

1960 PLYMOUTH

1960 PLYMOUTH VALIANT

1960 PLYMOUTH VALIANT

VEHICLE IDENTIFICATION NUMBER

PLYMOUTH
3303100551

The vehicle number (serial number) is stamped and embossed on a stainless steel plate attached to the left front door hinge pillar. It consists of car make symbol, series code, model year code, assembly plant symbol and a sequential production number.

FIRST DIGIT: Identifies the car make

CAR MAKE	CODE
Valiant	1
Plymouth (6 Cyl.)	2
Plymouth (8 Cyl.)	3

SECOND DIGIT: Identifies the series

SERIES	CODE
V-100, Savoy	1
Belvedere	2
V-200, Fury	3
V-100 Sta. Wgn., Savoy Sta. Wgn.	5
Belvedere Sta. Wgn.	6
V-200 Sta. Wgn., Fury Sta. Wgn.	7
Taxi	9
Fleet	0

THIRD DIGIT: Identifies the model year (1960)

FOURTH DIGIT: Identifies the assembly plant

ASSEMBLY PLANT	CODE
Detroit, MI	3
Los Angeles, CA	6
St. Louis, MO	7
Clairpointe	8
Canada	9

LAST SIX DIGITS: Represent the basic production numbers

BODY NUMBER PLATE

THE BODY PLATE is stamped and embossed on a stainless steel plate under the hood. It is attached to the right or left fender, cowl, or radiator cross member depending on the model and assembly plant. This plate indicates schedule date, body production number, body series, trim, paint, and accessory code.

CHRYSLER MOTORS
CORPORATION

SO	NUMBER	BDY	TRM	PNT
0224	0555	321	114	BB1

EXAMPLE:

0224	SON (Feb. 24)
0555	Production Sequence
321	Body Style (2-Dr. Sedan)
114	Trim
B	Lower Body Color
B	Upper Body Color

THE SHIPPING ORDER NUMBER is assigned prior to production. It consists of a four-digit planned delivery month/day date code, 0224 (February 24th), followed by a plant production sequence number (0555).

THE BODY NUMBER is a three-digit number which indicates the model and body style.

VALIANT V 100	CODE
4-Dr. Sedan	113
4-Dr. Wagon, 2-Seat	156
4-Dr. Wagon, 3-Seat	157

VALIANT V 200	CODE
4-Dr. Sedan	133
4-Dr. Wagon, 2-Seat	176
4-Dr. Wagon, 3-Seat	177

FLEET	CODE	
	6 CYL	8 CYL
2-Dr. Sedan	201	301
4-Dr. Sedan	203	303

SAVOY	CODE	
	6 CYL	8 CYL
2-Dr. Sedan	211	311
4-Dr. Sedan	213	313
2-Dr. Wagon	255	355
4-Dr. Wagon	256	356

BELVEDERE	CODE	
	6 CYL	8 CYL
2-Dr. Sedan	221	321
2-Dr. Hardtop Coupe	222	322
4-Dr. Sedan	223	323
4-Dr. Wagon	266	366
4-Dr. Wagon	—	367

FURY	CODE	
	6 CYL	8 CYL
2-Dr. Hardtop Coupe	232	332
4-Dr. Sedan	233	333
4-Dr. Hardtop Sedan	234	334
Convertible	—	335
4-Dr. Wagon	—	376
4-Dr. Wagon	—	377

THE TRIM NUMBER furnishes the key to the interior color and material.

VALIANT V-100

COLOR	CLOTH	VINYL	LEATHER	CODE
Silver	•	•		—
Silver/ Black	•	•		—

VALIANT V-200

COLOR	CLOTH	VINYL	LEATHER	CODE
Blue	•	•		751
White	•	•		751,752,753
Silver	•	•		751,752,753
Black	•	•		751,752,753
Green	•	•		752
Red	•	•		753

FURY

COLOR	CLOTH	VINYL	LEATHER	CODE
Blue	•	•		121
Green	•	•		122
Caramel	•	•		123
Red	•	•		124
Turquoise	•	•		125

CUSTOM

COLOR	CLOTH	VINYL	LEATHER	CODE
Blue	•	•		341
Green	•	•		342
Beige/Black	•	•		343
Turquoise	•	•		345
Red	•	•		347

BELVEDERE

COLOR	CLOTH	VINYL	LEATHER	CODE
Blue	•	•		111
Green	•	•		112
Beige/Black	•	•		113
Red	•	•		114
Turquoise	•	•		115

SAVOY

COLOR	CLOTH	VINYL	LEATHER	CODE
Blue	•	•		101
Green	•	•		102
Beige/Black	•	•		103

DELUXE SUBURBAN

COLOR	CLOTH	VINYL	LEATHER	CODE
Blue	•	•		331
Green	•	•		332
Beige/Black	•	•		333
Silver/ Black	•	•		244

THE PAINT CODE furnishes the key to the paint used on the car. A two-digit code indicates the top and bottom colors respectively. A number follows which designates two-tone, sports-tone, convertible top, etc.

COLOR	CODE
Buttercup Yellow	A
Jet Black	B
Sky Blue	C
Twilight Blue Metallic	D
Spring Green	F
Chrome Green Metallic	G
Aqua Mist	J
Turquoise Metallic	K
Platinum Metallic	L
Plum Red Metallic	P
Desert Beige	T
Oyster White	W
Caramel Metallic	Y

CONVERTIBLE TOPS	CODE
Black	331
White	332
Blue	334

ENGINE NUMBER

6-cylinder engine number is stamped on a boss on the left side of the cylinder block just below the head at the front or rear of the engine. The number provides the code to identify the series, block displacement, and month/day production date.

Other engine numbers are stamped on a boss on the top right side of the cylinder block just behind the water pump.

EXAMPLE:

P	38	2	24
YEAR	383	FEBRUARY	DAY

VALIANT

ENGINE CODE	NO. CYL.	CID	HORSE-POWER	COMP. RATIO	CARB	TRANS
P-17	6	170	101	8.5:1	1 BC	** M & A
P-17	6	170	148	10.5:1	4 BC	** M & A

PLYMOUTH

ENGINE CODE	NO. CYL.	CID	HORSE-POWER	COMP. RATIO	CARB	TRANS
P-22	6	225	145	8.5:1	1 BC	** M & A
P-318	8	318	230	9.0:1	2 BC	** M & A
P-318	8	318	260	9.0:1	4 BC	** M & A
P-36	8	361	305	10.0:1	4 BC	** M & A
P-36	8	361	310	10.0:1	2-4 BC	** M & A
P-38	8	383	325	10.0:1	4 BC	** M & A
P-38	8	383	330	10.0:1	2-4 BC	** M & A
P-38*	8	383	330	10.0:1	2-4 BC	** M & A

* Ram Ind
** MAN & AUTO

Other engine identifying marks are as follows:
A - Cylinders .020" oversize
B - Crankshaft journals .010" undersize
AB - Both above conditions exist
Maltese Cross - One or more crankshaft journals .001" undersize
Diamond - One or more valve lifters .008" oversize

1961 PLYMOUTH

1961 PLYMOUTH

1961 PLYMOUTH VALIANT

1961 PLYMOUTH VALIANT

VEHICLE IDENTIFICATION NUMBER

PLYMOUTH
3311100001

The vehicle number (serial number) is stamped and embossed on a stainless steel plate attached to the left front door hinge pillar. It consists of car make symbol, series code, model year code, assembly plant symbol and a sequential production number.

FIRST DIGIT: Identifies the car make

CAR MAKE	CODE
Valiant (6 Cyl.)	1
Plymouth (6 Cyl.)	2
Plymouth (8 Cyl.)	3

SECOND DIGIT: Identifies the series

SERIES	CODE
V-100, Savoy	1
Belvedere	2
V-200, Fury	3
V-100 Sta. Wgn., Savoy Sta. Wgn.	5
Belvedere Sta. Wgn.	6
V-200 Sta. Wgn., Fury Sta. Wgn.	7
Taxi	8
Special/Police	9
Fleet	0

THIRD DIGIT: Identifies the model year (1961)

FOURTH DIGIT: Identifies the assembly plant

ASSEMBLY PLANT	CODE
Detroit, MI	1
Los Angeles, CA	5
Newark, DE	6
St. Louis, MO	7

LAST SIX DIGITS: Represent the basic production numbers

BODY NUMBER PLATE

THE BODY PLATE is stamped and embossed on a stainless steel plate under the hood. It is attached to the right or left fender, cowl, or radiator cross member depending on the model and assembly plant. This plate will indicate schedule date, body production number, body series, trim, paint, and accessory code.

CHRYSLER MOTORS
CORPORATION

SO	NUMBER	BDY	TRM	PNT
0224	0555	311	501	BB1

EXAMPLE:

0224	SON (Feb. 24)
0555	Production Sequence
311	Body Style (2-Dr. Sedan)
501	Trim
B	Lower Body Color
B	Upper Body Color

THE SHIPPING ORDER NUMBER is assigned prior to production. It consists of a four-digit planned delivery month/day date code, 0224 (February 24th), a plant production sequence number follows (0555).

THE BODY NUMBER is a three-digit number which indicates the model and body style.

VALIANT V 100	CODE
2-Dr. Sedan	111
4-Dr. Sedan	113
4-Dr. Wagon, 2-Seat	156

VALIANT V 200	CODE
2-Dr. Hardtop Coupe	132
4-Dr. Sedan	133
4-Dr. Wagon, 2-Seat	176

FLEET		CODE
	6 CYL	8 CYL
2-Dr. Sedan	201	301
4-Dr. Sedan	203	303

SAVOY		CODE
	6 CYL	8 CYL
2-Dr. Sedan	211	311
4-Dr. Sedan	213	313
2-Dr. Wagon	255	355
4-Dr. Wagon	256	356

BELVEDERE		CODE
	6 CYL	8 CYL
2-Dr. Sedan	221	321
2-Dr. Hardtop Coupe	222	322
4-Dr. Sedan	223	323
4-Dr. Wagon	266	366
4-Dr. Wagon	—	367

FURY		CODE
	6 CYL	8 CYL
2-Dr. Hardtop Coupe	232	332
4-Dr. Sedan	233	333
4-Dr. Hardtop Sedan	234	334
Convertible	—	335
4-Dr. Wagon	—	376
4-Dr. Wagon	—	377

THE TRIM NUMBER furnishes the key to the interior color and material.

VALIANT V 100

COLOR	CLOTH	VINYL	LEATHER	CODE
Silver	•	•		103
Black	•	•		113
Blue	•	•		101,111
Green	•	•		102,112
White	•	•		103,113
Red	•	•		103,113

VALIANT V 200

COLOR	CLOTH	VINYL	LEATHER	CODE
Black	•	•		151
Blue	•	•		151
Green	•	•		152
Silver	•	•		155
Red	•	•		153
White	•	•		153

SAVOY

COLOR	CLOTH	VINYL	LEATHER	CODE
Maize	•	•		504
Black	•	•		501
Blue	•	•		501
Green	•	•		502
Turquoise	•	•		504
Silver	•	•		501
Red	•	•		504
Coral	•	•		504
Lavender	•	•		504
White	•	•		501

DELUXE SUBURBAN

COLOR	CLOTH	VINYL	LEATHER	CODE
Maize	•	•		604
Black	•	•		601
Blue	•	•		601
Green	•	•		602
Turquoise	•	•		604
Silver	•	•		601
Red	•	•		604
Lavender	•	•		604
White	•	•		601

BELVEDERE

COLOR	CLOTH	VINYL	LEATHER	CODE
Maize	•	•		514
Black	•	•		511
Blue	•	•		511
Green	•	•		512
Turquoise	•	•		514
Silver	•	•		511
Red	•	•		514
Lavender	•	•		514
White	•	•		511
Beige	•	•		513

CUSTOM SUBURBAN

COLOR	CLOTH	VINYL	LEATHER	CODE
Maize	•	•		614
Black	•	•		611
Blue	•	•		611
Green	•	•		612
Turquoise	•	•		614
Silver	•	•		611
Red	•	•		614
Lavender	•	•		614
White	•	•		611
Beige	•	•		613

FURY & SPORTS SUBURBAN

COLOR	CLOTH	VINYL	LEATHER	CODE
Maize				524
Maize		•		654
Black				521
Black		•		651
Blue				521
Blue		•		651
Green				522
Green		•		652
Turquoise				524
Turquoise		•		654
Silver				521
Silver		•		651
Red				524
Red		•		655
Lavender				524
Lavender		•		654
White				521
White		•		651
Beige				523
Beige		•		653

THE PAINT CODE furnishes the key to the paint used on the car. A two-digit code indicates the top and bottom colors respectively. A number follows which designates two-tone, sports-tone, convertible top, etc.

COLOR	CODE
Maize	A
Jet Black	B
Robins Egg Blue	C
Air Force Blue Metallic	D
Mint Green	F
Emerald Green Metallic	G
Twilight Turquoise	K
Silver Gray Metallic	L
Cardinal Red Metallic	R
Lavender Metallic	S
Alpine White	W
Fawn Beige	Y
Bronze Metallic	Z

CONVERTIBLE TOPS	CODE
Black	331
White	332
Blue	334

ENGINE NUMBER

6-cylinder engine number is stamped on the right side of the block below the cylinder head opposite the no. one cylinder. The number provides the code to identify the series, block displacement, and month/day production date.

8-Cylinder engine numbers are stamped on the boss on the top right side of the cylinder block just behind the water pump.

318 engine numbers are stamped on the front face of the left hand cylinder block.

EXAMPLE:

R	38	2	24
YEAR	383	FEBRUARY	DAY

VALIANT

ENGINE CODE	NO. CYL.	CID	HORSE-POWER	COMP. RATIO	CARB	TRANS
R-17	6	170	101	8.2:1	1 BC	*** M & A
R-17	6	170	148	8.2:1	4 BC	*** M & A
R-22	6	225	145	8.2:1	1 BC	*** M & A

PLYMOUTH

ENGINE CODE	NO. CYL.	CID	HORSE-POWER	COMP. RATIO	CARB	TRANS
R-22	6	225	145	8.2:1	1 BC	*** M & A
R-318	8	318	230	9.0:1	2 BC	*** M & A
R-318	8	318	260	9.0:1	4 BC	*** M & A
R-36	8	361	305	9.0:1	4 BC	*** M & A
R-38	8	383	325	10.0:1	4 BC	*** M & A
R-38*	8	383	330	10.0;1	2-4 BC	*** M & A
R-38**	8	383	330	10.0:1	2-4 BC	*** M & A
R-38+	8	383	340	10.0:1	2-4 BC	*** M & A
R-41	8	413	350	10.0:1	4 BC	*** M & A
R-41+	8	413	375	10.0:1	2-4 BC	*** M & A
R-41*	8	413	375	10.0:1	2-4 BC	*** M & A

+ Short Ram
* Runner
** Ram Ind
*** MAN & AUTO

Other engine identifying marks are as follows:

A - All cylinder bores .020" oversize
Maltese Cross - One or more bearing journals .001" undersize
Maltese Cross and X - One or more bearing journals .010" undersize
Diamond - One or more valve lifters .008" oversize
SP - Special Police
HP - High performance

1962 PLYMOUTH

1962 PLYMOUTH

1962 PLYMOUTH VALIANT

1962 PLYMOUTH VALIANT

VEHICLE IDENTIFICATION NUMBER

PLYMOUTH
3321100551

The vehicle number (serial number) is stamped and embossed on a stainless steel plate attached to the left front door hinge pillar. It consists of car make symbol, series code, model year code, assembly plant symbol and a sequential production number.

FIRST DIGIT: Identifies the car make

CAR MAKE	CODE
Valiant (6 Cyl.)	1
Plymouth (6 Cyl.)	2
Plymouth (8 Cyl.)	3

SECOND DIGIT: Identifies the series

V-100, Savoy	1
Belvedere	2
V-200, Fury	3
Valiant Signet, Sport Fury	4
V-100 Sta. Wgn., Savoy Sta. Wgn.	5
Belvedere Sta. Wgn.	6
V-200 Sta. Wgn., Fury Sta. Wgn.	7
Taxi	8
Police	9
Fleet	0

THIRD DIGIT: Identifies the model year (1962)

FOURTH DIGIT: Identifies the assembly plant

ASSEMBLY PLANT	CODE
Detroit, MI	1
Los Angeles, CA	5
Newark, DE	6
St. Louis, MO	7

LAST SIX DIGITS: Represent the basic production numbers

BODY NUMBER PLATE

THE BODY PLATE is stamped and embossed on a stainless steel plate under the hood. It is attached to the right or left fender, cowl, or radiator cross member depending on the model and assembly plant. This plate indicates schedule date, body production number, body series, trim, paint, and accessory code.

CHRYSLER MOTORS
CORPORATION

SO	NUMBER	BDY	TRM	PNT
0224	0555	131	501	BB1

EXAMPLE:

0224	SON (Feb. 24)
0555	Production Sequence
131	Body Style (2-Dr. Sedan)
501	Trim
B	Lower Body Color
B	Upper Body Color

THE SHIPPING ORDER NUMBER is assigned prior to production. It consists of a four-digit planned delivery month/day date code, 0224 (February 24th), followed by a plant production sequence number (0555).

THE BODY NUMBER is a three-digit number which indicates the model and body style.

VALIANT V 100	CODE
2-Dr. Sedan	111
4-Dr. Sedan	113
4-Dr. Wagon, 3-Seat	156

VALIANT V 200	CODE
2-Dr. Sedan	131
4-Dr. Sedan	133
4-Dr. Wagon, 2-Seat	176

VALIANT SIGNET	CODE
2-Dr. Hardtop Sedan	142

FLEET SPECIAL	CODE 6 CYL	8 CYL
2-Dr. Sedan	201	301
4-Dr. Sedan	203	303

SAVOY	CODE 6 CYL	8 CYL
2-Dr. Sedan	211	311
4-Dr. Sedan	213	313
4-Dr. Wagon	256	356

BELVEDERE	CODE 6 CYL	8 CYL
2-Dr. Sedan	221	321
2-Dr. Hardtop Coupe	222	322
4-Dr. Sedan	223	323
4-Dr. Wagon	266	366
4-Dr. Wagon	—	367

FURY	CODE 6 CYL	8 CYL
2-Dr. Hardtop Coupe	232	332
4-Dr. Sedan	233	333
4-Dr. Hardtop Sedan	234	334
Convertible	—	335
4-Dr. Wagon	—	376
4-Dr. Wagon	—	377
Convertible	—	335

SPORT FURY	CODE
2-Dr. Hardtop Sedan	342
Convertible	345

THE TRIM NUMBER furnishes the key to the interior color and material.

COLOR	CLOTH	VINYL	LEATHER	CODE
Gray/Blue	•	•		501,551
Gray	•	•		504,554,104
Gray	•	•		114,134
Gray		•		564,594,204
Gray		•		214,234,244
Gray		•		294
Gray/Red	•	•		505,555
Blue	•	•		521,101,111
Blue	•	•		121,131
Blue		•		571,201,211
Blue		•		231,241,253
Green	•	•		522,112,122
Green	•	•		132
Red	•	•		525,125
Red		•		573,575,245
Red		•		251
Cocoa	•	•		103,113,123
Cocoa	•	•		133
Cocoa		•		203
Black		•		254
Black/Gray	•	•		124

THE PAINT CODE furnishes the key to the paint used on the car. A two-digit code indicates the top and bottom colors respectively. A number follows which designates two-tone, sports-tone, convertible top, etc.

COLOR	CODE
Sun-Glo	A
Silhouette Black	B
Pale Blue	C
Luminous Blue	D
Pale Jade Green	F
Luminous Green	G
Luminous Turquoise	K
Pale Gray	M
Cherry Red	P
Luminous Cordovan	S
Sandstone	T
Ermine White	W
Luminous Brown	Y

ENGINE NUMBER

6-cylinder engine number is stamped on the right side of the cylinder block below the cylinder head opposite the no. one cylinder. The number provides the code to identify the series, block displacement and month/day production date.

8-cylinder engine numbers are stamped on the right side of the block below the distributor.

EXAMPLE:

R	38	2	24
YEAR	383	FEBRUARY	DAY

VALIANT

ENGINE CODE	NO. CYL.	CID	HORSE-POWER	COMP. RATIO	CARB	TRANS
S-17	6	170	101	8.2:1	1 BC	** M & A
S-22	6	225	145	8.2:1	1 BC	** M & A

SAVOY, BELVEDERE AND FURY (SPORT FURY NO 6-CYL.)

ENGINE CODE	NO. CYL.	CID	HORSE-POWER	COMP. RATIO	CARB	TRANS
S-22	6	225	145	8.2:1	1 BC	** M & A
S-318	8	318	230	9.0:1	2 BC	** M & A
S-318	8	318	260	9.0:1	4 BC	** M & A
S-36	8	361	305	9.0:1	4 BC	** M & A
S-36*	8	361	310	9.0:1	2-4 BC	** M & A
S-38	8	383	330	10.0:1	4 BC	** M & A
S-38*	8	383	335	10.0:1	2-4 BC	** M & A
S-41	8	413	365	11.0:1#	4 BC	** M & A
S-41*	8	413	385	11.0:1#	2-4 BC	** M & A
S-41+	8	413	410	11.0:1#	2-4 BC	** M & A

* Runner
** MAN & AUTO
+ Ram Ind
# Option 13.5:1

Other engine identifying marks are as follows:

A - .020" oversize cylinder bore
B - .010" undersize bearings
HD - 10 1/2" clutch
Diamond - .008" oversize tappets
Maltese Cross - .001" undersize bearing shells
X - 010" undersize crankshaft
LC - Low compression
HP - High performance
SP - Special police

1963 PLYMOUTH

1963 PLYMOUTH

1963 PLYMOUTH

1963 PLYMOUTH VALIANT

1963 PLYMOUTH VALIANT

VEHICLE IDENTIFICATION NUMBER

PLYMOUTH
3331100001

The vehicle number (serial number) is stamped and embossed on a stainless steel plate attached to the left front door hinge pillar. It consists of car make symbol, series code, model year code, assembly plant symbol and a sequential production number.

FIRST DIGIT: Identifies the car make

CAR MAKE	CODE
Valiant (6 Cyl.)	1
Plymouth (6 Cyl.)	2
Plymouth (8 Cyl.)	3

SECOND DIGIT: Identifies the series

SERIES	CODE
V-100, Savoy	1
Belvedere	2
V-200, Fury	3
Valiant Signet, Sport Fury	4
V-100 Sta. Wgn., Savoy Sta. Wgn.	5
Belvedere Sta. Wgn.	6
V-200 Sta. Wgn., Fury Sta. Wgn.	7
Taxi	8
Police	9
Fleet	0

THIRD DIGIT: Identifies the model year (1963)

FOURTH DIGIT: Identifies the assembly plant

ASSEMBLY PLANT	CODE
Detroit, MI	1-2
Los Angeles, CA	5
Newark, DE	6
St. Louis, MO	7

LAST SIX DIGITS: Represent the basic production numbers

BODY NUMBER PLATE

THE BODY PLATE is stamped and embossed on a stainless steel plate under the hood. It is attached to the right or left fender, cowl, or radiator cross member depending on the model and assembly plant. This plate indicates; schedule date, body production number, body series, trim, paint, and accessory code.

CHRYSLER MOTORS
CORPORATION

SO	NUMBER	BDY	TRM	PNT
0224	0555	211	325	BB1

1963 PLYMOUTH

EXAMPLE:

0224 SON (Feb. 24)
0555 Production Sequence
211 Body Style (2-Dr. Sedan)
325 Trim
B Lower Body Color
B Upper Body Color

THE SHIPPING ORDER NUMBER is assigned prior to production. It consists of a four-digit planned delivery month/day date code, 0224 (February 24th), followed by a plant production sequence number (0555).

THE BODY NUMBER is a three-digit number which indicates the model and body style.

VALIANT V 100	CODE
2-Dr. Sedan	111
4-Dr. Sedan	113
4-Dr. Suburban	156

VALIANT V 200	CODE
2-Dr. Sedan	131
4-Dr. Sedan	133
Convertible	135
4-Dr. Suburban	176

VALIANT SIGNET	CODE
2-Dr. Hardtop Sedan	142
Convertible	145

SAVOY	CODE	
	6 CYL	8 CYL
2-Dr. Sedan (Fleet)	201	301
4-Dr. Sedan (Fleet)	203	303
2-Dr. Sedan	211	311
4-Dr. Sedan	213	313
4-Dr. Wagon	256	356
4-Dr. Wagon	257	357
4-Dr. Sedan (Taxi)	283	383
4-Dr. Sedan (Police)	293	393
4-Dr. Wagon (Police)	296	396

BELVEDERE	CODE	
	6 CYL	8 CYL
2-Dr. Sedan	221	321
2-Dr. Hardtop Coupe	222	322
4-Dr. Sedan	223	323
4-Dr. Wagon	—	366
4-Dr. Wagon	—	367

FURY	CODE	
	6 CYL	8 CYL
2-Dr. Hardtop Coupe	232	332
4-Dr. Sedan	233	333
4-Dr. Hardtop Sedan	—	334
Convertible	—	335
4-Dr. Wagon	—	376
4-Dr. Wagon	—	377

SPORT FURY	CODE
2-Dr. Hardtop Sedan	342
Convertible	345

THE TRIM NUMBER furnishes the key to the interior color and material.

COLOR	CLOTH	VINYL	LEATHER	CODE
Gray/Blue	•	•		501
Blue	•	•		301,321,701
Blue	•	•		721,341
Blue		•		401,411,441
Blue		•		451,751,761
Blue		•		771,791,421
Blue		•		431
Tan	•	•		303,323,343
Tan		•		403,413,443
Tan		•		773,793,433
Alabaster/ Black	•	•		306,325,346
Alabaster/ Black		•		406,446,447
Alabaster/ Black		•		423,426
Gray	•	•		394,494,704
Gray		•		754
Green	•	•		322,702,722
Green	•	•		342
Green		•		442,752
Red	•	•		326,725,345
Red		•		445,455,775
Red		•		795,425
Copper/ Black		•		459

THE PAINT CODE furnishes the key to the paint used on the car. A two-digit code indicates the top and bottom colors respectively. A number follows which designates two-tone, sports-tone, convertible top, etc.

COLOR	CODE
Ebony	B
Light Blue	C
Medium Metallic Blue	D
Dark Metallic Blue	E
Light Green	F
Metallic Green	G
Light Beige	M
Ruby	P
Coppertone	R
Ermine White	X
Medium Beige	W
Metallic Brown	Y

1963 PLYMOUTH

ENGINE NUMBER

6-cylinder engine number is stamped on the right side of the block just behind the distributor or on a boss on the top side of the cylinder block behind the water pump. The number provides the code to identify the series, block displacement, and month/day production date.

318 engine number is stamped on the left front of block under the cylinder head.

361, 383, and 426 engine numbers are stamped on the right side of the block below the distributor, or on the left front of the block behind the thermostat housing.

EXAMPLE:

T	38	2	24
YEAR	383	FEBRUARY	DAY

VALIANT

ENGINE CODE	NO. CYL.	CID	HORSE-POWER	COMP. RATIO	CARB	TRANS
T-17	6	170	101	8.2:1	1 BC	* M & A
T-22	6	225	145	8.2:1	1 BC	* M & A

PLYMOUTH (NO SPORT FURY 6 CYL.)

ENGINE CODE	NO. CYL.	CID	HORSE-POWER	COMP. RATIO	CARB	TRANS
T-22	6	225	145	8.2:1	1 BC	* M & A
T-318	8	318	230	9.0:1	2 BC	* M & A
T-36	8	361	265	9.0:1	2 BC	* M & A
T-38	8	383	330	10.0:1	4 BC	* M & A
T-42	8	426	415	11.0:1	2-4 BC	* M & A
T-42	8	426	425	13.5:1	2-4 BC	* M & A

* MAN & AUTO

Other engine identifying marks are as follows:

Maltese Cross - .001" undersize crankshaft journals (M and R plus a number stamped on crankshaft counterweight indicates which main and rod journals are undersize).
X - .010" undersize crankshaft journals (M-10 and R-10 staped on crankshaft counterweight indicates all rod and main journals are undersize).
A - .020" oversize cylinder bores
Diamond - .008" oversize lifters
O/S - .005" oversize valves
LC - Low compression
HC - High compression
HP - High performance
MP - Maximum performance

1964 PLYMOUTH

1964 PLYMOUTH

1964 PLYMOUTH VALIANT

1964 PLYMOUTH VALIANT

VEHICLE IDENTIFICATION NUMBER

PLYMOUTH
2347100551

The vehicle number (serial number) is stamped and embossed on a stainless steel plate attached to the left front door hinge pillar. It consists of car make symbol, series code, model year code, assembly plant symbol and a sequential production number.

FIRST DIGIT: Identifies the car make

CAR MAKE	CODE
Valiant (8 Cyl.)	V
Valiant (6 Cyl.)	1
Plymouth (6 Cyl.)	2
Plymouth (8 Cyl.)	3

SECOND DIGIT: Identifies the series

SERIES	CODE
V-100, Savoy	1
Belvedere	2
V-200, Fury	3
Valiant Signet, Sport Fury, Barracuda	4
V 100 Sta. Wgn., Savoy Sta. Wgn.	5
Belvedere Sta. Wgn.	6
V 200 Sta. Wgn., Fury Sta. Wgn.	7
Taxi	8
Police	9
Fleet	0

THIRD DIGIT: Identifies the model year (1964)

FOURTH DIGIT: Identifies the assembly plant

ASSEMBLY PLANT	CODE
Detroit, MI	1-3
Los Angeles, CA	5
Newark, DE	6
St. Louis, MO	7

LAST SIX DIGITS: Represent the basic production numbers

BODY NUMBER PLATE

THE BODY PLATE is stamped and embossed on a stainless steel plate under the hood. It is attached to the right or left fender, cowl, or radiator cross member depending on the model and assembly plant. This plate indicates schedule date, body production number, body series, trim, paint, and accessory code.

CHRYSLER MOTORS
CORPORATION

SO	NUMBER	BDY	TRM	PNT
0224	5555	223	L1N	BB1

EXAMPLE:

0224	SON (Feb. 24)
5555	Production Sequence
223	Body Style (4-Dr. Sedan)
L1N	Trim
B	Lower Body Color
B	Upper Body Color

1964 PLYMOUTH

THE SHIPPING ORDER NUMBER is assigned prior to production. It consists of a four-digit planned delivery month/day date code, 0224 (February 24th), followed by a plant production sequence number (0555).

THE BODY NUMBER is a three-digit number which indicates the model and body style.

VALIANT V 100	CODE
2-Dr. Sedan	111
4-Dr. Sedan	113
4-Dr. Sedan	156

VALIANT V 200	CODE
2-Dr. Sedan	131
4-Dr. Sedan	133
Convertible	135
4-Dr. Wagon	176

VALIANT SIGNET	CODE	
	6 CYL	8 CYL
2-Dr. Hardtop Sedan	142	V42
Convertible	145	V45
Barracuda	149	V49

SAVOY	CODE	
	6 CYL	8 CYL
2-Dr. Sedan	211	311
4-Dr. Sedan	213	313
4-Dr. Wagon	256	356
4-Dr. Wagon	257	357

BELVEDERE	CODE	
	6 CYL	8 CYL
2-Dr. Sedan	221	321
2-Dr. Hardtop Coupe	222	322
4-Dr. Sedan	223	323
4-Dr. Wagon	—	366
4-Dr. Wagon	—	367

FURY	CODE	
	6 CYL	8 CYL
2-Dr. Hardtop Coupe	232	332
4-Dr. Sedan	233	333
Convertible	—	335
4-Dr. Wagon	—	376
4-Dr. Wagon	—	377

SPORT FURY	CODE
2-Dr. Hardtop Sedan	342
Convertible	345

THE TRIM NUMBER furnishes the key to the interior color and material.

COLOR	CLOTH	VINYL	LEATHER	CODE
Blue	•	•		L1B,L2B,L4B
Blue	•	•		K1B,K4B,M1B
Blue	•	•		M4B,H1B,H4B
Blue	•		•	H3B,H7B
Blue		•	•	M3B,M9B
Blue	•	•	•	M7B,M8B
Green	•	•		L1F,L2F,K1F
Green	•	•		H1F
Maroon	•	•		L1M,L2M,K1M
Maroon	•	•		M1M,H1M
Black/White	•	•		L1N,L4N,K1N
Black/White	•	•		K4N,M1N,H1N
Black/White	•	•		H2N
Turquoise	•	•		LIQ,L2Q,L4Q
Turquoise	•	•		H1Q,H4Q
Tan	•	•		L1T,L2T,L4T
Tan	•	•		K1T,K4T,M1T
Tan	•	•		M4T,H1T,H4T
Red		•		L4R,K4R,M4R
Red		•		H4R
Gray	•	•		K5A,K8A
Black	•	•		M4X,M8X
White		•	•	M4W,M8W
White		•		H4W
Gold	•		•	H3L,H7L
Blue/White		•	•	M9C

THE PAINT CODE furnishes the key to the paint used on the car. A two-digit code indicates the top and bottom colors respectively. A number follows which designates two-tone, sports-tone, convertible top, etc.

COLOR	CODE
Ebony	B
Light Blue	C
Medium Blue Metallic	D
Dark Blue Metallic	E
Sandalwood Metallic	H
Light Turquoise	J
Medium Turquoise Metallic	K
Dark Turquoise Metallic	L
Medium Gray Metallic	M
Ruby	P
Signet Royal Red	T
Chestnut Metallic	V
White	W
Light Tan	X
Medium Tan Metallic	Y

ENGINE NUMBER

6-cylinder engine numbers are stamped on the right side of the block on the top boss directly behind the ignition coil. The number provides the code to identify the series, block, displacement, and month/day production date.

273 and 318 engine numbers are stamped on the left front of the block under the cylinder head.

361, 383, 413, and 426 engine numbers are stamped on the right side of the block below the distributor.

EXAMPLE:

V	38	2	24
YEAR	383	FEBRUARY	DAY

VALIANT AND BARRACUDA

ENGINE CODE	NO. CYL.	CID	HORSE-POWER	COMP. RATIO	CARB	TRANS
V-17	6	170	101	8.5:1	1 BC	** M & A
V-22	6	225	145	8.4:1	1 BC	** M & A
V-273	8	273	180	8.8:1	2 BC	** M & A

PLYMOUTH (NO 6-CYL. FOR SPORT FURY)

ENGINE CODE	NO. CYL.	CID	HORSE-POWER	COMP. RATIO	CARB	TRANS
V-22	6	225	145	8.4:1	1 BC	** M & A
V-318	8	318	230	9.0:1	2 BC	** M & A
V-36	8	361	265	9.0:1	2 BC	** M & A
V-38	8	383	330	10.0:1	4 BC	** M & A
V-41	8	413	360	10.1:1	4 BC	** M & A
V-42	8	426	365	10.3:1	4 BC	** M & A
V-426*	8	426	415	11.0:1	2-4 BC	** M & A
V-426+	8	426	425	12.5;1	2-4 BC	** M & A

* VMP
\+ VMPHC
** MAN & AUTO

Other engine identifying marks are as follows:

Maltese Cross - .001" undersize crankshaft journals (M and R plus a number stamped on crankshaft counterweight indicates which main and rod journals are undersize).
X - .010" undersize crankshaft journals (M-10 and R-10 stamped on crankshaft counterweight indicates all rod and main journals are undersize).
A - .020" oversize cylinder bores
B - .010" undersize bearings
Diamond - .008" oversize lifters
O/S - .005" oversize stems

1965 PLYMOUTH

1965 PLYMOUTH

1965 PLYMOUTH

1965 PLYMOUTH BARRACUDA

1965 PLYMOUTH BARRACUDA

1965 PLYMOUTH VALIANT

1965 PLYMOUTH VALIANT

1965 PLYMOUTH

VEHICLE IDENTIFICATION NUMBER

PLYMOUTH
5157100551

The vehicle number (serial number) is stamped and embossed on a stainless steel plate attached to the left front door hinge pillar. It consists of car make symbol, series code, model year code, assembly plant symbol and a sequential production number.

FIRST DIGIT: Identifies the car make

CAR MAKE	CODE
Barracuda (8 Cyl.)	1
Belvedere (6 Cyl.)	3
Fury (6 Cyl.)	5
Fury (8 Cyl.)	P
Belvedere (8 Cyl.)	R
Barracuda (8 Cyl.)	V

SECOND DIGIT: Identifies the series

SERIES	CODE
V-100, Belvedere I, Fury I	1
Fury II	2
V-200, Belvedere II, Fury III	3
Signet, Satellite, Sport Fury	4
V-100 Sta. Wgn., Belvedere I Sta. Wgn, Fury I Sta. Wgn.	5
Fury II Sta. Wgn.	6
V-200 Sta. Wgn., Belvedere II	7
Fury III Sta. Wgn.	
Barracuda	8
Police	9

THIRD DIGIT: Identifies the model year (1965)

FOURTH DIGIT: Identifies the assembly plant

ASSEMBLY PLANT	CODE
Detroit, MI	1-2
Los Angeles, CA	5
Newark, DE	6
St. Louis, CA	7

LAST SIX DIGITS: Represent the basic production numbers

BODY NUMBER PLATE

THE BODY PLATE is stamped and embossed on a stainless steel plate under the hood. It is attached to the right or left fender, cowl, or radiator cross member depending on the model and assembly plant. This plate indicates schedule date, body production number, body series, trim, paint, and accessory code.

CHRYSLER MOTORS
CORPORATION

SO	NUMBER	BDY	TRM	PNT
0224	00551	R11	L1R	BB1

EXAMPLE:

0224	SON (Feb. 24)
00551	Production Sequence
R11	Body Style (8 cyl., 2-Dr. Sedan)
L1R	Trim
B	Lower Body Color
B	Upper Body Color

THE SHIPPING ORDER NUMBER is assigned prior to production. It consists of a four-digit planned delivery month/day date code, 0224 (February 24th), followed by a plant production sequence number (0555).

THE BODY NUMBER is a three-digit number which indicates the model and body style.

VALIANT V 100		CODE
	6 CYL	8 CYL
2-Dr. Sedan	111	V11
4-Dr. Sedan	113	V13
4-Dr. Wagon	156	V56

VALIANT V 200		CODE
	6 CYL	8 CYL
2-Dr. Sedan	131	V31
4-Dr. Sedan	133	V33
Convertible	135	V35
4-Dr. Wagon	176	V76

FURY I		CODE
	6 CYL	8 CYL
2-Dr. Sedan	511	P11
4-Dr. Sedan	513	P13
4-Dr. Wagon	556	P56
4-Dr. Sedan (Taxi)	583	P83
2-Dr. Sedan (Police)	—	P91
4-Dr. Sedan (Police)	—	P93
4-Dr. Wagon (Police)	—	P96

FURY II		CODE
	6 CYL	8 CYL
2-Dr. Sedan	521	P21
4-Dr. Sedan	523	P23
4-Dr. Wagon	567	P67

1965 PLYMOUTH

FURY III

	6 CYL	8 CYL CODE
2-Dr. Hardtop	532	P32
Convertible	—	P35
4-Dr. Sedan	533	P33
4-Dr. Hardtop	—	P34
4-Dr. Wagon	—	P76
4-Dr. Wagon	—	P77

SPORT FURY

	6 CYL	8 CYL CODE
2-Dr. Hardtop Sedan	—	P42

VALIANT SIGNET

	6 CYL	8 CYL CODE
2-Dr. Hardtop Sedan	142	V42
Convertible	145	V45

BARRACUDA

	6 CYL	8 CYL CODE
2-Dr. Sport Hardtop	189	V89

BELVEDERE I

	6 CYL	8 CYL CODE
2-Dr. Sedan	311	R11
4-Dr. Sedan	313	R13
4-Dr. Wagon	356	R56
2-Dr. Sedan (Police)	—	R91
4-Dr. Sedan (Police)	—	R93
4-Dr. Wagon (Police)	—	R96

BELVEDERE II

	6 CYL	8 CYL CODE
2-Dr. Hardtop	332	R32
Convertible	335	R35
4-Dr. Sedan	333	R33
4-Dr. Wagon	376	R76
4-Dr. Wagon	377	R77

SATELLITE

	CODE
2-Dr. Hardtop	R42
Convertible	R45

THE TRIM NUMBER furnishes the key to the interior color and material.

COLOR	CLOTH	VINYL	LEATHER	CODE
Blue	•	•		L1B,K1B,H1B
Blue	•	•		M1B,H2B,H4B
Blue		•		L4B,K4B,L5B
Blue		•		H1B,H4B,P4B
Blue		•		M4B,M5B,H5B
Red	•	•		L1R,K1R,M1R
Red	•	•		H1R,H2R,H4R
Red		•		L4R,K4R,L5R
Red		•		H1R,H4R,P4R
Red		•		M4R,M5R,H5R
Tan	•	•		L1T,K1T,L2T
Tan	•	•		K2T,M1T,H1T
Tan	•	•		H2T,H4T
Tan		•		L4T,K4T,L8T
Tan		•		K8T,T8T,L5T
Tan		•		H1T,H4T,M4T
Tan		•		M5T
Turquoise	•	•		M1Q,H1Q,H2Q
Turquoise	•	•		H4Q
Turquoise		•		H1Q,H4Q,P4Q
Turquoise		•		M4Q,H5Q
Black		•		H4X,P4X,H5X
Gold	•	•		H1Y,H2Y
Gold		•		H1Y,H4Y,P4Y
Gold		•		H5Y
Black/ Copper		•		P4U

THE PAINT CODE furnishes the key to the paint used on the car. A two-digit code indicates the top and bottom colors respectively. A number follows which designates two-tone, sports-tone, convertible top, etc.

COLOR	CODE
Gold Poly	A
Black	B
Light Blue	C
Medium Blue Poly	D
Dark Blue Poly	E
Copper Poly	H
Light Turquoise	J
Medium Turquoise Poly	K
Dark Turquoise Poly	L
Barracuda Silver Poly	N
Ruby	P
Ivory	S
Medium Red Poly	T
White	W
Light Tan	X
Medium Tan Poly	Y

ENGINE NUMBER

6-cylinder engine numbers are stamped on the right side of the block on a machined boss directly behind the ignition coil. The number provides the code to identify the series, block displacement, and month/day production date.

273 and 318 engine numbers are stamped on the left front of the block under the cylinder head.

361, 383, 413, and 426 engine numbers are stamped on the right side of the block below the distributor.

Hemi engine numbers are stamped on the left side of the cylinder block behind the thermostat housing.

EXAMPLE:

A	38	2	24
YEAR	383	FEBRUARY	DAY

VALIANT AND BARRACUDA (NO 170 C.I. BARRACUDA)

ENGINE CODE	NO. CYL.	CID	HORSE-POWER	COMP. RATIO	CARB	TRANS
A-170	6	170	101	8.5:1	1 BC	* M & A
A-225	6	225	145	8.4:1	1 BC	* M & A
A-273	8	273	180	8.8:1	2 BC	* M & A
A-273	8	273	235	10.5:1	4 BC	* M & A

BELVEDERE I AND II, SATELLITE (8-CYL.)

ENGINE CODE	NO. CYL.	CID	HORSE-POWER	COMP. RATIO	CARB	TRANS
A-225	6	225	145	8.4:1	1 BC	* M & A
A-273	8	273	180	8.8:1	2 BC	* M & A
A-318	8	318	230	9.0:1	2 BC	* M & A
A-361	8	361	265	9.0:1	2 BC	* M & A
A-383	8	383	330	10.0:1	4 BC	* M & A
A-426	8	426	365	10.3:1	4 BC	* M & A
AH-426	8	426	415	11.0:1	2-4 BC	* M & A
AH-426HC	8	426	425	12.5:1	2-4 BC	* M & A

FURY I, II, III AND SPORT FURY (8-CYL.)

ENGINE CODE	NO. CYL.	CID	HORSE-POWER	COMP. RATIO	CARB	TRANS
A-225	6	225	145	8.4:1	1 BC	* M & A
A-318	8	318	230	9.0:1	2 BC	* M & A
A-383	8	383	270	9.2:1	2 BC	* M & A
A-383	8	383	330	10.0;1	4 BC	* M & A
A-426	8	426	315	10.3:1	4 BC	* M & A

* MAN & AUTO

Other engine identifying marks are as follows:

Maltese Cross - .001" undersize crankshaft journals (M and R plus a number stamped on crankshaft counterweight indicates which main and rod journals are undersize).
X - .010" undersize crankshaft journals (M-10 and R-10 stamped on crankshaft counterweight indicates all rod and main journals are undersize).
A - .020" oversize cylinder bores
B - .010" undersize main and connecting rod bearings
Diamond - .008" oversize lifters
O/S - .005" oversize valve stems

1966 PLYMOUTH BARRACUDA

1966 PLYMOUTH BARRACUDA

1966 PLYMOUTH BELVEDERE

1966 PLYMOUTH BELVEDERE

1966 PLYMOUTH FURY

1966 PLYMOUTH FURY

1966 PLYMOUTH VALIANT

1966 PLYMOUTH VALIANT

1966 PLYMOUTH VIP

1966 PLYMOUTH VIP

VEHICLE IDENTIFICATION NUMBER

PLYMOUTH
PM21B65100551

The vehicle number (serial number) is stamped and embossed on a stainless steel plate attached to the left front door hinge pillar. It consists of car make symbol, series code, model year code, assembly plant symbol and a sequential production number.

FIRST DIGIT: Identifies the car make

CAR MAKE	CODE
Valiant	Y
Belvedere/Satellite	R
Fury	P
Barracuda	B

SECOND DIGIT: Identifies the series

SERIES	CODE
Valiant 100, Belvedere I, Fury I	L
Valiant 200, Signet, Belvedere II, Fury III	H
Fury II	M
Barracuda, Satellite, Sport Fury	P
Police	K
Taxi	T
VIP	S

THIRD AND FOURTH DIGITS: Identify the body style

BODY STYLE	CODE
2-Dr. Sedan	21
2-Dr. Hardtop	23
Convertible	27
2-Dr. Sport Hardtop	29
4-Dr. Sedan	41
4-Dr. Hardtop	43
Station Wagon, 6-Pass.	45
Station Wagon, 9-Pass.	46

FIFTH DIGIT: Identifies the engine

170	A
225	B
Special Order 6 Cyl.	C
273	D
318	E
361	F
383	G
426 Hemi	H
440	J
Special Order 8 Cyl.	K

SIXTH DIGIT: Identifies the model year (1966)

SEVENTH DIGIT: Identifies the assembly plant

ASSEMBLY PLANT	CODE
Lynch Road, Detroit, MI	1
Hamtramck, MI	2
Belvedere, IL	4
Los Angeles, CA	5
Newark, DE	6
St. Louis, MO	7
Windsor, Ont., CAN	9

LAST SIX DIGITS: Represent the basic production numbers

BODY NUMBER PLATE

THE BODY PLATE is stamped and embossed on a plate which is attached on the engine side of the cowl just above the master cylinder. On the Valiant, models the plate is located above the top hinge of the driver's side door. The plate shows the body type, trim code, schedule date, paint code, and some accessory codes.

CHRYSLER MOTORS
CORPORATION

SO	NUMBER	BDY	TRM	PNT
0224	05551	VL21	L4R	BB1

EXAMPLE:

0224	SON (Feb. 24)
05551	Production Sequence
VL21	Body Style (2-Dr. Sedan)
L4R	Trim
B	Lower Body Color
B	Upper Body Color

THE SHIPPING ORDER NUMBER consists of a three-digit month and day scheduled based on 01 through 31 days production date, and a five-digit production sequence number.

MONTH	CODE
JAN	1
FEB	2
MAR	3
APR	4
MAY	5
JUN	6
JULY	7
AUG	8
SEPT	9
OCT	A
NOV	B
DEC	C

THE BODY NUMBER is a four-digit number which indicates the car line, price class, and body style. Same first four digits as the VIN.

VALIANT 100	CODE
2-Dr. Sedan	VL21
4-Dr. Sedan	VL41
4-Dr. Wagon	VL45

VALIANT 200	CODE
4-Dr. Sedan	VH41
4-Dr. Wagon	VH45

SIGNET	CODE
2-Dr. Hardtop	VH23
Convertible	VH27

BARRACUDA	CODE
2-Dr. Hardtop+	BP29

+ Option Formulas

FURY I	CODE
2-Dr. Sedan	PL21
4-Dr. Sedan	PL41
4-Dr. Wagon	PL45

FURY II	CODE
2-Dr. Sedan	PM21
4-Dr. Sedan	PM41
4-Dr. Wagon, 2-Seat*	PM45
4-Dr. Wagon, 3-Seat	PM46

FURY III	CODE
2-Dr. Hardtop	PH23
4-Dr. Sedan	PH41
4-Dr. Hardtop*	PH43
Convertible*	PH27
4-Dr. Wagon, 2-Seat*	PH45
4-Dr. Wagon, 3-Seat*	PH46

SPORT FURY	CODE
2-Dr. Hardtop*	PP23
Convertible*	PP27

VIP	CODE
2-Dr. Hardtop	PS23
4-Dr. Hardtop	PS43

BELVEDERE I	CODE
2-Dr. Sedan	RL21
4-Dr. Sedan	RL41
4-Dr. Wagon	RL45

BELVEDERE II	CODE
2-Dr. Hardtop	RH23
4-Dr. Sedan	RH41
Convertible	RH27
4-Dr. Wagon, 2-Seat	RH45
4-Dr. Wagon, 3-Seat	RH46

SATELLITE	CODE
2-Dr. Hardtop	RP23
Convertible	RP27

* Indicates 8 cylinder only in these models

THE TRIM NUMBER furnishes the key to the interior color and material.

COLOR	CLOTH	VINYL	LEATHER	CODE
Blue	•	•		L1B,M1B,H1B
Blue	•	•		H2B
Blue	•			H8B
Blue		•		P4B,L4B,H4B
Blue		•		H5B,M4B
Black		•		P4X,H4X,H5X
Black	•			H8X
Citron	•	•		H1Y,H2Y
Citron		•		P4Y,H4Y
Red	•	•		L1R,M1R,H1R
Red	•	•		H2R,H1H
Red	•			H8R
Red		•		P4H,L4H,H4H
Red		•		L4R,H4R,P4R
Red		•		M4R
Tan	•	•		L1T,M1T,H1T
Tan	•	•		H2T
Tan		•		L4T,H4T,H5T
Tan		•		M4T
Tan/White		•		P4V
Turquoise	•	•		M1Q,H1Q,H2Q
Turquoise		•		H4Q,M4Q,H5Q

THE PAINT CODE furnishes the key to the paint used on the car. A three-digit code indicates the top and bottom colors respectively. A number follows which designates two-tone, sports-tone, convertible top, etc.

COLOR	CODE
Silver Metallic	A
Black	B
Light Blue	C
Light Blue Metallic	D
Dark Blue Metallic	E
Dark Green Metallic	G
Light Turquoise Metallic	K
Dark Turquoise Metallic	L
Bright Red	P
Dark Red Metallic	Q
Yellow	R
Soft Yellow	S
White	W
Beige	X
Bronze Metallic	Y
Citron Gold Metallic	Z
Light Mauve Metallic	6

ENGINE NUMBER

6-cylinder engine numbers are stamped on the right side of the block on a machined boss directly behind the ignition coil. The number provides the code to identify the series, block displacement, and month/day production date.

273 and 318 engine numbers are stamped on the left front of the block under the cylinder head.

361, 383, and 426 engine numbers are stamped on the right side of the block below the distributor.

440 engine numbers are stamped on the top of the water pump.

Hemi engine numbers are stamped on the left side of the cylinder block.

EXAMPLE:

B	38	2	24
YEAR	383	FEBRUARY	DAY

VALIANT AND BARRACUDA (NO 170 C.I.D.)

ENGINE CODE	NO. CYL.	CID	HORSE-POWER	COMP. RATIO	CARB	TRANS
B-170	6	170	101	8.5:1	1 BC	* M & A
B-225	6	225	145	8.4:1	1 BC	* M & A
B-273	8	273	180	8.8:1	2 BC	* M & A
B-273	8	273	235	10.5:1	4 BC	* M & A

BELVEDERE I, II AND SATELLITE 8-CYL.

ENGINE CODE	NO. CYL.	CID	HORSE-POWER	COMP. RATIO	CARB	TRANS
B-225	6	225	145	8.4:1	1 BC	* M & A
B-273	8	273	180	8.8:1	2 BC	* M & A
B-318	8	318	230	9.0:1	2 BC	* M & A
B-361	8	361	265	9.0:1	2 BC	* M & A
B-383	8	383	325	10.0:1	4 BC	* M & A
BH-426	8	426	425	10.25:1	2-4 BC	* M & A

FURY I, II, III AND SPORT FURY 8-CYL. AND VIP 8-CYL.

ENGINE CODE	NO. CYL.	CID	HORSE-POWER	COMP. RATIO	CARB	TRANS
B-225	6	225	145	8.4:1	1 BC	* M & A
B-318	8	318	230	9.0:1	2 BC	* M & A
B-383	8	383	270	9.2:1	2 BC	* M & A
B-383	8	383	375	10.0;1	4 BC	* M & A
B-440	8	440	365	10.1:1	4 BC	* M & A

* MAN & AUTO

Other engine identifying marks are as follows:

Maltese Cross - .001" undersize crankshaft journals (M and R plus a number stamped on crankshaft counterweight indicates which main and rod journals are undersize.
X - .010" undersize crankshaft journals (M-10 and R-10 stamped on crankshaft counterweight indicates all rod and main journals are undersize).
A - .020" oversize cylinder bores
Diamond - .008" oversize lifters
O/S - .005" oversize stems

 1967 PLYMOUTH

1967 PLYMOUTH BARRACUDA

1967 PLYMOUTH BELVEDERE GTX

1967 PLYMOUTH FURY

1967 PLYMOUTH VALIANT

1967 PLYMOUTH BARRACUDA

1967 PLYMOUTH SATELLITE

1967 PLYMOUTH FURY

1967 PLYMOUTH VALIANT

VEHICLE IDENTIFICATION NUMBER

PLYMOUTH
PM23F75100551

The vehicle number (serial number) is stamped and embossed on a stainless steel plate attached to the left front door hinge pillar. It consists of car make symbol, series code, model year code, assembly plant symbol and a sequential production number.

FIRST DIGIT: Identifies the car make

CAR MAKE	CODE
Valiant	Y
Belvedere/Satellite	R
Fury	P
Barracuda	B

SECOND DIGIT: Identifies the series

SERIES	CODE
Belvedere, , Fury I	E
Valiant, Belvedere I, Fury II	L
Signet, Belvedere II, Sport Fury	H
Fury III	M
Satellite, VIP, Barracuda	P
Police	K
Taxi	T
GTX, Sport Fury (2-Dr.)	S
Super Stock	O

THIRD AND FOURTH DIGITS: Identify the body style

BODY STYLE	CODE
2-Dr. Sedan	21
2-Dr. Hardtop	23
Convertible	27
2-Dr. Sport Hardtop	29
4-Dr. Sedan	41
4-Dr. Hardtop	43
Station Wagon, 6-Pass.	45
Station Wagon, 9-Pass.	46

FIFTH DIGIT: Identifies the engine

ENGINE	CODE
170	A
225	B
Special Order 6 Cyl.	C
273	D
273 (4-BBl) Hi Per	E
318	F
383	G
383 (4-BBl) Hi Per	H
426 Hemi	J
440	K
440 Hi Per	L
Special Order 8	M

SIXTH DIGIT: Identifies the model year (1967)

SEVENTH DIGIT: Identifies the assembly plant

ASSEMBLY PLANT	CODE
Lynch Road, Detroit, MI	1
Hamtramck, MI	2
Belvedere, IL	4
Los Angeles, CA	5
Newark, DE	6
St. Louis, MO	7
Export	8
Windsor, Ont., CAN	9

LAST SIX DIGITS: Represent the basic production numbers

BODY NUMBER PLATE

THE BODY PLATE is stamped and embossed on a stainless steel plate attached to the fender shield under the hood. The plate indicates the code for the body type, engine, transmission, schedule date, paint, trim and some option codes. The plate is read left to right, bottom to top, starting with the bottom row of numbers.

CHRYSLER MOTORS CORPORATION

		AX	TRM	PNT	UBS
		4	L4R	BB1	S
PM41	62	5	635	224	00551

EXAMPLE:

PM41	Body Style (4-Dr. Sedan)
62	Engine (383 1-4 BC, 8-Cyl.)
5	Transmission (3-Spd. Auto.)
635	Tire Size and Type
224	SON (Feb. 24)
00551	Production Sequence
4	Axle
L4R	Trim
B	Lower Body Color
B	Upper Body Color
S	Accent Color

THE SHIPPING ORDER NUMBER is the last right digit of the bottom row. It consists of a three-digit month and day scheduled production date, and a five-digit production order number.

THE BODY NUMBER is a four-digit number which indicates the car line, price class, and body style. Same first four digits of the VIN.

VALIANT	CODE
2-Dr. Sedan*	VL21
4-Dr. Sedan*	VL41

* Option V-200

SIGNET	CODE
2-Dr. Sedan	VH21
4-Dr. Sedan	VH41

BARRACUDA	CODE
2-Dr. Hardtop*	BP23
2-Dr. Special Hardtop*	BP29
Convertible*	BP27

* Option Formulas

BELVEDERE	CODE
4-Dr. Wagon, 2-Seat	RE45
4-Dr. Wagon, 3-Seat	RK45

BELVEDERE I	CODE
2-Dr. Sedan	RL21
2-Dr. Sedan	RL41
4-Dr. Wagon	RL45

BELVEDERE II	CODE
2-Dr. Hardtop	RH23
4-Dr. Sedan	RH41
Convertible	RH27
4-Dr. Wagon, 2-Seat	RH45
4-Dr. Wagon, 3-Seat	RH46
Super Stock	RO23

SATELLITE	CODE
2-Dr. Hardtop	RP23
Convertible	RP27

GTX	CODE
2-Dr. Hardtop	RS23
Convertible	RS27

FURY I	CODE
2-Dr. Sedan	PE21
4-Dr. Sedan	PE41
4-Dr. Wagon	PE45
4-Dr. Sedan	PT41
2-Dr. Sedan	PK21
4-Dr. Sedan	PK41
4-Dr. Wagon	PK45

FURY II	CODE
2-Dr. Sedan	PL21
4-Dr. Sedan	PL41
4-Dr. Wagon, 2-Seat	PL45
4-Dr. Wagon, 3-Seat	PL46

FURY III	CODE
2-Dr. Hardtop	PM23
4-Dr. Sedan	PM41
4-Dr. Hardtop	PM43
Convertible	PM27
4-Dr. Wagon, 2-Seat	PM45
4-Dr. Wagon, 3-Seat	PM46

SPORT FURY	CODE
2-Dr. Hardtop	PH23
Convertible	PH27
2-Dr. Fast Top	PS23

VIP	CODE
2-Dr. Hardtop	PP23
4-Dr. Hardtop	PP43

THE ENGINE CID CODE identifies the engine.

ENGINE CID	CODE
170 6 Cyl.	11
225 6 Cyl.	21
273 8 Cyl.	31
273 4-BBl HP 8 Cyl.	32
318 8 Cyl.	41
383 2-BBL 8 Cyl.	61
383 1-4 BBL 8 Cyl.	62
426 2-4 BBl HP 8 Cyl.	73
440 8 Cyl.	81
440 HP 8 Cyl.	83

TRANSMISSION	CODE
3-Spd. Manual Column Shift	1
3-Spd. Manual Column Shift	2
4-Spd. Manual Floor Shift	3
3-Spd. Automatic	5
3-Spd. Automatic	6
Special Order Transmission	9

The option which indicates tire size and type is not included.

The next row up there will be one-digit AXLE CODE found directly under the AX column.

THE UBS CODE identifies the upper door frame color and the accent stripe color.

THE TRIM NUMBER furnishes the key to the interior color and material.

COLOR	CLOTH	VINYL	LEATHER	CODE
Blue	•	•		L1B,H1B,E1B
Blue	•	•		M1B,P1B,X1B
Blue		•		E4B,L4B,H4B
Blue		•		P6B,X4B,L1B
Blue		•		M4B,H6B,H5B
Red	•	•		L1R,M1R,X1R
Red	•	•		H1R
Red		•		E4R,L4R,H4R
Red		•		P6R,M4R,H6R
Red		•		H5R
Tan	•	•		L1T,K1T,H1T
Tan	•	•		E1T,M1T,X1T
Tan		•		E4T,L4T,K4T
Tan		•		T4T,H4T,X4T
Tan		•		M4T,H6T,H5T
Tan			•	P9T
Copper	•	•		H1K,M1K,P1K
Copper		•		H4K,P6K,M4K
Copper		•		H6K,H5K
Turquoise	•	•		H1Q,E1Q,M1Q
Turquoise		•		E4Q,X4Q,L1Q
Turquoise		•		L4Q,M4Q,P1Q
Black	•	•		H1X,P1X
Black	•			P6X
Black		•		H4X,M4X,H6X
Black		•		X4X,X5X
White		•		H6W,H5X
White/Black		•		H4W,P6W,H5W
White/Black		•		H6W
White/ Turquoise		•		H4P
Copper/ Black		•		H4M
White/Red		•		P6V,H5V,H6V
White/Blue		•		H5C,H6C

THE PAINT CODE furnishes the key to the paint used on the car. A three-digit code indicates the top and bottom colors respectively. A number follows which designates two-tone, sports-tone, convertible top, etc.

COLOR	CODE
Buffed Silver Metallic	A
Black	B
Medium Blue Metallic	C
Light Blue Metallic	D
Dark Blue Metallic	E
Bright Blue Metallic	8
Light Green Metallic	F
Dark Green Metallic	G
Dark Copper Metallic	H
Light Turquoise Metallic	K
Dark Turquoise Metallic	L
Turbine Bronze Metallic	M
Bright Red Metallic	P
Dark Red Metallic	Q
Mauve Metallic	6
Yellow	R
Soft Yellow	S
Copper Metallic	T
White	W
Beige	X
Light Tan Metallic	Y
Gold Metallic	Z

ENGINE NUMBER

6-cylinder engine numbers are stamped on the right side of the block on the top boss directly behind the ignition coil. The number provides the code to identify the series, block displacement, and month/day production date.

273, 318, and 440 engine numbers are stamped on the left front of the block under the cylinder head.

383 engine numbers are stamped on the right side of the block below the distributor.

426 engine numbers are stamped on the left side on the horizontal surface behind the thermostat housing.

EXAMPLE:

C	38	2	24
YEAR	383	FEBRUARY	DAY

VALIANT

ENGINE CODE	NO. CYL.	CID	HORSE-POWER	COMP. RATIO	CARB	TRANS
C-170	6	170	115	8.5:1	1 BC	* M & A
C-225	6	225	145	8.4;1	1 BC	* M & A
C-273	8	273	180	8.8:1	2 BC	* M & A
C-273	8	273	235	10.5:1	4 BC	* M & A

BARRACUDA

ENGINE CODE	NO. CYL.	CID	HORSE-POWER	COMP. RATIO	CARB	TRANS
C-225	6	225	145	8.4:1	1 BC	* M & A
C-273	8	273	180	8.8:1	2 BC	* M & A
C-273	8	273	235	10.5:1	4 BC	* M & A
C-383	8	383	280	10.0;1	4 BC	* M & A

BELVEDERE, I, II AND SATELLITE 8-CYL.

ENGINE CODE	NO. CYL.	CID	HORSE-POWER	COMP. RATIO	CARB	TRANS
C-225	6	225	145	8.4:1	1 BC	* M & A
C-273	8	273	180	8.8:1	2 BC	* M & A
C-318	8	318	230	9.2:1	2 BC	* M & A
C-383	8	383	270	9.2:1	2 BC	* M & A
C-383	8	383	325	10.0:1	4 BC	* M & A
C-426	8	426	425	10.25:1	2-4 BC	* M & A

GTX

ENGINE CODE	NO. CYL.	CID	HORSE-POWER	COMP. RATIO	CARB	TRANS
C-440	8	440	375	10.0:1	4 BC	* M & A
C-426	8	426	425	10.25:1	2-4 BC	* M & A

FURY I, II, III

ENGINE CODE	NO. CYL.	CID	HORSE-POWER	COMP. RATIO	CARB	TRANS
C-225	6	225	145	8.4:1	1 BC	* M & A
C-318	8	318	230	9.0:1	2 BC	* M & A
C-383	8	383	270	9.2:1	2 BC	* M & A
C-383	8	383	325	10.0:1	4 BC	* M & A
C-440	8	440	375	10.0:1	4 BC	* M & A

SPORT FURY AND VIP

ENGINE CODE	NO. CYL.	CID	HORSE-POWER	COMP. RATIO	CARB	TRANS
C-318	8	318	230	9.0:1	2 BC	* M & A
C-383	8	383	270	9.2:1	2 BC	* M & A
C-383	8	383	325	10.0:1	4 BC	* M & A
C-440	8	440	375	10.0:1	4 BC	* M & A

* MAN & AUTO

Other engine identifying marks are as follows:

A - .020" oversize cylinder bores
B - .010" undersize bearings (273 and 318)
Maltese Cross - .001" undersize bearings
Maltese Cross and X - .010" undersize bearings
Diamond - Oversize tappets
LC - Low compression
HC - High compression
HP - High performance
MP - Maximum performance
R - Regular fuel

1968 PLYMOUTH BARRACUDA

1968 PLYMOUTH BARRACUDA

1968 PLYMOUTH FURY

1968 PLYMOUTH FURY

1968 PLYMOUTH GTX

1968 PLYMOUTH GTX

1968 PLYMOUTH ROAD RUNNER

1968 PLYMOUTH ROAD RUNNER

1968 PLYMOUTH SATELLITE

1968 PLYMOUTH VALIANT

VEHICLE IDENTIFICATION NUMBER

PLYMOUTH
PM41G8A100001

The vehicle number (serial number) is stamped and embossed on a stainless steel plate attached to the left front door hinge pillar. It consists of car make symbol, series code, model year code, assembly plant symbol and a sequential production number.

FIRST DIGIT: Identifies the car make

CAR MAKE	CODE
Valiant	V
Belvedere	R
Fury	P
Barracuda	B

SECOND DIGIT: Identifies the series

SERIES	CODE
Fury I	E
Valiant, Belvedere, Fury II	L
Signet, Satellite, Sport Fury	H
Fury III, Road Runner	M
VIP, Barracuda, Sport Satellite	P
Police	K
Taxi	T
GTX, Sport Fury Fast Top	S
Super Stock	O
Fury III 2-Dr. Fast Top	X

THIRD AND FOURTH DIGITS: Identify the body style

BODY STYLE	CODE
2-Dr. Sedan	21
2-Dr. Hardtop	23
Convertible	27
2-Dr. Sports Hardtop	29
4-Dr. Sedan	41
4-Dr. Hardtop	43
Station Wagon, 6-Pass.	45
Station Wagon, 9-Pass.	46

FIFTH DIGIT: Identifies the cubic inch displacement

CID	CODE
170	A
225	B
Special Order 6 Cyl.	C
273	D
318	F
383	G
383 Hi Per	H
426 Hemi	J
440	K
440 Hi Per	L
Special Order 8	M
340	P

SIXTH DIGIT: Identifies the model year (1968)

SEVENTH DIGIT: Identifies the assembly plant

ASSEMBLY PLANT	CODE
Lynch Road, Detroit, MI	A
Hamtramck, MI	B
Belvedere, IL	D
Los Angeles, CA	E
Newark, DE	F
St. Louis, MO	G
Windsor, Ont., CAN	R

LAST SIX DIGITS: Represent the basic production numbers

BODY NUMBER PLATE

THE BODY PLATE is stamped and embossed on a stainless steel plate attached to the fender shield under the hood. The plate indicates the code for the body type, engine, transmission, schedule date, paint, trim and some option codes. The plate is read left to right, bottom to top, starting with the bottom row of numbers.

CHRYSLER MOTORS
CORPORATION

		AX	TRM	PNT	UBS
		4	H4R	BB1	S
PM41	62	5	635	224	00551

EXAMPLE:

4	Axle
H4R	Trim
B	Lower Body Color
B	Upper Body Color
S	Accent Color
PM41	Body Style (4-Dr. Sedan)
62	Engine (383 4 BC 8 Cyl.)
635	Tire size and Type
224	SON (Feb. 24)
00551	Production Sequence

THE SHIPPING ORDER NUMBER is the last right digit of the bottom ros. It consists of a three-digit month and day scheduled production date, and a five-digit production order number.

THE BODY NUMBER is a four-digit number which indicates the car line, price class, and body style. Same first four digits as the VIN.

VALIANT	CODE
2-Dr. Sedan+	VL21
4-Dr. Sedan+	VL41

+ Option V-200

SIGNET	CODE
2-Dr. Sedan	VH21
4-Dr. Sedan	VH41

BARRACUDA	CODE
2-Dr. Hardtop+	BP23
2-Dr. Special Hardtop+	BP29
Convertible+	BP27
Super Stock	BO29

+ Option Formulas

BELVEDERE	CODE
2-Dr. Sedan	RL21
4-Dr. Sedan	RL41
4-Dr. Wagon	RL45

SPORT SATELLITE	CODE
2-Dr. Hardtop	RP23
Convertible	RP27
4-Dr. Wagon, 2-Seat	RP45
4-Dr. Wagon, 3-Seat	RP46

SATELLITE	CODE
2-Dr. Hardtop	RH23
4-Dr. Sedan	RH41
Convertible	RH27
4-Dr. Wagon, 2-Seat	RH45
4-Dr. Wagon, 3-Seat	RH46

ROAD RUNNER	CODE
2-Dr. Sedan	RM21
2-Dr. Hardtop	RM23

GTX	CODE
2-Dr. Hardtop	RS23
Convertible	RS27

FURY I	CODE
2-Dr. Sedan	PE21
4-Dr. Sedan	PE41

FURY II	CODE
2-Dr. Sedan	PL21
4-Dr. Sedan	PL41

FURY III	CODE
2-Dr. Hardtop	PM23
4-Dr. Sedan	PM41
4-Dr. Hardtop	PM43
Convertible	PM27
2-Dr. Fast Top	PX23

SPORT FURY	CODE
2-Dr. Hardtop	PH23
Convertible	PH27
2-Dr. Fast Top	PS23

VIP	CODE
2-Dr. Hardtop	PP27
4-Dr. Hardtop	PP23

FURY SUBURBAN	CODE
4-Dr. Wagon, 2-Seat	PE45

FURY CUSTOM SUBURBAN	CODE
4-Dr. Wagon, 2-Seat	PL45
4-Dr. Wagon, 3-Seat	PL46

FURY SPORT SUBURBAN	CODE
4-Dr. Wagon, 2-Seat	PM45
4-Dr. Wagon, 3-Seat	PM46

The two-digit ENGINE CID CODE identifies the engine.

ENGINE CID	CODE
170 6 Cyl.	11
225 6 Cyl.	21
273 8 Cyl.	31
318 8 Cyl.	41
383 2-BBL 8 Cyl.	61
383 4 BBL 8 Cyl.	62
426 2-4 BBl 8 Cyl.	73
440 8 Cyl.	81
440 8 Cyl. Hi Per	83

TRANSMISSION	CODE
3-Spd. Manual Column Shift	1
3-Spd. Manual Column Shift	2
4-Spd. Manual Floor Shift	3
3-Spd. Automatic	5
3-Spd. Automatic	6
Special Transmission	9

The tire size and type option is not included.

THE AXLE CODE is on the next row up. The one-digit found directly under the AX column.

THE UBS CODE identifies the upper door frame color and the accent stripe color.

THE TRIM NUMBER furnishes the key to the interior color and material.

COLOR	CLOTH	VINYL	LEATHER	CODE
Blue	•	•		H1B,L1B,E1B
Blue	•	•		M1B,P1B,P2B
Blue		•		L4B,H4B,H5B
Blue		•		H6B,D6B,D4B
Blue		•		P6B,S6B,E4B
Blue		•		M5B
Tan	•	•		L1T,H1T,E1T
Tan		•		L4T,M5T,D4L
Tan		•		H4T
Black	•	•		H1X,L1X,M1X
Black	•	•		P1X,P2X,P9X
Black	•	•		P0X,P7X,P8X
Black		•		L4X,H4X,M5X
Black		•		H6X,H5X,D6X
Black		•		B4X,P6X,S6X
Green	•	•		H1F,M1F,P1F
Green	•	•		P2F
Green		•		H6F,D6F,H4F
Green		•		P6F,S6F,L4F
Green		•		M5F,M5G
Burgundy		•		H4R,H6R,D6R
Gold	•	•		M1Y
Gold		•		H4Y,D6Y,H6Y
Gold		•		S6Y,P4Y,P5Y
Gold		•		M5Y
Red	•	•		E1R,M1R
Red		•		M5R,H4R,P6R
Red		•		S6R,L4R,P4R
Red		•		P5R,E4R,H6R
White/Blue		•		H6C,H5C,D6C
White/Blue		•		H4C,P6C,S6C
White/Green		•		H6D,H5D,D6D
White/Green		•		H4D,P6D,S6D
White/Gold		•		H6E,D6E
White/ Burgundy		•		H6V,H5V,D6V
White/Black		•		H6W,H5W,D6W
White/Black		•		P4W,P5W,M5W
Silver/Black	•		D4S	
Gold/Black	•	•		H1N,H4N
Gold/Black		•		P6N,S6N
White/Tan		•		H4H
White/Red		•		H4V,P6V,S6V

THE PAINT CODE furnishes the key to the paint used on the car. A three-digit code indicates the top and bottom colors respectively. A number follows which designates two-tone, sports-tone, convertible top, etc.

COLOR	CODE
Buffed Silver Metallic	A
Black Velvet	B
Mist Blue Metallic	D
Mist Green Metallic	F
Forest Green Metallic	G
Yellow Gold	H
Ember Gold Metallic	J
Mist Turquoise Metallic	K
Surf Turquoise Metallic	L
Turbine Bronze Metallic	M
Matador Red	P
Electric Blue Metallic	Q
Burgundy Metallic	R
Sunfire Yellow	S
Avocado Green Metallic	T
Frost Blue Metallic	U
Sable White	W
Satin Beige	X
Sierra Tan Metallic	Y

ENGINE NUMBER

6-cylinder engine numbers are stamped on the right side of the block below the number one spark plug. The number provides the code to identify the series, block displacement, and month/day production date.

273, 318, and 340 engine numbers are stamped on the left front on the block below the cylinder head.

383, 426, and 440 engine numbers are stamped on the pan rail at the rear corner under the starter opening.

EXAMPLE:

PM	383	2187	2401
PLANT CODE	CID	JULIAN DATE	DAILY SEQUENTIAL NUMBER

ENGINE PLANTS
PM-Mound Rd.
PT-Trenton

VALIANT

ENGINE CODE	NO. CYL.	CID	HORSE-POWER	COMP. RATIO	CARB	TRANS
PT-170	6	170	115	8.5:1	1 BC	* M & A
PT-225	6	225	145	8.4:1	1 BC	* M & A
PT-273	8	273	190	9.0:1	2 BC	* M & A
PT-318	8	318	230	9.2:1	2 BC	* M & A

BARRACUDA

ENGINE CODE	NO. CYL.	CID	HORSE-POWER	COMP. RATIO	CARB	TRANS
PT-225	6	225	145	8.4:1	1 BC	* M & A
PT-318	8	318	230	9.2:1	2 BC	* M & A
PT-340	8	340	275	10.5:1	4 BC	* M & A
PT-383	8	383	300	10.0;1	4 BC	* M & A
PT-426*	8	426	425	10.25:1	2-4 BC	* M & A

* Super Stock

BELVEDERE, SATELLITE

ENGINE CODE	NO. CYL.	CID	HORSE-POWER	COMP. RATIO	CARB	TRANS
PT-225	6	225	145	8.4:1	1 BC	* M & A
PT-273	8	273	190	9.0:1	2 BC	* M & A
PT-318	8	318	230	9.2:1	2 BC	* M & A
PT-383	8	383	290	9.2:1	2 BC	* M & A
PT-383	8	383	330	10.0;1	4 BC	* M & A

SPORT SATELLITE

ENGINE CODE	NO. CYL.	CID	HORSE-POWER	COMP. RATIO	CARB	TRANS
PT-318	8	318	230	9.2:1	2 BC	* M & A
PT-383	8	383	290	9.2:1	2 BC	* M & A
PT-383	8	383	330	10.0:1	4 BC	* M & A

ROAD RUNNER

ENGINE CODE	NO. CYL.	CID	HORSE-POWER	COMP. RATIO	CARB	TRANS
PT-383	8	383	335	10.0;1	4 BC	* M & A
PT-426	8	426	425	10.25:1	2-4 BC	* M & A

GTX

ENGINE CODE	NO. CYL.	CID	HORSE-POWER	COMP. RATIO	CARB	TRANS
PT-440	8	440	375	10.1:1	4 BC	* M & A
PT-426	8	426	425	10.25;1	2-4 BC	* M & A

FURY I, II, III

ENGINE CODE	NO. CYL.	CID	HORSE-POWER	COMP. RATIO	CARB	TRANS
PT-225	6	225	145	8.4:1	1 BC	* M & A
PT-318	8	318	230	9.2:1	2 BC	* M & A
PT-383	8	383	290	9.2:1	2 BC	* M & A
PT-383	8	383	330	10.0:1	4 BC	* M & A
PT-440	8	440	375	10.1:1	4 BC	* M & A

SPORT FURY AND VIP

ENGINE CODE	NO. CYL.	CID	HORSE-POWER	COMP. RATIO	CARB	TRANS
PT-383	8	318	230	9.2:1	2 BC	* M & A
PT-383	8	383	290	9.2:1	2 BC	* M & A
PT-383	8	383	330	10.0;1	4 BC	* M & A
PT-440	8	440	375	10.1:1	4 BC	* M & A

SUBURBANS (6 CYL. ON PE45 ONLY)

ENGINE CODE	NO. CYL.	CID	HORSE-POWER	COMP. RATIO	CARB	TRANS
PT-225	6	225	145	8.4:1	1 BC	* M & A
PT-318	8	318	230	9.2:1	2 BC	* M & A
PT-383	8	383	290	9.2:1	2 BC	* M & A
PT-383	8	383	330	10.0:1	4 BC	* M & A
PT-440	8	440	350	10.1:1	4 BC	* M & A

* MAN & AUTO

Other engine identifying marks are as follows:

L or LC - Low compression
HP - High performance
R - Regular fuel
A - .020" oversize cylinder bores
Diamond - Oversize tappets
Maltese Cross - .001" undersize bearing shells
X - .010" undersize crankshaft

1969 PLYMOUTH BARRACUDA

1969 PLYMOUTH BARRACUDA

1969 PLYMOUTH GTX

1969 PLYMOUTH GTX

1969 PLYMOUTH FURY III

1969 PLYMOUTH FURY III

1969 PLYMOUTH SATELLITE

1969 PLYMOUTH SATELLITE

1969 PLYMOUTH VALIANT SIGNET

1969 PLYMOUTH VALIANT SIGNET

VEHICLE IDENTIFICATION NUMBER

PLYMOUTH
PH29K9A100551

The serial number is stamped on a plate on the top left side of the dash panel visible through the windshield. It consists of car make symbol, series code, model year code, assembly plant symbol and a sequential production number.

FIRST DIGIT: Identifies the car make

CAR MAKE	CODE
Valiant	V
Belvedere	R
Fury	P
Barracuda	B

SECOND DIGIT: Identifies the series

SERIES	CODE
Fury I	E
Valiant, Belvedere, Fury II	L
Signet, Satellite, Sports Fury	H
Fury III, Road Runner	M
Barracuda, Sport Satellite, VIP	P
Police	K
Taxi	T
GTX	S
Super Stock	O

THIRD AND FOURTH DIGITS: Identify the body style

BODY STYLE	CODE
2-Dr. Sedan	21
2-Dr. Hardtop	23
Convertible	27
2-Dr. Sport Hardtop	29
4-Dr. Sedan	41
4-Dr. Hardtop	43
Station Wagon, 6-Pass.	45
Station Wagon, 9-Pass.	46

FIFTH DIGIT: Identifies the cubic inch displacement

CID	CODE
170	A
225	B
Special Order 6 Cyl.	C
237	D
318	F
383	G
383 Hi Per	H
426/Hemi	J
440	K
440 Hi Per	L
440 + 6	M
340	P

SIXTH DIGIT: Identifies the model year (1969)

SEVENTH DIGIT: Identifies the assembly plant

ASSEMBLY PLANT	CODE
Lynch Road, Detroit, MI	A
Hamtramck, MI	B
Jefferson Ave., Detroit, MI	C
Belvedere, IL	D

LAST SIX DIGITS: Represent the basic production numbers

BODY NUMBER PLATE

THE BODY PLATE is read left to right, bottom to top. For 1969 Chrysler Corp. started a new system on their body code plates. Each body code plate contains all the code numbers for every option on the car. If one plate didn't hold all the information, a second tag was used. Listed here will be the codes found (usually) on the bottom two rows.

CHRYSLER MOTORS
CORPORATION

			TRM	UBS
	A9	A9	H2R	W
BP29	E55	D21	P9A	100551

EXAMPLE:

A9	Lower Body Color
A9	Upper Body Color
H2R	Trim
W	Accent Colors
BP29	Body Style (2-Dr. Coupe)
E55	Engine (340 4 BC 8 Cyl.)
D21	Transmission (4-Spd. Man.)
P9A	Tire Size and Type
100551	Production Sequence

The first row includes a four-digit body model and style code, a three-digit engine code and a three-digit transmission code, and the last nine digits of the VIN NUMBER. The next row up is a four-digit plant code number, a three-digit trim code number followed by a special trim, stripping and door frame color codes if any.

THE BODY NUMBER is a four-digit number which indicates the car line, price class and body style. Same first four digits as the VIN.

VALIANT	CODE
2-Dr. Sedan+	VL21
4-Dr. Sedan+	VL41

+ Option V 200

SIGNET	CODE
2-Dr. Sedan	VH21
4-Dr. Sedan	VH41

BARRACUDA	CODE
2-Dr. Hardtop+	BP23
2-Dr. Sport Coupe+	BP29
Convertible+	BP27

+ Option Formulas
Option Cuda 340
Option Cuda 383

BELVEDERE	CODE
2-Dr. Coupe	RL21
4-Dr. Sedan	RL41
4-Dr. Wagon, 2-Seat	RL45

1969 PLYMOUTH

SATELLITE	CODE
2-Dr. Hardtop	RH23
Convertible	RH27
4-Dr. Sedan	RH41
4-Dr. Wagon, 2-Seat	RH45
4-Dr. Wagon, 3-Seat	RH46

SPORT SATELLITE	CODE
2-Dr. Hardtop	RP23
Convertible	RP27
4-Dr. Sedan	RP41
4-Dr. Wagon, 2-Seat	RP45
4-Dr. Wagon, 3-Seat	RP46

BELVEDERE (POLICE)	CODE
2-Dr. Coupe	RK21
4-Dr. Sedan	RK41
4-Dr. Wagon	RK45

BELVEDERE (TAXI)	CODE
4-Dr. Sedan	RT41

FURY I	CODE
2-Dr. Sedan	PE21
4-Dr. Sedan	PE41

FURY II	CODE
2-Dr. Sedan	PL21
4-Dr. Sedan	PL41

FURY III	CODE
2-Dr. Hardtop	PM23
4-Dr. Sedan	PM41
4-Dr. Hardtop	PM43
Convertible	PM27
2-Dr. Hardtop Formal	PM29

SPORT FURY	CODE
2-Dr. Hardtop	PH23
Convertible	PH27
2-Dr. Hardtop Formal	PH29

FURY I (POLICE)	CODE
2-Dr. Sedan	PK21
4-Dr. Sedan	PK41
4-Dr. Wagon, 2-Seat	PK45

FURY (TAXI)	CODE
4-Dr. Sedan	PT41

VIP	CODE
2-Dr. Hardtop	PP23
4-Dr. Hardtop	PP43
2-Dr. Hardtop Formal	PP29

ROAD RUNNER	CODE
2-Dr. Coupe	RM21
2-Dr. Hardtop	RM23
Convertible	RM27

GTX	CODE
2-Dr. Hardtop	RS23
Convertible	RS27

THE ENGINE CID CODE identifies the engine.

ENGINE CID	CODE
Special Order 6 Cyl.	E06
Special Order 8 Cyl.	E08
170 6 Cyl.	E11
225 6 Cyl.	E24
225 Special 6 Cyl.	E25
273 8 Cyl.	E31
318 8 Cyl.	E44
340 4 BBL 8 Cyl.	E55
383 2 BBL 8 Cyl.	E61
383 4 BBL 8 Cyl.	E62
426/Hemi	E74
440 4 BBL 8 Cyl.	E85
440 1 BBL 8 Cyl.	E86

TRANSMISSION CODE	
3-Spd. Manual	D11
3-Spd. Manual	D12
3-Spd. Manual	D14
4-Spd. Manual	D21
3-Spd. Automatic	D31
3-Spd. Automatic	D32
3-Spd. Automatic	D34

The tire size and type option is not included.

The last digits of the bottom row are a repeat of the last nine digits of the VIN plate.

THE UBS CODE identifies the upper door frame color and the accent stripe color.

1969 PLYMOUTH

THE TRIM NUMBER furnishes the key to the interior color and material.

COLOR	CLOTH	VINYL	LEATHER	CODE
Blue	•	•		H1B,D1B,P3D
Blue	•	•		M1D,L1B,E1B
Blue	•	•		P3B
Blue		•		H4B,H2B,D4B
Blue		•		D2B,L2B,H6D
Blue		•		M4D,E2B,D6B
Blue		•		H6B,P2B,M6B
Blue		•		P6D,F2Q,M2B
Gold		•		H4Y,H2Y
Green	•	•		H1G,P3G,M1G
Green	•	•		L1G
Green		•		H6G,M4G,D6G
Green		•		P2G,H2G,P6G
Green		•		M6G
Red	•	•		M1R
Red		•		H4R,H2R,D4R
Red		•		D2R,H6R,M4R
Red		•		L2R,E2R,D6R
Red		•		P6R
Black	•	•		H1X,D1X,P3X
Black	•	•		M1X
Black		•		H6X,H4X,H2X
Black		•		D4X,D2X,L2X
Black		•		P8X,P6X,H6X
Black		•		M8X,M4X,D6X
Black		•		P2X,M2X
Black		•	•	PPX
White/Black		•		H6W,H4W,P6W
White/Black		•		H2W,M6W
White/Blue		•		H6C,H4C,P6C
White/Blue		•		P2C,H2C,M6C
White/Gold		•		H6E
White/Green		•		H6F,H4F,P6F
White/Green		•		P2F,H2F,M6F
White/Red		•		H6V,H4V,P6V
White/Tan		•		P6H,P2H,H2H
White/Tan		•		M6H
Tan	•	•		H1T,P3T,L1T
Tan		•		L2T,P4T,H6T
Tan		•		M4T,D6T,P6T
Tan		•		P2T,H2T,M6T
Tan		•		M2T
Champagne	•	•		M1L,L1L,E1L
Champagne		•		E2L
Platinum		•		H6S,M4S
White		•		P4W,H6W,M4W
White		•		L2W
Yellow/Black		•		D6P
Tan/Green		•		D6J
Tan/Black		•		D6U
Pewter/ Black		•		P6S,P2S,M2S
Pewter/ Black		•		M6S,H2S

THE PAINT CODE furnishes the key to the paint used on the car.

PAINT	CODE
Buffed Silver Metallic	A
Black	B
Medium Blue Metallic	C
Light Blue Metallic	D
Dark Blue Metallic	E
Bright Blue Metallic	8
Light Green Metallic	F
Dark Green Metallic	G
Dark Copper Metallic	H
Light Turquoise Metallic	K
Dark Turquoise Metallic	L
Turbine Bronze Metallic	M
Bright Red Metallic	P
Dark Red Metallic	Q
Mauve Metallic	6
Yellow	R
Soft Yellow	S
Copper Metallic	T
White	W
Beige	X
Light Tan Metallic	Y
Gold Metallic	Z

ENGINE NUMBER

6-cylinder engine numbers are stamped on the right side of the block below the number one spark plug. The number provides the code to identify the series, block displacement, and month/day production date.

273, 318, and 340 engine numbers are stamped on the left front on the block below the cylinder head.

383, 426, and 440 engine numbers are stamped on the pan rail at the rear corner under the starter opening.

EXAMPLE:

PM	383	2187	2401
PLANT CODE	CID	JULIAN DATE	DAILY SEQUENTIAL NUMBER

ENGINE PLANTS
PM-Mound Rd.
PT-Trenton

VALIANT

ENGINE CODE	NO. CYL.	CID	HORSE-POWER	COMP. RATIO	CARB	TRANS
PT-170	6	170	115	8.5:1	1 BC	* M & A
PT-225	6	225	145	8.4:1	1 BC	* M & A
PT-273	8	273	190	9.0:1	2 BC	* M & A
PT-318	8	318	230	9.2:1	2 BC	* M & A

BARRACUDA

ENGINE CODE	NO. CYL.	CID	HORSE-POWER	COMP. RATIO	CARB	TRANS
PT-225	6	225	145	8.4:1	1 BC	* M & A
PT-318	8	318	230	9.2:1	2 BC	* M & A
PT-340	8	340	275	10.5:1	4 BC	* M & A
PT-383	8	383	300	10.0;1	4 BC	* M & A
PT-426*	8	426	425	10.25;1	2-4 BC	* M & A
PT-440	8	440	375	10.1:1	4 BC	* M & A

* Super Stock

BELVEDERE, SATELLITE

ENGINE CODE	NO. CYL.	CID	HORSE-POWER	COMP. RATIO	CARB	TRANS
PT-225	6	225	145	8.4:1	1 BC	* M & A
PT-318	8	318	230	9.2:1	1 BC	* M & A
PT-383	8	383	290	9.2:1	1 BC	AUTO
PT-383	8	383	330	10.0:1	4 BC	* M & A

SPORT SATELLITE

ENGINE CODE	NO. CYL.	CID	HORSE-POWER	COMP. RATIO	CARB	TRANS
PT-318	8	318	230	9.2:1	2 BC	* M & A
PT-383	8	383	290	9.2:1	2 BC	* M & A
PT-3838	8	383	330	10.0;1	4 BC	* M & A

ROAD RUNNER

ENGINE CODE	NO. CYL.	CID	HORSE-POWER	COMP. RATIO	CARB	TRANS
PT-383	8	383	335	10.0;1	4 BC	* M & A
PT-426	8	426	425	10.25:1	2-4 BC	* M & A
PT-440	8	440	390	10.1:1	3-2 BC	* M & A

GTX

ENGINE CODE	NO. CYL.	CID	HORSE-POWER	COMP. RATIO	CARB	TRANS
PT-440	8	440	375	10.1:1	4 BC	* M & A
PT-426	8	426	425	10.25:1	2-4 BC	* M & A
PT-440	8	440	390	10.11	3-2 BC	* M & A

FURY I, II, III

ENGINE CODE	NO. CYL.	CID	HORSE-POWER	COMP. RATIO	CARB	TRANS
PT-225	6	225	145	8.4:1	1 BC	* M & A
PT-318	8	318	230	9.2:1	2 BC	* M & A
PT-383	8	383	290	9.2:1	2 BC	* M & A
PT-383	8	383	330	10.0;1	4 BC	* M & A
PT-440	8	440	375	10.1:1	4 BC	* M & A

SPORT FURY AND VIP

ENGINE CODE	NO. CYL.	CID	HORSE-POWER	COMP. RATIO	CARB	TRANS
PT-318	8	318	230	9.2:1	2 BC	* M & A
PT-383	8	383	290	9.2:1	2 BC	* M & A
PT-383	8	383	330	10.0:1	4 BC	* M & A
PT-440	8	440	375	10.1:1	4 BC	* M & A

SUBURBANS (6 CYL. ON PE45 ONLY)

ENGINE CODE	NO. CYL.	CID	HORSE-POWER	COMP. RATIO	CARB	TRANS
PT-225	6	225	145	8.4:1	1 BC	* M & A
PT-318	8	318	230	9.2:1	2 BC	* M & A
PT-383	8	383	290	9.2:1	2 BC	* M & A
PT-383	8	383	330	10.0:1	4 BC	* M & A
PT-440	8	440	350	10.1:1	4 BC	* M & A

* MAN & AUTO

Other engine identifying marks are as follows:

R - .001" undersize connecting rod journals
M - .001" undersize main bearing journals
RX or MX - All main or rod journals .010" undersize
A - .020" oversize cylinder bores
Maltese Cross - .001" undersize crankshaft
Maltese Cross and X - .010" undersize crankshaft
Diamond - .008" oversize tappets
LC - Low compression
R - Regular fuel
P - Premium fuel
S - Special engine

1960 DE SOTO

1960 DE SOTO

VEHICLE IDENTIFICATION NUMBER

DeSOTO
7103100551

The VIN is stamped and embossed on a stainless steel plate attached to the left front door hinge pillar. It consists of the car make symbol, series code, model year code, assembly plant symbol and a sequential production number.

FIRST DIGIT: Identifies the car make

CAR MAKE	CODE
De Soto	7

SECOND DIGIT: Identifies the series

SERIES	CODE
Fireflight	1
Adventurer	2

THIRD DIGIT: Identifies the model year (1960)

FOURTH DIGIT: Identifies the assembly plant

ASSEMBLY PLANT	CODE
Detroit, MI	3

LAST SIX DIGITS: Represent the basic production numbers

BODY NUMBER PLATE

THE BODY PLATE is stamped and embossed on a stainless steel plate under the hood. It is attached to the right or left fender, cowl, or radiator cross member depending on the model and assembly plant. This plate indicates the schedule date, body production number, body series, trim, paint, and accessory code.

DeSOTO

SO	NUMBER	BDY	TRM	PNT
0224	0551	612	811	BB1

EXAMPLE:

0224	SON (Feb. 24)
0551	Production Sequence
612	Body Style (2-Dr. Hardtop)
811	Trim
B	Lower Body Color
B	Upper Body Color

THE SHIPPING ORDER NUMBER is assigned prior to production. It consists of a 4 digit planned delivery month/day date code.

THE BODY NUMBER is a 3 digit number which indicates the model and body style.

FIREFLITE	CODE
2-Dr. Hardtop	612
4-Dr. Sedan	613
4-Dr. Hardtop	614

ADVENTURER	CODE
2-Dr. Hardtop	712
4-Dr. Sedan	713
4-Dr. Hardtop	714

THE TRIM NUMBER furnishes the key to the interior color and material.

COLOR	CLOTH	VINYL	LEATHER	CODE
Blue	•			811,801
Green	•			812,802
Gray	•			814
Red/Gray	•			816
Tan	•			818,808
Black/ Silver	•			804
Black/Red	•			806

THE PAINT CODE furnishes the key to the paint used on the car. A two-digit code indicates the top and bottom colors respectively.

COLOR	CODE
Yuma Yellow	A
Black	B
Jamaica Blue	C
Arctic Blue	D
Willow Green	F
Cypress Green	G
Marine Aqua	J
Marine Turquoise	K
Silverglow	L
Smoke Pearl	N
Winterberry Red	P
Calcutta Ivory	T
Gabardine	U
Shell White	W
Adobe Rust	Y
Russett Red	Z

1960 DeSOTO

ENGINE NUMBER

THE ENGINE NUMBER is stamped on a machined boss on the engine, just behind the water pump at the right side of the engine. The number provides the code to identify the series, block, displacement, and month/day production date.

EXAMPLE:

P	36	2	24
YEAR	361	FEBRUARY	DAY

ENGINE NO.	NO. CYL.	CID	HORSE-POWER	COMP. RATIO	CARB	TRANS
P-36	8	361	295	10.0:1	2 BC	* M & T
P-38	8	383	305	10.0:1	2 BC	TORQ
P-38	8	383	325	10.0:1	4 BC	TORQ
P-38	8	383	330	10.0:1	2-4 BC	TORQ

* MAN & TORQ

Note: The following engine designation, when applicable, will also appear on this boss:

◊ = .008 Oversize Tappets
A = Oversize Cylinder Bore
U = Undersize Crankshaft Main Bearing Journals
+ = Undersize Crankshaft Rod Journals

Note: If one or more valves with oversize stems are used, it will be designated by either the letter "I" (intake) or the letter "E" (exhaust) stamped on a machined "flat" at the front of the particular cylinder head.

1961 DE SOTO

1961 DE SOTO

VEHICLE IDENTIFICATION NUMBER

DeSOTO
6113100551

The VIN is stamped and embossed on a stainless steel plate attached to the left front door hinge pillar. It consists of the car make symbol, series code, model year code, assembly plant symbol and a sequential production number.

FIRST DIGIT: Identifies the car make

CAR MAKE	CODE
De Soto	6

SECOND DIGIT: Identifies the series

SERIES	CODE
De Soto	1

THIRD DIGIT: Identifies the model year (1961)

FOURTH DIGIT: Identifies the assembly plant

ASSEMBLY PLANT	CODE
Detroit, MI	3

LAST SIX DIGITS: Represent the basic production sequence

BODY NUMBER PLATE

THE BODY PLATE is stamped and embossed on a stainless steel plate under the hood. It is attached to the right or left fender, cowl or radiator cross member depending on the model and assembly plant. This plate will indicate the schedule date, body production number, body series, trim, paint, and accessory code.

DeSOTO

SO	NUMBER	BDY	TRM	PNT
0224	0555	612	101	BB1

EXAMPLE:

0224	SON (Feb. 24)
0551	Production Sequence
612	Body Style (2-Dr. Coupe)
101	Trim
B	Lower Body Color
B	Upper Body Color

THE SHIPPING ORDER NUMBER is assigned prior to production. It consists of a 4 digit planned delivery month/day date code.

THE BODY NUMBER is a 3 digit number which indicates the model and the body style.

DESOTO	CODE
2-Dr. Coupe	612
4-Dr. Hardtop	614

1961 DeSOTO

THE TRIM NUMBER furnishes the key to the interior color and material.

COLOR	CLOTH	VINYL	LEATHER	CODE
Blue	•	•		101
Gray	•	•		104
Red	•	•		105

THE PAINT CODE furnishes the key to the paint used on the car. A two-digit code indicates the top and bottom colors respectively.

COLOR	CODE
Goldenrod Yellow	A
Black	B
Morning Blue	C
Mediterranean Blue	D
Spring Green	F
Jade Green	G
Tangier Aqua	J
Surf Turquoise	K
Platinum Gray	L
Regal Red	P
Glacier White	W
Tahiti Tan	Y
Bahama Bronze	Z

ENGINE NUMBER

THE ENGINE NUMBER is stamped on a machined boss on the engine, just behind the water pump at the right side of the engine. The number provides the code to identify the series, block, displacement, and month/day production date.

EXAMPLE:

R	36	2	24
YEAR	361	FEBRUARY	DAY

ENGINE NO.	NO. CYL.	CID	HORSE-POWER	COMP. RATIO	CARB	TRANS
R-36	8	361	265	10.0:1	2 BC	3-SP/ POWER

1960 STUDEBAKER HAWK

1960 STUDEBAKER HAWK

1960 STUDEBAKER LARK

1960 STUDEBAKER LARK

VEHICLE IDENTIFICATION NUMBER

STUDEBAKER
60S10551

The VIN is stamped on a plate welded to the left front door pillar.

FIRST AND SECOND DIGIT: Identify the model year (1960)

THIRD DIGIT: Identifies the engine

ENGINE	CODE
170 CID, 6 cyl.	S
259 CID, 8 cyl.	V

A letter "C" following the engine code indicates assembled in Canada.

LAST FIVE DIGITS: Represent the basic production numbers

BODY NUMBER PLATE

THE BODY CODE PLATE is stamped on a tag riveted to the cowl under the hood. This indicates the year, engine, body style, and trim.

STUDEBAKER-PACKARD
CORPORATION
SERIAL NO.
60S10551

60S - W6
671

EXAMPLE:

60	Model Year (1960)
S	Engine (170 CID, 6 cyl.)
W6	Body Style (Lark Regal, 4-Dr.)
671	Trim

LARK DELUXE	CODE
4-Dr. Sedan	W4
2-Dr. Sedan	F4
4-Dr. Sta. Wagon, 6-Pass.	P4
2-Dr. Sta. Wagon, 6-Pass	D4

1960 STUDEBAKER

LARK REGAL	CODE
4-Dr. Sedan	W6
2-Dr. Hardtop	J6
Convertible	L6
4-Dr. Sta. Wagon, 6 Pass.	P6

TAXI CAB	CODE
4-Dr. Sedan	Y1

HAWK	CODE
Coupe Sport	C6

THE TRIM NUMBER furnishes the key to the interior color and material.

LARK DELUXE TRIM

COLOR	CLOTH	VINYL	LEATHER	CODE
Red		•		552,551
Red/Black	•			472,471
Blue	•			422,421
Blue		•		522,521
Green	•			432,431
Green		•		532,531
Brown	•			442,441
Brown		•		542,541

LARK DELUXE WAGON TRIM

COLOR	CLOTH	VINYL	LEATHER	CODE
Red		•		556,557
Blue		•		526,527
Green		•		536,537
Brown		•		546,547

LARK REGAL TRIM

COLOR	CLOTH	VINYL	LEATHER	CODE
Red		•		751,759
Red/Black	•			671,679
Blue	•			621,629
Blue		•		721,729
Green	•			631,639
Green		•		731,739
Brown	•			641,649
Brown		•		741,749
Tan		•		761,769
Black		•		711,719

LARK REGAL CONVERTIBLE TRIM

COLOR	CLOTH	VINYL	LEATHER	CODE
Red		•		758
Blue		•		728
Green		•		738
Brown		•		748
Tan		•		768
Black		•		718

LARK REGAL WAGON TRIM

COLOR	CLOTH	VINYL	LEATHER	CODE
Red		•		757
Blue		•		727
Green		•		737
Brown		•		747
Tan		•		767
Black		•		717

HAWK TRIM

COLOR	CLOTH	VINYL	LEATHER	CODE
Red		•		753
Red/Black	•			673
Blue	•			623
Blue		•		723
Green	•			633
Green		•		733
Brown	•			643
Brown		•		743
Tan		•		763
Black		•		713

THE PAINT CODE furnishes the key to the paint used on the car. A two-digit code indicates the top and bottom colors respectively. It can be found on a piece of paper attached to the bottom of the glove box.

COLOR	CODE
Black Velvet	6010
White Sand	6011
Gulfstream Blue	6012
Oasis Green	6013
Williamsburg Green	6014
Sandalwood Beige	6015
Colonial Red	6016
Jonquil Yellow	6017

ENGINE NUMBER

The engines are stamped with a prefix code denoting the cubic inch displacement, plus a numeric production number.

6-cylinder engine numbers are located on a pad at the upper left front of the cylinder block.

8-cylinder engine numbers are located on a pad at the upper left front of the cylinder block.

ENGINE	CODE
170 Cid. 6-cyl.	S
259 Cid. V-8	V
289 Cid. V-8	P

Note: If a letter "C" follows the engine code, it designates Canadian manufacture.

ENGINE NO.	NO. CYL.	CID	HORSE-POWER	COMP. RATIO	CARB	TRANS
S	6	170	90	8.3:1	1 BC	
V	8	259	180**	8.5:1	2 BC*	
P	8	289	210***	8.5:1	2 BC*	

* Option: Carter WCFB — 4 BC available on all models except Taxi
** 195 H.P. with 4 BC carburetor
*** 225 H.P. with 4 BC carburetor

1961 STUDEBAKER

1961 STUDEBAKER HAWK

1961 STUDEBAKER HAWK

1961 STUDEBAKER LARK

1961 STUDEBAKER LARK

VEHICLE IDENTIFICATION NUMBER

STUDEBAKER
61S10551

The VIN is stamped on a plate welded to the left front door pillar.

FIRST AND SECOND DIGIT: Identify the model year (1961)

THIRD DIGIT: Identifies the engine

ENGINE	CODE
170 CID, 6 cyl.	S
259 CID, 8 cyl.	V
289 CID, 8 cyl.	P

A letter "C" following the engine code indicates assembled in Canada.

LAST FIVE DIGITS: Represent the basic production numbers

BODY NUMBER PLATE

THE BODY CODE PLATE is stamped on a tag riveted to the cowl under the hood. It indicates the year, engine, body style, and trim.

STUDEBAKER-PACKARD
CORPORATION
SERIAL NO.
61S10551

61S - P4
556

EXAMPLE:

61	Model Year (1961)
S	Engine (170 CID, 6 cyl.)
P4	Body Style (Lark Dlx., Sta. Wgn.)
556	Trim

LARK DELUXE	CODE
4-Dr. Sedan	W4
2-Dr. Sedan	F4
4-Dr. Sta. Wagon, 6-Pass.	P4
2-Dr. Sta. Wagon, 6-Pass.	D4

LARK REGAL	CODE
4-Dr. Sedan	W6
2-Dr. Hardtop	J6
2-Dr. Convertible	L6
4-Dr. Sta. Wagon, 6-Pass.	P6

LARK	CODE
4-Dr. Cruiser	Y6
Taxicab	Y1

HAWK	CODE
Sport Coupe	C6

THE TRIM NUMBER furnishes the key to the trim color and material. The trim code dictates the availability of exterior paint colors.

LARK DELUXE TRIM

COLOR	CLOTH	VINYL	LEATHER	CODE
Red/Black	•			472,471
Blue	•			422,421
Blue		•		522,521
Green	•			432,431
Green		•		532,531
Brown	•			442,441
Brown		•		542,541
Red		•		552,551

LARK DELUXE WAGON TRIM

COLOR	CLOTH	VINYL	LEATHER	CODE
Red		•		556
Blue		•		526
Green		•		536
Brown		•		546

LARK REGAL TRIM

COLOR	CLOTH	VINYL	LEATHER	CODE
Red/Black	•			671,679
Blue	•			621,629
Blue		•		721,729
Green	•			631,639
Green		•		731,739
Brown	•			641,649
Brown		•		741,749
Red		•		751,759
Tan		•		761,769
Black		•		711,719

LARK REGAL CONVERTIBLE TRIM

COLOR	CLOTH	VINYL	LEATHER	CODE
Red		•		758
Blue		•		728
Green		•		738
Brown		•		748
Tan		•		768
Black		•		718

LARK REGAL WAGON TRIM

COLOR	CLOTH	VINYL	LEATHER	CODE
Red		•		757
Blue		•		727
Green		•		737
Brown		•		747
Tan		•		767
Black		•		717

LARK CRUISER TRIM

COLOR	CLOTH	VINYL	LEATHER	CODE
Red/Black	•			675
Blue	•			625
Blue		•		725
Green	•			635
Green		•		735
Brown	•			645
Brown		•		745
Red		•		755
Tan		•		765
Black		•		715

HAWK TRIM

COLOR	CLOTH	VINYL	LEATHER	CODE
Red/Black	•			673
Blue	•			623
Blue		•		723
Green	•			633
Green		•		733
Brown	•			643
Brown		•		743
Red		•		753
Tan		•		763
Black		•		713

THE PAINT CODE furnishes the key to the paint used on the car. A two-digit code indicates the top and bottom colors respectively. It can be found on a piece of paper attached to the bottom of the glove box.

COLOR	CODE
Black Velvet	6110
Ermine	6111
Riviera Blue	6112
Green Jade	6113
Flamingo*	6114
Desert Sand	6115
Blaze	6116
Suntone	6117
Autumn Haze	6118

* Flamingo paint is optional on convertibles and Hawks only

ENGINE NUMBER

Engines are stamped with a prefix code denoting the cubic inch displacement, plus a numeric production number.

6-cylinder engine numbers are located on a pad at the upper left front of the cylinder block.

8-cylinder engine numbers are located on a pad at the upper left front of the cylinder block.

ENGINE	CODE
170 Cid. 6-cyl.	S
259 Cid. 8-cyl.	V
289 Cid. 8-cyl.	P

Note: If a letter "C" follows the engine code, it designates Canadian manufacture.

ENGINE NO.	NO. CYL.	CID	HORSE-POWER	COMP. RATIO	CARB	TRANS
S	6	170	112	8.5:1	1 BC	
V	8	259	180**	8.8:1	2 BC*	
P	8	289	210***	8.8:1	2 BC*	

* Optional: Carter WCFB — 4 BC available on all models except Taxi
** 195 H.P. with 4 BC carburetor
*** 225 H.P. with 4 BC carburetor

1962 STUDEBAKER HAWK

1962 STUDEBAKER HAWK

1962 STUDEBAKER LARK

1962 STUDEBAKER LARK

VEHICLE IDENTIFICATION NUMBER

STUDEBAKER
62S10551

The VIN is stamped on a plate welded to the left front door pillar.

FIRST AND SECOND DIGIT: Identify the model year (1962)

THIRD DIGIT: Identifies the engine

ENGINE	CODE
170 CID, 6 cyl.	S
259 CID, 8 cyl.	V
289 CID, 8 cyl.	P

A letter "C" following the engine code indicates assembled in Canada.

LAST FIVE DIGITS: Represent the basic production numbers

BODY NUMBER PLATE

THE BODY CODE PLATE is stamped on a tag riveted to the cowl under the hood. This indicates the year, engine, body style, and trim.

STUDEBAKER-PACKARD
CORPORATION
SERIAL NO.
62S10551

62S - Y4
445

EXAMPLE:

62	Model Year (1962)
S	Engine (170 CID, 6 cyl.)
Y4	Body Style (Lark Dlx., Sedan)
445	Trim

LARK DELUXE	CODE
4-Dr. Sedan	Y4
2-Dr. Sedan	F4

1962 STUDEBAKER

LARK REGAL	CODE
4-Dr. Sedan	Y6
2-Dr. Hardtop Coupe	J6
2-Dr. Convertible	L6

LARK DAYTONA	CODE
2-Dr. Hardtop Coupe	J8
2-Dr. Convertible	L8

LARK STATION WAGONS	CODE
4-Dr. Sta. Wagon, (Deluxe)	P4
4-Dr. Sta. Wagon, (Regal)	P6

LARK CRUISER	CODE
4-Dr. Sedan	Y8

TAXICAB	CODE
4-Dr. Sedan	Y1

POLICE	CODE
2-Dr. Sedan	F3
4-Dr. Sedan	Y3
4-Dr. Sta. Wagon	P3

GRAN TURISMO HAWK	CODE
2-Dr. Hardtop Coupe	K6

THE TRIM NUMBER furnishes the key to the trim color and material. The trim code dictates the availability of exterior paint colors.

LARK DELUXE TRIM

COLOR	CLOTH	VINYL	LEATHER	CODE
Taupe	•			442,445
Taupe		•		542,545
Blue	•			422,425
Blue		•		522,525
Green	•			432,435
Green		•		532,535
Red		•		552,555

LARK WAGON TRIM

COLOR	CLOTH	VINYL	LEATHER	CODE
Red		•		557
Blue		•		527
Green		•		537
Taupe		•		547

LARK REGAL TRIM

COLOR	CLOTH	VINYL	LEATHER	CODE
Taupe	•			645,649
Taupe		•		745,7451
Taupe		•		749,7491
Blue	•			625,629
Blue		•		725,7251
Blue		•		729,7291
Green	•			635,639
Green		•		735,7351
Green		•		739,7391
Black		•		715,7151
Black		•		719,7191
Red		•		755,7551
Red		•		759,7591
Tan		•		765,7651
Tan		•		769,7691

LARK REGAL WAGON TRIM

COLOR	CLOTH	VINYL	LEATHER	CODE
Red		•		757,7571
Black		•		717,7171
Blue		•		727,7271
Green		•		737,7371
Taupe		•		747,7471
Tan		•		767,7671

REGAL CONVERTIBLE TRIM

COLOR	CLOTH	VINYL	LEATHER	CODE
Red		•		758,7581
Black		•		718,7181
Blue		•		728,7281
Green		•		738,7381
Taupe		•		748,7481
Tan		•		768,7681

DAYTONA TRIM

COLOR	CLOTH	VINYL	LEATHER	CODE
Taupe	•			849
Taupe		•		949,9491
Blue	•			829
Blue		•		929,9291
Green	•			839
Green		•		939,9391
Black		•		919,9191
Red		•		959,9591
Tan		•		969,9691

DAYTONA CONVERTIBLE TRIM

COLOR	CLOTH	VINYL	LEATHER	CODE
Red		•		958,9581
Black		•		918,9181
Blue		•		928,9281
Green		•		938,9381
Taupe		•		948,9481
Tan		•		968,9681

LARK CRUISER TRIM

COLOR	CLOTH	VINYL	LEATHER	CODE
Taupe	•			845
Taupe		•		945,9451
Blue	•			825
Blue		•		925,9251
Green	•			835
Green		•		935,9351
Black		•		915,9151
Red		•		955,9551
Tan		•		965,9651

GRAN TURISMO HAWK TRIM

COLOR	CLOTH	VINYL	LEATHER	CODE
Taupe	•			644
Taupe		•		744
Blue	•			624
Blue		•		724
Green	•			634
Green		•		734
Black		•		714,7141
Red		•		754
Tan		•		764

1962 STUDEBAKER

THE PAINT CODE furnishes the key to the paint used on the car. A two-digit code indicates the top and bottom colors respectively. It can be found on a piece of paper attached to the bottom of the glove box.

COLOR	CODE
Black Velvet	6210
Ermine White	6211
Riviera Blue	6212
Metallic Green	6213
Metallic Silver	6214
Desert Tan	6215
Blaze Red	6216
Metallic Brown	6217

ENGINE NUMBER

Engines are stamped with a prefix code denoting the cubic inch displacement, plus a numeric production number.

6-cylinder engine numbers are located on a pad at the upper left front of the cylinder block.

8-cylinder engine numbers are located on a pad at the upper left front of the cylinder block.

ENGINE	CODE
170 CID 6-cyl.	S
259 CID 8-cyl.	V
289 CID 8-cyl.	P

Note: If a letter "C" follows the engine code, it designates Canadian manufacture.

ENGINE NO.	NO. CYL.	CID	HORSE-POWER	COMP. RATIO	CARB	TRANS
S	6	170	112	8.0:1	1 BC	112
V	8	259	180**	8.25:1	2 BC*	
P	8	289	210***	8.25:1	2 BC*	

* Option: Carter WCFB — 4 BC available on all models except Taxi
** 195 H.P. with 4 BC carburetor
*** 225 H.P. with 4 BC carburetor

1963 STUDEBAKER

1963 STUDEBAKER AVANTI

1963 STUDEBAKER AVANTI

1963 STUDEBAKER CRUISER

1963 STUDEBAKER CRUISER

1963 STUDEBAKER HAWK

1963 STUDEBAKER HAWK

1963 STUDEBAKER LARK

1963 STUDEBAKER LARK

1963 STUDEBAKER

VEHICLE IDENTIFICATION NUMBER

STUDEBAKER
63S10551

The VIN is stamped on a plate welded to the left front door pillar. On the Avanti, the plate is located under the hood on the top right frame rail.

FIRST AND SECOND DIGIT: Identify the model year (1963)

THIRD DIGIT: Identifies the engine

ENGINE	CODE
170 CID 6 cyl.	S
259 CID 8 cyl.	V
289 CID 8 cyl.	P
Avanti	R

A letter "C" following the engine code indicates assembled in Canada.

LAST FIVE DIGITS: Represent the basic production numbers

Note: Near the end of the 1963 production year, Avanti dropped the year designation from the VIN. Example: R-4835.

BODY NUMBER PLATE

THE BODY NUMBER PLATE is stamped on a tag riveted to the cowl under the hood. This indicates the year, engine, body style, and trim.

STUDEBAKER-PACKARD
CORPORATION
SERIAL NO.
63S10551

63S - F4
442

EXAMPLE:

63	Model Year (1963)
S	Engine (170 CID, 6 cyl.)
F4	Body Style (Lark Regal, 2 Dr.)
442	Trim

STANDARD	CODE
4-Dr. Sedan	Y2
2-Dr. Sedan	F2
4-Dr. Sta. Wagon, 6-Pass.	P2

LARK REGAL	CODE
4-Dr. Sedan	Y4
2-Dr. Sedan	F4

LARK CUSTOM	CODE
4-Dr. Sedan	Y6
2-Dr. Sedan	F6

LARK DAYTONA	CODE
2-Dr. Hardtop	J8
2-Dr. Convertible	L8

LARK STATION WAGONS	CODE
4-Dr. Regal	P4
4-Dr. Daytona	P8

LARK CRUISER	CODE
4-Dr. Sedan	Y8

GRAN TURISMO HAWK	CODE
2-Dr. Hardtop	VK6

AVANTI	CODE
Sport Coupe	RQ

TAXICAB	CODE
4-Dr. Sedan	Y1

POLICE	CODE
2-Dr. Sedan	F3
4-Dr. Sedan	Y3
4-Dr. Sta. Wagon	P3

THE TRIM NUMBER furnishes the key to the trim color and material. The trim code dictates the availability of exterior paint colors.

LARK REGAL TRIM

COLOR	CLOTH	VINYL	LEATHER	CODE
Chestnut	•			442,445
Chestnut		•		542,545
Blue	•			422,425
Blue		•		522,525
Green	•			432,435
Green		•		532,535
Red	•			452,455
Red		•		552,555

LARK WAGONS TRIM

COLOR	CLOTH	VINYL	LEATHER	CODE
Red		•		557
Blue		•		527
Green		•		537
Chestnut		•		547

REGAL CONVERTIBLE TRIM

COLOR	CLOTH	VINYL	LEATHER	CODE
Black		•		919,9191
Blue		•		929,9291
Green		•		939,9391
Chestnut		•		949,9491
Red		•		959,9591
Tan		•		969,9691

GRAN TURISMO HAWK TRIM

COLOR	CLOTH	VINYL	LEATHER	CODE
Black		•		714,7141
Blue	•			624
Blue		•		724,7241
Green	•			634
Green		•		734,7341
Chestnut	•			644
Chestnut		•		744,7441
Red	•			654
Red		•		754,7541
Tan		•		764,7641

LARK CRUISER TRIM

COLOR	CLOTH	VINYL	LEATHER	CODE
Black		•		915,9151
Blue	•			875,825
Blue		•		925,9251
Green	•			885,835
Green		•		935,9351
Chestnut	•			895,845
Chestnut		•		945,9451
Red	•			805,855
Red		•		955,9551
Tan		•		965,9651

DAYTONA CONVERTIBLE TRIM

COLOR	CLOTH	VINYL	LEATHER	CODE
Chestnut	•			849
Chestnut		•		948,9481
Blue	•			829
Blue		•		928,9281
Green	•			839
Green		•		938,9381
Red	•			859
Red		•		958,9581
Black		•		918,9181
Tan		•		968,9681

DAYTONA WAGON TRIM

COLOR	CLOTH	VINYL	LEATHER	CODE
Red		•		957,9571
Black		•		917,9171
Blue		•		927,9271
Green		•		937,9371
Chestnut		•		947,9471
Tan		•		967,9671

LARK CUSTOM TRIM

COLOR	CLOTH	VINYL	LEATHER	CODE
Black		•		712,7121
Black		•		715,7151
Blue	•			625,622
Blue		•		722,7221
Blue		•		725,7251
Green	•			635,632
Green		•		732,7321
Green		•		735,7351
Chestnut	•			645,642
Chestnut		•		742,7421
Chestnut		•		745,7451
Red	•			655,652
Red		•		752,7521
Red		•		755,7551
Tan		•		762,7621
Tan		•		765,7651

AVANTI TRIM

COLOR	CLOTH	VINYL	LEATHER	CODE
Black		•		813
Turquoise		•		823
Claret		•		833
Smoked Elk		•		843
Red		•		853

THE PAINT CODE furnishes the key to the paint used on the car. A two-digit code indicates the top and bottom colors respectively. It can be found on a piece of paper attached to the bottom of the glove box.

COLOR	CODE
Black Velvet	P6310
Ermine White	P6311
Blue Mist	P6312
Green Mist	P6313
Silver Mist	P6314
Champagne Gold	P6315
Regal Red	P6316
Rose Mist	P6317
Avanti Black	P6330
Avanti White	P6331
Avanti Turquoise	P6332
Avanti Gold	P6333
Avanti Red	P6334
Avanti Gray	P6335
Avanti Maroon	P6336

ENGINE NUMBER

Engines are stamped with a prefix code denoting the cubic inch displacement, plus a numeric production number.

6-cylinder engine numbers are located on a pad at the upper left front of the cylinder block.

8-cylinder engine numbers are located on a pad at the upper left front of the cylinder block.

ENGINE	CODE
170 CID 6-cyl.	S
259 CID 8-cyl.	V
289 CID 8-cyl.	P
R1 289 CID	R
R2 289 CID Supercharged	RS
R3S 304.5 Supercharged	R3S

Note: If a letter "C" follows the engine code, it designates Canadian manufacture.

ENGINE NO.	NO. CYL.	CID	HORSE-POWER	COMP. RATIO	CARB	TRANS
S	6	170	112	8.00:1	1 BC	
V	8	259	180**	8.25:1	2 BC*	
P	8	289	210***	8.25:1	2 BC*	

AVANTI ENGINE

ENGINE NO.	NO. CYL.	CID	HORSE-POWER	COMP. RATIO	CARB	TRANS
R	8	289	240	10.25:1		
RS	8	289	289	9.00:1		
R3S	8	304.5	335	9.75:1		

* Option: Carter WCFB — 4 BC available on all models except Taxi
** 195 H.P. with 4 BC carburetor
*** 225 H.P. with 4 BC carburetor

1964 STUDEBAKER

1964 STUDEBAKER

1964 STUDEBAKER AVANTI

1964 STUDEBAKER AVANTI

1964 STUDEBAKER HAWK

1964 STUDEBAKER HAWK

VEHICLE IDENTIFICATION NUMBER

STUDEBAKER
64S10551

The VIN is stamped on a plate welded to the left front door pillar. On the Avanti, the plate is located under the hood on the top right frame rail.

FIRST AND SECOND DIGIT: Identify the model year (1964)

THIRD DIGIT: Identifies the engine

ENGINE	CODE
170 CID, 6 cyl.	S
259 CID, 8 cyl.	V
289 CID, 8 cyl.	P
Avanti	R

A letter "C" following the engine code indicates assembled in Canada.

LAST FIVE DIGITS: Represent the basic production numbers

Note: Near the end of the 1964 production year, Avanti dropped the year designation from the VIN. Example: R-4835.

BODY NUMBER PLATE

THE BODY CODE PLATE is stamped on a tag riveted to the cowl under the hood. This indicates the year, engine, body style, and trim.

STUDEBAKER-PACKARD
CORPORATION
SERIAL NO.
64S10551

64 - F4
642

EXAMPLE:

64	Model Year (1964)
S	Engine (170 CID, 6 cyl.)
F4	Body Style (Commander, 2-Dr.)
642	Trim

CHALLENGER	CODE
2-Dr. Sedan	F2
4-Dr. Sedan	Y2
4-Dr. Sta. Wagon	P2

COMMANDER	CODE
2-Dr. Sedan	F4
4-Dr. Sedan	Y4
4-Dr. Sta. Wagon	P4

DAYTONA	CODE
4-Dr. Sedan	Y8
2-Dr. Hardtop	J8
2-Dr. Convertible	L8
4-Dr. Sta. Wagon	P8

CRUISER	CODE
4-Dr. Sedan	Y9

TAXICAB	CODE
4-Dr. Sedan	Y1

POLICE	CODE
2-Dr. Sedan	F3
4-Dr. Sedan	Y3
4-Dr. Sta. Wagon	P3

HAWK	CODE
2-Dr. Hardtop	K6

THE TRIM NUMBER furnishes the key to the trim color and material. The trim code dictates the availability of exterior paint colors.

CHALLENGER TRIM

COLOR	CLOTH	VINYL	LEATHER	CODE
Blue	•			422,421
Blue		•		522,521
Red	•			452,451
Red		•		552,551
Green	•			432,431
Green		•		532,531
Brown	•			442,441
Brown		•		542,541

CHALLENGER WAGON TRIM

COLOR	CLOTH	VINYL	LEATHER	CODE
Blue		•		527
Red		•		557
Green		•		537
Brown		•		547

COMMANDER TRIM

COLOR	CLOTH	VINYL	LEATHER	CODE
Blue	•			622,621
Blue		•		722,721
Red	•			652,651
Red		•		752,751
Green	•			632,631
Green		•		732,731
Brown	•			642,641
Brown		•		742,741

COMMANDER WAGON TRIM

COLOR	CLOTH	VINYL	LEATHER	CODE
Blue		•		727
Red		•		757
Green		•		737
Brown		•		747

DAYTONA TRIM

COLOR	CLOTH	VINYL	LEATHER	CODE
Blue	•			821,829
Blue		•		921,929
Red	•			851,859
Red		•		951,959
Green	•			831,839
Green		•		931,939
Brown	•			841,849
Brown		•		941,949
Black		•		911,919

AVANTI TRIM COLOR	CLOTH	VINYL	LEATHER	CODE
Black		•		813
Turquoise		•		823
Claret		•		833
Smoked Elk		•		843
Red		•		853

THE PAINT CODE furnishes the key to the paint used on the car. A two-digit code indicates the top and bottom colors respectively. It can be found on a piece of paper attached to the bottom of the glove box.

COLOR	CODE
Black Velvet	P6310
Ermine White	P6311
Blue Mist	P6312
Green Mist	P6313
Silver Mist	P6314
Champagne Gold	P6315
Regal Red	P6316
Rose Mist	P6317
Avanti Black	P6330
Avanti White	P6331
Avanti Turquoise	P6332
Avanti Gold	P6333
Avanti Red	P6334
Avanti Gray	P6335
Avanti Maroon	P6336

ENGINE NUMBER

The engines are stamped with a prefix code denoting the cubic inch displacement, plus a numeric production number.

6-cylinder engine numbers are located on a pad at the upper left front of the cylinder block.

8-cylinder engine numbers are located on a pad at the upper left front of the cylinder block.

ENGINE	CODE
170 CID 6-cyl.	S
259 CID 8-cyl.	V
289 CID 8-cyl.	P
R1 289 CID	R
R2 289 CID Supercharged	RS
R3S 304.5 Supercharged	R3S

Note: If a letter "C" follows the engine code, it designates Canadian manufacture.

ENGINE NO.	NO. CYL.	CID	HORSE-POWER	COMP. RATIO	CARB	TRANS
S	6	170	112	8.00:1	1 BC	
V	8	259	180**	8.25:1	2 BC*	
P	8	289	210***	8.25:1	2 BC*	

AVANTI ENGINE

ENGINE NO.	NO. CYL.	CID	HORSE-POWER	COMP. RATIO	CARB	TRANS
R	8	289	240	10.25:1		
RS	8	289	289	9.00:1		
R3S	8	304.5	335	9.75:1		

* Option: Carter WCFB — 4 BC available on all models except Taxi
** 195 H.P. with 4 BC carburetor
*** 225 H.P. with 4 BC carburetor

Studebaker operations ceased at the South Bend, Indiana Plant in 1965. All 1965 and 1966 Studebaker Vehicles were produced in Canada. Studebaker designated as 1965 and 1966 models differed very little from the 1964 models. Minor trim changes and reduction in the number of vehicles built in the individual model lines can be noted. Cars exported to the United States were powered by General Motors engines, as no Studebaker engine plant remained in production. Approximately 11,000 Studebakers were exported to the U.S. in 1965, and only 8,000 total units were produced in 1966 — the last year of production.